THE ENCYCLOPEDIA
OF
SEWING

By Adele P. Margolis

HOW TO DESIGN YOUR OWN DRESS PATTERNS

PATTERN WISE

THE COMPLETE BOOK OF TAILORING

THE DRESSMAKING BOOK

HOW TO MAKE CLOTHES THAT FIT AND FLATTER

DESIGN YOUR OWN DRESS PATTERNS

FASHION SEWING FOR EVERYONE

THE COMPLETE BOOK OF TAILORING, REVISED

MAKE YOUR OWN DRESS PATTERNS, REVISED

Adele P. Margolis

THE ENCYCLOPEDIA
OF
SEWING

Doubleday & Company, Inc.
Garden City, New York,   1987

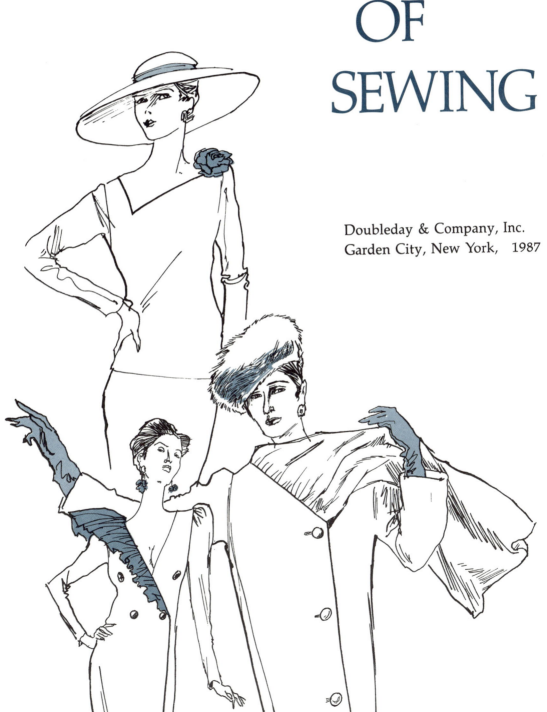

TO LINDA
AND JOHN AND PETER AND ANDREA

Selected illustrations adapted from *Reader's Digest
Complete Guide to Sewing.*
Copyright © 1976 by The Reader's Digest
Association, Inc. Used with permission.

Library of Congress Cataloging in Publication Data

Margolis, Adele P.
The encyclopedia of sewing.

   1. Sewing—Dictionaries. 2. Sewing. I. Title.
TT705.M29 1987   646.4'003'21   85–4342
ISBN 0-385-14989-1

Preface

Writing this book was wish fulfillment for its author, who hopes it will also be wish fulfillment for the reader. What sewer has not wished

for a book where one can look up specific information without having to extract it from a developmental text with what is, for the moment, extraneous material?

for an all-inclusive volume instead of having to plow through many separate books on as many different subjects?

for a book where one can find just that bit of information for much-used, little-used, or new techniques?

for a book where each subject is isolated and complete in itself, arranged alphabetically for easy reference?

A word about how to use this book. As with all encyclopedias, one must know precisely what to look for before being able to look it up. To help you, listings are under their familiar descriptive names or common usage as well as by type or technical name. For instance, a Peter Pan collar is listed by its commonly known name and as a flat collar, its type of construction. Cross-referencing throughout the book should enable you to find what you want either way.

Q.v. is Latin for *quod vide; q.q.v.* for *quae vide.* They mean "which see." Look up the entry or entries by the words immediately preceding.

I am very much indebted to all who through my long career added so immeasurably to my knowledge of clothing design and construction. I wish particularly to express my deep gratitude to

Phoebe Joslin Vernon, my dear, dear friend, whose "Why not an encyclopedia?" provided the form for my unordered ideas.

Harold Kuebler, my editor, whose confidence in me and guidance bolstered the effort.

Elfriede Hueber, the book's designer, whose skill made a work of art of the text.

Nan Grubbs, for her knowledgeable and sensitive editing of my complex manuscript.

ADELE POLLOCK MARGOLIS

Philadelphia, Pennsylvania

ABDOMEN PATTERN CORRECTIONS.

See PATTERN CORRECTIONS *for general information.*

A standard-size pattern may provide the necessary width at the hips but too much or too little shaping for the abdomen. Sagging fabric or poufs at dart points indicate too much length and too much shaping for a flat abdomen. Wrinkling or straining show that more length and more shaping are required for a large abdomen.

To make a correction for either, draw a vertical slash line from waist to hem through a single dart. If there are two darts, draw a slash line through one. Draw a horizontal slash line across the fullest part of the abdomen. Slash on each line.

Large Abdomen (a). Spread an equal amount vertically from waist to hem. Spread horizontally—equally from center front to vertical spread. Taper from vertical spread to nothing at the side seam. Fill in all spread areas with tissue. Pin or Scotch-tape to position. Make a small dart in the side section to control the amount of the vertical spread and to bring the side seam in line.

Make the existing waistline dart or darts larger to compensate for the addition at the waistline and to provide more shaping. If necessary, create another dart. Correct the side seam. Add length to the lower side. Correct the hemline with a slightly curved line starting at the original center front hemline and going to the original side-seam hemline.

Flat Abdomen (b). Reverse the above procedure.

Overlap the pattern lengthwise in the needed amount—equally from waist to

hem. Overlap horizontally—equally from center front to vertical slash line. Taper the overlap from the vertical slash line to nothing at the side seam. Pin or Scotch-tape in position. Make a small dart in the lower side section to control the amount of the overlap and to bring the side seam in line.

Make the waistline dart or darts smaller or eliminate one or all of them. Shape the garment at the side seam. Correct the side seam and the hemline.

ABUTTED DART.

A type of inner construction used to eliminate bulk in interfacings, interlinings, and the like.

Mark the dart and cut it out entirely (a). Cut a length of preshrunk tape as long as the dart plus 1/4 inch at each end for an underlay. (You could use a narrow strip of interfacing material instead.)

Bring one dart leg to the center of the strip (b). Pin. Bring the second dart leg to

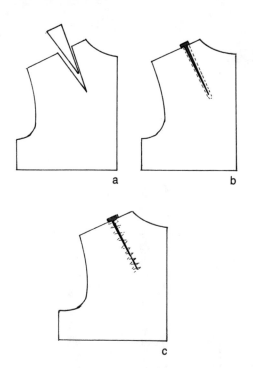

a   b

c

meet the first. Pin. Stitch close to each cut edge with short straight stitches (b) or through the center over the abutted line with a wide zigzag stitch, plain or multi-stitch (c). *See also* LAPPED DART *and* CATCH-STITCHED DART.

ABUTTED SEAM. A way to eliminate bulk from an interfacing or interlining seam. It is also an excellent method for stitching a shaping interfacing seam or one that needs special reinforcement.

Mark each seam line carefully. Trim away the seam allowance. Cut the required length of preshrunk tape or a narrow strip of interfacing for an underlay.

Bring one seam line to the center of the strip (a). Bring the second seam line to meet the first. Pin. Stitch close to each cut

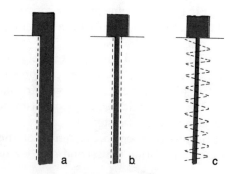

a   b   c

edge with short straight stitches (b) or through the center over the abutted line with a wide zigzag stitch, plain or multi-stitch (c). *See also* LAPPED SEAM *and* CATCH-STITCHED SEAM.

ACCORDION PLEATS. *See* PLEAT TYPES.

ACETATE. A synthetic fiber used to produce silk-like fabrics having a high luster and good draping qualities (satin, taffeta, lace, faille, tricot, brocade, crepe, jersey).

Advantages: Takes color well, resists mildew and moths, resists stretching and shrinking, is moderately absorbent.

Disadvantages: Tendency to wrinkle, is relatively weak, accumulates static electricity, is weakened by light, holds in body heat (good in cold weather, not so good in warm weather).

Care: Fabrics of acetate fiber are usually dry-cleaned, but they can be gently washed by hand or washing machine. Use a low setting for tumble dry and ironing.

ACRYLIC. A synthetic fiber used to produce a soft or fluffy fabric, often with a pile construction. It is frequently blended with other fibers, natural or synthetic.

Advantages: It is strong, quick-drying, wrinkle-resistant, lightweight; it holds shape well; is resistant to mildew, moths, chemicals, and sunlight; is colorfast, having a good affinity for dyes.

Disadvantages: It is heat-sensitive, tends to pill, accumulates static electricity, has low absorbency; it holds in body heat (good in cold weather, not so good in warm weather).

Care: Acrylic fabrics may be dry-cleaned or hand- or machine-washed with warm water. Use a fabric softener to reduce static electricity.

ALTERATION BASTING (SLIP BASTING). A basting stitch alternating between a fold of fabric (the alteration) and a single layer of cloth. It produces a line of basting on the wrong side that can be used as a guide for machine stitching. While done from the right side, the stitches are invisible when the thread is drawn up. *See* SLIP BASTING.

ALTERING A GARMENT. For perfect fit or to update a style. Often to do the one is to accomplish the other. Clothes may be too tight, too loose, too short, too long within the context of current fashion as well as the requirements of the wearer's figure.

Garments may be altered *if* the fabric and the darts and seams lend themselves to it. One has to determine whether modifications are possible. Some alterations are simple to make merely by taking in a bit here or letting out a mite there. Others are hard, if not impossible. For instance, lowering a neckline is easy; raising it is another story. Narrowing shoulders by resetting sleeves is comparatively simple; broadening them, almost impossible. Princess styles and long, fitted lines of jackets and coats can't be altered for short-waisted persons. The nipped-in waistline falling below the natural waistline is generally too tight to fit the hips of the short-waisted individual.

Determine how much reconstruction is involved in the alteration. It is often more work, more trouble, more time-consuming to remake a garment than to make it in the first place. Weigh the value of extensive or difficult alterations in terms of work, expense, and ultimate result.

When drastic changes are necessary (such as those caused by a considerable loss in weight), it is advisable to take the entire garment apart and recut it. Alterations on seams are only part of the needed change. Far more serious are changes in shaping necessitated by the new size.

Where ripping seams and darts is necessary, test a small section in an inconspicuous place to determine whether removal of stitching leaves needle holes. Make sure that letting down a hem or releasing a pleat does not leave permanent fold or soil marks.

All fitting is done from the right side so variations of left and right sides can be accommodated. Changes are transferred to the wrong side for stitching. Use tailor's chalk or basting thread of a contrasting color.

Pin, button, or zipper the garment on the correct closing line. Changes are made away from the center toward the side seams. While tempting, adding more ease at the center or making a single-breasted lap of a double-breasted garment displaces the position of darts, pockets, neckline, facings, collar, and lapels. Pin closed all slits, vents, and pleats. The garment should not depend on their released fullness for added width. In the case of pleats, the fullness can be used for extra width by eliminating them or reducing them in number or size.

Leave focal points of interest alone. Make any necessary changes above, below, beside, anywhere—but do not touch the lines that carry the design impact. Fitting is done on the part of the garment that can absorb the change. For instance: fit the dress in the illustration above and below the midsection, but do not alter *its*

size and shape. That band is *the* distinctive feature of the dress.

Changes in width can be made by releasing or taking in vertical seams or darts or creating new ones consistent with the overall lines of the design or compatible with the fabric. For example: too much fullness across the shoulders and chest can be absorbed in a new shaping seam from shoulder to waist incorporating the existing dart.

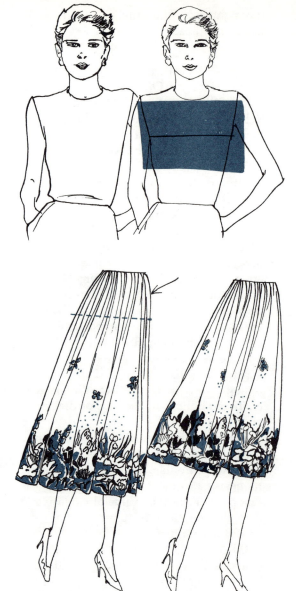

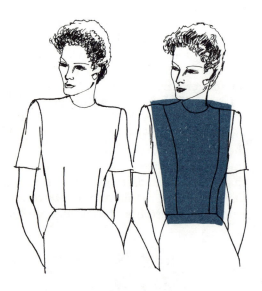

Changes in length can be made by releasing or taking in any cross seams or darts or by creating new ones if consistent with the overall lines of the design or compatible with the material. For instance: a yoke may be created by taking a tuck across the bust line or chest, thereby shortening a too long bodice.

Changes in length may also be made by lifting and recutting the top of the garment section. This would be the way to shorten any part that has style interest at one end—for instance: a skirt with a border print or a shirt sleeve with pleats and placket.

Lifting a bodice at the shoulders, however, is highly impractical. Involved are neckline, shoulders, sleeves, armholes, facing, collar, lapel, buttonholes or other fastening, interfacing or backing. In a suit or coat, there is the additional consideration of lining, shoulder pads, perhaps even an interlining.

Changes in width and length can also be achieved by insets of self- or contrasting fabric on any seam line.

For instance: a skirt can be lengthened by the insertion of a waistline band (the belt of the dress perhaps?) if the original waistline is wide enough to settle in its new position. A too tight sleeve can be relieved by the addition of a gusset at the underarm or by the insertion of a decorative overarm band.

Wrinkles in a garment are generally evidence of uncontrolled or inadequate shaping. Release the nearest seam or dart and smooth the material into it. Pin to fit. Where there is no dart or seam, create one.

Bulges or poufs at dart points mean the dart is too large for your contours. Eliminate some or all of it and shape the garment at the side seams. Or, for more subtle shaping, make several darts of the one bulging dart.

Where width as well as length adjustments are needed, make the length changes first.

General Procedure for Alterations. Try on the garment. Pin the centers closed when necessary. Pin-fit, following the same rules for grain, darts, and seams as in construction of a new garment.

Remove the garment. Replace the pins with slip basting (q.v.) *(see also* DRESSMAKER BASTING), which provides a guideline for machine stitching on the underside, or with thread tracing (q.v.) if the garment needs to be flattened for recutting. In the latter case, rip the stitching and press the garment flat. Repin or rebaste the darts and seams.

Try on the garment to check and refine the fit. When satisfied, machine-stitch the changes. *See also* FITTING.

APPLIED BAND NECKLINE FINISH. *See* SHAPED (APPLIED) BAND NECKLINE FINISH.

APPLIED CASING. A separate strip or band of fabric stitched to either the inside or the outside of a one-piece garment through which elastic or a drawstring may be threaded. *See* CASING.

Mark the placement line for the casing on the garment. Cut a straight or bias strip of fabric to the desired width and length with 1/4-inch seam allowances on all edges. Turning the ends first, turn under the seam allowances on all edges and press. In an open-ended casing, edgestitch the ends (a).

Pin casing to garment along the placement line. When ends abut, place the opening at a vertical seam (b).

Edgestitch the casing to the garment on

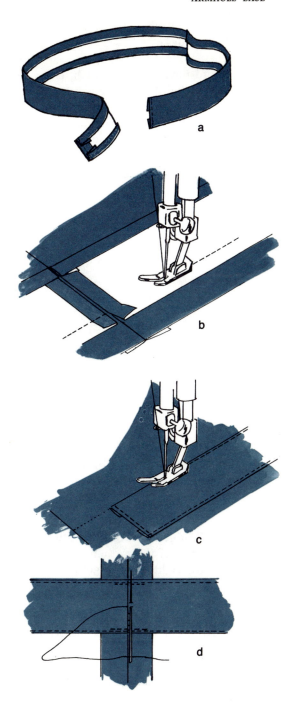

both long seams (b and c). Secure the ends of the stitching with backstitches. Insert the elastic or drawstring. In a closed casing, slip-stitch the ends (d).

ARMHOLE EASE. In some fabrics (wool particularly) a slight easing along the front and back underarm curves serves as supplementary shaping for the bust and shoulder blades.

Gather along the underarm seam line from front notch to back notch. Draw up the gathers slightly so the underarm of the garment fits against the body. Shrink out excess rippling over a tailor's ham (q.v.) or other suitable press pad. Use the tip of the steam iron.

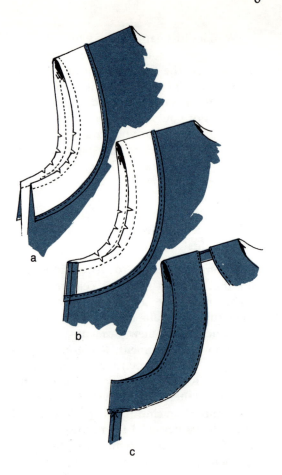

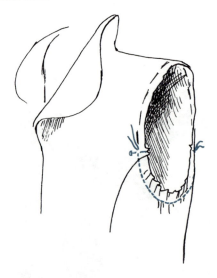

ARMHOLE FACING. This may be applied by either a mass production or a custom method. In either method, edge-finish the outer edge of the facing in a manner appropriate to the fabric.

Mass Production Method. Stitch the shoulder seam of the garment and press it open. With right sides together and all markings matched, pin, baste, then stitch the facing to the armhole. Leave the underarm seams of both garment and facing open. Trim, grade, and clip the seam allowances (a).

Open out the facing. With right sides of front and back together, pin and/or baste the underarm seam of facing and garment. Stitch in one continuous seam. Press the seam allowances open. Trim those of the facing.

Custom Method. Stitch the shoulder and underarm seams of the garment. Stitch the underarm seam of the facing and trim it to half width. Press all seam allowances open.

With right sides together, pin and/or baste the facing to the armhole, matching shoulder markings, notches, and underarm seams. With the facing side up, stitch the facing to the armhole, starting at the underarm. Trim, grade, and clip the seam allowances (b).

Both Methods. Turn the facing to the inside, rolling the seam to the underside. Press. Understitch (q.v.). Tack the facing to the shoulder and underarm seams (c).

ARMHOLE PATTERN CORRECTIONS. The armhole in a standard-size pattern should lie comfortably and correctly on the body. If the armhole is tight, it will bind. If it is too large, it will gap. Before making the following specific corrections, *see* PATTERN CORRECTIONS.

Gaping Armhole. A gaping armhole may be caused by sloping shoulders, rounded back or prominent shoulder

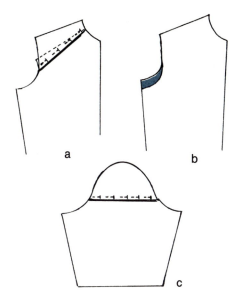

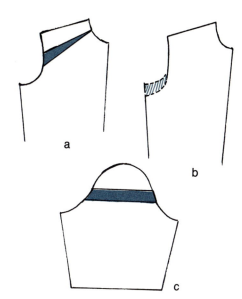

blades, erect back, bust with large cup. *See*
BACK, BUST *and* SHOULDER PATTERN CORRECTION.

Large Armhole. Make a dart in the pattern in the necessary amount at the armhole and taper to nothing at the neckline (a). Correct the armhole cutting line and seam line with smooth curved lines. Or slip a sheet of pattern paper under the pattern. Pin or Scotch-tape it to position. Raise the underarm curve on the front or back bodice patterns the desired amount by drawing new cutting and stitching lines from the notch to the underarm seam (b). Use a French curve #17 (a drafting tool useful for drawing any curved area on a pattern) or trace the underarm of a similar pattern.

Tuck the sleeve pattern across the cap in an amount equal to that of the armhole correction (c). Correct the cutting line and seam line with smooth curved lines. If the garment is sleeveless, make a corresponding correction on the facing.

Tight Armhole. Slash the bodice pattern from the neckline to the armhole. Spread the pattern at the armhole to the amount needed. Fill in the spread area with pattern paper. Correct the armhole cutting line and seam line with smooth curved lines (a).

Or lower the underarm curve on the front and/or back bodice patterns the desired amount by drawing new cutting and stitching lines from the front and/or back notch to the underarm seam (b). Use a drafting tool or trace the underarm of a similar pattern.

Make a corresponding correction on the sleeve pattern. Slash across the sleeve cap and spread in the amount of the drop at the underarm. Fill in the spread area with tissue paper and pin or Scotch-tape to position (c).

ARMHOLE SEAM. This seam starts from any point on the shoulder either currently fashionable or particularly becoming. Any fitting faults that extend to the armhole become much more obvious when sleeves are set in. Fit the garment carefully before setting and stitching the sleeve.

Natural Armhole Seam in a Dress. The top of the sleeve joins the shoulder seam at the outside of the prominent shoulder bone, curves over the top of the shoulder, continues in a slightly curved line—deeper in front, shallower in back—to the crease where arm and body join (there is some ease allowance at this point) to a depth of 1/2 to 1 1/2 inches below the armpit.

Many designers feel that more sleeve action is achieved by a high and close-fitting armhole seam. They point out that the lower the armhole drop the more the bodice is lifted when the arms are raised.

The exact position of the back armhole seam is best determined when the arms are brought moderately forward, to provide enough room for the forward movement of the arms.

Natural Armhole Seam in a Coat or Jacket. These sleeve seams are extended beyond those of a dress. The amount varies, depending on the current style, whether or not the shoulders are padded, and over what garments the coat or jacket is to be worn.

ARMHOLE STAY. This preserves the shape of the armhole. The stay may be stay stitching, tape, or chain stitching.

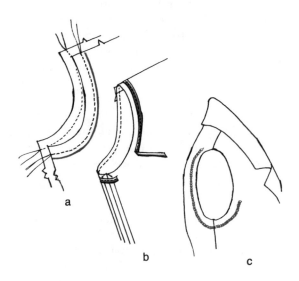

Stay Stitching (q.v.). Place a line of machine stitching in the seam allowance close to the seam line. Stitch front and back from shoulder to underarm (a). It is easier to do this before the shoulders and side seams are joined.

Tape Stay. Place a length of preshrunk, preshaped tape around the armhole, starting and ending at the underarm, with a slight overlap. Place one long edge of the tape slightly over the seam line and the other edge in the seam allowance. Pin or baste to position. Machine-stitch through the tape (b).

Chain-Stitch Stay. Start at the front notch and chain-stitch (q.v.) around the underarm to a point 1 inch below the back shoulder. Work in the seam allowance close to the seam line. Ease in any armhole fullness (c). Keep the stitches taut and even in tension.

ARROWHEAD TACK. A decorative triangular reinforcement used as a finishing touch at points of strain, at corners or ends of seams, tucks, darts, pleats, or joinings.

Mark the triangle with chalk or thread on the right side of the garment. Take several tiny running or backstitches within the triangle and bring the needle out at the lower left point. Take a small stitch from right to left at the upper point of the triangle (a). Insert the needle at the right point and bring it up at the left close to the first stitch within the triangle (b). Continue working down the sides and across the bottom (c) until the triangle is completely filled (d).

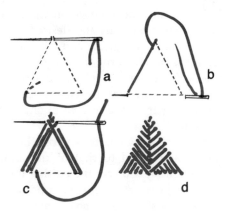

ASYMMETRIC. One-sided; not geometrically balanced. Asymmetric patterns are placed on the right side of the fabric in the position in which they will be worn, and cut in a single layer. The printed side of the pattern is up.

Asymmetric Designs

BACK-AND-FORTH STITCHING. *See* MACHINE BACKSTITCHING.

BACK HIP POCKET (MEN'S TROUSERS). This may be a single-welt pocket, a double-welt pocket (bound pocket), or a flap pocket. *See listing for each.* If there is only one back hip pocket, construct it on the left trouser back.

BACKING. *See* UNDERLINING.

BACK INTERFACING FOR TAILORED KNITS. The stretch quality of tailored knit garments calls for a back interfacing (when present) that will match the garment's free forward movement. This can be done in one of two ways. Use the one-piece back interfacing pattern included in the garment pattern or make your own. *See* INTERFACING FOR WOMAN'S JACKET—TRADITIONAL TAILORING. Cut the interfacing on the bias for a degree of stretch in keeping with a knit. Or make a two-piece back interfacing pattern (q.v.) cut on the grain of the outer fabric.

BACK INTERFACING PATTERN FOR TAILORED GARMENT. This may be in one piece (a) or in two pieces (b). For the for-

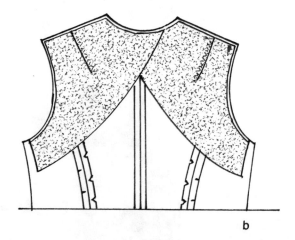

b

mer, *see* INTERFACING PATTERN FOR WOMAN'S JACKET—TRADITIONAL TAILORING. For the latter, *see* TWO-PIECE BACK INTERFACING PATTERN.

BACK PATTERN CORRECTIONS. Before making back changes, *see* PATTERN CORRECTIONS for general information.

Posture and bone structure may make body measurements alone insufficient for correct fit. The garment fabric should conform to the back contours without wrinkling, pulling, sagging, or gaping. If it doesn't, make the appropriate correction.

Broad Back. Draw an L-shaped slash line from a midpoint on the shoulder seam to the side seam just below the armhole. Slash from the side seam *to* but *not through* the shoulder seam. Spread to the desired amount and fill in the spread area with tissue paper. Pin or Scotch-tape to position. Redraw the side seam, tapering from the new armhole position to the waistline (a) or carrying the correction down to the waistline (b), depending on the figure needs. If necessary, make the shoulder and/or waistline darts larger.

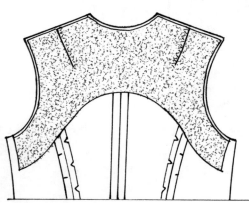

a

a   b

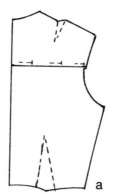
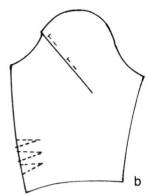

a   b

It is also possible to add a small amount (no more than 1/2 inch) at the center back. Such a change will affect the neckline and the waistline. Make corresponding changes in pattern sections that join them.

Narrow Back. Tuck the pattern from shoulder seam to waistline seam through the darts. Replace the shoulder and waistline darts, but make them smaller. Make corresponding changes in pattern sections that join the shoulder and waistline seams.

It is also possible to take off a bit (no more than 1/2 inch) at the center back and side seams. Such changes will affect the neck, waistline, and armhole seam. Make corresponding changes in pattern sections that join them.

Erect Back. Remove excess length by tucking the pattern from center back to armhole, either in an equal amount across the entire back or tapering to the armhole. Correct the center back or armhole as necessary. Make the neckline or shoulder dart smaller (a). If also necessary to remove sag,

make a lengthwise tuck from the shoulder down.

Slash and overlap the sleeve back in a corresponding amount (b). Straighten the grain line.

BODICE BACK LENGTH CORRECTIONS

To lengthen, slash and spread the pattern above or below the shoulder blades or in both places as necessary. Insert tissue in the spread area. Pin or Scotch-tape. Correct the pattern at the armhole and/or the side seam (a).

To shorten, tuck the pattern above or below the shoulder blades or in both places as necessary. Correct the pattern at the armhole and/or side seam (b).

If the armhole is involved in the change, make a similar correction in the sleeve cap.

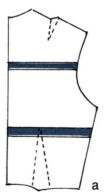
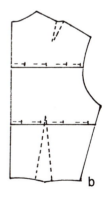

a   b

Rounded Back (Round Shoulders, Dowager's Hump). Slash the pattern across the back from center back to (but not through) the armhole seam. Spread the pattern at center back to the needed amount. Straighten the center back line to the neckline. Enlarge any existing neckline dart or create one to take up the same amount as that added at the center back.

When a dart is created on the back neckline in addition to one already at the back shoulder, ease the amount of the original shoulder dart into the front shoulder and stitch the newly created neckline dart as a dart. A good steaming over the tailor's ham (q.v.) should take care of the eased fullness. Too many darts in one small area are not pleasing from a design point of view.

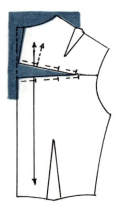

BACKSTITCH. The strongest of the permanent hand stitches. Before the invention of the sewing machine, it was *the* stitch that held clothes together. In fact, machine stitching closely resembles it.

To make the backstitch, start at the right-hand end. Bring the needle up on the right side one stitch ahead. Working back to the right, insert the needle at the point where the preceding stitch ended, slide it along the underside, and once more bring the needle out one stitch ahead. You are really encircling the cloth with stitches.

There are two variations of the backstitch: the half backstitch (q.v.) and the prick stitch (q.v.).

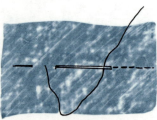

BALANCED (EVEN) PLAID. In this plaid, the stripes, spaces, and colors are the same both lengthwise and crosswise, forming a perfectly square repeat. *See* PLAIDS: TEST FOR EVENNESS OR UNEVENNESS.

BALANCED (EVEN) STRIPES. The stripes, spaces, and colors are the same going up or down in a horizontal stripe or to right or left on a vertical stripe. *See* STRIPES: TEST FOR EVENNESS OR UNEVENNESS.

BAND COLLAR. A collar made from a strip of fabric in the desired length and width on either straight or bias grain. Straight grain stands better; bias grain drapes better. The ends of the band may meet, overlap, button, tie, or loop. The band may be cut wide enough to double back against itself, as in the turtleneck or roll-over collars. It can be used as a convertible collar or as the stand of a shirt collar. *(See listing for each type.)* A deep band may hang softly like a cape or encircle the shoulders like a fichu. A long band may be gathered into a flounce, pleated, or laid in soft folds.

The band collar is constructed by a method appropriate for the design of the collar and the fabric of which it is made. In all cases, it is easier to attach the straight band to a curved neckline if you straighten the latter first. To do so, stay-stitch the neckline just inside the seam line. Clip the seam allowance almost to the stitching. Straighten the neckline to fit the band.

BAND CUFF THAT EXTENDS BELOW THE SLEEVE EDGE. *See* DETACHABLE CUFF.

BAND CUFF WITHOUT PLACKET. This is the simplest of all cuffs to make because no opening is involved (a).

Make the band long enough to slip over the hand easily (knuckle circumference plus ease). Make its finished width 1 inch to 1½ inches. Cut it on a fold for a one-piece construction. The grain may be straight or bias.

Prepare the cuff. *See* CUFF INTERFACING *and* CUFF CONSTRUCTION. Prepare the lower edge of the sleeve.

Band Collars

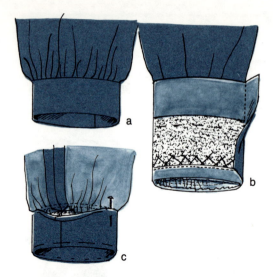

With right sides together, stitch the interfaced half of the cuff to the edge of the sleeve (b). Trim and grade the seam allowances and press them toward the cuff.

Turn the cuff to the inside along the fold line so wrong sides are together. Baste close to the fold. Turn under the raw edge and slip-stitch it along the seam line (c).

BAND CUFF WITH PLACKET. In this style of cuff, the placket (q.v.) is made first. The cuff may be applied in one of two ways.

1. Both ends of the cuff are flush with the placket edges, as in the shirt cuff (q.v.) (a) or the French cuff (q.v.).
2. The front end of the cuff, flush with the front placket edge, overlaps the end that projects beyond the back placket edge, as in the lapped band cuff (q.v.) (b).

BANDING. This can be strips of woven or knit fabrics, ornamental bands, braided,

embroidered, beaded, sequinned, or of metallic threads.

Banding can be used as a trim, as an insertion, as an extension, or as an edge finish. How it is applied depends on which of these it is and whether hand or machine stitching is more in keeping with the design and the character of the banding.

See DECORATIVE BANDING; MITERED DOUBLE BANDING; RIBBED BANDING; WOVEN AND KNITTED BANDINGS.

BAND NECKLINE FINISH. *See* SHAPED BAND NECKLINE FINISH *and* STRIP BAND.

BAR TACK. Used as a reinforcement at a point of strain. It may be made by hand or by machine. *See* OVERHAND BAR TACK, BLANKET STITCH BAR TACK, *and* MACHINE BAR TACK.

BASTING. A stitch that holds two or more layers of fabric together temporarily. It can also be used for marking. Basting may be done by hand or by machine. In either case, the stitches should be large enough to be seen readily and loose enough for easy removal.

Basting consists of a succession of stitches and spaces either small or large, even or uneven. The size of the stitch varies with the use, the amount of strain exerted on the seam, and the fabric. Where there is great strain, as in fitting, use small stitches; where there is no strain, use longer stitches.

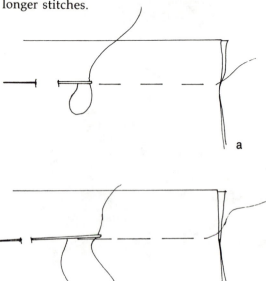

BASTING BY HAND

Even Basting (a) is used for seams subject to strain, long seams, and close control of curved edges, intricate seaming, or when easing fullness. Both stitches and spaces are of equal length on both sides of the fabric. The length of each depends on the kind of fabric and the degree of probable strain. For firm basting, take a backstitch every few inches.

Uneven Basting (b) is used on straight edges, for marking, and for holding fabric together at seams and edges that are not subject to strain. Stitches and spaces are unequal in length, being longer on the surface and shorter on the underside.

Both Types. Use a single thread in a contrasting color of convenient but not too long length for all but thread tracing (q.v.). The latter is done with a double thread for easy visibility. Use thread suitable for the fabric.

Start with a knotted end and finish with several over-and-over stitches (q.v.). The stitches should be "easy" so they can be readily removed. Baste beside the seam line to facilitate easy removal after permanent machine stitching. To remove, clip the basting at frequent intervals and remove the short threads. Pulling out a long basting thread through a length of fabric may injure or crease it. Tweezers are a fine instrument for this purpose.

See also DIAGONAL BASTING; DRESSMAKER BASTING; SLIP BASTING; TAILOR BASTING.

BASTING BY MACHINE

This may be done on fabrics that won't slip or show needle marks when the thread is removed and when no close control is required. Use the longest stitch on the machine and a slightly looser tension. To remove, clip the top thread at intervals and pull out the bottom thread.

BASTING TAPE. A narrow tape with paper-covered adhesive on one side that eliminates pinning or thread basting. Finger-press along or across the edges to be held together. Place the strips of tape across the seam to be held in place for stitching. Remove the tape when the sewing is complete.

It makes easier the application of zippers and the matching of cross seams, plaids, stripes. It is a good device for those places where basting is impractical, as in seams in leather.

BEADED FABRIC. A by-the-yard glamorous fabric that has beads sewn to a backing material. Opulent when used for an entire garment; sparkling when added to a garment section—a yoke, perhaps, or cuffs.

For a complete garment of beaded fabric, select a simple pattern with few seams and darts. Avoid fullness such as gathers or pleats. Avoid details such as buttonholes or pockets that require a slash in the material. For comfort, use a soft but closely woven lining to cover the rough underside of the fabric. For facings, use lining material.

A trial muslin (q.v.) is a must. There is little opportunity to correct errors in fitting after the material is cut. Cut with care. Remove the beads from the seam allowances. Make sure all thread ends are secured at the seam line, particularly in those fabrics (practically all of them) to which the beads are attached by a continuous thread in a chain stitch.

Baste the seams with small stitches, the better to hold the weighty fabric. Machine-stitch with a zipper foot resting in the seam allowance while one edge is close against the beads. Use a stitch length, stitch size, and tension appropriate for the texture of the backing fabric. Examine the stitched seam from the right side. If there are any broken or missing beads along the seam line, replace them. A fine touch is to hand-sew beads on the seam line to conceal it.

Press in the unbeaded seam allowance only. Because steam may affect the sheen of the beads, use a dry iron at a low heat setting.

BEADING TRIM (also called **VEINING** or **ENTRE DEUX**). An openwork edging or insertion through which ribbon may be run.

BELT. *See* BELT INTERFACED (HAND CONSTRUCTION); BELT INTERFACED (MACHINE CONSTRUCTION); BELT WITH CLASP BUCKLE; BELT WITH PASS-THROUGH BUCKLE; BELT WITH PRONG-AND-EYELET BUCKLE; BELT OR STRAP WITH RING BUCKLE; CONTOUR BELT; CORDED BELT; CUMMERBUND; OVERLAP BELT; SASH; TIE BELT.

BELT CARRIERS (BELT GUARDS, BELT LOOPS).
Thread or fabric loops through which a belt is passed and which hold it in place on the garment. Thread carriers (q.v.) are almost invisible and generally support lightweight belts. Because of the high visibility of fabric carriers they are often treated as design features. Those that must support the weight of heavy belts are made wider than those planned for lighter-weight belts. The carriers may be added either during construction or after.

BELTING. A rigid band used for stiffening belts and waistbands. It is available in white and black cotton or synthetics. Widths range from 3/4 to 2 inches. Other types of belting are French belting, and belting ribbon (q.v.).

BELTING RIBBON. A stiff grosgrain ribbon used for inside waistbands and for waistband and belt interfacings. *See also* GROSGRAIN RIBBON.

BELT INTERFACED (HAND CONSTRUCTION).
Cut the interfacing to the shape, length, and width of the finished belt. Pin, baste, or press (if iron-on) the interfacing to position on the wrong side of the upper belt. Turn the belt seam allowances over the interfacing, notching or clipping where necessary to make the fabric lie flat. Steam-press, sharply drawing the belt fabric tight over the interfacing. Tack the seam allowances to the interfacing only with long, permanent basting stitches (a) or catch stitches.

Turn under the facing seam allowances, shaping and notching as necessary. Press or baste close to the folded edge. Trim the seam allowances to 3/8 inch. (Seam allowances are unnecessary when using fabric with a finished or nonravelly edge such as ribbon or leather.) Baste the facing to position (b). Slip-stitch or topstitch the facing to the belt.

BELT INTERFACED (MACHINE CONSTRUCTION).
Cut a strip of fabric on the lengthwise grain twice the width of commercial belting by the required length of the belt plus seam allowances. Fold the fabric over the belting with the wrong side out. Using a zipper foot, stitch along the lengthwise seam, being careful not to catch the belting in the stitching. Trim the seam allowances to 1/4 inch (a). Slide the seam around so it is centered on the belting and press it open (b).

Stitch the shaped end of the belt, being careful to keep the stitching free of the belting. Trim the seam allowances. Remove the belting from the open end. Turn the belt to the right side and press.

a

b

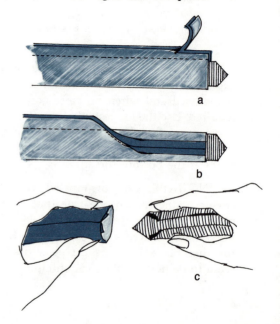

a

b

c

Cupping the belting slightly for easy insertion, slip it into the belt (c). Attach a buckle to the unfinished end. *See* BELT WITH PASS-THROUGH BUCKLE *and* BELT WITH PRONG-AND-EYELET BUCKLE.

BELT LOOPS. *See* BELT CARRIERS.

BELT OR STRAP WITH RING BUCKLE. A type of fastening used for cinch belts or straps on coats and sports clothes.

Make a tie belt or strap. Slip one end through the two rings and turn to the underside. Attach with hand or machine stitching.

To fasten this belt, weave the opposite end through the two rings and pull up. To hold ends in place, sew snaps or hooks and eyes far enough in from the ends so they won't show. (*See* BELT WITH PASS-THROUGH BUCKLE.)

BELT WITH CLASP BUCKLE. The two halves of the buckle hook at the center. Some buckles are sewn through holes at the edges or shanks on the underside. The directions below are for the more usual type, which has a bar at each end.

Make a tie belt (q.v.). Insert each end of the finished belt through the bar on each half of the clasp.

Try on the belt and adjust its length to fit the waistline. Pin. Remove the belt. Allow 1 inch for the turn-under and trim the excess. Stitch 1/4 inch from each end and overcast to prevent fraying. Slip the ends through the bars once more and whip-stitch to position, making certain the stitches are not visible from the right side.

BELT WITH PASS-THROUGH BUCKLE. A sash used for cinching a waist.

The finished width of the belt must fit the inside measurement of the buckle. Measure the length of the belt attachment bar to determine the width (a). The belt may be just this width or wider if the fabric is a soft material. Add seam allowances. Make the length of the belt the waistline measurement plus 1 1/4 inches for a turn-under at one end, plus a decorative extension at the other end consistent with the belt's shape and the design of the garment. Add seam allowances.

Construct a sash (q.v.). Make one end straight for the turn-under. The other end may be shaped.

Insert the straight end of the belt through the buckle (b). Turn it to the underside of the belt and sew securely in place by hand (c) or machine stitching.

Place the belt around the waist. Slip the shaped end through the buckle and pull up to fit the waist snugly. Mark the closing with pins. Remove belt. Sew snaps and/or hooks and eyes to each end of the closing to hold the belt in place. Place them far enough from the end so they will not show (d).

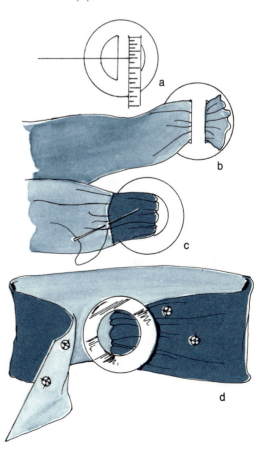

BELT WITH PRONG-AND-EYELET BUCKLE.

Make the belt. (See TIE BELT OR OVERLAP BELT.) Try on the finished belt and mark the center front position on both ends.

The Buckle End. Cut off the buckle end 2 inches from the center front marking. Stitch 1/4 inch from the cut edge and overcast. Pierce a hole at the center front marking large enough to fit the prong. Use an embroidery stiletto to punch the hole, then enlarge the opening with a scissors point to fit the prong. Work the opening as an eyelet (q.v.) (a). Another way to make an opening is to machine-stitch a small rectangle, then slash between the stitching (b).

Insert the prong in the opening, pull the end to the underside, and sew securely in place by either hand or machine stitching (c and d).

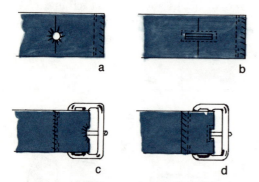

a   b

c   d

The Finished End of the Belt. On the other end of the belt, pierce and work one eyelet at the center front marking. Make one or more eyelets 1 inch apart on both sides of the first for variations in waist measurements.

There are several ways of handling the eyelets: with a special attachment for the sewing machine, with a tool that punches in metal eyelets (these come in a variety of colors), or worked by hand.

BEVELING SEAMS. *See* GRADING SEAMS.

BIAS.

The line that cuts diagonally across the warp and filler threads of a fabric. It is the hypotenuse of a 45° triangle.

Bias-cut fabric has considerable flexibility. It can be stretched, blocked, shaped. It can be used when body-conforming fit is desired in bodices, skirts, sashes, waistbands; wherever roundness or curviness is sought, as in collars, cuffs, trimmings; when easy movement or flare is wished in sleeves, skirts, capes. It can also be used for decorative effect in striped, blocked, or plaid fabric. It is essential for drapery, as in cowl necklines.

Because it can be molded to the body without using darts to do the shaping, it is a favorite of designers, who can then concentrate on line alone to achieve a sculptured form.

If you plan to use a pattern on the bias when it wasn't designed for bias use, establish the bias grain (q.v.) on each pattern piece. Bias tends to stretch either in width, making the garment shorter, or in length, narrowing it. To compensate, use more width, more length, and wider seam allowances—at least 1 inch.

A bias-cut garment requires a different fit than one cut on straight grain. It is more like the fit of a knitted garment.

Walking or sitting in a bias-cut skirt makes it ride up. A bias flared skirt is more practical than a bias straight one.

Choose an even plaid or stripe without any pronounced diagonal weave if you intend to use it on the bias. Sometimes, in order to dodge the intricate matching of stripes, plaids, or blocks, part of a garment may be cut on the bias. This also has the merit of adding design interest.

In addition to those uses listed under Bias, *see* BUTTON LOOPS; CASING; CORDING; COWL; EDGE FINISHES; PIPING; RUFFLE; TUBING; TRIMS AND TRIMMINGS; WAISTBAND.

BIAS BINDING.

A strip of bias material used as a finish for a raw edge, both strengthening and decorating it.

Commercial binding 1/2 inch wide is available in a range of colors, but it is often not as good in quality or as interesting as binding you can make for yourself. Use very lightweight silky or cotton material.

Cut strips four times the desired finished width plus 1/4 inch for stretching and turning. The width of the binding is

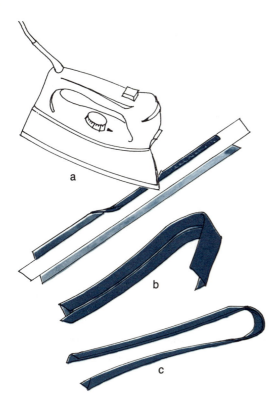

BIAS BINDING AS A DECORATIVE TRIM. A wide binding in a contrasting color or texture makes an effective trim.

Prepare the Binding. Use a material that can be stretched on the edges that require it and shrunk on the others. Cut strips of bias twice the desired finished width plus two 1/4-inch seam allowances determined by the texture of the fabric on which it is to be used. On sheer or transparent fabric, make it as narrow as possible, not exceeding 1/8 inch finished width. On firm fabrics, bindings may be as much as 1 inch. *See also* BIAS BINDING: DOUBLE-FOLD OR FRENCH.

In commercial single bias binding, both lengthwise raw edges are folded to the center of the underside and pressed. Do the same with made-by-you binding. Here is an easy and uniform way to do this. Cut a strip of firm paper twice the finished width. Place the bias strip wrong side up on an ironing board. Center the paper strip over the bias. Press both bias edges over the paper (a). Remove the paper (b). Fold the bias lengthwise and press (c).

The method of applying bias binding depends on the width of the binding, the fabric, and the shape of the edge to be bound. *See* BIAS BINDING AS A DECORATIVE TRIM; BIAS BINDING AT A VISIBLE EDGE; BIAS BINDING AT CORNERS; BIAS BINDING: DOUBLE-FOLD OR FRENCH; BIAS BINDING: MACHINE-APPLIED; BIAS BINDING ON A CURVED EDGE; BIAS BINDING: PRESHAPED; BIAS BINDING: SINGLE-FOLD.

plus an allowance for stretching or turning corners. Join the strips to equal the length of the edge to be bound plus 1/4-inch seam allowances at the ends. Turn under the lengthwise seam allowances and press. Preshape the binding. *See* BIAS BINDING: PRESHAPED.

Prepare the Edges to Be Bound. On the garment, make a guideline parallel to the finished edge to indicate where the inner edge of the binding is to be stitched. Stay-stitch 1/8 inch inside this line. Soft fabrics may require an interfacing along the edge to be bound.

Place the right side of the inner fold of the binding against the guideline on the right side of the garment. Pin and/or baste the binding to the garment. Machine-stitch.

Turn the binding toward and over the outer edge, bringing the remaining fold to the line of machine stitching on the inside of the garment. Slip-stitch. Press the binding lightly, leaving a slight fold where the binding joins the garment to avoid a flat look.

See BIAS BINDING AT A VISIBLE EDGE; BIAS BINDING AT CORNERS; BIAS BINDING ON A CURVED EDGE; BIAS BINDING: PRESHAPED.

BIAS BINDING AT A VISIBLE EDGE.

After the binding has been pinned to the garment edge, trim the garment seam allowances diagonally at the ends. Trim the ends of the bias binding 1/4 to 1/2 inch beyond the edge of the garment and fold

them so they are even with the edge (a). Stitch the binding to the garment. If the garment seam allowances have not already been trimmed, do so now.

Turn the binding over the seam allowances, bringing the folded edge to the line of stitching. Pin, then slip-stitch (b).

BIAS BINDING AT CORNERS.

The following directions are for standard or narrow bindings. When the binding is wide, it is best to miter the corner (q.v.) first.

Outward Corner. Open out the binding. Pin it in place as for bias binding: single- or double-fold (q.q.v.). Stitch along one side in the crease of the binding from the outer edge to the intersecting seam line at the corner (a). Secure the thread ends.

Fold the binding diagonally as for a miter. Stitch along the second side from one end to the other (b). On the right side, turn the binding up, form a miter at the corner (c), and fold the binding over the edge. On the underside, form a second miter with the fold in the opposite direction to avoid bulk. Bring the fold of the free edge of the binding to the seam and slip-stitch. If desired, slip-stitch the miters too.

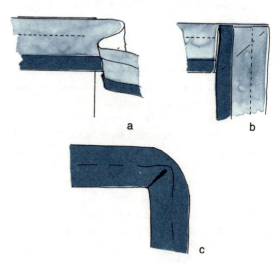

a   b

c

Inward Corner. Reinforce the corner on the seam lines. Clip the corner to the stitching (a). Open the clip to form a straight seam line.

Open out one folded edge of the binding and pin or baste it to the garment as

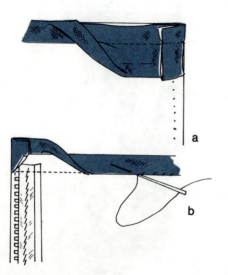

a

b

for bias binding: single- or double-fold (q.q.v.). Stitch from the garment side in a straight seam (b). On the right side, form a miter (c), pulling its fold to the wrong side through the clip (d). On the underside, form a miter in the opposite direction to avoid bulk (e). Bring the fold of the free edge of the binding to the seam and slip-stitch. If desired, slip-stitch the miters.

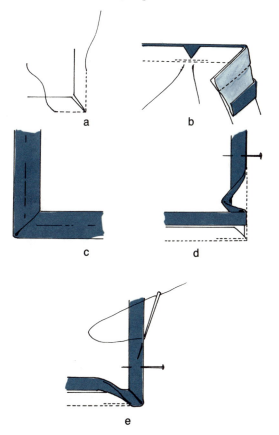

BIAS BINDING: DOUBLE-FOLD OR FRENCH. This is an excellent finish for lightweight and sheer fabrics.

Stay-stitch the edge to be bound in the seam allowance close to the seam line. Trim the seam allowance to slightly less than the finished width of the binding.

Cut bias strips four times the desired finished width of the binding plus 1/4 inch for stretching and shaping. Fold the bias strip in half lengthwise, right sides outside.

Place the folded binding against the right side of the garment with all raw edges aligned, stretching and easing as

necessary. Pin or baste to position. Stitch the binding to the garment along the seam line, keeping it an even width along the folded edge (a). Because bias widths can change with the slightest variations in tension or pressure, irregularities are a common hazard. Keep your eye on the width of the binding while stitching and correct as necessary.

Turn the finished (folded) edge of the binding over the raw edges, enclosing them. Bring the fold to the seam line on the underside. Hem or slip-stitch the fold to the seam (b). *See* BIAS BINDING; BIAS BINDING AT A VISIBLE EDGE.

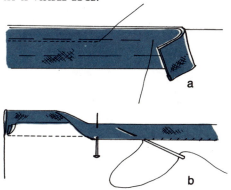

BIAS BINDING: MACHINE-APPLIED. Prepare the binding as for bias binding: single-fold (q.v.) with this exception: fold the binding lengthwise with the bottom half slightly wider than the top to make sure the loose under edge is caught in the machine stitching. Press. Enclose the raw edge with the binding. Pin or baste to position. Topstitch by machine. When basting is used, stitch beside it.

A machine application of binding may also be accomplished with the use of the binder, a sewing machine accessory. *See also* BIAS BINDING; BIAS BINDING AT A VISIBLE EDGE.

BIAS BINDING ON A CURVED EDGE. In stitching bias binding on a curved edge,

one must cope with the difference between the length of the line of stitching
and the length of the finished edge. Preshaping the binding makes it much easier
to apply. *See* BIAS BINDING: PRESHAPED.

When the finished edge is an *inward
curve,* stretch the binding as you stitch the
outer, longer line. The unstretched edge of
the binding will fit the shorter length of
the inner curve when the binding is turned
to position (a).

When the finished edge is an *outward
curve,* ease the binding as you stitch the inner, shorter line. The uneased edge of
binding will fit the longer outward curve
when the binding is turned to position (b).

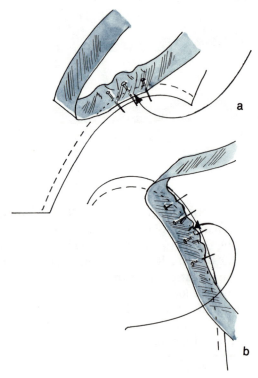

a

b

BIAS BINDING: PRESHAPED.

When a
curved edge is to be bound, the best effect
is obtained by preshaping the binding before applying it.

Place the binding on the ironing board
in a curve that corresponds to that of the
garment. Use the pattern for this or trace
the curve on firm paper. Keeping the side
of the iron parallel to the edge of the binding, swirl it to shape. Stretch the outside

edge while easing the inside. Follow the
arrow in the illustration.

BIAS BINDING: SINGLE-FOLD.

For firm
fabrics.

Trim the seam allowance from the garment edges to be bound. Make them
slightly narrower than the desired width
of the finished edge. Open out the binding
and place its right side against the right
side of the garment, raw edges together,
stretching and easing as necessary. When
the binding ends at a visible edge, leave
enough for an edge finish. Pin or baste the
binding to position. Machine-stitch along
the fold nearest the edge (a). Turn the
binding to the wrong side, enclosing the
seam allowances. Turn under the remaining raw edge of the binding and attach it
to the seam with slip stitches or hemming
stitches (b). *See* BIAS BINDING; BIAS BINDING AT
A VISIBLE EDGE.

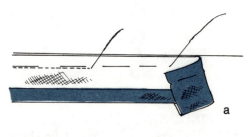

a

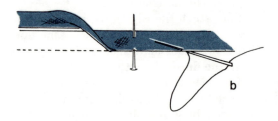

b

BIAS CUFF.

This fits more smoothly than a
cuff cut on straight grain. Because of the
flexibility of bias, it is possible for the upper layer of the cuff to stretch while at the

same time the underlayer eases into position. If an interfacing is used, it, too, must be cut on the bias.

Cut the bias cuff to fit the lower edge of the sleeve plus enough ease so it will fit over the sleeve when turned to position. Make it twice the width of the finished cuff plus 1¼ inches for a turnback. Add seam allowances. Mark the fold line with basting thread. Heavy fabrics may need a little more length to encircle the sleeve and a little more width for the turnback.

Apply the cuff interfacing (q.v.). Join the ends of the cuff on straight grain (a). Press the seam allowances open. Mark quarter divisions on sleeve and cuff.

With right sides together and raw edges aligned, slip the interfaced half of the cuff over the sleeve, centering the joined ends at the underarm seam (b). Distribute the ease evenly by matching the quarter division markings. Pin at right angles to the raw edges. Machine-stitch with the sleeve side up. Grade the seam allowances and press.

With the right side out, fold the cuff along the fold line and baste close to the edge. Turn the remaining raw edge into the sleeve, allowing enough length for a smooth turnback (c).

On thin fabrics, turn under the raw edge of the cuff and slip-stitch to the line of machine stitching on the underside. On heavy fabrics, finish the raw edge with binding or overcasting and fasten to the inside of the sleeve along the line of machine stitching.

BIAS-CUT PATTERN CORRECTIONS. *See* PATTERN CORRECTIONS.

BIAS-FACED HEM. This type of hem is suitable for curved, flared, or circular hems; when there is not enough self-fabric for a turned-up hem; or to eliminate the bulk of a turned-up hem in heavy fabric.

Use a strip of commercial bias binding or make your own bias facing (q.v.) of lightweight material cut to the desired length and width plus seam allowances. The width may be anywhere from ½ inch to 2½ inches. Mark the hemline on the garment. Allow at least ½ inch for a seam allowance plus a turn-under. Add more for heavy outer fabrics.

Join as many bias strips as are necessary for the length of the hem. Join the ends of the bias facing. All joinings are on straight grain. Press the seam allowances open. Turn under the lengthwise seam allowance of the outer edge and press. Preshape the facing to match the curve of the hem. *(See* BIAS BINDING: PRESHAPED.)

With right sides together and raw edges aligned, pin and stitch the facing to the

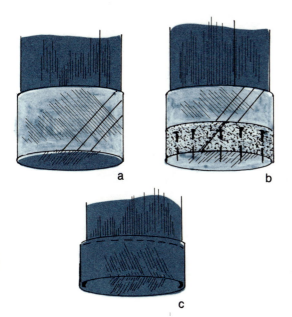

hem (a). Press the seam allowances open, clipping and notching where necessary so they will lie flat. Grade the seam allowances and press them toward the facing.

Turn the bias facing to the underside so the seam is at least 1/8 inch above the fold of the hem. Baste to position close to the fold and near the top of the facing. Fasten with blind hemming stitches or slip stitches, catching only a thread or two of the outer fabric (b).

BIAS FACING. Used in place of a regular shaped facing. In sheer fabrics a shaped facing shows through to the right side because of its depth. In bulky or scratchy fabrics, self-fabric facings may be too heavy or too uncomfortable. A bias facing is preferable in both cases.

Cut a strip of bias of some lightweight material. It should be equal in length to the length of the edge to be faced plus 2 inches for ease and finishing. Make it twice the desired finished width plus two seam allowances. The finished width of bias facing ranges from 1/2 inch to 1 inch.

Fold the strip lengthwise. This will provide a finished edge as well as a little more body (in lieu of an interfacing). If the edge to be faced is a curved one, shape the facing to conform to its shape. Be sure to keep both raw edges even and the strip an even depth throughout.

Pin and/or baste the folded bias strip on the right side of the garment, with raw edges aligned. Start at the center and work toward each end. Trim the excess facing at the ends but be sure to leave enough for a turned-under finish at a closure or for joining ends of a continuous facing.

Treatment of Ends of Facing. If the facing is a continuous one, join its ends on straight grain and press the seam allowances open.

When a closure is involved, complete the closure before applying the bias facing. Handle like bias binding at a visible edge (q.v.).

When this type of facing is used for an armhole edge, either treat it as a continuous facing or turn under one of the ends, lap it over the other, and slip-stitch.

To Apply the Facing. Machine-stitch the facing to the garment (a). Trim and grade the seam allowances, making those of the garment widest. Clip them to the stitching on all curved edges. Extend the facing up away from the garment and press the seam line (b). Finish the ends of the facing as necessary.

Turn the facing to the inside, bringing the joining seam to the underside. Press

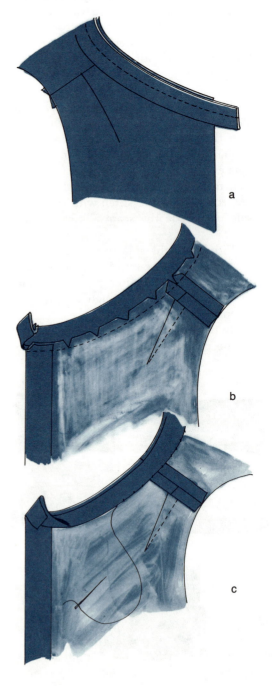

a

b

c

and pin to position. Slip-stitch invisibly through the fold of the facing (c).

BIAS FINISH FOR A FLAT COLLAR.

This type of finish produces a smooth roll. The seam allowances at the neckline are turned down into the garment rather than turned up into the collar as would be necessary without the bias finish. This is also a practical neckline treatment for children's clothing. It's much easier to handle than a tiny facing on a small size.

Use commercial bias binding or make your own of the collar fabric. Cut a strip of it to fit the neckline plus a 1/4-inch turn-under at each end. Construct the collar (q.v.) and baste it to the garment. Place the right side of the binding against the collar. Pin or baste it to the neckline seam. Start at center front or back and work toward the opening at each end. Stitch through all thicknesses along the neckline seam. Trim, grade, and clip the neckline seam allowances (a). Turn the binding well to the inside of the garment and pin. Fold under the ends. Hem or slip-stitch the binding to the garment (b). Though the hand stitching is done below the neckline, it will not be visible because the collar will cover it.

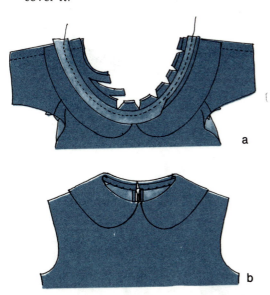

a

b

BIAS FITTING. For natural shaping, nothing is better than bias. Of itself, it molds, it clings, it moves, it defines. Its use is emi-

nently suited for slim-hipped, flat-chested types. For undeveloped figures, bias provides sufficient shaping without the use of darts and shaping seams. On developed figures, such designs at best provide inadequate shaping and at worst can be downright disastrous.

Dress (a) depends for its fit on the bias cut. It can be shaped at all its seams but the amount of fitting in these places is minimal. There is no provision for shaping in the bust area. Should one wish to use this design for a full-bosomed figure, one would have to create a bodice-front dart.

Dress (b) depends on its bias bodice for fit—an interesting design for one who needs little shaping.

In dress (c), the unrestricted movement characteristic of bias will reveal every body curve even in a semifitted dress like

a

b

c

d

You can expect bias-cut garments to stretch and dip on hanging out. That is the nature of bias and there is nothing you can do to prevent it. However, you can minimize this problem by letting the fabric sections hang out after cutting and before stitching. (You will find that a dart stitched before the fabric is stabilized will drop from the desired position in the settling process.) The amount of time it takes to stabilize a bias-cut fabric depends on the size and heaviness of the piece. To prevent stretching after the garment is completed, store it flat.

Bias cut calls for a complete pattern. (See BIAS LAYOUT.) It takes considerably more material. It requires expertise in cutting, stitching, pressing, and fitting. All this makes for limited use despite the drapability of bias, its ease of movement, its effortless shaping, its gracefulness.

BIAS-FOLD COLLARS. Bias strips of material, cut to the correct length and width and folded lengthwise, may be shaped into a variety of collars.

this one. To counteract this, bias clothes should be fitted with more than usual ease, as in dress (d).

Because bias can be so beautifully molded and shaped to fit, it is often used for sleeves and collars. When a sleeve is cut on the bias, it is comparatively easy to block into a cap for setting. Bias sleeves have a wonderful movability. They "give" with every motion of the arm.

A standing or turtleneck collar can be cut on the bias to give shape around the neck. The undercollar of the classic, tailored, set-on, notched collar is always cut on the bias. This makes it possible to pad-stitch and block the collar into a neck shape.

When a cowl or other drapery is part of a design, the fabric must be cut on the bias to provide the drape, either in its entirety, or confined to the area of the cowl.

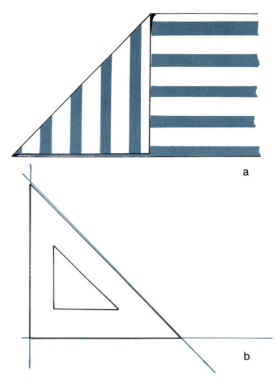

a

b

The raw edges are attached to the neck-line as for a flat collar (q.v.). The folded edge is the outer edge. Because of the bias cut, the outer edge can be manipulated to fit wherever the band falls on the body.

When attaching the bias-fold collar to the neckline, a higher stand may be pro-duced by stretching the neck edge to fit the neckline. A flatter collar may be ob-tained by easing the fullness of the collar neckline into that of the garment. Pre-shaping makes it easier to set and stitch the collar to the neckline.

BIAS FUNNEL COLLAR. This is really a bias turnover collar (q.v.) worn high with-out rolling over on itself.

BIAS GRAIN ESTABLISHED. There are two ways in which the grain can be estab-lished.

Bring the lengthwise grain to meet the crosswise grain. The fold is the bias (a). Or lay one straight edge of a 45° triangle along the lengthwise grain, the other edge of the triangle along the crosswise grain. Draw a line along the hypotenuse (b). This is the bias grain.

BIAS LAYOUT. Because of the stretchability of a bias fold, it is difficult to cut half a pattern on a fold as in the usual pattern layout. Therefore patterns for bias designs are generally complete patterns and pieces must be cut individually. The layout is on a single thickness of fabric opened right side up to a full width. *See* OPEN SINGLE LAY-OUT.

There is a difficulty with this arrange-ment, too. Even in a balanced weave, the lengthwise and crosswise grains may differ

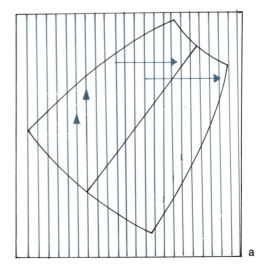

a

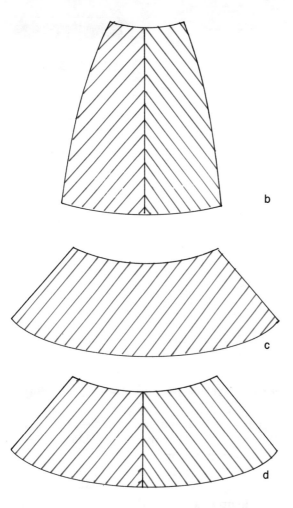

b

c

d

to some extent in appearance and in hanging qualities. Where the bias falls in the center of a complete section, the lengthwise grain is directed to one side of the body, the crosswise grain to the other (a). This is the problem with a one-piece bias collar (c).

Wherever feasible, a center straight seam rather than a center straight fold or a single pattern section makes it possible to place the pattern pieces so that the grain is in the same position on both left and right sides (b and d). A duplicate second pattern piece is helpful for this type of layout. *See* DIAGONAL PRINTS AND WEAVES (q.v.).

BIAS SASHES. Single- or double-thickness sashes cut on the bias wrap snugly around the waistline, fit well, and fall gracefully from waist to hem. Finish the edge of sin-

gle-thickness sashes with a hand-rolled hem (q.v.).

BIAS SEAMS. Allow bias-cut garments to hang out so the fabric settles into wearing position before fitting and permanent stitching. Recommended: at least overnight, up to a week.

Stitching a Bias-to-Bias Edge. Hand-baste the seam with loose stitches. Fasten the ends with loose backstitches, leaving several inches of thread. This permits the fabric to slip along the loose thread as it hangs out.

Loosen the top tension slightly. Use a shorter-than-usual stitch. For instance, if the fabric requires 10 stitches to the inch, use 15. Stretch the fabric slightly while stitching. These adjustments provide more elasticity and more thread to accommodate the stretch of the bias.

Or pin a strip of tissue paper along the seam line to stabilize it. With the tissue on top, stitch through both paper and fabric. When the seam is completed, tear away the paper.

Stitching a Bias-to-Straight Edge. With the bias on top, pin it to the straight edge, easing as necessary. Place the pins at right angles to the seam every few inches or as close as necessary to ease in the fullness of the bias. Pins give better control of the fabric and hold it more securely than basting.

With the straight edge on top, machine-stitch, removing the pins as you go along.

BIAS STRIPS. The flexibility of bias strips makes it possible to use them in many different ways—for tubing, binding, cording, trimming, button loops, frogs, or wherever some curviness is required of a strip or band of fabric.

To make the strips, start with a rectangle of fabric on straight grain and establish the true grain. *See* BIAS GRAIN ESTABLISHED.

Ideally, there should be one strip of bias long enough for the purpose. On firm, easily handled fabrics, rule off the strips to the desired width parallel to the bias and cut. For sheer or slippery fabric, rule bias lines on paper and match to the right-angled edges of the fabric. Place opaque fabric against the unlined side and pin. Place sheer or transparent fabric over the lined side and pin. Baste fabric to paper between the marked lines. Cut through both paper and fabric along the lines. It is helpful to leave the fabric on the paper until ready for use.

Often it is not possible to get a strip of bias of the necessary length, so piecing becomes necessary. Piecing may be done by joining individual strips (Method 1) or by continuous pieced strips (Method 2).

METHOD 1. INDIVIDUAL STRIPS JOINED

This is a good method when there is sufficient material to provide long strips with few joinings. When determining the length of the strips, plan the joinings in an inconspicuous place. So the joining will not hinder the flexibility of the strips, join them generally on the lengthwise grain. In fabrics with prominent crosswise ribs, such as faille, make the joining on the crosswise grain. Whether lengthwise or crosswise, all joinings should be on the same grain. To make them less noticeable, match any prominent weave, stripe, or design.

To Join the Strips. With right sides together, offset the width of the joining seam and stitch in a 1/4-inch seam (a). Press the seam allowances open.

If it is impossible to locate the joining accurately before attaching it to the garment, make it when you reach an appropriate place. Stop the stitching slightly before reaching the place of joining. Open out the strip. Join on straight grain and trim the excess fabric. Press the seam allowances open, then continue stitching.

For a lapped joining, stitch both lengths to within a short distance of the overlap. Fold the overlap to the inside on straight grain. Trim, leaving a 1/4-inch seam allowance. Trim the other end on straight grain so both raw edges will align. Pin or baste the overlap to position. Stitch across the joinings (b). If desired, the joining may be slip-stitched.

METHOD 2. CONTINUOUS PIECED STRIPS

This is the recommended method when a limited amount of suitable material is available. Measure a bias rectangle several times the width of the strip you want. Join the shorter ends, right sides together, with one strip width extending beyond the edge at each side (c). Stitch in a 1/4-inch seam. Press it open. Begin cutting on the marked line at one end and continue the cutting in a spiral (d).

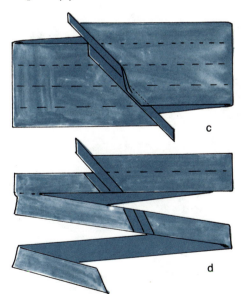

c

d

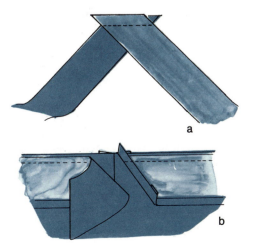

a

b

As you can see, this method saves the many individual joinings of small strips.

BIAS TAPES. Bias strips of lightweight fabrics in a variety of widths and colors with prefolded edges are commercially available. They are suitable for curved hems, facings, or casings where there is not enough self-fabric or when the self-fabric is so heavy that the casing would be bulky.

BIAS TUCKS. Mark the fold line of each tuck with thread tracing. Proceed as for tucks on lengthwise grain (q.v.), but handle more carefully because of the bias stretch.

BIAS TURNOVER COLLAR. You know this collar by its more familiar name: turtleneck. It is a one-piece standing collar cut on the bias and rolled or folded over to cover the neck seam.

Cut the interfacing on the bias without seam allowances and extending 5/8 inch

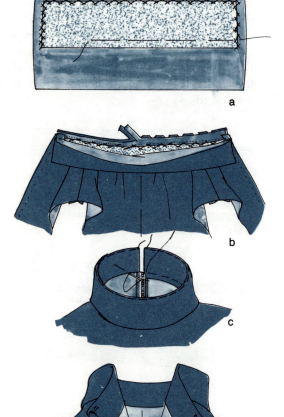

beyond the fold line of the collar. Apply the interfacing to the collar with catch stitching on all seam lines and long permanent basting along the fold line (a).

Fold the collar right sides together and stitch across the ends. Trim and grade the seam allowances. Press them open. Snip diagonally across the corner. Turn and press the ends of the collar only. Do not press the fold line.

Pin or baste the interfaced collar edge to the neckline of the garment. Stitch, trim, grade, clip as necessary (b). Press the seam allowances toward the collar. Lap the remaining open edge in place, matching seam lines. Baste loosely.

Try on the garment to establish the roll and fit of the collar. Make sure that the folded edge covers the neck seam. Stretch slightly to make it fit. Pin, then thread-trace (q.v.) the roll line of the collar through all layers.

Remove the loose basting at the neck seam. Clip, turn under the raw edge to cover the seam, and slip-stitch (c). For bulky fabrics, trim the seam allowance of the raw edge and overcast by hand or by machine. Attach the loose edge to the collar neckline.

Fold the collar to its wearing position. Sew hooks and eyes to the ends for a fastening (d).

BIAS UNDERCOLLAR. On tailored collars, the burden of fitting and shaping falls on the undercollar. The upper collar is just so much decoration. Because the molding and blocking can best be done on the bias, the undercollar and its interfacing are generally cut on the bias. *See* BIAS LAYOUT.

BIAS WAISTBAND. A bias waistband is valuable not only for design interest but because its moldability makes it settle comfortably into the natural indentation of the waist. The length of the waistband should be less than the actual waist measurement because of the bias stretch. The heavier the fabric and/or the fuller the skirt, the more the pull on the waistband and the more the bias will stretch.

To compensate for this, subtract 1 inch

from the waist measurement. If the fabric is very heavy or the garment very full, subtract a little more. Adjust the amount to fit. Because the stretch in length reduces the width, make the waistband a little wider than a straight band. Since it will conform to the shape of the waistline area, its extra width is no problem. In all other respects, the bias waistband is handled like the straight-and-narrow waistband (q.v.).

BLANKET STITCH. Originally used to bind the raw edges of blankets to prevent raveling. It is now used as an edge finish, as well as for a variety of hand-finishing details.

Work from left to right with the edge of the fabric toward you. Anchor the thread at the left. Insert the needle to the right the desired distance above the edge and from the anchoring stitch. Bring the needle out from under the edge and at right angles to it, looping the thread under its point. Draw up the thread and repeat. Keep the stitches uniform in size, spacing, and tension.

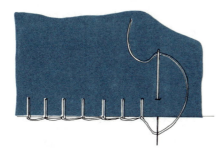

BLANKET-STITCH BAR TACK. This is used as a reinforcement at points of strain: for instance, at the ends of a hand-worked buttonhole.

Fasten the thread and bring it to the

right side. Take two or three foundation stitches (long threads) the length of the bar tack. Catching the fabric beneath, work closely spaced blanket stitches over the threads to cover them.

BLANKET-STITCH EYE. *See* THREAD EYE. Use matching double thread or a single strand of buttonhole twist or heavy-duty thread.

Take two or three foundation stitches (long threads) the desired length of a straight eye or the predetermined depth of a round eye (a). *See* HOOK AND EYE. Secure each end with tiny backstitches. With the same thread, work closely spaced blanket stitches over the entire length of the foundation stitches (b). Keep straight-eye foundation threads taut; they have a tendency to stretch in working.

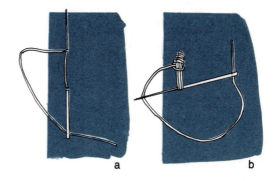

a   b

BLANKET - STITCH TACK. A blanket-stitch tack is used to join two layers of fabric: for instance, a facing and a garment front. It is a widely spaced (1- to 2-inch intervals) series of blanket stitches worked from left to right between two garment sections. Be sure to allow slack between the stitches.

BLIND CATCH STITCH. This stitch is made inside the garment in a series of small, invisible (only one thread of fabric lifted), loose backstitches. Work from left to right, alternating between the garment and the hem or facing. The slack between the stitches provides stretchability and prevents a hard, rigid, quilted look.

Because it is more secure than the blind hemming stitch (q.v.), which also alternates between hem and garment, it is more frequently used in tailoring, which generally uses firmer, heavier fabrics. *See* TAILOR'S HEM.

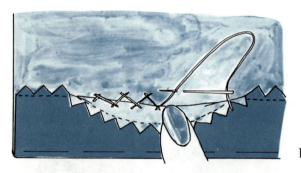

BLIND HEM. *See* BLIND-STITCHED HEM.

BLIND HEMMING STITCH (RUNNING HEMMING STITCH).

By Hand. A series of tiny, invisible, loose basting stitches running from right to left, picking up one thread of the garment, then one of the hem, alternating between the two (a).

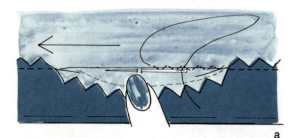

a

By Machine. A zigzag stitch pattern either built into the sewing machine or produced by use of a cam, a blind hemming guide, or a blind stitch foot. The stitch consists of 4 to 6 straight stitches followed by a single zigzag stitch (b) or several very narrow zigzag stitches followed by a wider zigzag stitch (c). Best results for the correct placement of the stitches are obtained with the use of a blind hemming guide or a blind stitch foot.

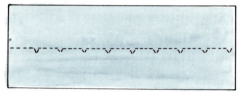

b

c

BLINDSTITCH. A hand or machine stitch worked inside the garment that is invisible (or nearly so) on the right side, used extensively for hemming or finishing.

There are several hand stitches used in this way: the blind hemming stitch, the slip stitch, the blind catch stitch. *(See listing for each.)* Machine blindstitching is done with a zigzag pattern. *See* BLIND HEMMING STITCH: BY MACHINE.

BLINDSTITCHED HEM.

By Hand. Finish the hem edge in any way desired or appropriate for the fabric and design. *See* EDGE FINISHES.

Fold back the edge of the hem toward the hemline to a depth of about 1/8 to 1/4 inch. Fold back the garment against itself. This places the folds of hem and garment opposite each other (a). Using a single strand of matching thread, lift one thread of the garment, then one of the hem, alternating between the two. Use either a blind hemming stitch (b) or a blind catch stitch (c). Fold back hem and garment to wearing position.

You'll be happy to learn that it's actually preferable to put up a hem with the least

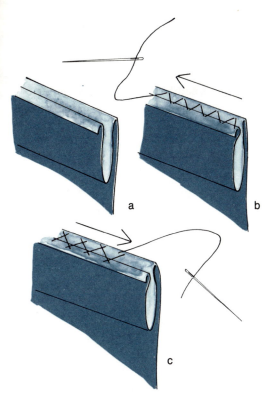

number of stitches that will hold it securely.

By Machine. This produces a strong hem for any clothing that gets hard wear. *See* BLIND HEMMING STITCH: BY MACHINE.

When needed, insert the cam or attach the blind hemming guide or blind stitch foot. Set the sewing machine for the blind

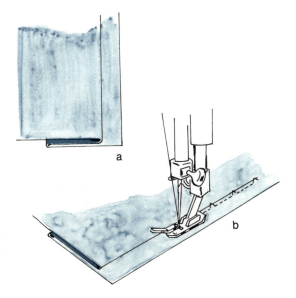

stitch pattern. Select the length and width of the stitches.

Finish the hem edge in any way desired or appropriate for the fabric and design. Turn up the hem and baste to position ¼ inch from the hem edge.

With the wrong side up, turn the hem under the garment along the line of basting, producing a soft fold and exposing the ¼-inch extension of the hem edge (a). Position the garment over the feed so the straight stitches (or narrow zigzag stitches) fall on the hem and the larger zigzag stitches pierce only one or two threads of the fold.

BLIND TUCKS. A series of tucks in which the fold of one comes to the stitching line of the next or overlaps it. *See* TUCKS.

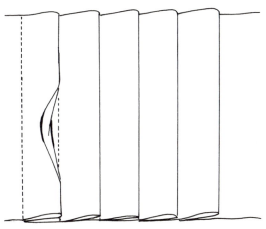

BLOCK. A mold, form, or rounded pad over which materials are shaped by steaming. *See* PRESSING EQUIPMENT.

BLOCKING. A method of molding or shaping by steam over an appropriately rounded press pad all curved areas of a garment that go over and around some part of the body (which is just about everywhere) and those straight pieces (like collars) destined to fit curved areas. *See* PRESSING.

BLOCK (MASTER) PATTERN. All patterns are created from a "staple," sometimes called a block, master, foundation, or basic pattern. This is drafted to body measurements plus ease and becomes the basis of all flat pattern designs.

BLOUSE HEM. If the blouse is a *tuck-in,* the hem must be as flat and unobtrusive as possible—a single-layer hem. On fabrics that will not fray, a pinked (or scalloped) and stitched edge is sufficient. On fabrics that tend to ravel, turn under the raw edge and stitch close to the fold. Make a second row of stitching close to the first. Trim excess fabric.

If the blouse is an *overblouse,* make a 1- to 1½-inch hand- or machine-stitched turned-up hem (q.v.).

BLOUSON. A type of fullness that creates the effect of a blouse held in at the waist by gathering, elastic, drawstring, a casing, or a fitted band. In some instances, the length and width of the fullness are held in place by a fitted bodice lining acting as a stay. It is made separately and is caught together with the blouson in a seam.

BLUNTING A CORNER. Only in very sheer materials can one get a sharp corner in an enclosed seam by stitching a 90° angle. In all other weights of fabric the sharpest corners obtainable result when they are blunted.

In lightweight fabrics, take 1 stitch diagonally across the corner (a); in medium-weight fabrics, 2 stitches (b); in heavy fabrics, 3 or more stitches (c). This technique is applicable in collars, cuffs, lapels, flaps, welts, and the like.

BLUNTING A POINT. Make a row of stitching that tapers to a point, take 1 stitch across the point, continue with the second row of stitching. This provides room for turning the fabric to the underside when it has been slashed.

BODICE TUCK. A practical device for providing extra bodice length for future growth (useful when making children's wear).

On the bodice pattern, draw a slash line at right angles to the center front. Slash on this line and spread the pattern 1½ inches. Insert paper in the spread area and Scotch-tape (a). Cut the bodice from this altered pattern.

On the wrong side of the cut-out bodice, mark the fold line of the tuck ¾ inch above the waistline seam (b). After the skirt has been stitched to the bodice, form the tuck at the waistline and press. Baste through the waist seam and the tucked bodice. Machine-stitch just below the waist seam line, using a large, easily removed stitch. Press the tuck and the seam allowance toward the bodice (c). Insert the zipper when there is one.

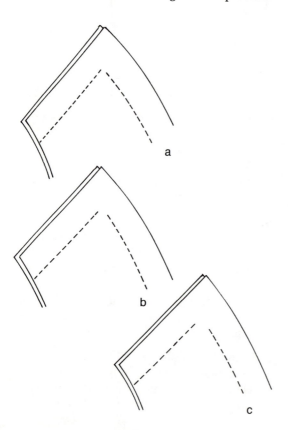

a

b

c

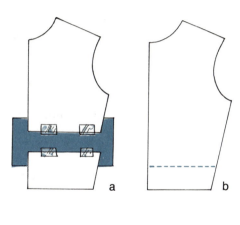

a   b

c

To release the tuck: remove the zipper from a point above the tuck to the bottom of the placket. Open out the tuck and press. Stitch the skirt seam, leaving a placket opening to accommodate the length of the zipper. Reinsert the lower portion of the zipper.

BODY MEASUREMENTS. Two sets of body measurements are needed. One is to help you select the correct size and figure type of pattern (starred below). The other set is needed to make pattern corrections for fit. Add ease (q.v.) to body measurements and compare the total with the pattern measurements.

You will need a tape measure, enough string to encircle the waist, and someone to do the measuring.

BODY MEASUREMENT CHART: CHILDREN

For small children and girls, the best measurements are taken over undergarments or leotards. For boys, measurements are taken over an undershirt and lightweight trousers. The same would be true for girls when measuring for pants.

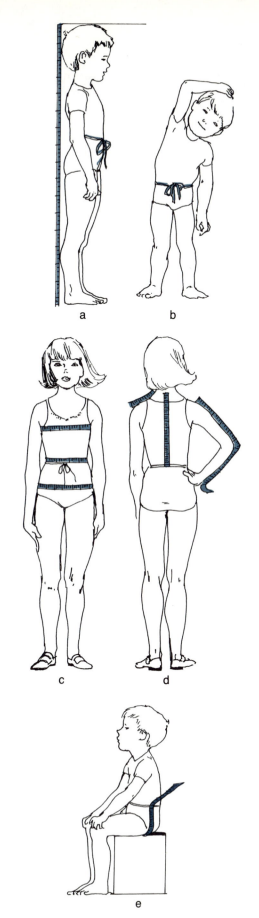

Body Measurement Chart—Children

Pattern corrections (q.v.) for children are done in the same way as for adults. The starred measurements are those that appear on patterns.

Weight (for babies).

Height (a): Stand the child, without shoes, with back against the wall. Place a ruler on top of the head at right angles to the wall. Mark where it touches the wall. Measure from mark to floor.

Tie a heavy string around the child's natural indentation at the waist. If this is hard to determine, have the child bend sideways. The string will settle into whatever indentation there is (b).

Waist: Take the waist measurement (c). A boy's waistline can also be measured at the waistline seam of trousers that have settled into wearing position.

Breast (girls) or *Chest* (boys): Measure under the arms over the fullest part of the chest in front, just under the shoulder blades in back (c).

Hips: Measure around the fullest part of the buttocks (c).

Back Waist Length: Measure from the prominent bone at the back of the neck to the waistline string (d). For boys, this could be the trouser waistline seam instead.

Front Waist Length: Taken from the hollow between the collarbones to the waistline string or trouser waistline seam. For shirts, add 1½ to 2 inches for a tuck-in allowance.

Shoulder Length: Measure from the base of the neck to the socket bone at the shoulder (d). To locate the base of the neck, have child shrug shoulders.

Arm Length: With arm bent, measure from the socket bone at the shoulder around the bent elbow to the wrist (d).

Shirt Sleeve Length for Boys. See BODY MEASUREMENT CHART: MEN AND TEEN/BOYS.

Neck: Girls—taken around the base of the neck from the socket (prominent) bone in back to the hollow between the collarbones in front. *Boys*—around the neck at the Adam's apple plus ease *(see* BODY MEASUREMENT CHART).

Measurements for Pants

Crotch Depth: Seat the child on a firm chair with feet flat on the floor. Measure from the waistline string to the chair seat (e). Allow ease. Or measure a pair of pants that fit the child well.

Inseam: Measure a pair of pants that fit well from the crotch seam to the hem on the inside seam.

Outseam: Measure a pair of pants that fit well from the waist seam to the hem on the outside seam.

Finished Length of Pants and Trousers: The back length comes to the top of the heel; the front, to the top of the instep. Or make the pants the desired length.

Finished Length of Skirt: For a small girl, the skirt comes midway between the hip and knee. As the child grows older, the skirt is set at a fashionable length.

BODY MEASUREMENT CHART: MEN AND TEEN/BOYS

Take the measurements over a thin shirt and pants with no belt. Stand in a natural posture.

The starred measurements below are those that appear on patterns and determine pattern size. The other measurements are needed when making pattern corrections for fit (q.v.). Tie a heavy string around the waist or where one would like the waistline to be. Clue: where one likes to wear one's trousers.

Overall Height: Without shoes, stand with back against the wall. Place a ruler on top of the head at right angles to the wall. Mark where it touches the wall. Measure from mark to floor.

Neck: Measure around the neck at the Adam's apple (a). Add ½ inch for ease.

Chest: Measure around the fullest part of the chest (a).

Waist: Measure around the natural waistline or where the string is positioned (a).

Hip or Seat: Measure around the fullest part of the hips. Note how far below the waistline this measurement is. This is the *hip depth* (a).

Back Waist Length (b): Measure from the

Body Measurement Chart—Men and Teen Boys

prominent bone at the back of the neck to the back waistline. (Bend the head forward to locate the socket bone.)

Front Waist Length (c): Measure from the base of the neck at the shoulder to the front waistline. (Shrug the shoulders to locate the base of the neck.)

Shoulder Length (c): Measure from the base of the neck to the top of the arm (shoulder socket bone).

Back Width (b): Measure straight across the back over the shoulder blades from arm to arm. If wearing a shirt that fits well, take this measurement from sleeve armhole seam to sleeve armhole seam.

Arm Measurements

Length measurements are taken with the arm bent at a right angle.

Shirt Sleeve Length (b): Measure from the prominent bone at the back of the neck along the shoulder, around the bent elbow, to the wristbone.

Overall Arm Length: Measure from shoulder socket bone, around the bent elbow, to the wristbone. With the tape measure in this position, note the measurement from *shoulder to elbow* and from *elbow to wristbone* (c).

Circumference Measurements (c): Measure the *biceps* around the fullest part of the arm. Measure the *wrist* at the bone.

Measurements Needed for Pants

In addition to the waist and hip measurements already taken, measure the following.

High Hip Measurement (c): This measurement is taken at the top of the hipbones.

Inseam (b): Measure from the crotch seam to the hem on the inside seam of well-fitted pants.

Outseam (b): Measure from the waistline to the hem on the side seam of well-fitted pants.

Thigh (c): Measure the fullest part of the thigh just under the crotch.

Knee (c): With knee bent, measure around the knee.

Crotch Depth: See CROTCH MEASUREMENTS or measure the crotch seam of a pair of comfortable pants.

BODY MEASUREMENT CHART: WOMEN AND MISSES

The best measurements are taken over a slip and/or bra and girdle if you wear them. Length measurements for figure type are taken without shoes. Circumference measurements are snug but not tight.

The starred measurements below are those that appear on patterns and determine the size and type of pattern. The other measurements are needed when making pattern corrections (q.v.). Tie a heavy string around the waist or where you would like the waistline to be.

Overall Height: Measure from the top of the head (not the hairdo) to the floor (a).

Back Waist Length: Measure from the socket bone to the waistline string (a). (To locate the socket bone, bend your head forward. The socket bone is the prominent bone on which the head is hinged.)

High Bust: Bring the tape measure around the body directly under the arms (b).

Bust: Bring the tape measure around the body across the fullest part of the bust, slightly raised in back (b). Measure the distance this line is above the waist. It will locate the bust point height (apex of the bust) and will determine the length of the waistline darts.

Waist: Measure in the hollow of the waist or where you would like the waistline to be—slightly above or below the natural waistline (b).

Hips: Measure around the fullest part (b). Note the distance from the waistline. This is the hip depth and will help determine the length of skirt and pants darts.

Biceps: Measure around the heaviest part of the upper arm. Usually this is about midway between the shoulder and the elbow.

Elbow: With arm bent, measure around the elbow.

Wrist: Measure around the wristbone.

Knuckles: Measure around the fullest

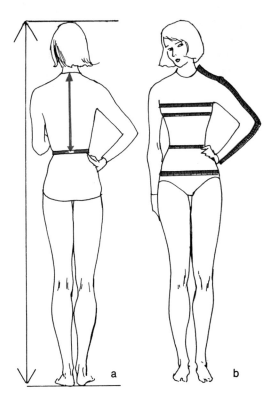

a   b

Pants Measurements

part of the hand as you would slip the hand through a sleeve.

Overarm Length: With arm bent, measure from the shoulder socket to the elbow, then to the wrist at the little finger position (b). While the tape is still in position, note the shoulder-to-elbow measurement and the elbow-to-wrist measurement. This will locate the position for the elbow dart.

Shoulder Width: Measure from the base of the neck to the socket bone (b). Shrug the shoulders to locate the base of the neck.

Pants Measurements

Pants length is best determined while wearing shoes. Use the same waist and hip measurements as above. You will need the additional measurements below.

Outseam: Measure the length of the side seam from the waistline to the top of the shoe heel or to the desired length.

Inseam: Measure from the crotch depth to the top of the shoe heel (or the desired length) on the inside of the leg.

Thigh: Measure at the fullest part of the upper leg. Note how far below the waistline you are taking this measurement.

For fitted styles, you may need the measurements for the *knee* (taken around bent knee), the *calf,* and the *ankle.* Measure around each.

To determine the *crotch depth* and *full crotch length, see* CROTCH MEASUREMENTS.

For all body measurements, it is a good idea to date them and take new ones from time to time. Small figure changes creep up unnoticed even when weight remains stable. This could affect the size, perhaps even the figure type, and of course the necessary pattern alterations.

BONDED AND LAMINATED FABRICS. These terms are often used interchangeably, though there is a difference. What they have in common is that both are made of two or more layers of fabric permanently joined by adhesive or heat-setting to form a bond.

In *bonded fabrics,* almost any fabric can be used as a face fabric. The backing or lining is usually acetate tricot or loosely woven cotton.

In *laminated fabrics,* almost any face fabric is bonded to a thin layer of chemical foam. Sometimes a third layer of lining material is bonded to the underside of the foam to protect it. If it is not already so covered, a lining should be added to the garment for protection.

While the appearance of both bonded and laminated fabrics may still be that of the original face fabric, the new fabric performs like its backing. This has some advantages and some limitations.

Advantages: Stability, body, opaqueness, reinforcement. Garments are speedy to sew, for usually only a single cutting and sewing of a simple pattern is required. There is very little fitting and none of the handwork or more complex techniques of dressmaking or tailoring. In the case of the laminates, there is the further advantage of warmth without weight and insulation against the weather. Further, the resilience of the foam makes it uncrushable.

Limitations: Largely style. Choose simple, unfitted designs with few pattern pieces, few darts and seams, few details—no gathering, easing, draping, pleating, or circularity. *See* BONDED FABRIC: CONSTRUCTION *and* LAMINATED FABRIC: CONSTRUCTION.

BONDED FABRIC: CONSTRUCTION. *See also* BONDED AND LAMINATED FABRICS.

Trim away the pattern tissue at the cutting line. (It is easier to cut beside the line rather than through it.) Straighten the grain on the face of the fabric by following one rib of a knit or a lengthwise thread of a woven material. Square off the crosswise grain with any 90° angle.

Fold the fabric with the right side outside so the grain line is clearly visible. Place pins parallel to the seam line. Cut as you would any other fabric.

Mark with tailor's tacks. Interface with preshrunk lightweight material for dresses and hair canvas for suits and coats. Hand-baste all seams and darts to prevent slipping while machine-stitching. Don't pull the fabric as it is being fed into the machine. Let it ease through.

For stitching, use a fine machine needle and silk, mercerized, or synthetic thread. Regulate the tension for the fabric. Use medium pressure and 10 to 12 stitches to the inch.

Blunt all corners. Make welt, flat fell, or double topstitched seams. Slash all darts, grade all seams, eliminate bulk wherever possible. Stay all crosswise, curved, and angled seams with stay stitching and/or seam binding to prevent stretching. Steam-press all darts and seams on the wrong side, using a press cloth, moistened if necessary.

Reinforce all areas to be slashed, such as buttonholes and pockets, with iron-on or lightweight interfacing. Make bound or machine-worked buttonholes. Make a French or tailor's hem. *(See the listing for each of the techniques mentioned above.)*

BONING. *See* FEATHERBONING.

BORDER PRINT. One whose design is printed along or parallel to one or both selvages.

There are many design possibilities for use of a border print. The obvious one is at the hem. It can also be used at the wrist, as a ruffle, for a strapless bodice, collar, cuffs, patch pockets, peplum, apron effect, and other interesting placements. Nor need it always be used horizontally. A border print can be quite effective worked either vertically or diagonally.

Easiest to use is a pattern designed for a border print. Buy the suggested yardage. If you are going to be innovative about your use of the border design, you had best make a trial layout to determine just how much fabric you will need.

Since the border can be used only in a straight line, avoid A-line, flared, or circular designs. If you use a pattern with slightly curved lines, you will have to straighten them.

If you plan to use the border at a hem, the length of the garment will have to be predetermined. It can be only as long as the width of the fabric, but it can be seamed where necessary. Wherever possible, match the motifs at the seams.

BOUCLÉ. A woven or knitted fabric made of bouclé yarns. It has a curly, nubby, looped, or knotted surface and a springy hand.

Since this is a directional fabric, use a "With Nap" layout. Thread, needle, ten-

Border Print Designs

sion, and pressure are dictated by the texture of the fabric. To prevent the presser foot from catching on the loops of the fabric, use strips of tissue paper over it, directly under the presser foot. Steam-press from the wrong side with the right side of the material against a strip of self-fabric or any other raised-surface material. Use a very light touch.

Facings of smooth, silky fabric are more comfortable and less bulky. Interfacing, when used, depends on the style of the garment and the weight of the fabric.

BOUFFANT. A puffed-out design usually for a skirt or sleeve. Fabrics firm enough to sustain the puff are best to use. When soft materials are used, they need the support of a crisp underlining (q.v.) or layers of crisp fabric (such as petticoats under a skirt).

To achieve the bouffant effect, gather, lay in pleats, or stitch darts to fit the unfull bodice. A good way to control a great deal of fullness is to lay the fabric in deep pleats first, then gather the pleated edge.

BOUND BACK HIP TROUSER POCKET. A double-welt bound pocket with topstitching in the grooves formed by the welt seams as in the inside bound pocket (q.v.). This pocket is easier to construct if sewn before the back trouser sections are joined.

If there is only one back hip pocket, place it on the left trouser back, 3½ inches below the waistband for easy accessibility. It may be secured by a buttonhole and button (made when the pocket is completed) or by a buttoned tab. (See POCKET TAB.)

Cut narrow bindings and a strip of pocket facing from the trouser fabric. Cut the pocketing long enough so the under pocket folds up and extends to the waistline.

Stitch the facing to position on the right side of the under pocket (a). Turn in ⅛-inch seam allowances on the long edges of the pocketing and press. Stitch close to the fold. Baste the pocket to position on the

wrong side of the trouser back (b). Wrong sides of both are together.

On the right side, construct the bound pocket (q.v.) through both thicknesses—trouser and pocketing (c). Topstitch in the grooves formed by the welt seams (d).

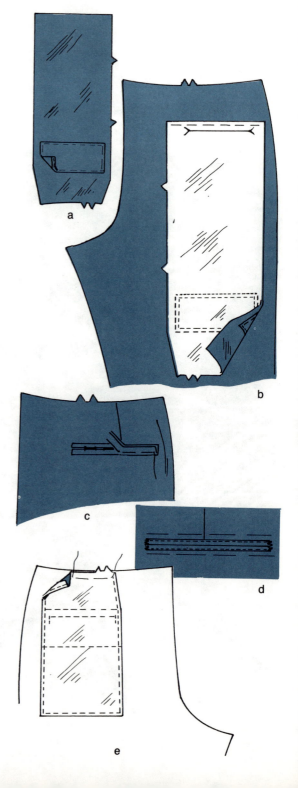

Turn up the pocket to position so the facing is directly behind the pocket opening and the top of the pocket extends to the waistline. Baste along the waistline (e). Make a second line of machine stitching joining the pocket along the sides and bottom 1/8 inch from the first stitching. Include the top of the pocket when the waistband is attached.

BOUND BUTTONHOLE. While bound buttonholes do take time and a degree of skill, their presence on a garment lifts it out of the realm of the ordinary. Their attractiveness amply repays the sewer for the time and effort.

There are a number of ways to make a bound buttonhole. Choose the one that will work best on your material and that you feel most comfortable in handling. All methods are acceptable if well done.

Bound buttonholes are made on the right side of the garment and turned to the inside. Therefore, markings must be made on the right side. Thread tracing (q.v.) is safest.

Bound buttonholes are always made on the garment *before* the facing is turned back or attached. The facing is finished separately for the underside of the buttonhole.

When making a series of buttonholes, the work is quicker and more accurate if you do the same operation on each buttonhole before going on to the next step, rather than completing one buttonhole at a time.

Match any stripes, checks, or plaids of the binding to the area in which the buttonholes are located. The binding may be cut on the bias to avoid matching if this is consistent with the design of the garment.

BOUND BUTTONHOLE: ONE-STRIP METHOD. This method works well on light- to medium-weight fabrics.

Cut a strip of garment fabric 1 inch wide by the length of the buttonhole plus 1 inch. *Optional:* To make a sturdier buttonhole, reinforce the buttonhole strip by pressing on a 1/2-inch strip of iron-on material, centered lengthwise. Or enclose a

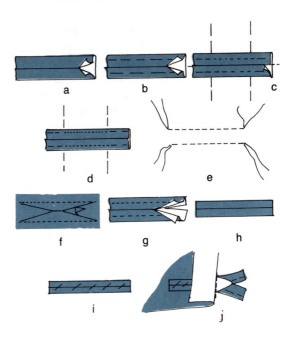

length of cording, heavy yarn, or string in each of the lengthwise folds.

Fold the strip in half lengthwise, right side outside. Crease or press along the fold. Open out and fold each lengthwise raw edge to meet the center line or crease (a). This now makes the strip 1/2 inch wide. Using matching thread, place a line of hand or machine basting slightly more than 1/8 inch in from each folded edge (b). When cording, yarn, or string is used for the reinforcement, it is enclosed by this stitching. Place the binding on the right side of the garment, centering the strip on the slash line. Baste to position through the center of the strip (c).

Starting a stitch or two beyond the cross markings, machine-stitch the binding to the garment 1/8 inch in from each folded edge (d). Do not stitch across the ends. Do not lock-stitch at the beginning and end of stitching. The use of the zipper foot rather than the regulation presser foot makes it easier to stitch corded strips or strips of heavy fabric.

Turn to the wrong side. You will see two parallel lines of machine stitching and the unsecured thread ends at each corner. Pull all four sets of thread ends through to the wrong side. Pull them back to the cross markings (e). Tie each pair in a square knot and trim close to the knots.

Working from the underside, make a *tiny snip* in the material at the center of the space between the parallel rows of stitching. Use very sharp trimming or embroidery scissors. From the small opening, slash diagonally to all four corners to the middle of each last stitch. Come as close to the stitching as you safely can (f). Be careful not to cut the binding on the other side. Note the long triangular flaps that form at each end.

Turn to the right side. Slash through the center of the binding strip without cutting the garment (g). Grasp the pair of strips at each end (one pair at a time) and very gently push them through the opening to the wrong side. The binding will assume its rightful position. Adjust the strips so the folds just meet at the center without any overlapping (h). You may have to do a little coaxing to get them into position.

On the right side of the garment, close the lips of the buttonhole with diagonal basting (i). This is very important because the basting holds the binding in place for securing the ends. Omit the basting and you end up with gaping buttonholes.

Once again, turn to the underside. Fold back the garment against itself so you can see the triangular flaps as they lie against the end of the binding. Stitch each triangle to the strip across each end of the buttonhole. Stitch close to the fold but not over it (j). Were you to stitch over the fold, you would get a tuck on the right side. Stitch too far away from it and you will find a hole at each end. Trim the excess binding to about 1/4 inch from the stitching. Remove the basting that holds the lips together.

This method of making a bound buttonhole is basic, easy, and practically foolproof. The preparation of the binding guarantees the evenness of the lips of the buttonhole. Centering the binding on the slash line automatically puts the stitching lines in the right position. The buttonhole is bound to be good.

In all honesty, however, one must admit that in very heavy or very lightweight materials it is extremely difficult to handle the tiny strips produced by the one-strip method. For such fabrics, the two-strip method (q.v.) of making bound buttonholes is preferable.

BOUND BUTTONHOLE: ORGANZA PATCH METHOD. *See* BOUND BUTTONHOLE: WINDOWPANE METHOD.

BOUND BUTTONHOLE: PATCH METHOD. In this buttonhole, a patch of garment fabric is used for a facing which is folded into an inverted pleat that forms the lips of the buttonhole. It is a method suitable for light- to medium-weight fabrics that crease well and do not ravel.

Cut a patch of garment fabric 2 inches wide and 1 inch longer than the buttonhole. With right sides together, center and pin the patch over the buttonhole placement marking on the right side of the garment (a). The rectangle for the buttonhole opening may be marked and stitched on either the patch or the wrong side of the garment. The long sides are 1/8 inch above and below the opening line. This will make the finished buttonhole 1/4 inch wide. In heavy or bulky fabrics, 3/16 inch above and below the opening line will make the finished buttonhole 3/8 inch wide. It should not be any wider than that even in heavy fabric. The ends of the buttonhole are at the exact size of the buttonhole (b).

Stitch the rectangle along each of the four sides, pivoting at the corners and finishing with several overlapped stitches. *(See* OVERLAP STITCHING.) Count the stitches for a perfect rectangle. Make a short snip in the garment and patch in the center of the space formed by the stitching and long cuts diagonally to each corner to the center of each last stitch (c).

Push the rest of the patch gently through the opening to the wrong side (d). Finger- or steam-press so the stitching is on the edge of the opening.

Fold both long sides of the facing to form the lips of the buttonhole. Crease sharply along stitching at the corners to

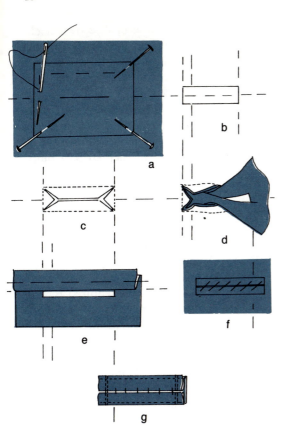

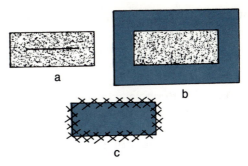

make the buttonhole in the reinforced outer fabric first before applying it. The reinforcement may be a patch of iron-on material, organza, muslin, or any other lightweight material. (An iron-on is particularly good, not only because it saves time in application but because it holds the yarns in place—a boon in loosely woven or ravelly fabrics.)

After the interfacing is applied to the garment, mark the opening of the buttonhole carefully on the in-place hair canvas. Draw, then cut out, a rectangle of the canvas 3/8 inch away from the buttonhole marking on all sides. Don't make the opening any larger than this or you will lose the benefit of the interfacing. It should be just large enough to pull the binding of the buttonhole through the opening, which you now do.

Should you (for fitting purposes) apply the hair canvas interfacing before making the buttonholes, follow this procedure. Transfer the buttonhole markings from the right side to the underside. Draw, then cut out, a rectangle of the canvas 3/8 inch away from the markings on all sides (a). Place the cut-out rectangle on new backing material as a guide. Trace around it. Draw, then cut out, a new larger rectangle, making it at least 1/4 inch larger all around for an overlap (b). Cut out the replacement material. Either insert it in the opening of the interfacing or place it on top of it. You may use the markings of the original rectangle as a placement guide. Fasten with catch stitching (c). Iron-on replacements need only be ironed on.

make them clean-cut. Each of the lips fills one half the open space and continues as a pleat beyond it. Adjust as necessary. Baste along the center of each lip (e).

On the right side, close the lips with diagonal basting (f). When the underside of the buttonhole is completed, the stitching should hold the lips of the buttonhole in place. However, for buttonholes that get hard usage, it is advisable to turn the garment back on itself, exposing the long triangular ends against the binding. Stitch through all thicknesses close to the fold (g). *See* BOUND BUTTONHOLE: ONE-STRIP METHOD.

BOUND BUTTONHOLE: REINFORCEMENT FOR THE SLASH LINE. Any area that is to be slashed should be reinforced before a cut is made in the material. With the exception of hair canvas, the interfacing or underlining can be that reinforcement. Hair canvas is too tough, too resilient, and too bulky to be incorporated into a buttonhole.

When hair canvas is the interfacing,

BOUND BUTTONHOLE: TWO-PIECE PIPED METHOD. *See* BOUND BUTTONHOLE: WINDOWPANE METHOD.

BOUND BUTTONHOLE: TWO - STRIP METHOD.

Two separate strips are necessary for each buttonhole. Make them 2 inches wide by the length of the buttonhole plus 1 inch. *Optional:* To make a sturdier buttonhole, reinforce each strip by pressing on a 1/2-inch strip of iron-on material, centered lengthwise. Or enclose a length of cording, string, or yarn in each of the lengthwise folds.

With the right side outside, fold each buttonhole strip in half lengthwise. Using matching thread, make a line of thread tracing (q.v.) slightly more than 1/8 inch from the folded edge (a).

Additional guidelines are necessary to place these larger strips in the same relative position for stitching as in the bound buttonhole: one-strip method (q.v.). Make a line of thread tracing above and below the slash line equal to the total width of the finished buttonhole (b), that is, for a 1/4-inch-wide finished buttonhole, 1/4 inch above and 1/4 inch below the slash line; for a 3/8-inch-wide buttonhole (for heavy or bulky fabric), 3/8 inch above and 3/8 inch below the slash line.

Because of the size of the strips, only one at a time is basted and stitched to the right side of the garment. Place strip no. 1 in such a position that the folded edge is against the upper marking. Baste in place (c). Stitch 1/8 inch (or 3/8 inch in heavy fabric) below the fold, starting and ending a stitch or two beyond the cross markings. The use of the zipper foot rather than the regulation presser foot makes it easier to stitch corded strips or strips of heavy fab-

ric. Fold back the binding strip over itself. Pin it securely in this position (d), revealing the rest of the buttonhole marking. Position and stitch binding strip no. 2 in the same way.

The rest of the construction for this buttonhole is the same as that for the bound buttonhole: one-strip method (q.v.). Note the wide extensions of each strip of binding on the underside of the buttonhole (e). Grade the thicknesses, making the inner thickness narrower than the outer one. Trim the ends.

BOUND BUTTONHOLE: UNDERSIDE FINISH.

Whatever method you choose to make a bound buttonhole on the right side of the garment, a finish is required for the underside, through the facing. There are several ways to do this. All methods start the same way.

After the facing has been turned to the inside, pin or baste around each buttonhole through all thicknesses (a). From the upper side, push a straight pin through each end of the buttonhole at the line of the opening. On the facing side, draw a line for the opening with pencil, tailor's chalk, or a line of basting (b).

Make certain that the opening is the same distance in from the edge on both the outside and the facing. Make sure that the length of the buttonhole is the same on both sides. Make sure there is the same distance between buttonholes. Measure!

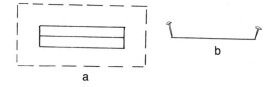

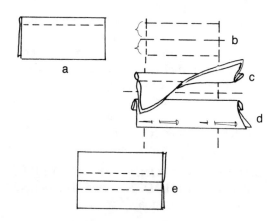

METHOD 1: EASIEST OF ALL METHODS

Slash from one end of the marking to the other (a). Turn under the raw edges of the facing to form an ellipse (b). Hem to position. In loosely woven fabrics, it is even possible to push the opening into the shape of a rectangle with the point of the needle (c). Hem quickly to prevent fraying.

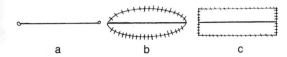

a   b   c

Method 2: A Little More Work

Make a short slash through the center of the marking and clip diagonally to each corner to a depth equal to the width of the binding (a). Turn under each of the four little flaps to form a rectangle, exposing the binding (b). With hemming stitches, fasten the rectangular opening to the stitching lines of the binding (c). Take several tiny reinforcing stitches at each corner.

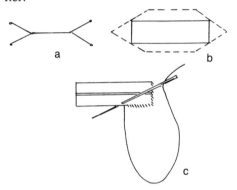

a   b

c

Method 3: Windowpane Method

By this method, a faced "windowpane" becomes the opening that reveals the buttonhole binding. The buttonhole has the same finished look on both outside and underside. It is a good method for a convertible collar style where both sides of the closing must look identical. It is also a good method for fabrics that ravel readily. It is a soul-satisfying method for those who respect perfection.

Construct the "windowpane" on the facing over the buttonhole marking. *See* BOUND BUTTONHOLE: WINDOWPANE METHOD— THE FACED OPENING.

Place the faced rectangular opening against the underside of the bound buttonhole. Slip-stitch to the stitching lines.

Method 4: Twin Buttonholes

This is a good method for heavy or tough fabrics. Make two identical bound buttonholes—one on the outer fabric, the other on the facing. The trick is to position them so accurately that they function as one buttonhole opening.

BOUND BUTTONHOLE: WINDOWPANE METHOD (ORGANZA PATCH METHOD, TWO-PIECE PIPED METHOD).

By this method, the bindings (lips of the buttonhole) are applied to a faced opening. It is a method particularly suited for bulky fabrics or those that ravel easily. Since this method provides its own reinforcement, the garment interfacing is applied after the buttonholes are made.

The Faced Opening. Cut a patch of organza or any other sheer, crisp material. (Organza is ideal for this purpose, for it is practically weightless, adding no bulk to the buttonhole.) Any color will do since it won't show if properly done, but a matching color is a safeguard and a nice touch. Make the patch 1 inch larger than the finished buttonhole on all sides.

On the right side, center the patch over the buttonhole marking. Pin it to position. Stitch the organza to the garment in a rectangle equal to the desired length and width of the finished buttonhole. Use small stitches. Start the stitching at the center of one long side, pivot at the corners, finish with overlap stitching (q.v.). Count the stitches, particularly at each end, to get a perfect rectangle. Slash through the center of the rectangle and diagonally to each corner (a).

Turn the organza to the wrong side, working it gently through the slash. Press the seam allowances and the triangles at each end away from the opening. Make sure to square the corners and that none of the organza shows from the right side. The "windowpane" is the faced rectangular opening. It is the exact size of the finished buttonhole (b).

The Bindings. For the bindings (pipings), cut two 1½-inch-wide strips of garment fabric the length of the buttonhole plus 1 inch. With right sides of the strips together, machine-baste through the center (c). Fold each strip back upon itself (d)

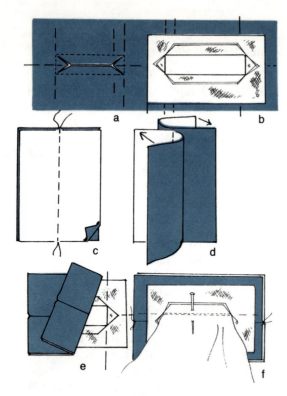

so the basting is concealed and the right sides of the fabric are exposed. Press.

Working from the right side so you can adjust the evenness of the lips, center them in the faced openings and pin to position (e).

On the wrong side, fold back the garment in turn on each of the four sides. (Remove the pins and repin as necessary.) Stitch the binding to the fabric and organza seam allowances that result from the slashing of the buttonhole opening. Make the new line of stitching a hair's width from the previous line of stitching. Use small stitches (f). Begin and end the stitching at the raw edges of the organza patch. The lines of stitching cross to form sharp corners. Trim the binding at each end to 1/4 inch. To open the buttonhole, remove the basting.

BOUND EDGES. Effective for unlined garments of loosely woven fabrics, materials that tend to ravel, and machine-washable garments. The bindings protect the fragile edges in a decorative way. *See* BIAS BINDING: DOUBLE-FOLD; BIAS BINDING: SINGLE-FOLD; NET-BOUND EDGE FINISH; *and* SEAM BINDING.

BOUND (PIPED) BUTTONHOLE PLACKET. This is an excellent finish for a neck opening to be made in a slash in the material. The placket is worked like the bound buttonhole: patch method (q.v.), except that one end is open to form the placket.

With right sides together, place the patch of garment fabric over the marked slash line. Stitch on three sides for the length and width of the opening. Slash through the center and diagonally to each end (a).

Turn the binding to the inside and form the lips of the opening like the lips of a buttonhole. Close them with diagonal basting (b). On the underside, tack the lips to the triangular flap at the point where they form an inverted pleat.

In sheer or lightweight fabrics, turn under the free edges on the underside, bringing the folds to meet the machine stitching, and slip-stitch (c). In medium-weight fabric or fabric that won't ravel, edge-finish the raw edges and blindstitch the opened-out seam allowances to the machine stitching (d).

Fold back the garment against itself, exposing the triangular flap against the binding. Stitch across flap and binding close to the fold.

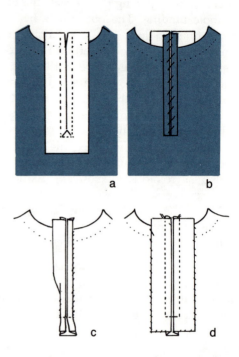

BOUND POCKET. As in a bound buttonhole, the binding of a bound pocket is used to finish and protect the slash in the fabric. The easiest way to construct the binding for the pocket is by the bound buttonhole: two-strip method (q.v.). Then all one need do is attach the upper and under pockets. Turn under the seam allowance of the upper pocket and hem or whip it to the lower seam allowance of the binding. Attach the under pocket to the upper seam allowance with backstitches (a). Hand stitching is easier, but you may use machine stitching if you prefer.

Use lining material for the upper pocket and outer fabric for the under pocket so there will be no break in color or texture at the pocket opening. Or face a lining under pocket with a strip of outer fashion fabric in the opening area only (b). The latter is a good method for heavy or bulky fabric. Make the facing strip wide enough to extend to a safe depth. Use a selvage where possible so there will be no need to turn under a seam allowance for a finish. Lap the facing over the lining material and stitch around all sides.

A very attractive *curved bound pocket* (c) can be made by this method with two bias strips for the binding in either self or contrasting fabric. Curve the upper edges of under and upper pockets to match the curve of the bound pocket.

AN ALTERNATIVE METHOD FOR MAKING THE BOUND POCKET

Cut the pocket and binding all in one piece of garment fabric. Place the upper end of it over the marking for the pocket opening, right sides together. Make the binding for the pocket by the bound buttonhole: patch method (q.v.). Pull the fabric through the opening to the underside and form the lips of the opening. Bring the free end of the pocket to meet the upper-end seam allowance. Stitch across the two ends and down the sides.

BOUND POCKET WITH FLAP. To hide the opening of the pocket, a flap may be added. The flap may be inserted in the upper seam over the binding to cover it (a) or under the binding to reveal it (b).

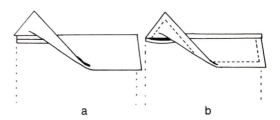

a   b

TO CONSTRUCT THE FLAP OVER THE BINDING (a)

Make the flap and stitch it to the garment 1/8 inch above the pocket opening (slightly more if the fabric is heavy) (b). Trim the seam allowances close to the stitching.

Place the upper binding over the flap so that its stitching line is directly over the stitching that fastened flap to garment (c). *(See illustration on next page.)* Place and stitch the lower binding to position. Construct the bound pocket (q.v.).

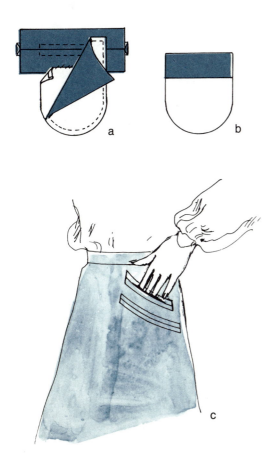

a   b

c

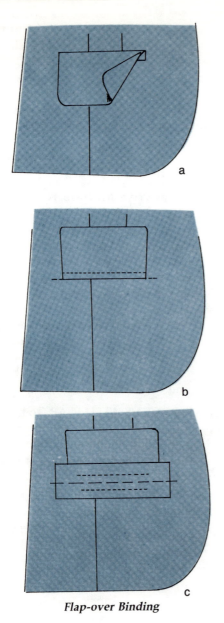
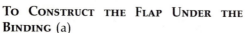

Flap-over Binding

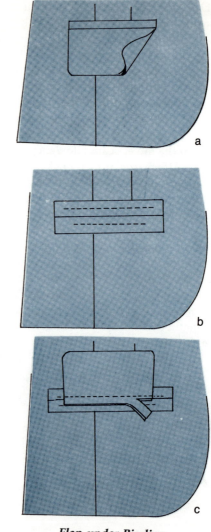

Flap-under Binding

To Construct the Flap Under the Binding (a)

Place and stitch the upper binding the full length of the opening. Stitch the lower binding parallel to the first, tapering in 1/8 to 1/4 inch at each end (b) so that when the flap is turned to wearing position, it will cover the opening.

Make the flap and stitch it in place directly over the stitching line of the upper binding (c). Construct the bound pocket (q.v.).

BOX PLEAT. *See* PLEAT TYPES.

BREAK. *Of a collar,* it is the point at which the collar or garment turns back to form a lapel. When a garment buttons, the first, or top, button is located at the break. *Of a skirt,* it is the point where the fitted upper part of the skirt breaks away from the body into movement on a fuller, lower part.

BREAST POCKET. A welt pocket (q.v.) made on the upper left side of a jacket. It is constructed through the jacket front and the interfacing. It may or may not be top-stitched.

BROADCLOTH. A closely woven fabric in plain or twill weave. It is made in many weights, fibers, and blends. Because the fabric is so closely woven, it is better used for styles that call for little or no easing—shirt sleeves rather than set-in sleeves, tailored details, lapped or fell seams, pleats, tucks, and the like.

Broadcloths of cotton, silk, rayon, or blends, with their soft, semigloss finish, resemble poplin. The wool and worsted broadcloths are napped fabrics with a lustrous appearance and a velvety feel. To preserve the glossy surface, *do not* sponge or preshrink. There is no home method for renewing the fabric finish. To maintain the sheen, use as little pressure and moisture as possible in pressing. Press with the nap and brush it up after pressing. Use a self-fabric press cloth. Treat broadcloth as a napped fabric (q.v.) for layout, cutting, and stitching.

BUCKLES. *See* BELT WITH PASS-THROUGH BUCKLE; BELT WITH PRONG-AND-EYELET BUCKLE; BELT OR STRAP WITH RING BUCKLE; CLASP BUCKLE CLOSURE; SASH.

BULLION-STITCH LOOP. This is made like a French knot but with more coils, to

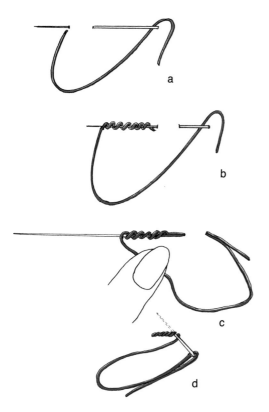

a

b

c

d

form a short bar. Use a short double thread pulled up evenly and a round-eyed needle so the winding slips off easily.

Fasten the thread on the underside. Bring the needle to the surface at the bottom of the loop. Take a backstitch in the ground material the size of the loop. Bring the needle up *partially* at the original point of entry (a).

Using the thread at the point of the needle, wind it closely but not tightly around the exposed end of the needle to the depth of the loop (b). Holding the winding thread securely with your thumb, slip the needle and thread through the coils and draw up tightly so the coils reach the top end of the loop (c). Insert the needle at this point to form the bar (d). Fasten the thread on the underside.

BUST AREA. Generally the size of a pattern that includes a bodice is determined by the bust measurement. However, this is only an overall width measurement and may not be sufficient information for the proper fitting of the bust area. For instance, it may not tell you how much is front and how much is back, how flat or how full the bust bulge, how high or how low in relation to the shoulders and waist. There is this, too, to consider: patterns are usually designed for a B cup whether they have darts or not. If your bust is smaller or larger than this, some pattern correction may be necessary.

Those problems that are known or can be anticipated may be handled by making the necessary pattern alterations before cutting. *See* BUST PATTERN CORRECTIONS. Those that show up in the fitting must of necessity be taken care of then.

In general: the right amount of shaping seams and darts in just the right places is the secret of successful shaping. All darts must head toward the apex, or high point, of the bust whatever their point of origin on the bodice. All darts are stitched just short of the high point to cup smoothly over the bosom. Curved darts produce a closer fit than straight darts, though the latter may produce a sharper bulge. All shaping seams must pass directly over the high point or within 1 inch on either side. If darts or shaping seams *(see* PRINCESS SEAM**)** produce bulges above, below, or beside the high point, they must be relocated to fit the curve of the bosom.

Bulges or poufs at the dart point mean the dart is too large. Make a smaller dart and/ or reshape the garment at the nearest seam. *Wrinkles or folds* mean that a larger dart is needed. Push the excess material into the nearest seam or dart. Or, where there is no dart or seam, create one consistent with the style and the fabric.

Sometimes *out-of-position grain* is a clue to the need for a larger or smaller dart. *Drooping grain* with its unsightly wrinkles and folds calls for a dart or shaping seam. *Off-grain straining* requires release from a too deep dart or a steeply shaped seam.

BUST DART CREATED WHERE NONE EXISTS. Creating a bust dart will provide more width and length across the bust as well as more shaping.

Determine and mark the apex of the bust on the pattern (a). Draw three lines: one, the position of the new dart (1), the

second, from the dart point to the armhole notch (2), the third, from the dart point to the bottom of the pattern (3) (b).

Slash all three lines. Cut line 2 *to* the armhole notch but not through it. Spread the pattern from armhole to bust point, allowing a 1/2-inch space for a C cup, a 3/4-inch space for a D cup, and a 1 1/4-inch space for a DD cup. Spread the underarm dart in the new position. Make it as large on the seam line as the opening at the bust point (c).

Correct the seam line or hemline. Draw the new underarm dart (d).

BUST DART ELIMINATED. Reverse the procedure for bust dart created (q.v.). Overlap the slash lines instead of spreading them.

BUST PATTERN CORRECTIONS. Before making any pattern changes, *see* PATTERN CORRECTIONS for general information.

Because the bust area is the most difficult to fit, most patterns that involve a bodice are chosen by the bust measurement. However, there is this to consider: patterns are designed for a B cup. If the pattern fits everywhere except over a full or small bust, it is advisable to buy the pattern that fits most measurements and make the pattern adjustment for an A, C, D or DD cup rather than going to another size. *(See* BUST DART CREATED WHERE NONE EXISTS.)

All darts and shaping seams must line up with the fullest part of the bust (the apex, high point).

Bust with Large Cup. In the following pattern correction, note that it takes length as well as width to encompass a full bust.

Draw a vertical slash line from the shoulder to the waist seam (to the hem in styles that extend below the waist) through any existing darts. Draw a horizontal slash line at the bustline starting at and at right angles to the center front and extending to the side seam through any existing darts (a).

Slash both slash lines and spread to the needed amount. The vertical spread is equal from bust to waistline or hem and

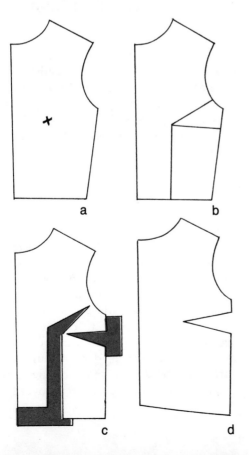

a   b

c   d

tapers from bust to shoulder. The horizontal spread is equal from center front to bust point and may or may not taper to the side seam depending on the figure requirements (b). If there is no underarm dart in the pattern, it may be necessary to create one in the spread area.

Fill in the spread area with tissue. Pin or Scotch-tape to position. Redraw the enlarged darts, bringing the points to the centers of the spread areas (b). If this change results in too large a dart, which distorts the grain or printed design of the fabric, divide it into two or more darts.

Correct seams as necessary.

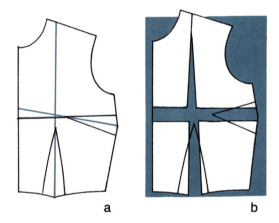

a   b

Bust with Small Cup. Reverse the procedure for bust with large cup (q.v.). Overlap the slashed lines instead of spreading them.

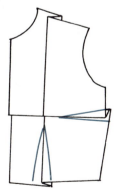

High Bust. Raise all underarm bust darts regardless of angle. Shorten any shoulder or neck darts. Lengthen all waistline darts (a). *See* DART SHORTENED; DART LENGTHENED; DART RELOCATED.

In a style with a horizontal shaping seam, shorten the upper bodice section and lengthen the lower bodice section (b). The broken lines represent the original pattern; the solid lines, the correction.

See PRINCESS STYLE PATTERN CORRECTIONS for any changes necessary for that style.

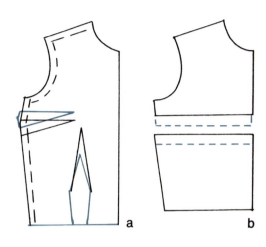

a   b

Low Bust. Lower all underarm bust darts regardless of angle. Shorten the waistline darts (a). Lengthen any shoulder or neck darts. *See* DART LENGTHENED; DART SHORTENED.

In a style with a horizontal shaping seam, lengthen the upper bodice section and shorten the lower bodice section (b). The broken lines represent the original pattern; the solid lines, the correction.

See PRINCESS STYLE PATTERN CORRECTIONS for any changes necessary for that style.

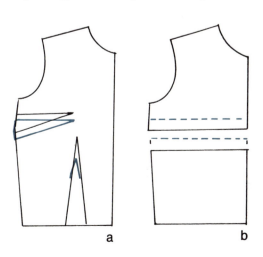

a   b

BUTTOCKS PATTERN CORRECTIONS.

Before making these corrections *see* PATTERN CORRECTIONS for general information.

Fitting problems in this area manifest themselves in wrinkling, pulling, sagging, and uneven hemline.

Flat Buttocks. Draw a vertical slash line in the skirt pattern from waist to hem. Draw a horizontal slash line from the center back to the side seam at the fullest part of the buttocks. Slash the pattern on both slash lines.

Remove the excess width across the buttocks by overlapping the pattern lengthwise in the needed amount. Overlap equally from waist to hem. Remove the sag by overlapping the pattern horizontally from the center back to the side seam at the fullest part of the buttocks. Overlap equally from the center back to the vertical slash line. Taper the overlap from the vertical slash line to nothing at the side seam.

Pin or Scotch-tape all overlaps. Make a small dart in the lower side section to control the amount of the overlap in the lower section of the skirt and to bring the side seam in line. Make the existing dart or darts smaller. If there are two darts, the skirt may fit better if one is eliminated. Correct the side seam and the hemline.

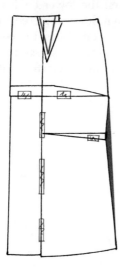

Large Buttocks. Make vertical and horizontal slash lines, as above for FLAT BUT-

TOCKS. Spread the slashes in the amounts necessary to go around the bulge of the buttocks—equally from waist to hem; equally from center back to vertical spread, tapering to nothing at the side seam.

Fill in the spread areas with tissue paper. Pin or Scotch-tape to position. Make a small dart in the lower side section to control the amount of the spread and to bring the side seam in line.

Make any existing waistline dart or darts larger to compensate for the addition at the waistline and to provide more shaping. If necessary, create another dart. Correct the side seam. Correct the hemline with a slightly curved line, starting at the original center back hemline and going to the original side seam hemline.

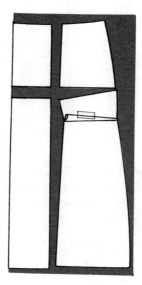

BUTTONHOLE. That every sewer is just a bit apprehensive about making a buttonhole is understandable. After all, it involves a slash in the garment and that is so final! If it can be said there is a trick to making a beautiful buttonhole it is to measure carefully, mark carefully, and stitch as directed.

There are several ways in which buttonholes can be made. The most frequent types are bound buttonholes (a), hand-worked buttonholes (b), and machine-worked buttonholes (c). Choose the type that will be suitable for the design of the

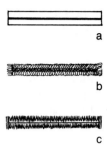

garment, the character of the fabric, and your sewing skill.

Bound Buttonholes (q.v.) are the choice for all good tailored women's clothing—suit, coat, dress, shirt, blouse—for all fabrics except those that are too sheer (transparent material reveals the inner workings) or too heavy (resulting in a bulky buttonhole). They demand a degree of sewing skill.

Hand-worked buttonholes (q.v.) are *the* classic closing on men's tailored garments (also acceptable on women's), on fabrics too transparent for bound buttonholes or too fragile for machine-worked button-holes.

Machine-worked buttonholes (q.v.) have long been used on clothes that get hard wear, on sportswear, work clothes, washable garments, children's clothes. Because the method is easy and quick, re-quiring a minimum of skill to make the buttonhole, more and more machine-made buttonholes make their appearance even in expensive bought clothes. Machine-worked buttonholes are functional and these days are apparently also acceptable. *See also* IN-SEAM BUTTONHOLE, CORDED BUTTON-HOLE, TAILOR'S BUTTONHOLE.

BUTTONHOLE GUIDE MARKINGS. One of the secrets of successful buttonholes is very accurate marking. Using a double thread of contrasting color, mark the posi-tion of the opening of the buttonhole (slash line). Place cross markings (vertical basting) to indicate the beginning and end of each buttonhole. When making a series of buttonholes, make certain that they line up, are identical in size, and are evenly spaced.

BUTTONHOLE PLACEMENT. In a but-toned garment, the closing line is generally a button's width from the open edge. In order to ensure that the garment buttons directly on the closing line, a slight correc-tion must be made for the thickness of the shank of the button. The standard amount for this correction is 1/8 inch. Therefore the buttonhole begins not at the closing line where you would expect it to begin but 1/8 inch beyond, toward the outer edge in a horizontal buttonhole and 1/8 inch toward the upper edge in a vertical buttonhole. Even for small buttons, buttonholes are not usually placed closer than 5/8 inch from a closing edge.

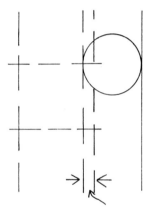

Buttonholes work best when made on the horizontal or crosswise grain of the material. This is the direction of the stress on them. Buttonholes on an angle may look pretty but present a problem in the cutting and making. Bias buttonholes tend to ripple. However, in a bias garment, but-tonholes on an angle really place them on straight grain, which is fine. In a narrow band (for instance a shirt or shirtwaist), the buttonhole must be made vertically on the straight grain to fit the space.

Whatever the buttonhole placement, the closing lines of both sides must match to locate the position of the buttons. *See also* BUTTONHOLE SIZE.

BUTTONHOLE SIZE. This depends on the size and type of button. It must be slightly larger than the button for easy slide-through. Here's the rule: for a *flat button,* the width of the button plus 1/8 inch for ease (a); for a *bumpy button,* the width of the button plus its height. An easy way to determine this is to wrap a tape measure completely around the button (b) and note the total length. Half this amount is the size the buttonhole should be.

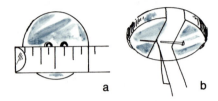

a   b

In heavy coat or suit material, the buttonholes have a tendency to end up a little smaller than anticipated. Allow a bit of extra ease to compensate.

Make a test slash in an extra bit of the material to see if the button can slide through easily. Better yet, make a test buttonhole through your fabric, interfacing and/or underlining to discover any unforeseen problems in size and the handling of the material.

BUTTONHOLE STENCIL. A useful device for ensuring uniformity of buttonhole size in a series of buttonholes.

Draw a rectangle on a strip of cardboard or stiff paper. Make it the width and length of the finished buttonhole. Cut out the rectangular opening. Center the stencil over the buttonhole placement line. Trace the opening with tailor's chalk or thread.

BUTTONHOLE STITCH. This is both a decorative and protective finish for the opening of a hand-worked buttonhole.

Work the stitch from right to left. Slip the knotted end of a length of buttonhole thread between the outer fabric and the facing. Hold the needle vertically and bring it through a loop of thread. Form the loop by placing the thread behind the eye of the needle and under its point. Each

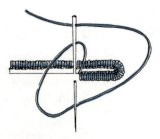

purl (the knot that is formed by pulling up the intertwisting thread) should be on the edge of the slit. Make the stitches close together and even in depth.

The buttonhole stitch is similar to the blanket stitch (q.v.). The difference is that the blanket stitch has a single purl, while the buttonhole stitch has a double purl, providing better protection for the cut edge of the buttonhole.

BUTTON LOCATION ON FINISHED GARMENT. In order to maintain the design and fitting of a garment, the button must be properly located. In an unfitted garment, the location of the buttons can be done on a flat surface. In a fitted garment, the button placement is best done over a slightly curved surface—over you, a dress form, a tailor's ham, or a rolled up towel.

Pin the garment closed. Match the closing lines and all cross lines: edges, stitching, and fabric design. Using a safety pin (this won't fall out as a straight pin may), pin through the buttonhole opening. Close the safety pin. This locates the position for the button. This technique also has the merit of correcting any discrepancies between the original marked placement and the actual completed opening of the buttonhole.

In *horizontal buttonholes,* the button is placed 1/8 inch in from the closing end of the buttonhole directly on the closing line. In *vertical buttonholes,* the button is placed 1/8 inch below the top end of the buttonhole directly on the closing line.

Mark and sew the first button, centering it on the closing line. Button the garment. Locate the next button. Sew it on. This locate-and-sew procedure assures an accurate placement of each button.

BUTTON LOOPS. These are substitutes for buttonholes that can be made of tubing (self-filled) or corded tubing (q.v.) in contrasting or self-fabric; braid; or any other tubular material.

Make a length of tubing 1/8 inch or less in width (in all but heavy fabrics, where it may be slightly wider). In chiffon or other sheer fabrics, the tubing may be as narrow as 1/16 inch. Button loops can also be made of thread. *See* THREAD LOOP.

Loops may be individual (spaced) (a) or continuous (not spaced) (b) depending on the weight of the fabric and the desired spacing.

Mark the seam (closing) line the length of the closure. Mark a line in from and parallel to the seam line the distance the loops are to extend from the finished edge (approximately half the button's width plus the thickness of the tubing). Rule short lines at right angles to these lines to mark the spread of each loop. The loops should be large enough to take the buttons with ease (test to see that they do), identical in size, and evenly spaced, beginning and ending exactly at the top and bottom of the closing (c). For thick buttons, spread the loops rather than extend them farther in from the edge.

Form and position the loops within the markings, keeping the seamed side up. Keep the loops turned away from the closing line in a position opposite to that of the finished loop. Use narrow masking tape to hold the loops in position. Machine-baste them close to the stitching line. Remove the tape. Loops can be spaced quickly and accurately by stitching them to a paper guide, which is in turn applied to the garment.

For *single loops*, cut equal lengths of tubing to fit the markings plus two seam allowances. Form and position the loops (a).

For *continuous loops*, use a long strip of tubing to form the continuous row of loops (b). Extend them 1/2 inch into the seam allowance. After machine-basting, clip and trim to 1/4 inch the short looped ends in the seam allowance (c).

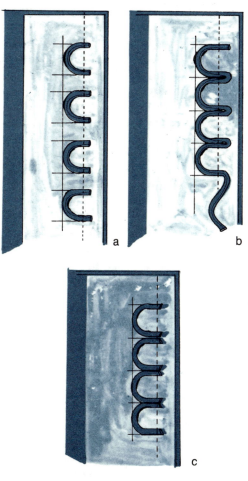

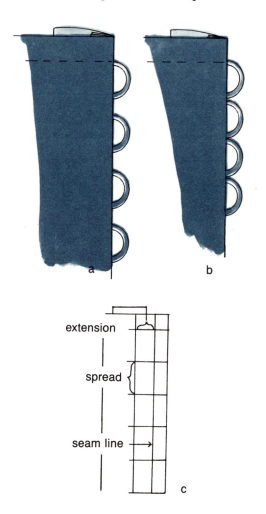

Apply the Facing. Place the right side of the facing over the right side of the garment with the loops sandwiched between them. Stitch directly on the seam line. Grade the seam allowances. Fold the facing to the inside along the seam line. Understitch, then press.

The finished loops now extend beyond the edge of the garment. Lap them over the opposite side, bringing the finished edge of the garment to the button position line. Mark the button placements and sew them to the garment. *See* LOOP-AND-BUTTON CLOSING.

BUTTON PLACEMENT. The easiest and safest thing to do is to stick with the button placement on a pattern. However, some liberties can be taken for the sake of design or fit so long as you observe the basic design of the garment and the size of the button planned for it. *See* BUTTON SIZES.

You may use more or fewer buttons than the pattern calls for. The buttons may be placed singly, in a series, or in groups. The size of the button may help determine this. Large buttons are spaced farther apart than small buttons. Experiment with cut-out circles of paper and judge the effect.

If you've lengthened or shortened a pattern, adjust the number and placement of the buttons.

In a fitted garment, buttons should be so placed that the garment does not pop open at the bust or chest nor gap at the waist. Space the remaining buttons accordingly.

In an unfitted or semifitted garment, the buttons may be widely spaced. Such designs look better when the garment is held closed between the buttons with snaps covered to match. *See* COVERED SNAPS.

If a belt is used at the waistline, place the buttons sufficiently above or below so they don't interfere with the belt.

Do not change the position of the top button in a style with a lapel. This would alter the width of the lapel, the roll line of lapel and collar, and the fit of the collar.

When a garment is buttoned to the neckline, the top button is placed a button's width below the finished neckline. The last button on a dress should be 3 to 4 inches from the bottom—never through the hem.

BUTTON SHANK OR STEM. This is the bridge between the upper and under parts of a closing. It floats the button on the surface of the garment. Without it, the garment would bunch rather than button. So important is this bridge, particularly for heavy or bulky fabrics, that when a button doesn't have a shank a stem must be created with the thread by which the button is sewn to the garment (a). In a shank button, the shank (neck, loop) appears on the underside of the button (b).

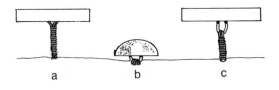

The length of the shank or stem depends on the several thicknesses of the opening edges—outer fabric, interfacing, facing. The thicker the area through which the button is to pass, the longer the shank must be; the thinner the area, the shorter the shank. In a heavy overcoat, it may be necessary to lengthen the shank by adding a thread stem to the metal shank (c). Only when buttons are used decoratively rather than as a fastening is it permissible to omit the shank or stem. *For sewing directions, see* SEW-THROUGH BUTTON; SHANK BUTTON; OVERCOAT BUTTON.

BUTTON SIZES. Buttons come in sizes from 1/4 inch to 2 inches or more in diameter. The size increments are 1/8 inch. Size is based on a system of "lines"—forty to an inch. Illustrated is a button gauge in actual size. It will help you convert the known inch size to lines.

It is wise to purchase the size button recommended on the pattern since the closing extension was planned for it. To change the extension may involve the collar, a neckline facing, a lapel and/or other style details.

When a garment is buttoned, its two sides must overlap each other for a secure closing. The overlap is an extension of the material beyond the closing line toward the outer edge. There is a rule governing this width: the width of the extension equals the width of the button to be used. When the garment is buttoned, there should be half a button's width between the rim of the button and the finished edge of the garment. In addition to a good over-lap, this bit of mathematics ensures a proper setting for the button. A cramped setting detracts from the design interest.

You may use a slightly smaller button in the same space. When an outsize button is used, make certain that there is at least 1/2 inch left between the rim of the button and the finished edge of the garment.

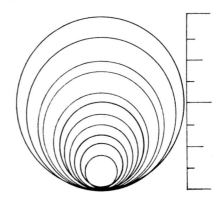

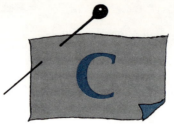

CABLE CORD. A cord composed of several strands of cotton, loosely twisted to resemble a cable, string, twine, or rope. Covered with a bias strip or tubing, it is used wherever firmness is desirable; for instance: through the lips of a buttonhole, for button loops, for string belts, or where the definition of an edge or seam would be decorative. *Caution:* the ridges and twistings of the cord will show through thin or soft materials.

Cable cord is available by the yard in thicknesses ranging from 1/16 to 1/2 inch. Select the size according to its use and the texture of the fabric with which it is used.

CAP SLEEVE. A short sleeve just covering the shoulder but not continued as a sleeve (a).

To Add a Cap Sleeve to a Sleeveless Bodice, trace the bodice front and back. Extend the shoulder lines to the desired length of the cap—only deep enough to cover the shoulders. Mark a point 1 to 2 inches below the armhole on the side seam. Connect the extended shoulder to this point. Use either a straight line (b) or a curved line (c).

On some figures such cap sleeves have a tendency to strain and tear at the armhole. In that case connect the extended shoulder to the waistline (d). Stitch the side seam to a point 1 to 2 inches opposite the lowest point of the armhole.

CARRIERS. Loops of thread or fabric through which a belt, scarf, or sash is passed and which holds it in place on the garment. *See* BELT CARRIERS; THREAD CARRIERS; *and* FABRIC CARRIERS.

Cap Sleeve

CARTRIDGE PLEATS. Rounded pleats, extending out from the garment rather than lying flat against it as most pleats do. They resemble a cartridge belt. When the extension is deep, the pleats are called pipe organ folds. The pleats may be stiffened with crinoline or filled with a roll of stiff paper to hold their shape.

Fold under the top edge of the section to be pleated. Determine the spacing and the depth of each pleat. Mark with a line of basting. Mark the position and spacing on the garment with lines of basting.

Set the pleats in position on the garment, matching basted markings. Use a cording foot and stitch between the pleats

just beside the basting. In fine fabrics, stitch by hand, using tiny running stitches.

CASING. A "tunnel" created by two parallel lines of stitching through two layers of fabric and through which an elastic or drawstring can be drawn. It is a device both decorative and practical for controlling fullness. As fabric is pulled up in graceful folds, the fullness can easily be adjusted to body measurements.

Any existing or specially created hem, tuck, facing, seam allowance, or applied straight or shaped strip or band can serve as a casing. It may be stitched to the inside or outside of a garment along a placement line.

The casing is equal in length to the area to which it is to be applied plus 1/4-inch turn-under at each end. The band is as wide as the drawstring or elastic plus 1/8 to 1/4 inch for ease in drawing up plus 1/4 inch seam allowance on each long side. It may be cut on straight grain or bias. The bias is easier to manipulate on any curved placement line.

When applied to the inside of a garment, the casing should be of some thin or lightweight material to avoid bulk when drawn up into gathers or folds. Prepackaged bias tape will do, as will self-fabric if it is lightweight enough. When applied to the outside of the garment, self-fabric or any decorative band may be used for the casing. Whether an inside or outside application, leave an opening for the drawstring or elastic.

Before the casing is stitched to position, any seam allowances within it must be treated in such a way that they do not prove to be obstacles to the threading of drawstring or elastic. Any of the following methods will take care of the situation.

1. Trim the seam allowances close to the stitching and overcast what's left.
2. Baste the pressed-open seam allowances and remove the basting after the threading.
3. Catch-stitch the seam allowances to the garment, making sure they do not show on the right side.

4. Place narrow strips of fusible web between the seam allowance and the outer fabric and press into permanent position.

The drawstring may be of cord, string, fabric, tubing, braid, ribbon, strips of leather or pseudoleather, strips of anything appropriate to the design of the garment and its use. The drawstring should be narrow enough to move freely within the casing. Its length should be equal to the body measurement at the casing position plus the amount needed for the loop, bow, or knot used to tie the ends.

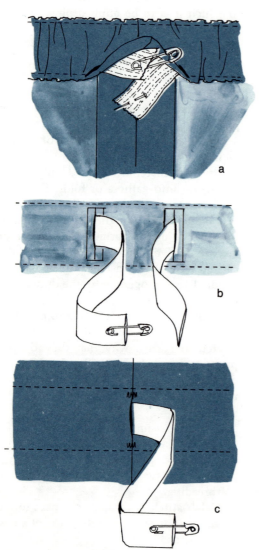

a

b

c

When elastic is used, it must be firm, flat, and narrow enough to slide easily through the casing. Its length is slightly less than the body measurement at the casing placement. How much less depends on the stretchability of the particular elastic—just enough less so the garment fits snugly and does not droop. Add 1/2 inch for seam allowances. Pin one end to the garment on the underside so it will not be pulled through the casing when the other end is drawn up. Attach a safety pin of a size that can go through the casing to the other end and thread it through the casing, taking care not to twist it (a). The ends of the elastic may be joined by a 1/2-inch overlap. See SELF-CASING.

A drawstring can be pulled to the outside of the garment through a buttonhole (bound or worked) or an eyelet. These must be made in the outer fabric before the casing is applied (b). Another way in which a drawstring may be pulled to the outside is through an in-seam opening (c). When stitching the seam, leave an opening large enough for the drawstring. Secure each end of the opening with lock stitching or bar tacks (q.v.).

A combination of elastic plus decorative tie ends can be both comfortable and decorative. Construct the tie ends. Fasten them securely to the elastic. Make certain that the joining is well hidden beyond the opening in the casing. See also SHAPED CASING; APPLIED CASING; FACING-CASING; CASING WITH A HEADING; CASING AT ZIPPER OPENING; CASINGS UTILIZING SEAM ALLOWANCES, NARROW HEMS, AND TUCKS.

CASING AT ZIPPER OPENING. See CASING before beginning.

Apply the casing. For standard zipper installations, the casing ends at the zipper seam line (a). For invisible zipper installations, extend the casing 1/4 inch beyond the seam line into the seam allowance (b).

Insert the elastic or drawstring. Tack its ends to the ends of the casing, keeping the garment free. Insert the zipper. Press the zipper tapes flat over the casing and whipstitch them to the casing, elastic, or drawstring (c).

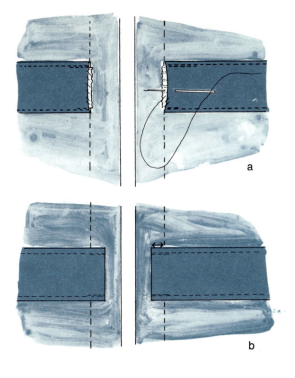

a

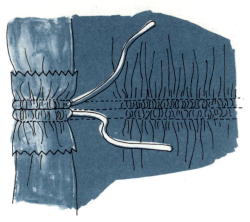

b

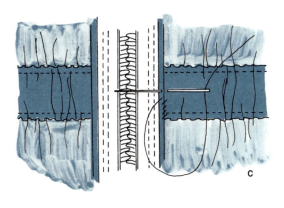

fullness. Adjust the gathers. Secure the ends or tie them.

CASING WITH A HEADING. A ruffle tops the casing for design interest (a). This type of heading may be added to either a turned-down self-facing or a facing-casing. Allow an amount beyond the casing equal to twice the width of the ruffle.

Turn down an amount deep enough for both casing and ruffle. Pin and stitch the lower edge of the casing, leaving an opening for the elastic or drawstring. Make a second row of stitching an even distance

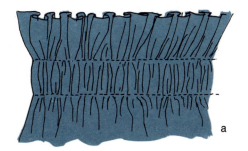

a

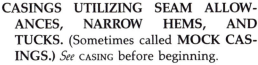

c

CASINGS UTILIZING SEAM ALLOW-ANCES, NARROW HEMS, AND TUCKS. (Sometimes called MOCK CAS-INGS.) *See* CASING before beginning.

Press the *seam allowances* of a plain seam open. Stitch them to the garment an equal distance from the seam line on each side. The distance from the seam line should be deep enough to accommodate the elastic or drawstring. Thread either through the casings and secure the ends by tying or stitching over them. Adjust the shirring.

Thread cord, string, or heavy yarn through a *narrow hem* or *tuck.* Draw up the

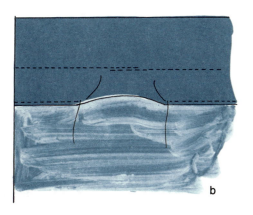

b

from the first to the desired depth of the casing. Finish with backstitching or overlap stitching since no opening is needed on this row (b). Thread and finish the casing as for a self-casing (q.v.). The ruffle will form when the casing is drawn up. *See* CASING.

CATCH STITCH. A permanent hand stitch resembling a cross-stitch that joins layers of fabric securely, invisibly, yet with a degree of stretchability. It is used extensively in dressmaking and tailoring in all its versions. *See* BLIND CATCH STITCH; CATCH-STITCH TACK; FLAT CATCH STITCH.

The stitch is worked from left to right. Bring the needle out at the lower left. Take a tiny backstitch on an imaginary upper line a little to the right with the thread below the needle. Pick up only a thread or two of the outer fabric. Complete the stitch by taking a similar backstitch on an imaginary lower line to the right with the thread above the needle. The movement is always to the right. The needle points to the left shoulder. The stitches are loose to provide flexibility.

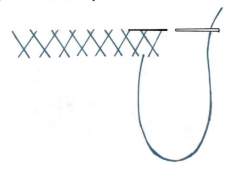

CATCH-STITCHED DART. A way of eliminating bulk in the construction of an interfacing or interlining. There are two ways in which this can be done. Both methods call for careful marking of the stitching lines of the dart.

METHOD 1. THE OVERLAP METHOD

Slash one dart stitching line to the dart point. Overlap the slashed edge on the other dart stitching line. Reinforce the point of the dart with a patch of tape or interfacing material. Join with flat catch stitches over the cut edge of the dart (a).

Trim away the excess interfacing on the underside.

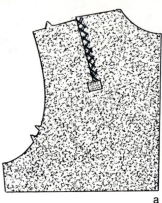

a

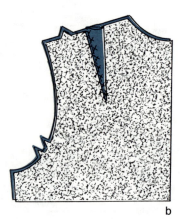

b

METHOD 2. THE CUT-AWAY METHOD

Cut out the entire dart of the interfacing or interlining. Place piece over the garment. Pull the stitched garment dart through the cut-out dart. Pin the interfacing or interlining alongside the seam of the garment dart and catch-stitch the cut edges along the seam (b).

CATCH-STITCHED SEAM. Used to guarantee the flatness of a seam or to prevent the seam edges from rolling when the garment is worn or cleaned.

Make a plain seam and press it open. Catch-stitch the edges of the seam allowances to the garment so the stitching will not be visible on the right side. Lift only a single thread of the outer fabric.

If the garment interfacing or underlining has been included in the seam, trim it close to the stitching. Press the seam open.

Catch-stitch the seam allowances to the interfacing or underlining. Make sure that no stitches go through to the right side.

CATCH-STITCH METHOD OF ELIMINATING HAIR CANVAS (and Other Heavy Interfacing Materials) FROM THE CONSTRUCTION SEAMS.

By this method, the hair canvas is trimmed away at the seam allowances of the construction seams and catch-stitched to the outer fabric.

The trimming can be done before the interfacing is applied to the garment but you would have to be certain that the construction seam is exactly where you wish it to be (a). When uncertain, fit the interfaced garment first, mark the exact position of the construction seams, then trim away the interfacing and catch-stitch. Directions follow.

Open the seam allowances between the outer fabric and the interfacing. Using tailor's chalk, mark the seam lines as pinned on both the hair canvas and the outer fabric (b). Unpin the seams.

Trim away the seam allowances of the hair canvas, as marked. Catch-stitch the cut edges of the interfacing to the seam lines of the fashion fabric (c). Use a matching single thread and pick up only one thread of the outer fabric so the hand stitches do not show on the right side. Do not pull up the thread too tightly—just enough to secure the interfacing.

With the right sides of the outer fabric together, pin and stitch the construction seam. Stitch *beside* the interfacing, not through it. Press the seam allowances open as flat as possible, using the pressing technique determined best for the fabric.

Optional: If you'll feel more secure about it, catch-stitch the opened seam allowances to the interfacing (d). *See also* FOLD-BACK METHOD AND STRIP METHOD OF ELIMINATING HAIR CANVAS FROM CONSTRUCTION SEAMS; TAPING METHOD OF ELIMINATING HAIR CANVAS FROM OUTSIDE SEAMS.

CATCH-STITCH TACK. A widely spaced series of catch stitches worked from left to right at intervals of 1/2 to 1 inch between two garment sections. Be sure to allow slack between the stitches.

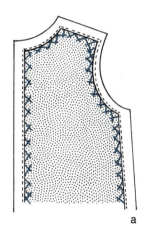

a

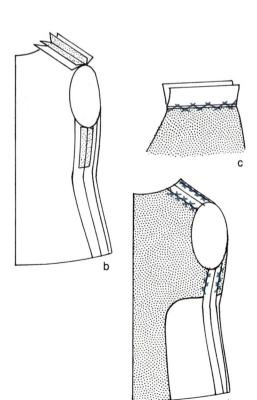

b

c

d

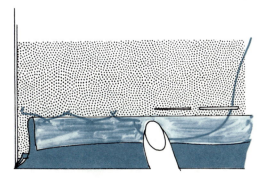

CENTERED (SLOT-SEAM) ZIPPER.

The zipper is concealed by two folds of material centered over it. There are two visible lines of stitching, one on each side of the closing. The zipper may be installed by hand or by machine. Before proceeding with the setting and stitching of this zipper, *see* ZIPPERED CLOSINGS.

Hand Method. When putting in a zipper by hand, it is easiest to leave open the seam to which it is applied.

Mark the seam line of the placket opening with thread. Turn under each seam allowance along the thread marking and press.

Working from the right side, place one folded edge *slightly beyond the center of the zipper* to offset the tendency of the stitching to pull the fold away from the center, thereby exposing the zipper teeth. When a facing is used at the garment edge, place the top stop of the zipper 1/2 inch below the cross seam of the garment. This allows for turning the seam and facing to the underside. Allow a little more if the fabric is heavy, a little less if the fabric is lightweight. Pin to position.

Using a half backstitch or a prick stitch (q.v.) start at the top of one side and work down the length of the zipper.

Pin the second side in the same way as the first. Stitch across the bottom below the bottom stop and continue up the second side. Make the welts even on both sides.

Machine Method. When putting in a zipper by machine, application is neater and easier if the seam to which it is attached is closed. Close the placket opening on the seam line with hand or machine basting. Press the seam allowances open. Leave the basting in until the placket is completed.

On the underside, place the zipper face down on the seam allowance with the teeth or coil directly over the seam line. Pin the zipper tape to one seam allowance. Open the zipper. Using the zipper foot, machine-baste the zipper tape to the seam allowance along the woven guideline of

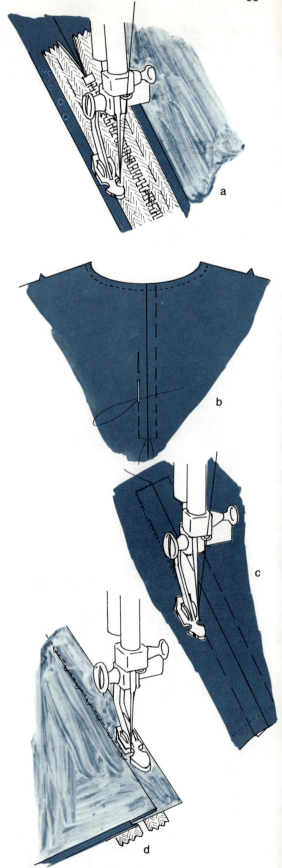

a

b

c

d

the tape. Stitch from the bottom of the zipper to the top. Close the zipper, keeping the pull tab up. Baste the second side of the zipper in the same way (a).

On the right side, hand-baste ¼ inch from each side of the seam line and across the bottom, catching all thicknesses (b). Starting at the bottom of the placket at the seam line and using a regular stitch length, stitch beside the basting through all thicknesses along one side. (The machine stitching may be done from either the right side or the underside of the garment.) Pull the bottom thread ends through to the wrong side and tie. Repeat the procedure for the second side (c).

Make the welts even on both sides. Clip and remove the basting along the center seam.

Variation Machine Method. Instead of the standard machine stitching, use a blindstitch to simulate a hand application (d). *(See* BLINDSTITCH.*)* To place the zipper foot in the correct position requires that you work from top to bottom on one side of the zipper and from bottom to top on the other side.

CHAIN STITCH.
A useful stitch that may be used decoratively or functionally. It consists of a continuous series of interlocking looped stitches that form a chain. It can be made by hand or by machine.

By Hand. Fasten the thread on the underside and take a ¼-inch stitch on the right side. Loop the thread under the needle. Draw it up (a). Make successive links, beginning each new stitch inside the previous loop to form the chain (b). Use the thumb to hold the thread in place while working. Keep the stitches even in tension and in size. The stitch may be worked vertically, horizontally, at an angle, or curved. Finish by fastening the thread on the underside with tiny backstitches.

By Machine. This requires the use of a chain-stitch attachment. The interlocking loops of the chain stitch are visible on the underside (c). On the right side, only a regular machine stitch appears. Because there is no locking of stitches, the machine chain stitch is easily removed by simply pulling a thread, making it a useful *temporary* stitch. It is a convenient way to baste seams, mark guidelines, make "growth" tucks in children's clothing, apply removable trimming and the like—anything that requires quick and easy removal of stitches.

CHAIN WEIGHTS.
Used to assure the proper hang of a hem, particularly in lightweight fabrics and unconstructed garments. Such chains come in light and heavy weights, in brass or silver-colored metal. They are generally available in 24-inch pieces but some dressmaker and tailoring supply stores carry them by the foot or yard.

Stitch the chain every other link along the top and bottom at the lower edge of a garment (a) or just below the lining when there is one (b). Where there is tuck ease

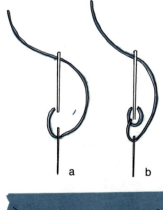

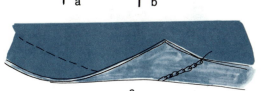

a   b

c

a

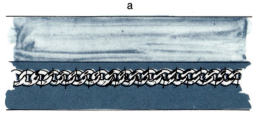

b

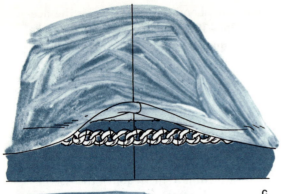

c

d

in the lining, the chain will be hidden by a fold (c). If no tuck ease, the chain remains visible. When there is a faced opening edge, tuck the ends of the chain under the edge of the facing (d).

CHAIN ZIPPER. A closure consisting of individual metal teeth attached to a cotton or cotton-blend tape. The chain pattern is formed by the interlocking of the teeth when the zipper is closed. Such zippers are used on medium to heavy fabrics, for they tend to be too rigid and too heavy for lightweight, supple, or limp fabrics.

If the chain zipper is difficult to work, run a piece of soap or beeswax over the teeth.

When ironing, always use a press cloth to protect the teeth of the zipper.

Close the zipper before storing, handling, laundering, or cleaning to prevent excess strain on it.

CHANGE (WATCH OR TICKET) POCKET IN MEN'S TROUSERS. This is a 4-inch in-seam pocket on the right trouser front. It is constructed after the waistband has been attached to the trousers but before it is finished on the inside.

Mark the pocket position on the right-front waist seam. The outside edge will be 3/4 inch from the outside seam. Cut two 5-inch squares of pocketing material. Cut a

2-inch-by-5-inch facing of trouser material. Trim the trouser waist and waistband seam allowances to 3/8 inch.

With right sides up, place the facing over one pocket section. Align the top edges and pin. Stitch the lower edge of the facing.

With wrong sides together, stitch the two pocket sections in a 1/4-inch seam. Start and end 1 inch from the top on each side. Clip to the stitching. Trim the seam allowances to 1/8 inch. Trim corners diagonally (a). Press. Turn the pocket to the right side. Press. Stitch in a 1/4-inch seam.

Fold under the faced edge toward the pocket and pin out of the way. Observing the placement marks, place the right side of the unfaced end of the pocket against the trouser waist. Align the edges of the pocket and the waist seam allowance. Stitch 1/4 inch from the edge (b).

Fold the pocket down and press it to position. Stitch close to the fold through the pocket and the seam allowance (c). Unpin

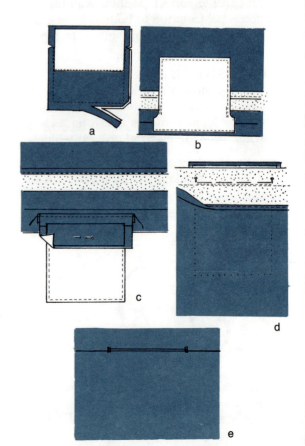

a

b

c

d

e

the faced end of the pocket. Baste, then stitch it to the waistband seam allowance from one end of the pocket opening to the other as marked. Make the stitching as close as possible to the waistband seam (d).

On the right side, bar-tack (q.v.) each end of the opening. To make the pocket opening, carefully rip the waist-seam stitches between the bar tacks (e). Or you could leave the marked opening un-stitched when attaching the waistband.

CHECKED FABRIC. How much of a problem checked fabric is in layout, cutting, and stitching depends on the size of the check and how meticulous the sewer is. Ideally, whether printed, woven, or knit, all checks should be matched not only horizontally at the construction seams but vertically as well in the same way as are plaids (q.v.). If the check is smaller than 1/4 inch, you could get away without the matching.

Choose a design with straight rather than curved style lines. They are more consistent with the angularity of the check. Choose horizontal or vertical darts that can be balanced on the straight lines of the fabric. Diagonal darts can be down-right disastrous, as they cannot but result in a complete mismatching of fabric.

Remember that matching checks calls for more yardage than when a fabric is a solid color. How much more depends on the size of the check, the number of seams that must be matched, and whether there is directional movement (as in hound's-tooth check).

CHEST PATTERN CORRECTIONS. Before making these corrections *see* PATTERN COR-RECTIONS for general information.

Whether sitting or standing, this portion of the garment, along with the neckline and sleeves, is always on view. Therefore a smooth fit across the chest is essential.

Hollow Chest. Fold a dart across the chest in the needed amount with the widest part at the center front and tapering to nothing at the armhole. Correct the center front as necessary.

Pigeon Chest. Draw an L-shaped slash line from a midpoint on the shoulder seam to the notch at the armhole. Slash, starting at the armhole and cutting *to* but not through the shoulder seam. Spread the pattern in the desired amount across the chest.

Draw a new underarm curve, starting at the point of spread and ending beyond the side seam in the same amount as that added at the chest. Correct the side seam by tapering from the new underarm. Correct the shoulder seam.

CHEST PIECE (MEN'S TAILORING). Used to fill in and round out the hollow in front of the shoulders. It gives the man-tailored garment its characteristic smooth, subtle chest shaping.

A chest piece consists of graded layers of interfacing and padding material, joined loosely together by catch stitching or machine zigzag stitching. It is attached to the front interfacing (a).

Ready-made chest pieces are commercially available but customized ones have the advantage of meeting the particular needs of a figure and the lines of a design. Most patterns for men's jackets include one upper front reinforcement pattern

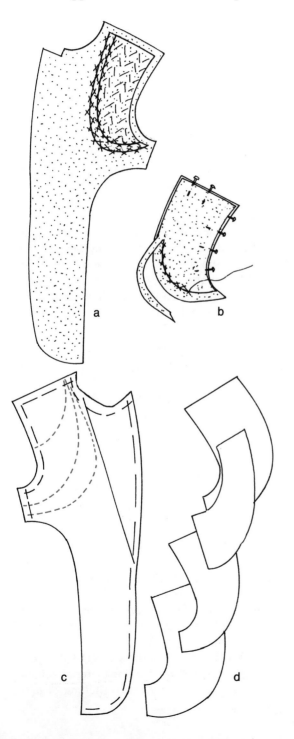

a

b

c

d

piece. This may be used to create additional graded patterns by trimming away a bit on all edges (b).

If there is no pattern for a chest piece, make your own, using the interfacing pattern as a guide (c). Draw in the shape of each piece. The standard chest piece consists of 4 layers—2 chest pieces (keep 1/2 inch from the roll line of the jacket), 1 armhole reinforcement, and 1 shoulder piece (shoulder pad pocket) (d). However, the number of pieces can be varied to accommodate figure requirements and the style of the jacket. Use as many layers as seem indicated.

Trace each pattern section. Since chest pieces are used in pairs, remember to reverse the patterns for the other side.

The materials generally used for this purpose are hair canvas for all four pieces or hair canvas in combinations with felt, wool interfacing fabric, lamb's-wool padding, heavy cotton flannel, or cover cloth. Use whichever appears suitable to create the degree of padding desired or whichever is available.

To Assemble: Place two large chest pieces to face in opposite directions. Place an armhole piece on top of each. Fuse or zigzag to the chest piece along the curved and armhole edges. If zigzagged, use the largest and widest stitch (a). Or wait until all pieces are in place and tailor-baste them through all thicknesses (b).

Place a shoulder piece on top of the first two. If this is to be used as a shoulder-pad pocket, leave the shoulder and armhole edge open. Once more, fuse, zigzag, or wait until all pieces are in place and tailor-baste. Cover all with the second chest piece, graded along the curved edge. Tailor-baste to the rest of the layers.

Position the completed chest piece on the interfacing so the largest piece will be toward the interfacing and the smallest piece will be toward the body. Armhole and shoulder edges are aligned with armhole and shoulder seams. Pin and tailor-baste in place with long, wide stitches that come through to the interfacing only. Catch-stitch the curved edge next to the

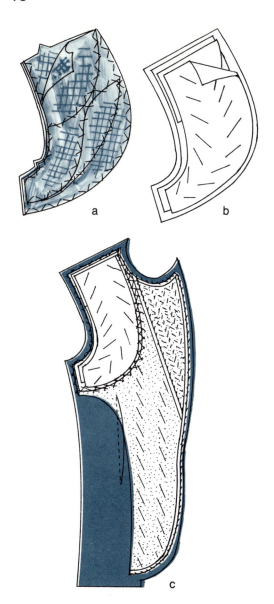

a   b

c

roll line (c). This last step is easier to do before the interfacing is applied to the garment, though, from the standpoint of fitting, this may not always be possible.

When a commercial chest piece is used, position it on the interfacing with the felt side up. Attach it in the same way as suggested for the custom chest piece.

CHILDREN'S CLOTHES. Sewing is sewing, whether it be for children or for grown-ups. Most of the sewing techniques for adult clothing are also applicable for children's clothes. However, since the life expectancy of the latter is considerably less than the former and since the wear given children's garments is considerably harder, it appears logical to simplify, speed up, and adapt the standard sewing techniques to the construction of children's clothing. *(See* UNIT CONSTRUCTION.*)* For instance, machine stitching for most operations is speedier and stronger. Limit the handwork to details of high visibility.

Check the pattern measurements against the child's measurements. *(See* BODY MEASUREMENT CHART: CHILDREN.*)* Make the necessary pattern corrections (q.v.) in the same way as for an adult.

Because the sections are small, keep them flat or open as long as possible. This makes it much easier to handle the garment. For example: in making a one-piece dress or shirt, complete the front and back by stitching all the darts and seams, applying any interfacing, attaching the pockets, tabs, or other details, and making the machine buttonholes. Join the front and back at the shoulders.

Make and apply the collar. Since the tiny neck facings are difficult to handle, use bias strips at the neck edge for attaching the collar. *(See* BIAS FINISH FOR A FLAT COLLAR.*)* Stitch the sleeve into the armhole. In a sleeveless garment, a combination neckline and armhole facing (q.v.) makes construction easier. The work is flat up to this point.

Then, in one continuous line of stitching, join the underarm sleeve seam and the side seam of the garment. Make the hem. Add the finishing hand details.

Make sturdy seams—strong enough to withstand repeated washings and rough wear. French seams (q.v.) are fine on little girls' clothing, flat fell seams (q.v.) for boys' shirts and shorts. To avoid the job of repeated repairs, stitch twice all areas of stress like armholes, crotch seams, pockets.

Finish seam edges with binding, edge-stitching, or overcasting (q.q.v.) so they won't fray in washing. Hem finishes should be durable. Blindstitch by machine (q.v.) for everyday clothes; hand-stitch for dress-up clothes.

In making pants (which are really joined

tubes), the flat-as-long-as-possible rule becomes open-as-long-as-possible. First join the inseams on both legs. Then stitch the crotch seam. Finally close the tubes by stitching the outseams. Add the circumference seams at the waistline-waistband or casing and the hems.

While the size will be smaller, the proportionate amount of ease should be greater. For comfort, children's clothes must be roomy, particularly at the armholes and the crotch. All-in-one garments such as snowsuits, creepers, or pajamas need a low crotch to provide ample room for sitting (particularly if there are diapers beneath). Necklines should have plenty of ease.

Here are a few things to keep in mind about children's clothing.

Make them attractive, not just practical. Children are just as responsive as grown-ups (sometimes more so) to pretty things. If you've ever had the experience of permitting them their choice you know how insistent they are upon colors and styles that appeal to them. Decorative details like appliqués, patches, monograms delight them. Pockets are wonderful places to hide treasures. Add pockets even if the pattern doesn't call for them.

Make them easy to get into. Elasticized pull-on pants and skirts. Large enough buttons for little hands to manipulate. Zippers that slide easily, particularly decorative ones with interesting pulls. Snaps that work quickly and easily.

Make them practical. Keep in mind ease of laundering. Allow generous hems. Allow room for growth by making hem or bodice tucks (q.q.v.) and expandable waistlines.

CHILDREN'S COATS AND JACKETS. As with other children's clothes (q.v.) and for the same reasons, it makes sense to strip down the time-consuming handwork of traditional tailoring to a minimum when making children's coats and jackets.

Skip the laborious pad stitching. Use a fusible interfacing instead and keep that minimal. Make machine buttonholes. Make and attach the pockets, collar, and

lining by machine. *See listings for all machine methods for tailoring.*

If you have the time and are willing to put it into a child's garment, go ahead and make that beautiful coat or jacket, using all the classic tailoring techniques. After all, gems come in small sizes.

CHILDREN'S SIZES. Patterns for children's clothes come in a variety of types and sizes.

Babies': for infants who don't yet walk. Diaper allowance is included in the pattern. Choose size by weight, height, and age—from newborn to 6 months. (Age alone is not a good determinant.)

Toddlers': between baby and child. Diaper allowance is included in the pattern. Sizes 1/2 to 4 are suitable for both boys and girls.

Children's: for both boys and girls. In general, they have the same breast and waist measurements as toddlers' but are designed for taller children. Sizes 1 to 6X.

Girls': designed for growing girls with figures that have not begun to mature. Sizes 7 to 14.

Chubbie: designed for growing girls who are above average weight for age and height and whose figures have not yet begun to mature. Sizes 8½c to 14½c.

Boys': for growing boys in sizes 7 to 14.

Teen sizes for girls and boys are for maturing figures not yet grown to adult proportions.

In order to make a correct size selection of a pattern, measure the child. (*See* BODY MEASUREMENT CHART.) When measurements fall between two sizes, choose the larger size for a child with husky build, the smaller size for a child of slender build. If providing room for growth concerns you, choose the larger size. Choose boys' sizes according to the chest measurement, girls' sizes according to the breast measurement. Adjust other pieces as necessary.

Shirt sizes go by the neckband measurement; pants and skirts by the waist measurements; jackets and coats by chest measurement for boys, by breast measurement for girls. The same is true for a pattern that includes separates—a jacket plus trousers, a shirt plus pants, and the like.

CHINESE BALL (KNOT) BUTTON. An ornamental button made of a single or double strand of cord, round braid, self-filled, or corded tubing woven and drawn up to form a ball or knot.

Though the actual knot uses up only about one third of a length of cord or tubing, that extra length is needed to interlace the loops of which the knot is formed. For a single knot, 12 to 14 inches is a comfortable length to start with. Another third of length is needed for a double knot; an additional third for a triple knot. The size of the finished ball depends not only on the number of knots but on the thickness of the material and whether one or two strands have been used for the weaving. To be sure of the desired size, make a test button.

To Form the Ball. About one third of the way up on the cording, form a loop (a). You can pin it to paper if you wish but a small knot can easily be held in place by hand. Make a second loop over the first, bringing the second end under the first (b). Make a third loop with the long end, weaving it through the previous two loops (c). *Caution:* If tubing is used, keep the seam either up or down but be consistent throughout. Never allow it to twist.

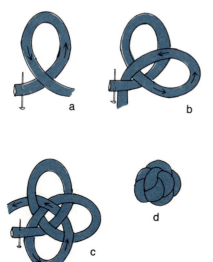

To draw up the cord into a knot, begin at the center, keeping ends 1 and 2 about equal in length. Pull each end toward the side. (When the loops are drawn up but still flat, the knot forms a frog and can be so used.) Continue to draw up the ends until the outer edges pull inward. At this stage, the seam of tubing should be on the underside so it will be completely hidden when the knot is tightened. The trick to forming a symmetrical ball is in the easing and shaping of the loops as you work.

Cup the knot over your finger and pull up all loops tightly, bringing the ends underneath to form the ball (d). Trim the ends and sew them flat to the underside of the button. Attach the ball to the garment with a button stem. *(See* BUTTON SHANK OR STEM.)

For a *double knot,* follow the weaving pattern twice around. For a *triple knot,* follow the weaving pattern three times around.

CHINESE COLLAR. An ever popular, close-fitting standing collar (q.v.) variously

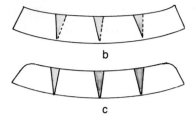

b

c

termed mandarin, Nehru, or Mao depending on your age and point of view (a).

For closer fit at the upper edge, draw
slash lines in several places. Slash and
overlap the pattern to fit the neck measurement at the upper edge of the collar
(b). For more length at the upper edge,
slash and spread the collar to the desired
length. Fill in the spread area with tissue
(c).

CIRCULAR HEM. The depth of a turned-
under circular hem is never more than
what can be eased at its upper edge. The
more circular the hem edge, the narrower
the hem.

There are a number of ways in which
this narrow turned-under hem can be
treated: as a rolled hem, a bias-faced hem,
a turned-and-topstitched hem, or a
turned-up hem. Nor need the hem edge be
a turnunder. Try a lettuce edge, a shell-
stitched edge, or picot edge finish. *See listing
for each of the above.*

CIRCULAR SKIRT. A considerable portion
of a circular skirt is bias. All bias areas
stretch. There is the additional pull on the
waistline of the weight of the material.
Therefore, in reckoning the length of the
waistline, make it 1 to 2 inches less than
the actual body measurement. How much
will depend on the amount of fullness and
the heaviness of the fabric. This corrected
measurement also tends to make the skirt
fit more smoothly over the hips by lowering the point at which the folds or ripples
start.

Stretch the adjusted skirt waistline to fit
the waistband, the measurements of which
are in no way changed—unless the band,
too, is cut on the bias. In that case, the
measurement for the bias band would be

that of the corrected circular-skirt waistline.

Use soft fabric for a very full circular or
circle skirt. Unless the fabric is extremely
wide, the size of the pattern extremely
small, or the skirt very short (skating
skirt), the fabric will need to be pieced for
extra width. *See* PIECING FABRIC *and* CIRCULAR
HEM.

CLAPPER. Another name for the pounding
block (q.v.).

CLASP BUCKLE CLOSURE. A clasp buckle
can be used for a closure as well as for its
more usual use as a belt fastening. Attach
each half to each side of the closing. Use
heavy-duty thread or buttonhole twist
and whipstitch the entire length of the
bar. When a bar is in an exposed position,
cover it completely with thread either before attaching it or while doing so. *See* BELT
WITH CLASP BUCKLE.

CLASSIC TAILORING ("HARD" TAILOR-
ING, CONSTRUCTED TAILORING). The
method for producing a traditional tailored
garment featuring notched collar and lapels, set-in sleeves, subtle built-in and
blocked-in shaping, flat seams, crisp edges,
and, above all, flawless fit. It requires
firmly woven, hard-surfaced woolens.

Classic tailoring starts with the outer
fabric and works in toward the figure with
an understructure consisting of interfacings, linings, paddings, and weights.

The classic tailored look is the result of
meticulous cutting, a network of tiny hand
and machine stitches that firm and shape
its sculptured form, skillful snipping and
slashing, perfect pressing, and flawless fit
that subtly skims the body it covers.

Considering what goes on underneath,
its characteristic trimness is a miracle of
construction and workmanship. This is the
tailoring for those who love well-con-
structed, expertly crafted, timeless clothes.
Lots of work but worth it!

CLEAN-FINISHED SEAM. For light- and
medium-weight nonbulky fabrics.

Make a line of machine stitching 1/8
inch from the cut edge of the seam allow-

ance. Turn under along the line of stitching and press. Stitch again close to the folded edge.

CLIP. A short snip in the seam allowance at right angles to the stitching line and just short of it. Use sharp-pointed trimming scissors.

CLOSURE. A means by which an opening can be closed. This is a prime example of how one can make decorative use of a structural necessity. If a closing there must be, make it beautiful or interesting. Though the simpler, less gadgety fastenings are always acceptable, there are times when your imagination can run free. Almost anything can do for a closing. *See* BUTTONHOLES; BUTTONS; BUCKLES; FLY CLOSING; HOOK AND EYE; LOOP-AND-BUTTON CLOSING; SNAPS; TAPE FASTENER; ZIPPERED CLOSING.

COAT. Use the same size pattern as for other garments. The necessary ease is built into the pattern.

COAT-AND-JACKET PRESS BOARD. If this piece of pressing equipment (a) is not available for purchase, make one from the following directions.

Make patterns for the board and its stand (b). Cut two 24-inch pieces out of 3/4-inch lumber or plywood. Cut a 7-inch length of four-by-four. Countersink screws in the designated positions (b) and attach one side of the four-by-four to the board, the other to the stand (c).

Following the outline of the board, draw a pattern for the largest layer of padding (q.v.). Make patterns for a series of similar shapes, each slightly smaller than the other, until you reach the smallest (about 6 to 8 inches long). Make a pattern for a top layer that extends over the edges of the board.

Cut out the layers of padding from the patterns. Center the smallest piece on the board. Place each slightly larger layer over the preceding for the gradual shaping of the board (d). Keep in mind that the pressure of pressing will flatten the shape somewhat.

Trace and cut out a cover of strong, coarse twilled cotton to enclose all the padding and the edges of the board. Bind it with a double-fold bias tape so it can be used as a casing. Enclose a length of string.

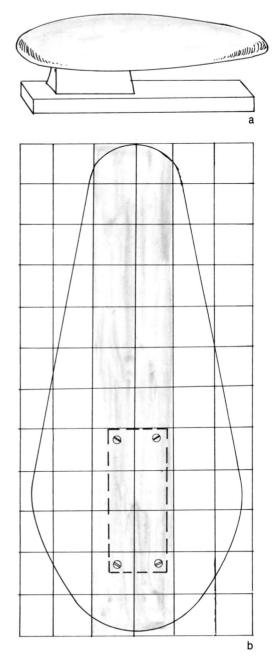
a

b

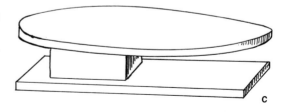
c

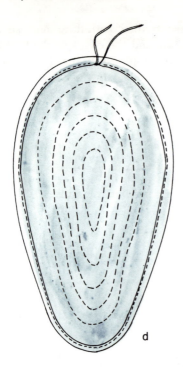

d

Place the cover over the padding and the edges of the board and draw it up to fit snugly.

COIL ZIPPER. A continuous synthetic strand (nylon or polyester) twisted into a spiral and dyed to match the woven or knit tape to which it is attached. It comes in various lengths and in many colors.

Its light weight and flexibility make it desirable for many garments that do not need the strength of the metal-toothed chain zipper.

If the zipper sticks or is difficult to work, run a piece of soap or beeswax over the coil. Take care in pressing. Use a press cloth to protect it. Since it is made of synthetic fiber, keep the heat low. Close the zipper before hand laundering or cleaning to prevent excess strain.

COLLAR. The construction of a collar depends on the type of collar, its design, the texture of the fabric, and whether it is a dressmaking or tailoring project. Because of the variety of construction possibilities, each type of collar is dealt with separately (see COLLAR TYPES). There are, however, certain considerations common to them all.

Do not cut out the collar until all the seams and

darts that intersect the neckline are completed. A final fitting of the body of the garment may indicate a necessary change in the position and length of the neckline that will necessitate a corresponding collar adjustment. It is even wise to test the adjusted collar in interfacing material or muslin before cutting out the collar.

Because of its curved edge, the neckline stretches very easily, making the collar setting difficult and often inaccurate. To prevent any stretching or distortion, staystitch the neckline as soon as the garment is cut.

When the opening is a zippered one, insert the zipper before attaching the collar to the garment. (There are a few exceptions, such as band collars that extend above the neckline.)

In a button-to-the-neck style, it is advisable to postpone the making of the buttonholes until after the garment and its collar are fitted. Should you need to raise or lower the neckline, you would also need to place and space the buttonholes and buttons accordingly.

To preserve the overall shape of a collar, do not make too large an alteration in any one place. This distorts the shape of its neckline and style line. Up to a seam-allowance adjustment may be made on the center back. When more than this is needed, slash and spread the collar pattern; when less is needed, slash and overlap the collar pattern in several places.

In a collar that consists of two layers (most collars do)—an undercollar and an upper collar—the seam that joins them is rolled to the underside, out of sight. To accomplish this, an extra amount of material is added to the length and width of the upper layer. *See* PATTERN PREPARED FOR CUTTING *and* COLLAR ROLL ALLOWANCE.

To guarantee that the seam that joins the two layers never slips into view, the two thicknesses are further held in place with either topstitching (q.v.) or understitching (q.v.), depending on which is appropriate to the design and the fabric.

Since two layers of fabric are involved in the construction of the collar, study carefully the directions for an enclosed (encased) seam (q.v.).

Every bit of sewing skill you possess goes into the making of a collar. Observe particularly the directional hand and machine stitching, the squaring or blunting of corners, the trimming and pressing, the elimination of bulk by grading and diagonal snipping at the corners, the notching and/or clipping of all curved seam allowances and the pressing of them in the direction of least bulk, the collar roll allowance, and the pressing to shape.

COLLAR INTERFACING. What to use for the collar interfacing and how to apply it depends on many factors: the type of collar; whether its style is soft or firm, dressmaker or tailored; the texture of the fabric, whether it is washable or dry-cleanable. Since the interfacing is there to provide body and shape, some collars (washable, soft styles) may not require it. Many designers choose not to interface, preferring a very soft appearance.

Since there so many possibilities and choices, the interfacing of collars and the method of application is best dealt with by specific directions for particular types of collar (q.v.).

In General. The interfacing used for a collar is the same as that used for the rest of the garment. *(See* INTERFACING.*)* The exceptions to this rule are the interfacings for the tailored notched collar (q.v.) and the standing collar (q.v.).

In *opaque materials,* the interfacing is applied to the wrong side of the under collar (a). In *thin or transparent materials,* interface the upper collar (b). This places the interfacing in such position that, when stitched and turned to the right side, the seam allowances won't show.

If the *collar and facing are in one piece,* the interfacing may be applied to the entire collar in nonbulky material (c). Either the upper collar or the undercollar may be interfaced, depending on how opaque or how transparent the material is. Such interfacing is brought to the fold line for a

crisp edge (d) or ½ inch beyond the fold line for a soft edge (e).

Transfer all pattern markings to the interfacing. Choose a method for marking that will not show through the collar fabric.

The methods for *applying the interfacing to the collar* depend on the weight of the interfacing and whether it is fusible.

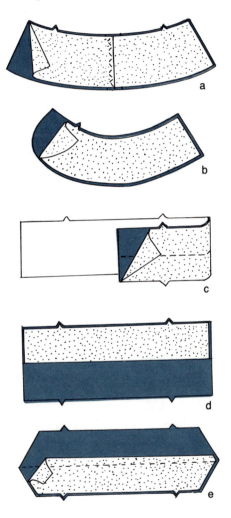

Lightweight Interfacings. Trim the outer corners to about ¼ inch beyond the seamlines. Apply the interfacing to the wrong side of the undercollar or the upper collar. Pin and baste to position. Include the seam allowances in the seams. Trim them close to the stitching.

Medium to Heavy Interfacings. Trim away all seam allowances and across the outer corners. Pin and baste to the wrong side of the undercollar. Catch-stitch all edges.

Fusible Interfacings. Trim all seam allowances and corners. Fuse to the wrong side of the undercollar either before or after the center back seam, when present, is stitched in the fabric.

Center back seams in woven or nonwoven interfacings are joined by a lapped or abutted seam construction (q.v.).

COLLAR NECKLINE. An important part of the design and fit of the collar.

Any collar that conforms to the shape and length of the garment neckline lies flat (a). When a collar neckline is shortened slightly and stretched to fit the unshortened garment neckline, it is pushed into a soft roll. To shorten the collar neckline, add tissue to a depth of about 1/8 inch. The broken line is the original neckline; the solid line, the raised neckline (b).

When the neckline of a collar curves in a direction opposite to the curve of the garment neckline, the collar is pushed into a stand (c). The shallower the opposing curves, the lower the stand. The deeper the opposing neckline curves, the higher the stand.

When a collar neckline is more curved than the garment neckline, the collar will ripple (d).

A straight band whose neckline is the exact length of the garment neckline will stand (e).

COLLAR ON A STAND. For shirt, dress, jacket, or coat. *See* SHIRT COLLAR WITH SELF-BAND *and* SHIRT COLLAR WITH SEPARATE BAND.

COLLAR PRESS PADS. Somewhere on the rounded surface of the tailor's ham (q.v.), that all-purpose shaping pad, is an area that can be used for collar shaping (a). However, there are two press pads that are designed specifically for that purpose.

Collar Press Pad No. 1: Cut two circles of firmly woven material 6 inches in diameter and one 1-inch bias strip to join them.

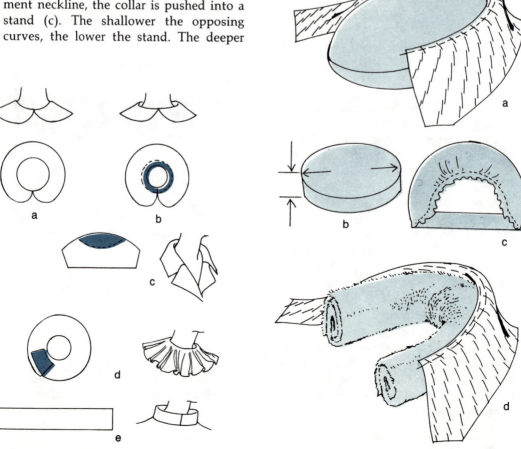

Stitch the circles to the bias strip, leaving an opening for the stuffing. Pack tightly with hardwood sawdust. Close the opening with hand stitches (b).

Collar Press Pad No. 2: Cut a bias strip of firmly woven material 6 inches wide by 12 inches long. Fold this rectangle lengthwise and stitch the long side. Stuff tightly to within 2 inches of each end and hand-stitch across the pad. Overlap the un-stuffed ends and stitch them securely to each other. These 2-inch ends can be stiffened with cardboard or buckram, which makes it easier to hold the press pad. If you wish, the ends may be tacked to a heavy piece of cardboard or plywood 2 inches by 4½ inches, so that the pad can sit upright (c).

If none of these is available, a Turkish towel rolled and curled into a neck shape can also be used as a collar-shaping device (d).

COLLAR ROLL ALLOWANCE. Allowances must be made to accommodate the various rolls of a collar.

The collar rolls *around the neck.* Its outside curve, being longer than the inside curve, requires more length (a).

The collar rolls *from the neckline over the roll line, to the style line.* The curve of the upper collar, being longer than that of the undercollar, requires more depth (b).

In addition, when there are *two layers* of collar—an upper and an under—extra length and width are required so the seam that joins the layers can be rolled to the underside, out of sight.

To provide these needed lengths and widths, add the necessary amount to the outer edges of the upper collar and taper to the neck edge. Do not alter the edge that joins the garment (c). How much to add depends on the weight and texture of the fabric. Many patterns provide an average amount for these rolls but this may not be a right amount for your fabric, particularly if it is heavy or bulky. Check the pattern first. Test the turn in the material you are using to determine just how much is needed.

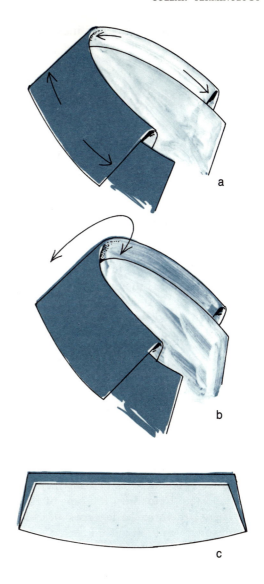

a

b

c

COLLAR—SINGLE-LAYER. *See* SINGLE-LAYER COLLAR.

COLLAR STYLE LINE. *See* COLLAR TERMINOLOGY.

COLLAR TERMINOLOGY. A collar has parts and each part has a name.

The neckline is the part of the collar that is stitched to the garment neckline. Notches indicate the points that are matched.

The style line is the outer edge of the collar. As with any other style line, this may be anything the designer dreams up. The style line always finds that part of the shoulders which equals it in measurement, pushing the rest into a stand. As the outer edge is shortened, the stand increases. As the outer edge is lengthened, the stand decreases.

The stand is the amount the collar rises from the neckline to the roll line.

The roll line is the line along which the collar turns down.

The fall is the depth of the collar from the roll line to the style line. The fall must be deep enough to hide the neckline seam plus a little extra.

The break is the point at which a collar turns back to form a lapel.

The gorge line is the horizontal seam line on a jacket or coat at which a notched collar joins the lapel.

The upper collar is the top portion or upper layer of a collar that has two thicknesses. It is often called *the* collar.

The undercollar is the bottom portion or bottom layer of a two-thickness collar. It is often called the collar facing or simply facing.

COLLAR TYPES. Whatever the style, size, shape, or descriptive name, collars are classified by type. You may know them by their more familiar names (Peter Pan, sailor, Bertha, ring, turtleneck, and so on). However, for purposes of construction, it is important to identify the type of collar.

There are three basic types of collars with some variation within each.

A flat collar (a) is almost identical to the shape and length of the garment neckline and shoulders, though it has a slight roll. It may be a one-piece collar with a front or back opening (b) or in two sections, a right-hand and a left-hand (c). It is generally faced, though in children's clothing it is often a bound single layer.

A rolled collar (d) rises from the neck seam and turns down to create a rolled edge around the neck. The neckline of the collar varies from straight (as in a convertible collar) to an opposing curve like that of the classic notched tailored collar or the shawl collar. The upper layer and the underlayer of a rolled collar are generally cut separately (e), though they are sometimes cut all in one piece (f).

a

b

c

d

e

f

g

i

h

A standing collar (g) extends up from the neckline in either a soft or stiff manner. The collar may be rectangular (cut in one piece and folded over lengthwise) (h) or slightly curved, in which case it must be cut in two pieces (i). A curved standing collar hugs the neck like a Chinese collar. A rectangular standing collar stands away from the neck like a ring collar (q.v.) unless it is cut bias and pressed into a curve.

Collar listings in this book are both under their familiar descriptive names and by collar type. The latter provides the directions for construction.

COMBINATION LAYOUT. One in which part of a garment is laid on one type of fold, another part on a different fold. Since you can fold fabric only one way at a time, pin the pattern on the fabric for the first layout (a). Cut it out. Arrange the fabric for the second layout. Place the pattern in the new layout and cut it out (b). Repeat the procedure as many times as necessary.

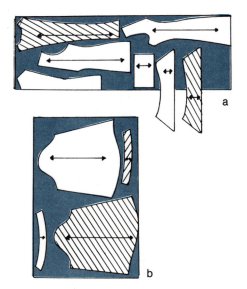

COMBINATION NECK AND ARMHOLE FACING. This is a shaped facing in which the neck and armhole facings are cut as one piece. Facings for sleeveless and collarless styles are often cut in this way.

While the machine application of this type of facing may look complicated, it is in fact simple if you leave one seam open.

The open seam may be at the shoulder or the underarm (side).

With the Shoulder Seam Open. Stitch the side seams of the garment but leave the shoulder seams open. Stitch the side seams of the facing but leave the shoulder seams open. Press all seam allowances open. Trim and grade them. Free them of cross-seam bulk.

Place the right side of the facing against the right side of the garment. Match centers, seams, and outside edges, stretching as necessary. Pin a tiny tuck in each garment shoulder. This represents the extra fullness that permits the joining seam to be rolled to the underside. Pin to position.

With the facing side up, stitch around the neck and around the armholes but do not stitch the shoulders (a). Trim, clip, and grade all seam allowances. Unpin the tuck on the garment shoulder. Turn the facing to the underside through the opening at the shoulder.

Turn in the raw edges of the front shoulder about a seam allowance (b). Slip the back shoulder into the turned-in opening (c). Make certain the right sides of the outer fabric are together and the right sides of the facing are together. Neckline and armhole seams must match. Stretch the facing to match the garment.

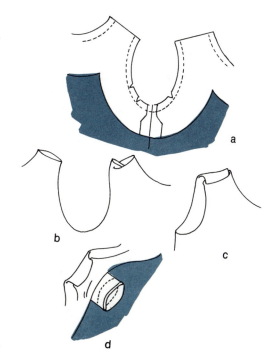

Reach up under the facing, grasp the open shoulders, and pull them down far enough between the facing and garment so you can work with them. With right sides together, raw edges and seams matching, stitch the shoulder opening in one continuous circle of a seam (d). Trim the seam allowances and finger-press them open with nail of thumb or forefinger. Carefully pull the shoulder back to its correct position. Press all outside edges, remembering to roll the neckline and armhole joining seams to the underside.

With the Side Seams Open. This kind of construction can be used when the length and bulk of the garment are not too great and when there is a center front or center back opening.

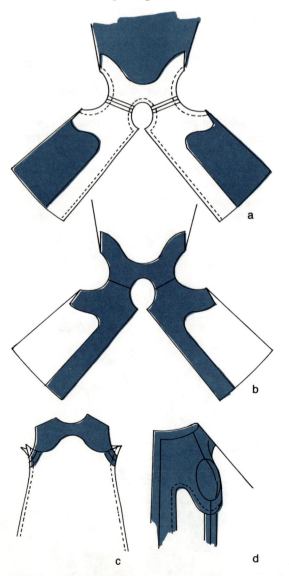

Stitch the garment at the shoulders but not at the side seams. Stitch the facing at the shoulders but not at the side seams. Press all seam allowances open. Trim and grade them.

With right sides together, stitch the facing to the opening and neck edges. Stitch the facing to the armhole edges (a). Ease and/or stretch as necessary to make the smaller facing fit the garment. Grade the seam allowances and clip all curves.

Turn the facing to the underside, bringing the opening edges through the shoulders (b). Open out the facing so it extends the side seams.

With right sides together, seams matching, make one continuous line of stitching to form the underarm seam from the edge of the facing to the hem of the garment (c). Press the seam allowances open. Trim and clip them where necessary. Turn the armhole facing to its correct position (d). Press all the outside edges, being careful to roll the neckline and armhole joining seams to the underside.

COMBINATION NECK AND PLACKET BAND. A decorative finish for a collarless neckline as well as a placket opening. Combine the techniques for a shaped (applied) band neckline finish (q.v.) and straight placket band (q.v.).

CONTINUOUS BOUND PLACKET (CONTINUOUS LAP).

This is an inconspicuous finish consisting of one strip of self-material inserted in a slash or seam from one end of the opening to the other. The front edge of the finished placket laps over the back edge.

Cut a straight strip of self-fabric to be used for the binding. Make it 1½ inches wide by twice the length of the slash. Fold under and press ¼ inch along one side of the strip. This could be a selvage instead of a fold-under to reduce the bulk somewhat. Should you plan to use the selvage, make the strip ¼ inch narrower. In lightweight or sheer materials, the strip can also be made a little narrower—about 1¼ inch or less.

In a Slash. Reinforce the stitching line of the opening with small machine stitches, blunting the point. Slash to the point, taking care not to cut the stitching (a). Spread the slash open all the way until it forms a continuous straight line. With right sides together, place the line of reinforcement stitching against the binding ¼ inch in from the unfolded edge.

With the garment side up and using small stitches, stitch beside the previous line of stitching (b). Turn the binding to the wrong side, bringing the folded edge (or selvage) to the stitching, and slip-stitch to the seam (c).

Turn the front edge of the completed binding to the wrong side and press. To assure that the binding remains in position, make a diagonal line of stitching on the inside at the top of the fold (d).

In a Seam. Stitch the seam, leaving the opening for the placket. Clip the seam allowances at the end of the opening. Press the seam allowances of the garment, leav-

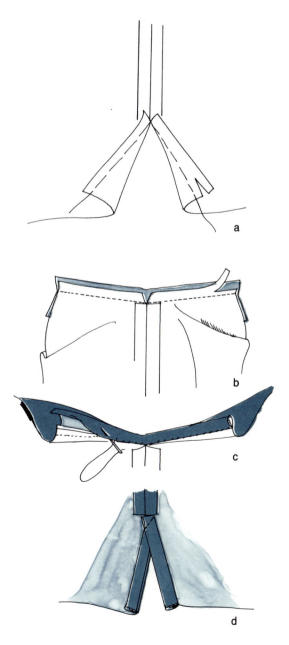

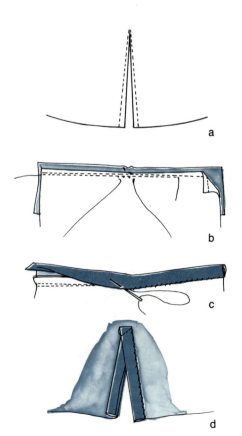

ing the placket seam allowances un-pressed. Trim the latter to 1/4 inch (a).

Spread the placket open until it forms a straight line. With right sides together, stitch the unfolded edge of the binding to the placket in a 1/4-inch seam. Use small stitches. Grade the seam allowances (b).

Turn the binding to the wrong side, bringing the folded edge to the stitching, and slip-stitch to the seam (c). Turn the front edge of the binding to the wrong side and press. Finish with a line of diagonal stitching on the inside across the top of the fold (d).

CONTINUOUS-THREAD DART. A dart stitched so there are no thread ends at dart point. This is a technique used wherever a thread knot would be unsightly, as on a right-side decorative dart or a wrong-side dart in sheer or transparent material. In this operation the threading of the machine and the stitching of the dart are the reverse of the usual procedure.

Bring the bobbin thread up through the throat plate. Unwind enough bobbin thread to complete the stitching of the dart. Rethread the machine with the bobbin thread, starting at the eye of the needle and working up through the various thread guides and moving parts to a spool of thread on the spool pin. Tie the ends of bobbin and spool threads. Bring the needle down into the dart point and stitch to the wide end of the dart.

CONTINUOUS-THREAD TUCK. Construct a released tuck (q.v.) by the same method as that for the continuous-thread dart (q.v.).

CONTOUR BELT. A belt shaped to conform to the natural curve of the waistline. Because it requires precise fit, a trial fitting in heavy muslin or similar material is essential. Transfer all changes from the muslin to the pattern.

Cut all layers of the belt on the lengthwise grain. The facing may be of self-fabric or any suitable lining material. The interfacing (cut without seam allowances) may be of crinoline or similar stiff fabric or

of two layers of heavy canvas pad-stitched in lengthwise rows 1/4 inch apart (a).

Optional: Stay all edges of the interfacing with 1/8-inch twill or bias tape.

Stay-stitch the belt on all outer edges. Miter all corners. Ease-stitch the outer curved edges of both facing and belt.

Place the interfacing on the wrong side of the belt, bringing the edges to the seam line. Baste to position. Turn the seam allowances of the belt over the interfacing, drawing up the ease stitching so the belt fabric fits tightly over the interfacing (b). Steam-press the edges sharply. Clip, notch, and trim the seam allowances. Fasten them to the interfacing *only* with permanent basting or catch stitching.

Turn under a 3/4-inch seam allowance on the facing, clipping, notching, and easing as necessary. Baste close to the fold. Trim the seam allowances to half width. Place the facing in position on the interfaced belt, wrong sides together, keeping the folded edges slightly inside the belt. Pin at right angles (c). Slip-stitch the

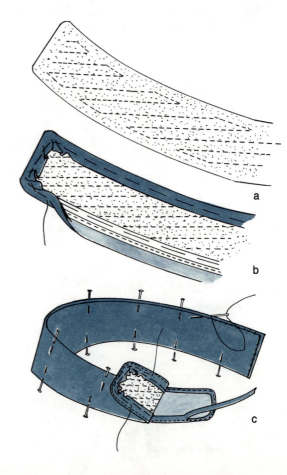

a

b

c

facing to the belt. Or baste the facing to the belt, then topstitch from the right side.

All pinning and stitching must be done very carefully to preserve the grain of the belt and facing fabric. Off-grain pulling and wrinkling will disfigure the belt. Remove all visible bastings. Attach the belt fastening.

CONTOUR DART. *See* WAISTLINE DART *and* DOUBLE-POINTED DART.

CONTOUR WAISTBAND. One that follows and settles into the natural contour of the waistline. Not only is it the best fitting of the waistbands but its graceful curve adds design interest. It is particularly important to establish the exact line of the waistline seam to which the contour waistband is attached. *See* WAISTLINE LOCATED.

Because of its shape (and often its width), this waistband requires a separate facing and a firm interfacing. Use any stiff or stiffened interfacing.

Cut the interfacing from the facing pattern. Trim away the seam allowances. Place the interfacing on the wrong side of the waistband facing. Attach in either of the following ways: catch-stitch all edges to the seamlines (a) or machine-pad-stitch the interfacing to the facing (b). Stay the upper and lower seamlines with preshaped bias or twill tape (c).

With right sides together, pin and baste the waistband to the interfaced facing along its upper edge and ends to within a seam allowance of the edges. Stitch as basted through the center of the tape. Press the seams open over a point presser. Trim the corners. Trim, grade, and clip the seam allowances. Turn the waistband to the right side. Baste around all outside edges, rolling the joining seam to the underside (d). Press.

With right sides together, pin and baste the waistband to the garment waistline, matching all markings and adjusting the ease as necessary. Stitch. Trim, grade, clip, and notch the waistline seam allowances and press them toward the waistband (e).

Turn under the seam allowance of the

free edge. Slip-stitch the fold to the stitching, continuing across the underlap. Remove all basting and press. Sew fasteners to the ends. The number of sets of fasteners depends on the width of the waistband.

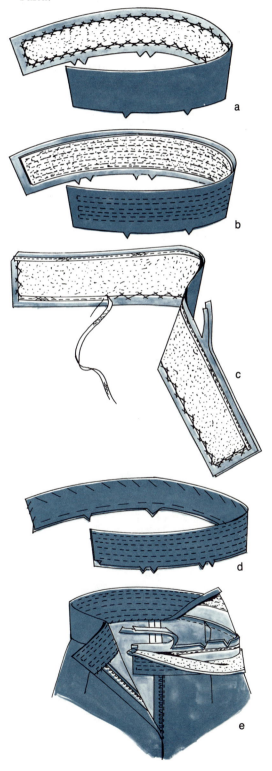

CONVERTIBLE COLLAR. A notched flat collar that can be worn either buttoned at the neck or open with lapels. *See* FLAT COLLAR *and* SHIRT COLLAR.

CORDED BAND TRIMMING. A decorative way of stiffening an edge.

Cut bands of self-fabric long enough for the amount of desired shirring and wide enough to allow for a casing on each long side that will accommodate the cording. Turn under a casing on each long edge, enclosing the cording and allowing sufficient ease to draw it up. Use the cording or zipper foot. *Alternative method:* Stitch the casing. Draw a length of Germantown yarn through it.

By either method, draw up the cording (or yarn) to the desired degree of shirring. Place the corded, shirred band on the right side of the garment in a straight or scalloped pattern. Slip-stitch the cording to the garment. To finish the ends of the corded band, *see* CORDED SEAM.

CORDED BELT. A narrow string belt made of one or more lengths of purchased cord or self-fabric tubing (q.v.). Finish the ends with a knot, a Chinese ball button, a tassel, a bead, or the like.

CORDED BUTTONHOLE. Cording adds body, strength, and durability to buttonholes, though it does reduce their flexibility. It produces a soft, plump, rounded edge.

In bound buttonholes, the cording may be inserted while making the bindings or just after the lips are formed.

1. Enclose cable cording, string, or yarn with the strips of buttonhole binding, right side out. Baste close to the cording by hand or by machine (a). *(See* CORDED TUBING.) Cut the filler even with the ends of the binding. Continue with the buttonhole construction.
2. Draw cable cording, string, or yarn through the lips of the buttonhole (b).

a

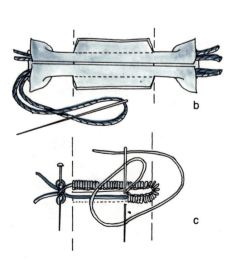

b

c

Use a loop turner or a blunt-pointed needle (tapestry or bodkin). Cut the filler even with the ends of the binding. Stitch across the end of the buttonhole.

In hand-worked buttonholes, work the buttonhole stitch over buttonhole twist or gimp secured at one end by a pin (c). Clip the cording, fasten it, and cover with a bar tack.

In machine buttonholes, stitch over the cording. The cording may be embroidery floss, crochet thread, pearl cotton, or a double strand of mercerized thread. How the cording is inserted depends on the type of buttonhole foot used for the button-hole. It may be looped over a toe at the front (a), at the back (b) of the buttonhole foot, or it may be threaded through an eyelet in the foot (c).

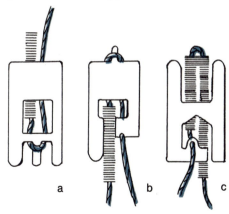

a   b   c

The cording loops around one end of the buttonhole. The loose threads at the other end are tied, trimmed, and hidden under a bar tack.

CORDED FACED EDGE. *See* CORDED SEAM.

CORDED SEAM. A seam in which cording has been inserted for firmness or decorative purposes. Buy or make the necessary length of corded tubing (q.v.).

To Insert Cording in a Straight Seam. Baste the cording on the right side of one layer of fabric, aligning the raw edges and seam lines of cording and fabric. Hold the cording taut so the seam won't buckle. If the seam involves one gathered and one straight edge, attach the cording to the lat-

ter. Place the second layer of fabric over the first, right sides together, cording be-tween them. Match all seam lines and raw edges of all fabric layers. Using the cording or zipper foot, machine-stitch through all thicknesses directly against the cording (a). Trim the cording seam allowance to 1/8 inch and grade the others.

To Apply Cording to a Curved Seam. Place and pin the cording as for a straight seam. On an *inside curve,* clip the seam al-lowances of the cording almost to the stitching to relieve it for the turn (b). On an *outside curve,* notch the seam allowance of

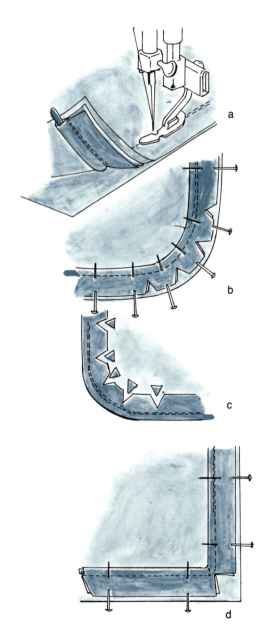

a

b

c

d

the cording almost to the stitching to remove excess fullness or rippling (c).

To Apply Cording to a Corner. Place and pin the cording as for a straight seam. At the corner, clip its seam allowance almost to the stitching to release it for the 90° turn (d). Continue as for a straight seam. Use short stitches at the corner for reinforcement.

To Finish the Ends of a Corded Seam

At a Placket Opening. Trim the cording just outside the placket seam line. Release enough stitching of the bias fabric enclosing the cording to open the end. Cut the cord even with the finished edge. Trim the fabric ends to ¼ inch and fold them to the inside even with the cord (a). Rewrap the fabric around the cord and restitch. Slip-stitch the fabric ends of the cording

and fasten with hook and eye or a hanging snap (q.q.v.). If the cording is heavy enough, attach snaps to the ends (b).

When There Is No Placket Opening. Overlap the cording at the least conspicuous place. Trim the ends for a short overlap. Release enough stitching of the fabric to open each end. Trim the cords as if to abut them (c). Overlap the empty ends of fabric, easing them toward the raw edge. Close the stitching across the ends through all layers (d).

CORDED SELF-FINISHED EDGE. A combination of cording and facing.

Cut a bias strip of fabric wide enough to enclose the cording plus 1 inch. A wider strip will not lie flat when turned to the inside to form the self-facing. Wrap one lengthwise end of the bias strip around the cord so that ¼ inch is left for a narrow seam allowance (a). Finish the outer edge of the self-facing with overcasting or by an edgestitched turn-under.

Pin the corded facing to the right side of the garment with its wider edge up, seamlines matching. Finish the ends of the

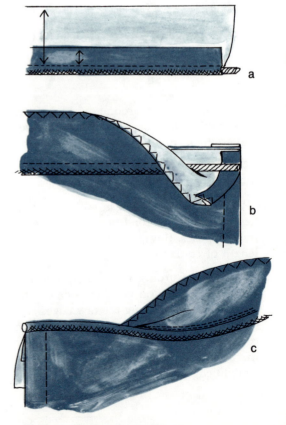

corded seam (q.v.) (b). Using the cording or zipper foot, stitch the corded facing to the garment. Trim the garment seam allowance. Clip or notch both graded seam allowances as necessary.

Turn the self-facing to the inside (c). Press. Tack where necessary.

CORDED SHIRRING. A decorative use of cording for controlling fullness. The shirring is produced by drawing up the cording through tucks. *See* CORDED TUCKS. For flexible shirring, use rounded elastic instead of cording.

CORDED TUBING. Such tubing is made of cable cord or twine enclosed in bias strips of fabric whose seam allowances are contained within the tube. Because of its finished appearance it can be used for button loops, frogs, Chinese ball buttons, ties, trimming, and the like.

Cut a length of bias fabric wide enough to cover the cord plus two seam allowances. If necessary, join sufficient lengths of bias strips for your purpose. However, there are times when it may be easier to use and make several short strips rather

than one long one. Cut a length of cord or twine *twice* as long as the bias strip. The extra length is needed to facilitate the turning.

Midway through the cord, fold the bias strip over it, right side against the cord, wrong side out. Using a cording or zipper foot, stitch across the bias strip (a). Continue stitching close to the cord but leave a little room for the seam allowances when turned. Make the beginning of the tubing somewhat wider so the turning will be easier. Trim the seam allowances (a).

To turn the tubing to the right side, start at the open end and reverse it over the other half of the cord, smoothing it as you work the tubing down over the cord (b). Cut away the surplus cord, including the stitched end.

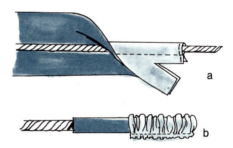

This type of tubing has the firmness provided by the cord. For a softer tubing, *see* TUBING: SELF-FILLED.

CORDED TUCKS. A right-side decorative trim made by drawing cording or twine through a series of tucks.

To determine how much fabric will be required for each tuck, make a test. Pin the fabric closely around the cording. With chalk or pencil mark the position of the pins on both sides of the tuck. Remove the cording, open the tuck, and measure from marking to marking.

On the garment, mark the tuck lines carefully on the right side of the fabric with thread tracing (q.v.). Working from the right side, wrap the tuck around the cording, matching the thread tracings. Pin, baste, and stitch, using a cording or zipper foot.

Since cording produces a stiff tuck, this

is best used at edges rather than within the garment.

CORDING. Bias-covered cable cord with exposed seam allowances, which are incorporated in joining seams and edges. Such cording provides a decorative way to give seams definition and firmness.

Cording can be bought by the yard but the choice is limited in color, fabric, and width. In most instances, you are better off making your own cording of self-fabric or one of contrasting color or texture.

To Make Cording of Woven Fabric. Cut a strip of bias fabric. Make it wide enough to cover the cording plus two seam allowances. Join sufficient lengths of bias strips for your purpose. Fold the strip, right side out, and slip the cording into the fold. Either backstitch close to the cording with matching thread or machine-stitch, using a cording or zipper foot.

To Make Cording of Knit Fabric. Cut strips of fabric on the crosswise grain, which has more stretch than the vertical grain. Or cut the strips on the bias. Proceed as for woven material.

CORDING USED FOR OUTLINING DESIGNS. An interesting decorative trim.

Trace the design on the wrong side of the garment with dressmaker's carbon paper (a). Transfer the markings to the right side with thread tracing (q.v.).

Make the needed length of corded tubing (q.v.). Place the tubing along the lines of the design. Pin or baste in place. Stitch in place from the underside with running stitches. Be sure to catch only the underside of the tubing so no stitches will be visible (b).

CORNER AT HEM OF COAT OR JACKET. When the facing is turned back to its true position after the hem has been completed, bulk is apt to form at the corner because of the many (often thick) layers of fabric superimposed one on another. There are several methods of handling this bulk. Choose the one best suited to the design, the fabric, and your personal needs—that is, whether you plan to lengthen the garment at some future time.

METHOD 1

Many patterns are cut with a seam allowance rather than a hem at the lower edge of the facing (a). If the pattern doesn't provide this feature, draft it yourself. Just be sure to allow enough length for rolling the joining seam to the underside.

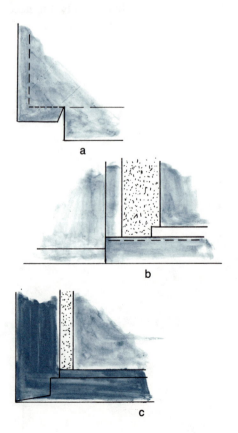

a

b

c

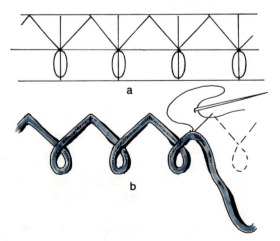

a

b

METHOD 2

Grade the facing hem (b). Fold the facing to position. Clip the seam allowance of the facing at the top of the hem. Fold under the seam allowance of the facing from the clip to the hemline and along the hemline (c). Slip-stitch the folded edges to the hem.

METHOD 3

Coat facings are often treated in the following manner if there is the least possibility that the coat will need lengthening at some future time.

Turn up the entire hem of both coat and facing (a). Fasten it to the coat in a tailor's hem. Fold the facing to position. If the fabric does not ravel, it needs no further finish. Simply make a French tack from the underside of the facing to the hem (b). If the fabric does ravel or if a finished edge is desired, clip the facing at the top of the hem. Turn under the seam allowance from the clip down and slip-stitch it to the hem.

a

b

METHOD 4

Sometimes, to avoid bulk, corners are mitered (q.v.) (c).

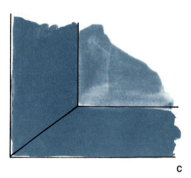

c

CORNER BLUNTED. *See* BLUNTING A CORNER.

CORNER SEAM. Stitch the seam to the corner, ending with the needle in the fabric. Raise the presser foot and pivot a 90° angle. Lower the presser foot and proceed with the stitching in the new direction. To reinforce such a corner, take small stitches —15 to 20 to the inch—for about 1 inch on either side.

This method of stitching a corner is reserved for sheer and very lightweight fabrics. In fabrics heavier than this, blunt the corner by taking 1 to 3 or more stitches across or around the corner.

CORNERED STYLE LINE. When a cornered seam occurs within the body of a garment, as it would in a style line like that in the illustration, it's easier and more accurate to stitch it by the following method.

Mark the matching points and seams very carefully. If necessary, reinforce the corner with stay stitching or an organza facing on the seam allowance that is to be clipped.

With right sides together, match the markings of both sections. Bring the needle down directly on the matched points. Stitch away from the point of precision to the end of the first seam. Pull the thread ends at the corner through to the underside and tie them in a square knot. Clip the seam allowance (as indicated) at the corner to the stay stitching in order to facilitate

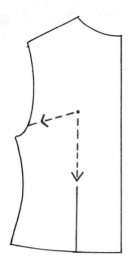

the matching and stitching of the second seam.

Once more, bring the needle down into the marking at the point where the previous stitching started. Stitch away from the marking in the opposite direction to the end of the seam. Again pull the thread ends at the corner through to the underside and tie in a square knot. Make sure that the two lines of stitching just meet at the corner.

For any cornered style-line stitching, a good rule to follow is this: lower the needle at the point of precision each time and stitch away from it.

CORNERED STYLE LINE OF A MACHINE-STITCHED TAILORED COLLAR. Start the stitching at the point where

the collar and lapel meet, stitch to the center back of the collar. *Do not include the seam allowances of the gorge line in the stitching.* Pull the thread ends at the corner to the underside and tie them in a square knot. Once more, bring the needle down at the point where collar and lapel meet and stitch around the lapel, down to the hem. Pull the thread ends to the underside and tie in a square knot.

CORNER PRESSING. Slip the pointed end of the point presser (q.v.) into the corner of the garment section and press the seam allowances open along one seam. Set the second side in position in the same way and press.

CORNER TRIMMED. To free a corner of bulk, it should be trimmed. Make three slashes—one diagonally across the corner, a second diagonally farther into the seam allowance on one side, a third diagonally farther into the seam allowance on the other side. Cut close to the stitching. If you're worried about the stitching coming apart at this now fragile corner, reinforce it with very small machine stitches.

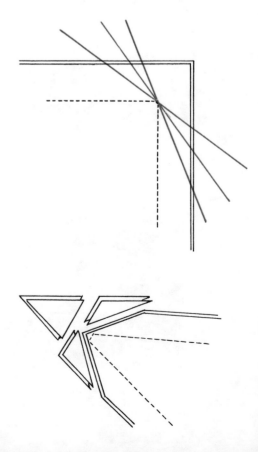

COVERED BUTTONS. Buttons can be covered commercially by services that specialize in such matters, or they can be covered by you with the help of molds or plastic or bone rings. *See* COVERED RING BUTTON; COVERED MOLD BUTTON.

COVERED DOUBLE-RIM BUTTON. *See* COVERED RING BUTTON.

COVERED HOOKS AND EYES. These provide a fine finishing touch. They can be purchased ready-made or you can make your own. The latter is preferable because the choice of size and thread color is greater.

To Cover Before Attaching to the Garment. A suitable method for large hooks and eyes. Using a double strand of matching thread or a single strand of matching buttonhole twist, work blanket stitches (q.v.) very close together over the hooks and eyes until they are completely covered (a). You may have to pry the hook open a bit to compensate for the extra thickness of the stitches. Sew to the garment by either the overlap or abutted method. *See* HOOK AND EYE.

To Cover While Attaching to the Garment. By this method you can both cover and attach the hooks and eyes at the same time. Sew the hooks and eyes to the garment by either the overlap or abutted method. Using a double strand of matching thread or a single strand of matching buttonhole twist, cover the hook and eye with closely spaced buttonhole stitches (b). The stitches will catch some of the fabric on all but the actual hook and eye. Obviously these must be so worked that they are left free. You may have to pry the hook open a bit to compensate for the extra thickness of the stitches.

COVERED MOLD BUTTON. Button molds of wood, metal, or plastic can be covered in practically any pliable fabric. Buy the type and size required of a material strong enough to support the fabric.

When covering buttons in loosely woven, sheer, or transparent fabric, use either a double thickness of the fabric or a thin, opaque liner. For instance: a lace button could have a crepe lining; an organza button could have either a double layer of the organza or a single layer over a lawn liner.

One-Part Mold. Cut a circle of fabric twice the diameter of the button. Using a double thread, gather the edges of the circle but do not cut the thread at the end. Center the button mold on the wrong side of the fabric. Draw up the gathering to fit. Fasten with backstitches. When attaching this button, create your own shank.

Two-Part Mold. A two-part mold consists of a button shell and button back. Easiest to use is the kind in which the covering fabric tucks under the back rather than over prongs around the rim. The button shank may be attached to either the shell or the back, depending on the brand. When the shank is attached to the shell, the button back has a slot through which it fits.

A number of button-mold kits are available. They vary in the equipment they provide to fit the back into the shell. Most include a pattern for the needed circle of cloth. Convenient features are a holder for the button while it is being covered and a metal pusher, the size of the button back, which assures even pressure around the rim of the button.

If there is no pattern for the button

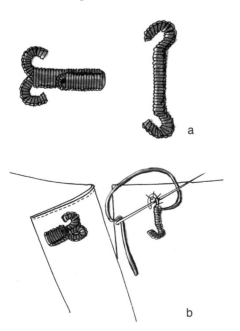

a

b

cover, cut a circle of fabric large enough to cover the button shell, fold over the rim, and tuck under the button back.

To Cover the Mold. Place the fabric wrong side up. Center the button form on it. Fold the fabric edges to the inside of the shell. (It may be a help to gather them and draw them up to fit.) If necessary, trim excess fabric, particularly if it is heavy.

Place the button back over the shell. Make sure all the fabric is tucked in and that the cover fits smoothly over the mold. Press down on the button back with the metal pusher or a spool. If the latter, it should be of a size to fit the button back and have a hole large enough to slide over the shank. Use a small hammer to tap the spool until the button snaps into place.

COVERED RING BUTTON. An easy-to-make button. It has the advantage of being rustproof, a boon for washable fabrics. The rings are not too hard to come by, since they are sold at many variety stores.

Choose rings the size of the button needed. Cut circles of fabric slightly less than twice the diameter of the ring (a). Using a double thread, gather the edges of the circle but do not cut the thread at the end. Insert the ring (b). Pull up the gathering thread tightly and fasten with several backstitches (c).

For a decorative touch, run a line of stab stitches directly against the bone ring to form a rim (d). The stitches may be either half backstitches or prick stitches (q.q.v.). Use buttonhole twist or embroidery floss.

A double-rim button has interest. It consists of a small ring inside a larger one (a). Cut the circle of fabric for the larger ring slightly larger than twice the diameter to allow for stitching the inner as well as the outer ring.

Use the same procedure as for the single ring. Run lines of decorative stitches around and against both rings (b).

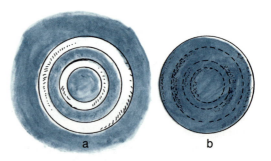

COVERED SNAPS. Metal snaps in an exposed position can be a jarring note. A more pleasing and finished appearance results when snaps are covered in a color to match the garment.

Cut two circles of matching organza, organdy, thin lining material, or self-fabric (if it is thin enough). Make the circles twice the diameter of the snap plus a small seam allowance.

To Cover the Ball. Pierce a tiny hole in the center of one circle and force the ball through it (a). Gather the outer edge of the circle and draw up the gathering until it fits taut over the snap (b). Wind the thread

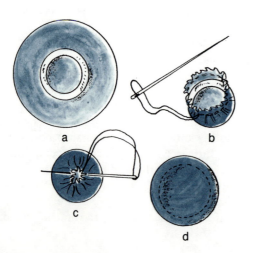

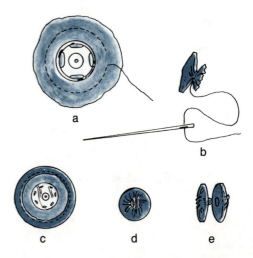

around the drawn-up material once or twice. Fasten with several secure stitches through the drawn-up material. Trim away the excess fabric.

Optional method for large snaps: Turn under the seam allowances and gather the outer edges close to the fold (c). Draw up the gathering until it fits taut over the snap. The gathered edges just meet at the center of the underside. Use a cross-stitch or several backstitches to secure the closing (d).

To Cover the Socket. Enclose the socket with the second circle of cloth in the same way as the ball but *do not pierce* the hole at the center. Snap the ball and socket together (e). As the ball is forced into the socket, the needed hole for the latter is created.

Attach the covered snap to the garment in the same way one would an uncovered snap. *See* SNAPS.

COWL. A soft fold or drape of material. In women's clothing, it generally appears at the front neckline, though it may also appear on the back neckline, at the shoulder of a sleeve, even at the sides or back of a skirt. Cowl necklines range from a single, high, front drape to the multiple folds of a low, deep, dramatic back drape.

Since bias drapes best, the cowl is cut from a straight length of bias material. Use a fabric that will fall in soft folds—chiffon, velvet, jersey, crepe, satin, voile, batiste, or the like.

Bias calls for a complete pattern. Half a pattern on a bias fold may result in inaccuracies in cutting. Furthermore, a seam at center front or back in bias is not only too conspicuous, detracting from the beauty of the cowl, but stitching the bias seam in the soft, stretchy fabric presents a problem.

Use a self-fold for a facing rather than a separate facing. Stitching a separate facing on straight grain at the cowl's edge produces a rigid line that restricts the drape.

In testing any of the cowl drapes, use a test material that will be soft enough to drape. Voile, batiste, nylon tricot are all good for this purpose.

Designs with fullness such as the cowl

often call for a stay to keep the fullness in its rightful place. Cut a lining stay to fit the basic, unfull shape of the garment or to fit the body of the wearer. Tack the drapes to this undercover control at strategic points.

Other ways of holding cowl drapery in position are weighting in one spot or weighting along a fold. *Dressmaker's weights* (q.v.) covered in self-fabric are tacked in place on the underside of the garment at any spot that controls the *drop* of the drape. *Weighted tapes* (q.v.) are tacked to the underside of the garment along a fold to define the line of the drape.

COWL SKIRT. A design with cowl drapery at the sides or back of a skirt. *See* COWL.

COWL SLEEVE. A design with cowl drapery at the shoulder of a sleeve. *See* COWL.

CREPE. A soft fabric whose texture and moldability are due to its tightly twisted yarns, which expand and contract like so many invisible little springs. (Its crinkly surface may also be achieved by embossing, weaving, or chemical treatment.) Made in a seemingly endless variety of fibers—wool, silk, cotton, rayon, and synthetics—and in many weights from *chiffon crepe* to *crepe Elizabeth*. It comes in degrees of sheerness from *georgette* to *marocain*. Surface textures range from the smooth *flat crepe* to the rough-textured *bark crepe;* from the matte-finished *cotton crepe* to the lustrous *crepe de chine*. Whatever the variety, crepe is a fabric that is generally hard to cut, hard to stitch, hard to press, hard to fit. But it is at the same time a fabric so fluid and so flattering that it is worth the effort to master the necessary techniques.

Layout and cutting should be done on a large surface. A cutting board is fine, for the fabric can be pinned to it to provide stability. Lacking that, pin the fabric to tissue paper. Use plenty of pins so the crepe doesn't crawl away in cutting or creep away in stitching. *Stitch slowly* over tissue paper (if necessary) to prevent stretching, particularly on curved, angled, or bias seams.

Machine Stitching. Tension: light; pressure: light; stitch size: 12 to 15 stitches per inch; needle: fine; thread: appropriate for the fiber. Seams and seam finishes should be as flat and as unobtrusive as possible.

Pressing is a very touchy job. Two bits of advice: test-press a sample seam first and quit when you're ahead. Too much pressing and you'll flatten the crinkled surface, which is the charm of the cloth. Not to mention ending up with a garment several sizes too big, enlarged by the flattening and straightening process. If you steam-press the fabric you'll end up with a doll's dress.

The way to press crepe is with a dry iron over a dry press cloth on the wrong side of the fabric. No steam. Don't overpress.

Closings. A hand-stitched zipper is safest. One has more control over the fabric than with machine stitching. A self-fabric loop-and-button closing is preferable to a buttonhole-and-button closing. If the latter must be used, be sure to reinforce the buttonhole opening with organza or a lightweight iron-on material.

CREW NECKLINE. A round neckline that hugs the throat like the sweaters worn by boat crews. The crew neckline is often achieved by banding, by 1-inch ribbed banding, or by Bias Binding: Single Fold (q.q.v.).

CROCHETED BUTTON. An interesting way to get a perfect color match in a different texture. Use yarn unwoven from a remnant of the garment fabric. Starting with a button mold or an old button, crochet a tiny cap to cover it. Fasten the yarn on the underside of the button.

CROCHETED CHAIN OR CHAIN STITCH. A series of interlocking loops producing a chain. It may be created by hand or by crochet hook. *See* CHAIN STITCH *and* THREAD CHAIN.

CROSSED-BAND NECKLINE FINISH (a). Stay-stitch the neckline of the garment, blunting the point. Fold the band lengthwise along the fold line, right side out.

a

b

c

d

Press. Pin-mark the center backs of band and neckline.

With right sides together and center backs matching, pin and stitch one side of the neckline (right-hand side for women, left-hand side for men) from the center back to the point of the V. Break the threads. Pull them to the underside and tie in a square knot. Slash the seam allowance at the V to the stay stitching.

Sew the second side in the same way but end the stitching leaving an opening a few stitches wider than the band (b). Turn the garment to the right side. Slip it over the end of an ironing board or over a tailor's ham. Extend the seam allowances into the garment. Cross the ends of the band at the V. Slip the upper band through the opening on the unstitched side. Smooth the bands so they lie flat. Carefully pin them in this position (c). Press lightly, avoiding the pin.

Slip-baste both bands through the neckline fold of the garment. Turn the garment to the inside and stitch along the slip basting. Make a second line of stitching through all thicknesses just outside the neck seamline in the seam allowance. Finish the raw edges of the seam allowance with zigzag or overedge stitches (d).

CROSS (INTERSECTING) SEAMS. Seams that cross one another when sections of a garment are joined, as at a shoulder, waistline, underarm, and so forth. *See* JOINING CROSS SEAMS.

CROSS-STITCH. A stitch composed of two diagonal stitches of equal size crossing at the center to form an X. It may be used decoratively or in construction, either as a single stitch or in a series.

As a Single Stitch. Fasten the thread on the underside. Bring the needle up at the lower left corner of an imaginary square. Insert it at the upper right corner to form one diagonal stitch (a). Bring the needle out at the upper left and insert it at the lower right to form the second diagonal stitch crossing at the center to form an X (b).

This single-stitch method can be worked in a series in the same way. Start each new stitch in the lower left corner and end in the lower right. The wrong side will show two parallel rows of stitches (c).

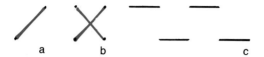

a   b   c

In a Series. Here is an easy way to do a series of cross-stitches. Fasten the thread on the underside. Bring the needle out at 1, insert it at 2, bring it out at 3, insert it at 4, bring it out at 5, insert it at 6. This makes 3 diagonal stitches going in the same direction (a). (There may be any number of stitches in a series worked the same way.) To complete the stitches, make 3 diagonal stitches going in the opposite direction. Bring the needle out at 7, insert it at 8, bring it out at 9, insert it at 10, bring it out at 11, insert it at 12 (b). Fasten the thread on the underside.

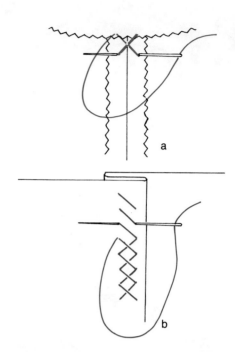

a

b

worked in a series for a predetermined length (b).

CROSS TUCKS. Make a series of lengthwise tucks and press them in one direction. Make a second series of crosswise tucks at right angles to the first. Press them in one direction. *See* TUCKS.

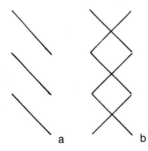

a   b

CROSS-STITCH TACK. Used to hold an edge or a fold of fabric in place.

Where *one spot on an edge* needs to be held in position (as a facing edge to a seam), make a single cross-stitch over the edge to be tacked. Work 1 or 2 more cross-stitches, one directly over the other, to look like a single strong stitch (a).

Where *a fold* needs to be held in place (as at the front-shoulder, center-back, or waistline fold of a coat or jacket lining), pin or baste the fold to position. Tack the fold in place with several cross-stitches

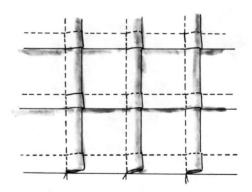

CROSSWISE FOLD LAYOUT. For unusually wide pattern pieces and/or for more economical use of fabric.

Straighten both crosswise cut edges. With the fabric opened to its full width, fold it in half crosswise, right sides inside. Align the selvages and the straightened ends. *Use only for non-directional fabrics.* For di-

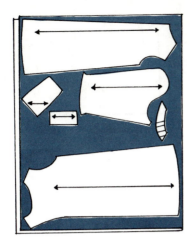

rectional fabrics, use the open double lay-out (q.v).

CROSSWISE GRAIN. A horizontal thread of the fabric. This grain usually needs to be re-established before layout and cutting because (for one reason or another) it comes to the sewer imperfect.

CROTCH FITTING. It is best to perfect the fit of pants in a trial muslin. It may be too late to make the necessary changes after the pattern has been cut out in fashion fabric. There is little, if any, fabric to work with. For known figure requirements, *see* PANTS PATTERN CORRECTIONS.

To test fit in the crotch area, stay-stitch the crotch. Baste the crotch seam. Clip the seam allowance of the crotch almost to the stay stitching. The pants must fit at the seamline, not at the edge.

After pinning or basting the remaining seams and darts, try on the pants. Examine the crotch for fit. Remember that all parts of a garment are interrelated. Adjustments made to the crotch may also affect the waistline, outseams, and inseams. Changes in these seams may also affect the crotch seam.

Check the crotch seam for length and ease, adding or subtracting as necessary. It should not be too tight or too loose, too high or too low, for comfort. Adjust by taking in or letting out at the crotch seam and the inseam.

If the pants are too tight across the legs at the crotch, let out the crotch seam and add a strip of muslin at the inseam (a). If there are wrinkles, release the nearest seams and darts. Repin to fit.

If the abdomen or seat is too baggy or too low, pin a horizontal tuck across the buttocks or abdomen, thereby shortening the crotch seam, and/or take in some of the pants on the inseam (b).

If the waistline drops at the center back or center front, build it up with strips of muslin, in effect adding length to the crotch seam (c). If the waistline needs dropping, trim some way.

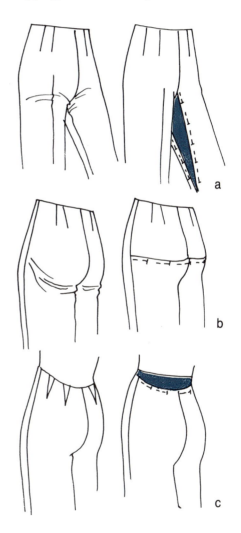

When all the needed changes have been made, mark them clearly in colored pencil. Then transfer the muslin changes to the pattern for cutting.

CROTCH LINE. The line drawn across the pants pattern at the widest part of the crotch at right angles to the grain line. *See* CROTCH MEASUREMENTS.

Length changes in pants patterns are made above or below the crotch line as necessary.

CROTCH MEASUREMENTS. Two measurements are essential for fitting the crotch area—*crotch depth* (the distance between the waist and the bottom of the hips) and *crotch length* (the length of the crotch seam from back waistline to front waistline). The former is necessary to determine whether the pattern needs adjusting between the waist and hips. The latter is necessary to determine what, if any, changes need to be made to accommodate any unusual back or front figure requirements.

CROTCH DEPTH MEASUREMENT

Sit on a hard chair. Measure the distance from the waistline to the chair along the side seam (a). The seated position provides the necessary ease. On the pants pattern this measurement is represented by the distance from the waist to the crotch line (b).

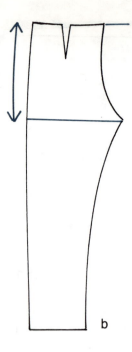

b

CROTCH LENGTH MEASUREMENT

Total Crotch Measurement: While standing, measure the distance from the front waistline to the back waistline between the legs (a). Add 1½ to 2 inches for ease.

a

a

Front Crotch Length: The front portion of the preceding measurement to the center of the inner thigh plus half the ease.

Back Crotch Length: The difference between the total crotch length and the front crotch length plus half the ease.

The corresponding seams on the pants pattern: the front crotch seam extends from the front waistline to the inseam (b); the back crotch seam extends from the back waistline to the inseam (c).

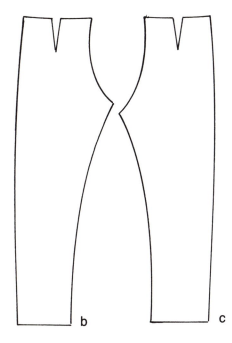

By measuring a pair of pants that fit well, one can also arrive at the necessary crotch measurements. *Crotch depth:* subtract the inseam measurement from the outseam measurement. *Crotch length:* measure the length of the front and back crotch seams from the waistline to the inseam.

Keep in mind that pants are drafted so that the center back seam is longer and the curve deeper than the center front seam. This longer, deeper center back seam provides the length required to accommodate the buttocks when seated.

CROTCH POINT. The point at which the crotch seam and the inseam meet.

CROTCH REINFORCEMENT (STAY). Because of the considerable stress in wearing,

it is wise (though not necessary) to strengthen the crotch seam with a stay. Many pants patterns include a pattern for this. If not, you can make your own.

When There Is a Pattern for the Stay: Cut the reinforcement section of lining material or pocketing (q.v.). Turn under the outside edges of the stay and stitch close to the edge (a). Set it in place against the crotch and inseams (b). Wrong sides of stay and pants are together. Continue the construction of the pants, including the stay in the seams.

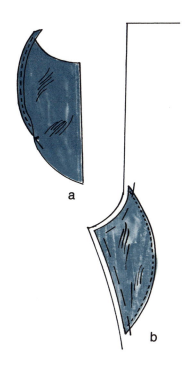

To Make Your Own Reinforcement (Stay): Cut two 6-inch squares of pocketing or lining material. Fold each diagonally to form a triangle, right side outside (a).

Place a triangle at the crotch point on the wrong side of each trouser front. Set it so that the fold extends about 2¼ inches in from the crotch point and tapers to the inseam 6 inches below the crotch. Trim the triangles to match the contours of the crotch and inseams (b). Proceed with the pants construction, including the stays in the crotch and inseams.

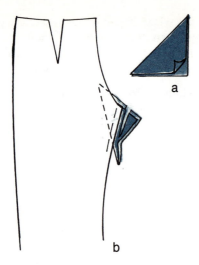

CROTCH SEAM. The crotch seam is stitched after the inseams have been stitched. To facilitate the stitching, turn one pant leg right side out. Slip it inside the other pant leg. Stitch the crotch seam.

Stitch again on the curve of the crotch seam, using a smaller straight stitch or a very small zigzag stitch as a reinforcement. Clip at each end of the curve. Trim the seam allowance between the clips to 1/4 inch. Overcast this edge with hand or machine stitching. Press open the seam allowances above the clips. *See also* CROTCH REINFORCEMENT.

CROW'S-FOOT TACK. Used on tailored garments as a reinforcement or as decoration. It is similar to an arrowhead tack (q.v.) except that the triangle has indented sides. Its raised center is formed by the pattern of the closely spaced satin stitches.

Mark the triangle with its indented sides

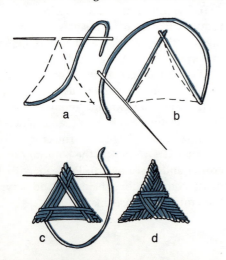

on the right side of the garment (a). Fasten the thread on the underside and bring it out at one of the points of the triangle. Take a small stitch from right to left at each point of the triangle (b). This stitch grows slightly larger each time as the sides of the tack are filled in. Work the stitches around the triangle (c), following its indented outline, until all sides are completely filled in. (d). Turn the work to make it easier if you wish.

CUFF. What a collar is to a neckline, a cuff is to a sleeve. And, like the collar with which it is frequently paired and coordinated, it ranges from a modest band to one that matches the collar in drama.

There are a number of factors that determine the construction of the cuff.

1. Is the cuff attached to the bottom of the sleeve, an extension of it, or detachable?
2. Is the cuff meant to be slipped over the hand without an opening or is a placket involved?
3. Are cuff and facing cut in one piece or in two?
4. Are the ends of the cuff flush with the edge of the placket or are they lapped?
5. Are buttonholes, when present, bound or worked by hand or machine?

Prepare the bottom of the sleeve to receive the cuff. Prepare the cuff. How the cuff is attached to the sleeve will depend on the style of the cuff and the answers to the above questions. *See* BAND CUFF WITH PLACKET; BAND CUFF WITHOUT PLACKET; CUFF CONSTRUCTION; CUFF INTERFACING; DETACHABLE CUFF; FRENCH CUFF; LAPPED BAND CUFF; SHIRT CUFF; TURNBACK BAND CUFF; TURNBACK CUFF: EXTENSION OF THE SLEEVE; TURNBACK SHAPED CUFF.

CUFF CONSTRUCTION. In general, cuffs are constructed like collars. The main difference is in the way they are attached to the bottom of the sleeve. Slight variations of the following two methods are dictated by the style of the cuff. *(See the listing for a particular cuff.)*

A cuff may be simply a rectangle of fabric folded in half so cuff and facing are cut in one piece on straight or bias grain. Or a cuff may be cut in two pieces—a cuff and its facing. This provides opportunity for shaping, for contrasting color or texture, and (whenever there is a seam) for insertion of trimming.

One-Piece Cuff. Interface the cuff section. Turn under the seam allowance of the facing section to the wrong side. Trim it to half width (a). Press and baste to position.

With right sides together, fold the cuff along the fold line. Pin and stitch each end. Leave open the edge that joins the sleeve. Treat as an enclosed (encased) seam (q.v.) (b).

Press the seam allowances open over the point presser. Turn the cuff to the right side and press (c).

With right sides together, pin and stitch the cuff and the facing around all outside edges. Leave open the edge that joins the sleeve. Treat as an enclosed seam (q.v.) (b). Press the seam allowances open over the point presser. Turn the cuff to the right side and press (c).

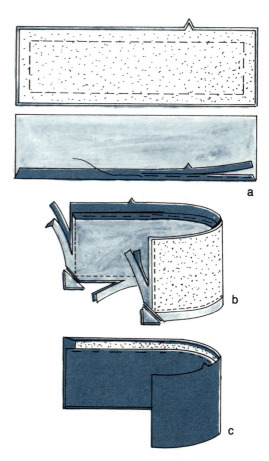

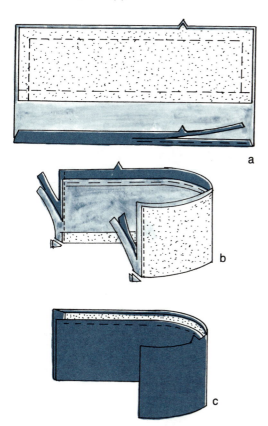

Two-Piece Cuff. Interface the cuff section. Turn under the seam allowance of the facing section to the wrong side. Trim the seam allowance to half width (a). Press and baste it to position.

Both Types. Attach the cuff to the bottom of the sleeve according to the style of the cuff and sleeve.

CUFF INTERFACING. It is the *outer layer,* the cuff itself, that gets interfaced. Use the cuff pattern if there is no interfacing pattern. A bias-cut interfacing, particularly for a turnback cuff, provides a graceful roll.

In a *one-piece cuff,* interface the cuff section to the fold line for a crisp edge or for cuffs that will be topstitched. Extend the interfacing a seam allowance beyond the fold line for a softer edge.

In a *two-piece cuff*, apply the interfacing to the cuff section.

For Both Types. Use any interfacing material—woven, nonwoven, or fusible—consistent with the garment fabric and the desired style of the cuff.

If fusible interfacing is used, trim 1/2 inch from all edges and cut diagonally across corners. The remaining material is included in the seam. Fuse to the wrong side of the material. (Follow product directions.) *See* FUSIBLES.

If nonfusible interfacing is used, it may be cut like the cuff, machine-basted 1/2 inch from all edges, and trimmed close to the stitching. Be sure to cut diagonally across all corners before applying it (a and c).

Freeing the corners of bulk in either of these ways makes for neater, sharper corners when the cuff is turned to the right side.

In fine dressmaking and classic tailoring, when interfacing medium to heavy fabrics, trim all seam allowances away before ap-plying the interfacing. Catch-stitch all edges (b and d).

When the interfacing extends beyond the fold line of the cuff, attach it to the facing, close to the fold line, with permanent uneven basting (c and d). Pick up as little of the facing fabric as possible.

CUMMERBUND. A broad sash worn as a waistband, originally by men but adopted by women in various styles. Directions for making a popular type follow.

Cut the cummerbund on the bias for an easy drape around the waist. Make it at least 9 inches wide. Its length is the measurement of the rib cage plus 1/2 inch for ease. Finish the long edges with a 1-inch hem. Make two rows of gathering stitches at each end (which will be a back opening) and at the sides. Draw up the gathers to the desired depth and fasten the threads on the underside (a).

Featherboning (q.v.) is used to support the gathered areas. Cut four lengths of the featherboning slightly shorter than the width of the cummerbund. If the featherboning is covered, remove the cas-

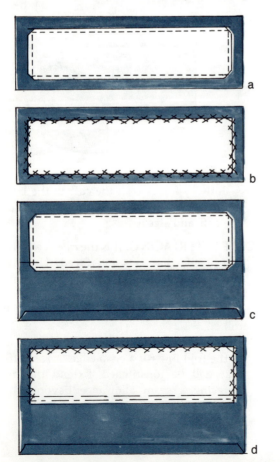

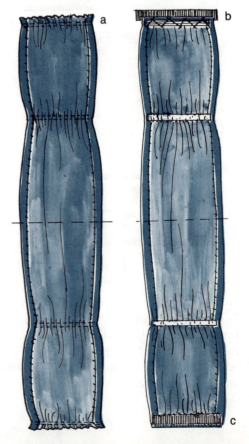

ings. Cover the side lengths with seam binding or strips of self-fabric. Sew them in place with hand stitches.

Cut two lengths of 1/2-inch grosgrain ribbon equal to the width of the cummerbund plus 1/2-inch extensions at top and bottom. Lap the grosgrain over the right side of each gathered end. Pin and stitch. Catch-stitch the featherboning over the gathers at each end (b). Fold under the top and bottom extensions to the inside. Fold the grosgrain ribbon to the inside, covering the boning and hand stitching (c).

For a closing, fasten the ends of the cummerbund with hooks and eyes that just meet. Or make and attach a grosgrain underlap to one end. Sew hooks and eyes as for a lapped closing.

CURVED LAPPED SEAM. On the edge to be turned and overlapped, make a row of stay stitching in the seam allowance close to the seam line. Turn under the seam allowance, clipping it in a sufficient number of places so the seam line curves as planned (a). Press to position.

Overlap the upper section and undersection, matching raw edges. Pin or baste to position. Topstitch on the right side an even distance from the fold and close to it (b).

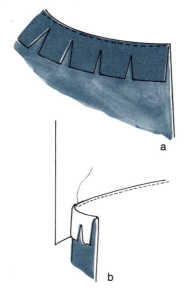

CURVED OPPOSING SEAM LINES. Joining an inward curve to an outward curve is made easier by clipping the one and notching the other.

Stay-stitch each seam line. Clip the seam allowance of the outward curve almost to the stay stitching. Notch the seam allowance of the inward curve almost to the stay stitching. Notch between the clips so there will not be too much stress on the seam.

With right sides together, pin and/or baste the matching seam lines. Ease and stretch as necessary. Stitch. Press the seam open over the tailor's ham (q.v.). *See* CURVED PLAIN SEAM.

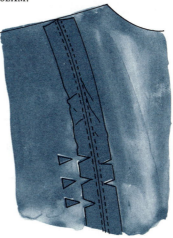

CURVED PLAIN SEAM. *(See* PLAIN SEAM *for stitching directions.)* It is the clipping and notching that produce the flat finish of a curved seam. The depth of the clips or notches and their number depend on the degree of the curve and the "give" of the fabric. Start with short ones at even intervals of 1/2 to 1 inch and adjust accordingly. Keep the cutting to a minimum on loosely woven fabrics or those that ravel easily.

Make a row of stay stitching in the seam allowance of each side 1/8 inch from the seam line.

When a seam line curves inward (a), clip the seam allowance almost to the stay stitching so its cut edge can spread the amount necessary to fit the longer length of its now outward curve.

When a seam line curves outward (b), notch the seam allowance almost to the

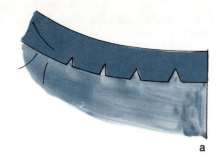

a

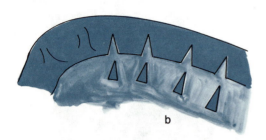

b

stay stitching so its cut edge can be closed up to fit the shorter length of its now inward curve.

For treatment of other curved seams, *see* CURVED LAPPED SEAM; CURVED OPPOSING SEAM LINES; CURVED SEAM LINE STITCHED TO A STRAIGHT SEAM LINE; CURVED TUCKS; CURVED TUCK SEAM; FEATHERBONING; PRINCESS SEAM; SCALLOPS; SHARPLY INDENTED SEAM.

CURVED SEAM LINE STITCHED TO A STRAIGHT SEAM LINE. Stay-stitch the curved edge.

If the seam line is an outward curve, clip the seam allowance almost to the stay stitching. Open out the clips until the curved seam line becomes a straight line (a). With right sides together and seam lines matching, stitch a straight seam.

If the seam line is an inward curve, notch the seam allowance almost to the stay stitching. Close the remaining seam allowance until the curved seam line becomes a straight line (b). With right sides

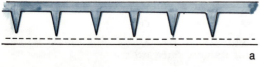

a

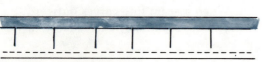

b

together and seam lines matching, stitch a straight seam.

CURVED TUCKS. Mark the position of each tuck with thread tracing (q.v.). Gather the underside of each tuck. Draw it up to fit the upper side, distributing the gathers evenly. Baste and stitch with small running stitches or with machine stitching. Take care not to stretch or twist the tucks. *See* TUCKS.

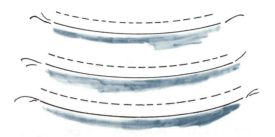

CURVED-TUCK SEAM. This is really an overlap seam stitched to resemble a tuck. It requires a facing for the upper edge in the same shape and on the same grain as the upper section.

Stitch the facing to the curved upper edge. Clip the seam allowances to the depth of the tuck only. Grade them. Turn the facing to the underside, rolling the joining seam out of sight. Press.

Overlap the faced upper section on the under section matching seam lines. Pin and/or baste. Topstitch an even distance from the faced edge.

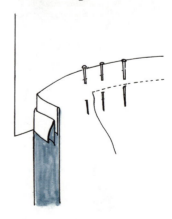

CUTTING OUT A GARMENT. Cutting out the garment is one of the hard, backbreaking, tedious parts of sewing. Be comforted by the thought that, once the garment is cut, you're well on your way. Cut when you are fresh and alert and least likely to be distracted. You will be less apt to make mistakes.

Keep the cloth as flat and smooth as possible. Move around the layout rather than shifting the fabric to meet you. The cutting surface should be accessible from at least three sides, preferably four.

Use sharp scissors or shears. Use long, firm strokes for the straight edges, short strokes for the curved edges. Do not use pinking or scalloping shears. Save them for edge finishes.

As in the layout, start at one end of the fabric while the other end is supported or rolled up. The weight of the fabric can be a drag—literally.

Cut with the grain. Many patterns indicate the direction of the stroke with a scissors symbol. When the fabric has a pile or nap, cut with the nap.

Notches may be cut into or out from the cut edge, depending on the amount of seam allowance needed or the character of the cloth. *See* NOTCHES. To leave the seam allowances intact, notches may also be marked in thread after the garment has been cut.

Where the pattern reads "Clip" or "Slash," it is the fabric, not the pattern, that is to be clipped or slashed. This should not be done until the seam line is first reinforced or stitched.

It is difficult to cut accurately through two or more layers of very heavy or very bulky fabric. Sometimes it is necessary, after the section has been cut, to correct the cutting of the underlayer. Use the pattern or the upper layer as a guide.

As the pieces are cut, lay them flat or hang them on a hanger. If folding is necessary, use as few folds as possible. Keep the pattern side out for easy identification and for protection of the fabric.

DARNING STITCH. A running or even basting stitch worked so it resembles weaving. It is used to reinforce or replace worn areas or as a filling stitch in embroidery.

DART. There is variety in even so simple a device as a dart. A dart may be single-pointed (q.v.) (a), like one originating at some seam. It may be double-pointed (q.v.) (b), like the one that shapes the waistline area of a garment without a waistline seam. It may be stitched only part way, as in a dart tuck (q.v.) (c).

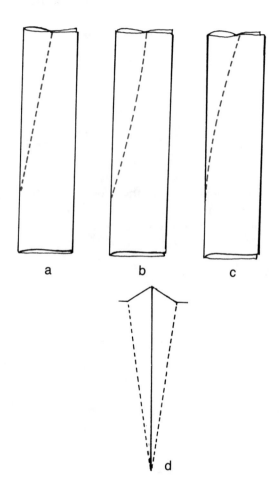

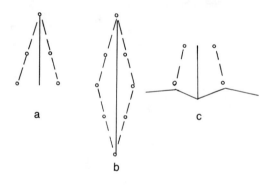

Most darts have straight legs (a). Some, for purposes of design or fit, may have concave (b) or convex (c) stitching lines.

They all have in common the following features: two stitching lines, a fold line, and a dart point (d). The *stitching lines* (dart legs) are equally spaced on both sides of a fold line. The *fold line* may be indicated on the pattern or created when the dart legs are brought together for stitching. All three lines meet at the *dart point.* In addition, there is a little *jog* at the wide end of a single-pointed dart that provides enough extra material to include the dart in the seam (d).

See following entries under individual DART *topics for answers to specific questions. See also* DESIGNER'S DART *and* DRESSMAKER'S DART.

DART CONTROL AND FITTING. *See* DART—CREATING ONE WHERE NONE EXISTS; DART ELIMINATED; DART LENGTHENED; DART RELOCATED; DART SHORTENED. *See also* PATTERN CORRECTIONS *that involve shaping.*

DART—CREATING ONE WHERE NONE EXISTS. There may be times when the addition of a dart to a dartless pattern will improve the fit of the garment.

For instance, to create a waistline dart in a bodice: draw a slash line across the pattern from the point on the seam line where you wish to locate the dart to the opposite side of the pattern (a). Slash to but not through the shoulder and spread the pattern to the amount you wish to put into the dart. For a starter, be guided by the amount in one of your favorite garments. You may have to do a little adjusting in the trial fitting.

Fill in the spread area with tissue or pattern paper (b). Place a mark for the dart point (q.v.) in the center of the spread area at the desired height of the dart (c). Draw dart legs (q.v.), starting at the waistline seam and ending at the dart point. Draw a fold line through the center of the dart (d).

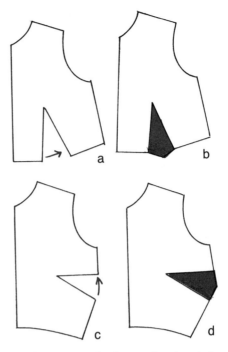

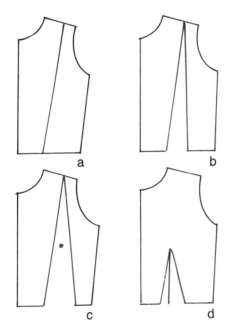

Working on the right side, fold the dart on the underside of the pattern in the position in which it will be pressed in the garment. (Vertical darts are pressed toward the center, horizontal darts are pressed down.) Here is an easy way to do it. For a *vertical dart:* crease the dart leg nearest the center; bring it over to meet the other dart leg (a). This closes the dart as if it were stitched and pressed to position. For a *hori-*

zontal dart: crease the lower dart leg; bring it up to meet the upper dart leg (c).

Using a tracing wheel or scissors, trace or cut the seam line of the pattern over the folded dart. When the pattern is opened out, you will see a pointed shape. This represents the amount of material necessary for including the dart in the seam (b and d).

By using this method, darts can be created on any outside seam of a dartless pattern.

DART ELIMINATED. Often for purposes of design, fabric, or fitting it may become necessary to eliminate an existing dart.

Divide the dart in half by drawing a line midway through it to the other side of the pattern (a). Draw new lines, starting at each dart end, to the new point at the opposite side of the pattern (b). Crease on

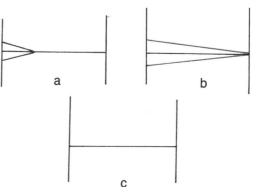

one line and bring it to meet the other (c). Pin or Scotch-tape to position.

Should this make the pattern too bulky, cut out the excess along each new line in (b). Make the newly cut edges meet and Scotch-tape them to position.

DART LEGS. These are the stitching lines of the dart. Generally, they are equal in length. In those rare instances when one dart leg is a trifle longer than the other (as in some French darts), its extra length must be eased to fit.

DART LENGTHENED. Measure directly up (or over) from the dart point the amount you wish to lengthen the dart. Mark the new dart point (a). Draw new dart legs, starting at the ends of the original dart and ending at the new dart point (b).

The broken line in (b) represents the original dart. The solid line, the new lengthened dart.

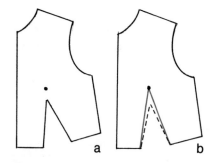

a   b

DART POINT. The point at which the stitching lines (dart legs) meet.

DART PRESSING. *See* PRESSING DARTS.

DART RELOCATED. An easy way to relocate a dart on the *same seam line* where it would serve better in its new position.

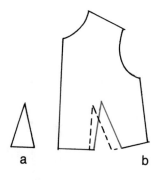

a   b

Trace the dart on another piece of paper. Cut it out (a). Place the cut-out dart on the pattern in the desired new position and trace (b). The broken line is the original dart; the solid line is the newly placed dart.

DART SHORTENED. Reverse the dart-lengthening process. Measure down from the dart point the amount you wish to shorten the dart. Mark the new dart point in the center of the space. Draw new dart legs, starting at the ends of the original dart and ending at the lowered dart point.

DARTS IN A REVERSIBLE GARMENT MADE OF REVERSIBLE FABRIC. Such darts are stitched to resemble a welt seam (q.q.v.).

Press a *narrow dart* to one side and stitch along the folded edge (a).

Trim one side of a *wide dart* to a narrow width. Fold under a narrow seam allowance on the second wider side. If it will improve the appearance of the finished dart, trim a bit of the other side too. Press the wider side so it encloses the narrower (b). Stitch from the wide end to the dart point close to the folded edge. Pull the thread ends through to the underside and tie them in a square knot.

This method is also applicable for unlined tailored jackets and coats.

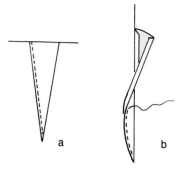

a   b

DARTS IN FUR, LEATHER, ULTRA-SUEDE, OR OTHER SPECIAL FABRICS. *See individual fabric listings.*

DARTS IN SHEER FABRICS. Stitch in the same way as seams in sheer fabrics (q.v.) or as continuous-thread dart (q.v.).

DARTS IN UNDERLINED GARMENTS.

Use whichever of the following methods produces the least bulky results in your fabric and the most accurate stitching as it comes off the dart point.

METHOD 1: FOR SHEER AND VERY LIGHTWEIGHT FABRICS

By this method, no construction details are visible from the right side of the garment.

Cut the fabric and the underlining from the same pattern. Transfer the pattern markings to the underlining only. With both right sides up, stay-stitch or baste the outer fabric to the underlining.

Machine-stitch directly down the center of the dart, ending at its point, through both thicknesses of the material (a). This prevents the layers from slipping. In a French dart, stay-stitch the layers just inside the dart stitching line (b).

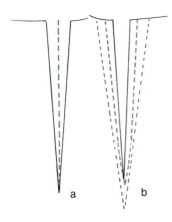

Pin and stitch the dart through all layers of the material. Stitch from the wide end of the dart to its point, being particularly careful to smooth the fabric at the point and to taper the stitching off the fabric for a perfect blend. If the finished dart is not too bulky, leave it uncut. If bulky, slash the dart and press it open. Press over a tailor's ham.

METHOD 2: FOR LIGHTWEIGHT OUTER FABRIC AND UNDERLINING

Cut the fabric and underlining from the same pattern. Transfer the pattern markings to the outer fabric and the underlining. Pin and stitch the dart in each, separately. If the finished dart is not too bulky, leave it uncut; if bulky, slash the dart and press it open. When the darts are cut, place them one over the other. If uncut, press the garment dart in one direction, the underlining dart in the opposite direction, to avoid bulk.

Place the backing (underlining) over the tailor's ham wrong side up. Since this section has now been shaped by darts, it can no longer be worked as a flat section. Place the outer fabric over the underlining right side up. This places the material and backing in the same relative position and shaping in which the garment will be worn—fashion fabric topping foundation fabric, with the tailor's ham representing the body. Match the darts and pin (a). Using the dart point as a hub, smooth the fabric toward the outer edges in strokes like the spokes of a wheel; pin (b). Baste or tailor-baste (q.v.) the two thicknesses with rows of diagonal stitching about 2 to 3 inches apart (c). Start with the dart and work to the outer edges.

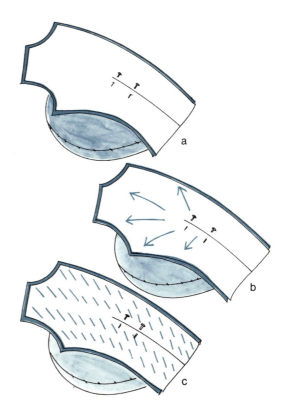

METHOD 3: FOR MEDIUM TO HEAVY OUTER FABRIC AND CRISP OR SPRINGY INTERFACING (LIKE HAIR CANVAS) OR UNDERLINING

Cut out the outer fabric and the underlining or interfacing. Transfer the pattern markings to each. Pin and stitch the dart in the outer fabric; slash and press it open.

Stitch the dart in the underlining or interfacing by the abut or overlap method (*see* LAPPED DART *and* ABUTTED DART). Press over the tailor's ham. Join the two thicknesses in the same way as in Method 2.

DARTS: RIGHT-SIDE DECORATIVE.

Darts need not always be hidden on the underside. Groups of small darts can be quite decorative when stitched on the outside and incorporated into the design.

When stitched by the standard method, pull the thread ends at the dart point to the underside and tie each pair in a square knot. To avoid the problem of thread ends, stitch as a continuous-thread dart (q.v.). Leave the darts uncut. Press in the direction as designed.

DART STITCHED. *See* SINGLE-POINTED DART; DOUBLE-POINTED DART; *and* CONTINUOUS-THREAD DART.

DARTS: TRIMMING, CLIPPING, SLASHING.

These are important steps for smooth, flat construction.

Narrow darts and *darts in lightweight fabrics*

are the only darts that can remain uncut. They are pressed to one side. *See* PRESSING DARTS.

Wide darts are trimmed to seam-allowance width or less, slashed, and pressed open.

When *slashing open a dart,* cut to within 1/4 to 1/2 inch of the dart point, depending on the thickness of the fabric (a). Snip across the unslashed end of the dart almost to the seam line. Press the dart open where slashed; press to one side where unslashed (b).

To make stitching easier, clip *curved darts* before stitching or after stitching to make them lie flat when pressed open (c).

Clip *double-pointed darts* at the waistline to relieve strain and to do the shaping for which they were intended. Slash and press the dart open above and below the clip as if each were a single-pointed dart (d).

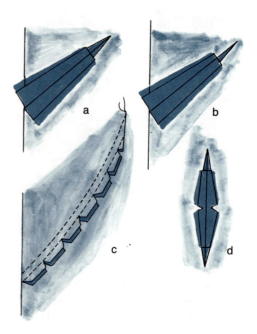

DART TUCK.

A tuck that begins as a dart but is stitched only part way (a). Sometimes the stitching continues across the end of the dart tuck (b). Fullness released by this construction produces a soft, full, draped effect. Do not press the released fullness flat or you will lose the main fea-

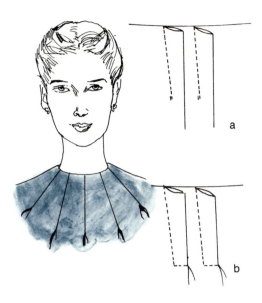

ture of this tuck. For construction, *see* RE-
LEASED TUCK.

DÉCOLLETÉ. A strapless or low-cut dress
exposing the neck, back, and shoulders.
The more the exposure, the greater the en-
gineering required to anchor or support
the neckline.

A low V neckline (a) can be anchored to
a bra with a covered hook of boning or
zigzag wire. One end is stitched to the
point of the décolletage and the other
hooked into the bra.

A wide, square neckline (b) can be held
in place with a length of narrow elastic. It
should be long enough to encircle the
body from one corner of the neckline to
the other and fit snugly. Stitch the elastic
to one corner against the neck facing. Sew
the ball of a snap to the free end of the
elastic; sew the socket to the facing of the
opposite corner of the neckline.

An off-the-shoulder décolletage (c) is
held within bounds with a narrow elastic
run through a hem casing around the entire neckline—front, back, sleeves, or just
inside the sleeve edge of the dress from
the front to the back. While this looks
gathered off the person, the elastic
stretches to fit snugly and flat when the
dress is worn.

DECORATIVE BANDING. Used as an edge
finish, an extension, or as an ornamental
band within the garment. Banding comes
with one or both edges finished. If only
one edge is finished, turn under a narrow
seam allowance on the unfinished edge.
Baste and press to position.

As an Edge Finish. On the garment,
fold a narrow seam allowance to the right
side of the fabric along the edge (a). Baste
and press.

If necessary: turn under the ends of the
band or join them. Press seam allowances

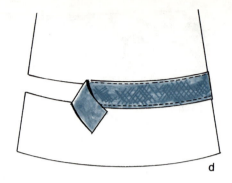

open and trim to half width. Preshape the band and miter the corners.

Lap the wrong side of the band over the right side of the garment along the folded edge, covering it (b). Slip-stitch or top-stitch the band to position (b). On the underside, tack the fold of the seam allowance to the banding with invisible stitches.

Banding used as an extension is handled in the same way.

Bands Within the Garment. Mark the position of the banding on the garment (a). Prepare the band. Place the band in position on the right side of the garment. Slip-

stitch or topstitch both long edges of the band to the garment (b).

If the *band is used as an insertion* to lengthen the garment, mark the line for the insertion (c). Cut the garment along this line. Fold a narrow seam allowance to the right side of the fabric along both cut edges. Press and baste. Lap the band over the right side of the garment along both long edges. Treat each edge in the same way as for an edge finish (d).

DECORATIVE FACING. Instead of stitching the facing to the underside in the usual way (where it won't be seen) apply it to the outside where it can become a decorative detail of the design. The facing may be an unusual shape (a), a contrasting color (b), or a different texture (c). The construction method that follows works in the same way at any outside edge of a garment.

About the easiest and most effective way to cope with a decorative top facing is

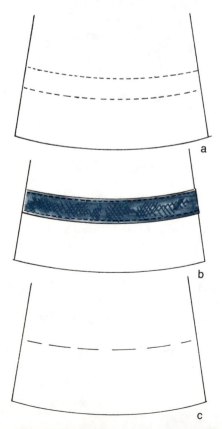

to face it first and then attach it. There are two bonuses to this method. The 'facing edge is finished before being fastened to the garment. (It's much less bulky this way.) The facing's facing functions as an interfacing.

In attaching the facing to the outside of the garment, some of the operations are the reverse of those used for applying it to the underside. Since the facing must fit the outside measurement of the garment, make it slightly larger than the area it is to face. To enlarge the facing, add a bit at the seams or slash and spread the facing pattern in several places to preserve the overall shaping of an unusual style line.

Cut out the facing. Cut a facing for it of a lightweight material in a matching color. Make the facing's facing just a little smaller than the facing itself. With right sides together, stitch the facing to its facing on all outside edges. Press the seam allowances open. Trim and grade them. Clip or notch as necessary. Turn the facing to the right side. Press the edges flat, being careful to roll the joining seam to the underside. Baste to position on the outside edges and at the raw edges.

The underside of the facing must be handled in such a way that no seam allowances are visible at the finished edge of the garment. Treat all seams that enter that edge as follows:

Mark a point on the seam line just short of the width of the decorative facing. Clip the seam allowances at the marking. With *wrong* sides together, pin, then stitch the seam in the facing area from the outside edge to the marking. Trim the seam allowances to half width (a). Reverse the procedure for the remainder of the seam: with *right* sides together, pin, then stitch the seam from the marking to the opposite edge. Press all seam allowances open.

Place the right side of the facing against the wrong side of the garment. Match raw edges, centers, shoulders, and notches. Ease the facing to the garment seam line. Pin it to position.

With the garment side up, stitch the facing to it an even distance from the raw

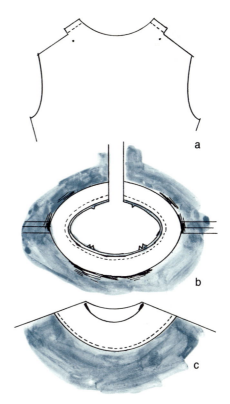

edges (b). Trim and grade the seam allowances. Notch or clip as necessary. Turn the facing to the right side of the garment, rolling the joining seam to the underside. Pin or baste it to position. Topstitch or slip-stitch the outer edge of the facing to the garment (c).

DECORATIVE TACK. *See* ARROWHEAD TACK *and* CROW'S-FOOT TACK.

DESIGNER'S DART. One that extends to the apex of a body curve or bulge. It is used by the designer or pattern maker to create a new design by shifting this dart. *See also* DRESSMAKER'S DART.

DESIGN UNITS OR MOTIFS. A real consideration in the use of your fabric is the judicious placement of its design units. Drape the fabric over yourself and study the effect in a mirror. Choose what is most effective or most flattering.

Centering a unit makes for formal balance (a). The unit placed to one side results in an asymmetric balance (b). An unexpected placement produces a dramatic effect (c). The placement of these floral

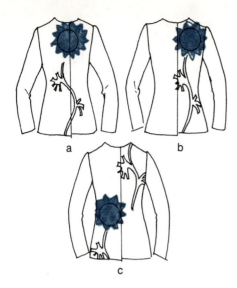

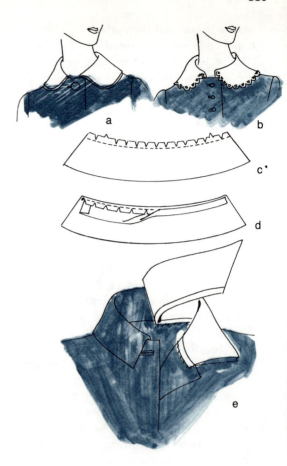

units is obvious. Not so apparent but equally important is the placement of geometric units and of the dominant lines or color bars in plaids and stripes (q.v.).

When a fabric has a repeat of a design unit, whether woven or printed, floral, geometric, plaid, checked, or striped, the repeats must be matched at all joining seams. Study the direction and movement of the design units. If they are moving in one direction, a one-way placement must also be observed.

DETACHABLE COLLAR. A collar that lies on top of an existing collar (a) or that fits inside a collarless neckline (b).

Whether or not you interface this collar depends on the desired effect. If the collar is a washable one, omit the interfacing.

The Collar That Lies on Top of an Existing One. Trace the collar pattern. Determine how much extra material is needed to cover the existing collar. Add that amount to the pattern at all outside edges. Do not add anything to the neck edge.

Construct the collar (q.v.). Stitch the neck edges together a little beyond the seam line in the seam allowance. Clip so the collar neckline can spread to fit the garment neckline (c). Cover the raw edges with bias binding (q.v.) (d). Pin the collar to the neck edge. Attach it to the garment with snaps (for easy removal) or slip stitching (e).

The Collar That Fits Inside a Collarless Neckline. Trace any collar in your collection that has the same neckline as the garment it is to trim. Construct the collar (q.v.). Finish and attach it in the same way as the above collar.

Make detachable cuffs (q.v.) to match.

DETACHABLE CUFF. This cuff provides a removable, washable trim when used over a sleeve or an existing cuff (a). A band cuff, simulating a shirt cuff that extends below the sleeve edge, adds a crisp, fresh touch (b).

The Cuff That Goes Over a Sleeve or Other Cuff. This cuff must fit both the measurements of the outer layer that goes over the sleeve or other cuff and the measurement of the inner circumference of the sleeve. Cut the cuff to the necessary length and width at the outer edges and taper them to the inner circumference of the sleeve.

sleeve (with cuff in place) inside out. Slip-stitch the cuff in place (b). If you prefer, sew snaps to both cuff and sleeve hem or facing for easy removal.

Turn the sleeve and cuff to the right side. Roll the cuff to position. *Optional:* Anchor the corners of the cuff to the sleeve with bar tacks (q.v.) (c).

The Cuff That Extends Below the Sleeve. Cut the band cuff to fit the inner circumference of the sleeve. With right sides together, stitch the ends of the cuff. Press the seam allowances open and trim them to half width. Fold the band with wrong sides together and raw edges matching. Pin. Baste close to the fold (a). Turn in the seam allowances along the open edge and slip-stitch.

From the right side, lap the sleeve over the cuff, leaving the desired amount showing. Be sure it is even all around. Pin to position (b). From the wrong side, slip-stitch the cuff in place (c). Or sew snaps to the edge of the cuff and the sleeve hem for easy removal.

With right sides together, stitch the ends of a one-piece cuff or all outer edges of a two-piece cuff. Leave the hem edge open for turning. Trim and grade all seam allowances. Clip or notch as necessary. Free corners of bulk. Turn to the right side and press.

Pin or baste the raw edges together. Encase them with a strip of bias binding (a). Edgestitch the binding, overlapping the ends.

The cuff may be worn with free ends (a) or with a slit at the outer end (b). For the latter cuff, slip-stitch the ends part way.

Slip the bound edge of the cuff into the sleeve to the desired depth, with right sides of both up. Pin to position. Turn

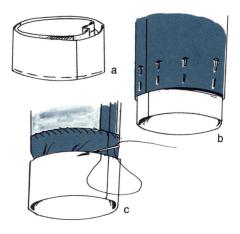

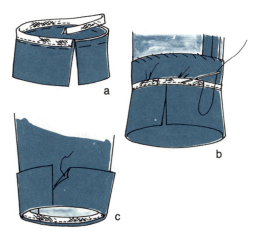

DETACHABLE SHANK BUTTON. Any shank button may be made detachable. It is a good way to use a particularly ornamental or valuable button for a fastening in more than one garment or for easy removal for laundering or dry cleaning.

Work matching pairs of eyelets (q.v.) on both sides of a closing. Make them large enough to take the shank inserted through them. Slide the toggle through the shank.

DIAGONAL BASTING (TAILOR BASTING).

Used during construction to hold two or more layers of material together. It consists of a series of horizontal stitches taken parallel to each other on the underside, producing long, diagonal floats on the right side. For greater control, take short, diagonal stitches spaced close together; for less control, longer stitches with more space between them.

Short diagonal basting is used to hold edges flat or the lips of bound buttonholes together for finishing (a). *Long diagonal basting* (tailor basting) is used to hold interfacing or underlining in place under the outer fabric (b).

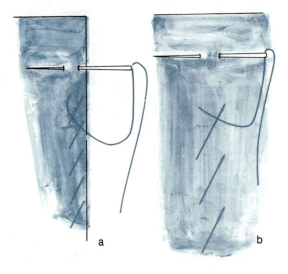

a   b

There are two permanent hand stitches used in tailoring that are variations of diagonal basting. *See* DIAGONAL TACKING *and* PAD STITCHING.

DIAGONAL PRINTS OR WEAVES. If the

diagonal print or weave is inconspicuous there is little problem in pattern selection, layout, and cutting. Handle the fabric like a plain weave. When a diagonal print or weave *is* obvious, the choice of pattern is limited, layout and cutting more complicated. In fact, many patterns are labeled "Not suitable for obvious diagonals." Better heed that advice or you may end up with diagonals mismatched at seams, distorted at darts, and going in opposite directions at center front or back of a collar.

For Obvious Diagonals. Choose patterns with few seams, few darts, and few structural details. Avoid gored sections, darts that distort, collars cut in two pieces or on a fold. If, despite the difficulties, you have lost your heart to a bold and dramatic diagonal, plan to make the stripes part of the design.

When in doubt, lay out and cut diagonals on a single thickness of fabric, opened to its full width, right side up. If a pattern piece needs to be used more than once or reversed, it is helpful to trace and cut out a second piece. In this way you can have the complete layout before you so you can see exactly how the diagonal stripes will fall in the garment.

A single pattern section placed on a lengthwise fold will produce stripes going in one direction because the center is on a straight, vertical line and right and left halves are a continuation of each other (a). However, gores placed on a lengthwise fold will result in mismatching when joined (b) because of the angle of the seams.

A complete collar placed on a single layer of fabric along a stripe will produce similar stripes at the center back and on both front ends (c). This avoids the mismatching that results at the front and back when half a collar is placed on a double thickness of cloth (d).

Two fronts placed on a lengthwise grain and cut separately on a single thickness of fabric—one with the printed side of the pattern up, the other with it down—will produce diagonals that go around the body in the same direction. One pattern piece placed on a crosswise fold of fabric will also produce diagonals that go in the same

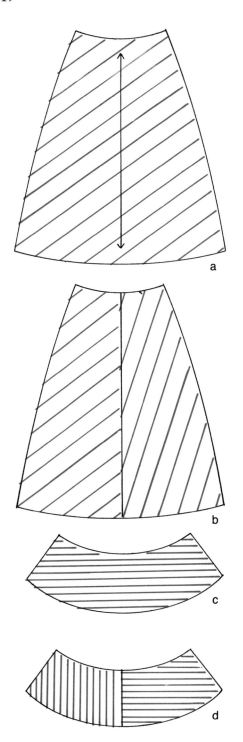

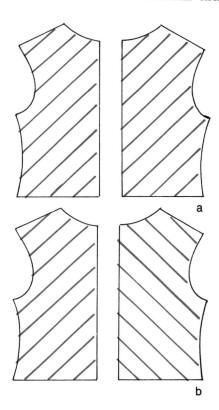

forms a chevron design. *See* DIRECTIONAL FABRICS.

DIAGONAL TACKING. A variation of diagonal basting (q.v.). It is a permanent stitch used to join interfacing and underlining when both are used to support the fashion fabric.

Make very small horizontal stitches through the interfacing and underlining and long, diagonal floats 3/4 to 1½ inches between. Keep the stitches loose. Do not allow any of them to come through to the outer fabric.

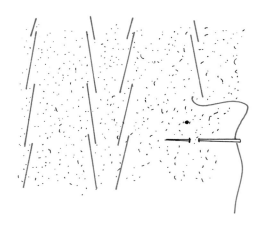

direction (a) if the diagonal is nondirectional.

In a reversible fabric, cut two identical pieces. Reverse one to create a mirror image (b). The meeting of the diagonals

DIRECTIONAL FABRICS. Those that have some feature that "moves" in one direction only and therefore requires a one-way placement of all pattern pieces. The following are considered directional fabrics: napped, short- or deep-pile fabrics, long-float or shaded fabrics, one-way designs, uneven plaids, unbalanced stripes, and diagonals.

Study the direction of the movement and observe the "With Nap" layout of the pattern. *See* DIRECTIONAL LAYOUT.

DIRECTIONAL LAYOUT. A one-way placement of all pattern pieces, from neck to hem. In pattern directions this is referred to as "With Nap." All directional fabrics (q.v.) require a directional layout.

Directional layouts often take more yardage. How much more depends on the number, size, and shape of the pattern pieces. When, in addition, the matching of one-way design units is involved, the number of seams that need matching and the size of the repeats (q.v.) must also be considered. A trial layout on paper of the same width as your fabric is the only way to determine accurate yardage.

DIRECTIONAL PRESSING. This means pressing the fabric with the grain or nap. Off-grain pressing pushes the material out of shape or stretches it. Pressing against the nap or across it will distort the directional surface texture of the cloth.

Press all woven fabrics with the lengthwise or crosswise grain. Press all knit fabrics with the lengthwise rib. Pressing across the ribs stretches the fabric. Press all napped materials with the nap.

DIRECTIONAL STITCHING. Stitching with the grain. This preserves the length and shape of a seam. When in doubt, use the cut fabric edge as a guide to the direction of the stitching. When the threads point down (a), stitch down. When the threads point up (b), stitch up.

You will be stitching with the grain if you stitch from a high point to a low one; from a wide point to a narrow one. On a long, shaped seam, stitch in the direction that stays longest with the grain. Or break

 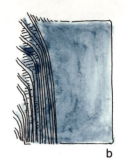

a   b

the thread at the point where the direction changes and start at the other end.

DOLMAN SLEEVE. A variation of the kimono sleeve (q.v.). While similar in silhouette, the true dolman is a combination of sleeve and part of bodice. Unlike the kimono sleeve, whose front and back bodices are joined in a shoulder seam, front and back bodices and dolman sleeve are

joined by a bodice seam. The underarm of the sleeve may be as deep as desired, often starting at the waistline. Like the kimono sleeve, the dolman sleeve is a comfortable sleeve to wear, dramatic in its fullness. While it looks (and is) easy to sew, it requires careful fitting.

Make whatever adjustment one would normally make in a bodice and kimono sleeve. This style generally does not have darts; it looks better without them. Such shaping as is necessary can be done on the bodice seam. However, if there are darts, check them for size and position.

Fit the shoulder seams. Stitch and press them open. With right sides together, pin and/or baste, then stitch the dolman sleeve to the bodice in one continuous seam from back to front. Clip or notch as necessary. Press the seam allowances open. With right sides together, join the front to the back at the underarm seams. Since these are curved seams and the necessary clipping and trimming may weaken them, they should be reinforced. (See KIMONO SLEEVE WITHOUT A GUSSET.) Continue the construction.

DOUBLE-BREASTED. A front closing that has enough overlap to allow two rows of buttons equidistant from the center line. Both overlap and underlap are identical. Usually only the outer closing edge of the overlap actually buttons through a buttonhole (a). You may make a second inner row of buttonholes for design balance should you desire to do so (b). The latter may or may not open through to the underside.

The outer button placement line on both overlap and underlap is a button's width in from the finished edge. Buttonholes on the overlap are *squared off the center line* whatever the outer style line may be. They start 1/8 inch beyond the placement line toward the finished edge (c). The buttonhole ends a button's width plus ease toward the opposite side.

Buttons are stitched directly on the inner button placement line of overlap and underlap. When not buttoned, hold the finished edge of the underlap in place with covered snaps (q.v.).

DOUBLE-CORD SEAM. A double-topstitched seam with the topstitching 1/8 inch or closer to the seam line, producing a cordlike effect in wool fabric. On thinner fabrics, it reinforces seams that get hard wear and are subjected to great strain, as in children's clothes or active sportswear.

DOUBLE-FACED FABRIC. A two-layered fabric held together by fine threads woven at right angles to the layers or by bonding. Though the design may be different on each side, both sides of the fabric are equally usable. There is no right or wrong side, making the fabric reversible. You have the choice of constructing a garment made of it as a reversible one or disregarding its double identity and treating it like any other single-layer fabric.

Almost any simple pattern can be used for a reversible garment of double-faced fabric even if it hasn't been designed as such. The best choice is an unfitted style with no intricate seaming or details. Seams are preferable to darts for shaping, since they are easier to handle in the stitching. A kimono or raglan sleeve is easier to stitch than a set-in sleeve. When a set-in sleeve is used, it is stitched into the armhole first, then, like the kimono sleeve (q.v.), the underarm of sleeve and side seam of garment are stitched in one operation. Use patch pockets applied to one or both sides of the garment or in-seam pockets that can be pulled to either side.

Bound buttonholes are impossible. Even were you to use hand-embroidered or machine-made ones, there would still be the problem of where to put them, since right and left fronts are reversed when the garment is worn inside out. There are two possibilities for buttoning. Make buttonholes on both the right and left fronts; use a set of link buttons to join them. Or make the buttonholes on the right front and sew two sets of buttons to the left front, one on each side. Of course, the closing would then be in the opposite direction, but that is not of major consequence. If you belt the garment, you will eliminate the buttonhole problem.

There is no inner construction and no lining. Use one layer throughout—no facings, no hems. All marking is done with thread tracing (q.v.) and tailor's tacks so the exposed surfaces are in no way marred. There are two ways in which the seams can be handled: a hidden seam (described immediately following) or a flat-fell or welt seam (q.q.v.).

Hidden Seams. Separate the two layers of fabric for about 1½ inches at all edges to be stitched. Slice through the perpendicular threads that join the layers with a seam ripper, a sharp razor, or small scissors (a). Only material that can be pulled apart can be used for this technique.

Machine-stitch the seams of one layer (b). Press the seam allowances open as best you can with the tip of the iron. (Being small, a traveling iron can be used for this purpose.) Trim and turn under the seam allowances of the second side so the folds meet directly over the seam line. Slip-stitch (c) and press.

Set the hem. Add seam allowances. Trim the excess fabric. For the hem and all outside edges: separate the two layers of fabric and slice the perpendicular joining threads as for the other seams. Turn under both seam allowances toward each other. Slip-stitch along the edge and press.

Slice back about 1½ inches of all collar edges. Turn under and slip-stitch all outside edges. Turn under both seam allowances of the collar neck edge but leave it open. Slip the garment neck edge into the collar opening. Slip-stitch the folds of the collar edges to the neck seam of the garment (d). Cuffs can be attached in the same way. Zippers can be sandwiched between the folded edges of sliced-back layers.

All hidden-seam edges can be top-stitched for a decorative trim. Raw edges

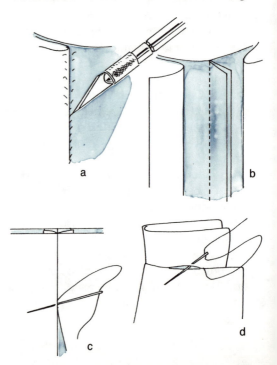

a

b

c

d

can be bound with bias, ribbon, braid, or leather. *See* BOUND EDGES.

Half the material can double the fun. Instead of limiting yourself to the seams and edges, separate the entire two layers of fabric. Now each layer is a complete and usable length. Though half the original, it has double the possibilities. Use half for a skirt and half for a top or in any other way you can devise.

Admittedly it's a chore to put asunder what the factory hath joined together, but where would you ever find such matching fabrics otherwise?

DOUBLE-FOLD BIAS BINDING. *See* BIAS BINDING: DOUBLE-FOLD OR FRENCH.

DOUBLE-FOLD HEM. One used in sheer and lightweight fabrics. The extra layer provided by the double fold acts as an interfacing, weighting the hem slightly for a better hang.

Mark the hemline. Allow an even amount below the hemline equal to twice the depth of the hem. For the first fold, bring the raw edge up to the hem fold line on the inside. Pin on the outside. Fold the turned edge again along the fold line. Pin. Slip-stitch the hem to the garment through the upper fold of the hem.

DOUBLE-FOLD LAYOUT. Sometimes each of several pattern pieces needs to be on a fold: for instance, the center front *and* center back of a skirt.

Measure the widest part of one of the pattern pieces that needs to be on a fold. Mark this measurement in from the selvage in a sufficient number of places to provide an accurate fold line. Use pins or a line of thread tracing (q.v.) for the marking. With right sides inside, fold along the

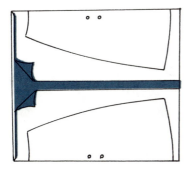

marked line. Do the same for the fold on the other side.

If the fabric has a visible stripe, you won't need to measure. Simply fold along it.

DOUBLE-FOLD TAPE. A strip of bias fabric with prefolded edges, folded in half lengthwise slightly off center. *See* BIAS BINDING: MACHINE-APPLIED.

DOUBLE KNIT: produced by two yarn-and-needle sets working simultaneously. Face and back of the fabric may look alike or different.

Some of the common fears in sewing with single knits are absent when working with double knits. In many ways they handle more like woven cloth. They are firm and stable. (Don't choose a pattern designated "For Stretchable Knits Only.") They should be sponged or dry-cleaned before cutting. They are easy to cut because they lie flat without edges curling. They are easy to stitch. (Use a plain seam, straight stitch, medium pressure and tension.) They are pressed with a steam iron over a dry press cloth and shaped over the tailor's ham. A softly padded ironing board is better than a firmly padded one.

Double knits take beautifully to welt seaming and topstitching. They tailor well: use an interfacing appropriate for the weight; make bound or machine-worked buttonholes through an interfaced area; finish with a tailor's hem.

See KNIT FABRICS *for general information.*

DOUBLE-POINTED (CONTOUR) DART. A long, single dart that shapes the front contour at bust, waist, and hips and the back contour at shoulder blades, waist, and hips. The widest part of the dart is at the waistline. It tapers off in two opposite directions—toward the bust and hips in front and toward the shoulder blades and hips in back. It acts as (and takes the place of) two separate darts.

Transfer the pattern markings to the wrong side of the fabric. With right sides together, fold the dart along the fold line and pin or baste the dart, matching the stitching lines and easing as necessary. It's easier to do this if you start the matching at the waistline first, the two dart points next, then dart legs between these points.

Start the stitching at the widest part of the dart (the waistline) and stitch to the dart point in one direction (a). Do not backstitch at either start or finish of stitching. Clip the threads. Bring them through to one side and tie both sets in square knots.

Once again, bring the needle down into the wide part of the dart, starting where the first stitching ended. Stitch to the second dart point in the opposite direction (b). Repeat the procedure for tying the thread ends.

If one is very careful, it is possible to overlap the stitching for a short distance at the widest part of the dart instead of tying the thread ends (c). But this takes precision stitching.

Clip the dart at the waistline to within 1/8 inch of the stitching to release the shaping for which the dart is intended (c). If the dart is a deep one, trim some of the seam allowance. If the dart is a curved one, it may be necessary to clip in several places above and below the waistline too. Press over the tailor's ham. *See* PRESSING DARTS.

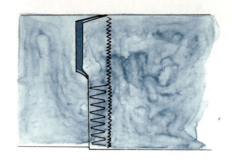

Press the seam to one side. On the right side of the garment, stitch along the first seam with a wider zigzag. Trim the excess material from the underside.

DOUBLE-STITCHED HEM. A method that lends support to very wide hems or hems in knits or heavy fabrics.

Finish the hem edge. Turn up the hem and baste it close to the fold line. Baste again halfway up the hem (a). Fold back the hem to the upper line of basting and sew the supporting line of stitching with blind catch stitches or blind hemming stitches (b).

Turn the top of the hem to position and make a second line of blind catch stitching or blind hemming stitches (c). Press. Remove both rows of basting.

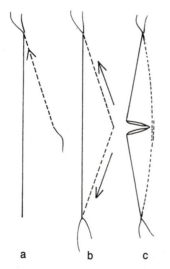

a   b   c

DOUBLE-STITCHED FLAT SEAM. A good seam for cotton jersey underwear. With right sides together, stitch a plain seam with a row of narrow zigzag stitching.

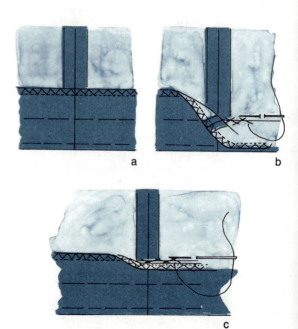

a

b

c

DOUBLE-STITCHED SEAM. Provides flexibility with minimum bulk. It is an excellent seam for knits, lightweight, or see-through fabrics in which seam allowances are unnecessary or undesirable.

Stitch a plain seam. In the seam allowance, stitch a second row close to the first, using either straight stitching (a), zigzag stitching (b), or overedge stitching (c). Trim the seam allowance close to the stitching either before (d) or after the second row of stitching, depending on the desired edge finish.

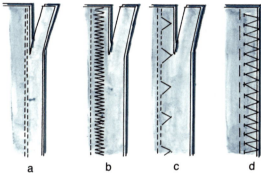

a   b   c   d

DOUBLE-STITCHED WELT SEAM. Make the welt seam (q.v.) (a). Make a second row of topstitching close to the original seam line (b).

DOUBLE-TOPSTITCHED SEAM. Make a plain seam and press it open. On the right side of the fabric, make two rows of topstitching equally distant from each side of the seam line. The seam allowances are caught in the stitching. The topstitching adds strength and decorativeness to the seam.

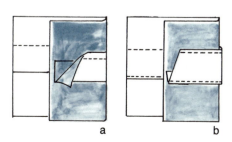

a   b

DOUBLE-WELT (BOUND) BACK HIP POCKET—Men's trousers. *See* BACK HIP POCKET.

Mark the position of the pocket on the trouser back with thread. Cut the pocket of pocketing either in one piece, deep enough to be folded up into a pocket that extends to the waistline seam, or in two pieces, one of which will reach the waistline seam. Cut three strips of trouser fabric the width of the pocket opening plus seam allowances and 2 inches in length. Two of these strips will be used to form the welts (bindings) of the pocket. The third will be used as an underlay.

On the section of the pocket that will reach the waistline seam (the underpocket), place the underlay so it will be directly behind the pocket opening. Stitch or fuse it in place (a).

On the underside of the trouser back, place and baste the upper pocket (the section without the underlay). Keep the right side up. Make the top edge extend 1 inch above the pocket opening (b).

On the right side of the trouser back,

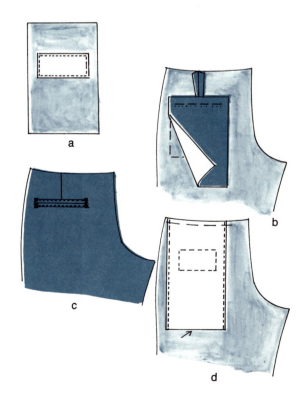

a

b

c

d

construct a bound buttonhole with the two-strip method (q.v.) through the trouser fabric and the pocketing. When completed, topstitch in the seam grooves and bar-tack (q.v.) the ends (c).

To Complete the One-Piece Pocket: Fold up the underpocket so its end reaches the waistline edge. Pin and baste to the waistline seam allowance. Double-stitch the sides together in a narrow seam (d).

To Complete the Two-Piece Pocket: With right sides together, place the underpocket in position against the upper pocket. The top edge of the underpocket reaches the waistline edge, the raw edges of the sides and bottom are aligned. Baste the upper edge to the waistline seam allowance. Double-stitch the sides and bottom in a narrow seam (d).

The waistline edge of the pocket will be stitched when the waistband is attached.

DRAWSTRING. A length of cord, fabric tubing, braid, leather strips, ribbon—anything narrow enough and firm enough to be drawn through a casing and used for a tie or bow. The length of the drawstring should be equal to the body measurement at the casing position plus enough extra for tying in a bow or knot.

DRESSMAKER BASTING. One long stitch and two short ones; can be used as a quick way to join long seams having little or no strain, or as a guideline.

DRESSMAKER'S DARTS. These are darts that don't quite reach the high point of certain body curves or bulges. Their shortening produces a soft effect and a little more ease in the area. Were the darts to be stitched to the high point, the result would be a sharply defined figure. *See* DESIGNER'S DART.

DRESSMAKER'S DUMMY—PAPIER-MÂCHÉ. This individualized dress form is made of strips of moist gummed tape applied to a skin-tight tricot or jersey foundation worn over the figure. The moist, glued paper hardens as it dries to produce a firm duplicate of one's figure.

If you can endure the ordeal of standing in a clammy, gooey mess for at least two hours you will be rewarded with a highly personalized dress form at very little cost. Better make this form when you are feeling spry on a warm day in a warm place.

In addition to several devoted friends and great determination, you will need a thin, tubular jersey or tricot foundation to which gummed paper will adhere, a large roll of 1-inch gummed tape, a bowl of water, a sponge, and scissors.

Slit the tubular jersey to form armholes. Slip the jersey over your body or over your best-fitting foundation garments if you wear them. Shape the jersey to fit your neck and shoulders. See that it fits snugly around the armholes. Lap and tape the seam allowances to position. If any further adjusting must be done to provide a close fit, slash, overlap, and tape the jersey to the new position.

Have one of your helpers prepare the strips of gummed tape. Cut them to length, moisten them with a damp sponge, and keep the fitter supplied. The fitter applies the tapes as quickly as they are fed to her. Work goes faster if you can persuade a third helper to lend a hand.

The strips of moist gummed tape can be worked vertically, horizontally, diagonally, or crosshatched. Use short strips for deep curves; longer strips for more gradual curves.

SUGGESTED SEQUENCE FOR APPLYING THE TAPES

Foundation Tapes: Apply these tightly around the waist, the diaphragm under the bust, and the hips. Define the armholes and the neck in similar fashion. Use short strips to define the bust separation. Work short strips over the bust, shaping and *lifting* as the work progresses. This is particularly important or the dress form will end up with a squashed and flattened bust line. Work tapes well over the shoulders.

Overlay Tapes: Apply longer strips to the upper back, the bust, the chest, the lower front, the lower back. Often one layer of tape is not sufficiently firm to hold the shape. Reinforce any area that needs it with crosshatching but take care not to pile up too many layers. While the buildup is necessary, each added layer increases the size of the dress form.

TO COMPLETE THE FORM

When the form is completely taped (but still moist), cut it open along the center back. Slip out of it *very carefully*. Using a tape measure, pull in the waistline and hipline to actual body measurements. Tape the center back closed.

To make certain that the form hardens in shape, prop up the bust or any other curve in danger of collapse with wads of tissue paper, cardboard strips, or cardboard cut to shape. When thoroughly dry, apply a coat of shellac both inside and outside. Hang the form over a coat hanger and suspend the two from any convenient rod. Or mount the form on a stand.

DRESSMAKER'S HEM. *See* FRENCH DRESSMAKER'S HEM.

DRESSMAKER'S TRACING (CARBON) PAPER. A paper that is carbon-coated on one or both sides. It is used in conjunction with a tracing wheel, either blunt or pronged. It is available in white and colors. *Note:* Dressmaker's carbon paper is *not* typewriter carbon.

Choose white when possible or a color close to but sufficiently contrasting to leave visible marks. Test the color on a scrap of your fabric for visibility. Also test for easy removal by washing or steam pressing. Some tracing papers leave permanent marks. *Use with care.* Always make carbon markings on the *wrong side* of your material.

DRESSMAKER'S TRACING (CARBON) PAPER AND TRACING WHEEL MARKINGS.

GENERAL DIRECTIONS

Unpin a small section of one pattern piece. Slip the tracing paper into position. Carefully replace the pattern and pin it in just enough places to hold it in position.

Slip a sheet of cardboard or a magazine under all. It provides a firm base that won't resist the tracing wheel. It will also protect the surface on which you are working.

Using the tracing wheel, carefully mark the seam line. Use a ruler for straight lines; it's easier as well as more accurate to trace with one. Trace the curved lines freehand, carefully following the lines of the pattern.

Unpin the pattern, remove the tracing paper, slide it and the cardboard base along to a new section, and repeat the procedure until the entire piece is marked. Make sure the new marking is a continuation of the old.

TO MARK DOUBLE THICKNESSES OF CLOTH WITH RIGHT SIDES INSIDE

Slip a sheet of tracing paper between the pattern and the upper layer of the fabric with the coated side against the wrong side of the material. Slip a second sheet of carbon paper under the lower thickness with the coated side against the wrong side of the fabric. In effect you are enclosing the fabric with the tracing paper so both layers of fabric can be marked simultaneously. Using the tracing wheel, mark the seam lines.

To Mark Double Thicknesses of Cloth with Wrong Sides Inside

Use a sheet of tracing paper coated on both sides, or put two sheets of tracing paper together with the carbon-coated sides outside, the uncoated sides against each other inside.

Slip the tracing paper between the two thicknesses of fabric with the coated sides against the wrong sides of the material. Proceed as for double thicknesses with right sides inside.

To Mark a Single Thickness of Fabric

There are times when a simultaneous marking of a double thickness is ineffective or impossible (as would be true in heavy or bulky fabrics) or unnecessary (as when a section is cut singly with the right side up). In such instances, mark one side at a time. Place the coated side of the tracing paper against the wrong side of one thickness of fabric and mark with the tracing wheel.

When Right-Side Markings Are Necessary: Mark with the carbon tracing paper on the wrong side and transfer the markings to the right side with thread. *See* THREAD TRACING *and* MARKING METHODS.

DRESSMAKER'S WEIGHTS. Lead disks that come in a range of sizes up to 1½ inches in diameter. They are generally round (a), though some come in square shapes.

Weights are used in dressmaking and tailoring wherever an anchor is needed to hold a detail in place—the drape of a cowl neckline, for instance. In a circular gar-

ment (skirt, cape, coat) a dressmaker's weight stitched to the garment at each deep fold will guarantee that the ripples will always fall into their planned positions.

So they will never be seen, the weights are inserted into a hem (b) or enclosed in a fabric sack (c). They are attached to the inside of the garment at the spot to be weighted. *See also* WEIGHTED TAPES.

DRESS PLACKET. An underarm placket that substitutes for a zippered closing. Use it where a zippered closing might be unsightly, where tugging at a zipper would prove hazardous, or when a zipper is not available. Equally good for sheer, very lightweight, or lace fabrics and for very heavy or very shaggy fabrics.

The following method produces a flat, inconspicuous closing. It consists of a faced opening set in the side seam to form an underlap and overlap, centered at the waistline and closed with snaps and a hook and eye.

Stitch the underarm seam of the dress, leaving an opening for the placket as marked—usually 9 to 11 inches. Press the seam allowances open. Mark the closing lines of the opening with thread tracing (q.v.). Ease-stitch 1/16 inch inside the seam allowance on each side of the opening to prevent gaping.

Prepare two strips of self-fabric on straight grain (on bias grain should a deep indentation at the waistline call for shaping). Make them 1½ inches wide and 2 inches longer than the placket opening.

With right sides together and raw edges matching, center the front facing strip between the markings. Stitch it to the opening edge in the seam allowance, enough inside the closing line to allow for rolling the seam to the underside. Trim and grade the seam allowances, making those of the garment wider. Fold the facing to the underside to form the *overlap* (a). Press. Understitch the seam allowance to the facing. Sometimes the front facing is further reinforced by placing under the facing a length of seam ribbon or a selvage strip of light-

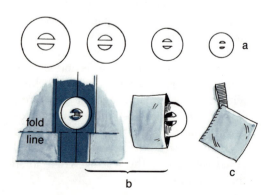

fold
line

a

b

c

weight material through which to sew the fasteners.

Clip the garment-back seam allowance 1/2 inch beyond each end of the opening. With right sides together and raw edges matching, center the back facing strip between the markings. Stitch the back facing to the opening edge in the seam allowance 1/4 inch from the edge. Press both seam allowances and facing forward. This extension becomes the *underlap* (b). As a reinforcement on which to sew the fasteners, stitch the seam allowance that has been pressed forward.

From the right side, lap the front edge over the back, thread-tracing and closing lines matching. This should completely cover the seam of the underlap. Baste to position close to the edge.

through to the right side. Sew the ball snaps 1/16 to 1/8 inch in from the front edge and about 1 inch apart. Directly under the ball of each snap, mark the center of its socket and sew it in place. Place a hook and eye at the waistline where the strain is greatest (c).

DROPPED NECKLINE. Any neckline that drops below the natural neckline. If you have any doubt how far the neckline will plunge you had better test the drop. Before cutting the neck facings and the garment, cut test facings and join them at the shoulders. Clip and turn under the seam allowances at the neck edge and baste. Try on the facing, settling it at the shoulders. See where it comes to rest on the body.

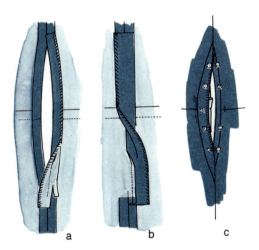

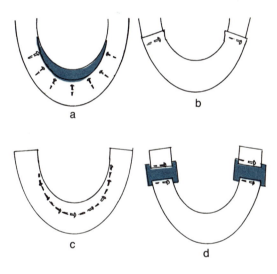

Turn to the inside. If necessary, trim the strips so they are flush with the edges of the garment seam allowances. Finish their raw edges in the same way as the garment seam allowances are finished. Stitch both facings to the front seam allowances at the top and bottom of the placket, keeping the garment free. It is easier to do this with catch stitching or backstitching than with machine stitching. Blindstitch the long, free edge of the front strip to the front of the garment.

Fasten the opening with snaps, preferably covered (q.v.), stitched to position on the overlap and underlap. *Do not come*

If the décolletage is too low, fill in the drop with a scrap of fabric and pin it carefully to position (a). Or tuck the facing at each side until the neckline is where you want it. Pin to position (b).

If the drop is not low enough, mark the desired depth on the facing with a chalk or pencil line or a line of pins (c). Remove the facing and cut out the new neckline. Or slash the facing on each side. Spread until the neckline reaches the desired depth. Fill in the spread with strips of fabric (d).

True up all lines of the altered neckline, balancing both sides. Transfer the changes to the garment and facing patterns.

DROPPED-SHOULDER SLEEVE. A loose-fitting, kimono-style sleeve with the bodice and the upper part of the sleeve cut as one and dropping over and below the shoulder like a cap sleeve. To this is stitched the lower part of the sleeve. The dropped-shoulder line creates the illusion of an extended shoulder.

EASE. The quality that makes you reach for a particular garment because it is so livable. Ease gives you room to move, but it is different from just plain big. It concerns where a garment touches and how it glides over the body. There should not be so much as to make the garment look sizes too large for you or so little that you can't move in it. You are the only one who can determine just the right amount, for it is a matter of feel as well as appearance. However, there are some factors that must be considered in making your determination.

1. The Fabric. The more elastic the fabric, the less ease is necessary. The more rigid the fabric, the more ease is necessary. Most fabrics don't have sufficient "give" to permit body movements if fitted strictly in accordance with body measurements.

Some fibers have more stretch than others. Except when used in knits, synthetic fibers tend to have less stretch than natural fibers. Some weaves have a tendency to make any fiber stiffer. For instance, firmly woven menswear suiting has less give than loosely woven fabrics. The structure of the fabric makes a difference too: knit fabrics have considerably more elasticity than woven fabrics.

2. The Function of the Garment. Active sportswear requires more ease than spectator clothes. Styles for relaxed moments can have as much ease as one may require for the relaxing, while show-off clothes can be fitted as tightly as the figure can stand the showing.

3. The Design and the Designer of the Garment. Since fullness, or lack of it, is so much a matter of style, it is the designer who determines the amount any given garment is to have over and above the basic amount of ease in the master pattern.

4. You, Yourself. Some folks aren't comfortable unless they are wearing clothes at least two sizes larger than they really need, while others are never happy unless their clothes look as if they were two sizes too small for them.

Here is an easy way to tell how much ease you like in your clothes. Try on a favorite dress or skirt or jacket. Pinch out the excess fabric until the garment fits tight at chest, bust, waist, hips. Measure the amount of the "pinch." Add this amount to your body measurements.

5. The Pattern Company. The "staple" or block that most pattern companies use as a basis for all pattern making is based on a set of standard body measurements issued by the U.S. Bureau of Standards. Even though they start with the same measurements, pattern companies have different policies in regard to ease. Some add a little more, some less. Some pattern companies will tell you what their policy is in regard to ease. That can be very helpful, since different amounts of ease may be provided for different sizes and different styles even within the same company.

The difference in the amount of ease added to body measurements accounts for the difference in the fit of patterns produced by the various pattern companies. This may explain why you prefer one above the others.

6. Whether the Garment Is to Be Worn Under or Over Another Garment. When it comes to jackets, capes, coats, and ensembles, it is difficult to predict the exact amount of ease. That depends on what the garment is to be worn over. For instance, if a jacket is meant to be worn over one layer (a blouse or a nonbulky sweater) it will have less ease than if it is to be worn over two layers (say, a blouse and sweater or a blouse and vest). A coat designed to be worn over a blouse and jacket will have more ease than one designed to be worn over a dress alone. If, in wearing, you depart from the planned coordinates, the outer garment will fit with more or less ease.

The pattern you buy has the ease built right into it. Should you decide that you want a little more or less ease than the pattern provides, you can add or subtract the amount you choose. *See* EASE ADDED OR SUBTRACTED.

EASE ADDED OR SUBTRACTED.

You will find ease in the following places in a garment or pattern in varying amounts:

Circumference Ease: At the bust (women's clothing), chest (men's clothing), the waist, hips, biceps, elbow, wrist.

Width Ease: Across the chest, across the shoulder blades (from crease where arm and body meet to opposite crease).

Length Ease: Bodice or shirt at center front and center back, over the bust (women), over the chest (men), over the shoulder blades, overarm, crotch.

Pants: In addition to the ease at the waistline, hips, and crotch mentioned above, there may also be ease at the thigh, knee, calf, ankle.

Ease may be added or subtracted in any of the above-mentioned places. If you know your problem or preference, it is easier to make changes in the pattern than in your garment. If you are uncertain, make the needed changes in a trial muslin.

Pattern Changes for Ease

Ease may be added at any existing seam line, at center front or back in length or in width. The amount involved may be equal throughout the pattern or in one place only.

For instance, along the entire side seam of a skirt—waist to hem (a); from hip to hem but not at the waist (b); at the seams of a princess-style dress (c).

Ease may be added or subtracted *within* the pattern on the principle of slash and spread or its reverse, slash and overlap. The change may be equal in width or length across the entire pattern or in one place only. For instance, less ease across the pants from crotch seam to side seam (d); more ease at the crotch seam only (e).

If darts fit well, don't tamper with them in making changes for ease. You may alter the shaping of the garment.

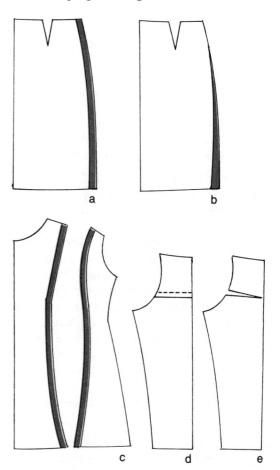

a   b

c   d   e

Changes for Ease in the Trial Muslin

When fitting a trial muslin, small changes may be made on any outline seam by using some of the seam allowance. Be mindful of the fact that any change on an outline seam alters the shape and size of that seam. For instance, to add at a side seam will affect the length and shape of the armhole. Corresponding change will need to be made on an armhole facing or a sleeve. Wherever possible, make the change *within* the garment section so the outline seams remain unaltered. For instance, if more or less ease is required across the bosom or the shoulder blades, make the change within the front or back section rather than on the side seam.

Slash the muslin from the shoulder point to the high point of the bust or shoulder blades through any waistline dart to the waist and across to the side seam (a). Spread the slash to the needed amount at the bust or shoulder blades (b). Fill in the spread area with a strip of muslin and pin (c).

Reposition the dart. Correct the side seam (d). At the hemline, trim away the length added by the slash and spread to the side seam. Taper the trimming to the center front or back.

This slash-and-spread-insert-muslin-strip method can be used anywhere when more size or ease is indicated in the muslin fitting. To decrease the ease, reverse the procedure: slash and overlap the muslin.

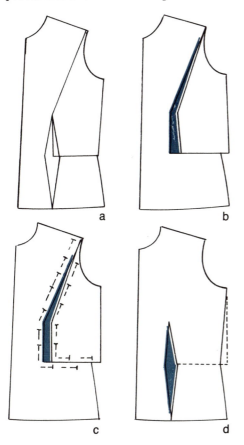

a   b

c   d

EASE STITCHING (OFF-GRAIN STITCH-ING). A useful technique for working in a slight amount of fullness in a top layer. It is also a good way to prevent that layer from slipping forward while stitching.

Place the forefingers on either side of the presser foot. Pull the fabric horizontally as it feeds into the machine. Stitch a little bit at a time, slowly, easing in the fullness. *See* EASING.

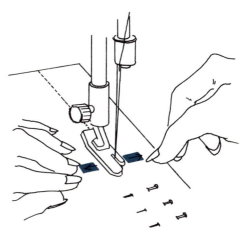

EASING. When one seam line of two that are to be joined is longer than the other, the additional length of the longer edge must be worked into the shorter edge without visible fullness.

When the amount to be eased is slight and the fabric obliging, the easing can be accomplished by ease stitching (q.v.) or steam pressing. Stretching the shorter length to match the longer length is another good method. Stitch with the shorter side up so the feed can "work in" the underlayer. In hand stitching, try cupping the layers over the hand with the longer side up and basting with short even stitches or backstitches.

When there is more fullness than can be eased by any of these methods, the additional length can be controlled by gathering (q.v.).

EDGE AND POINT PRESSER. An essential piece of pressing equipment. It is used for getting into and pressing the points of collars, cuffs, lapels, welts, flaps, and the like. It is also used to prevent seam imprints on

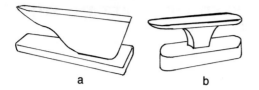

a   b

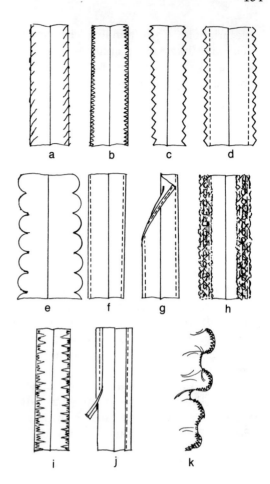

a   b   c   d

e   f   g   h

i   j   k

the right side of the fabric when the seams are pressed open over its long, narrow surface. The pressing is done in the well of the seam and not on the edges of the seam allowances.

The edge and point presser is made of wood, either alone (a), in combination with a pounding block (b), or as part of a tailor's board. The first two types are useful for straight seams; the last one can be used for curved seams too.

EDGE BASTING. A line of basting stitches made close to a rolled edge to hold it in place.

EDGE FINISHES (SEAM FINISHES). An attractive finish for a raw edge may enhance its appearance; it also prevents the edge from raveling. There are as many types of finishes as there are functions, fabrics, and fancies of creative sewers.

When a lining is used, no special finish is necessary unless the fabric tends to ravel. When a lining is not used, the finish must not only be functional, it should also be attractive. Here are some commonly used edge finishes.

Overcasting by hand (a) or by machine (b) (q.v.).

Pinked edge (c) (q.v.); *stitched and pinked edge* (d) (q.v.).

Scalloped edge finish (e) (q.v.).

Row of machine stitching along the edge (f).

Edgestitched finish *(see* CLEAN-FINISHED SEAM) (g).

Edgestitched finish—fancy: *lace, rickrack, or any other* decorative *edging* or *edging trim* (h).

Machine overedge finish—any of the decorative *overedge finishes* your machine is capable of (i).

Bound edges—*bias-bound edge* (j), *net-bound edge* (q.v.).

Lettuce edge—a frilly edge for knit fabrics (k) (q.v.).

EDGING TRIM. A narrow length of lace, ornamental banding, cording, ruching, ruffles, and the like used to finish or decorate an edge. There is an extensive variety of commercially available edgings in addition to those that a sewer can create. *See the listing for each.*

To apply, turn under the raw edge of the fabric. Press and/or baste. Place the turned-under edge over or under the edging trim and pin. *To attach,* use straight or zigzag stitching.

ELASTIC BRAID (TUNNELING ELASTIC). The familiar, lengthwise-ridged elastic that is run through casings. It looks the same on both sides; both edges are finished in the same way. Made of rubber or spandex, it comes in varying widths—1/4, 3/8, 1/3, 3/4, 1 inch—that narrow when stretched. The yarn may be of rayon, nylon, cotton, or a blend. For threading, *see* CASING.

ELASTIC DECORATIVE WAISTBAND.

There is a wide variety of decorative stretch waistbands in solid colors, stripes, plaids, prints. They come in a number of widths and can be woven, braided, or shirred. Choose one that is close to the weight and color of your fabric and whose stretchability will suit your needs. How it is applied depends on whether one or both edges are finished and whether the garment has or does not have a closure.

The length of the waistband should be enough for a snug fit plus 2 inches for finishing the ends. Stitch across the cut ends with straight or zigzag stitching to prevent raveling. Stitch all garment seams that enter the waistline and press the seam allowances open.

If no closure is used, stitch the waistband ends together in a 1-inch seam, right sides together. Press the seam allowances open and tack them to the waistband (a). *If a closure is used,* turn under the ends of the elastic to fit and whipstitch them to position (b).

Divide the waistband and waistline of the garment into equal parts and pin-mark.

If both edges of the waistband are finished, lap the wrong side of one edge over the right side of the garment, matching pin marks and seam lines (c). *If one edge only is finished,* place the unfinished edge against the garment edge, right sides together. Match pin marks and seam lines (d).

Stitch, using 12- to 14-per-inch straight stitches or medium-length-and-width zigzag stitches. The zigzag stitches are preferred because of their elasticity. Stretch the elastic between the pins as you sew. Stitch under tension *(see* TAUT STITCHING) beside or between the rows of elastic thread, close to the edge or where indicated on the waistband. Trim the garment waistline seam allowance. When the stretched waistband relaxes, the garment will be brought to size.

When there is a great deal of fullness in

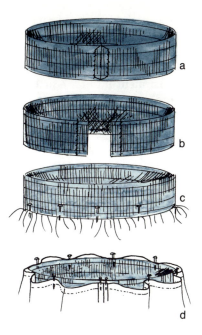

the garment, it is preferable to gather the fullness first, draw it up to the desired length, and stitch it to the waistband without stretching the elastic. Use a zigzag stitch to provide the necessary elasticity.

ELASTIC EDGING FOR LINGERIE.
Available in webbing (a), frill edge (b), picot edge (c), or fold-over binding (d). It is applied to the outside or the inside edge of the garment.

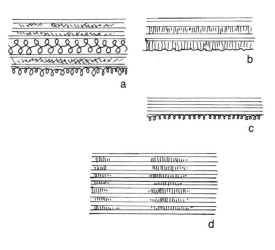

Cut the elastic to a comfortable waistline (or leg) measurement plus 1 inch for joining. With wrong sides together, stitch across the ends of the elastic. Open the seam and stitch ¼ inch on each side of it. Trim the elastic to the outer stitching (a).

Place the seam at the center front (or back) of the garment. Divide the elastic and the garment into an equal number of parts and pin-mark. Overlap the elastic edging on the right side of the garment edge, matching the markings. The bottom edge of the elastic touches the seam line. Stitch the edging to the garment with narrow zigzag stitches (b). Trim the garment seam allowance close to the stitching.

Cover the elastic joining with a length of ½-inch satin ribbon folded over it. Topstitch on both sides and along the lower edge (c).

The elastic may be concealed except for its decorative edge. With right sides together, place the decorative edge on the seam line of the garment. Stitch close to the edge with narrow zigzag stitching. Trim the seam allowance of the garment to ¼ inch. Turn the elastic to the inside of the garment. Topstitch through all thicknesses with a multistitch zigzag (d).

produces a result somewhat similar to that of a casing.

METHOD 1. WITH A LENGTH OF NARROW ELASTIC

Mark the position of the line where the elastic is to go on the underside of the garment. Cut a narrow length of elastic to fit the figure snugly plus 1 inch for finishing the ends. Divide the elastic and the garment into eighths and pin-mark. Allow ½ inch at each end of the elastic. If there is no closure, lap and stitch the ends securely. If there is a closure, turn under the ½-inch ends and whipstitch them to the closure after the elastic has been stitched in place (c).

Match the pin marks of elastic and garment. Pin in place on the underside of the garment (a). Stretch the elastic between the pins as you stitch under tension. (See TAUT STITCHING.) Use a narrow multistitch zigzag (b) or two rows of straight stitching (c).

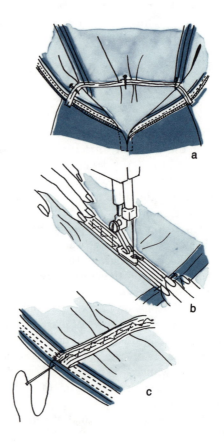

ELASTIC GATHERING WITHOUT A CASING. A type of elastic application on the underside of a no-seam garment. It

137

METHOD 2. WITH ELASTIC THREAD

Wind the elastic thread on the bobbin. When winding by hand, stretch the elastic slightly. When greater strength is needed wind bobbin with double elastic thread. Use mercerized or silk thread for the top threading of the machine. Use a stitch length of 10 to 12 stitches per inch, depending on the fabric. Test the fullness on a scrap of fabric. For best results, stitch several rows 1/4 inch apart. As you sew, stretch the elastic so the shirring will be even. The more you stretch, the more the fabric will gather. Tie the ends of the thread in a square knot.

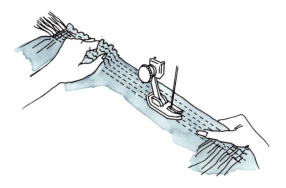

With Elastic Thread Through a Zigzag Casing. Set the machine for a zigzag stitch wide enough and close enough to form a casing for the elastic thread. Use an appropriate thread for the bobbin and the top threading. Place the elastic on the line of marking on the underside of the garment. In some machines, the elastic can be threaded through a hole in the embroidery foot—a good guide for the feeding. Pull the elastic while you stitch. The more you pull, the more the fabric will gather. For a second row, pull the material until it is straight while sewing to produce even shirring.

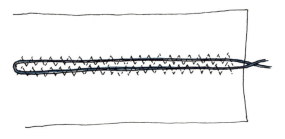

ELASTICIZED GATHERING. *See* ELASTIC GATHERING WITHOUT A CASING.

ELASTICIZED SHIRRING. Several rows of elastic gathering (q.v.).

ELASTIC WAISTBAND. *See* CASING *and* ELASTIC DECORATIVE WAISTBAND.

ELBOW DARTS CONVERTED TO GATHERS OR EASE STITCHING.
Often gathers or ease stitching in your garment fabric are more easily handled than the elbow darts that appear in the pattern.

To Convert Elbow Darts to Gathers or Ease Stitching. Cut the dart out of the pattern. Locate the outside limits of the fullness on the seam line above and below the cut-out dart—points A and B (a). A total area of 2 1/2 to 3 inches should suffice.

Draw slash lines from A and B to the dart point. Draw one or more slash lines on either side of the cut-out dart. Slash and spread so the spaces between the sections are equal (b). Scotch-tape them to position. Correct any irregularities on the seam line. On your pattern note the area to be gathered or eased (c).

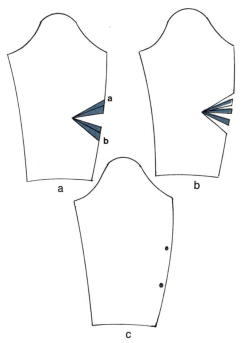

ELBOW SHAPING. A close-fitting sleeve that extends below the elbow requires some shaping to accommodate the bulge formed when the arm is bent. The shaping of a one-piece sleeve may be by darts (a) or ease stitching (b). Which to use depends on the fabric and/or the design of the sleeve.

If there is one dart, it is located at the elbow. Two darts are located on either side of the elbow about 1 inch apart. When there are three darts, the center dart is at the elbow.

Ease stitching (q.v.) is another way of handling the shaping. This is designated by markings on the back seam line, an area about 2 1/2 to 3 inches, which must be eased into the shorter front seam line at the elbow position. The easing is centered at the elbow.

In a two-piece sleeve (c) the elbow shaping is contained in the fullest part of the curve of the sleeve seam. There is often some easing involved here too.

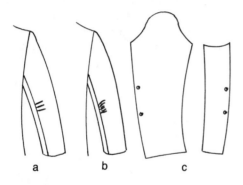

a   b   c

For correct shaping, the exact location of the elbow is extremely important. To preserve the sleeve shaping of the pattern while providing for the proportion of the arm, all sleeve corrections must be made above or below the elbow.

If you are unsure about the exact location of the elbow shaping by measurement, pin or baste the sleeve seam from the underarm to a point slightly above the elbow. Gather the sleeve cap. Pin, then baste it into the armhole. Try on the garment. Check the sleeve setting. With arm bent, mark the position of the elbow darts or ease stitching on the sleeve. Remove the garment.

ELIMINATE BULK. In all fine dressmaking and tailoring there must be nothing in the construction of the garment that detracts from the beauty of the fabric or diverts attention from the lines of the design. Many things contribute to a smooth appearance, but none is more important than the elimination of excess fabric once the darts and seams have been stitched. This makes the trimming scissors a very important piece of equipment, and the courage to cut an essential attribute of any sewer.

Because the necessity for such cutting is so pervasive in clothing construction, it is dealt with throughout this book in context with the technique described. However, it would be wise to see the following specific listings: TRIM A CORNER; TRIM A DART; CLIP; NOTCHES; GRADING SEAMS; SLASHED NECKLINE OPENING.

ENCLOSED (ENCASED) SEAM. One that is enclosed when the outer fabric and its facing are joined. Such seams appear in collars, lapels, flaps, welts, at the neckline, hem, front or back closings, and so on.

They call for placing the actual line of stitching beside the seam line rather than on it, so that the seam can be rolled to the underside, out of view.

Press the seam open. (Use the edge and point presser, tailor's ham, or tailor's press board as needed.) Grade the seam allowances, clip or notch them as necessary, free the corners of bulk. Turn the two layers to the right side, easing the facing to the underside. Press to position. Hold the seam firmly in place with edge or diagonal basting.

To guarantee that the seam that joins the outer layer and its facing never slips into view, the two thicknesses are held in place with either topstitching or understitching, depending on which is appropriate to the design and the fabric.

ENCLOSED HEM EDGE. Hem edges may be enclosed by banding or binding.

Banding (q.v.) becomes an extension of the hem. Cut wide enough, it becomes a decorative edge. It is also a good way to lengthen a garment.

Binding wraps around the hem. It is a good edge for reversible styles and sheer fabrics and as a decorative trim.

EXPANDABLE WAISTLINE. One in which extra fabric is added to the waistline. The fit is then controlled by elastic run through a waistline casing. This can be done for any waistline—in clothing for children or adults who have variable waistlines. The fullness may be controlled around the entire waistline or partially—at front or back.

Use any darts or vertical seam allowances in the bodice and skirt. Add extra fabric to the side seams at the waistline of bodice and skirt, front and back. Taper to the original underarm and hips.

Construct the garment. Sew a bias casing in place along a marked seam line in a one-piece garment or at the waist seam of a two-piece garment. Run a length of narrow elastic through the casing. Overlap and fasten the ends of a complete waistline elastic. Or attach the elastic ends of a partial casing at any darts, side seams, or opening. *(See* CASING.)

EXPOSED ZIPPER. The exposed zipper, which often becomes a decorative element in a closure, may be installed in a seam or slash. Instead of being covered as in the more usual installations, the zipper teeth are brazenly exposed.

Measure the width of the zipper teeth. Add enough room for slide-fastener clearance. From the center line of the closure, measure over this amount on each side of it for the entire length of the zipper. Mark with thread tracing (q.v.). Turn under the closure seam allowances along the thread tracing and press. Remove the basting. Place the exposed zipper, face up, under one opening edge. Stitch the turned-under edge to the zipper tape close to the fold. Repeat for the second side. *See* EXPOSED ZIPPER ENCLOSED AT BOTH ENDS; EXPOSED ZIPPER SET IN A SLASH; EXPOSED ZIPPER WITH TRIMMING; *and* SEPARATING ZIPPER.

EXPOSED ZIPPER ENCLOSED AT BOTH ENDS. A type of application used for pockets, pillowcases, handbags. The zipper installation is the same as that of the exposed zipper (q.v.) except that *both* ends of the zipper opening are enclosed.

Close the zipper tapes above the top stop with several back-and-forth machine stitches or with a bar tack. Set and stitch the zipper in a seam or slash, with or without a stay.

EXPOSED ZIPPER SET IN A SLASH. This zipper is installed where there is no seam.

Mark the center line of the opening on the garment. Measure the width of the zipper teeth or coil. *See* EXPOSED ZIPPER. Continue the marking across the end of opening.

With a Stay. Cut a stay 2 inches longer than the opening by 4 inches wide. Mark the center. With right sides together and center lines matching, place and baste the stay over the garment (a).

Stitch the stay to the garment on each side of the center and across the bottom as marked. Slash along the center line and diagonally to each corner (b). Turn the stay

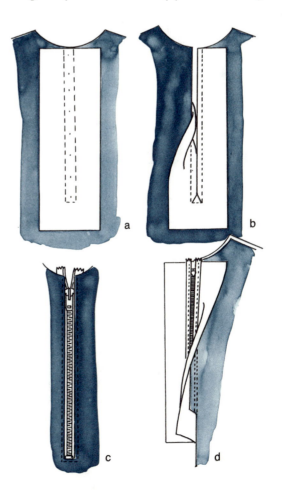

to the inside, rolling the joining seam to the underside. Press. Pin or baste the stay to position.

Center the zipper in the opening and baste to position. If consistent with the design of the garment, topstitch close to the folded edge (c). If no visible stitching is desired, slip-baste the fold at the opening to the zipper tape. Turn back the garment, exposing the zipper tape, the stay, and the slip basting. Machine-stitch the zipper tape to the stay over the slip basting (d) along each side and across the triangle at the bottom.

Without a Stay. Reinforce the corners of the opening with small machine stitches. Slash the center line of the opening and diagonally to each corner (a).

Working from the right side, turn under the seam allowance along the thread tracing (q.v.) at sides and bottom. Press (b). Center the zipper in the opening and baste to position. Topstitch close to the folded edge (c).

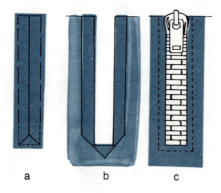

a   b   c

EXPOSED ZIPPER WITH TRIMMING. Disguise the zipper with trimming of braid, ribbon, beaded or sequined bands, embroidery, anything that strikes your fancy. Add a bit of glitter to the pull or dangle a tassel or pompon. It all could be *the* decorative touch for an otherwise unadorned dress.

Position the zipper and mark the opening with thread or tailor's chalk. Stay-stitch 1/8 inch from the marking on both lengthwise edges and across the bottom of the placket. Slash down the center to

within 1/2 inch of the ends. Clip diagonally to each corner. Turn this narrow seam allowance to the *right side.* Baste and press (a).

Center the zipper in the opening and edge-baste close to the fold (b).

Baste the trimming around the zipper, covering the fold of the placket opening with the inner edge of the trim. Miter the bottom with a square (c) or pointed end (d). *See* MITERED TRIM FOR A PLACKET OPENING. Stitch both inner and outer edges of the trimming by hand or by machine—whichever appears most suitable for the trimming.

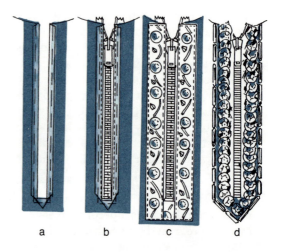

a   b   c   d

EXTENDED FACING. This is the simplest of facings. It is cut all in one piece with the garment and is turned to the underside along a fold line (a). There is no particular virtue in having a seamed facing. The seam does not make it hang better. In fact, if you eliminate the seam, you may eliminate a stitching or matching problem. There are many times when one would prefer not to cut into a beautiful fabric for a seam that has no apparent advantage. *(See also* EXTENDED WAISTLINE FACING.)

If the pattern does not have an extended facing, it is possible to create one if the extension line is straight, on vertical or cross grain, the material is wide enough, there is enough fabric for the layout, and the seam line is not essential to the design.

When there is a facing pattern, add it to the garment pattern by overlapping seam

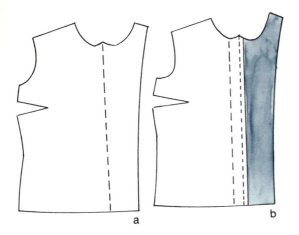

lines (b). Pin or Scotch-tape to position. Mark the new fold line. Treat like any other facing.

When there is no facing pattern and you wish to create an extended facing, *see* FACING PATTERN FOR A STRAIGHT EDGE; FACING PATTERN FOR A CLOSING EDGE.

EXTENDED SNAP. A useful closing device for garment edges that abut at collars, neckbands, necklines, waistlines, and the like.

With whipping stitches, sew the socket to one side of the garment through *one* hole only, extending it from the edge. On the inside of the opposite edge, locate the exact placement of the ball for a perfect closing. Sew it in place with whipping stitches through all holes at the edge of the snap.

EXTENDED WAISTLINE FACING. Some patterns are so designed that the waistline facing is cut all in one with the skirt.

Mark the fold line at the waist with thread tracing (q.v.). Stitch the darts and seams of both skirt and facing. Slash the darts open (when possible). Press open all seam allowances and darts. Finish the fac-

ing edge by a method appropriate for the fabric (a).

Cut a length of ribbon seam binding or twill tape the length of the waistline from one edge of the garment to the other for a stay. Apply it to the underside of the facing with one long edge along the fold line. The ends of the stay are even with the opening edges of the closure. Stitch through stay and facing close to the fold line (b).

Turn the facing to the inside of the skirt along the fold line. Press to position. Insert the zipper. Turn in the ends of the facing diagonally against the zipper tape and slip-stitch them. Tack the facing to the garment at all seams and darts (c). Sew a hook and eye or a hanging or extended snap (q.q.v.) at the top of the closing.

If interfacing is used, apply it to the underside of the facing.

EXTENSION CLOSING. An extension of the material beyond the closing line of the garment toward the outer edge. This provides sufficient overlap of the two sides of the closing. When the closing is a buttoned one, the width of the extension is determined by the size of the button. *See* BUTTON SIZES; EXTENSION CLOSING OF WAISTBAND.

EXTENSION CLOSING OF WAISTBAND.
The standard extension closing of a skirt or pants waistband measures 1½ inches beyond the closing line at its front or back end. The extension may appear as an overlap (a) or an underlay (b).

a   b

In the *overlap extension closing*, the 1½ inches extend beyond the closing line of the garment front while the back waistband ends flush with the back closing line. The band is fastened (usually) with a buttonhole and button. A bound buttonhole is made in the band before it is attached to the garment; a machine-made buttonhole, after.

In the *underlay extension closing*, the 1½ inches extend beyond the closing line of the garment back waistband while the front ends flush with the front closing line. This band may also close with a buttonhole and button but looks trimmer if closed with snaps or hooks and eyes— large or small, covered or uncovered.

EYELET. A small hole or perforation used in belt fastenings, for cuff links, studs, drawstrings, lacing of ties. It may also be used decoratively as in eyelet embroidery. The hole is reinforced with hand or machine stitching or with a metal ring.

Hand-worked Eyelet. Mark the position of the eyelet. If used for studs or cuff links, mark matching pairs on the right and left sides of the closing. Cut an opening the desired size, using sharp scissors to cut away the excess fabric. Or punch a hole in the material with an awl or stiletto, an orange stick, darning needle, or any similar sharp tool that won't injure the fabric. Overcast each eyelet to hold the layers of fabric in place or sew around the eyelet with small running stitches.

Using a single strand of silk, mercerized thread, or buttonhole twist, bring the needle up through the fabric from the underside about ⅛ inch from the edge of the hole, leaving a 1-inch end. Work the stitches around the hole and over the 1-inch end. Use a buttonhole stitch (q.v.), forming the purl on the inside edge (a) or the outside (b) of the hole. Keep the stitches even and closely spaced. Edges may also be covered with blanket stitches or satin stitches (q.q.v.). Fasten the thread end securely on the underside. You may need to insert the stiletto or awl from time to time to keep the eyelet open and to make sure it is the right size. Fabric has a tendency to creep back to cover the hole.

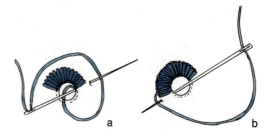

a   b

Machine-worked Eyelet. This requires a special foot, needle plate, and slide. Set them in place (a). *(See the instruction book for your machine.)* Set the machine for a satin stitch. Mark the position of the eyelet. Set the fabric taut in an embroidery hoop. Punch a hole with an awl or stiletto. (Use a round awl for fabric, a square awl for felt or leather.) Place the opening on the prong of the plate (b). Sew the eyelet—twice

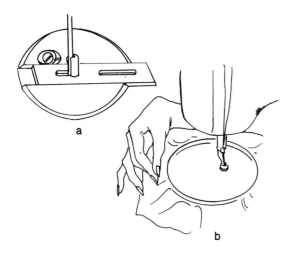

a

b

varying the speed. Start the turning as soon as the machine is in position. Stop the machine at the end of one complete turn without overlapping stitches, which make for uneven thickness.

Tool-worked Eyelet. This eyelet is made with special pliers that punch a hole and set the metal eyelet in one operation. The pliers and metal eyelets are sold in packaged units. Eyelets are available in nickel and gilt-finished aluminum and enameled brass.

Mark the position of the eyelet. Insert the metal eyelet in the punch. Locate the punch under the marking and squeeze firmly to set the eyelet. For special directions, follow the instructions that come with the equipment.

around for small holes, three times around for large holes. Hold the work so it can be turned without stopping the machine or

F

FABRIC AND PATTERN COORDINA-TION. The pattern has a design, largely realized by its darts and seams. The fabric has a design built into it by the way in which it was woven, knitted, or printed. The sewer must anticipate what will happen to the fabric design when the darts and seams of the pattern are stitched into it. If the effect is pleasing, one can safely go ahead. If not, something must be changed—either pattern or fabric. For example, note what happens to a waistline dart in various materials.

In a solid-color, plain-weave fabric there is no problem (a). In (b), the waistline dart cuts right into the design unit, *the* attraction of the fabric. Horizontal stripes are easily matched and balanced on the vertical waistline dart (c). Vertically striped material produces a chevron shape (d). This may or may not be objectionable, depending on the width, color, and location of the stripes. A vertical waistline dart in diagonal material is hopeless. It produces an unsightly distortion of the fabric design (e).

Having trouble visualizing the effect of the darts on the fabric? Try one of the following. When buying fabric, fold the material into a dart or seam similar to that of the pattern. Note what happens to the fabric design. Or trace the prominent lines or motifs of the fabric on the pattern. (Don't try to copy the whole design.) Pin the darts or seams closed. Note what happens to the fabric design.

More garments are spoiled by lack of coordination between pattern and fabric than by anything else in sewing. When the fabric and pattern work together, the result is a success. When the fabric and pattern fight each other, the result is a flop.

FABRIC CARRIERS.

FABRIC CARRIERS. Loops made of strips of self-fabric. The carrier is made as wide or as narrow as the design requires and long enough for the belt to pass through easily. *See* BELT CARRIERS; TROUSER BELT LOOPS; WAISTBAND CARRIER.

The carrier may be a complete loop or turned under at each end. The fabric strips may be constructed and attached in one of several ways. The strips may be made individually or in a single long strip, cut to individual lengths. If making the latter, take the precaution of securing a few stitches at the beginning and end of each carrier.

To Construct the Fabric Strips

Method 1. Cut a strip of fabric along the selvage, three times the desired finished width of the carrier by the predetermined length. With right side outside, fold the strip in thirds lengthwise so the raw edge is inside, the selvage slightly in from the edge on the underside. Either hem the selvage to position or topstitch both long edges (a).

Method 2. Cut a strip of fabric along the selvage twice the desired finished width of the carrier plus 1/4 inch for an underlap by the predetermined length. Turn under and press the 1/4-inch underlap. Lap the selvage over the turned edge, right side outside, slightly in from the edge on the underside. Slip-stitch to position (b).

Method 3. When the selvage is not available or is undesirable, cut a strip of fabric twice the width of the finished carrier plus two narrow seam allowances by the predetermined length. Turn under the narrow seam allowance on each long edge

a   b   c

and press. Fold the strip not quite in half, right side outside, with the slightly narrower part on the underside. Topstitch along both long edges (c). If carriers are made of fabric that tends to ravel, overcast the short edges. Otherwise, they need no special finish, for the ends are either whipstitched or turned under when attached to the garment.

To Attach the Fabric Carriers

Establish the belt position on the garment. Make placement marks at the desired intervals.

The Complete Loop Carrier. Make the carrier length twice the width of the belt plus ease. Heavier fabrics require more ease. Bring the ends of the carrier together and whipstitch them (a). Pin the carrier to position on the garment and sew it securely at both ends with backstitches on the inside of the loop.

The Turn-under Strip Carrier. Make each carrier as long as the width of the belt plus ease. Add 1 inch for two 1/2-inch turn-unders. Allow more ease and more turn-under for heavy fabrics.

Fold under the turn-under allowance and press. Pin to position on the garment. Attach by hand stitching: slip-stitch the turn-unders and folds at the top and bottom of the carrier (b); or attach by machine: topstitch across the folds at top and bottom (c).

a   b   c

FABRIC CHOICES. A garment is only as exciting as the fabric that makes it. And there are plenty of exciting fabrics today, even among the inexpensive ones.

If you don't enjoy the material while you are working on it, you probably won't enjoy wearing it. Chances are you may not even want to finish it. On the other hand, you will discover what a delight it is to work on something that is a joy to look at and a pleasure to handle.

The first creative step in sewing is selecting a fabric that best interprets the style. Some fabrics are better able to do this than others. The designer refers to this as "hand," meaning its quality of smoothness or roughness, its softness or stiffness, its flexibility or drapability, its dryness or luxuriousness. For instance, gathering, shirring, smocking, or draping call for soft fabrics that can fall in graceful folds. Sharp pleats require firm, close weaves, while unpressed pleats are better in soft fabrics.

If a garment is a structured one, the choice of fabric is limitless, since the understructure can supply what the material lacks by way of firmness. If the garment is an unstructured one, the fabric must have enough body to sustain the lines of the design, since there is no help from an understructure.

Generally, the difficulty in choosing a fabric is not so much its suitability for a particular style as its relation to the shaping of the garment. *See* FABRIC AND PATTERN COORDINATION.

These fabrics are *easy to handle:* solid colors, medium weights, plain weaves, firmly woven, small all-over surface designs, two-way design units, cottons, linens, and some woolens.

These fabrics are *hard to handle* in layout, stitching, pressing, and the like: stripes, plaids, checks, blocks; some woolens, such as ribbed ottoman; silks; many synthetic fibers, such as polyesters and Qiana; raised surfaces, looped, fuzzy, furry fabrics; nap or fleece fabrics, corduroy, velveteen, velvet (all of which tend to "creep" in stitching); very stretchy, very loosely woven, very sheer, very heavy, *very anything.* If you have sufficient eagerness, determination, and patience (it takes lots of this!) to carry you over the rough spots, a choice of any of these will reward you with an exciting-looking garment. Hard work, but worth it!

FABRIC CUT OFF GRAIN. This is the problem most frequently encountered in piece goods. The cut may be made straight across the material but if that has been pulled off-grain to begin with, the cut will also be off-grain. The heavy line in the illustration shows the true grain. Then, too, the cut may be in a straight line but that straight line may be at an angle. (It's wise to buy a little extra fabric to take care of such contingencies.)

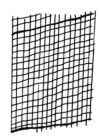

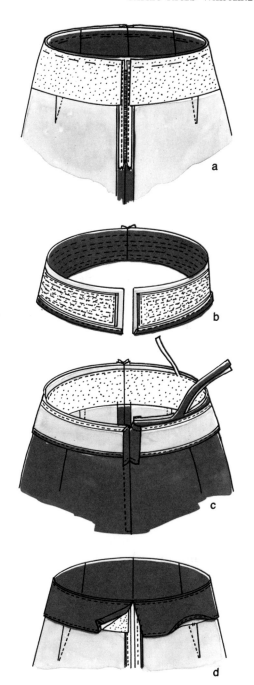

The best thing to do is to supervise the cutting of the material and insist that it be cut on-grain. This may not endear you to the one behind the counter, for it does take time and more care. Also, the seller may lose those few inches of fabric instead of you. If the first length was cut off the bolt on-grain, all subsequent cutting can easily be made accurate too.

FABRIC-FACED WAISTLINE. There are many times when the design of a skirt would be greatly improved by eliminating its waistband. Instead face the waistline with self- or lightweight fabric. This is also a good alternative to a bulky waistband of heavy fabric. *See also* RIBBON-FACED WAISTLINE.

Cut a facing for the waistline area of the skirt. Make it 1½ to 2 inches wide plus seam allowances. Stitch front and back seams to conform to the closure. Finish the outside edge of the facing in any way appropriate for the facing material.

Interfacing is optional but it does support the waistline area and provides a firm fit. To interface: cut a single layer of interfacing material from the facing pattern. Make lapped seams. Apply the interfacing to the underside of the skirt and baste along the waistline (a). Alternate method: pad-stitch a single or double layer of interfacing minus seam allowances to the

wrong side of the facing with rows of machine stitching (b).

With right sides together, pin and/or baste the facing to the garment, easing as necessary. Stay the facing waist seam line with ribbon seam binding or twill tape, centered over the seam line on the wrong side.

Stitch, trim, clip, and grade the seam allowances (c). Understitch the facing to the seam allowances of the skirt. Turn the facing to the inside and press along the waistline edge, rolling the seam to the underside. Turn in the ends of the facing diagonally and sew to the zipper tape (d). Tack the facing to the garment at all seams and darts. Attach a hook and eye, an extended or hanging snap (q.q.v.) at the top of the closing.

FABRIC FINISHED OFF GRAIN. Sometimes the fabric is pulled off-grain in the finishing process (a) in much the same way that you might press a handkerchief out of its rectangular shape. Just as you can pull or press your handkerchief back into shape, so you can correct your material in the same way. Pull the grain on the bias in the opposite direction (b) until the threads are restored to their original rectangular position (c).

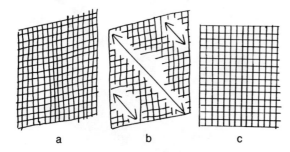

a   b   c

If pulling dry fabric doesn't realign the grain, dampen the cloth first by sponging, steam pressing, or simply moistening with a sponge or spray. If the fabric can take it, press it dry. If not, lay it on a flat surface to dry.

Caution: Don't dampen silk. It waterspots. You will have to pull and press the dry silk material into position as best you can.

Test your straightened fabric against any right angle to make sure you have reestablished the grain to its true position.

FABRIC FINISHES. The beautiful fabric that lured you into purchasing it may be quite different from that same fabric as it came off the loom. Between that point and your purchase the fabric may have been subjected to a number of treatments that affected its appearance, its texture, its wear. In fact, the processing may have begun even earlier, with the fiber or the yarn. All of these treatments and processes are called *finishes.* There are so many of them, it is practically impossible to list them all or to project those that will be developed in the future.

Finishes That Affect Wear. The best known are those that make fabrics crease-resistant, colorfast, flame-resistant, permanent-press, stain- or spot-resistant, wash-and-wear, drip-dry, waterproof, water-repellant, and those that impart crispness or prevent shrinkage.

Finishes That Affect Texture and Appearance. You may recognize many of the following terms: beetling, calendering, ciréing, embossing, fulling, glazing, moiréing, plisséing, sizing, tentering, weighting, mercerizing.

FABRIC FOR A CONSTRUCTED GARMENT. *See* FABRIC CHOICES.

FABRIC FOR AN UNCONSTRUCTED GARMENT. *See* FABRIC CHOICES.

FABRIC INSET WAISTBAND. *See* INSET WAISTBAND.

FABRIC PREPARED FOR CUTTING. Before one can proceed with the layout and cutting of any garment, the fabric must be prepared for it. This also applies to every material that goes inside the garment—interfacing, underlining, lining, interlining.

The true grain of the fabric must be established. *See* FABRIC CUT OFF GRAIN; FABRIC FINISHED OFF GRAIN; FABRIC PRINTED OFF GRAIN; GRAIN; GRAIN ESTABLISHED IN KNIT FABRIC; GRAIN ESTABLISHED IN WOVEN FABRIC.

Unless the fabric has already been treated for shrinkage, it is wise to sponge it, launder it, or dry-clean it before cutting. Knits should be stabilized before cutting. *See* KNITS: TO STABILIZE.

FABRIC PRINTED OFF GRAIN. This does not happen often (there are frequent checks at the factory), but it does happen often enough to make some yardage imperfect. Even when the imperfection is spotted and the factory rejects the fabric, such goods often find their way into mill-end stores or onto bargain counters. If the imperfection is not spotted, the fabric may even appear in fine fabric stores.

Off-grain printing presents a real problem for the sewer. When you follow the print, the fabric will not hang on-grain. If you follow the grain, the printed design may march itself uphill and down dale. What to do? Of the two evils, the lesser is to follow the printed design and hope for the best. Moral: examine fabric carefully before buying.

FABRIC WIDTH CONVERSION CHART.

Use this as a guide for estimated yardage when the width of your chosen fabric is not included in the yardage requirements listed on the pattern envelope.

FACED (FALSE) HEM.

A good device for a shaped edge when there is not enough hem allowance, when the fabric is too bulky for a turned-up hem, when smoothness is more desirable than the original textured fabric.

If there is no pattern for the facing, trace the hemline of the garment on a piece of paper. Measure up the width of the facing (generally up to 2½ inches) in a sufficient number of places to provide the line for the upper edge of the facing. Trace the grain line. Construct like any other facing.

If the curve of a flared or circular hem is not too deep, a bias facing may be used instead of a shaped one. *See* BIAS-FACED HEM.

FACED PLACKET.

The finished edges of this placket meet at the opening.

Mark the slash line (opening) on the garment. Cut a rectangle of self-fabric for a facing about 2½ inches wide and 1 inch longer than the length of the opening. Finish all edges but the one to be placed against the garment edge.

With right sides of garment and facing together, center the facing over the slash line. Pin or baste to position in the

Fabric Width	32"	35"–36"	39"	41"	44"–45"	50"	52"–54"	58"–60"
Yardage	1⅞	1¾	1½	1½	1⅜	1¼	1⅛	1
	2¼	2	1¾	1¾	1⅝	1½	1⅜	1¼
	2½	2¼	2	2	1¾	1⅝	1½	1⅜
	2¾	2½	2¼	2¼	2⅛	1¾	1¾	1⅝
	3⅛	2⅞	2½	2½	2¼	2	1⅞	1¾
	3⅜	3⅛	2¾	2¾	2½	2¼	2	1⅞
	3¾	3⅜	3	2⅞	2¾	2⅜	2¼	2
	4	3¾	3¼	3⅛	2⅞	2⅝	2⅜	2¼
	4⅜	4¼	3½	3⅜	3⅛	2¾	2⅝	2⅜
	4⅝	4½	3¾	3⅝	3⅜	3	2¾	2⅝
	5	4¾	4	3⅞	3⅝	3¼	2⅞	2¾
	5¼	5	4¼	4⅛	3⅞	3⅜	3⅛	2⅞

Reprinted courtesy of New Jersey Cooperative Extension Service, Rutgers, The State University

Fabric Width Conversion Chart

V-shape indicated (a). With small stitches sew along one side of the marking, starting 1/4 inch from it at the edge, taper to almost nothing at the point, take one stitch across the point, then down the other side in the same way as the first.

Slash between the lines of stitching to the point, being careful not to cut the stitching (b). Turn the facing to the inside and press. Tack lightly at each corner (c) or slip-stitch facing to garment.

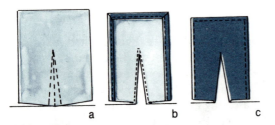

a   b   c

FACING. A second layer of material, generally applied to the underside of a garment. The exception is a decorative right-side facing (q.v.). The facing acts as both a finish and a support. It adds body, sustains the shape, and reinforces every outside edge subject to stress and wear.

When the edge to be faced is a *straight* one, the facing is often an extension of the garment turned back at a fold line, like a hem. *(See* EXTENDED FACING.) When the edge to be faced is a *shaped* one, the facing is generally a separate piece of fabric cut in the same size, shape, and grain.

A strip of bias is another way of handling a narrow, not deeply curved facing. *See* BIAS FACING.

What to Use for a Facing. When the garment fabric is opaque, smooth, and light to medium weight, use self-fabric. When of fabric sheer enough so the design on its surface will show through if self-fabric is used, make it of a matching solid color instead.

If the garment fabric is transparent, cut a facing of flesh-colored net, tulle, marquisette, horsehair braid, or another transparent material. For heavy-weight, rough, shaggy, pile or other raised-surface fabric, use a lightweight lining material.

In plaid, striped, or checked fabric, the facing should match the outer fabric at the seam.

Necessary Pattern Adjustments. Wherever a change has been made in the garment fitting or in the pattern, a similar change must be made on the facing. Facings joined to an upper layer by a seam should be slightly smaller than the edge to be faced. This shortened length does several important things: it makes the facing fit the shorter length of the inside curve; it makes the faced area lie better against the body; it makes it possible to roll the seam that joins facing to garment to the underside—out of sight. *(See* FAVORING; ENCLOSED [ENCASED] SEAM; FACING CHANGES IN SIZE.)

Construction Suggestions. When a garment is unlined, the outer edge of the facing is treated in any of the ways suggested for edge finishes (q.v.) appropriate for the fabric. If the garment is to be lined, this is unnecessary unless the fabric frays.

To tack a facing to a garment, use a blind hemming stitch or a blind catch stitch (q.q.v.), keeping the stitches very loose so there will be no telltale signs on the right side. Better yet, to avoid any possibility that this may happen, tack the facing to any of the construction seams, darts, pockets, or the like that it covers. When there is an underlining, tack the facing to it. When there is a lining (as in a jacket or coat), it is not necessary to tack it at all. The lining will hold it in place.

A facing correctly sewn in never shows from the right side, is smooth (no bumps) and flat (no drawing up). This is the result of precise stitching, trimming, grading, clipping, and notching of seam allowances, and careful pressing before and after turning the facing to the underside.

FACING AT ZIPPERED CLOSING (NECKLINE, WAISTLINE, OR THE LIKE). Some think it is easier to apply a facing first and then put the zipper in. Others feel it easier to fit the garment if the zipper is inserted before the facing is attached. (There is this too: it is easier to work on a flat section than on an assembled garment.) Whatever the sequence of the zipper insertion, the application of the facing is such as to prevent bulk above the zipper pull tab and to avoid catching the ends of the facing in the zipper teeth.

METHOD 1

Can be used before or after the zipper installation.

With the right sides together, pin and/or baste the facing to the garment, matching centers, shoulders, notches, seam lines. Make sure the seam lines at each side of the closing align with each other (a). Stitch the seam and treat it as an enclosed seam (q.v.).

Open out the facing. Open the seam at the ends to within 1/4 inch of the closing edge. Clip the facing at a slight angle so that, when turned in, the facing ends will clear the zipper teeth (b). Understitch the facing to the garment seam allowances. Turn the facing to the inside. Slip-stitch the folded ends to the zipper tape (c).

METHOD 2

Before the zipper installation.

Turn back 1 inch at each end of the facing. With right sides together, pin and/or baste the facing to the neckline. Machine-stitch facing to garment, continuing the stitching to the end of the opening.

Trim, grade, and clip the seam allowances. Stop just short of the unfaced portion (a). Press the seam first closed, then open over the tailor's ham. Understitch the facing to the neckline seam allowances. Turn the facing to the inside and press (b). Insert the zipper. Slip-stitch the facing ends to the zipper tape (c).

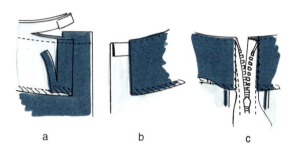

a   b   c

To Eliminate Bulk of Zipper Tape at the Faced Edge. After the zipper has been installed, clip into the tape almost to the cord at zipper's edge. Trim close to the cord up to the end of the tape. Fold the cord over the cut ends of the tape and whipstitch, using matching thread. Trim any excess cord that extends beyond the zipper tape.

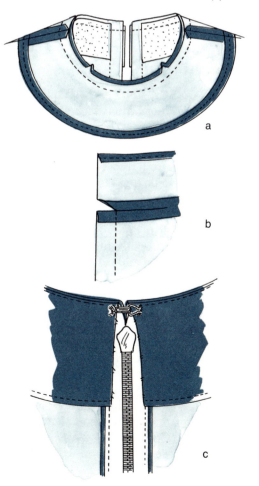

a

b

c

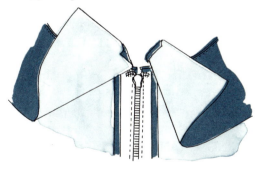

FACING-CASING. As the name implies, this is a facing that will also serve as a casing.

Cut a strip of fabric to the desired width and length of the finished facing-casing plus 1/4-inch seam allowances on all edges.

Trim the seam allowance of the garment edge to be faced to 1/4 inch. Turn in the 1/4-inch seam allowances on both ends and along the lower edge of the facing and press.

Starting at a vertical seam, with right sides together and edges aligned, pin, then stitch the facing to the garment 1/4 inch from the edge (a). Press the seam open. Grade the seam allowances. Turn the casing to the inside, rolling the joining seam to the underside. Pin the casing to position. Stitch along the lower edge close to the fold (b). After threading the casing with elastic or drawstring, close the opening with slip stitches.

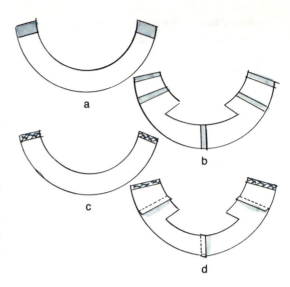

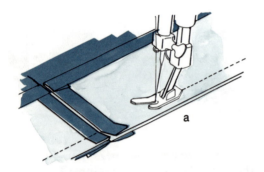

Alternative Method: With right sides together, stitch the ends of the facing and press the seam allowances open. Apply like a self-casing (q.v.).

FACING CHANGES IN SIZE. The facing pattern may be made larger or smaller at the seam allowances or within the pattern.

To Make the Facing Larger. Add a small amount at the joining seams (a). To preserve the overall shape of an unusual style line or if considerable enlarging is necessary, slash and spread the pattern in

several places. Fill in the spread with paper (b).

To Make the Facing Smaller. Take a bit off the joining seams (c). To preserve the overall shape of an unusual style line or if considerable reduction in size is necessary, tuck the pattern in several places (d).

FACING MATERIALS. *See* FACING.

FACING—NECK AND ARMHOLE ALL IN ONE. *See* COMBINATION NECK AND ARMHOLE FACING.

FACING PATTERN FOR A CLOSING EDGE. A pattern for a single-layer style or one meant to be lined to the edge does not include a pattern for a facing. Should you wish to add a facing to the closing edge, this is how it is done. The following procedure is for a bodice but the same general principle can be applied wherever there is a closing.

Trace the bodice, leaving plenty of room along the straight edge for a facing. Measure 1 1/2 inches over on the shoulder from the neckline. On the waistline, measure over 2 1/2 to 3 inches from the center line. These are standard measurements. You may make the facing any suitable width. Just be sure to make it wide enough to cover any buttonholes completely plus a little over. Connect the two points with a slightly curved line (a).

For an extended facing (q.v.), fold the pattern along the straight edge. Using a tracing wheel, trace the neckline, the shoulder line to the facing, the outer edge of the facing (the curved line), and the waistline. Unfold the paper and, following the marks of the tracing wheel, draw the facing (b).

For a separate facing, cut along the straight edge of the above pattern (b), separating garment and facing (c). Be sure to trace the grain line. Add notches and seam allowances along the straight edges.

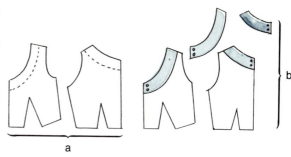

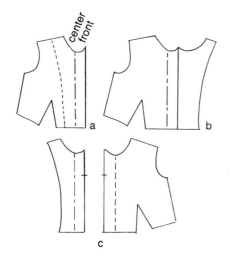

This type of facing is used when the straight line is diagonal, when the edge is shaped, when the material is not wide enough or for an extended facing, if the layout is more economical by the use of a separate pattern, or if you plan to use a contrasting fabric for the facing.

FACING PATTERN FOR A SHAPED EDGE. Start with the garment pattern. From the edge to be faced, measure over on the pattern the width of the facing in a sufficient number of places to provide the line for the outer edge (a). The width is usually 1½ to 2 inches. Draw the facing edge by connecting the markings.

Keep facings simple in shape. Eliminate style details and darts. The width of the facing is so narrow that shaping by small darts and seams is unnecessary. Besides, they would prove too bulky when

stitched. If the pattern includes any seams or darts that enter the edge to be faced, eliminate them in the facing pattern by overlapping.

Trace the facing pattern onto another sheet of paper. Trace the grain line, which should be the same as for the garment. Place pairs of similar notches on the garment and facing edges. Indicate any fold of fabric. Add seam allowances where necessary (b).

Make a slight adjustment in the length of the facing so it fits the inside rather than the outside of the garment. *See* FACING CHANGES IN SIZE.

FACING PATTERN FOR A STRAIGHT EDGE. This type of facing may be made in one of two ways: all in one with the edge to be faced or as a separate piece. Either trace the pattern, allowing enough room at the straight edge for the facing, or Scotch-tape an additional piece of paper for the purpose.

Measure and mark on the pattern the width of the facing—the broken lines in (a). Fold the pattern on the original straight edge. Trace the facing on all remaining sides, using a tracing wheel. Unfold the pattern and, following the marks of the tracing wheel, draw all outside edges (b). Mark the fold line on the pattern.

For a separate facing, cut the pattern away at the original straight edge. Add seam allowances, a grain line (the same as that of the original pattern), and notches

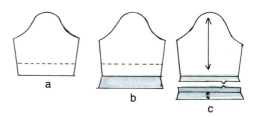

at the edges to be joined (c). *See also* EX-TENDED FACING *and* FACING PATTERN FOR A CLOS-ING EDGE.

FACING SEAMS MATCH GARMENT SEAMS.

If, in fitting, you changed the position of a seam, you must make a similar change on the facing. Facing seams must match garment seams to provide identical shape and fit.

With right sides together, place the facing over the garment, matching center front and back. Working out from the center, smooth the facing toward the seams. Pin to position. When you reach the seams, fold back the facing against itself. The folds follow the seam lines of the garment, just touching. Slip-stitch the folds as a guide for the machine stitching.

Unpin and remove the corrected facings. Stitch the seams. Take a slightly deeper seam allowance, making the facing a bit smaller than the edge to be faced. Trim the seam allowances and press them open. Apply facing to garment in the usual manner.

FAGOTED SEAM.

On a strip of paper as a guide, draw a seam line. Draw parallel lines on either side of the seam line to represent the width of the openwork.

Fold each edge of fabric back from its seam line to the corresponding parallel line. Pin and baste to the paper. Join the folds of fabric with hand fagoting stitches (q.v.) or by machine zigzag stitches. If the latter, make a test stitch to determine its width. Make sure that each folded edge is caught in the machine stitching.

Press lightly before removing from the paper guide.

FAKE FLAPS OR WOULD-BE WELT POCKETS.

They look like real pockets but they're only fake flaps and would-be welt pockets. Their function is purely decorative. There are two ways in which you can make and apply these great pretenders.

METHOD 1

Complete the three sides of the welt or flap. Attach the fourth side to the garment with machine stitching as one would any flap (q.v.).

METHOD 2

Complete all four sides. (Machine-stitch three sides, turn to the right side, and tuck in and slip-stitch the fourth side.) Slip-stitch the finished welt or flap to position.

The second method makes a flatter application by avoiding the turnover essential to the first method. In some fabrics this is a decided advantage.

FALL OF COLLAR. *See* COLLAR TERMINOLOGY.

FALSE HEM. *See* FACED (FALSE) HEM.

FAVORING. Wherever there are two thicknesses of cloth, an upper and a lower, the seam that joins them is rolled to the underside so it will be out of sight. It could be said that one "favors" the upper layer in this respect. *See* PATTERN PREPARED FOR CUTTING.

FEATHERBONING. Flexible strips of featherbone, available by the yard, ranging in width from 1/8 to 5/8 inch, either uncovered or muslin-encased.

Featherboning is used for stiffening seams, darts, edges, or wherever the lines of a garment require rigid support. For in-

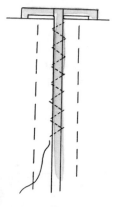

stance: in a fitted, strapless bodice, a drop-shoulder décolletage, a high-standing collar, wide belt, hoopskirt, or the like. It is easy to handle, for it can be cut with scissors and stitched either by hand or by machine.

Cut the necessary length of covered featherboning. If encased, include a narrow seam allowance at each end. Trim the featherboning from the seam allowances at the ends and turn the empty covering to the underside for a finish.

On the wrong side of the garment, center the featherboning over the seam line and stitch along both long edges. For a curved, boned seam, place the featherboning over the curved seam line, holding it in an arched position to fit the contour of the seam, and stitch.

If the boning is uncovered, stitch tape or binding to the underside of the fabric or lining to form a casing of the necessary length. Insert the boning and secure both ends of the tape.

FELLED SEAM. *See* FLAT FELL SEAM.

FIGURE TYPES: WOMEN AND MISSES.

In an effort to accommodate the many variations in height, weight, and figure development of women's and misses' figures, patterns now come in figure types as well as sizes. You'll need a lot less pattern alteration if you buy the right size within the right figure type.

Figure types are decided by height, length of bodice (a good indicator of the proportion of bodice to legs within the overall height), and the degree of figure development.

Misses	5'5" to 5'6"	the so-called average figure
Miss Petite	5'2" to 5'3"	an overall shorter Miss figure
Women's	5'5" to 5'6"	a longer, larger, well-proportioned figure
Half-size	5'2" to 5'3"	a short-waisted, heavier-than-average figure
Junior	5'4" to 5'5"	a shorter-waisted Miss figure
Junior Petite	5' to 5'1"	a petite figure
Young Junior/ Teen	5'1" to 5'5"	a not fully grown figure

Misses and *Miss Petite* have similar sophisticated styling. *Women's* and *Half-sizes* are styled for heavier figures. *Junior* and *Junior Petite* sizes provide a young fashion image. *Young Junior/Teen* caters to a very young fashion image.

The greatest range of styles is in the *Misses* group. If you have another figure type but crave the more sophisticated styling, choose the Misses size that comes nearest to your measurements and do a little changing.

FITTING. If what you make doesn't fit, forget it! Anybody can do exercises in stitching. The trick is to make what is stitched fit. And fit in a flattering way, at that.

Familiarize yourself with current styles. Chic in this year's look may be a subtle change in line and proportion, a mere pinch here or there. Look at the fashion magazines, look in the shops. Observe well-dressed women. Train your eye to see small niceties. Make mental calculations as to how to achieve an effect. As your perception grows, you'll grow more and more demanding about fit.

Be fastidious but not hypercritical of your fitting. Many a sewer worries herself through every last 1/8 inch. There is a point at which you can get too much of a good thing. Quit while you're ahead.

Pace yourself. Work quickly with materials that ravel. Take your time with stretchy fabrics. Give them time to stabilize themselves before the final fitting.

If you are one who depends on a bra and girdle for shape, wear for the fitting exactly what you plan to wear with the finished garment. A different bra and girdle will produce a different shape and all those carefully fitted darts and shaping seams will be dislocated.

When fitting or being fitted, stand in a natural position. Clothes must fit your posture as well as your measurements. If you "stand up straight" or "pull your shoulders back" or "tuck your stomach in" for a fitting (frequent admonitions), the garment may not fit you when you are at ease and in your normal posture.

Allow sufficient ease to be comfortable. Remember that more fabrics won't give than will, particularly when they are underlined or interfaced. Remember that the garment may get interfacing, underlining, facing, lining, and possibly interlining. Allow a little ease for these.

When shoulder pads are to be used, set them into position for the fitting.

In fitting a jacket, try it on over a blouse or sweater similar to one that will be worn under it. This will give a more accurate idea of the necessary ease. In fitting a coat, try it on over the garment or garments to be worn under it.

While most fitting can be done in the fabric alone, some styles are absolutely dependent on the understructure for support before one can attempt a fitting. In that event, test the garment over a suitable underlining and/or interfacing.

Be mindful of the fact that even unfitted clothing must be long enough and wide enough and must touch the body at certain crucial points.

Don't overfit! Contrary to popular notion, tight fitting is not slimming. It outlines the figure and focuses attention on all one's figure faults.

If you fit yourself, use safety pins rather than straight pins for strategic marking. They won't fall out as you maneuver your fitting and remove the garment.

All fitting is done from the right side. Corrections are transferred to the wrong side for stitching. Were you to do your fitting inside out you would be fitting the opposite side of you—inside right becomes outside left, inside left becomes outside right. If you fit in reverse, you defeat the whole purpose of fitting.

Pin the garment closed on the correct line. This is fixed by the design and you must not take liberties with it. There are too many style details dependent on the closing—extensions, collar, lapel, neckline, facings, even the position of the darts. While it may be tempting to give oneself a little more ease on this line or to make a double-breasted lap of a single-breasted garment, the pattern changes involved are too difficult for anyone unacquainted with patternmaking.

When a pattern calls for a stay to control the fullness of a design, fit the stay before adding the fullness. It is the relation of the stay to the figure that produces the actual fit of the garment. The fullness or drapery is just so much decoration held in place by the stay.

Pin all slits and pleats closed. The garment should fit without relying on their released fullness for added width.

Tentatively pin up the hems of skirt and sleeve. You will get a much better idea of how to fit in proportion to the length.

Examine the fit. If changes need to be made, start at the shoulders and work down, checking the grain, ease, shaping, outline seams. Starting at the neckline and working down, check the style features of neckline, collar, sleeves, and so on. Locate the position of buttons and buttonholes. Locate the position of applied pockets and trimmings.

Organize the sewing sequence to include the fitting. Most home sewers follow (indeed, depend on) the printed directions in the pattern for putting the garment together. These pattern directions deal with construction, not fitting. That is left to the sewer. No pattern company could possibly anticipate or have room for a consideration of all the individual fitting problems involved.

From the standpoint of fitting, the suggested step-by-step sewing directions may not be a logical or satisfactory order of work for some individuals. The sewer must then reorganize the sewing sequence to include her fittings as they are needed.

Stitch and press each unit of outer and supporting fabrics, following the pattern directions for construction as far as possible, before a try-on. Join what seems reasonable or essential for a fitting.

Do as much fitting as you feel will be fruitful at one time. When you are satisfied that you have gone as far as you can with a fitting, remove the garment carefully. Transfer the right-side corrections to the wrong side for stitching. (Use basting thread or tailor's chalk.)

Do as much sewing as possible between fittings to make the garment ready for the next examination. Always check the stitching lines from the right side. Correct any wavy lines or bulges with slip basting. Restitch on the wrong side. The line of stitching will affect the fit of the garment.

WHAT TO LOOK FOR

Ease (q.v.). Ease is what provides movability in your clothing.

Grain (q.v.). This is the most obvious clue to fit. Fabric hangs with the grain and fits with it.

Outline Seams (q.v.). The neck, the shoulders, the armholes, the side seams, the waistline, and the hem outline the garment.

Shaping Seams and Darts. The amount necessary, in just the right places, to convert a flat length of cloth into one that fits the curves of your body.

Style Lines. (See FITTING STYLE LINES.) The subtleties of design that give a garment its particular charm or interest must be preserved, though many of them offer possibilities for fitting.

Fit where you can, fake where you must, flatter everywhere. As important as knowing when to follow the rules of fitting is knowing when not to follow them. Clothes must not only fit, they must flatter as well. It is not a slavish reproduction of your figure that one is after, nor is it a slavish adherence to the lines of the design at the expense of the figure. The real trick in fitting is to *strike a balance between the lines of the design and the lines of the figure.* The ability to do this is often more felt than learned. But give yourself a chance. Follow what rules there are. Train the eye to see and the hand to act. Most of all, develop the courage to do what needs doing. Many sewers know

what is necessary but immobilize themselves by fear of moving a dart or seam.

Fitting is like sculpturing: it creates a three-dimensional form. Just as you can push clay around until you get what you want, so you can manipulate the fabric until you get the form you want.

FITTINGS—HOW MANY?

How many times should a garment be fitted? As many times as it takes to make it fit. This varies with the experience of the fitter, the complexity of the design, and the waywardness of the figure.

Why is all the fitting necessary when one has already gone to such lengths to guarantee good fit? Measurements, a basic pattern perhaps, pattern alterations, a dress form, a trial muslin—all extremely helpful. Yet, in the end, nothing can take the place of fitting the garment fabric on the person. Each fabric has its own unique qualities. Only the cloth can exploit the illusions created with color and texture.

The *first fitting* is a pin fitting (q.v.), or basting if you prefer or if the fabric is easily bruised by pins. It locates the exact position of the darts and seams within the garment sections and tentatively locates the outline seams.

A *second fitting* (q.v.) is necessary when the garment has been stitched, pressed, and the interfacing and/or underlining put in place. This fitting refines and perfects the fit of the seams and darts within the garment sections and locates the final position of the outline seams.

From then on you're on your own. Do as many fittings as you need until all the elements in combination make for a garment that looks good, feels comfortable, and is as lovely in motion as in standing still. Often after a first wearing you may decide some small changes are necessary. This is a common experience. If you are a perfectionist, this refining and polishing will go on until you get that cherished project to fit precisely as you desire it.

FITTING A BODICE. With the vertical grain in the correct position, pin the center front and center back to your slip, a waistband, a ribbon, or anything that passes for a waistband. This will hold the bodice at fixed points.

Clip the neckline as far as safe or as far as is necessary to bring the bodice into position at the base of the neck. Check the horizontal grain across the chest, across the bust, across the back, across the shoulder blades.

Fit both shoulders first, then work down. Fit the bust. Fit the shoulder blades toward the shoulder and toward the waistline. Fit the side seams.

Often shoulders, bust, neck, and side seams are pinned tentatively until the fitting is worked out.

Establish the neckline with chalk or a line of pins around the base of the neck from center front to center back. Duplicate the curve on the other side. This fitting is for a natural or jewel neckline. For a neckline below this, *see* DROPPED NECKLINE. For one above it, *see* RAISED NECKLINE.

Establish the curve of the armhole. Start at the correct position on the shoulder. Mark the armhole with a line of pins from the shoulder point down the front armhole to the underarm curve. Do the same for the back armhole. Duplicate the armhole fitting for the second armhole. *See* SET-IN SLEEVE.

Establish the waistline. Pin a tape or tie a length of heavy string pushed into the indentation of the waist or where you have decided you would like the waistline to be. Place a line of pins along the bottom of the tape or string. Or mark with tailor's chalk. Do the entire waistline; right and left sides may need different fitting.

Remove the garment. Mark all changes in the fitting on the wrong side with chalk or basting thread. This will assure that right and left sides of the fitting will remain so when stitched.

Correct any "jumpiness" of pin markings. See that all corresponding seams and each pair of dart legs match in length.

True up all seam lines with a ruler or curved drafting instrument. If the latter is not available, use a similar curve on the pattern. Baste the garment. Try it on again

to check the fit. Make any necessary refinements. *See* FITTING.

FITTING A MAN'S SHIRT. The same principles of pattern correction and fitting apply to both men's and women's clothing. *See the listings for specific figure problems.*

A man's shirt fits the body smoothly. It doesn't bag, pull, wrinkle, strain, or gap. The sleeve covers the wristbone. The sleeve seam is where arm and shoulder meet. The waist fits snugly but has sufficient wearing room. The collar fits comfortably around the neck. *See* FITTING.

FITTING A MAN'S TAILORED SUIT. Fit is one of the most important aspects of men's custom tailoring. In many ways, it is easier to accomplish than in women's clothing, since there aren't the dramatic curves to fit. The original straight lines of tailored clothing were designed to conform to the straight lines of a man's figure.

Take careful personal measurements and compare them with the pattern measurements. Make such pattern changes as are needed. *See* PATTERN CORRECTIONS. Further refinements in fit can be made directly in the garment fabric cut from an adjusted pattern. *See* FITTING *for general information.* The same principles apply to both men's and women's clothing. For problem figures or for first tailoring projects it is wise to make a trial muslin (q.v.). You may be unfamiliar with the fit of men's clothing.

How a Man's Tailored Suit Should Fit

Jacket. The collar fits low and close with $1/2$ inch of the shirt collar showing. Shoulders should lie straight. There is no pulling or wrinkling across the back. The collar and lapels roll easily from the center back to the first button. The waist is slightly tapered at the natural waistline. (This varies with the current style.) Sleeves are full across the cap and taper to the wrist. The sleeve hem is set so that $1/2$ inch of shirt cuff shows. The jacket is long enough to cover the seat. The hem edge hangs parallel with the floor.

Trousers. The legs hang straight with no twisting. Width and flare depend on style. There is enough ease through the crotch and hips for comfortable sitting or crossing of one's legs. The trousers touch the shoe in front without breaking, reach the heel seam in back. The grain of the fabric, the ease, the shaping, the outline seams follow the same general rules as for women's pants. *See* FITTING PANTS.

FITTING A SKIRT. The crucial area in fitting a skirt is waist to hips (a). The rest of the skirt is merely an extension of the seams from hips to hem.

When there are any fitting problems below the hip line, look for the cause above it. It could be that, for your figure, this area of your skirt (or pants) is not long enough or short enough, not wide enough or narrow enough. Perhaps there is too much or too little shaping by darts and seams. When skirt seams swing forward or backward, poke out or hike up, look for the origin of the trouble in the waist-to-hip area.

To prevent skirt fitting problems, first cut to measure. Pin a length of grosgrain ribbon, tape, or waistband into position at the waist as a stay. Pin the center front and center back of the skirt to position on the waist stay.

Pin the side seams at the hips. Make certain that the center-front and center-back vertical grain lines hang at right an-

gles to the floor and that the horizontal grain lines, both front and back, are parallel to the floor (b). Pin the side seams, fitting the curve of the hips.

Check the front and back darts or seams for correct shaping. Unsightly bulges indicate the darts are too large. Spanning across the abdomen and buttocks indicates darts that are too long or incorrectly placed. Repin the darts, making the needed correction. Or more width may be needed.

Continue pinning the side seams from hips to hem. Should the side seams tend to swing forward or backward, unpin each seam, check the grain line, check the darts, correct as necessary, and repin. Determine the correct waistline seam and mark it. Set the approximate length and pin. *See also* FITTING.

FITTING BIAS GARMENTS. *See* BIAS FITTING.

FITTING PANTS. Stay-stitch the crotch. Baste the crotch seam. Clip the seam allowance of the crotch almost to the stay stitching. Pin or baste the remaining seams and darts. Pin a waistband in place and pin the pants to the waistband.

Fitting the waist-to-hip area of pants and skirts is similar. *See* FITTING A SKIRT.

Check the grain lines, making certain that the grain at center front and center back of each pant leg hangs at right angles to the floor and that the horizontal grains of both front and back are parallel to the floor.

Check the front and back darts and/or seams for correct shaping. Release for added width where spanning occurs. Reduce the size of the darts where bulges appear.

Check the side seams and the inseams, making sure they hang at right angles to the floor. Should they swing forward or backward, unpin the seam, check the darts and the grain line. Repin the darts if necessary and reposition the seam.

Check the crotch seam for length and ease, adding or subtracting as necessary. The crotch should not be too tight or too

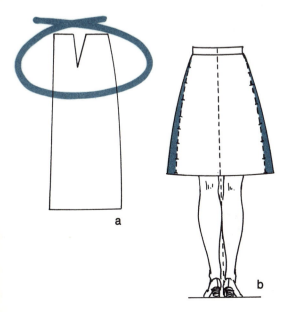

a

b

loose, too high or too low, for comfort. *See* CROTCH FITTING *and* CROTCH SEAM.

Test the pants for ease in sitting. Does the thigh area bind? Is it possible to cross one's legs? Note the position of any pull or strain and add ease accordingly.

Knit and stretch fabrics are fitted with less ease because of their elasticity. Suede, leather, canvas, duck, denim, and like fabrics need more ease because of their nonstretchability.

Determine the length of the pants.

To handle some of the most common fitting problems, *see* CROTCH FITTING *and* FITTING.

FITTING STYLE LINES. You choose a pattern because you like the design. In your overzealousness to make it fit, don't destroy or distort the style lines that attracted you. If you tamper with the proportions and the shape, you must pit your artistry against the designer's.

Leave the focal points of interest alone. Make any necessary changes above, below, beside, anywhere—but do not touch the lines that carry the design. Fitting can be done on that part of the garment that can absorb the change.

In (a), it is possible to make the yoke slightly shorter or longer, narrower or wider but don't touch its intriguing shape. Fit the dress below the yoke seam.

In (b), you could run into real trouble if you attempted to change the X-seaming and the front panel. The logical place to do the fitting is beside this intricate detail, at the side or shoulder seams.

In all designs, preserve the distinctive details that engaged your interest.

FITTING WOMEN'S JACKETS AND COATS. Everything one can say of fitting in general and in particular can also be said of jackets and coats. The only difference is the question of ease. Just remember that jackets and coats are worn over other garments. It is also likely that they will contain more understructure, for which an ease allowance must be made.

In the main, coats are the easiest of all garments to fit. They hang from the shoulder (this requires careful fitting) and are generally unfitted or semifitted. Even fitted coats are not quite as fitted as dresses. Unfitted jackets are as easy to fit as unfitted coats.

Suggested Sequence for Fitting Jackets or Coats. Try on the garment. Pin the center fronts closed. Check the vertical and horizontal grains. Start the fitting at the shoulders and work down. Check the ease and the shaping (darts and shaping seams). Fit the side seams. Check the neckline. Set the approximate length of the garment.

Set the sleeve cap, starting at the shoulder and working down, front and back, to the notches. Check the grain. Remove the garment. Pin in the underarm. Check the elbow dart for correct position and ease. Set the approximate length of the sleeve. *See the listing for* COLLAR TYPES; *tailored lapel; and sleeve types other than set-in sleeve.*

FLAP (TAB). A flat, thin section of a garment that is attached only at one edge while the other hangs free. When the flap is a double thickness of fabric plus an interfacing, every bit of sewing skill you possess goes

a   b

into the making of it. The test of your expertise is here in microcosm.

Flaps are generally made of the same fabric as the garment, cut on the same grain and same nap. All checks, stripes, or plaids must match the part of the garment where the flap is to be located. The only way to avoid doing so is by cutting it on the bias if the design will permit.

For a One-Piece Flap. Cut a strip of fabric the length of the flap by twice its width plus seam allowances on all outside edges. Interface the under half of it (a). Fold it in half lengthwise, right sides together. Set the end raw edges of the upper thickness down a little from the end raw edges of the under thickness. Stitch across the ends (b).

For a Two-Piece Flap. Allow enough fabric on the upper thickness so the joining seam may be rolled to the underside. Interface the facing (c). With raw edges matching and wrong sides together, stitch the upper layer to the facing, easing in the fullness. Leave the lower edge open (d).

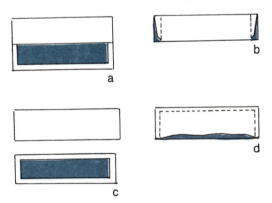

Both Types. Press all seam allowances open before turning to the right side. Use the point presser (q.v.). Grade the seam allowances. Free all corners of bulk. Clip and/or notch as necessary. Turn to the right side and press.

With the upper side of the flap on top and the underside against the hand, roll it over the fingers, making the needed adjustment in length (a). Pin to position. Baste both thicknesses across the lower edge (b). This *establishes the roll of the flap* so

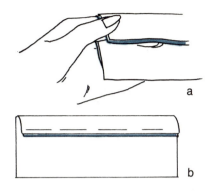

that, when stitched to the garment and turned to its proper position, it will lie flat. To attach flaps to garment, *see individual listings for each type of flap pocket.*

FLAP POCKET. To both hide the opening and enhance its appearance, a flap may be placed over the opening of any kind of pocket—patch (a), in-seam (b), bound (c). A flap may be used decoratively to simulate a pocket opening (d). *See listing for each type of pocket.*

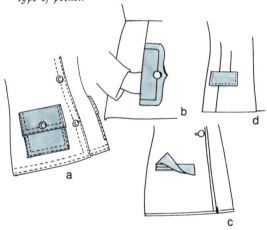

The completed flap (q.v.) is placed on the garment in a position for stitching in a direction opposite to the way it will appear when finished. When turned to its rightful position, the opening of the pocket is concealed. The exception to this rule is the patch pocket with self-flap (q.v.).

FLAP PRESSING.

In Construction: Press open all enclosed seams before turning the flap to the right side. Use the point presser (q.v.). When the flap has been turned, press all edges flat by the method deemed best for the fabric.

After the Flap Has Been Attached to the Garment: Slip a double thickness of brown wrapping paper somewhat larger than the flap between flap and garment. This acts as a cushion to prevent the imprint of the flap on the garment. Press by the method deemed best for the fabric.

If, inadvertently, an imprint has been made, lift the flap and press out the mark.

FLARED SKIRT. The grain line in a flared skirt is an important consideration for the design of the skirt. Where you place it depends on the effect you would like in your skirt and/or the material you are using. Just remember that straight grain will hang straight and flat. Ripples or folds will fall at the flare.

When you wish straight sides and rip-

pling at the front and back, place the side seams on the straight of goods (a). If you are using a plaid or striped material, this placement of the grain will result in straight lines at the side seams and chevrons forming at front and back (b).

If you wish the center front and back to hang straight with flare at the sides, place the center front or back on the straight of goods (c). In striped or plaid material this will result in straight lines at the front and back and chevrons formed at the side seams (d).

Should you want even flares at front, back, and sides of a four-gore skirt (e), fold each gore of the skirt in half. The fold line becomes the straight of goods (f).

To preserve the shape of the flare, stitch with the grain. This means stitching from hem to waist. Were you to reverse the direction (waist to hem), the action of the feed and the presser foot on the angle of the flared seam line would tend to stretch and distort the grain.

FLAT BRAID TRIM. An effective and decorative border for outlining necklines, pockets, panels, openings, hems, and the like. Flat braid trims are available in a range of colors, materials, weaves, and widths. They may be used in single or multiple rows, in combinations of widths, weaves, and colors.

Cut the braid to the desired length plus 1/2 inch at each end for a seam allowance. To prevent the cut end from raveling, overcast it by hand immediately upon cutting. Stay-stitch it with backstitching to keep it from spreading. If the ends are not included in some seam, turn under the 1/2-inch seam allowance and pin or baste to position.

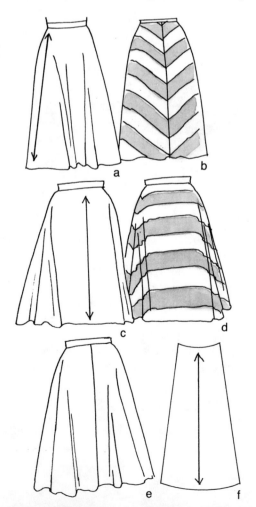

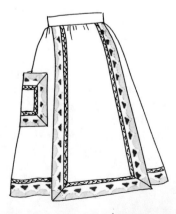

Apply the braid to the garment by pinning and/or basting. Stretch on outside curves, ease on inside curves, miter all corners. Stitch along both edges of the braid by hand or by machine.

FLAT CATCH STITCH. A catch stitch (q.v.) worked over a garment edge to hold it flat. *See* CATCH-STITCHED DART *and* CATCH-STITCH METHOD OF ELIMINATING HAIR CANVAS FROM THE CONSTRUCTION SEAMS.

FLAT COLLAR. When the shape of a collar closely approximates the shape of the garment neckline, it will lie flat. Not completely flat; there will be a slight roll when its somewhat shorter length is stretched to fit the garment neckline.

The flat collar consists of an upper and under collar usually cut on straight grain from the same pattern piece. It may consist of one unit (a) or two units (b). If the latter, the units are joined to form a complete

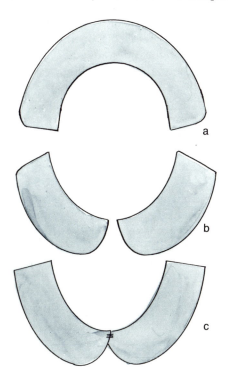

collar where the neck seam lines meet (c). The seam allowances will overlap. Fix the point of the overlap with several backstitches.

Construct the collar. *See* COLLAR.

Prepare the Garment for the Collar Application. Stitch and press all seams and darts that enter the neckline. Staystitch the neckline. When interfacing is used, apply it to the underside of the garment. If a placket opening or a zipper is involved, this is completed before the collar is attached. If the closing is a buttoned one, there will be a facing, which should be stitched to the point where collar joins garment.

How the collar is attached to the garment depends on whether there is a complete neckline facing, a front facing only, or no facing at all, and whether, when there is a facing, it is shaped to fit the neckline or is simply a strip of bias binding. The collar will fit with a smoother roll when the seam allowances are turned down into the garment, as would be the case when a facing—shaped or bias—is used. Choose the method that produces the least bulk in your fabric.

How to Apply the Collar with a Complete Facing. Edge-finish the outer edge of the shaped facing in a manner appropriate for the fabric.

Pin the collar neck edge to the garment neck edge in the same relative position in which it will be worn—the right side of the garment is up, facing you; the right side of the collar is up, facing you. Match the neck edges at the center front, center back, the shoulders or notches, and the point at which the collar joins the garment (a). Clip and stretch the collar as necessary to make it fit the neckline of the garment. Baste the collar to the garment. Take several backstitches in place to fasten the collar at the point where the ends of the collar join the front or back of the garment. This will prevent it from slipping when the collar is stitched to the neckline.

Place the right side of the facing against the right side of the garment with the col-

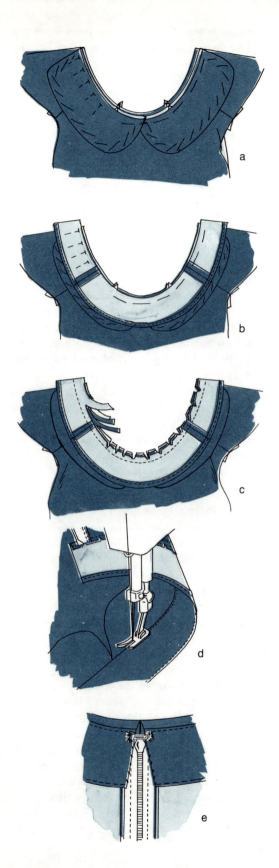

lar sandwiched between the two. Once more, match center fronts, center backs, shoulder seams, notches. Ease, stretch, clip as necessary to make it fit. Pin or baste the facing to position (b).

Stitch through all layers—garment, collar, facing, and interfacing, if any, in one seam that goes from one end of the neckline to the other. Trim, grade, and clip the seam allowances (c). Press the seam open over the tailor's ham. Turn the facing to the inside and press. Understitch the facing to the neckline seam allowance (d).

Tack the edges of the facing at the shoulder seams and at any other darts and seams. Do not hem the facing to the garment. Besides being unnecessary extra work, hemming produces an outline of the facing on the right side of the garment that detracts from the appearance of the garment.

At the zipper closing, turn under the ends of the facing to clear the zipper and slip-stitch to the zipper tape (e).

How to Apply the Collar with a Front Facing Only. This is the type of application that would apply to a convertible or similar collar.

Edge-finish the outer and shoulder edges of the front facing. Attach the facing to the closing edge of the garment but *not* at its neck edge. Construct the collar (q.v.), leaving the neck edge open.

With right sides together, pin and/or baste the under collar to the garment from shoulder seam to shoulder seam. Machine-stitch (a). Clip the neck seam allowance and seam allowances of both upper and under collars at the shoulders. In ravelly fabrics, reinforce the points of the clips with small machine stitches.

Baste both upper and under collars from the front ends to the shoulders (b). With right sides together, pin the front facing to the garment over the collar from the outside edges to the shoulder clips through all layers. Machine-stitch (c). Treat the seam as an enclosed seam (q.v.).

Turn the facing to the underside and press. Press the back neck and under-collar seam allowances into the collar, clip-

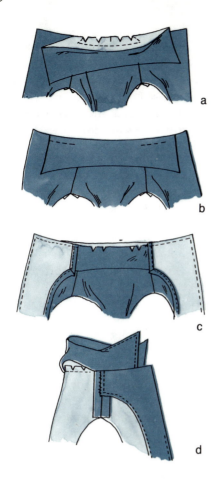

ping as necessary. Turn under the free edge of the **upper collar,** clipping as necessary. Slip-stitch the upper collar through its fold so it covers the stitching of the neck seam (d).

To Apply the Collar with a Bias Binding. *See* BIAS FINISH FOR A FLAT COLLAR.

To Apply the Collar When There Is No Facing. Stitch the under collar to the garment neck edge, keeping the upper collar free. Trim, grade, and clip the stitched seam allowances and press them into the collar. Clip and turn under the seam allowance of the upper collar and slip-stitch it so it covers the neck seam line.

FLAT FELL SEAM. A self-enclosed seam with no exposed raw edges. This is an excellent seam for unlined garments, reversible garments, garments that get rough wear, like play clothes, or much laundering, like tailored shirts. It is *the* classic seam

for sportswear, menswear, boys' wear, shorts, pants, and the like.

The fell may be formed on the right side or the wrong side of the garment. If the fell is on the inside, there is only one visible row of stitching. If the fell is on the right side, there are two visible rows of stitching. The direction of the fell does not matter if you are consistent. It is best to blend the fell in the direction that will produce the least bulk or that will preserve the style line of the seam.

Stitch the seam—with the right sides together for a fell on the inside of the garment, with the wrong sides together for a fell on the right side. Press the seams to one side—the direction of the blend.

Trim the under-seam allowance. Turn under some (from a little up to half) of the upper-seam allowance and press. Pin to position and topstitch.

When two rows of visible stitching are involved in the fell, keep the right side of the first row of stitching on top while doing the second row.

FLY CLOSING. A "fly" produces a flat, inconspicuous closing. Fabric is used as a lap to conceal an opening or fastening. In women's clothing, the lap is right over left; in men's, the lap is left over right. The fastening under the lap may be by buttons, snaps, or zipper.

The fly-front closing is the traditional closing of men's trousers. Because it is such a strong construction, it is also used (with variations) for sportswear, skirts, shirts, jackets, coats, and dresses. The finished fly of men's trousers may look the same as other fly constructions but is more complicated because it involves a facing and a fly shield (q.v.).

FLY CLOSING BUTTONED. In this closing, an overlap conceals a strip of buttonholes. The buttons are sewn to the familiar extension of all buttoned closings. The fly may extend throughout the garment from neck to hem or be limited to a small area.

Neck-to-Hem Closing. Construct the front edges of the garment from neckline to hem in the usual manner.

Cut the fly of self-fabric on the lengthwise grain. Make it the length of the closing plus two seam allowances. If buttonholes are to be worked horizontally, make it as wide as the buttonhole plus the button, plus two seam allowances for a one-piece strip folded at the closing edge or four seam allowances for a two-piece strip seamed at the closing edge. On a narrow fly, the buttonholes are worked vertically. Make the strip twice the width of the button plus seam allowances as above. Bound buttonholes are made before the fly is constructed; hand- or machine-worked buttonholes, after.

Construct the fly, making it as flat as possible. Finish the long raw edges with pinking or overcasting so they, too, remain flat.

With the closing edge of the garment on a flat surface, pin the fly to position on the underside of the overlap. Set it back 1/8 to 1/4 inch from all finished edges so that it will not be visible from the right side. Buttonholes are in line with the center front (a). Baste to position.

From the right side, topstitch through all thicknesses (b). Cut the ends of the thread long enough to thread a needle and work them into the machine stitching on the underside as a secure fastening.

A single or double length of preshrunk grosgrain ribbon of a suitable width can be used for the fly in women's shirts and dresses, following the same general procedure as for self-fabric (c). Since the edges are already finished, there will be no need for lengthwise seam allowances. Machine-worked buttonholes are appropriate for this treatment of a fly.

Closing in a Limited Area. Because this type of fly closing is not carried to the neckline or the hem, a convertible collar and the lower portion of the garment will look well when worn either open or closed. It is a type of closing often used on coats (a).

Prepare the underlay edge of the garment as usual. Cut a pair of fly facings. Make them long enough and wide enough to contain the buttonholes comfortably. Add seam allowances.

Mark the position of the fly opening on the garment overlap edge and on its facing edge. With right sides together, pin and/or baste one fly facing to the garment edge and the other fly facing to the facing edge in the area of the fly opening. Stitch. Clip the seam allowances above and below the stitching. Treat as enclosed (encased) seams (q.v.). Turn the first fly facing to the underside of the garment and press (b). Turn the second fly facing to the underside of the facing and press. Work buttonholes through both garment facing and fly facing (c).

With right sides together, pin and/or baste the garment facing to the front edge of the garment above and below the fly opening. Stitch. Treat as enclosed seams. Turn the facing to the underside of the garment and press.

On the underside of the garment, pin and/or baste the outer raw edges of both fly facings and stitch. Keep the fly facings free of both the garment and the garment facing. It's as if you were forming a pocket between them.

If you wish no visible stitching on the right side of the garment, tack the raw edges of the fly facings to the interfacing

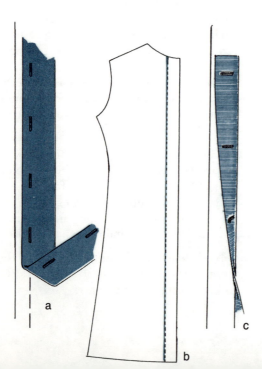

a

b

c

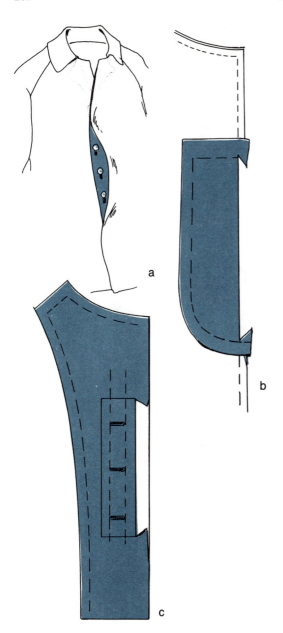

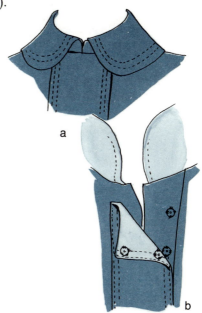

ment and its facing. Covered snaps hold the closing edge of the free side in place (b).

FLY CLOSING ZIPPER INSTALLATION—MEN'S TROUSERS.
Should you wish to use this tailored construction for women's pants, reverse the directions, making the right lap over the left instead of left over right.

Patterns for men's trousers generally include all the pieces necessary for the fly construction. Should they be missing or should you choose to make others than those provided, *see* FLY PIECE.

It is easier to construct the fly if the trousers are worked flat. Join the pants for only 2 inches on the front crotch seam, starting at the end of the fly markings.

There are many variations of procedure for installing the zipper. The directions included below start with the right front. However, you could start the construction with the left front instead. Some pattern directions have you first attach the zipper to the separate facings before joining them to the pants. Some designs call for facings that extend to the top of the waistband instead of to the waist. In that case, one would have to attach the waistband before completing the fly front. What all variations have in common is that the zipper is

of the garment. If visible stitching is consistent with the design of the garment, topstitch through garment and fly facings.

FLY CLOSING WITHOUT AN OVERLAP.
This resembles a slot seam or an inverted pleat. The opening edges meet at the center front under a finished overlay, which is the fly strip.

The fly strip is fastened to the garment along one side with rows of topstitching (a). Matching rows of topstitching are made on the second side through the gar-

firmly attached with multiple rows of machine stitching and that the neat, trim closing looks deceptively simple.

Whenever possible, use a special trouser zipper of either metal or nylon. The metal zippers are 11 inches long but a 9-inch, 10-inch, or 12-inch nylon zipper can be used. The nylon zippers are more flexible and lighter in weight. If a trouser zipper of appropriate length, weight, and color is not available, use a neck or skirt zipper.

Carefully transfer all pattern markings to facilitate the work.

Right Front Opening Edge. Clip the right front seam allowance at the fly marking. Turn it under to form a 1/4-inch extension into the opening. (When the fly is closed, the left front lap will then completely conceal the zipper.) Baste the seam allowance close to the fold (a).

Place the closed zipper, right side up, under the right front opening with the bottom stop 1/4 inch above the end of the fly marking. Note that the zipper will extend above the upper edge the depth of the waistband. Baste (b). Remove the first basting.

Construct the fly shield (q.v.).

On the inside of the trousers, place the fly shield over the zipper at the right front edge. Keep all raw edges even. The curve of the fly shield matches the curve of the topstitching on the left side. Pin in place. Baste along the straight edge through all thicknesses (c). Open the zipper. From the right side, topstitch close to the fold at the edge (d).

Left Front Opening Edge. With right sides together, pin the fly facing to the left front edge and baste. Stitch from the fly

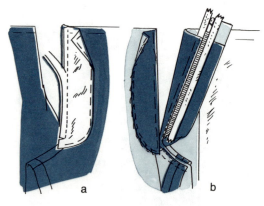

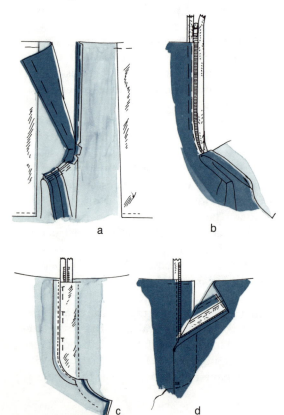

marking to the upper edge. Clip the seam allowances at the fly marking. Trim and grade them, clipping where necessary (a).

Open out the facing and press the seam allowances, first open, then toward the facing. Turn the fly to the inside, press, and baste close to the turned edge. Overcast the remaining raw edges (b). If the facing is cut all in one with the pant leg, turn under the extension along the fold line. Press and baste.

Lap the left front opening edge over the right front, matching centers. Baste close to the edge through all thicknesses (c).

On the inside, turn the fly shield back out of the way and pin it. Pin and baste the other side of the zipper to the left fly facing *only.* Keep the pants free. Stitch close to the zipper teeth (d). Make a second row of stitching 1/4 inch away from the first. Turn the left fly down against the pants and baste to position. Open the zipper.

On the right side of the trousers, topstitch the left front along the characteristically curved stitching line through all thicknesses (e). Do not catch the right zipper tape in the stitching. *Optional:* Since the base of the opening is subjected to considerable strain, secure it with a bar tack (q.v.) through all thicknesses (f).

FLY CLOSING ZIPPER INSTALLATION— WOMEN'S GARMENT. A variation of the regulation zipper installation plus fly-shaped topstitching on the right front. This is the easiest type of zippered fly closing. The fly closing of men's trousers takes a little more doing.

On patterns designed for this type of installation, the front facings are usually cut as extensions of the garment. Separate facings may be added to any straight seam edge for the fly front even if the pattern has been designed without it.

Mark the center lines, the fold lines, and the topstitching lines. Stitch the pants sections together to the fly marking. Clip the seam allowances at the end of the fly marking. Turn under the left front seam allowance so that it creates a 1/4-inch extension above it. Baste across the upper

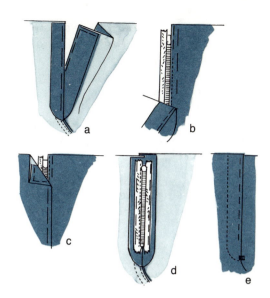

edges and close to the front folds (a) of both right and left sides.

Place the closed zipper, face up, under the left front extension with the folded edge close to the teeth and the pull tab 1/4 inch below the cross seam. Pin or baste to position. Stitch close to the folded edge (b).

Overlap the right front opening edge on the left front, matching center lines. Baste to position through all thicknesses close to the edge (c).

On the underside, baste the zipper tape to the right front through all thicknesses (d). On the right side, topstitch through all thicknesses, catching in the zipper tape. The topstitching has the familiar characteristic fly-front curve. Add a bar tack (q.v.) at the bottom, through all thicknesses (e).

FLY FACING. The left front edge of a trouser opening requires a facing for a finish. Some patterns are cut with a front extension which, when turned to the underside along the fold line, becomes the facing for the opening. Most often, the facing is a separate piece cut from the pattern for the fly piece (q.v.).

FLY PIECE. This serves as a facing for the left front trouser opening edge, as the fly shield, and as the shield lining (facing). Most trouser patterns include a pattern for a fly piece. Should you wish to substitute your own simple piece, use the left trouser pattern as a guide.

On a fresh piece of paper, trace the straight front edge, the curved line of the topstitching, and the waist edge. Add seam allowances on all sides. Midway on the piece, draw a grain line parallel to the long, vertical front line.

FLY SHIELD. An extension or underlap attached to the right front opening edge of men's trousers. It acts as a covering, concealing and protecting any garment worn beneath.

Using the fly piece pattern, cut the shield of garment fabric. Cut its lining (facing) of pocketing (q.v.) or any other lining fabric cut on the cross grain. If the garment fabric is lightweight, it may be used for both shield and facing.

With right sides together, pin the shield and lining. Stitch along the curved side. Trim and grade the seam allowances. Notch the curved edge. Turn the shield to the right side and press.

Finish the straight edge by trimming 3/8 inch from the shield of trouser fabric. Encase its raw edge with the lining. Stitch close to the fold.

FLY STAY. An interfacing that reinforces and supports the fly. Cut it from the fly piece pattern and baste it to the wrong side of the left trouser facing.

FOLD-BACK METHOD OF ELIMINATING HAIR CANVAS FROM CONSTRUCTION SEAMS. This is the method to use when one wishes to retain the hair canvas yet does not wish to involve it in a seam. A good example of this treatment is stitching a sleeve into an interfaced armhole.

Fold back the hair canvas from the armhole seam (a). Pin it out of the way. Stitch the sleeve into the armhole in the usual way. Bring the hair canvas back to position. Permanently baste it to the seam allowances just beyond the seam line (b). Trim away the underarm seam allowance close to the stitching. *See also* CATCH-STITCHED METHOD, STRIP METHOD, TAPING

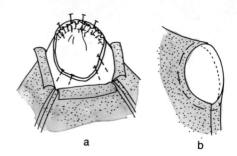

a   b

METHOD OF ELIMINATING HAIR CANVAS FROM CONSTRUCTION SEAMS.

FOLD-DOWN CASING. *See* SELF-CASING.

FOLD-OVER BRAID. A decorative braid available in a variety of colors, widths, and designs that can be bought by the yard or prepackaged. Both long edges are finished. The braid is prefolded slightly off center, making the top a bit narrower than the bottom. This is to ensure that, when topstitched, both edges are included in the one seam.

Cut the needed length plus 1/2-inch seam allowance at each cut end. Overcast or stay-stitch the ends to prevent fraying. When the ends of the braid are not included in the seams, turn them under for a finish. *(See* BIAS BINDING AT A VISIBLE EDGE.)

For Bound Edges: Place a line of stay stitching along and close to the seam line on the garment side of the edge to be bound. Trim the seam allowance close to the stitching. Slip the trimmed edge of the garment into the fold of the braid with the narrower side on top. Pin or baste through all thicknesses. It facilitates the application if the braid is preshaped by steam pressing to match all curved edges and is mitered at all corners. This is similar to the treatment of bias binding (q.v.).

To Attach the Braid by Machine: With right side on top, stitch close to the edge of the braid, making certain that the underside is caught in the stitching.

To Attach the Braid by Hand: Slipstitch each edge of the braid to the garment on both outside and underside. A hand application provides better control of the braid on difficult fabrics and produces an invisible finish.

FRENCH BINDING. A narrow bias binding: double-fold (q.v.) made of sheer fabric used as an edge finish chiefly for sheer fabrics but also for velvets, metallics, silks, and other fine materials.

FRENCH CUFF. A wide, faced band that turns back to form a double cuff. It extends rather than laps at the ends (a).

There are four buttonholes on each cuff fastened together in pairs through which cuff links are passed. On fabrics and styles that require bound buttonholes, they are generally made on the outermost cuff only after the interfacing has been applied. The remaining buttonholes, which will not show, may be machine- or hand-worked to prevent bulk. Should you think that four bound buttonholes are a finer touch, go right ahead and make all four of them for each cuff.

In planning the layout and cutting of the French cuff, be mindful of the fact that the inside layer of cuff when turned to position becomes the outside of the cuff. In

a

b

c

d

directional fabrics, it is particularly important to keep this in mind.

Prepare the Lower Edge of the Sleeve. Finish the placket opening by whatever method seems best for the material. Check for even lengths on the front and back edges of the placket. If the pattern does not have notches and underarm seam markings on the lower edge of the sleeve and the upper edge of the cuff, section off each into quarters. Mark each quarter with pins, thread, or notches.

Prepare the Cuff. The circumference of the cuff is a loose wrist measurement from buttonhole to buttonhole plus an extension equal to the diameter of the cuff links (at least) plus seam allowances. For facing and cuff cut all in one: cut the cuff four times its depth plus seam allowances. For separate cuff and facing: cut each twice the depth plus seam allowances.

The cuff may be made with or without an interfacing but it looks and turns better with one. Cut an appropriate interfacing the depth of the band and the turnback cuff without seam allowances. Place the interfacing on the wrong side of the inside cuff section. Catch-stitch around all outside edges. Sew along the fold line with long running stitches (a).

With right sides together, stitch the cuff sections, ending a seam allowance from the long, notched or marked edge. Trim and grade the seam allowances. Free corners of bulk (b). Press the seam allowances open over the point presser. Turn the cuff to the right side and press the edges.

With right sides together and cuff ends flush with the edges of the placket, pin and/or baste the noninterfaced side of the cuff to the lower gathered edge of the sleeve. Match all markings. Pull up the gathers to match the length of the cuff. Distribute the fullness (c). Stitch the seam as basted with the sleeve uppermost. Trim and grade the seam allowances, making those next to the cuff the widest. Press the seam allowances toward the cuff.

Turn under the raw edge of the underside of the cuff. Slip-stitch over the seam (d). Finish the underside of the bound buttonholes. Make any remaining buttonholes. Turn the lower edge of the cuff to the outside along the roll line so that the buttonholes meet. Fasten with cuff links.

FRENCH DRESSMAKER'S HEM. Bind the hem edge with a double-fold strip of net or sheer bias binding. Blindstitch it to the garment. *See* BIAS BINDING: DOUBLE-FOLD.

FRENCH FOLD. Fold a bias strip lengthwise so the edges meet at the center. Press. Fold again slightly off center so the upper double layer is a bit narrower than the under. Press. *See* BIAS BINDING: MACHINE-APPLIED; FOLD-OVER BRAID.

FRENCH GATHERING. *See* GAUGING.

FRENCH HEM. One that is used chiefly on a straight edge of sheer or lightweight fabric that frays.

Turn the raw edge of the hem to the wrong side of the garment. Pin or baste (a). From the right side, fold the garment over the hem along its raw edge. Stitch a tuck in the garment that encloses and conceals the raw edge (b). Press to one side.

This is a useful device for dropping a hem when the crease at the fold cannot be pressed out. By this method, the hem crease becomes the tuck crease.

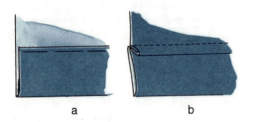

a   b

FRENCH PLACKET. *See* TAILORED PLACKET.

FRENCH SEAM. This is *the* classic seam for sheer materials. It is a narrow, self-enclosed seam, twice stitched—first from the right side, then from the wrong side.

With *wrong sides together,* stitch the seam on the right side about 1/4 inch in from the raw edge. Trim the seam allowance fairly close to the stitching (a). Press the seam.

Fold the seam so the *right sides are together.*

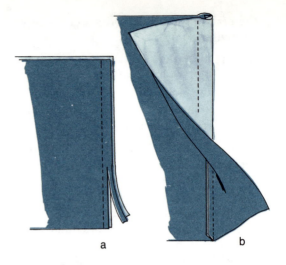

a   b

Crease or press so the stitched line is directly on the edge of the fold. Stitch a second seam 1/4 inch from the fold, completely enclosing the first seam allowances (b). Press to one side.

The trick is to keep the second seam even and quite narrow without catching any of the first seam allowance.

FRENCH SEAM SIMULATED. *See* MOCK (SIMULATED) FRENCH SEAM.

FRENCH TACK. A free-swinging tack made of several long, loose stitches that link together two separate parts of a garment while allowing each a certain amount of movement. For instance, the bottom edge of a coat to the bottom edge of its lining.

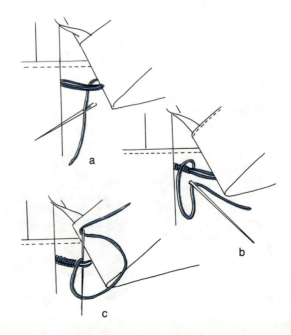

a

b

c

Take a tiny stitch on one part, then another directly opposite on the part to be joined. Pull up the thread to the desired length (generally 1 to 2 inches). Repeat, making 2 to 3 stitches between the layers (a).

Because of its exposed position, the French tack is protected, strengthened, and beautified by wrapping thread around it (b) or by working blanket stitches over it (c).

FRENCH WHIPPED SEAM. Useful for lace, embroidered fabrics, and curved seams on sheer fabrics.

Stitch a plain seam. Make a second line of stitching 1/8 inch away from the first into the seam allowance. Trim 1/8 inch from the second line of stitching. Overcast the raw edges by hand or by machine.

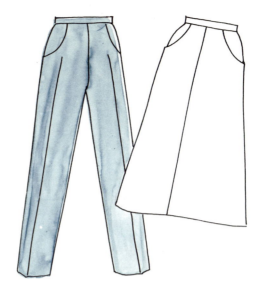

FRONT HIP (FRONTIER) POCKET. A variation of the in-seam pocket frequently found in skirts and pants. The pocket opening follows the style line of the main garment section. The upper pocket is part of the style-line facing. The under pocket is a continuation of the remaining garment section.

Cut out the garment sections. Cut the facing for the main garment section. Use either the fashion fabric if it is not too heavy or a lining material.

Cut an interfacing, following the shape of the style line. Make it a 2-inch-wide strip and baste it to the underside of the front garment section (a).

With right sides together, pin and stitch the pocket facing along the style line. Press the stitching line to blend it. Grade the seam allowances, making those of the garment widest. Clip and notch as necessary (b). Press the seam allowances open. Turn the facing to the inside. Press, rolling the joining seam to the underside.

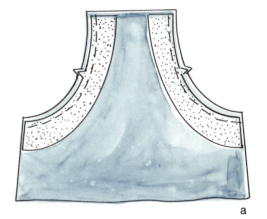

a

b

If the style line is not to be topstitched, understitch the facing to the seam allowances close to the line of stitching (c). Turn the facing to position on the underside and baste close to the opening edge. When

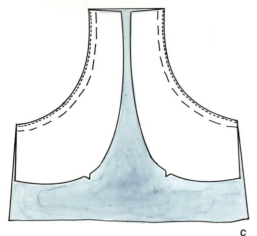

c

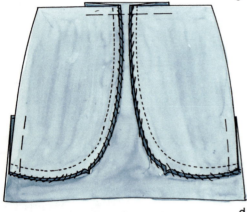

d

even more important, you can wear them with a free conscience, knowing that the animals they resemble are alive and well and romping in field and forest with their friends and families.

Sometimes the fake furs are handled like the fabrics they are. And sometimes they are handled like the furs they pretend to be. To carry out the illusion of authentic fur, choose a design with style lines and details that one would commonly find in a true fur garment. Choose a pattern with few seams and darts and no topstitching. In the long-haired or deep-pile fabrics there will be less bulk at the edges if you plan to face them with a smooth fabric. Or eliminate the facing. Instead, bind the edges or bring the lining almost to the edge. Use any of the fastenings characteristic of real fur garments.

FUR-FABRIC HEM. If the fur fabric is *short-haired,* handle the hem like any medium-weight fabric. Mark and turn up the hem. Pin or baste it to position. Finish the hem edge in an appropriate manner. Attach the upper edge of the hem to the backing of the fabric with hemming stitches.

Hems in *long-haired* fabrics are less bulky when faced. Mark the hemline. Add 1½ inches for a seam allowance and a turnback. Cut a length of bias facing for the hem.

topstitching is to be used, do it now (without the understitching).

Pin the under pocket to the pocket facing around the outside edges. Stitch. Trim the seam allowance. Finish the edges in an appropriate manner and press them. Pin and baste the two garment sections that complete the front of the garment along the seam lines (d).

From this point on, treat the pocketed front section as a one-piece unit and join it to the back unit of the garment in the usual way.

FUR FABRIC. Among the most exciting of the new fabrics are the fake furs, look-alikes for the skins they ape but with virtues of their own. They have nap, sheen, realistic or wildly imaginative color, shading, and markings. They're warm, they're comparatively inexpensive, they're fun, and presently they're high fashion. What's

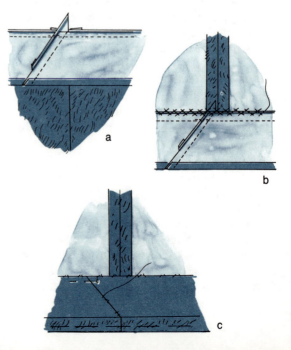

a

b

c

With right sides together, pin the facing to the edge of the garment. Pin the short ends of the facing on straight grain. Trim the excess facing from the joined short ends, leaving narrow seam allowances for lapping, remove pins, and finger-press seam allowances to one side. Stitch the facing to the garment edge (a).

The facing-hem is handled as a Double-Stitched hem (q.v.). Catch-stitch the facing to the fur fabric (b). Slip-stitch the lapped ends. For a finish, turn under the raw upper edge of the hem. Attach it to the backing with hemming stitches (c).

FUR FABRIC: LAYOUT, CUTTING, AND MARKING.

Use a "With Nap" layout. Place the pattern so the nap or pile runs down—neck to hem (as you would stroke a pet).

Only smooth, flat fur fabrics can be cut on a fold with the fur side outside. Those with deep pile require that each section be cut separately and in its entirety. This means that you must convert each half pattern to a full pattern and make a duplicate for every pattern piece that says, "Cut 2."

Place the pattern on the fur side so you can match any shading or distinctive markings. Pay particular attention to the grain, which should hang in a plumb line. Pin the pattern to the fabric, using long, sturdy pins or T pins. If pinning produces puckering of the pattern, use dressmaker's weights (or any other weights) instead of pinning it. Cutting is easier if done from the wrong side. Outline the pattern by placing pins along the cutting edge. Show darts and notches with pins. Turn to the wrong side and trace the pin marking with chalk or pencil if it will not show. Remove the pins and the pattern.

Smooth Fur Fabric: Cut with sharp shears. Mark notches with thread loops on the edge of the fabric.

Long-haired Fabric: Cut with a single-edge razor blade. In this way you will cut only the backing and avoid cutting the hair or pile. The uncut hair is used to cover the seam, making the joining invisible.

FUR FABRIC: PRESSING.

Fur fabric requires little or no pressing. When pressing is done, press over a needle board, a strip of self-fabric, or a Turkish towel. All pressing is done on the wrong side. Press lightly in the direction of the nap. A dry iron is best since steam may mat some fur fabrics. Where steam is necessary, protect the fabric with a press cloth. Brush up the nap after pressing. Finger-press *narrow seams* to one side.

FUR FABRIC: STITCHING.

Fur fabrics may be stitched by hand or by machine. The latter is more usual. It's a good idea to make a test seam or dart so that you can get the feel of the fabric and determine the best method for stitching it.

Stitch in the direction of the nap. Keep tension and pressure light. Use a coarse machine needle and heavy-duty thread. Stitch slowly, stretching the fabric slightly as it feeds into the machine. Since most fake furs have a knit backing, it is not too difficult to ease the fullness of one thickness into another (when stitching the cap of a set-in sleeve, for instance, especially if the pile is shaved from the seam allowance). Should the fabric creep or pucker when stitched, baste or backstitch to hold it in place. An even-feed mechanism or roller foot is helpful in feeding top and bottom layers at the same pace.

All hemming and tacking stitches catch only the backing of the fabric. They should never come through to the right side.

If you want to give your fake fur the full fur treatment, tape the seams and darts to reinforce them. Before stitching, baste preshrunk twill tape over the seam line so it extends 1/8 inch beyond the stitching line into the seam allowance. Include it in the seam.

SHORT-PILE FABRIC

With fur sides inside, align the edges to be joined. Pin the seam. Stitch, using 8 to 10 stitches per inch (a). Open the seam allowances. Holding sharp scissors parallel to the fabric, shear the pile from the seam allowances (b). If you choose to retain the

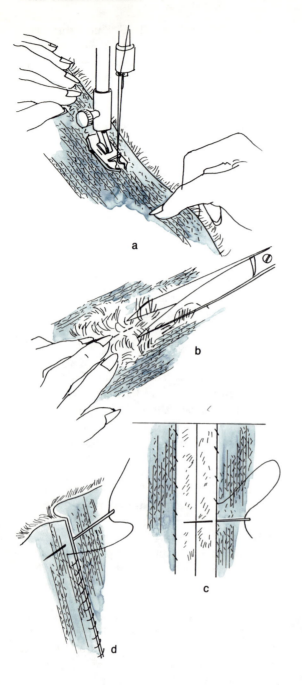

Fold a dart with fur side inside and stitch. Slash open to the point of the dart. Trim, shave off pile, and finish edges as for the seam.

DEEP-PILE FABRIC

Trim seam allowances to 1/4 inch. With fur sides inside, align the edges to be joined and hold in place with large paper clips (a). Machine-stitch with wide zigzag stitches, 12 to 15 per inch, removing clips as you sew. If you prefer hand stitching, use small blanket stitches (b). Finger-press the seam to one side. On the right side, work the hair out of the seam with a blunt needle.

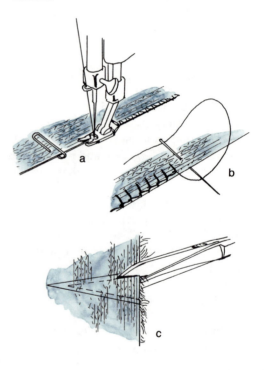

seam allowances, flatten them against the garment and fasten with flat catch stitches or hemming stitches (c).

Alternate Method of Handling Seam Allowances. Trim them to 1/8 inch. Stitch the edges together (including pile) with hand or machine overcasting stitches (d). Use medium-width, short-length zigzag stitches. Finger-press seam to one side.

Alternate Method of Handling Seams. Eliminate bulk in the seam by shaving off the pile in the seam allowance before stitching a plain seam. It is helpful to use a zipper or cording foot to accommodate the difference in the thickness between the shaved and unshaved fabric. When the seam has been stitched, work the hair out of it on the right side until the seam is completely concealed.

Cut out the dart, leaving narrow seam allowances (c). Fold the dart with the pile inside and stitch with hand or machine overcasting.

FUR FABRIC: TAILORING TECHNIQUES. Use any of the tailoring techniques that seem appropriate for the style of the garment and the fur fabric.

FUR FABRIC: ZIPPER INSTALLATION. *See* ZIPPER IN HIGH PILE, SHAGGY FABRIC, OR FAKE FUR.

FUR FIBERS AND BLENDS. These add surface interest and warmth to wool and other fibers. Some of the pelts used are beaver, chinchilla, fox, angora hare, muskrat, nutria, opossum, raccoon, mink, marten, and sable.

FUSIBLE INTERFACING FOR UNSTRUCTURED TAILORED GARMENTS. Cut the necessary fusible interfacings. Pinked outside edges make the demarcation line less visible. Trim away all seam allowances. Trim away the fusible from the tips of all corners—lapels, collars, welts, flaps, and the like. This will facilitate the turning of the corners.

Reinforce buttonhole and slashed-pocket areas with patches of fusible interfacing. Apply the fusible to the underside of welts, flaps, patch pockets, and so on.

To compensate for the omission of the traditional pad stitching, cut a second layer of fusible material for the stand of a collar and a triangular piece for the lapel from the roll line to the point of the lapel.

Transfer all necessary pattern markings and proceed with the construction. *See* FUSIBLES.

FUSIBLES (IRON-ONS). These adhesive-backed materials are pressed rather than stitched onto a garment. There are many types, many forms, many weights and widths, many brands, and they are useful for many purposes. Fusibles can be purchased by the yard, in strips, in rolls, in patches, in packaged precut lengths and widths designed for specific areas. They are both machine-washable or dry-cleanable, though they have a tendency to come free of the garment fabric in cleaning.

Some fusibles are woven, retaining some of the characteristics of woven fabric plus their fusibility. The nonwoven variety do not have the moldability of the wovens. On some, the adhesive is applied to one side only. These are used for interfacings, patches, appliqués. Fusible webs (q.v.) have adhesive on both sides, making them useful for joining double thicknesses of fabric (such as hems).

Always check the instructions that come with a particular fusible. Test the fabric before applying it to the garment to see if it can take the heat or steam required for the fusing.

To prevent rippling of either the fusible or the garment fabric, preshrink the fusible by placing it in hot water for 10 minutes. Do not wring; the adhesive granules may come loose if you do. Do not preshrink in a washer-dryer for the same reason. Do *not* preshrink the fusible webs.

Because of the ease and speed of application, it is tempting to use the iron-ons to replace traditional interfacings. Indeed, many simplified tailoring methods call for fusible interfacing. When so used, it can only be for reinforcement and firmness and not for shaping, which it cannot do. Use it if time is important to you but don't expect the same fine tailored results you will achieve with the classic tailoring methods.

Because *fusibles change the texture of the fabric,* it is wise to confine them to small areas and preferably to an undersurface. They are excellent for stiffening collars, cuffs, belts, waistbands, shirtbands, and the like. Use them as reinforcements for areas to be slashed, like buttonholes and bound or welt pockets. In addition, they are a necessary part of the construction of Ultrasuede (q.v.) and similar materials. Avoid using them on silks.

Fuse before the pattern markings are transferred to the garment. Wrong-side markings will be covered by the fused interfacing. Right-side thread markings will be too difficult to remove after the interfacing has been fused.

Place the fusible in position on the

wrong side of the fabric. Pin at intervals. Steam-baste by lightly touching the tip of the steam iron to the fusible at a few points on the edges to anchor it. Remove the pins. Set the iron at the fusing temperature. Fuse according to the directions for the particular fusible material. Let the fabric cool and dry before checking the bond.

FUSIBLE WEB. A fusing material with adhesive on both sides, making it a fast, inconspicuous way of joining double thicknesses of fabric. Since removal is messy at best and impossible at worst, be sure that second layer is just where you will want it forever.

Cut a strip of fusible web of an appropriate width and length. The outside edge should be just short of the fabric. Slip it between the two thicknesses and pin at intervals.

Steam-baste on the wrong side between the pins by touching the tip of the iron lightly at the edge in enough places to anchor it. Remove the pins. Using a press cloth to cover the fabric, fuse the layers with the steam iron, following the directions that come with the fusible web. Press a section at a time, making sure the layers are firmly joined and dry before moving on to the next section. Press a hem from the fold to the top. Press a facing from the faced edge to the outer edge. Press seam allowances in the direction in which they have been stitched and whichever way they will produce least bulk. *See* FUSIBLES.

GATHERING. Fullness (small, soft folds) drawn up by thread into a desired length. It may be done by hand or by machine. Gathering is generally done after the construction seams have been stitched and pressed. However, it is often easier to gather each section first before joining them to each other.

While gathering may be done in any direction, gathers fall best on the lengthwise grain. Two rows of gathering stitches make for a more even distribution of fullness (a).

The first row is made in the seam allowance close to the seam line. The second row is made 1/4 inch above the first toward the raw edge.

To eliminate bulk at all cross seams, notch the seam allowance almost to the stitching lines where the rows of gathering will be made (b). Or, when making continuous rows of hand gathering, do not stitch through the seam allowances. Allow them to hang free (c). *See also* JOINING GATHERED EDGE TO GATHERED EDGE *and* JOINING GATHERED EDGE TO STRAIGHT EDGE.

GATHERING BY HAND. Using a double thread, make rows of running stitches. Weave the needle through the material with an up-and-down hand motion while holding the fabric still. When the needle is full of stitches, draw the thread through.

GATHERING BY MACHINE. There are several ways in which gathering can be done by machine.

1. Use a basting stitch (6 to 8 to the inch); the longer stitches for heavy fabric, the shorter for medium- and lightweight fabric. For easy pulling of the bobbin thread, loosen the tension and use buttonhole twist or heavy-duty thread.

2. Use a large zigzag stitch over a length of crochet cotton, pearl cord, or several strands of double-duty thread. Pull up the strands to form the gathers. This is a good method for long strips or for bulky fabrics. It provides both the necessary easing and the hem finish for a very flared skirt.

3. For *elasticized gathering,* wind the bobbin with elastic thread by hand, stretching it slightly. For heavy fabric where greater strength is required, wind double strands of elastic thread. Use mercerized thread for the top threading. Experiment with the stitch size. Hold the fabric taut while stitching. The more pull on the elastic, the more the gathers. For the second row, pull the material straight while sewing. Tie the thread ends.

It is a good idea to test the stitching on a scrap of fabric to determine the best stitch size, the best tension, and the amount of gathering desired. *(See also* ELASTIC GATHERING WITHOUT A CASING.)

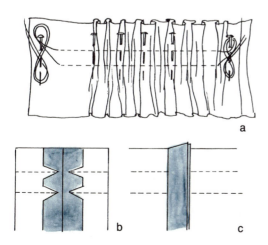

a

b   c

4. Use the gathering foot or ruffler. These accessories automatically gather with each stitch.

GATHERS IN A DART. Mark the seam line. Reinforce the dart with a very lightweight facing. *(See* REINFORCE A SLASH LINE.) Slash the opening. Press both edges of the facing up toward the top of the garment. This creates an extension of the lower edge of the dart. Gather this edge to within 1/4 inch of the end of the slash. Make one row of gathering on the dart seam line and the second row on the extension 1/8 inch above the seam (a).

To Stitch the Dart with a Plain Seam: Place the right sides of the upper and lower edges together. To prevent bulging, stitch on the dart seam line from the wide end, tapering to 1/4 inch beyond the dart point (b). Tie the thread ends.

To Stitch the Dart as a Lapped Seam: Place and baste the upper edge of the dart (which has been folded under on the seam line) over the gathered lower edge. Top-stitch close to the edge from dart end to dart point (c). Pull the thread ends to the underside and tie.

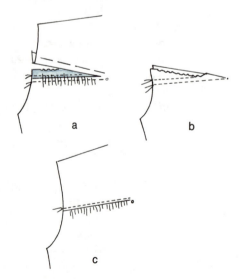

GAUGING (FRENCH GATHERING). Used when a great deal of material is to be gathered into a small length. The first row is unequal basting—long stitches on the right side, short ones on the wrong side.

The stitches of the second row are directly under the first row (a). When the fullness is drawn up it lies in deep folds (b).

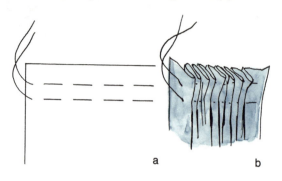

The folds may be caught in a seam. For a decorative effect, finish the edge of the garment section before gauging. Apply it to the surface by attaching the inner end of each fold with an overhand stitch.

GODET. Fullness added to the edge of a skirt, sleeve, peplum, or collar by setting a section of cloth into a seam, a dart, a slash, or a cutout of the garment. Godets lend flounce, flair, and flip to an otherwise simple style.

A godet can be pie-shaped to semicircle (an arc of a circle whose radius is the length of the godet; the curve of the arc supplies the hemline) (a). The top of the godet can be pointed (the usual type) (b), rounded (c), or squared (d). It can be pleated (e) or contain another godet (or godets) within its folds (f).

The center of the godet is generally on straight grain, though it could be bias for design purposes. Two procedures call for particular care: stitching a perfect point at the end of a slash or seam and stitching the bias or near-bias edges of the usual triangular godet to the straight sides of a seam, dart, or slash. To facilitate the latter, insert and baste the godet into the garment seam, dart, or slash. Work down from the top for a few inches on both sides. Let the remainder of the bias edges hang out for at least twenty-four hours. You will probably end up with a little extra length because of the settling. Remove the basting. Pin the godet to the straight sides of seam, dart, or slash without forcing the extra length to

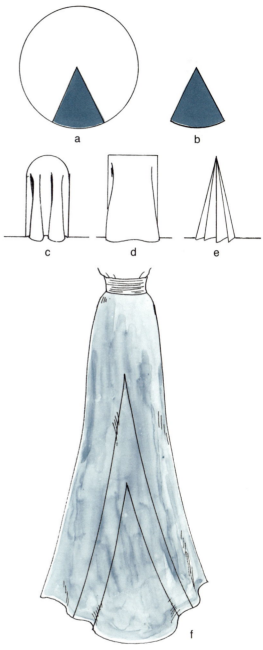

match. Trim away the excess length at the hemline. *See* BIAS SEAMS—*Stitching a Bias-to-Straight Edge.*

Stitch the Godet in a Slash of Fabric. Reinforce the slash line with small stay stitching. Face the point with a small patch of sheer fabric (a). Slash on the marked line. Turn the facing to the inside and press. Pin the point of the godet to the point of the slash, matching seam lines (b).

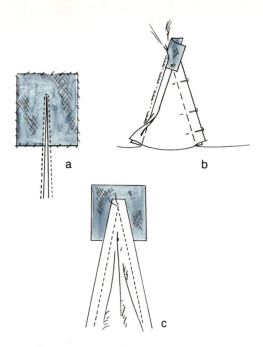

Baste to position, then stitch, keeping the slashed section on top.

Start the stitching at the point (the reverse of the usual rule) and stitch toward the end. Pull the thread ends at the point to the underside and tie them. Stitch the second side of the godet in the same way. It is easier and more precise to stitch each side separately than to try to pivot at the point of the slash. Press the seam allowances toward the garment (c).

Stitch the Godet in a Seam or Dart. Stay-stitch the seam lines of dart or seam. Stitch the seam or dart to the marking for the godet insertion. Pull the thread ends to the underside and tie. Slash the dart to with 1/2 to 1 inch of its point. Press the seam allowances open and the dart point

flat to one side (a). Press seam allowances of seam open.

Pin the godet to the garment, matching seam lines. Baste, then stitch, keeping the garment seam on top. Stitch each side separately in the same way as for the godet in a slash (q.v.). Press the seam allowances toward the garment (b).

Stitch the Godet in a Cutout of the Garment. A squared or rounded godet can be set into a cutout of a garment.

Stay-stitch the cutout along the seam line. Clip into the corners of a squared godet (a). Clip the curved seam allowances of a rounded godet (b).

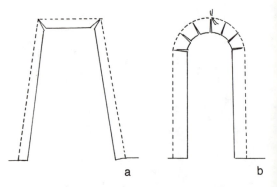

With right sides together, pin the godet into the cutout. Match centers first. Work down to the lower edges. Baste. With garment side on top, stitch the godet to the garment. (*See* CORNERED SEAM; CURVED LAPPED SEAM; CURVED OPPOSING SEAM LINES; CURVED PLAIN SEAM.) Press seam allowances toward the garment.

Topstitching a Godet. For a casual look, topstitch the godet through all thicknesses. It is done on the garment rather than the godet side of the seam.

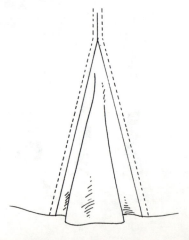

If you plan to use topstitching, consider the possibility of using it for your construction seams. It makes the insertion of the godet much easier. To do so, turn under the garment seam allowances in the godet area. Lap them over the godet, seam lines matching. Pin, baste, topstitch close to the fold.

Staying the Fullness of the Godet. The godet looks prettier if there is some slight control in the way its fullness breaks. A stay at the point of a godet provides such control.

Cut a triangle of some sheer or lightweight fabric. (Self-fabric will do if it is lightweight.) Extend the stay several inches down from the point. You may have to experiment with the size of the stay for the proper hang of the godet. Stitch the stay in the seam allowance close to the previous line of stitching.

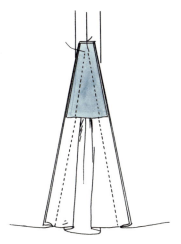

Squared or rounded godets may or may not be stayed, depending on how full they are. Generally the fullness is distributed over a wider area than in the triangular godet, making the stay less necessary. If the godet has considerable fullness, treat the squared or rounded godet in the same way as the triangular godet.

The Godet Hem. Allow the garment to hang out at least twenty-four hours before setting and stitching the hem.

Consider any special effect you would like for the hem of the godet. Stiffen it

with horsehair braid. For soft folds kept close to the body, use lead weights in the hem on either side of the godet.

GORE. A tapered section of a garment. Fullness at its lower edge without additional bulk at the upper makes this a favorite styling device for graceful movement.

Generally, the center of each gore is on straight grain, but it can be cut on the bias for design purposes.

Flare may originate at any point between the top and bottom of the gore. In order to preserve the grain and shaping of each gore, start at the wide end and stitch to the narrow.

GRADING SEAMS. The gradual diminution of bulk in a seam. Trim away one seam allowance so that it is narrower than the other, giving a staggered or layered appearance (a).

If there are more than two seam allowances, each of the several is trimmed to a different width so the effect is that of beveled thicknesses (b).

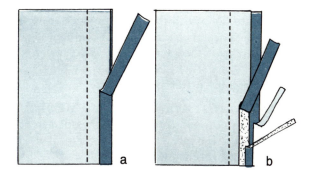

The width of each trimmed seam allowance is determined by the thickness of the fabric and where the grading occurs in the garment. In general, lightweight fabrics can be trimmed to a narrower width than can heavy fabrics.

GRAIN. A lengthwise or crosswise yarn or thread of woven fabric. In knitted fabric, it is a lengthwise rib (wale) or a horizontal course. In patterns, grain is referred to as "Straight of Goods."

Whatever the fiber, whatever the texture, whatever the weave or knit, cloth has *grain.* All woven or knit fabrics, therefore all such garments, hang with the grain. (In fact, they'll persist in hanging with the grain whether you cut them that way or not.) The designer utilizes the natural "hang" of the material in his or her design. The patternmaker who provides the blueprint for construction designates on each pattern piece the position of the grain that will achieve the designer's intent. You must observe these pattern markings religiously if your finished garment is to look the way it was planned. If you don't, you may end up with an effect you hadn't anticipated and a fit you cannot rescue.

Before one can proceed with the layout and cutting of fabric, its true grain must be established. This holds for every material that goes inside the garment as well—interfacing, underlining, lining, interlining. To establish the grain in single or double knits, *See* GRAIN ESTABLISHED IN KNIT FABRIC. To establish the grain in woven fabrics, *see* GRAIN ESTABLISHED IN WOVEN FABRIC.

To preserve grain perfection once it has been ascertained or established, all layout and cutting, all stitching, pressing, and fitting are done with the grain. So necessary to the appearance and fit of the garment is the grain of the fabric that a wise sewer must regard it with respect in every phase of the construction of the garment.

GRAIN AND PATTERN PLACEMENT.
The grain of the pattern is always placed parallel to the selvage of a woven fabric or the lengthwise wale of a knitted one.

The layout chart that comes with the pattern shows how it is to be placed on the fabric. Whatever the layout—lengthwise, crosswise, or bias—it shows an arrangement of pattern pieces *on grain.* You must position them that way. Don't trust your eye. For accuracy, use a yardstick or ruler (a tape measure is too unreliable) and measure each pattern piece from grain line to selvage or an established vertical grain in as many places as will ensure correct placement throughout the garment section.

GRAIN—CLUE TO GOOD FIT. Fabric
hangs with the grain and fits with it. This

is how the grain should appear in your garment.

The center-front and center-back grain hang at right angles to the floor. This places the horizontal grain parallel to the floor. The check points are across the chest, across the bust, across the shoulder blades, across the hips (a).

The vertical grain of the sleeve hangs at right angles to the floor from shoulder to elbow. This places the horizontal grain parallel to the floor. Check across the biceps (b). The lower portion of the sleeve (elbow to wrist) will not follow this line, since it is shaped by elbow darts in a one-piece sleeve or by the shaping seams in a two-piece sleeve.

Use any prominent lengthwise or crosswise yarns, stripes, plaids, or checks to locate the grain (c).

If the garment is cut on the horizontal or bias grain, your only guide is a line of

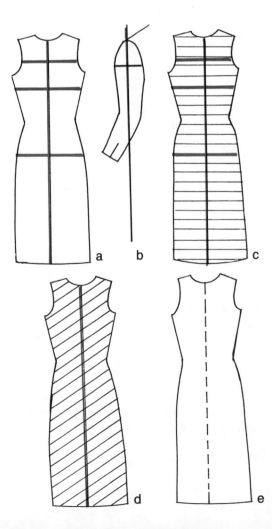

thread tracing (q.v.) (d). It is helpful to mark the vertical grain at the center front or center back with thread tracing (e).

For instance: if the crosswise grain slants out of its horizontal position (a), release the shoulder seams, set the grain aright, and repin (b). If the crosswise grain droops (c), release the side seams, set the grain aright, and repin (d). This same procedure is followed in each part of the garment.

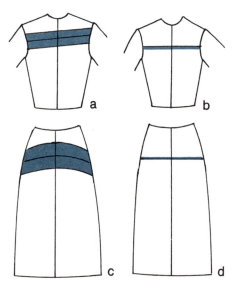

If the lengthwise grain of the sleeve tilts forward (a) or backward (c), unpin the sleeve and *dial* the cap to its correct position (b).

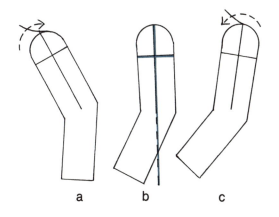

When the entire garment is fitted correctly for grain, it is possible to trace the horizontal grain completely around the bodice front, sleeve, and bodice back in a

continuous line that is parallel to the floor. The same can be done for a skirt or pants.

Sometimes out-of-position grain indicates the need for more shaping. When this is so, the drooping grain is accompanied by a deep wrinkle or fold just crying out to be put into a dart or seam. Wrinkles or folds like these are in reality uncontrolled darts.

So you see the correct grain is more than a question of aesthetics—the weave or design motif in an upright position. It also indicates the proper placement of outline seams and the proper amount and placement of the shaping. In a very real sense it is the key to good fit.

GRAIN ESTABLISHED IN KNIT FABRIC. You can't assume that the fold of a tubular knit is the lengthwise grain, any more than you can assume that a straight cut across woven material is the horizontal grain.

Sometimes knits that come to you flat have been produced on a circular loom and cut at the factory or by the merchandiser. Unfortunately, the cut may not be along a lengthwise rib. Check all knit goods for vertical straight grain. If not on grain, you must establish it so.

The Lengthwise (Vertical) Grain. Find the lengthwise wale and follow it throughout the length of the fabric. Unless the knit has a prominent wale or line, you may have to work on it a few inches at a time. Cut or baste along one lengthwise wale near the edge of the material, then cut along the marking. Don't worry about losing that convenient fold that you had hoped to use for the layout. One shouldn't use it anyway.

In raschel knits (warp knits made of thick and thin yarns held in place by a chain or series of loops), follow the lengthwise chain for the vertical grain.

The Horizontal Grain. This is a crosswise course. When the course is a prominent line, cut along it. When it is not, establish the horizontal grain at right angles to the vertical grain.

Lay the fabric on a flat surface with the lengthwise grain along one straight edge.

Place the fabric in such manner that you can use a corner to determine the right angle (a). Or, better yet, use a drafting tool—a right-angle triangle, an L-square, a T-square. Square the horizontal grain off the vertical grain (b).

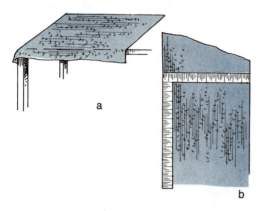

Weight the material with any safe, weighty object to hold the fabric in position. Using tailor's chalk or basting thread, mark, then cut along the horizontal grain near the edge of the fabric.

It is easier to establish the grain of shaggy, looped, or other raised-surface knits on the wrong side where the wales and courses are more clearly visible.

If, when the vertical and horizontal grains have been established, a knit fabric is not in a perfect rectangle, it can usually be pulled diagonally into one. Knits with permanent press finish cannot be handled in this way. In such fabrics it is best to cut each piece individually on grain rather than on a fold.

GRAIN ESTABLISHED IN WOVEN FABRIC. The selvage is the true vertical grain of woven fabric and generally needs no further treatment. The exception would be a puckered selvage. In this case, clip every few inches to release the strain but do not cut the selvage away. If you do, you will have to re-establish the vertical grain. Use the same method as for the horizontal grain.

The Horizontal Grain. If the fabric has a prominent horizontal yarn, rib, line, or stripe, simply cut along one of these. Just as easy and just as quick is tearing the material on the horizontal grain. Many fabrics tear easily without any ill effects. Some, however, are damaged by tearing. You had better test. Close to the cut end of the cloth, make a short snip through the selvage and into the fabric with the points of a pair of sharp scissors. Tear a short distance. If it works, tear across the width.

When fabric does not tear easily (as often happens in complex weaves and firm or fuzzy fibers) or if tearing will harm it in any way, then you must establish the grain by the following method.

Pull a crosswise thread. Make it a gentle but firm pull. Don't expect to do the whole row at one time: there are only a few fabrics in which this is possible. Pull a short distance. Hold the fabric up to the light so you can see the space left by the drawn thread, and cut (a). Repeat until you are clear across the width.

Sometimes the material gathers along the pulled thread. Cut following the line of gathers (b) instead of the drawn thread, as above.

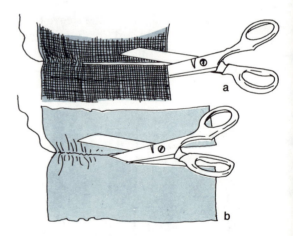

In either case, you know you've been successful when you can lift one horizontal thread across the entire width. If straightening the grain in the ways suggested takes you forever, you're doing something wrong. Start again. It should not be too lengthy a process.

GRAIN MARKING ON PATTERN. Every pattern piece, no matter how small or how large, must fit into a general plan the designer had in mind for the hang of the fabric. It has its grain marked on it.

The grain is indicated by a line with an arrowhead at each end. If the grain line does not run the entire length of the pattern piece, you must elongate it so it does to assure accurate placement of the pattern on the fabric throughout its length. Use a yardstick (rather than a tape measure, which is more flexible and consequently less reliable for this particular purpose) to do so.

GROSGRAIN RIBBON. A firm ribbon with heavy crosswise ribs corded from selvage to selvage. It is available in a variety of widths and colors.

Because of its firmness it is useful for waistband and waistline facings or wherever similar firm facings are necessary. It can be used as backing for belts as well as for trimmings.

When used in the construction of the garment, it is wise to preshrink the grosgrain. Set it in a basin of hot water and leave it there until the water cools off completely. Allow it to dry naturally. Press.

GUIDE BASTING. *See* THREAD TRACING.

GUSSET. A small piece of fabric set into an underarm slash that cuts from front to back. It is a hinge that permits freedom of movement in a fitted kimono sleeve. For maximum flexibility, it is cut so that its length is on the bias.

The one-piece diamond is the basic gusset shape (a). It may or may not have a shaped dart at the underarm (b). It is the most difficult of the gussets to sew because it must be set and stitched into an opening after the side and sleeve seams have been stitched. Because of this, four points of precision are involved in the stitching. This has frightened many a sewer off styles that incorporate gussets in the design.

The two-piece triangular gusset (c) is somewhat easier to handle. For one thing,

each triangle is set and stitched before the sleeve and side seams are stitched; the entire underarm—sleeve, gusset, and side—is stitched in one seam. For another, there are only two precision points to cope with, halving the difficulties of construction.

To make things easier for yourself, you may convert a one-piece diamond-shape gusset into a two-piece triangular gusset. Cut the gusset in half lengthwise, dividing front and back into two sections. Add seam allowances to the cut edges.

Sometimes, for purposes of design, part of the sleeve or bodice is combined with the gusset (combination gusset) (d).

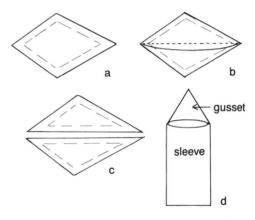

Reinforcing the Point of the Slash. Whatever the type of gusset and whatever the method of insertion, the point of each slash must be reinforced. Transfer the gusset markings precisely from pattern to garment. Reinforce each point in one of the following ways.

METHOD 1

Stay-stitch on both sides of the slash line, tapering toward the point. Blunt the point (q.v.) (a). Use 15 to 20 stitches per inch. Slash through the center to the point of the stitching.

METHOD 2

Reinforce each point with a 4-inch length of seam binding, folded into a V-shape (b) or a 2-inch bias patch of organza (or other very lightweight fabric) (c) placed and stay-stitched on the right side of the garment. Slash through the center of the opening and turn the facing or binding to the wrong side and press (d).

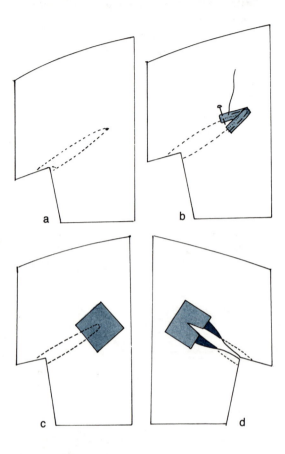

Stitching the One-Piece Gusset. This may be done by hand or by machine.

By Hand

It's easy enough to sew the gusset if you do it by hand. (In sewing, this is always a good rule to follow: if it's too difficult to do it by machine, do it by hand.)

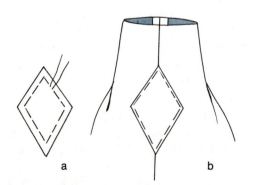

Mark the seam line of the gusset with thread tracing (q.v.) (a). Turn under the seam allowance of the reinforced, slashed sleeve opening along the seam line, rolling it slightly to the underside, and baste. Lap the folded edge of the slash over the right side of the gusset, bringing the fold to the thread tracing. Pin or baste to position (b). Using a single strand of thread, slip-stitch the fold to the gusset. Reinforce the points with tiny whipping stitches. Slip stitching is strong enough if the stitches are small and the garment does not get hard wear. Perhaps you would feel more secure with a second row of slip stitching. Or combine hand and machine stitching by using the slip stitching as a guide for machine stitching on the underside.

By Machine

The One-Piece Diamond-shaped Gusset. Stitch the sleeve and side seams to the markings for the gusset opening. Press the seam allowances open. Turn under the slash seam allowances and press. Treat the reinforcement patch or seam binding as seam allowance.

On the wrong side, place the right side of the gusset over the diamond-shape opening. Match front, back, and seam lines (a). Pin or baste.

With right sides together and garment side up, stitch the gusset into the garment (b). It's easier if you stitch one side at a time and break the thread at the end of each row, which is carried to the end of the fabric rather than to the marked points. Pivoting at a point, an academically approved method, is not only difficult for most home sewers but can be inaccurate and downright hazardous. Press all seam allowances toward the garment (c).

A practically foolproof machine method is topstitching, if it is consistent with the design of the garment (d). It is also a good method for garments that get hard wear. Topstitch on the garment side of the gusset in one continuous line of machine stitching. Blunt the points. Bring the thread ends through to the underside and tie.

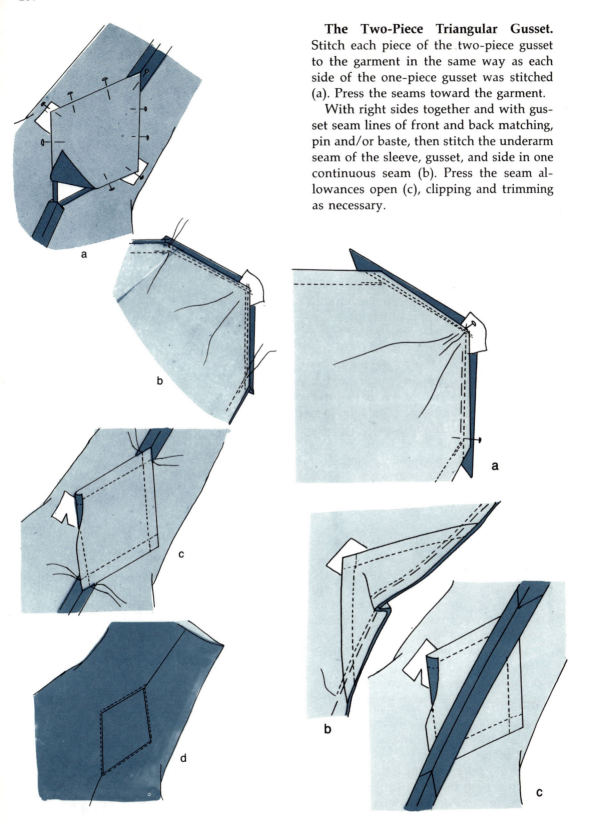

The Two-Piece Triangular Gusset.
Stitch each piece of the two-piece gusset to the garment in the same way as each side of the one-piece gusset was stitched (a). Press the seams toward the garment.

With right sides together and with gusset seam lines of front and back matching, pin and/or baste, then stitch the underarm seam of the sleeve, gusset, and side in one continuous seam (b). Press the seam allowances open (c), clipping and trimming as necessary.

HAIR CANVAS. *The* classic interfacing material for tailoring. What makes it so very special is the goat's hair or horsehair wound around its filler yarns. The hair gives the canvas its springiness, its resilience, its ability to cling to wool.

Hair canvas comes in light, medium, and heavy weights and in a variety of fibers—cotton, wool, linen, synthetic, and blends. The softest hair canvas is made of wool. Use this for any soft style and for any soft fabrics: cashmere, camel's hair, and the like. The stiffest hair canvas is that made of synthetic fiber. Use it only in places where considerable stiffening is necessary. The most generally used are those of medium-weight linen, cotton, or blends. The texture of these falls somewhere between the two extremes. They are firm yet pliable. They provide the shaping of most jackets and suits.

Because of its texture, when included in a construction seam, hair canvas produces too much bulk, impossible to press flat. For this reason, it should be eliminated from the construction seams. (*See* CATCH-STITCH METHOD, TAPING METHOD, FOLD-BACK METHOD, STRIP METHOD OF ELIMINATING HAIR CANVAS FROM CONSTRUCTION SEAMS.) Special stitching methods are required for its darts and seams. (*See* INTERFACING SEAMS AND DARTS.)

HAIRLINE SEAM. A very narrow, closely spaced overedge seam designed for flexibility, minimum bulk, and no visible seam allowances.

Set the sewing machine for a very narrow (no more than 1/4 inch), short zigzag stitch. Test the length and width before stitching. With right sides together, stitch the garment on the seam line indicated on

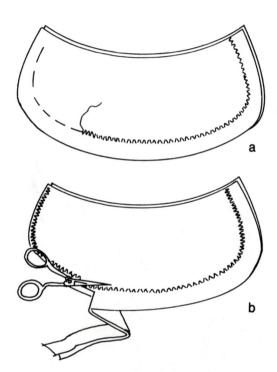

the pattern so the size of the section will be maintained (a). Trim close to the stitching (b). Turn to the right side, work the seam to the very edge, and press.

HALF BACKSTITCH. A delicate-looking strong stitch.

Fasten the thread on the underside of the material at the right end. Bring the needle to the right side one small stitch toward the left. Working back to the right, insert the needle half the distance of the

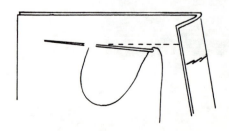

first stitch, slide it along the underside, and once more bring the needle out one stitch ahead. Repeat for the length of the seam.

HALF-SIZES. Patterns for half-sizes range from size 10½ to 24½. They are designed for a fully developed woman who stands 5'2" to 5'3" without shoes. She has a short back waist length, waist and hips larger in proportion to her bust than in other figure types.

HAND-ROLLED HEM. A suitable finish for soft or sheer fabrics.

Stay-stitch ¼ inch from the marked hemline. Trim close to the stitching a few inches at a time to prevent fraying of the entire edge (a). With wrong side up, roll the edge toward you with thumb and forefinger. Moistening the fingers a little helps the roll. Do a small section (½ to 1 inch) at a time. Fasten with slip or hemming stitches, catching only a thread or two of the fabric (b).

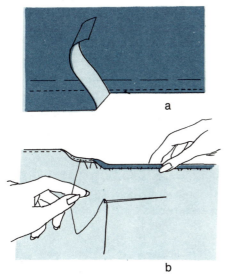

a

b

HAND STITCHES. Left over from the day when all sewing was done by hand are a considerable number of hand stitches for every conceivable need. The trick is to choose the right stitch for the right place.

Hand stitches may be temporary or permanent. Temporary hand stitches are used while the garment is in process of con-struction and removed when the permanent stitching is completed. Permanent hand stitches are *the* construction. They must remain for the life of the garment.

Temporary hand stitches are all variations of the basting stitch. *See* ALTERATION BASTING; BASTING; DIAGONAL BASTING; DRESS-MAKER BASTING; EDGE BASTING; SLIP BASTING; TAILOR BASTING, THREAD TRACING. *See also* GATHERING, GAUGING, SHIRRING.

Permanent hand stitches held garments together long before the sewing machine was dreamed of. They can be as strong as machine stitching. This is not to suggest that you revert entirely to hand stitching. Often, however, hand sewing does accomplish the construction of details more easily, more quickly, more precisely, and more effectively. A good rule to follow: if it's too difficult to do by machine, do it by hand.

See the following permanent hand stitches: BACKSTITCH; BLANKET STITCH; BLIND CATCH STITCH; BLIND HEMMING STITCH; BUTTON-HOLE STITCH; CATCH STITCH; FLAT CATCH STITCH; HALF BACKSTITCH; HEMMING STITCHES; OVER-AND-OVER STITCH; OVERCASTING; OVERHAND STITCH, PAD STITCHING; PRICK STITCH; SLANT HEMMING STITCH; SLIP STITCH; VERTICAL HEM-MING STITCH; WHIPSTITCH.

HAND-WORKED BUTTONHOLE. A classic decorative method of covering and protecting the edges of fabric slashed for a buttonhole opening.

Hand-worked buttonholes may be made either horizontally or vertically and are much easier to work if they are on straight grain. This buttonhole is made *after* the facing is attached to the garment and is worked through both garment and facing.

The *vertical buttonhole* is made with a bar at each end as a reinforcement (a). The *horizontal buttonhole* may be worked in a similar manner or be reinforced with a bar at one

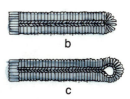

b

c

a

end and a fan at the other, the end nearest the finished edge of the garment (b).

The *tailor's buttonhole* (q.v.) is usually found on men's suits and coats but it is also used on women's tailored clothing. The buttonhole is made with an "eyelet" nearest the finished edge of the garment to reinforce the point of stress (c).

How to Make the Hand-worked Buttonhole. Mark the exact placement and length of the buttonhole. Mark the slash line with tailor's chalk, the ends with basting thread. Or mark the entire rectangle to be worked with machine stitching or small running stitches.

Slash the opening with a thin, single-edge razor blade or buttonhole blade, either of which is preferable to scissors because the cut can be made in one stroke to ensure accuracy and prevent fraying. So that no interfacing or underlining material will show in the opening of the buttonhole, trim away a very narrow rectangle of it.

With matching thread, overcast the slashed edges (a) to prevent raveling. Make the overcasting stitches a scant 1/16 inch deep for a 1/16-inch finished buttonhole. A deeper stitch can be used on loosely woven fabric or a large buttonhole. On sheer or ravelly materials, overcast (or work buttonhole stitches) before cutting the buttonhole. Carefully trim away any extraneous threads along the edges.

For the buttonhole stitch, use a slender needle, medium length, the smallest size suited to the thread you use. This makes it possible to place stitches close together and close to the edge in depth. For the buttonhole thread, use a single strand of buttonhole twist or heavy-duty cotton thread of matching color. Another possibility is a double strand of matching mercerized thread run through beeswax to keep the strands from separating. Start with a 24-inch length of thread for the first buttonhole. You'll be better able to judge just how much length will be needed for the next buttonhole when you've completed the stitching. Rethread the needle for each buttonhole.

Anchor the thread with backstitches on the wrong side of the fabric or slip the knotted end of the thread between the outer fabric and the facing. If new thread is needed, run the end under a few stitches and bring it up through the last purl.

Work buttonhole stitches (q.v.) over the overcast edges (b). Make a bar for a finish on each end beyond the opening by covering 2 or 3 straight stitches with small overhand stitches. Or, fan the stitches around the end against which the button will rest (c). Keep all stitches close together and even in depth.

HANGING SNAP. A neat and effective closing for garment edges that abut.

Sew the socket section to position on the inside of the garment at one edge of the closing. Attach the ball section to the opposite side with a thread chain (q.v.) just long enough to span the closing. *See also* EXTENDED SNAP.

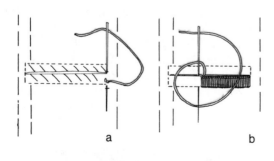

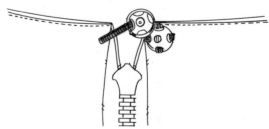

a   b

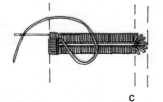

c

HEADED RUFFLE. A variation of a double ruffle in which the gathering is off center, an even distance from one edge. *See* RUFFLES.

HEADING. A finished edge an even distance above a line of gathering or casing (q.v.). It forms a ruffle when the gathering is drawn up.

HEAVY-DUTY SLIDE TYPE HOOK AND EYE. Use an overlap application. *(See* HOOK AND EYE ON EDGES THAT OVERLAP.) Using overhand stitches, fasten the hook and the eye through the holes (a). In long-bar types, fasten across the bars in a sufficient number of places to hold securely (b).

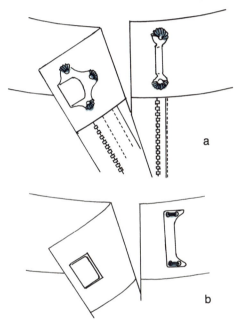

HEAVY-DUTY TACK. A sturdy tack used for joining areas of a heavy garment.

Fold back the edge to be tacked. Work from the bottom to the top. Fasten the

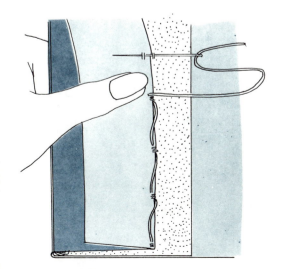

thread at the bottom of one layer. Working from right to left, take two or three short stitches directly above (or to the side of) one another. Catch only a few threads of the fabric. Keep the stitches relaxed, not tight. Make another set of stitches 1 to 2 inches above (or to the side of) each completed group.

HEM. It matters not whether one lets down, puts up, or evens out; whether it's a first-time job or a retread—there are certain general procedures applicable to all hems. There are also certain criteria for judging well-handled hems.

When properly set and stitched, skirt hems are an even distance from the floor all around. Turned-up hems are a uniform width throughout. The hem is either deep enough to provide a proper hang to the garment or narrow enough not to interfere with its appearance. If the hem is meant to be unseen, the hand or machine stitching must be inconspicuous. If the hem is planned to be a decorative note, it should be highly visible. Whatever else it is or isn't, a hem is smooth and flat—no lumps, no bumps, no pleats, no puckers.

For general procedures applicable to all hems, *see* HEM DEPTH; HEM-EDGE FULLNESS REMOVED; HEMMING STITCHES; HEM RESETTING; HEM SETTING.

For hem types, *see* BIAS-FACED HEM; BLIND-STITCHED HEM; BLOUSE HEM; CIRCULAR HEM; DOUBLE-STITCHED HEM; FACED (FALSE) HEM; HAND-ROLLED HEM; KNITS: HEMS; MACHINE-ROLLED HEM; NARROW HEM; SHIRT HEM; TAILOR'S HEM; TURNED UP HEM; WHIPPED HEM.

For special techniques relating to hems, *see* HEM AT A CLOSING; HEM AT A CORNER; HEM TUCK; INTERFACED HEM; SPLICED HEM; UNDERLINED HEM. *See also* FUSIBLE WEB; HORSEHAIR BRAID; PLEATS: HEM TREATMENT; WEIGHTS AT A HEMLINE.

For hems with covered edges, *see* BIAS BINDING; DOUBLE-FOLD HEM; EDGE FINISHES; FRENCH DRESSMAKER'S HEM; FRENCH HEM; HEM FACING; NET-BOUND EDGE FINISH; SEAM BINDING.

For hems with uncovered edges, *see* EDGE FINISHES.

For decorative hems, *see* BANDING; CORDING; LETTUCE EDGE; PIPING; REVERSED SEAM;

SHELL–STITCHED (SCALLOPED) EDGE; TOPSTITCHED HEM.

For hems in special fabrics, *see listing under the fabric name.*

HEM AT A CLOSING. Compare both open edges from top to bottom, allowing a bit of extra length for the side that overlaps. How much will depend on the thickness of the fabric. Turn up the hem. Pin on the closing line. Make sure the overlap covers the underlap.

The hem at a closing is always completed *before* the facing is turned back.

HEM AT A CORNER. When a facing is turned to its true position, bulk forms at the corner of the hem because of the many (often thick) layers of fabric superimposed one on another. There are a number of ways of handling this bulk. All of them begin with trimming away any interfacing at (or in) the hemline. Catch-stitch the cut edge to the garment at the hem fold line. *Choose one of the following methods.*

Hems That May Be Lengthened Later. If there is any possibility that the garment will need lengthening at some future time, turn up the entire hem of both garment and facing (a). Finish the hem edge in a way best suited to the fabric and whether or not the garment will be lined. *(See* EDGE FINISHES.*)* If the fabric does not ravel and the garment will be lined, the hem and facing edges need no finish.

Fold the facing to position and pin it parallel to its edge. Note: All facings along opening edges of garments are brought *over* the hem to keep the closing edges smooth. In a coat, simply make a French tack (q.v.) from the underside of the facing to the hem (b). In very heavy coat fabrics, treat like a double-stitched hem (q.v.) (c).

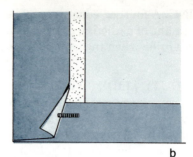

b

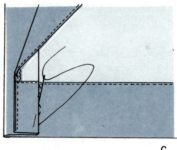

c

If the fabric ravels or if a finished edge is desired, clip the facing at the top of the hem, turn under the seam allowance from the clip down, and slip stitch the facing to the hem (a).

If the facing does not ravel, finish the edge of the facing without the turn-under and catch-stitch (b), whipstitch, slip-stitch, or blindstitch the facing to the hem, depending on the fabric and the desired finish.

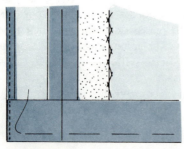

a

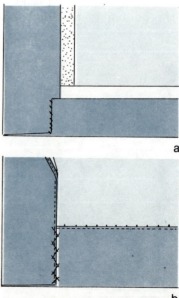

a

b

Hems That Will Not Be Lengthened.
While these methods permit no lengthening, they are excellent ways of avoiding bulk at a corner.

1. Grade *(see Grading Seams)* the facing and the hem in the corner area (a).
2. Miter (q.v.) the corner where hem and facing meet (b).
3. Join facing and hem by a seam rather than a turn-under (c). Many patterns provide this feature. If your pattern doesn't, you can achieve the same result by stitching the facing to the garment at the hemline and trimming away the excess material.

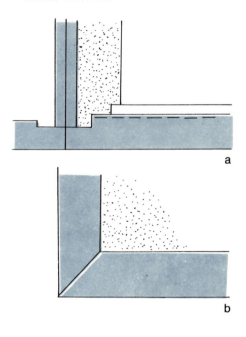

a

b

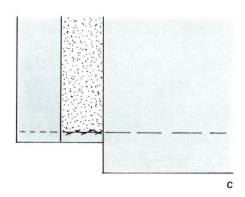

c

HEM DEPTH. The depth of a turned-up hem should be no more than can be made

to lie flat against the inside of the garment. If it does not, the fullness must be removed *(see* HEM EDGE FULLNESS REMOVED*)* or the width of the hem reduced. In recent years, some designers have dispensed with hems altogether.

The depth of the hem also depends on the fabric and the style. Lightweight or gauzy fabrics generally need wider hems than heavy fabrics. Stretchy fabrics require narrow hems. Opaque fabrics can have narrower hems. Sheer fabrics can have it both ways—either very narrow or very deep hems.

Straight Hems. On *skirts,* these may range from 2 inches in opaque fabric to 12 inches in sheer fabric used in evening wear. On *coats,* the hems are generally 2½ to 3 inches. On *jackets,* the hems are 1½ to 2 inches. On overblouses, hems vary from ½ inch to 2 inches.

Straight Sleeve Hems. On *dresses* or *blouses,* sleeve hems are generally 1 inch. *Jacket* sleeves have 1½-inch hems; *coat* sleeves have 2-inch hems.

Unless one is following the straight line of a stripe or plaid, even a straight hem is slightly curved. That is because all circumference seam lines are curved to follow the natural contour of the body. (This is one reason why a hemline is set on the wearer.) However, a slight curve does not affect the classification of the hem as straight.

Flared Hems. On any of the above, flared hems are narrower, depending on the degree of flare. When there is much flare, a facing is used in place of the hem.

Circular Hems. Have little (1 inch at most) or no turnback, in which case some decorative edge finish (q.v.) is required.

HEM-EDGE FULLNESS REMOVED.
When the upper edge of the hem does not lie smoothly against the garment, the excess fullness must be removed. This can be done by one of the methods described below.

Ease the Fullness. Make a row of machine basting or hand gathering close to

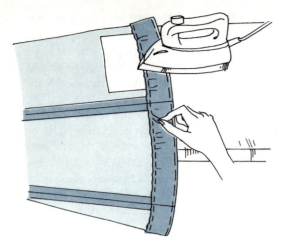

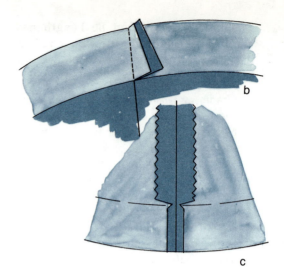

the raw edge of the hem. Slip the hem over the ironing board, wrong side out. Pull up the basting or gathering thread to fit the garment. Steam-press the hem with short strokes, using an upward motion of the iron from the fold to the upper edge. (Pressing parallel to the fold stretches the edge.) Remove any bastings at the fold line as you do a small section at a time.

To shrink out the hem without shrinking the fabric beneath, as well as to prevent a hem imprint, insert a wrapping-paper strip as a shield between the hem and the garment.

Rebaste or pin the hem when dry.

Remove Fullness at a Seam. By this method, the shape of the hem becomes the reverse of the shape of the garment at the hemline (a).

Turn the hem to the outside of the garment. Pin the hem seam close to and matching the corresponding garment seam. Stitch (b). Trim away excess material. Notch the seam allowances at the fold line to prevent bulk when the hem is turned up to its correct position. Trim the hem seam allowances to half width and press open (c). Turn the fitted hem to the

underside of the garment and finish as one would any other hem.

Wedge the Hem. A very good method for very curved hems of fabrics that won't ravel. *See* SPLICED HEM.

HEM FACING. A prepackaged 2-inch-wide bias strip of cotton or rayon. The edges are prefolded to the inside. The facing may be used for hems (*see* FACED HEMS), as wide casings, or, when folded in half lengthwise, as a binding. There are also stretch lace types available. Both come in a range of colors.

HEMMER. A sewing machine accessory that automatically turns under a raw edge and stitches it without previous pinning, basting, or pressing. It is useful on any long edge where a narrow, machine-stitched hem is acceptable.

Replace the presser foot with the hemmer. Form a 1/8-inch double fold at the edge of the fabric. Crease it for about 2 inches. Place the folded edge under the hemmer and sew a few stitches through the creased fold. Leaving the needle in the fabric, lift the foot. Hold the thread ends with one hand and guide the edge into the scroll with the other. When guiding work, hold it taut and lift it slightly. Soft fabrics enter the scroll best with the foot down; firm, crisp fabrics with the foot up. Run the fabric through the machine in a straight line. Feed the fabric evenly and

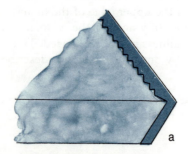

keep the same width in the scroll throughout.

Corners are done in two operations. Before doing any stitching, trim the corner
diagonally (a). Sew the first side as directed above.

Make a double fold on the second edge
and anchor it with needle and thread (b).
Feed the second edge into the scroll in the
same way as the first. Stitch the second
side.

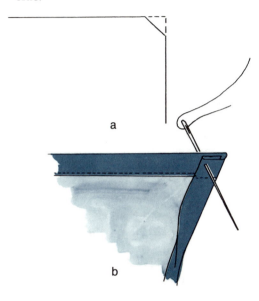

To facilitate the start of the stitching,
grasp the corner and threads. Pull gently
until the presser foot is off the corner and
the fabric has entered the scroll.

HEMMING STITCHES. Tiny inconspicuous stitches that fasten the finished edge
of a hem to the outer fabric. For most
hemming, only one or two threads of fabric are caught so that the stitching is practically invisible from the right side.

Use a single length of matching thread.
For most purposes, keep the stitches
"easy" and "relaxed" rather than drawn
up tightly. Hemming stitches are either
flat or blind.

The *flat stitches* pass over the hem edge
from hem to garment, fastening the edge
against the garment in such a way that it
can't catch or curl. *See* FLAT CATCH STITCH;
SLANT HEMMING STITCH; SLIP STITCH; VERTICAL
HEMMING STITCH.

The *blind stitches* are taken inside the hem
between it and the garment. The positioning of the two for the stitch provides sufficient length of thread between them to
produce a slack stitch. Combined with the
inconspicuous stitch itself, this makes for
a hem that hardly reveals its presence. *See*
BLIND HEMMING STITCH (RUNNING HEMMING
STITCH) *and* BLIND CATCH STITCH. The latter is
a stronger stitch, more suitable for heavy
fabrics.

HEM RESETTING. To reset the hem in a
finished or ready-to-wear garment, first
rip the old hem. If it is uneven, remove
any seam binding. If the hem is even and
does not need cutting, the seam binding
may remain for the new hem. Note: Not
all hem edges need binding. Many are better off without it. *See* EDGE FINISHES.

Brush out the lint that gathers in the
fold of the hem. Clean the crease mark at
the fold line and press it to remove the
crease. Unfortunately, in many fabrics,
once a fold has been pressed it is almost
impossible to eliminate the crease. Even if
that can be done, it is probable that there
will be some discoloration and some wear
visible along the edge. This is what makes
lengthening a skirt so much more difficult
than shortening one. If the original hemline remains as a permanent marking, plan
to hide it with some decorative detail like
topstitching, braid, or ribbon. Mark a new
hemline and turn up the new hem. *See* HEM
SETTING.

When there is a *band or flounce at the hemline,* it is possible to shorten it at the hemline but not to lengthen it there. Length
must be added some other place on the
garment. *(See* ALTERING A GARMENT.)

To shorten such a garment, remove the
band or flounce. Decide the finished
length of the garment. Subtract the depth
of the band or flounce. Set the new seam
line and add a seam allowance.

With right sides together, pin the upper
edge of the flounce or the upper layer of
the band to the garment, then stitch the
seam. Grade the seam allowances, making
those of the garment wider. Press them toward the flounce or band.

For the band, turn under the seam allowance of the under layer. Bring the fold to the seam (enclosing the garment seam allowance), and hem. For the flounce, turn under the wider garment seam allowance, bring it to the stitching for a self bound seam (q.v.). *See also all listings under* RUFFLE.

HEM SETTING. For all fabrics and for all styles, this is done after the garment is otherwise completed, the fit perfected, and the final pressing administered.

Before setting the hem, allow sufficient time for the fabric to "hang out." It must do all the stretching, dipping, sagging, and settling it's going to do. "Hanging out" overnight will do for most fabrics and styles. Bias-cut, knits, flared, or circular garments take longer—often as much as a week.

It's a good idea to hang up the garment each time you have finished working on it. Use a tissue-paper-padded hanger or a dress form. By the time you are ready to set the hem, the fabric will have settled.

Make any final (we hope) adjustments in the fit of the garment. To refit after the hem is set will affect the hang of the hem and, in turn, the hemline.

A good final pressing of the garment is essential. Smooth out all mussed areas and wrinkles. Block the garment to shape over an appropriate press pad. To do so after the hem is set may cause an uneven hemline.

Hems are marked on the right side of the garment. Hems at hipline or above may be set and marked on a flat surface. Hems below the hipline are marked on the wearer.

Hems Marked on a Flat Surface. Try on the garment and determine the desired length at several points. Remove the garment. Check the marking against the hemline of the pattern. If adjustments are necessary, use the pattern hemline as a guide for the new hemline and alter the depth of the hem. Trim any excess width of the hem.

Hems Marked on the Wearer. Bedeck yourself *exactly* as you plan to when wearing the garment. This means the bra, the girdle, the slip, the stockings, the shoes, the belt. Top-to-toe color continuity affects the length you choose for the garment as does the wearing of a belt. There is also the very real matter of heel height. This not only affects the number of inches from the floor a hem is to be, it also affects one's posture, which in turn involves the evenness of the length.

If it is a coat hem you are setting, wear the dress or sweater or suit over which it will be worn. If you set a hem without doing so, you may discover your garment is a different length when you do add the underneath layer.

Try on the garment and turn up a tentative length. Consider whether the length is both fashionable and becoming to you. Test the length at rest and in motion.

There are ways of setting a hem by yourself but each such method has its drawbacks. This is one time when someone to set the hem for you can be a big help. Set the skirt marker for the number of inches from the floor you've decided the hem is to be.

Stand naturally. If you stand stiffly at attention for the marking when that is not your natural posture, your hem will be uneven when you lapse into your usual stance. Stand still while your helper and skirt marker move around you.

With the hemline at your helper's eye level, have him or her place pins 2 to 3 inches apart for straight hems, closer for curved hems, almost continuously for circular hems. (To position oneself so that the hem will be at the eye level of your helper means that you may have to stand in some elevated position—on a stool, a platform, on a table or desk. Lacking any appropriate raised surface, your assistant may have to kneel or sit on the floor.)

Using the pins as a guideline, turn up and pin the hem tentatively to position. These pins are placed at right angles to the fold. Correct any irregularities or jumpiness that may have occurred in the pinning.

Both you and your helper examine the

hem for evenness. Reset it in whole or in part if necessary. When satisfied with the setting, remove the garment for finishing the hem.

How the hem is treated from this point on depends on the kind of fabric and the design of the garment. *See the listing for your particular type of hem.*

HEM TUCK (in Skirt). Provides growing room in children's clothing. *See also* BODICE TUCK.

Add 1 to 4 inches extra allowance at the bottom of the pattern. Mark the hemline originally designated in the pattern. Make a tuck within the extra fabric far enough above the fold line of the hem so the fold of the tuck won't be seen from the right side. Use a large machine stitch so it can be easily removed when needed.

Press the tuck toward the hemline. Complete the hem as usual. To lengthen the skirt, release the tuck and use as much or as little as desired. Make a new tuck if necessary.

HIDDEN HOOKS. You can do a real disappearing act with hooks by hiding them in the weave of the fabric. To be consistent, instead of a metal eye, use a thread eye (q.v.).

Mark the position of the bill end of the hook on the facing. Make a small opening in the weave of the fabric by carefully pushing the threads apart with a blunt instrument. In tightly woven fabric, make a tiny slit for this purpose.

Gently work the rings of the hook into the opening, one ring at a time (a), until only the bill of the hook is exposed (b). Slip the thread in the opening and fasten

a   b

the rings with tiny, inconspicuous stitches. Fasten the bill. When the fabric has been slit to make the opening, sew up the ends to prevent tearing or fraying.

HIDDEN SEAMS. Used in construction of reversible garments of double-faced fabric (q.v.).

HIDDEN ZIPPER CLOSING. *See* INVISIBLE ZIPPER INSTALLATION.

"HIKING UP" OR "POKING OUT" (of Bodice, Skirt, or Sleeve). Such fitting problems are the result of insufficient length and/or insufficient shaping. Check both. If this is a problem you often encounter in your fitting, learn to alter the pattern before cutting out your material. If you must fit cut-out material, all you can hope to do is salvage what you can of seam allowances and darts.

Bodice Pattern Correction. Measure center-front and/or center-back bodice

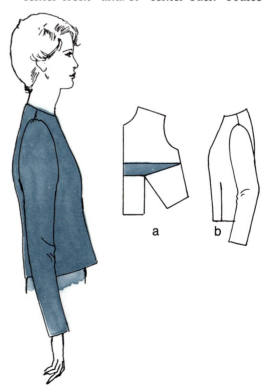

a   b

length. Compare with the pattern length. Slash and spread the pattern for additional length (a). Fill in the spread area with tissue or pattern paper.

Bodice Fitting Correction. Release the shoulder and side seams. Straighten the center front or back, dropping the waistline as necessary. Add length by using as much as possible of the seam allowances at the shoulder, neck, and waistline. Check the darts and shaping seams. If necessary, make the darts larger or add darts (b). Take more in on shaping seams. Establish a new waistline.

Skirt Pattern Correction. Determine the necessary additional length. Slash and spread the pattern for additional length at the center front or back (a). Fill in the spread area with tissue or pattern paper.

Skirt Fitting Correction. Release the side seams. Straighten the center front or back, dropping the waistline as necessary. Fit the hip-to-waist area, making the darts larger or adding darts if needed (b). Refit and repin the side seams, adding or subtracting at front or back as much as necessary to preserve the correct position of the center front or back. Establish a new waistline.

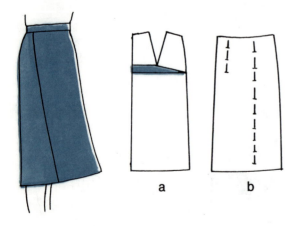

a b

Sleeve Pattern Correction. Determine the necessary additional length. Slash and spread the sleeve cap for the additional length. Fill in the spread area with tissue or pattern paper (a).

Sleeve Fitting Correction. Release the armhole seam. Reset the sleeve, using the horizontal grain as a guide. It should be parallel to the floor. Use as much seam allowance as you can salvage from the cap of the sleeve (b).

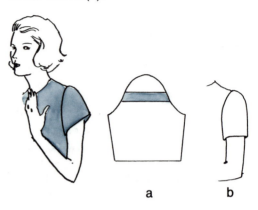

a b

HIP PATTERN CORRECTIONS. A garment that extends to or below the hips must not only have sufficient circumference but should fit smoothly over the buttocks, the hipbones, and the abdomen without pulling or wrinkling.

Big-hipped Figure. There are several ways in which corrections for this figure type can be made.

METHOD 1

Slip a sheet of fresh paper under the pattern out from the side seam. Add the necessary amount at the fullest part of the hip. Draw a new side seam, starting from the enlarged hip and tapering to nothing at the waistline. Carry the correction to the hem (a).

METHOD 2

This method preserves the shaping at the side seam while adding width. Draw a vertical slash line from the waistline to the hem. Slash and spread the pattern to the needed amount at the hips. Make a small tuck in the side section to reduce the flare at the hem. Some fullness at the hem is necessary to balance the additional width at the hips (b). Fill in the spread area with tissue. Correct the hemline.

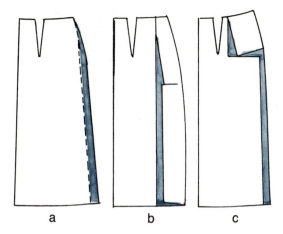

a   b   c

METHOD 3

(An alternate method that provides the same correction as Method 2.) Draw an L-shaped slash line from the waist to the fullest part of the hips. Slash and spread the pattern to the needed amount at the hips. Insert tissue paper in the spread area and at the side seam. Carry the hip correction to the hem (c).

Slim-hipped Figure. The corrections for this figure type are the reverse of those for the big-hipped figure.

Draw a vertical slash line from waist to hem and a short horizontal slash line from it to the side seam at the hipline. Slash and overlap the pattern in an equal amount from the hips to the hem. Taper the amount from the hips to the waist.

Check the darts. They may be too deep for a slim-hipped figure in the original pattern. If so, make them smaller.

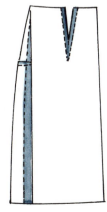

HOOK AND EYE. A fastening for closing where there is considerable strain. There

are two parts to the fastener—the hook or bill (a) and the eye. There are straight eyes for edges that overlap (b) and round eyes for edges that abut (c). Thread eyes (q.v.) can substitute for the metal variety when used in exposed positions.

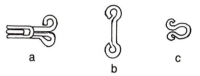

a   b   c

Hooks and eyes come in a variety of styles and sizes depending on the use to which they are put. *Standard types* are made of brass, nickel, or black enamel-coated metal in sizes 00 to 5 (a). *Special-purpose* hooks and eyes are covered, larger, heavier, and can withstand considerable strain, as would be the case in heavy-weight fabrics or fur (b). *Heavy-duty* (slide type) hooks and eyes (q.v.) are used for waistbands (c). When multiple hook-and-eye application is necessary, there is a *hook and eye tape* (q.v.) (d).

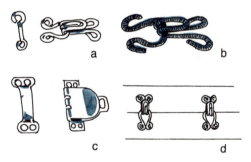

a   b

c   d

Those fastenings that will be exposed at some time in the wearing should be covered. Silk-covered hooks and eyes are available in an assortment of standard colors. If your garment is a nonstandard color, cover your own hooks and eyes for an exact color match. *See* COVERED HOOKS AND EYES.

Another way to keep hooks and eyes inconspicuous is to hide them. *See* HIDDEN HOOKS.

HOOK AND EYE ON EDGES THAT ABUT. Sew both the hook and round eye to the underside of the closing. Position

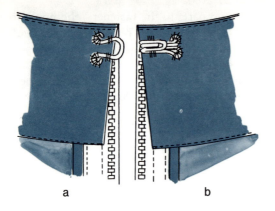

a   b

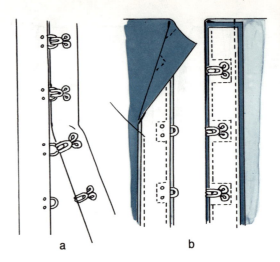

a   b

the hook slightly in from the edge. Work overhand stitches around the first ring. Slip the needle through the fabric and bring it up at the second ring. Sew the second ring, working overhand stitches around it. Slip the needle through the fabric and bring it up at the hook end. Work overhand stitches just under the bill. It is just as important to anchor the bill as to secure the rings (b). Fasten the thread with tiny backstitches and cut it.

Position the round eye so that the loop extends a bit beyond the edge. Fasten the rings with overhand stitches. Whipstitch both sides of the loop slightly above the rings to secure it (a).

HOOK AND EYE ON EDGES THAT OVERLAP.

Position the hook on the inside of the garment, setting it close to the edge. Stitch it to the garment in the same manner described above, for edges that abut.

On the outside of the underlap where the end of the hook falls, place the straight eye. Stitch the eye with overhand stitches around each ring.

HOOK AND EYE TAPE.

A convenient way to apply multiple hooks and eyes at one time. The hooks are attached to one length of cotton tape, the eyes to the other (a). Hook and eye tape is sold by the yard and comes in neutral colors.

Since the hooks and eyes must abut to be fastened, this calls for a centered application.

Mark the fold line for the edge finish or facing, which should be wider than the

tape. Place the hook tape on the right side of the facing along the edge with the hooks just inside the fold line. Stitch the tape to the facing only, going around the hooks. Use the zipper foot to avoid hitting the hooks. Fold the facing to the underside and stitch through all layers along the free edges.

Stitch the eye half of the tape to the opposite edge in the same way (b). Be sure to align the eyes with the hooks.

HORSEHAIR BRAID.

A stiff, loosely woven braid, originally of horsehair, now mostly of transparent nylon strands. It is used for extra stiffness without extra weight at hems, edges, and trimmings. It is often used as the hem itself for lace, sheer fabrics, or where a transparency is needed. Very lightweight, it comes in varying widths from 1/2 inch to 5 inches and in many colors, though the one most frequently used is translucent, clear, almost no-color. The wider braids have a shirring thread along one edge which makes it possible to curve the braid to shape.

When used at a hem edge, set the hemline and add 1/2 inch for a hem allowance. Cut the necessary length of horsehair braid plus two seam allowances. Overlap the ends and stitch. Trim the excess material close to the stitching. Because the cut ends of the braid are so scratchy against the skin, they should be covered. Use strips of appropriate fabric and attach with two rows of machine stitching (a).

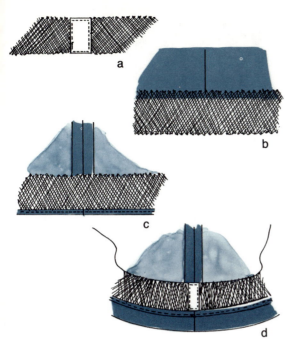

a

b

c

d

To attach the braid at a hem edge or as a facing to a straight edge, overlap one edge of the braid 1/4 inch on the cut edge of the fabric. Pin or baste to position. Edgestitch along the overlapped braid, using thread that matches the garment fabric

(b). Turn the braid to the inside, bringing the seam 1/4 inch in from the fold line of the hem (c). Slip-stitch or catch-stitch the upper edge of the braid to the outer fabric or the underlining.

To attach the braid as a facing to a flared or circular edge, use a horsehair braid that has a shirring thread along one edge. Use this edge as the upper edge of the hem. Follow the directions for the straight edge with this additional step: when the braid has been turned to the inside, draw up the shirring thread to fit the garment (d). When the garment has been hemmed, trim away the excess shirring thread.

When horsehair braid is used as an interfacing for a hem, select a braid of the same width as the hem. On the wrong side of the garment, place one edge along the fold line of the hem and the other at the raw edge. Pin at right angles to the hem from the fabric side. Overcast the raw edge of the hem to the upper edge of the braid. Baste the interfaced hem to position. Finish as a tailor's or French dressmaker's hem (q.v.).

IN-A-DART SLEEVE PLACKET. An easy-to-make sleeve placket. *(See* SLEEVE PLACKET.*)*

With right sides together, pin the dart. Stitch the dart at the upper end with its point at the fold line (a). Slash the stitched dart part way and press it flat. Turn in the opening edges to form a narrow hem (b) and slip-stitch it.

a   b

INSEAM. The seam on the inside of the trouser leg from the crotch to the hemline. It should hang at right angles to the floor. If it swings forward or backward, unpin the seam, check the grain line, and reposition the seam, taking off or adding to the front or back pant leg as necessary. Repin the seam.

IN-SEAM BUTTONHOLE. This is the easiest to make of all types of buttonholes. Simply leave the seam unstitched at intervals to provide the openings for the button. Any seam may be utilized for this purpose.

Mark the buttonhole placement on the seam (a). Stitch the seam, starting and ending the stitching at the markings. Secure the thread by backstitching or tie the thread ends. Press the seam open. Work bar tacks (q.v.) on the wrong side at the ends of the buttonhole (b).

If facings or linings are involved in the buttonhole area, leave similar openings in the seams. Slip-stitch the facing or lining to the garment opening.

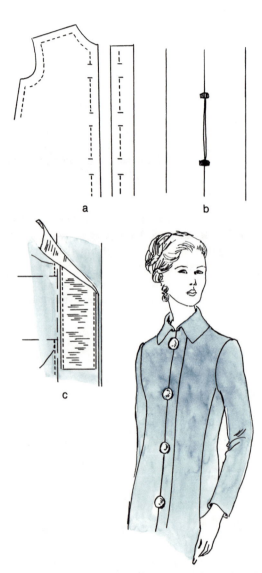

Optional: Reinforce the buttonhole on the underside with strips of seam binding or narrow cotton tape. Cut each strip 1 inch longer than the buttonhole and center it along the opening next to the seam line. Stitch the binding (or tape) to the seam allowance close to both its edges (c).

IN-SEAM POCKET. A designer often
utilizes a seam to conceal a pocket. For instance, the front or side seam of a skirt or
dress. No one may know the in-seam
pockets are there until you plunge your
hands into them. Or you may advertise
their presence with topstitching.

There are three types of in-seam pockets. In the *all-in-one in-seam pocket*, pocket
and garment are cut as one (a). A *separate in-
seam pocket* is joined to the garment at a
seamline (b). An *extension in-seam pocket* consists of a separate pocket piece joined to
garment-plus-small-extension (c). Any of
these pockets can be put into any seam
whether the pattern calls for it or not.

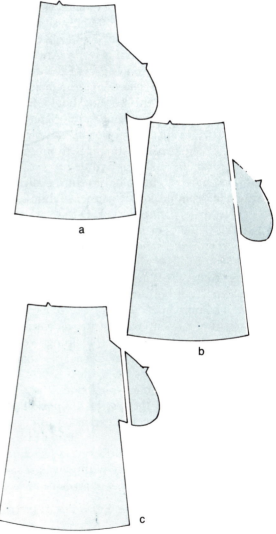

a

b

c

You can make your own patterns for
these pockets. Draw a pocket to the desired size and shape. Add seam allowances. Mark the position for the pocket
placement on the garment seam.

For the all-in-one in-seam pocket, add

the entire pocket to the garment section with Scotch tape. Overlap the seam allowances at the joining.

For the separate in-seam pocket, use the pocket as is.

For the extension in-seam pocket, draw the depth of the extension on the pocket. Cut the pocket apart on this line. Add seam allowances to both cut edges. Scotch-tape the extension to the seam allowance of the garment pattern at the pocket opening. Overlap the seam allowances. The pattern for the remainder of the pocket becomes correspondingly smaller.

The *opening of the in-seam pocket* will reveal the material of which it is made. Anything seen, as this is, becomes part of the design of the garment. Therefore, the material you choose for the pocket should fit in with the total concept of the design. You could add a splash of color or pattern for drama. The usual treatment is to preserve the continuity of color and texture.

You have no choice but to cut the all-in-one in-seam pocket of garment fabric.

For the separate pocket, if the garment fabric is light- or medium-weight, cut the pocket of the same material. Or cut the under pocket of the outer fabric and the upper pocket of lining material. For heavy material, cut both upper and under pockets of lining material. Face the edges that join the garment with strips of garment fabric deep enough so the lining won't show when the pocket opens. *See* BOUND POCKET.

Cut the garment-plus-extension of outer fabric and the rest of the pocket of lining material for the extension in-seam pocket.

All in-seam pockets: Reinforce the seamline of the front pocket only with woven seam tape. *See* IN-SEAM POCKET REINFORCEMENT.

To Set and Stitch In-Seam Pockets to the Garment

All-in-One In-Seam Pocket. With right sides together and pocket extended, baste along the pocket opening. Pin and/or baste the garment and pocket seams, then stitch in one continuous seam. Reinforce the pocket opening markings with backstitches. Clip the back seam allowance at the corners where garment and pocket meet. Press the garment seam allowances open above and below the pocket. Press the pocket toward the garment front. Remove all bastings. Trim the pocket seam allowances and overcast the edges together.

Separate In-Seam Pocket. Pin front and back pockets to front and back garment sections, matching the markings for the opening. Use only 3/8 inch of the usual 5/8-inch seam allowance. This will give 1/4 inch for rolling the pocket seam to the inside. Grade the front pocket seam allowance only. Edge-finish each seam allowance separately. Press the back pocket seam allowance open and the front pocket seam allowance toward the pocket. Continue the construction in the same way as for the all-in-one in-seam pocket.

Extension In-Seam Pocket. With right sides together, pin, then stitch the front pocket piece to the front garment extension and the back pocket piece to the back garment extension. Press seams flat toward the pocket. Trim the seams and overcast the edges together. Continue the construction as for the all-in-one in-seam pocket.

IN-SEAM POCKET REINFORCEMENT.
An area that gets as much use as a pocket opening needs some reinforcement. Further, its length and shape should be preserved with a stay.

Use a length of woven seam tape or similar firmly woven material. Make either one the length of the opening plus 2 inches—1 at each end.

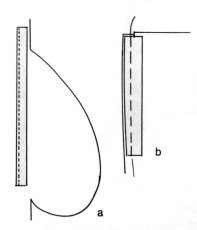

Whether the in-seam pocket is all-in-one, separate, or extension, position the stay on the wrong side of the pocket opening, centering it. Place the tape in the seam allowance beside the seam line and stitch 1/8 inch from it (a).

More generally used in men's trousers is a 1 1/2-inch-wide strip of pocketing placed directly over the seam line and included in the separate-pocket seam (b).

IN-SEAM SLEEVE PLACKET. An easy-to-make sleeve placket.

Stitch the seam, leaving the opening for the placket. Clip the seam allowances slightly beyond the end of the opening. Press them open, continuing into the placket seam allowances (a). Turn under the raw edges of the placket seam allowances and hem or slip-stitch them (b).

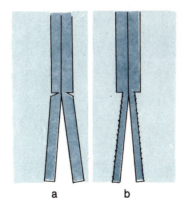

a   b

IN-SEAM TROUSER POCKET. This pocket in a seam varies with the design of the trousers but essentially it is a piece of self-fabric-faced pocketing material set in the side seam or in a side front section.

Cut four pocket sections of pocketing (q.v.) to form a pair of pockets. Cut four pocket facings of trouser fabric about 2 1/2 inches wide by the length of the pocket opening plus two seam allowances. If the inside edge of each facing is cut along a selvage, it will provide a fine finished edge. Notch to indicate the pocket opening.

Place the front and back pocket sections right side up. Place a facing on each, right side up, matching notches. Pin and/or baste. The front facing and pocket edges

are aligned. The back facing is set 3/8 inch in from the edge. Stitch each facing to the pocket along the inside edges (a). Repeat for the second pocket, remembering to reverse the pocket position for the second side.

With right sides together, pin and stitch the front pockets to the trouser fronts between the notches (or other markings) and 1/2 inch in from the edges. Clip the seam allowances to the stitching (b) and press them open.

Fold the pockets to the wrong side of garment, rolling the seams to the underside. Press to position. Topstitch each pocket in the groove of the seam (c).

Reinforce the back pocket opening. *(See* IN-SEAM POCKET REINFORCEMENT.) Stitch the back pockets in the same way as the front.

Pull the front and back pockets away from the trousers and join each pair in a French seam (d). Stitch the front and back trouser sections along the outseams above and below the pocket opening. Press the seam allowances open.

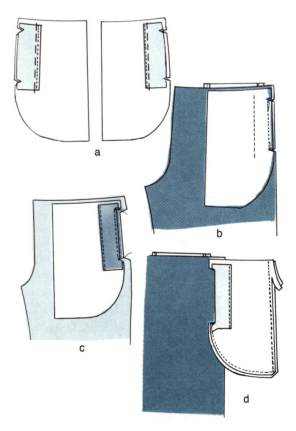

a

b

c

d

On the underside, trim the back-garment seam allowances and the pocket facings to 1/4 inch in the area of the pocket opening. Fold the pocket-stay seam allowances over the trimmed garment-back seam allowances and press to position. Fold the pocket seam allowances over the trimmed pocket-facing seam allowances and press (a). Bring these two folded edges together and stitch them along the edge (b). This both finishes the seam and strengthens it.

On the right side of the trousers, and with pockets in wearing position, reinforce the ends of the openings with bar tacks (q.v.) at top and bottom (c).

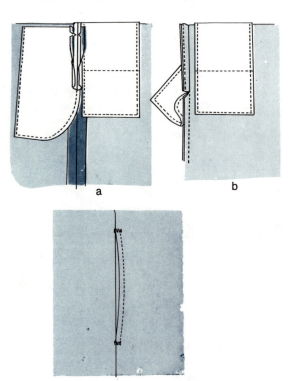

INSERTION. Narrow lace or embroidery with a plain edge on each side so that it can be set into fabric as a trimming. Place it over the fabric and stitch along each edge. Cut away the under section of the fabric. Or attach each edge of the insertion to a cut and finished edge of fabric.

INSET WAISTBAND. A band of fabric, generally shaped, is inset at the waistline for design purposes or for fit. The inset may be of fabric (a) or of ribbed banding (b).

FABRIC INSET WAISTBAND

The fabric is generally faced and often interfaced. If interfaced, apply the interfacing to the wrong side of the band. If the inset band has side seams, match them to the side seams of the garment. Leave an opening for the zipper placket to match that of the garment. The inset band may be applied with either a lapped seam or a plain seam.

Lapped Seam Application. Turn under the seam allowances at the upper and lower edges of the inset band. Pin the upper edge of the band over the lower edge of the bodice and the lower edge of the band over the upper edge of the skirt (a). Bring the folds of the band to the seam lines of the garment. Topstitch (b). Trim, grade, and notch the seam allowances as necessary and press them toward the inset band.

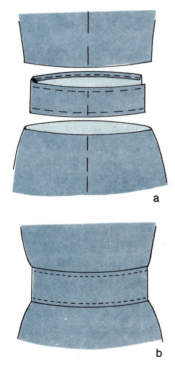

Plain Seam. With right sides together, stitch the upper edge of the inset to the bodice, the lower edge of the inset to the skirt. Trim, grade, or notch the seam allowances as necessary. Press the seam allowances toward the band.

Both Types. Turn under the seam allowances of the facing and baste or press them. Place the wrong side of the facing against the wrong side of the inset band, matching centers, side seams, and any notches between. Match the placket ends. Slip-stitch each edge of the facing to the seams at bodice and skirt.

RIBBED BANDING INSET WAISTBAND

Cut a length of ribbed banding. The length will depend on the degree of stretch of the banding. It should fit snugly around the waist. Add seam allowances. If the garment has no placket, the length must be sufficient to slip the garment over the shoulders and bust and the ends must be joined so they form a circle.

Section the banding into halves, quarters, eighths. Section the bodice and skirt into the same number of parts and pin-mark (a). When there is a placket, mark off the seam allowance at each end of the ribbing before dividing the band into sections (b).

With right sides together, pin the band-

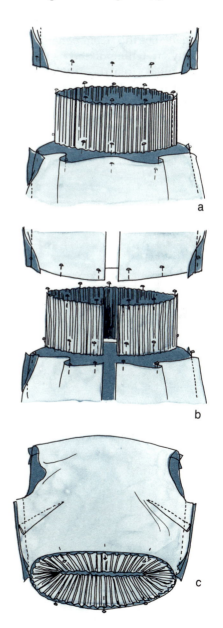

ing to the bodice, matching pin marks and stretching as necessary (c). Match the joining seam of the banding to a seam of the bodice either back or side. Or pin the ends of the banding to the placket opening.

With the banding side up, stitch the inset to the bodice, stretching the band to fit. Make a second row of either straight or zigzag stitching about ¼ inch away from the first in the seam allowance. Trim the seam allowances close to this last stitching.

Attach the banding to the skirt in the same way. Carefully align the center fronts, backs, side seams of bodice, inset, and skirt so the ribs of the band run vertically. Turn the seam allowances toward the garment. Hold a steam iron above each inset seam. Let the steam penetrate and restore any stretching of the band that may have resulted from the stitching. Insert a zipper in the placket opening, being careful to match the cross seams of the inset.

INSIDE BOUND POCKET (MEN'S TAILORING). This pocket is generally made on the right front, though it can be made

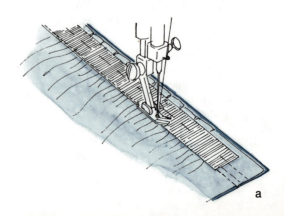

a

b

c

on both fronts if desired. Use lining fabric for the pocket.

In a lined jacket with narrow lapels and narrow facing, the pocket is made entirely on the lining (a). If the lapels are wide, a small portion of the pocket extends into the wide front facing (b). In an unlined jacket, the pocket is made in the extrawide facing (c). In any case, the pocket is made before the facing is stitched to the jacket. If the pocket goes through facing and lining, these must be joined before the pocket can be constructed.

Make the bound pocket (q.v.). From the right side, topstitch in the two horizontal grooves formed by the welt seams. Do not topstitch across the ends.

INSIDE WAISTBAND. A lifetime of self-fabric waistbands can be pretty dull stuff. Why not try for something a little different? Like no visible waistband. Instead, a ribbon- or fabric-faced waistline (q.v.).

INSIDE WAIST STAY. Used in fitted dresses, it assures fit at the waistline and relieves the strain on the closing and all seams and darts in the waistline area. Apply it to the inside of the garment either before or after the zipper has been installed. Use ½-inch- to 1-inch-wide preshrunk grosgrain ribbon or French belting.

If applied before the zipper insertion (a), cut a length of stay that measures from placket seam line to placket seam line. Place the stay over the skirt side of the waistline seam allowances with one long edge at the waistline seam and ends at the placket seam lines. Pin and/or baste to position. Machine-stitch through the stay

a

and both waistline seam allowances beside the waistline seam. Trim and grade the seam allowances. Press all toward the bodice. Continue the construction, catching the ends of the stay in the zipper seam.

If applied after the zipper insertion (b), cut a strip of stay long enough to fit the waistline snugly but comfortably. Add 1 inch for finishing the ends.

b

Turn under the ends of the ribbon and stitch. Sew hooks and eyes to the ends of the ribbon that just meet at the garment closing. Tack the stay at all seams and darts along the waistline. Leave 2 inches free at each side of the placket.

This latter method is the one used for a garment without a waistline seam.

INTERFACED FACING. The general rule for interfacing is that the garment, not the facing, gets interfaced. As with most rules, there are exceptions. When the fabric of the garment and the interfacing are both lightweight (some cottons and some silks) and when buttonholes (if present) are to be hand-worked or machine-made after the facing is applied, then it is possible to interface the facing rather than the garment.

Cut out the facing and the interfacing. With right sides together and raw edges matching, stitch the interfacing to the facing at the outer edges (a). Press the seam allowances open. Trim and grade them. Clip or notch as necessary. Turn the facing/interfacing unit to the right side and press carefully along the edge. Treat the interfaced facing as one fabric and stitch it to the garment in the usual manner (b).

When the front facing is cut all in one

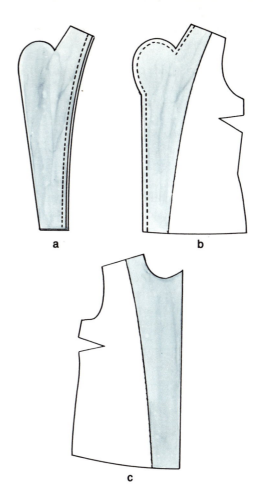

a   b

c

with the garment, tack the interfacing lightly to the facing close to the fold line. Turn the interfaced facing to position along the front fold line (c). Pin or baste to position.

INTERFACED HEM. Because a hem adds a second layer of cloth to an edge, it adds body. As a result, the garment hangs better. In many fabrics and in many styles an interfacing is required to provide even more weight. This is particularly true of hems in tailored garments. How the interfacing is applied depends on whether it is desired that the hem edge be crisp or soft.

Note that in the hems described below 1/2 inch of the interfacing extends above the hem in order to grade the thicknesses. It is the method used when a lining is brought down over the hem edge. When there is no lining, the grading is reversed:

make the interfacing ½ inch narrower than the hem depth.

For a Crisp Edge. Cut a bias strip of interfacing the width of the hem plus ½ inch and as long as needed plus two seam allowances. Overlap the straight-grain ends of the bias strip, stitch, and trim the seam allowances close to the stitching (a).

Place the interfacing against the garment with the lower edge along the fold line of the hem. Lightly and invisibly blind-catch-stitch the lower edge to position (b).

Turn up the hem along the fold line. Fasten the upper edge of it to the interfacing with permanent basting or catch stitching (c). Pin the interfaced hem to the garment. Fasten the upper edge of the interfacing to the garment with a blind hemming or blind catch stitch.

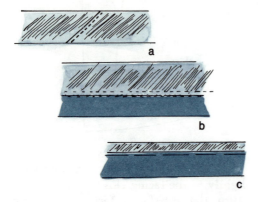

For a Soft Edge. *(See* PADDED EDGE *for a super-soft hem edge.)*

Cut a bias strip of interfacing the width of the hem plus 1 inch and as long as needed plus two seam allowances. Overlap the straight-grain ends of the strip. Stitch. Trim the seam allowances close to the stitching.

Place the interfacing against the garment with the lower edge ½ inch beyond the fold line into the hem (a). Permanently baste the interfacing to the hem slightly down from the fold line toward the hem (b). Pick up only one thread of the hem fabric in loose stitches. *Alternate method:* Cut the interfacing as for a 1-inch soft fold. Turn up the fold and fasten its upper edge to the interfacing with running stitches (c).

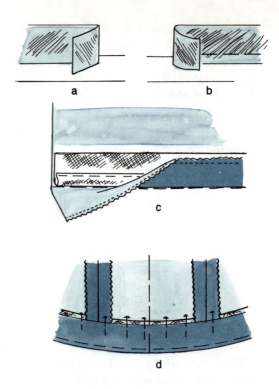

Turn up the hem along the fold line. Pin it to the garment (d). Fasten the upper edge of the interfacing to the garment with blind hemming or blind catch stitches.

INTERFACING. A layer of supporting material used to reinforce, to stiffen, and often to shape.

In dressmaking, the interfacing is limited to the same size and shape as the facing and placed between it and the outer fabric. This is also the limit of interfacing in many "soft," unconstructed, shirt-shaped jackets and coats.

In traditional tailoring (constructed), the interfacing assumes more importance. It is extended to include part (for women) or all (for men) of the front shaping and often a back reinforcement as well. In addition, for women, the shaping can be as subtle as the shieldlike shape of a man-tailored jacket. Or it can be frankly feminine, as curvaceous as style and figure dictate.

In both dressmaking and tailoring, all important design details are interfaced: collars and cuffs (a), pockets, welts, and flaps (b), yokes (c), peplums and other hip

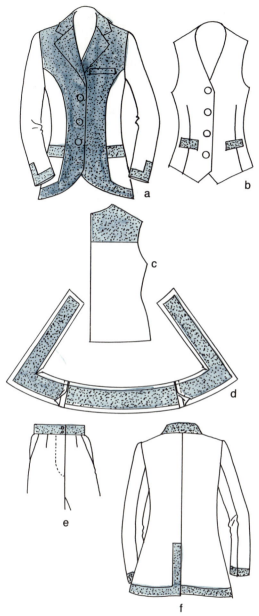

interest (d), belts and waistbands (e). In addition, in tailoring, all outside edges that have not already been interfaced are interfaced with bias strips of interfacing material: hems, sleeve closings, vents (f). What you choose to do with the interfacing depends largely on the effect you want.

In general, choose an interfacing compatible with the outer fabric in weight and cleanability. While the interfacing should be no heavier than the fashion fabric, it can be crisper. *See* INTERFACING MATERIALS.

Unless labeled "Preshrunk," all interfacings should be preshrunk or sponged. *See* PRESHRINKING UNDERSTRUCTURE MATERIALS.

The interfacing is cut with the same meticulous care for grain as the outer fabric. Mark carefully with dressmaker's tracing (carbon) paper (q.v.) and a tracing wheel.

So as not to detract from the lines of the outer fabric, the inner construction of a garment must be as smooth and as unobtrusive as possible. This calls for a bulkless construction of all darts and seams in the interfacing. *See* INTERFACING SEAMS AND DARTS.

Only light- to medium-weight interfacings can be included in the construction seams. Heavy interfacings are never included. They are eliminated by the CATCH-STITCH METHOD, THE FOLD-BACK METHOD, THE STRIP METHOD, THE TAPING METHOD (q.v.).

Fusible interfacings, like other interfacings, come in various weights and fibers. They may be woven or nonwoven. Bear in mind that fusibles change the texture of the fashion fabric by stiffening it and sometimes even rippling it. *See* FUSIBLES; FUSIBLE INTERFACING FOR UNCONSTRUCTED TAILORED GARMENTS; FUSIBLE WEB.

Press and, when necessary, shape each interfacing unit before applying it to the garment. *See* PRESSING: BLOCKING THE UNDERSTRUCTURE.

To join the interfacing and outer fabric of tailored garments *see* INTERFACING APPLIED TO OUTER FABRIC; INTERFACING APPLIED TO OUTER FABRIC OF FITTED TAILORED GARMENT; INTERFACING APPLIED TO OUTER FABRIC OF UNFITTED TAILORED GARMENT.

When there is considerable shaping via hair canvas, make the buttonholes and bound pockets in the outer fabric before the hair canvas is applied. *See* BOUND BUTTONHOLE: REINFORCEMENT FOR THE SLASH LINE *and* INTERFACING APPLIED TO OUTER FABRIC.

When there is minimal shaping via hair canvas, the interfacing can be joined with the outer fabric first. *See* BOUND BUTTONHOLE: REINFORCEMENT FOR THE SLASH LINE.

INTERFACING APPLIED TO OUTER FABRIC. The interfacing and fashion fabrics of all garments, shaped or unshaped, are best joined in the same relative position in which they will be worn (fashion fabric topping foundation fabric) and over a tailor's ham to simulate the body contour. This is the order: tailor's ham representing the body, then the supporting fabric, and lastly the outer fabric, right side up.

Because an inside curve is smaller than an outside curve, some of the foundation fabric will extend slightly beyond the edges of the fashion fabric. This positioning automatically adjusts the necessary length and width of the supporting material. The excess can be trimmed away after the layers are joined.

If both underlining *and* interfacing are used, first join them to each other with stay stitching, then join them to the garment fabric with tailor basting (q.v.). The underlining is placed directly against the wrong side of the outer fabric. This method of joining ensures that the shaping of both fabric and understructure correspond.

Caution: If needles and pins leave permanent marks or bruises on the fashion fabric (velvets, brocades, satins, and so on) do not join the units with tailor basting. Baste the sections together in the seam allowances of all outside edges. Work over the tailor's ham, of course.

INTERFACING APPLIED TO OUTER FABRIC OF FITTED TAILORED GARMENT.

In matching the *front outer and supporting fabrics,* start at the dart (a) and work toward the outer edges. Pin. When matching shaping seams, start at the crest of each curve and work toward the outer edges (b). Pin to position. You can see how this procedure makes for exact shaping.

Working from the right side, tailor-baste the two thicknesses. The first line of basting goes over the dart or shaping seam—up toward the shoulder, down toward the hem, stopping several inches short of each (a). This line of basting may also run through an upper and lower pocket when they are present.

When there are pockets involved, turn back the side-front outer fabric section against itself so the seam allowances of any welt or bound pockets are visible. Fasten them to the interfacing with hemming stitches (b). Replace the side-front fabric. Turn back the front outer fabric against itself, exposing the second side of any welt or bound pockets. Fasten the seam allowances to the interfacing with hemming stitches. Return the fabric to position. In the same way, you may fasten the seam allowances of any waistline darts.

Locate the exact position of the buttonhole and pocket openings on the interfacing. Cut out rectangles of the hair canvas just large enough to expose the openings. Slip the canvas under the seam allowances of pocket and buttonholes. Fasten the

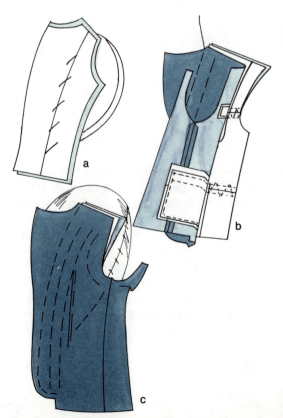

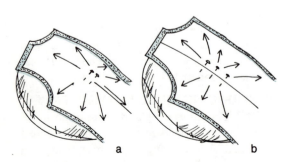

seam allowances to the interfacing with catch stitching.

Working from the right side, continue the tailor basting, making several lines of it several inches apart toward the side and toward the front. Smooth the fabric toward the outer edges as you work. Make the last rows 1 inch in from the front and side edges (c).

In matching the *back outer and supporting fabrics,* start at the center back and work toward the outer edges. Make a line of tailor basting down the center, starting 1 inch down from the neck edge. Run a line of basting 1 inch in from and along the shoulder and neck edges. Run a line of basting at each armhole about 2 inches from the armhole edge, starting about 1 inch below the shoulder and ending about 1 inch from the side seams (a).

Optional: If it will hold your fabric more securely, you may run another line of tailor basting between the center and armhole edge (b).

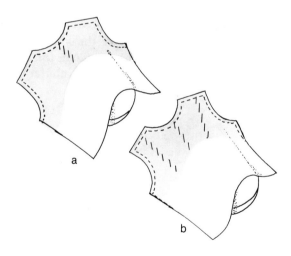

INTERFACING APPLIED TO OUTER FABRIC OF UNFITTED TAILORED GARMENT.

Since an unfitted garment requires minimal interfacing, it can be applied without regard to shaping, of which there is little or none.

Place the front interfacing on a flat surface. Place the completed front unit of fashion fabric over it, matching front edges. Pin to position. Make a line of bast-

ing 1 inch in from and along the front edge (a).

Place the two joined layers over the tailor's ham, fashion fabric right side up over the interfacing. Smooth the fabric toward all outer edges. Pin to position. Make a line of basting 1 inch in from and along all other outer edges that are interfaced (b).

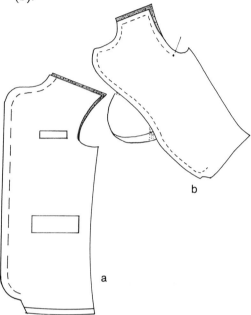

INTERFACING AT A FOLD LINE.

When garment and facing are cut in one piece, the interfacing may end at the fold line or extend a short distance beyond it.

When the interfacing ends at the fold line, the finished edge of the garment will be *crisp.* Catch-stitch the edge of the interfacing along the fold line. The stitches of the upper row of the catch stitch should lift only a thread or two of the outer fabric. Those on the lower row go through the interfacing only (a).

For a *very sharp* and somewhat *stiffer* front closing edge, as in a straight-hanging box jacket, extend the interfacing beyond the fold line about 1/2 to 3/4 inch. Turn the extension under at the fold line. Stiffen the double thickness with rows of machine stitching. Attach the edge of the stiffened interfacing to the outer fabric with catch stitching (b).

For a *soft edge* at a fold line, extend the

a

b

c

interfacing beyond the fold line about 1/2 to 5/8 inch. Attach the interfacing to the outer fabric along the fold line with short, permanent basting stitches that go through the interfacing and pick up a thread or two of the outer fabric in the same way that a pad stitch does (c).

Fusible interfacings may end at the fold line or beyond it, depending on the desired degree of stiffness or softness.

INTERFACING FOR COAT. This follows the same general rules as for jackets. *See* INTERFACING FOR MAN'S JACKET; INTERFACING FOR STRAIGHT-HANGING BOX JACKET; INTERFACING FOR UNLINED JACKET OR COAT; INTERFACING FOR WOMAN'S JACKET.

INTERFACING FOR COLLARS AND CUFFS. For dresses, blouses, shirts, *see* COLLAR INTERFACING; CUFF INTERFACING. For tailored garments, *see* INTERFACING FOR SHAWL COLLAR; INTERFACING FOR STANDING COLLAR; INTERFACING FOR TAILORED COLLAR.

INTERFACING FOR KIMONO STYLE. The charm of the kimono style is its easy, natural shoulder line. To keep that soft-shoulder look, cut the interfacing like the facing (a). If the garment is to be lined, extend the interfacing 1/2 inch beyond the facing edge. If unlined, keep it 1/2 inch within the facing edge.

For a firm shoulder line in a lined garment, make an interfacing pattern like that for a woman's jacket. Since the kimono-sleeved garment has no armhole for a guide as a stopping place for the interfacing, you'll have to create one.

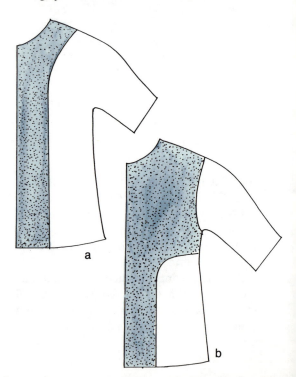

a

b

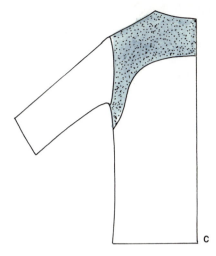

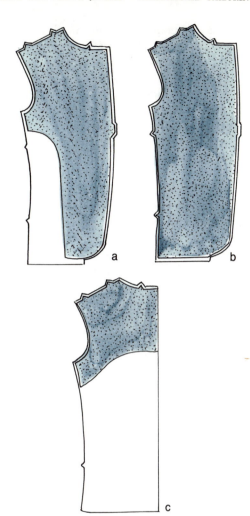

Mark the length of the shoulder seam 1/2 inch beyond the prominent shoulder bone. Draw a slightly curved line from this point to the underarm seam (b). Draw the back armhole curve in the same way (c). Now the interfacing pattern can follow the same outline as for the set-in sleeve of the tailored woman's jacket. *(See* INTERFACING FOR WOMAN'S JACKET.)

INTERFACING FOR MAN'S JACKET— TRADITIONAL TAILORING.

The traditional tailored man's jacket is a very structured affair. Layers of interfacing and padding material create that subtly sculptured line. How much goes inside the jacket depends on the style, the fabric, and the man. Currently, in men's as well as women's tailoring, the classic structure has been reduced to conform to the new softer lines.

The easiest but not necessarily the best way to handle the whole front inner construction is to buy a commercially available packet of preassembled, shaped, and pad-stitched hair canvas interfacing. It can be trimmed down to size or padded out additionally if need be.

However, most patterns for men's clothing provide a pattern for the front interfacing. It is quite easy to make your own and has the added advantage of customized size and shaping.

The basic interfacing, generally made of hair canvas, may be a partial front (a) or a complete front unit (b).

A *partial interfacing* reinforces the armhole, the shoulder, and front areas. Starting from a point 3 inches down on the side seams, the interfacing proceeds in a curved line toward the front, then straight to the hemline. It may avoid the front dart entirely or it may include 1 inch of the dart point and come down through the center of the dart to the hemline.

A *complete front interfacing* includes all darts and seams within the perimeter of the interfacing.

To this basic unit are added extra layers of graded interfacing and padding material to build up the shoulder and armhole areas and to fill in and round out the hollow in front of the shoulders. *(See* CHEST PIECE and SHOULDER PADS.) Use as many layers in as many suitable kinds of material as will create the lines of the design.

b

The materials generally used for this purpose, either alone or in combination, are hair canvas, wool interfacing fabric, lamb's wool padding, heavy cotton flannel, cotton wadding. *(See individual listings.)* With the exception of hair canvas, these materials are not always easily available for home sewers. Use the ones that are, or order from a mail-order supply house. (Such services are often advertised in the pattern books.)

Many schools of tailoring omit the *back interfacing* entirely. Should you choose to use one when none is provided in the pattern, it's easy enough to make your own.

A back interfacing reinforces the entire back across the shoulders, around the armholes from the neck edge to a point 10 inches down on the center back, 3 inches down on the side seams. The lower edge is a curved line (c). Since the movement of the arms is forward and the interfacing should not restrict the motion, cut the interfacing on the bias or make a two-piece back interfacing (q.v.). Use muslin or any other lightweight woven interfacing material.

For figures that require it, the back armhole may be further supported and padded with extra layers of interfacing and padding material in the same way the front was with a chest piece.

When all layers of interfacing and padding material are set in place, shape by pad-stitching (q.v.) them together.

INTERFACING FOR RAGLAN-SLEEVE STYLE. Like the kimono sleeve, the line of

this sleeve also follows the natural contour of the shoulder. *(See* INTERFACING FOR KIMONO STYLE.)

To preserve the soft-shoulder look, interface the front only to the raglan style line (a). For a firm shoulder, add interfacing across the shoulder from neck to shoulder bone at both front and back (b).

INTERFACING FOR SHAWL COLLAR. For soft styles, whether dressmaking or tailor-

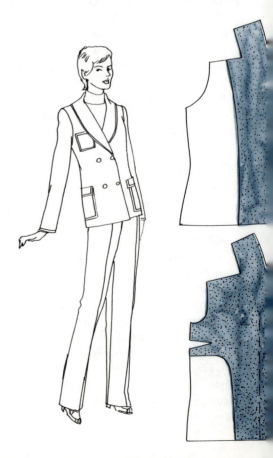

a

c

ing, cut the interfacing for the shawl collar from the facing pattern. If the garment is to be lined, extend it ½ inch beyond the facing edge; if unlined, ½ inch within the facing (a).

For firm, tailored styles, interface the front of the garment in the same way as for a woman's jacket—traditional tailoring (q.v.) plus the collar extension (b). If the undercollar is cut as a separate piece, treat it like a tailored collar (q.v.) (c).

INTERFACING FOR SHIRT JACKET. Interface collars and cuffs, front bands or edges, pockets, flaps (or welts), other design details, hems, and vents.

INTERFACING FOR STANDING COLLAR. There are several ways to make a

standing collar really stand. Use a length of firm iron-on material minus seam allowances. Cut a length of stiff interfacing material minus seam allowances. Cut a length of interfacing material, either single or double thickness, minus seam allowances. Make diagonal rows of machine stitching until the interfacing is the desired degree of stiffness. The smaller the stitches and the more closely spaced the rows of stitching, the stiffer the interfacing will be.

INTERFACING FOR STRAIGHT-HANGING BOX JACKET. This usually has little or no shaping.

Extend the front interfacing to include the shoulder and armhole area. Mark a point 3 to 4 inches down on the underarm seam. Make the front interfacing ½ inch wider than the front facing. With a curved line, connect the underarm point with the inner edge of the front interfacing. Extend the interfacing to the hemline in a straight line (a).

When the facing is cut all in one with

a   b

c

the front of the garment, extend the interfacing ½ inch beyond the fold line of the front edge (b). To firm the front edge of the interfacing, turn under the front extension at the fold line and stiffen with close rows of machine stitching (c).

INTERFACING FOR STRAP-SHOULDER STYLE.

In this sleeve style, interface the strap to or slightly beyond the shoulder with a double thickness of interfacing material. Stiffen it with close rows of machine stitching.

INTERFACING FOR TAILORED COLLAR.

The best interfacing for the neck-hugging tailored collar is tailor's linen or tailor's canvas. When cut on the bias from the undercollar pattern, these materials mold and fit beautifully.

For a similar collar on a slightly dropped neckline (more usual in women's tailoring), use hair canvas, the interfacing for the rest of the garment.

For some types of construction, melton cloth is recommended. When melton cloth is not available in suitable colors, try firm felt instead.

INTERFACING FOR UNLINED JACKET OR COAT.

Interface only the areas with facings. Make the interfacing slightly narrower than the facing. In that way, not only will you make certain that the interfacing won't peep out from under the facing but you will have graded the two thicknesses, making for a smoother construction. Interface all design details.

Use a softer or lighter-weight interfacing than one would normally use for a lined garment. This avoids too much difference in thickness or stiffness between the interfaced parts and the rest of the garment. The interfacing may be of woven, nonwoven, or fusible material.

INTERFACING FOR WOMAN'S JACKET —TRADITIONAL TAILORING.

In the traditional man-tailored woman's jacket the interfacing is extended to include the bust area in addition to the shoulder and armhole area. Even if your pattern does not provide an interfacing that includes this extension, you can make your own. While this may be a little extra work, it pays off by providing elegant shaping and support.

On the adjusted style pattern, draw the overall outline of the interfacing. Either cut the original pattern apart (if you don't intend to use it again) or trace the interfacing pattern on a fresh piece of paper (if you do intend to use the pattern again).

The Overall Outline of the Front Interfacing. Carry the interfacing across the

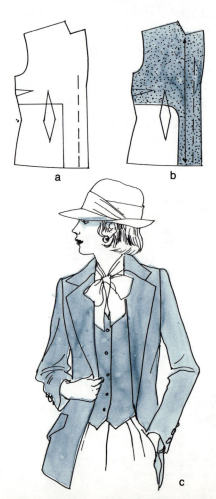

a   b

c

shoulder and chest to the armhole and across the bust to the side seam (a). Bring the interfacing 3½ to 4 inches down from the armhole on the side seam (excluding darts), or as far down as may be necessary to include any underarm shaping.

Make the remainder of the interfacing, from the cross line to the hem, ½ inch wider than the facing itself. With a curved line, correct the corner where the horizontal and vertical edges of the interfacing meet (b). Trace the grain line, the center-front line, and the notches.

The front interfacing is always cut on the lengthwise grain. When the interfacing is hair canvas, this takes advantage of the crosswise roll of the hair-wound filler threads. This is what produces that soft turnback so characteristic of a tailored lapel (c).

Should the width of the above interfacing bring the inner edge close to a dart or seam, carry the interfacing all the way over to the center of a vertical dart (a) or to the nearest seam (b). These are logical stopping places.

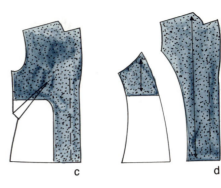

c   d

interfacing as there are sections of outer fabric (d).

When the facing is cut all in one with the jacket, cut the interfacing only to the fold line for a crisp edge (a), or extend it ½ to ⅝ inch beyond the fold line for a soft edge (b). Keep in mind that it is the garment that gets interfaced, not the facing.

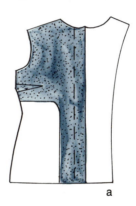 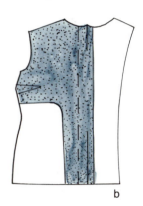

a   b

a   b

Include any darts that lie completely within the overall outline (a). Include 1½ to 2 inches of the tops of any vertical darts (b) or any angled darts (c).

Include any shaping seams that lie within this area. Cut as many sections of

The Overall Outline of the Back Interfacing. Bring the back interfacing 3½ to 4 inches down on the center back and a distance down on the side seam to match that of the front interfacing. Join these two points with a flattened S curve from the center back to the underarm seam (a).

The long, bias sweep of the S curve provides "give" for the forward movement of the arms. A no-stretch straight line would

a   b

a   b

restrict such action. Often the back interfacing is cut on the bias to provide even more ease of movement.

Some schools of tailoring omit the back interfacing, but it has its obvious advantages, not the least of which is that it blocks out the shoulder-pad ridge so that it doesn't show through. Some tailors use a two-piece back interfacing (q.v.) for tailored knits. They feel it provides freer forward movement consistent with the stretch of knit fabrics.

Include any darts or seams that lie within this overall outline (b). Cut as many on-grain sections of interfacing as there are sections of outer fabric.

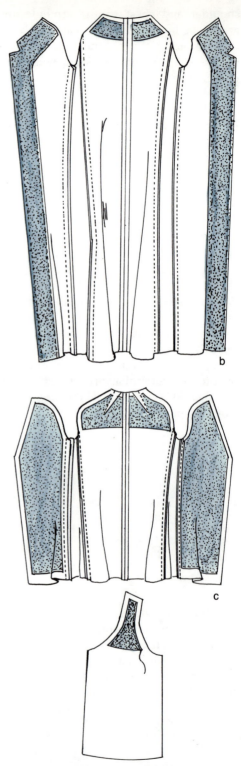

b

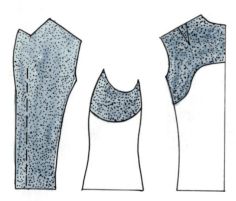

When there is an underarm section rather than an underarm seam, follow the same general outline as for the front and back interfacings but divide the area into its several parts.

To soften the "hard" effect of this much interfacing, subtract some of it. For instance, one way to deal with bust shaping is to circumvent it (a). In this raglan-sleeve coat, only the decorative bands are interfaced (b). The effect is soft shoulders.

c

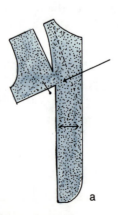

a

When a firm effect is desired in a raglansleeve garment, the entire front, the entire shoulder, and part of the back are interfaced (c).

INTERFACING FOR WRAP STYLES. Since these are generally "soft" styles there is a minimum of shaping in the interfacing.

Make the front interfacing ½ inch wider than the front facing. Extend the front interfacing to include the shoulder and armhole down to the point at which the armhole swings into an underarm curve. Generally a notch appears here in the pattern. With a curved line, connect this point with the inner edge of the front interfacing (a). Extend the interfacing to the hemline in a straight line.

When a back interfacing is used, draw a slightly curved line, starting 4 to 5 inches down from the neckline at the center back to the point on the armhole seam that swings into the underarm curve (b). Back notches will appear here on the pattern.

a   b

INTERFACING MATERIALS (FOUNDATION OR SHAPING MATERIALS).

Theoretically, almost any fabric can be used as an interfacing (or underlining). (Every sewer has drawers full of odds and ends that can be pressed into service for such purposes.) However, a number of supporting materials have been developed for such purposes. These are divided into three classes: the wovens, the nonwovens, and the fusibles (iron-ons). They vary in character—limp to stiff. They vary in weight—light to heavy. They vary in width—18 inches to 72 inches. They vary in price. They vary in cleanability: some are washable, some are dry-cleanable. Some come in an array of colors, some come in neutrals.

Woven fabrics can be eased, stretched, and blocked to fit the figure. Nonwoven materials cannot. For example, wool, a woven fabric, can be molded into a figure-conforming shape, while the nonwoven felt cannot. The same holds true for interfacings and underlinings. Since shaping is a very important part of dressmaking and tailoring it is wise to choose woven interfacings and underlining for this purpose. Save the nonwovens for design details that require more stiffness.

Generally, the fusibles are best used in small areas. Use them to stiffen standing collars, cuffs, and belts, and as reinforcement for areas to be slashed, like buttonholes and bound pockets. There are many of these iron-ons. They come in varying weights: sheer webs to canvas.

Interfacings are generally compatible in weight with the fabric they interface. That is, lightweight fabric—lightweight interfacing; medium-weight fabric—medium-weight interfacing; heavyweight fabric—heavyweight interfacing.

Underlinings, however, may be of any weight or texture that will give the desired effect.

Interfacing and underlining materials are used interchangeably. What is underlining in one garment may be interfacing in another; what is interfacing in one can be underlining in another.

Since there is such a variety of interfacing and underlining materials to choose from, it isn't always easy to make a decision as to which to use. The safest thing to do when you shop for supporting material is to take with you a sample of your fabric and a picture of the design. Slip the interfacing or underlining under the fashion fabric. Study the effect. Decide whether the weight, finish, degree of flexibility, softness, firmness, or crispness of the supporting material will produce the design of the pattern in your chosen fashion fabric. There are no hard and fast rules. The only test is whether or not *this* material will produce and hold the lines of *this* particular fabric. You must be the judge. *(See* LIGHT- TO MEDIUM-WEIGHT INTERFACINGS.)

INTERFACING SEAMS AND DARTS. If the interfacing is very lightweight, its seams and darts may be included in all construction seams. They are treated as if they were underlining material rather than interfacing. *(See* UNDERLINING: CONSTRUCTION.)

Standard seams in heavy, springy, or resilient interfacing produce considerable bulk that often cannot be pressed flat to produce an unobtrusive construction. Special stitching methods are required. *See* ABUTTED DART; ABUTTED SEAM; LAPPED DART; LAPPED (OVERLAP) SEAM; CATCH-STITCHED DART; CATCH-STITCHED SEAM.

INTERLINING. Any coat or suit may be winterproofed for warmth by the insertion of an interlining between the interfaced garment and the lining. You may interline as much or as little of your coat or jacket as you would like. If you are the type that never thaws out till the end of spring, better interline the whole coat, sleeves and all. If a double layer of interlining will help you face the winter winds, here's your chance. (The usual bought coat never does seem to have enough interlining for warmth.) Just make sure there is sufficient room in your garment for the insertion of the interlining.

Lamb's wool is the traditional interlining material. It comes in several colors and weights. Very lightweight wool blends or polyester fleece are new but much-used interlining fabrics. The care requirements of the interlining should be compatible with the rest of the garment. Since everything else in the garment has been sponged, play it safe and sponge the interlining too.

Another presently fashionable way to add warmth is via a quilted, knit, or pile lining. Such bulky fabrics double as lining

and interlining. They contain features of both.

INTERLINING INSERTION. In addition to warmth, an interlining also adds weight and bulk. The trick is to get the coat as warm as possible with as little weight and bulk as possible. There are several ways in which this can be done, depending on how much time and patience you have and the style and bulk of the garment.

Whichever method you choose, it is best to work over a dress form or tailor's ham. This will provide just the amount of ease necessary to preclude any pulling or buckling of the outer fabric.

METHOD 1. EACH SECTION SEPARATELY INSERTED

The ultimate in interlining insertion is a complete hand operation in which each section of the interlining is set and stitched into position individually. It is trimmed in such a way that the edges of interlining just meet the edges of all seam and dart allowances, all facings and hems. All edges are joined by catch stitching.

By this method, there is never any place on the garment that has more than two thicknesses of fabric—not even a small overlap.

Perhaps you are thinking this is carrying the flatness fetish a bit too far. Consider this: in addition to the trimness of this type of insertion, it has another advantage. It is often much easier to handle one piece of interlining at a time than to insert another great coat into what may already be a voluminous garment.

It may be the most work, but Method 1 is the most precise and the least bulky of the several suggested methods.

Method 2. Interlining-Lining Inserted as One Fabric

By this method, the interlining is applied to the lining rather than to the garment. The two layers are then treated as one fabric.

Cut out the lining and interlining. When there is a center-back seam in the interlining, either cut the center back on a fold instead or join the back sections with a lapped (overlap) seam (q.v.).

Form the pleat at the back of the lining

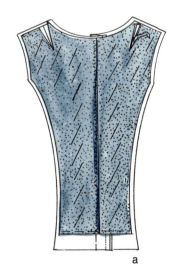

a

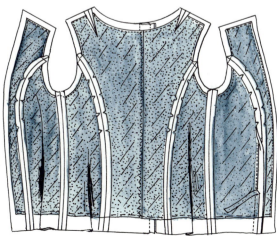

b

but *not* the interlining. The loosely woven interlining has a degree of "give," making the pleat that provides "give" in the lining unnecessary.

Tailor-baste (q.v.) each section of interlining to the wrong side of each section of lining and handle as one layer (a). Pin and stitch all darts and seams by the standard method. Slash the darts open. Trim the seam allowances of the interlining close to the stitching. Press the darts open.

With right sides together, stitch all vertical seams of the lining-interlining sections, leaving the shoulder seams open (b). Trim the interlining seam allowances close to the stitching. Press them open.

Stay-stitch the two layers along the front, shoulders, neck, and armhole edges. Trim the interlining seam allowances close to the stitching (b).

Remove all bastings. Insert the interlining-lining as a lining (q.v.).

Method 3. Interlining and Lining Inserted Separately

Cut out and construct the lining. (*See* lining.) Cut out and construct the interlining as follows.

Overlap and stitch all vertical seams and all darts in the interlining in the same way as interfacing seams and darts (q.v.). Use a longer straight or zigzag stitch and a looser tension. (Interlining material, being loosely woven, tends to be stretchier.) Trim the seam allowances on both sides close to the stitching (a).

Turn the coat inside out. Place the interlining in position against the wrong side of the outer fabric. Match the side seams. Match any shaping seams and darts. Smooth the fabric so there is no rippling.

The interlining may go in before the shoulder pads are attached (a preferable method) or may be put in place over the shoulder pads.

Fasten the side seams with permanent basting. Overlap the shoulder seams and fasten them with catch stitching (b).

Trim the interlining seam allowances of all outside edges. Trim the interlining to meet the top of the hem (b). Fasten all outside edges with catch stitching.

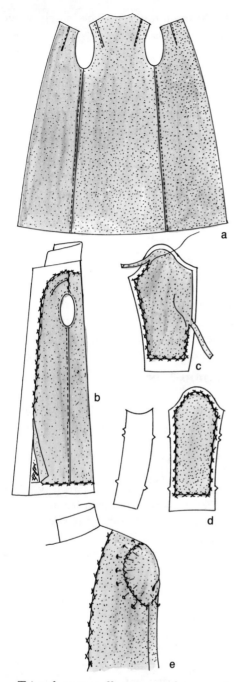

as the one-piece sleeve and its interlining (d).

If the sleeve interlining is put in as a separate unit after the sleeve has been stitched, overlap it on the armhole seam (e) and catch-stitch.

Turn up the sleeve hem to meet the interlining. Catch-stitch the edge of the hem to the interlining.

When the interlining has been completed and inserted, put in the lining by the usual method. *(See* LINING.)

INTERLINING PATTERN. Even if the pattern doesn't call for it, it is possible to interline a coat or jacket. Patterns rarely include a pattern for an interlining. Generally one must work out one's own pattern and layout.

Use the adjusted lining pattern with the modifications described here for an unfitted coat or jacket and the adjusted original pattern for a fitted garment. In the latter case you will, in effect, be backing the garment with a layer of interlining material. Make certain that your pattern has sufficient ease to accommodate this extra layer.

One-piece sleeves may be completely interlined. In a two-piece sleeve, generally only the upper sleeve is interlined. In a kimono sleeve, gussets (when present) are *not* interlined.

Start with the lining pattern. Eliminate the center-back pleat. Extend the lines of the front-shoulder dart-tuck until they converge to form a dart. Retain the back shoulder dart. Trim away the interlining at all outside edges so it will just meet the front facings, the back facing, and the hem. Allow only 1/4-inch seam allowances at the shoulder, the armhole, and the sleeve cap for overlapping seams.

In most coats, these days, the lining is attached to the hem, thereby covering the interlining. If the lining is to hang free of the coat, cut the interlining sufficiently shorter so that it won't be visible.

INVERTED PLEAT. *See* PLEAT TYPES.

INVISIBLE ZIPPER INSTALLATION. With this type of installation, the only break in

Trim the seam allowances of a one-piece sleeve interlining. Apply to the underside of the sleeve before stitching the underarm seam. Catch-stitch the interlining edges to the sleeve seam lines (c). Proceed with the usual sleeve construction.

In a two-piece sleeve, generally only the upper sleeve is interlined. Handle the upper sleeve and interlining in the same way

the continuity of the fabric design is that of a normal seam.

There are two types of invisible zippers. One is a featherweight nylon coil for lightweight fabrics. The other is a metal-tooth chain for heavier-weight fabrics. They are both installed in the same way.

The easiest installation by machine is with a special zipper foot designed for this purpose, though the zipper may also be stitched with the regulation zipper foot or by hand.

Before setting, flatten the nylon coil (it has a tendency to curl up). Press it flat with your finger or with an iron. Only the tape should be visible when the zipper is being set.

In all other installations, the seam in which a zipper is set is stitched first, leaving an opening for the zipper. One does just the opposite with the invisible zipper. It is installed first; then the seam below it is stitched.

Place the opened zipper face down on the right side of the fabric. The coil or teeth are placed on the seam line, while the zipper tape is in the seam allowance. The top stop of the zipper is placed 1/2 inch below the cross seam line.

Slide the special zipper foot into position so the coil or metal fits into the appropriate groove and the needle can be lowered into the hole. Insert the needle in the fabric. Lower the presser foot. Stitch from the top of the tape until the foot touches the slider at the bottom (a). Lock with backstitching.

Pin the second side of the zipper to second side of the opening on the right side of the fabric. The tape is set the same distance from the top as on the first side. Set the groove of the zipper foot over the coil or metal. Bring the needle down into the tape through the hole. Lower the presser foot. Stitch the second side like the first (b).

Close the zipper. Place the right sides of the fabric together below the zipper, with seam lines matching. Pin. Slide the zipper foot to the left of the zipper so it clears it, making it operate like a regulation zipper

foot. Insert the needle through the outside notch, 1/2 inch above the zipper end and 1/16 inch to the left of it. Lower the foot and stitch to the end of the seam (c). There will be 1 inch of zipper tail extending below the installed zipper. Stitch each side of the tail tape to the seam allowance. This stitching must not show on the right side.

No stitching shows on the right side. Successfully done, this closing looks just like another seam (d).

Theoretically, it should be easy enough to stitch the garment seam below the zipper. In reality, it is hard to be precise because of the bulk of the zipper. Some sewers find it easier to stitch the seam below the zipper with the regulation zipper foot, then come back and backstitch that half-inch length above the zipper end by hand.

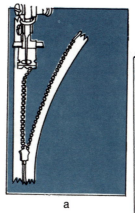

a

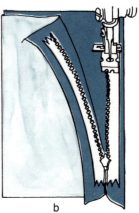

b

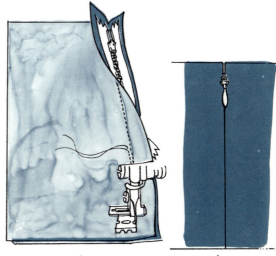

c   d

The invisible zipper can be installed in the same way *with the use of a regulation zipper foot.* The placement of the zipper is the same. However, it is helpful to baste it to position before stitching. Stitch close to the coil or teeth.

Though it may take a little more time, the *hand-stitched installation* of even this zipper is much easier to manage. The placement is the same. Instead of machine stitching, use backstitching very close to the zipper teeth. This installation also eliminates the problem at the lower end of the zipper.

IRONING TECHNIQUES. Fabrics that can be laundered are ironed smooth. All others are pressed. Ironing is a gliding motion; the iron is pushed along. Because of the long stroke, ironing is always done on a flat surface.

All the general rules for pressing (q.v.) are also applicable to ironing. Some of the pressing equipment (q.v.) can also be used for ironing. In addition, there are the following hints for ironing.

1. Iron with the grain. Iron *with,* not across, seams and pleats.
2. Suit the heat setting to the fabric. Generally, if the work wrinkles under the iron, the iron is too hot or too cool. If the fabric gets glazed or shiny, the iron is too hot.
3. Smooth and guide the work with one hand along seams, hems, sleeve lengths, yokes, and so on, while the other hand glides the iron along.
4. If seams are puckered, hold one end firmly, stretch the work slightly, and iron in the direction of the stitching. This should distribute the thread throughout the length of the seam.
5. As you iron, pull taut all straight edges of collars, cuffs, lapels, and the like to keep them straight. Iron from the points or corners toward the center of each to avoid wrinkles.
6. Iron shaped sections of the garment (darts, shaping seams) over the tailor's ham.

7. In all double thicknesses, iron on the wrong side first till semidry, then finish on the right side.
8. Nose the iron around buttons, buckles, or other projections.
9. Iron raised surfaces (embroidery and so on) face down on a soft, padded surface with a slight rotary motion.
10. Keep all zippers closed while ironing. Iron along each side of the zipper with the point of the iron but do not iron the zipper itself.
11. Iron skirt hems harder along the fold and lighter at the stitched top of the hem. Iron the hems from the bottom up rather than around.
12. Prevent imprints of seam allowances, darts, tucks, pleats, and the like by using a brown wrapping-paper cushion. *(See* PRESSING: PREVENT IMPRINTS.) If imprints do occur in ironing, lift the edge that produced the imprint and iron beneath it.

SUGGESTED ORDER FOR IRONING COMPLETED GARMENT

Iron all *interior* parts—facings, pockets, inside of hems, seams, darts, bands, and so on.

Iron all *dangling* parts—sleeves, belts, bows, ties, pockets, flaps, and the like. If there is a cuff, iron the underside first, then the right side.

Iron all *trimmings:* ruffles, edgings, applied pockets, appliqués, and the like.

Iron the shoulder and yoke areas (if the design includes this).

Iron the tops of long garments before the lower parts.

If there is a back or front opening, start at one opening side and iron around the garment to the second side of the opening.

Iron the collar last, beginning with the collar facing, then the right side of the collar.

Touch up any creases or wrinkles resulting from handling the garment. Be sure to use a press cloth on all right-side touch-ups.

For ironing pants, *see* PRESSING PANTS.

JERSEY. A single-filling knit of wool, worsted, cotton, silk, or synthetic fibers. It is made with the stockinette stitch on a circular loom, which produces a tubular cloth. The face of the fabric is smooth, though lengthwise wales are visible. The wrong side of the fabric shows purl stitches.

Because of the considerable crosswise stretch, it is wise to use the fabric on the vertical grain. Avoid crosswise or diagonal seams and flared or circular skirts. Take great care in cutting, for the edges tend to curl. *See* KNIT FABRICS.

JEWELED BUTTON. A beautiful but impractical closing. Because of its setting, a jeweled button functioning like a regular button can do damage to itself or to the garment fabric. In continually sliding in and out of the buttonhole, the stones can come undone and the prongs eventually snag the fabric.

The solution? Sew the button to the end of the buttonhole, which may be completed or unfinished on the underside (a). The garment actually closes with covered snaps sewn in place under the fake operation (b).

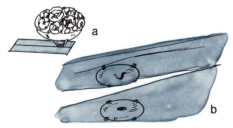

JOINING BIAS-CUT FABRIC TO BIAS-CUT FABRIC. *See* BIAS SEAMS.

JOINING BIAS-CUT FABRIC TO STRAIGHT FABRIC. *See* BIAS SEAMS.

JOINING CROSS SEAMS. Stitch each seam and press it open. Free the cross-seam areas of bulk by trimming away some of the seam allowances in either of the two ways shown (a).

Place the fabric with right sides together and cross seams matching. Put the point of a pin through both thicknesses of the matching seams (b). Slide it along the seam line of the under surface and bring it up on the seam line of the upper surface. The pin spans the cross seam. Pin the seam allowances on each side of the matched seam line to hold it in place while stitching.

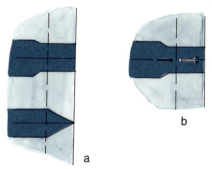

Stitch across the pins very slowly and very carefully to run less risk of striking them. They truly are the best way to hold the matching seams in place. If you insist on using thread to hold the cross seam in place, use a backstitch rather than a basting stitch. It holds more securely.

JOINING FITTED BODICE TO FITTED SKIRT. With right sides together, slip the bodice into the skirt (a). Match the waist seam lines, the side seams, center fronts and backs, and any notches. Pin at frequent intervals, placing the pins at right angles to the seam. Stretch or ease as necessary to make the skirt and bodice fit each other. Diagonally trim the seam allowances of darts and cross seams to eliminate bulk.

With the bodice inside the skirt, stitch the waistline seam from one placket edge to the other (b). Press the seam as stitched. Finish the edges of the seam allowances with zigzag or overedge stitching.

Pull the bodice out of the skirt. Press the seam allowances toward the bodice. If necessary to prevent stretching, stay the waistline seam.

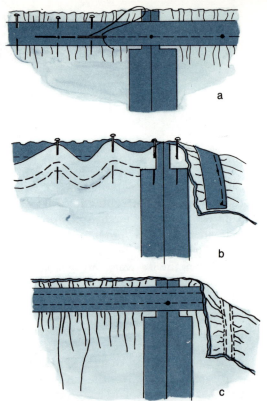

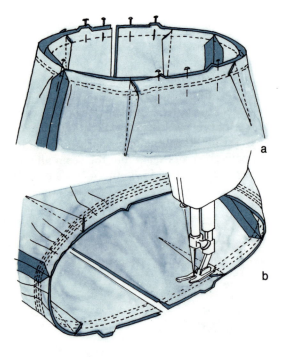

stay, distributing the fullness evenly between the markings. Baste (a).

Divide, mark, and gather the second garment unit in the same way as the first.

With right sides together, pin (at right angles to the seam) the second garment unit to the first, matching all markings (b). Draw up the gathers to fit. Distribute the fullness evenly between the markings. Baste.

Stitch through all thicknesses on the seam line. Make a second row of stitching in the seam allowance. With the stay uppermost, press the seam allowances (c).

JOINING GATHERED EDGE TO GATHERED EDGE. Cut a stay of seam binding the length of the finished seam. Section it into halves, quarters, eighths. Mark with pins or basting thread. In a similar manner, section the first of the garment units to be gathered. Make two rows of hand or machine gathering, one on the seam line, the other in the seam allowance.

Pin the stay to the wrong side of the first unit over the seam line, matching the markings. Place the pins at right angles to the seam. Draw up the gathering to fit the

JOINING GATHERED EDGE TO STRAIGHT EDGE. Section off the length to be gathered into halves, quarters, eighths, and as many other sections as convenient for the length. Mark with pins, notches, or thread loops. In a similar manner, section off the straight length to which the fullness is to be joined. Place two rows of hand or machine gathering, one along the seam line, the other in the seam allowance.

With right sides together, place the gathered edge against the straight edge, matching markings. Pin at right angles to the seam (a). Draw up the fullness until it equals the straight edge. Distribute the fullness evenly between the markings.

Secure the gathering with pinning, basting, or backstitching. If the fabric is light- to medium-weight, simply pinning or basting may be enough before machine stitching. If the fabric is heavy, slithery, or pile, backstitch. This locks the folds of the gathers in place. Fullness controlled in this way is not likely to be dislodged by subsequent machine stitching.

With gathered side up, stitch on the seam line, correcting and redistributing the fullness where necessary (b). Hold the fabric taut on either side of the needle so the gathers do not get stitched into little pleats.

Trim and/or finish the seam edge with a zigzag or overedge stitch.

On the wrong side, press the seam allowance toward the straight edge. Do not press the gathers flat. Use lengthwise strokes, working the tip of the iron into the gathers (c).

JOINING INWARD CORNER TO OUTWARD CORNER.

The trick to easy joining of these opposing corners is a simple clip.

Reinforce the inward corner with stay stitching in the seam allowance just inside the seam line for about 1 inch on both sides of the corner (a). Clip the corner almost to the stitching, being careful not to cut into it (b).

Spread the clipped corner to fit the outward corner, raw edges aligned. Pin and/or baste. Stitch on the seam line, pivoting at the corner (c). Use small stitches as a corner reinforcement.

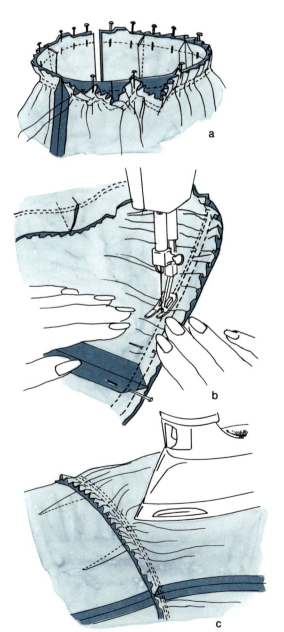

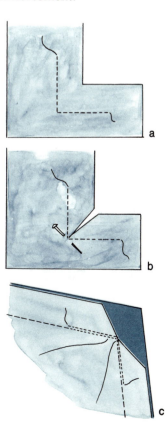

JOINING KNIT TO WOVEN FABRIC. Usually the knit section of a garment is cut slightly smaller than the woven section to which it will be joined. Divide into eighths and pin-mark both sections of fabric. With right sides together, match the markings. Pin and/or baste, stretching the knit fabric to fit the woven. Stitch with the knit side up.

JOINING MATCHING CROSS SEAMS, PLAIDS, STRIPES, CHECKS, OR MOTIFS AT ZIPPER OPENINGS. When a zipper is installed by hand stitching, one has perfect control in matching cross seams, plaids, stripes, checks, and motifs. It takes a little more doing when the stitching is done by machine.

Machine-stitch the first side of the zipper as usual. Fold under the seam allowance of the second side. Match exactly all cross seams, plaids, stripes, motifs (a). Using narrow strips of basting tape, apply them horizontally, at intervals, across the closing on the right side of the garment.

When a *standard zipper* is used, topstitch. Remove the tape.

When an *invisible zipper* is used, turn to the wrong side. Pencil-mark the zipper tape at each seam line or unit (b). Remove the tape from the right side. Open the zipper. Match the markings on the zipper tape with the seams, lines, or motifs of the fabric. Stitch as usual.

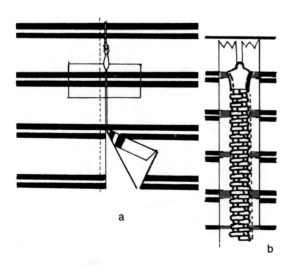

a

b

JOINING MATCHING PLAIDS, STRIPES AND CHECKS. Use the same method as that for joining cross seams (q.v.).

JOINING PILE OR NAP TO SMOOTH, UNNAPPED FABRIC. Place the smooth fabric on the napped fabric and hand-baste with short even stitches or backstitches. Adjust the pressure on the sewing machine for the fabric. With the smooth fabric uppermost, stitch in the direction of the nap.

JUMPSUIT. An all-in-one garment that has bodice and pants joined. The joining may be as one piece (a) or by a waistline seam (b). It is easier to adjust the pattern and fit of the latter type. Choose your pattern size as usual by bust, waist, and hip measurements. You will, in addition, need the following measurements to make the pattern fit.

One-Piece Jumpsuit. To determine the overall fit, take body measurements from the shoulder at the neckline to the center-front waistline, through the crotch, up the center-back waistline to the back shoulder at the neckline. Add 1 inch for lengthwise ease, half in front, half in back.

Compare your measurement with the pattern measurement. The pattern will have built into it the 1-inch ease.

If your hips measure more than 35 inches, add more lengthwise ease—enough for sitting, bending, and so on. There is 1 inch ease at the thigh circumference in a standard-size pattern. Add more if necessary. *(See illustration on next page.)*

Jumpsuit with a Waistline Seam. Measure the bodice length at the center back. Add 1/2 inch ease in length. Measure the crotch depth *(see CROTCH MEASUREMENTS).* Add 1/2 inch ease in length. If hips measure more than 35 inches, add more lengthwise ease.

Compare your measurements with the pattern measurements. *(See illustration on next page.)*

Both Types. Make the usual pattern adjustments for bodice and pants. Transfer

the corrections to a trial muslin and test
the fit before cutting into the material. *See*
BODY MEASUREMENT CHART; PANTS PATTERN
CORRECTIONS.

One-piece Jumpsuit

Jumpsuit with Waistline Seam

KEYHOLE BUTTONHOLE (TAILOR'S BUTTONHOLE) (q.v.). Hand-worked, with an eyelet or hole at the end nearest the closing edge, making it look like a keyhole.

KICK PLEAT. *See* PLEAT TYPES.

KILT PLEAT. *See* PLEAT TYPES.

KIMONO SLEEVE. A sleeve cut all in one with the bodice. It is easy to understand the universal and timeless appeal of this sleeve: it is easy to cut out, easy to sew, easy to wear. There is an ample grace to its appearance.

An unfitted kimono sleeve is comfortable to wear and problem-free to construct (a). The deeper it is, the more freedom (b) but difficult to wear under a coat.

There is an inevitable amount of wrinkling on the underarm of a deep kimono sleeve. This is the nature of the sleeve. The looseness prevents tearing under the arm.

As a kimono becomes more fitted, the wrinkles disappear. Its freedom of movement lessens while the sewing problems

b

increase. With the insertion of a hinge (*see* GUSSET), movement is restored.

Don't be fooled by the deceptively simple appearance of the kimono sleeve. It calls for subtle, careful, and precise fitting to hang right. *See* KIMONO SLEEVE PATTERN CORRECTIONS *and* SHOULDER SEAM.

KIMONO SLEEVE CUT IN ONE WITH A YOKE. This is a frequent theme in design because it provides the kimono sleeve with a closer fit while dispensing with the construction of a gusset.

Reinforce the corner of the yoke/sleeve at the point where yoke ends and sleeve begins. Clip the seam allowance to the corner (a).

a

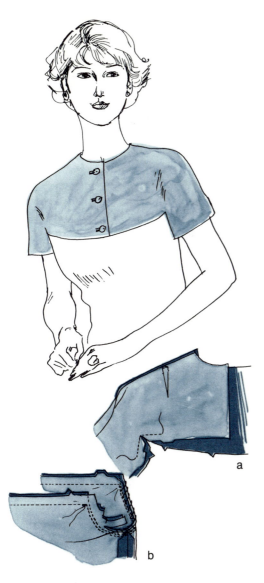

a

b

seam allowances close to the stitching. Finish the raw edges with hand or machine overedge stitching.

Trim and grade the yoke/garment seam allowances, making the yoke seam allowance the narrower of the two. Press them toward the yoke. Leave the underarm seam allowances unpressed.

KIMONO-SLEEVE PATTERN CORRECTIONS. *See* PATTERN CORRECTIONS for general directions.

Broad Shoulders. Draw a slash line on the pattern from the underarm to the shoulder point. Slash the pattern. Spread to the needed amount. Insert pattern paper in the spread area. Redraw the shoulder line, starting at the neck and merging with the new shoulder line.

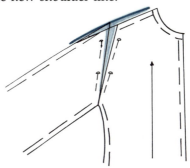

Bust with Large Cup. Draw a vertical slash line on the pattern from shoulder to hem. Draw a horizontal slash line across the bustline. Spread the upper vertical slash at the bustline to the needed amount, tapering to nothing at the shoulder. Spread the lower vertical slash at the bustline to match the upper section and taper to nothing at the hem. Spread the horizontal slash

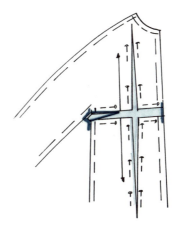

With right sides together, stitch the shoulder and underarm sleeve seams of the front and back yoke/sleeve sections. Press the seam allowances open.

With right sides together, drop the yoke/sleeve sections into the garment, matching the yoke and underarm seams. Pin and/or baste. Stitch the yoke to the garment. Break the thread. Stitch the underarm sections of yoke/sleeve and garment (b). This procedure is easier and more accurate than stitching one continuous seam and pivoting at the corners.

Make a second row of stitching close to the first at the underarm in the seam allowance. Secure all thread ends. Trim the

evenly across its length. Insert pattern paper in the spread area. Create a dart in the spread space.

Bust with Small Cup. Tuck the pattern vertically, tapering toward the hemline. Tuck the pattern at the bustline, tapering to the underarm seam. Redraw the shoulder and underarm seams.

Prominent Shoulder Blades. Draw an L-shaped slash line on the pattern from the shoulder seam to the underarm seam. Spread vertically evenly to the cross line in the needed amount. Insert pattern paper in the spread areas. Create a shoulder dart in the spread space. Redraw the shoulder and underarm seams.

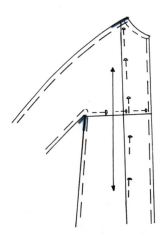

Large Arm. Draw an L-shaped slash line on the pattern into the sleeve, beginning at the overarm seam and ending at the shoulder seam. Slash and spread the pattern at the upper end, taper to nothing at the lower end. For a large lower as well as upper arm, taper to a smaller amount rather than to nothing. Insert pattern paper in the spread area. Redraw the shoulder/overarm seam.

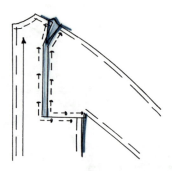

Sloping Shoulders. Draw a slash line on the pattern from underarm to shoulder point. Slash the pattern. Set the sleeve down from the shoulder line in an amount sufficient to provide the needed slope. Redraw the shoulder seam, starting at the neckline and merging with the new dropped shoulder line. Redraw the underarm seam.

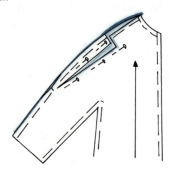

Narrow Shoulders. Draw a slash line on the pattern from the underarm to the shoulder point. Slash the pattern. Overlap the needed amount on the shoulder. Pin or Scotch-tape. Redraw the shoulder and underarm seams.

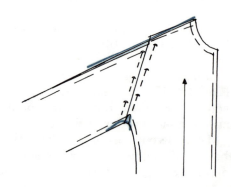

Square Shoulders. Draw a slash line on the kimono sleeve pattern from the underarm to the shoulder point. Slash the pattern. Raise the sleeve pattern up in an amount sufficient to accommodate the square shoulders. Redraw the shoulder seam, starting at the neckline and merging with the raised shoulder seam. Redraw the underarm seam.

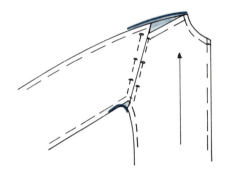

Thick Elbow. Draw an inverted L-shaped slash line on the pattern from the sleeve underarm seam to the shoulder seam. Slash and spread at the elbow. Insert pattern paper in the spread area. Redraw the underarm seam line.

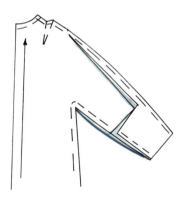

Thin Arm. Take off some of the pattern at the shoulder and underarm seams.

KIMONO SLEEVE: SHOULDER SEAM FITTING.

The same rules apply to the fitting of the shoulder of a kimono sleeve as for fitting the shoulder seam (q.v.).

The shoulder seam line is set from the neck to the shoulder point and carried down the length of the sleeve. When properly placed, the side seam appears as a continuation of this line. Take off or add some of the front or back sleeve in order to bring the sleeve seam into line. Carry the correction down from shoulder to hem.

KIMONO SLEEVE WITH GUSSET. *See* GUSSET.

KIMONO SLEEVE WITHOUT A GUSSET.

When there is no gusset, there is considerable strain on the underarm seam of the kimono sleeve. Some reinforcement is required to keep the seam from breaking open. Use one of the following methods. Methods 1 and 2 produce reinforcements not visible from the right side. Methods 3 and 4 are visible from the right side. The tape or seam binding is placed over the seam line of the *back* garment section.

All Methods Start the Same Way. With right sides together, pin and/or baste the underarm seam. Cut a 4- to 5-inch length of bias seam binding or twill tape for each sleeve. This may be used as a single thickness or be folded lengthwise to be used double. The latter is a stronger reinforcement—good for heavier fabrics—but it is a bit bulkier. Using the steam iron, shape the binding or tape to fit the curve of the underarm seam.

METHOD 1

Center the single (a) or double (b) seam binding or tape over the seam line. Baste, then stitch through all thicknesses. Use a shorter stitch on the curved section of the seam. Remove the basting.

Press the seam flat. Clip the seam allowances along the curve (b), being careful not to clip the tape or binding. Press the seam allowances open over the tailor's ham.

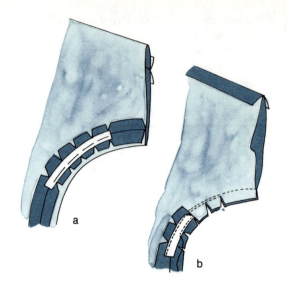

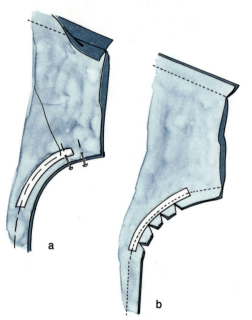

METHOD 2

Stitch the underarm seam, using smaller stitches on the curve. Remove any basting. Clip the seam allowances along the curve. Press the seam flat, then open over a tailor's ham. Center the shaped length of

bias seam binding or tape over the open seam and baste it through the seam line (a).

Spreading the clips to fit the curve, stitch the seam binding or tape to the seam allowances on each side of the seam line. Remove the basting (b). For extra strength, make another row of stitching beside the first. *Note:* The stitching goes through seam allowances and seam binding or tape *only*. It does not come through to the right side of the garment.

METHOD 3

Stitch the underarm seam, using smaller stitches on the curve. Clip the seam allowances along the curve. Press the seam flat, then open over a tailor's ham.

Center the shaped length of bias seam binding or tape over the open seam and baste through the seam line to the right side.

From the right side, stitch through all

thicknesses along the curve on each side of the seam line and fairly close to it. Remove the basting.

METHOD 4

After the underarm seam has been stitched, clipped, and pressed open, center the shaped seam binding or tape over the open seam. Baste through all thicknesses on both sides of the seam line (a).

From the right side, stitch through all thicknesses directly over the seam, using a narrow zigzag stitch and 12- to 15-stitch length (b). Remove the basting.

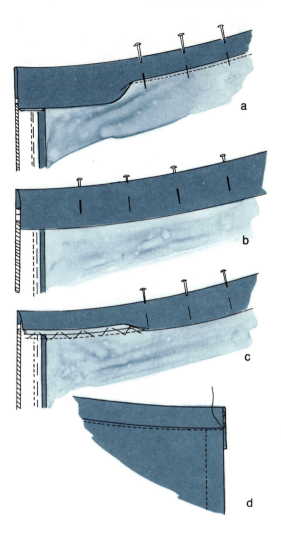

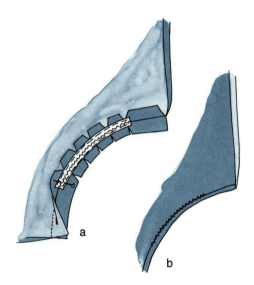

KNIFE PLEATS. *See* PLEAT TYPES.

KNIT BANDING. If used as an extension, *see* WOVEN AND KNITTED BANDINGS USED AS EXTENSIONS. If used for close fit, *see* RIBBED BANDING.

KNIT BINDING. Available by the yard in a variety of colors and widths. Or cut a strip of binding from knit fabric on the crosswise grain.

With right sides together, stitch the binding to the garment along the seam lines. Press the seam flat. Bring the binding over the seam allowances, folding it to the wrong side.

If the binding is made of *knit fabric,* turn under its raw edge along the seam line (a). Pin to position and slipstitch. Or treat like the commercial binding.

If the binding is a *commercial knit binding,* let the edge lie flat, extending beyond the seam line (b). There are two ways of fastening the underside.

By Hand. Using a blindstitch (q.v.), fasten the underside of the binding to the garment along the seam line (c). Do not permit the stitches to come through to the right side.

By Machine. From the right side, topstitch through all thicknesses along the well of the seam (d).

KNIT FABRIC AS LINING. As a way of adding warmth to a garment in a decorative way, use knit fabric as a lining. *See* PILE LINING for suggestions.

KNIT FABRICS.

No wonder they're so popular! All the ease of movement one could want (no need to add any), all the shape without stitching one needs (the figure does all the work), all the mobility desired (they remain unruffled and unmussed by travel). They're supple, they're shapely, they're sensational, they constitute a major part of today's wardrobes.

Whereas woven cloth is made by interlacing horizontal and vertical yarns, knitted fabric is made by intermeshing a series of continuous rows of loops in such a way that each loop interlocks with the preceding loop. A vertical series of loops is called a *wale;* a horizontal series of loops is called a *course. The fact that loops can straighten out when stretched and return to loops when released gives knits their elasticity and flexibility.*

Two stitches, *knit* (a) and *purl* (b) are the basis of knit construction whether by hand or by machine.

The knit stitch produces a flat surface. The purl stitch produces a slightly raised surface. Alternating knit and purl stitches in the same row produces vertical ridges or ribs (c). A rib knit is reversible and provides an excellent, snug fit often used in waistbands, collars, and cuffs.

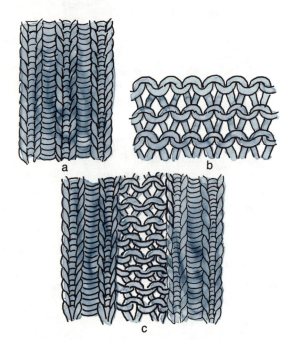

FILLING (WEFT) KNIT

In knitting, when the yarn runs horizontally across the fabric in a series of loops (a), it is called a filling knit (b).

The crosswise yarns are interlocked in a chain of stitches. When a link (loop) in the chain breaks, the fabric "runs" or "ladders." (This is what happens to filling-knit stockings.) For this reason care is required in cutting filling knits.

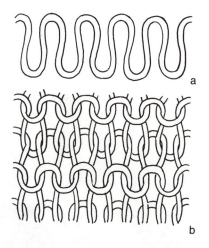

Single-filling knit: usually made on a circular machine that produces a tubular cloth. There is a right and wrong side. The right side is smooth, while visible wales appear on the wrong side. When a filling knit is made with a rib stitch it is the same on both sides.

Filling knits have a moderate to great amount of stretch and tend to sag in areas of stress.

Double knit: (q.v.) filling knit made on a rib-knitting machine. Two yarn and needle sets work simultaneously and cast off stitches in opposite directions so they interlock. The face and back of the fabric may look alike (in which case there is no right or wrong side) or they may be different (use the side you prefer). Unlike single-filling knits, which are made on a circular loom, the double knits are generally knitted flat like woven cloth.

The double-knitting process produces a heavier, firmer, more stable cloth with limited stretch. For this reason, avoid patterns designated "Stretchable Knits Only."

WARP KNIT.

When the loops run vertically, the fabric is a warp knit. In warp knits, the yarn follows a zigzag path and forms a loop at each change of direction (a). These loops interlock with other loops formed by adjoining warp yarns following a similar zigzag path (b).

Fabrics of warp knits aren't as sheer as the filling knits but they are much stronger. (Mesh stockings are an example of a warp knit.) Because they don't run or snag, they are easier to cut.

Variations of warp knits are tricot and raschel knits.

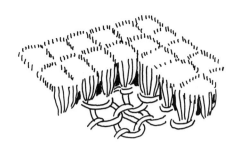

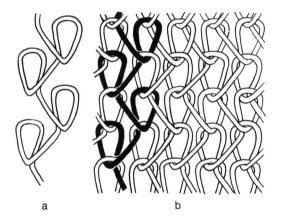

a   b

Pattern Knit: A complex variation of knit and purl stitches made by rearranging, dropping, adding, alternating, and crossing stitches or groups of stitches in much the same way that hand knitting forms intricate patterns. The cable knit and fisherman's knit are examples of pattern knits.

Sliver Knitting. A knit-pile construction, just as velvet is a woven-pile construction. Fake furs are made by this construction.

Sliver knitting produces both the plain jersey backing and the pile at the same time. Bunches of loose fibers are locked in place by the looping action of the backing yarn over the knitting needle.

Like woven materials, knitted fabrics are produced in great variety. This is achieved by using different fibers, different yarns, a variety of patterns, a variety of colors, in-genious and intricate methods of interlocking, and combinations of any of these.

KNITS AND SEWING MACHINE CARE.

Knits demand greater care of the sewing machine than do woven fabrics because they tend to drop more lint, fibers, and finishing granules along the upper threading, the feed, and the bobbin case. Frequent cleaning and oiling are important.

Remove the throat plate, the face plate, and the bobbin case. Where necessary, brush with a lint brush. Wipe with a piece of soft cloth. Oil lightly with sewing machine oil at points indicated in your sewing machine instruction book.

KNITS: CLOSURES. To prevent stretching, stay-stitch all closure areas. Like other fabrics, knit closures may be by zipper, by buttonhole and button, by loop and button.

By Zipper. For lightweight knits, choose a lightweight nylon coil and insert by hand. Avoid invisible zippers, which tend to be too heavy and too rigid. For medium to heavy knits, use light- or medium-weight zippers. If the fabric is firm enough, an invisible zipper can also be used.

By Buttonhole and Button. Limit the size and weight of the button to what the knit can support. Interface all buttonhole areas. Trim the interfacing when the buttonhole is completed. The buttonhole may be bound or hand- or machine-worked. Reinforce the button areas with small scraps of interfacing placed on the underside. Sew the buttons through all layers.

By Loop and Button. Rather than cutting into the knit for a buttonhole, use this closing. The loops may be of either self-fabric or thread.

See listing for each type of closure.

KNITS: FITTING. Patterns for knit fabrics contain a minimum of ease and shaping, relying for these on the elasticity of the fabric. Garments of knit fabrics can, therefore, be fitted closer to the body than a similar design of woven fabric.

If the pattern has been designated for knits, get the same size as you would were you choosing a pattern for a woven fabric. If your knit is loosely woven or stretchy you may be able to get away with a pattern one size smaller than usual. Should you plan to use a pattern designed for woven fabric, you may also be able to use one a size smaller than usual. If you plan to use a pattern you already have in your size, it may be wise to remove some of the ease *(see* EASE ADDED OR SUBTRACTED*)*.

Make all the necessary pattern corrections. For a trial fitting, cut the corrected pattern of tricot material rather than the usual muslin. Its knit construction provides a truer test.

Where stretch would distort a seam or dart, stay the seam with seam binding or narrow twill tape.

Follow the same general rules for fitting as for woven fabrics with the exception of the ease and shaping mentioned above.

KNITS: GAUGE. Used to determine the degree of crosswise stretchability and recovery of the knit fabric. This is an important factor in choosing the right pattern for the material, the kind of stitch, thread, seam construction, and the amount of ease needed in fitting.

Patterns designated "For Knits Only" generally have a gauge like the one in the illustration but you can make one for yourself should you wish.

Fold the fabric 2 inches in from the crosswise edge. Hold the fold of fabric against the gauge. Brace one end of the fabric against one end. Hold the knit at the 4-inch mark and gently stretch. Note the point at which the knit stretches comfortably without distortion and compare this

with the amount of stretch suggested for the particular pattern.

If the 4 inches has stretched to a little less than 5 inches, the knit has minimum stretch.

If the 4 inches has stretched to 5 inches, the knit has moderate stretch.

If the 4 inches has stretched to more than 5 inches, the knit has maximum stretch.

Also note whether the knit returns to its original dimensions when released. This will indicate whether and how much the fabric will stretch out of shape in wearing and whether it should be lined or underlined to prevent sagging. It will also help to determine whether and which seams should be stayed to prevent stretching.

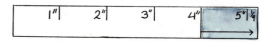

A reading for the amount of lengthwise stretch is valuable in deciding how much lengthwise ease is necessary for a bodice in a garment with a waistline seam or in the crotch length of pants.

KNITS: HAND STITCHING. Hand stitches must have enough play to match the stretch of the fabric without breaking the thread. Whatever the hand stitch, make it "easy," "relaxed," nonrestrictive. Stretch the fabric from time to time both to test the hand stitches and to provide enough thread to accommodate the stretch.

Use the correct ball-point needle and thread. *See* NEEDLE/THREAD/STITCH LENGTH GUIDE.

KNITS: HEMS. Since the greatest amount of stretch in a knit fabric is across the width, a hem must be so handled as to "give" with the crosswise stretch of the fabric. *See* KNITS: HAND STITCHING.

Allow the garment to hang out at least twenty-four to forty-eight hours before setting the hem.

Finish the raw edge with a line of straight stitching 1/4 inch in from the edge or overcast the edge.

In lightweight single-knit fabrics, a narrow hem, hand- or machine-stitched, is preferable to a wide hem. Double-knit fabrics may have the usual 2- to 3-inch turned-up hem. In heavy or firm knits, make a double-stitched hem (q.v.). Fasten all hems with blindstitches (q.v.).

Alternatives to a turned-up hem are a narrow topstitched hem, a hand- or machine-rolled hem, a shell-stitched hem, or a lettuce edge. *See* HEM *and listing for each of the hem types.*

KNITS: LAYOUT, PINNING, CUTTING. The loop construction of knit fabrics gives them an up-and-down movement that calls for a *"With Nap" layout.* In raschel knits made of thick and thin yarns held in place by a chain or series of loops, the end that "unchains" is the top; place the pattern pieces accordingly.

The vertical grain of knit fabric has the least stretch, so most pattern pieces are placed on the lengthwise grain. The maximum stretch is crosswise. If you need strips for bindings, cut them across the width rather than on the bias, which has less stretch. *(See* GRAIN ESTABLISHED IN KNIT FABRIC.)

Don't use the sharp fold of fabric for a fold-of-fabric layout. It may not be the straight vertical grain. Furthermore, the fold cannot be pressed out. If you need a fold of fabric for the pattern layout, refold the fabric along a vertical wale, avoiding the original fold. Fold raschel knits along a vertical chain.

If you can't straighten the knit material (some of it can't be), use a complete pattern on grain on a single layer of material, right side up. (You will need to trace and add the second half of the pattern.) Use ball-point or fine sharp-pointed pins placed in the seam and dart allowances.

The edges of lightweight single knits have a tendency to curl to the right side. Pin the pattern to the wrong side. If curling persists after cutting, overcast all raw edges so they lie flat.

Use sharp shears and long cutting strokes. Cut extended notches on firm knits. Mark the notches on loosely knit fabrics with tailor's tacks. Use basting

thread for all other markings as well. Double knits can take dressmaker's carbon paper for marking but take care that the color does not come through to the right side.

KNITS: LINING. Linings in knits are optional. They add stability to the fabric, making it hang more like a woven fabric, at the cost of losing some of the elasticity. To minimize this loss, use a lining of another single knit (like tricot), add more than usual ease to the lining, or cut it on the bias.

KNITS: MACHINE STITCHING. When stitching knit fabrics all seams must have enough "give" to match the stretch of the fabric and yet not break the thread. There are several ways in which this can be done: by straight stitching, by zigzag stitching, or by stretch stitching. Which method you choose depends on the weight and character of the knit fabric and the capabilities of your sewing machine.

Because *straight stitching* has no give, some stretch comes by providing sufficient length of thread to accommodate the pull. To do this, use shorter stitches and a little less tension. Hold the fabric firmly and pull it slightly both in front of and behind the presser foot as you stitch. *Caution:* Too much stretch makes a wavy seam; too little stretch puckers the seam. Knits with moderate stretch require such stitching. Knits with minimum stretch can be stitched like woven fabrics. Maximum-stretch knits require a light pressure.

The side-to-side movement of the *zigzag stitch* does provide some give and needs no stretch while stitching. For normal sewing, use the narrowest of the zigzag stitches, a reduced tension, and a stitch length appropriate for the fabric. Use this stitch for all the big construction seams—never for top-stitching, which requires the straightest of seams.

Variations and combinations of straight and zigzag stitching appear as stitch patterns on many of the newer sewing machines.

The *stretch stitch* (q.v.) is built into many

of the newer machines and is a great boon to those who love to work with stretch fabrics. Simply set the sewing machine as directed for stretch stitching.

For *all types of machine stitching*—straight, zigzag, or stretch—use the correct ball-point needle and thread. *See* NEEDLE/THREAD/STITCH LENGTH GUIDE.

Avoid ripping, which is difficult and hazardous in knit fabrics.

KNITS: PATTERNS FOR.

A good rule for the selection of a pattern for a knit fabric is this: the fewer the seams the better, and those preferably on the vertical grain, since knits stretch more in a crosswise or diagonal direction. For this reason, avoid crosswise or diagonal seams and flared or circular skirts. Avoid side-seam pockets, which tend to droop. The pattern companies are very helpful in this matter by indicating which patterns are suitable for knit fabrics.

Some patterns are designed primarily for woven fabric but may also be used for some stable, firm knits. Such patterns include standard basic ease allowances and certain design ease allowances for the particular style. Keep this in mind when fitting garments made of knit fabrics from these patterns.

Patterns designated "Recommended for Knits" or "Suitable for Knits" are designed mainly for wovens but from the standpoint of design would be equally suitable for knits. These patterns contain standard basic ease and design ease for the particular style. There are pattern suggestions for specific knit fabrics that can be used.

Patterns labeled "Stretchable Knits Only" are designed to utilize the stretchability of the fabric for shaping and ease. Their measurements are the same as body measurements without ease. Patterns so labeled should not be used for woven fabrics or for firm or medium knits. It is a good idea to follow the pattern suggestions for types of knits.

KNITS: PRESSING.

A softly padded ironing board is preferable to a firmly padded one for knits. Observe all the general rules for pressing (q.v.). Press with the lengthwise rib or wale. Pressing across the ribs stretches the fabric.

KNITS: SEAMS.

There are as many different seam possibilities for knits as there are for wovens. The choice depends on the type of garment, the style, the fiber, the weight and texture of the fabric, the amount of stress on the seam (its location and the tightness of the garment), and the degree of stretch of the knit.

Most seams are not stayed, so they can stretch with the rest of the fabric. It is advisable, however, to stay-stitch the neck, armhole, and waistline seams to prevent their stretching. Do not stay-stitch loosely woven knits. Instead, stitch them 1/4 inch from the cut edge to prevent raveling.

PLAIN SEAMS

Plain Seam with Straight Stitch. *(See* TAUT STITCHING.) Press the seam allowances as stitched, then open.

Plain Seam with Narrow Zigzag Stitch. Using the narrowest zigzag stitch on the machine, stitch under tension. Press the seam allowances as stitched, then open.

If stitching tends to be wavy or if cloth has tendency to stretch, place a thread on one seam, then zigzag over it for stability. Hold it taut while sewing. Press the seam before removing the extra thread.

Overlock and overedge seams take advantage of stitch patterns that both join and finish in one operation.

Overlock Seam. Set the machine for the overlock stitch. Trim the seam allowances to 1/4 inch. Stitch the seam (a). Press. Note that this stitch is a combination straight stitch (along the seam line) and a zigzag stitch over the raw edges.

Overedge Seam. Set the machine for any overedge stitch. Trim the seam allow-

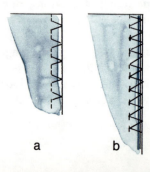

a   b

ances to 1/4 inch. Stitch the seam (b). Press. This stitch encloses the raw edges.

DOUBLE-STITCHED SEAMS

These consist of two rows of stitching, the first of which is generally a straight stitch. For the second row there are three possibilities.

1. Make another row of straight stitching 1/8 inch from the first (a).
2. Make a row of overedge stitching 1/8 to 3/8 inch beyond the first. Trim the seam allowances close to the second row of stitching (b) and press as stitched to one side.
3. Trim the seam allowances before stitching the second row. Make the second row of any overedge stitch (c).

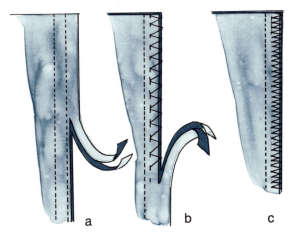

a   b   c

KNITS: SLEEVE SETTING AND STITCH-ING.

Raglan, kimono, strap, and set-in sleeves in firm or medium-firm knit fabrics are all set and stitched by standard methods.

Set-in sleeves in loosely woven or stretchy knits are best set like shirt sleeves. Stitch the sleeve cap to the open armhole. Start the stitching at the shoulder marking and stitch toward the underarm seam, first one side, then the other. Stitch the underarm seam of sleeve and garment in one continuous seam.

To set and stitch by this method, there should be less ease and less cap width. *See* SET-IN SLEEVE CAP EASE *and* SHIRT SLEEVE.

KNITS: TO ESTABLISH GRAIN. *See* GRAIN ESTABLISHED IN KNIT FABRIC.

KNITS: TO REMOVE EXCESS SHRINK-AGE BEFORE CUTTING.

One can't rely on the elasticity of knits to guarantee fit after cleaning or laundering. It is best to remove the excess shrinkage before cutting out the garment.

Most fabrics have some designation as to whether they can be dry-cleaned or washed either by hand or by machine. Handle the fabric in accordance with the fabric label instructions. If the fabric is likely to fray in the process, stay-stitch any straightened edges.

Bonded fabrics generally do not have to be preshrunk.

Silk knits need dry cleaning. *Wool knits* can be sponged like any other woolen fabric. *Knits of synthetic fibers* can be laundered.

Machine Washing. Handle in the same way you plan to launder the completed garment. Use warm to cool water, a mild detergent, and a gentle cycle. An antistatic water softener is also recommended. Put the washed fabric into the dryer along with a *dry* Turkish towel to absorb the moisture. Set the dryer for a low temperature. Remove the fabric before completely dry. Dry over a padded shower rod or on a flat surface. Turn the fabric to dry both sides as you would a sweater.

Hand Washing. Wash the fabric by hand in warm to cool water, using a mild detergent. Roll in a Turkish towel to remove moisture and dry as suggested above.

KNITS: TO STABILIZE.

If you do not stabilize your knit fabric before cutting it out, you may find that darts and seams carefully fitted and stitched will eventually drop from the desired positions in the settling process.

To stabilize a knit, lay it opened out on a flat surface and let it stay that way overnight.

KNITS: UNDERSTRUCTURE (INTERFAC-ING, UNDERLINING).

How much, whether, where, and what kind of understructure you use or don't use depends on the style of the garment, the character of the knit fabric, and the effect you are striving for.

The possibilities range from the no-understructure of sweater-type construction to the full treatment of a classic tailored garment; from the use of practically weightless organza to firm hair canvas; from settling for quick and easy iron-on interfacing to more traditional time-consuming handwork on standard interfacing fabrics.

Remember, an understructure may deprive you of the elasticity of the knit and its easy comfort but will in exchange provide the hang and stability of firm woven fabric—if that's what you want.

KNITS: ZIPPERS IN. *See* ZIPPER IN KNIT FABRIC.

LABEL. A way of saying you made it and are proud of what you have created. The final, ultimate touch—your signature.

You could order commercial labels; there are such available. Or give it the personal touch by making your own. Embroider your name or initials on your favorite color ribbon. Cross-stitch it in place at the center of the back neckline. It will write "finish" with a flourish.

In lieu of a label, embroider your initials on the lining of a tailored garment a few inches above the right front hipline.

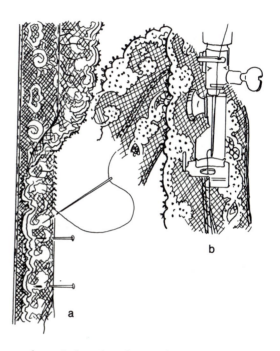

LACE EDGING AND LACE INSERTION JOINED ON A STRAIGHT EDGE. Match the lace patterns when cutting the lengths of lace edging and insertion.

To Join by Hand. With right sides of edge and insertion together, patterns matching, and edges aligned, pin to position. Join the edges with small, shallow overhand stitches (a). Make the stitches just loose enough so the edging and insertion will lie flat when spread.

To Join by Machine. Replace the presser foot with the edge stitcher. Place one length of lace in slot 1 and the other in slot 4, so the edges barely overlap. Adjust the lug for stitching close to the edges of the lace. Stitch (b). When finished, open the seam so the lace lies flat. If you have no edge stitcher, barely overlap one length of lace on the other and stitch.

LACE EDGING APPLIED TO A CURVED EDGE SO OUTER EDGE OF LACE LIES FLAT. Stay-stitch the curved edge of the garment close to the seam line. Pin it to paper.

Pin the lace edging to the paper at the seam line, following the curve of its edge. Keep the fullness at the upper edge of the

lace evenly spaced. Keep the outside edge of the lace flat. Draw up the top thread to fit the curve. Lap the upper edge of the eased lace on the seam line of the fabric. Pin or baste to position.

Join by hand or by machine in the same way as applying lace edging to a straight edge (q.v.).

LACE EDGING APPLIED TO A FINISHED EDGE.

By Hand. With right sides together and edges aligned, place the lace over the finished edge. Working from the lace side and easing the lace slightly, whip the two edges together with small, shallow, somewhat loose overhand stitches (a). Spread the seam open when finished.

By Machine. Replace the presser foot with the edge stitcher. Place the finished edge in slot 1. Adjust the lug so the stitching will be close to the edge. Insert the lace edging in slot 4 with the edge overlapping it slightly. Stitch (b). If you have no edge stitcher, lap the finished edge over the lace and stitch close to the edge.

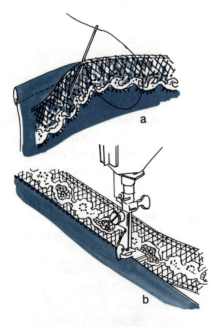

a

b

LACE EDGING APPLIED TO STRAIGHT EDGE. It may be applied over or under a rolled edge. Which you choose is a matter of design.

By Hand. Trim the seam allowance of the fabric edge to 1/4 inch. To position the lace over the rolled edge, place the right side of the lace over the right side of the fabric on the seam line and baste (a). To position the lace under the rolled edge, place the right side of the lace against the wrong side of the fabric on the seam line and baste (b).

With the fabric toward you, roll its edge lightly between the thumb and forefinger. Whip the lace over the rolled edge, catching only the edge of the lace. Pull up the stitches just tight enough to hold the roll in place.

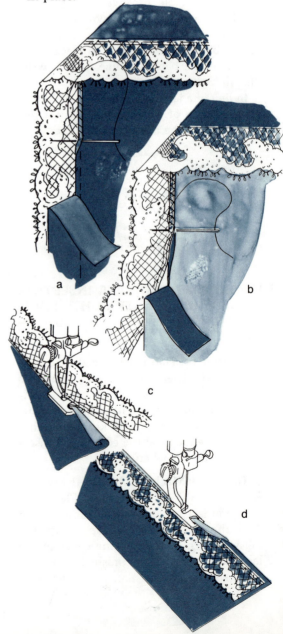

a

b

c

d

By Machine. The lace edging and a narrow hem are stitched in one operation with the use of the hemmer foot. As with the hand operation, the lace may be stitched in place by slipping it over (c) or under (d) the hem. If you do not have a hemmer foot, roll the hem edge by hand and apply the lace edging over or under the hem.

LACE EDGING GATHERED AND APPLIED TO A CURVED EDGE.

Mark the seam line on the right side of the fabric. Stay-stitch the curved edge close to it. Draw up the top thread of the lace edging to fit the curve and to the desired degree of fullness evenly distributed. Apply and stitch to the garment edge in the same way as for lace edging applied to a straight edge (q.v.).

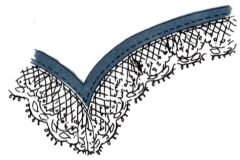

LACE EDGING GATHERED AND APPLIED TO A CURVED POSITION WITHIN THE GARMENT.

Mark the curved position line on the right side of the fabric. Draw the top thread of the lace edging to fit the curve and to the desired degree of fullness evenly distributed. With fabric and lace right side up, pin and baste to position.

Join by hand with small, shallow overhand stitches.

Join by machine with a straight stitch, a narrow, open-spaced zigzag stitch, or one of the other decorative zigzag stitches.

LACE EDGING GATHERED AND APPLIED TO A STRAIGHT EDGE.

Gathered lace may be applied over or under a rolled hem in the same way as lace edging applied to a straight hem (q.v.).

Gather the lace edging by pulling the selvage thread to the desired fullness. Ease the lace back on the thread and distribute the fullness evenly. Stay-stitch the fabric close to the seam line. Trim the seam allowance to 1/4 inch.

Gathered Lace Under the Rolled Edge. Roll the fabric hem to the underside. Place the lace over the rolled hem, right side of lace against wrong side of fabric. Whip stitch the roll catching the edge of the lace (a).

Gathered Lace Over the Rolled Edge. With right sides of gathered lace and fabric together, baste on the seam line. On the underside, roll the edge of the fabric.

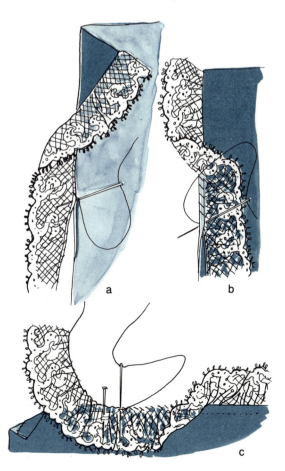

Whipstitch the roll, catching the edge of
the lace (b).

Gathered edging may be *applied to a finished
edge* (c) in the same way as lace edging applied to a finished edge (q.v.).

**LACE EDGING OR INSERTION APPLIED
TO A CORNER.** Miter the lace insertion
or edging at the corner. Pin. Cut away the
excess lace at the miter (a). Use overhand
stitches to join the cut edges by hand or a
narrow zigzag stitch to join by machine.

When the lace insertion is joined to the
lace edging at a corner, miter the lace insertion first. Gather the lace edging around
the mitered corner (b) by pulling the top
thread of lace edging for about ½ inch on
either side of the corner—just enough fullness to make the edging lie flat while making the turn. With right sides together,
join the edging to the insertion (q.v.).
Make the stitches go over the loop of
selvage thread used for the gathering.

a

b

c

a
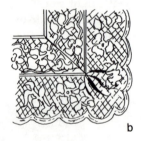
b

LACE EDGINGS AND INSERTIONS. Soft,
dainty, delicate touches that can be added
to blouses, dresses, lingerie, handkerchiefs,
infants' wear, children's clothes, hem
edges, edges of seam allowances, and so
on. They resemble each other and in some
cases can be used interchangeably. *(See also*
LACE INSERTIONS.)

Edgings are designed to be applied to an
edge. One lengthwise edge of the lace (the
edge to be attached to the fabric), the
selvage, is straight. The other edge is decoratively shaped. The top thread of the
selvage can be drawn up for gathering (a).

Insertions are applied like bands within
the length or breadth of the fabric. Both
lengthwise edges are attached to the fabric. Generally both edges are straight (b)
but often they are shaped or scalloped (c).

Press all lace edgings or insertions before applying them to the fabric.

Both edgings and insertions come in a
variety of widths, patterns, types, and fibers. Special sewing techniques consistent
with the delicacy of the lace are required.
They may be stitched by hand or by machine, depending on the garment, the
openness or fragility of the lace, the fabric
to which it is to be joined, the position of
the edging or insertion on the garment,
and how much work you wish to put into
the garment.

Scalloped edges of insertions are easier
to sew by hand. Edgings and insertions applied to delicate fabrics look prettier when
sewn by hand.

Free-hanging ends of edgings are finished with narrow rolled hems (q.v.). Ends
that need joining can be stitched in a
French seam (q.v.) or an overlock seam
(one stitched with an overlock foot). The
couturier method of joining ends is to appliqué the lace along a motif. For both
handwork and machine work, use short
stitches, fine needles, and fine thread.

LACE FABRIC. The loveliest of lace in the
simplest of styles—a formula for a very

special dress that requires very special treatment.

Lace comes in a great variety of types, widths, weights, fibers, and cost. Treat your by-the-yard lace as if it were the precious handmade sort.

Somehow it takes more derring-do to cut into lace than into other fabrics. The obvious solution: cut as little as possible. Choose a style with few seams, few darts and dressmaking details—certainly nothing that requires a slash into the lace like buttonholes or pockets.

Eliminate seams where you can. When the pattern has straight on-grain edges, overlap the seam lines. Pin or Scotch-tape them to position (a). When the pattern has flared edges, remove the flare by drawing new, straight edges parallel to the grain (b). Join the new straight edges as in (a).

The openwork of lace is a net ground having no grain that must be observed. From this standpoint, the lace can be used lengthwise or crosswise. However, lace may have an up-and-down movement of the design or floral units and many do have shaped self-edges or borders. So, while grain is not a consideration in the layout, the directional design of the fabric will require a directional layout. Further, in lace as in other fabrics where design

motifs are involved, strategic placement of the design units and their matching need special consideration.

When possible, use a crosswise layout so there are fewer seams to match and sew (c). This may alter the design of the dress but it has its own plus factors: you can use any shaped self-edge as a trim for the hem, the lower edge of the sleeves, and even, with judicious cutting, for the waistline, hipline, or neckline of the bodice.

Everything below the surface of the lace must preserve the transparent quality that is one of its chief beauties. This means that the understructure (facings, hems, edges, finishes) and the structure (seams, darts, fastenings) must be so planned and worked as to be as inconspicuous as possible. Moreover, wherever possible, structure and understructure should be incorporated in the design of the garment.

LACE FABRIC: APPLIQUÉ TECHNIQUE FOR MOTIFS. A beautiful effect is achieved by the appliqué of cutout lace motifs instead of by a regulation seam. The irregular joining, done as invisibly as possible, preserves the overall design of the lace (a).

Place the lace motifs where they will look best in the garment. Cut around the design motifs that may land on any seam. Leave a 1/8-inch seam allowance around each motif (b).

By Hand. Turn under the seam allowance and baste. Overlap the motifs on the

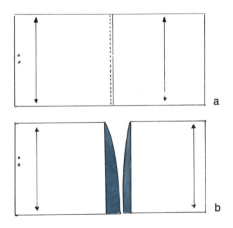

a

b

c

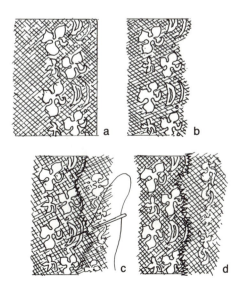

a

b

c

d

adjoining section. Attach with whip-stitches (c). Trim away any excess lace on the underside close to the hand stitching.

By Machine. Overlap the motif on the adjoining section. Sew around the motif with a fine zigzag stitch (d). Trim the excess lace on both upper and under sides close to the stitching.

LACE FABRIC: CONSTRUCTION

Layout. The safest layout is the use of a complete pattern (rather than the usual half pattern) placed on the right side of the fabric to take best advantage of the design motifs. When a fold of fabric is feasible, fold the lace right side outside, either lengthwise or crosswise, matching design motifs. Observe a directional layout where necessary. Utilize any self-shaped edge or border where possible.

Pinning. Use sharp, fine pins or needles to avoid snagging the lace. Pin within the seam allowances.

Cutting. Use sharp scissors. Cut notches outward. For standard seams, cut along the cutting line. For appliquéd lace motifs (see LACE FABRIC: APPLIQUE TECHNIQUE), cut around the design motifs that land on any seam or dart. Leave a 1/8-inch seam allowance around each motif.

Marking. Use thread markings only.

Machine Stitching. Tension: slightly loose. Pressure: adjust to fabric. Stitch size: delicate lace—15 to 20 stitches per inch; lightweight lace—12 to 15 stitches per inch. Needle: delicate lace—size 9; lightweight lace—size 11. Thread: appropriate for the fabric with this exception—it is best not to use synthetic thread even though the fabric is synthetic. If the lace puckers, stitch it over strips of tissue paper. Use the straight-stitch throat plate. The hole is smaller, so you won't risk the possibility that the lace will be drawn into it. A roller foot or an even-feed attachment is helpful in keeping the layers of fabric even.

Hand Stitching. Use a fine crewel needle, size 10, and fine matching thread.

Darts. Avoid when possible. Convert the shaping into gathers or soft folds. When darts are absolutely necessary, use the appliqué method for lace fabric preferably. Stitch darts by the standard method only when opaque underlining is used.

Seams. The most beautiful and practically invisible joining is by the hand or machine appliqué technique. Use a French seam or any other enclosed seam type (q.q.v.) or, to eliminate bulk, any of the double-stitched seams (q.q.v.). As suggested for darts, stitch seams by the standard method only when the lace is underlined with an opaque material.

LACE FABRIC: FASTENINGS. Use the finest, sheerest, narrowest standard or invisible zipper. To make the fastening as unobtrusive as possible, settle for nothing less than a perfect color match. If the color does not match perfectly, use another type of fastening. Apply the standard zipper by a lapped (regulation) zipper application (q.v.).

Other Fastening Possibilities. Consider matching thread loops and small, lace-covered buttons. (The lace should be over a matching lightweight fabric.) Snaps covered (q.v.) in lightweight matching silk or organza are good. Or use matching thread-covered hooks and thread eyes (q.q.v.).

LACE FABRIC: HEMS. The hem treatment depends on the lace itself and how it is used in the garment.

Ideally, the self-shaped or bordered edge of the lace used for a finish needs no further treatment. Next best, and providing a similar effect, is a length of border or lace edging (q.v.) appliquéd to the lace as a trim.

If the garment has been underlined, make a turned-up hem (q.v.). The hem finish for a lace edge is a facing of tulle, net, marquisette, organdy, organza, or horsehair braid. A lightweight lace may have a rolled hem (q.v.).

LACE FABRIC: PRESSING. To preserve the raised surface of the lace, place it over a thick padding of Turkish towel or a wool-faced press pad. Use a steam iron over a dry, thin press cloth. If additional moisture is needed, use a moist cheesecloth over a dry, thin press cloth and press with a dry iron.

LACE FABRIC: UNDERSTRUCTURE. Lace, like other sheer fabrics, can be made like a cage or shell to be worn over its own underdress or slip. If the style calls for more firmness, it can be underlined.

To retain sheerness and transparency, underline lace with tulle, net, or marquisette in a matching color. For an opaque effect, underline the lace with taffeta, crepe, satin, China silk, peau de soie, or any other suitable fabric. For a truly intriguing look, combine the "now-you-see-it" of flesh-colored tulle, net, or marquisette in strategic places with the "now-you-don't" of an opaque underlining or underdress.

When an underlining is used, place its right side against the wrong side of the lace so that both right sides face outward and both wrong sides face the body. In this way, no seams or darts will be visible.

Interfacings are unnecessary in lace. Avoid facings whenever possible but, when essential, make them of net, tulle, marquisette, organza, or organdy in a matching or flesh color. When an underlining is used, it is brought all the way out to the edge so that no further facing is necessary.

Avoid shoulder pads or shapes that make their presence known even in underlined laces.

LACE INSERTIONS. Narrow bands of lace finished on both edges.

With right sides up, pin the lace insertion in place on the fabric. Machine-stitch close to the edge on each long side of the insertion.

On the underside, trim the fabric under the lace, leaving very narrow seam allowances (a). Turn the seam allowances away from the lace insertion and press to position. Make a second row of very narrow zigzag stitches over the straight stitching. Trim away the excess seam allowances close to the zigzag stitching (b).

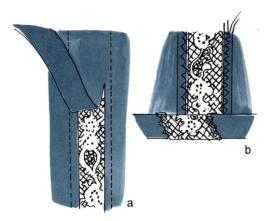

LAMB'S WOOL PADDING. A soft, fuzzy, loosely woven material used as an underlining to produce a padded look in a sleeve cap, along the front edges, in hems, or throughout a silk or brocade garment (an extravagant technique but effective). Do not confuse with lamb's wool *interlining,* which is a different material. *See also* SLEEVE HEAD.

LAMINATED FABRIC. Two or more layers of fabric permanently joined by adhesive and heat setting to form a bond. Almost any face fabric can be laminated to a thin layer of chemical foam. Sometimes a third layer of lining material is bonded to the underside of the foam to protect it. If not already so covered, a lining should be added to the garment for the same reason. *See also* BONDED AND LAMINATED FABRICS.

LAMINATED FABRIC: CONSTRUCTION. To compensate for the thickness of the foam backing, alter the pattern to provide additional ease. Trim away the tissue of the pattern at the cutting line; it is easier to cut beside the line rather than through it. Straighten the lengthwise grain on the face of the fabric by following one rib of knit material or a lengthwise thread of woven material. Square off the crosswise grain with any 90° angle.

For accuracy in cutting, place each pattern piece on the right side of the fabric and cut individually. If the laminate is a lightweight material, it is possible to fold it with the foam sides together and the right sides outside for cutting. Note: Foam resists pinning. Use long pins, firmly placed parallel to the seam line. Cut with sharp shears. Mark with tailor's tacks or basting thread only. As soon as the fabric is cut, stay all crosswise, curved, or angled seams with stay stitching and/or seam binding to prevent stretching.

Because of the body of the fabric, interfacings are not necessary. Cut facings of matching plain fabric to avoid the double thickness of foam. Hand-baste all seams and darts to prevent slipping while machine stitching.

For stitching, use a fine machine needle and silk, mercerized, or synthetic thread. Adjust the tension for the fabric. Use medium pressure and 10 stitches per inch. Place strips of tissue paper on both sides of the seam to prevent the foam from sticking to the feed and the presser foot. Bring

the needle down into the fabric before lowering the presser foot. Stitch at a moderate speed. Blunt all corners and points (q.v.). Welt, flat-fell, or double-stitched seams are best. Eliminate bulk wherever possible. Generally no seam or edge finishes are necessary since the fabric will not ravel. Where necessary, overcast.

Since hand stitching will pull away from the foam, all hand stitches must go through the foam to the face of the fabric.

Make machine-worked or bound buttonholes. Reinforce all areas to be slashed with a strip of firmly woven light- or medium-weight interfacing material.

Laminates require little or no pressing. In many instances, finger pressing is sufficient. Steam-press on the right side protected by a press cloth. Never touch the iron to the foam side of the fabric or you may find you don't have any foam left.

Don't overfit. Strain weakens the foam.

When lining a garment, follow the usual procedure.

LAP. The width of an extension from closing line to finished edge. The lap should be sufficient so there is no gaping.

In women's clothing the right side laps over the left both front and back. In men's clothing, left over right. At a side placket, the front laps over the back, as it also does in a sleeve placket. Unusual designs sometimes disregard these general rules for dramatic effect.

LAPPED BAND CUFF. In this cuff, the front end is flush with the front placket edge while the underlap projects from the back placket edge (a).

Prepare the lower edge of the sleeve (pleated or gathered) and the sleeve placket (q.v.). Prepare the cuff. *See* CUFF INTERFACING *and* CUFF CONSTRUCTION.

With right sides together, pin and/or baste the interfaced half of the cuff to the lower edge of the sleeve. The underlap edge projects from the back placket edge. The overlap edge is flush with the front placket edge. Match all markings. Stitch the cuff to the sleeve slowly, taking care that pleats or gathers stay in position. Trim

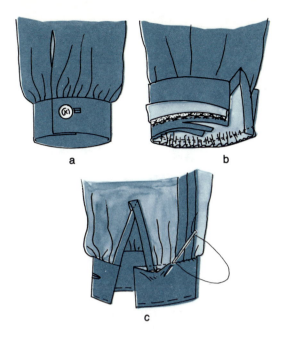

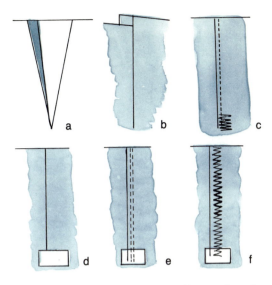

stitching line on the other. Proceed as for the above dart.

LAPPED (OVERLAP) SEAM. One in which the sections to be joined are positioned and stitched from the right side.

Turn under the seam allowance of the upper section and press to position. Overlap the turned edge on the lower section, raw edges matching. Pin and stitch from the right side an even distance from the fold. Variations of this basic lapped seam are the tucked straight or curved seam and the curved lapped seam (q.q.v.).

LAPPED (OVERLAP) SEAM IN INTERFACING AND UNDERLINING. Mark each seam line carefully. Overlap the seam line of one section on the seam line of the other. Pin to position. Stitch in any of the following ways. *(See illustrations on next page.)*

1. Make two rows of straight stitching, the first directly on the seam line, the second right beside it (a).
2. Make a row of zigzag stitching directly over the seam line (b).
3. Join by hand stitching, using cross-stitches (c).

and grade the seam allowances (b). Press them toward the cuff. Turn under the seam allowance on the free end of the cuff facing and press.

On the underside of the sleeve, bring the folded edge of the cuff facing to the seam and slip-stitch (c). Remove the bastings. Press the finished cuff. Complete the underside of bound buttonholes or make worked buttonholes by hand or by machine. Sew on the button.

LAPPED DART. A bulkless construction of a dart in interfacing or underlining material.

Mark the dart stitching lines (legs) carefully. Slash one dart leg to the dart point (a). Overlap the slashed edge on the other dart leg (b). Reinforce the point of the dart with either zigzag stitching (c) or, what is preferable, a patch of tape or interfacing (d). Start the stitching at the dart point and stitch to its end. (This is the opposite of a standard dart.) Stitch close to the cut edge. Use either two rows of straight stitching (e) or one row of zigzag stitching (f). Trim away the excess fabric close to the stitching.

An alternate method is to slash the dart through the center, then overlap one dart

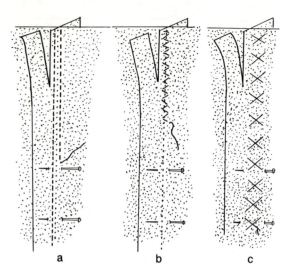

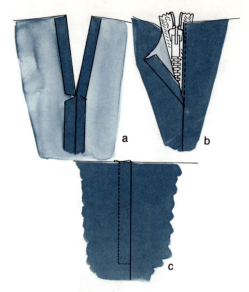

On all seam types, trim away excess fabric on both sides close to the stitching

LAPPED (REGULATION) ZIPPER INSTALLATION: HAND METHOD.

Before setting and stitching the zipper, *see* ZIPPER for general information.

Prepare the Placket. Mark the placket seam lines with basting thread. Turn under and press the overlap seam allowance. Clip the underlap seam allowance slightly below the end of the placket to the seam line (a). Fold the under seam allowance to make a 1/8-inch underlap extension. Press along this fold.

Apply the Zipper. Working from the right side, place the folded edge of the extension (underlap) over the right side of the zipper tape, allowing enough room to work the slider (b). When a facing finish is used at the garment edge, place the top stop of the zipper 1/4 inch below the cross seam line of the garment. This allows for turning the seam and facing to the underside. Allow a little more if the fabric is heavy. Pin to position. Starting at the top, backstitch the extension to the zipper close to the fold (b).

Bring the fold of the overlap to the seam line (basting) of the underlap. Pin to position. This placement of the overlap should completely conceal the zipper. Using a half backstitch or prick stitch (q.q.v.), sew the overlap in place, attaching the left zipper

tape to it. Stitch across the end below the bottom stop and continue to the top. Keep the welt even all the way up. As you approach the top stop, pull the tab down. This makes it easier to preserve a narrow welt in the slider area. Complete the stitching (c).

When installing a zipper in a curved seam —as in the hip-fitting side seam of skirt or pants—hold the seam in a curve over the hand.

LAPPED (REGULATION) ZIPPER INSTALLATION: MACHINE METHOD.

Machine-baste the placket closed (a). Clip the basting at intervals for easy removal. Press the seam allowances open.

On the underside, place and pin the zipper face down against the opened seam allowances with the teeth or coil along the seam line. Using the zipper foot positioned to the right of the needle, machine-baste the zipper tape to the seam allowance from the bottom to the top along the woven guideline of the zipper tape (b).

Turn the zipper face up with its tape directly under the seam allowance. Smooth the fabric away from the zipper. Note the underlap extension that forms in the seam allowance. Position the zipper foot to the left of the needle and stitch from the bottom to the top close to the fold through all thicknesses (c).

On the right side, smooth the fabric flat.

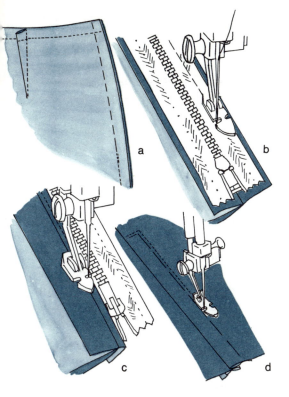

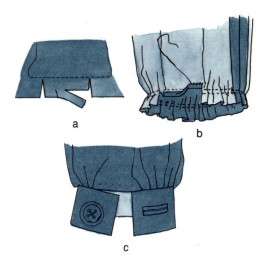

Baste across the bottom of the zipper and up the remaining side, placing the basting close to the woven guideline of the zipper tape. Machine-stitch close to the basting from either the right side (d) or the underside. Keep the stitching an even distance from the folded edge.

Pull the thread ends at the bottom of the zipper through to the wrong side and tie. Remove all bastings to open the placket.

Variation: Instead of topstitching, use machine blindstitching (q.v.) to simulate a hand installation. *See also* CENTERED (SLOT SEAM) ZIPPER.

LAPPED SLEEVE CLOSING WITH A ROLLED HEM.
Generally used with a buttoned cuff. When the sleeve band is attached, the placket is folded into a pleat for a closing. *(See also* SLEEVE PLACKET.)

Mark the position of the 1³/8- to 1¹/2-inch opening centered over a line that would extend to the little finger. Reinforce the opening with stay stitching that goes across the seam line of the opening and slightly beyond the ends. Clip the seam allowance to the corners beside the stay

stitching (a). Trim the seam allowance to ³/8 inch between the clips. Make a rolled hem across the opening (b). Whipstitch the ends. Proceed with the band construction (c).

LAYOUT CHART OF PATTERN.
All commercial patterns provide a layout chart that shows how the pattern is to be placed on the fabric. This is a photostatic copy (in scale) of all actual pieces necessary to complete the garment. This particular placement makes an economical use of the fabric while strictly respecting the grain that provides the "hang" intended by the designer.

The layout contained in the pattern may not be the only possible one. Sewers have been known to invent their own, either because they don't have enough fabric or because the pattern has been altered in some way. *See* LAYOUT CHART OF YOUR OWN DEVISING.

You will notice that a number of layouts are offered for each design. This is to accommodate the variety of shapes of pattern pieces, the varying widths of cloth as well as the varying widths of sewers as represented by the size of the pattern.

Select the layout planned for your size, the view of the design you are making, and the width of your fabric. Circle the chart with colored pencil so you will have no trouble remembering which layout you are using.

The standard layout arrangements are

the following: lengthwise fold, crosswise fold, open double, open single (full width), double-fold, partial lengthwise fold, combination. *See listing for each.*

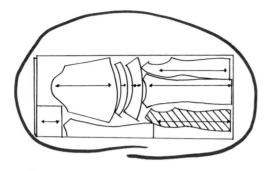

LAYOUT CHART OF YOUR OWN DEVIS-
ING. In every sewer's experience there are times when one cannot follow exactly the layout chart that comes with a pattern. The fabric may be wider or narrower, the figure requirements less or more. The garment may have been shortened or lengthened, widened or narrowed. You may simply have lost your heart to a remnant with less yardage than the pattern calls for. Whenever your needs or your conception of a design depart from the original pattern, you may have to modify the layout or devise your own.

It takes time and doing to dovetail all the pieces of pattern tissue. It's like playing with a giant puzzle. The game is to place your altered pattern pieces on grain in such fashion as to use the width and length of the material most economically.

For such purposes, it is a good idea to keep on hand several lengths of wrapping or shelf paper cut to standard widths of fabric—35, 39, 45, 54, 60 inches—opened out, doubled, or folded.

In devising your own layout chart, be mindful of the following:

Wherever possible cutting is by twos. One cuts either two of a kind or two halves (to be joined by a seam for a whole) or a half pattern placed on a fold of fabric (to become a whole when unfolded).

Half a pattern is better than a whole pattern for large or balanced sections. It ensures that both sides of the garment are cut alike. It saves time. Folded fabric is not so unwieldy as fabric opened to full width.

Note which twos are to be cut in pairs— a right and a left, like sleeves—and which are just duplicates, like patch pockets.

Place the largest pieces first, then those that need to be on a fold. Fit in the smaller pieces. Fit shapes against each other, locking them wherever possible. Be sure to *observe the grain line* in placement.

If the fabric you are planning to use has nap, pile, or a directional weave or print, arrange all pattern pieces so they go in the same direction, neck to hem. The repeat of design units on prints, weaves, plaids, or stripes must match.

When you are satisfied with the layout, make a little working chart. Incidentally, this is also a good way to estimate yardage for a particular design.

LEATHERLIKE FABRICS. You get a reasonable facsimile of the real thing plus all the advantages of cloth in the leatherlike fabrics. Their shiny, sleek, or grained surfaces have an attractiveness all their own, so one need not feel as if one were settling for second best.

The fake leathers consist of a plastic layer of polyurethane or vinyl over a knitted or woven base of cotton or polyester. Polyurethane produces a soft, spongy fabric while vinyl tends to be more rigid. The knit backing makes for a more supple, flexible fabric than those that are woven-backed.

These fabrics look best in tailored styles. Avoid gathers, sharp pleats, tucks. Shaping by seams is preferable to darts. However, darts are preferable to easing; convert ease to darts.

Choose a style with simple lines that requires little or no easing. For instance, raglan or kimono sleeves, which don't require easing, are preferable to set-in sleeves, which do. Because there is no ease in the fabric, there must be plenty of ease in the garment.

It is important to test-fit the garment before cutting into the fabric. You get no second chances for refitting once the garment has been cut and stitched. Use muslin or, better yet, a nonwoven material that more nearly approximates the hang of leather-like fabric.

Needles and pins leave permanent puncture marks. Stitching must be sure; you can't rip and start again. *For layout,* use pins sparingly and only in seam and dart allowances. Instead of pins, use weights or basting tape. *To hold thicknesses together* for stitching, use basting tape or paper clips. When coated surfaces are inside, match the edges and press them lightly by hand. They don't need much holding because the surfaces tend to stick together.

Coated surfaces tend to adhere to those with which they come in contact. *For storage:* keep the fabric rolled rather than folded. *For layout:* fold with the right side out when double layers are necessary. When *stitched from the right side,* dust the surface with talcum powder or cornstarch. (Better test for complete removal before stitching.) Alternate methods: Use an even-feed attachment or strips of tissue paper to keep the fabric from sticking to the throat plate or the presser foot.

For wrong-side marking, use chalk or marking pencil. *For right-side marking,* use a grease-base china marking pencil. It should wipe off without leaving a smudge. Test. CAUTION: Do not use tracing wheels; they leave permanent marks.

Leatherlike fabrics do not require edge finishes or stay stitching. However, stay seams where necessary with preshrunk tape.

For machine stitching, use size 14 leather-sewing needles for medium-weight fabrics, size 16 for heavyweight fabric. Make certain they are new and sharp-pointed. Use a light to medium tension, light to medium pressure. If stitches appear smaller than set, increase the pressure slightly. If feed marks show, decrease the pressure. Stitch size: 8 to 10 per inch. Smaller stitches tend to tear—like tearing paper along a perforated line. Use spun polyester or polyester-core thread. Make a test seam.

These fabrics require some flattening but *not with an iron.* Finger-press the seam allowances. Pound flat with a mallet or pounding block or roll with a small roller. Another possibility: glue seam allowances with fabric glue.

Topstitching is a good way to avoid any type of pressing. Make a topstitched plain seam, a double-stitched seam, a welt seam, or a double-topstitched seam (q.q.v.).

Interfacings are optional. Leatherlike fabrics have enough body to hold their shape. Should you wish to use interfacings, choose hair canvas for sharp support, a nonwoven for soft support. *Underlining* is unnecessary. *Interlining* may be added for warmth. *Linings* for comfort are recommended. *See listing for each of the above.*

Turned-up hems may be glued with fabric glue, topstitched by machine, or blind-stitched by hand. Keep all hand stitches loose and pick up only a thread or two of the backing. Do not let them come through to the right side.

Each leatherlike fabric varies somewhat in the way it handles. It is best to test any special construction technique before sewing on the garment.

LEFT-HANDED SEWERS. The left-handed sewer has her problems. The sewing machine is designed for the right-handed. There is nothing one can do about that but adjust to the machine. Most sewing tools can be used with either right or left hand. Shears are an exception but, fortunately, there are left-handed shears available.

Sewing techniques are the same for right- and left-handed sewers. The only problem here is with the instructions and illustrations for handwork, which are written for the right-handed.

What to do? When the instructions say "right," change the wording to "left." When the directions say "left" substitute "right."

A mirror image is the easiest (and most accurate) way to handle the illustrations. Hold a small hand mirror in position beside the illustration and adjust it until you get a clear image in reverse. The position of hand, needle, thread, scissors will then be that for the left-handed sewer. Letters and numbers will also be in reverse but they can be read from the original illustration.

Another way to handle the illustrations is to turn them upside down. While this procedure will give you the hand, needle, and thread position, it is not a true picture of the work, since that will be upside down. Often this doesn't matter and one can get enough information to proceed with the work. If a sequence of numbers or letters is involved, these will have to be transposed.

LEG-OF-MUTTON SLEEVE. One shaped like a leg of mutton. The cap of the sleeve is puffed, extending up and out from the shoulder. It tapers toward the elbow and is slim and fitted below the elbow.

Make the sleeve of material stiff enough to sustain the puff. The puff can be further bolstered by underlining with a stiff interfacing or underlining material. *See also* SLEEVE CAP SUPPORT *and* PUFF SHOULDER PAD.

LENGTHWISE FOLD. A term used in pattern layout. With right sides inside (generally), fold the fabric in half lengthwise,

aligning the selvages and the straightened ends.

LETTUCE EDGE. A decorative, rippled finish for knit or bias-cut fabric that takes advantage of its stretchiness.

Set the hemline and trim any excess material beyond it. Set the machine for a close, zigzag stitch of a width appropriate for the fabric. Use matching or contrasting thread. Stitch the edge, stretching the fabric as you do so. The more the stretch, the more rippling will result.

For a firmer edge, add 1/4 inch to the hemline for a narrow hem. Fold the hem to the inside. Do the overedge stitching over the fold. Trim any excess fabric on the underside.

LIGHT- TO MEDIUM-WEIGHT INTERFACINGS. These may be applied to the wrong side of the fabric either as a complete unit (a) or as separate parts (b). In both cases, the interfacings are included in the construction seams. Which of these two methods you choose depends on the type of fabric, the kind of interfacing, and the sewing sequence.

Cut the interfacing from the facing pattern. Trim away half of the seam allowances of the outer edges so the facing and interfacing will be graded. Baste the interfacing to the wrong side of the outer fabric. Proceed with the construction, in-

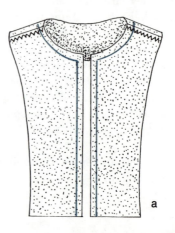

a

b

c

cluding the interfacing in the seams. Trim and grade the seam allowances, trimming the interfacing close to the stitching (c).

An exception to the general rule of interfacing the garment is made if the fabric and interfacing are lightweight enough. The interfacing may then be applied to the facing. This has the merit of providing a finished outer edge for the interfaced facing (q.v.).

LINEN. Always an understandably cherished fabric because of its strength, beauty, absorbency, and washability. Its natural luster and crispness give it its beauty. Its long, strong, smooth, and pliable fibers give it practicality. The variety in size of its fibers, from very fine to very coarse, makes it possible to produce a range of fabrics from sheer handkerchief linen to heavy suiting material.

Linen does have one drawback—its lack of elasticity. This makes it wrinkle easily. Crease-resistant finishes remove this difficulty but also remove the absorbency.

Shrink-resistant finishes reduce shrink-

age to a minimum. Since even the slightest shrinkage may affect the fit of the garment, particularly if it is a close one, it is wise to treat linen in some way before cutting. Dry cleaning retains the crisp finish. Linens may be sponged in the same way as woolens (q.v.) or rinsed in cold water. The use of a fabric softener in the water helps preserve the finish and makes linen easier to iron. Crispness may be restored by the use of spray sizing or starch.

Linen responds easily and beautifully to ironing. The linen should be well dampened, the iron hot. Iron until dry or the linen may muss or wrinkle. Work on the wrong side. If right-side ironing is necessary, press over a press cloth to prevent shine.

LINGERIE SEAM. A dainty but durable seam. With right sides together, make a plain seam. Press as stitched, then press both seam allowances in the same direction.

Turn to the right side. Using a very narrow zigzag stitch, make a row of stitching directly over the seam line. Trim the seam allowances on the underside.

LINGERIE: TRICOT KNIT. For general information, *see* KNIT FABRICS.

Many·lingerie patterns are now available. Buy the same size and figure type as for other patterns. Alter as necessary in the usual way. You could make your own pattern. Either cut apart an old garment that you would like to replace or make a muslin pattern by "tracing" the seam lines. *(See* PATTERN COPIED FROM A FAVORITE GARMENT.)

Before laying out and cutting, launder the fabric to remove excess finish and static. Pressing is generally not needed. If it is desired, press at a low temperature. Stabilize the fabric by allowing it to lie flat overnight.

Fold the fabric with right sides together. If in doubt as to the right side, stretch a crosswise edge. Tricot will roll to the right side. Lay out the pattern with the stretch running across the figure. In crotch sections, the stretch should run from back to front. Use ball-point pins (preferably) in the seam allowance. Observe the grain markings. Cut with sharp shears. Cut all notches outward. Mark any internal details with thread.

For stitching, use size 11 ball-point or regular fine machine needles and a fine but strong thread (nylon, silk, spun polyester labeled "For Lingerie"). Make a test seam on scraps of fabric to determine the best stitch size, tension, and pressure. Adjust as necessary.

For seams, use a regular straight stitch or any of the stretch stitches (q.v.). Trim the seam allowances. For seam finish, use any of the overedge stitches available on your machine. An overedge foot can provide this feature if it is not built into your machine. *See also* LINGERIE SEAM.

Interfacings are generally not necessary. Double layers of tricot add the necessary degree of firmness at the crotch, collar, and so on.

Finish the hem with machine blind-stitching, shell-stitched (scalloped) edging, a narrow turned-up hem, lace edging (nylon or polyester), or bias binding. *See listing for each.*

The waistline of panties or briefs may be finished with elastic edging, topstitched elastic braid (q.v.) or elastic in a casing (q.v.).

LINING. There is no denying the feeling of luxury that comes when one slips on a dress or jacket or coat lined in a silky material. It takes more time than a single-layer garment, to be sure, but is worth the effort.

In addition to the obvious use of a lining as a cover-up for the considerable internal workings of well-made garments, it protects them from the abrasion that comes with wear. It adds body to the outer fabric, making the garment hang better and wrinkle less.

The lining must support but not interfere with the lines of the design and the shaping of the garment. It is designed, stitched, and inserted in such a way as to permit freedom of movement. Therefore you will find considerable ease in a lining

in both width and length. It should be smooth, easy, and unobtrusive in construction.

The very nicest way to handle a lining—for dress, skirt, jacket, coat, pants, vest, and so on—is to make the lining separately by machine, slip it into the garment, and attach it by hand.

If the lining extends to the edge of the garment, a neater and stronger finish is made by machine. Should time and patience be limited or should you be making a garment that will get hard wear, you may also want to insert the lining by machine. *See* LINING A TAILORED GARMENT (MACHINE APPLICATION).

For the lining, use some soft fabric compatible with the care requirements of the outer fabric and strong enough to withstand the strain and abrasion of the putting on and taking off it will be subjected to.

LINING A DRESS. Complete the dress except for a collar. Complete the lining, leaving the placket opening.

With wrong sides of dress and lining facing each other, slip the lining into the dress. Match side seams (or any seams that come near the side of the dress). Pin together the seam allowances of dress and lining and join them with permanent basting stitches that are loose and easy. Stop about 6 inches from the hem. Match the shoulder seams and pin.

If the dress is collarless and/or sleeveless, clip and turn under the lining seam allowances at neckline and/or armhole. Slip-stitch the lining to the garment either at its edge or at the lower edge of any facings present. For a machine lining insertion, *see* LINING A SLEEVELESS, COLLARLESS GARMENT TO THE EDGE.

If the dress has a collar and/or sleeves, match the raw edges of lining and dress and baste in the seam allowances close to the seam line. Attach the collar, including the lining in the seam. Insert the sleeve lining in the dress in the same way as in a jacket. *See* LINING A TAILORED WOMAN'S GARMENT.

Fold under the lining seam allowance

against the zipper tape and slip-stitch. Turn up the hems in the dress and lining separately. Make the lining 1 inch shorter than the dress. Use an appropriate finish for each hem. Or, if you choose, attach the lining to the hem. *See* LINING HEM: ATTACHED TO GARMENT.

LINING A SKIRT. If there is no lining in the pattern, use the skirt pattern pieces to cut out the lining. For a half lining, cut it to extend well below the seat area, about mid-thigh length.

Complete the skirt except for the waistband and the hem. Complete the lining in the same way. Make a narrow machine-stitched hem along the bottom of a half lining.

Turn the skirt to the wrong side. Slip the lining over it, wrong sides together. Pin to position at the waistline, matching center front and back, all seams, all darts, and the placket opening. Turn under the lining seam allowances at the placket. Pin, then slip-stitch or hem the lining to the zipper tape. Baste the skirt and lining together across the waistline, easing as necessary.

Stitch the waistband to the skirt, including the lining in the seam. Loosely and permanently baste together the seam allowances of skirt and lining to within 6 inches of the hem. Turn up the hems in the skirt and lining separately for a free-hanging hem. Or attach the lining to the hem. *See* LINING HEM: ATTACHED TO GARMENT.

LINING A SLEEVELESS, COLLARLESS GARMENT TO THE EDGE (BY MACHINE). The lining in such a garment is attached in the same way as the combination neck and armhole facing (q.v.). This procedure is applicable to dresses, blouses, vests, and the like.

LINING A TAILORED GARMENT (MACHINE APPLICATION). This is a method suitable for garments that get rough wear, for children's clothing, for any but fine, custom-tailored garments.

Machine-stitch all darts and seams that complete the body of the lining. Stitch the sleeve seams. Press all seam allowances open. *(See directions on next page.)*

a

b

c

Ease-stitch the cap of the sleeve. Pin it into the lining armhole and sew with a double-stitched seam. Lay a soft pleat at the center back and machine-baste across the top and bottom of the lining (a).

With right sides together, pin and baste the lining to the entire facing, front and back. With the facing side up, stitch them together. Start the stitching at the center back and stitch to within 4 inches of the front hem. Repeat for the second side (b).

Turn the lining to the right side. Turn the sleeve lining into the sleeve. Lift the lining and fasten the side or underarm seam allowances of garment and lining with permanent basting or running stitches to within 4 inches of the hem (c). Turn under the lining seam allowances at the hem and sleeve. Slip-stitch them in place. At the front facings, smooth the lining down over the hem so the tuck ease forms a soft fold. Close the remaining front edges with slip stitching.

LINING A TAILORED MAN'S GARMENT (HAND APPLICATION). *See* LINING for general information. If you prefer to apply the lining by machine, *see* LINING A TAILORED GARMENT (MACHINE APPLICATION). *See also* LINING A TAILORED WOMAN'S GARMENT.

Classic men's tailoring calls for a complete lining to cover all construction. Unstructured garments may be unlined (q.v.) or have partial linings (q.v.).

The traditional lining material for men's suits and coats is a rayon twill that comes in standard neutral colors—black, gray, beige, brown, white, navy. The sleeve lining may be of the same material or a white rayon twill. Also used are taffeta, satin, acetate twill, or polyester fabrics. Pocket linings can be made of the lining material or of silesia.

For nontraditional suits, the sky's the limit! Flashy colors, elaborate weaves. But however grand the rest of the lining, choose for the sleeves any smooth fabric that will slide on and off easily.

In men's tailoring, when and how the lining is put into a garment is determined in part by the inside bound pocket construction and in part by the collar applica-

tion. In some modes of tailoring, the lining (all but the sleeves) is inserted before the shoulders are stitched, the collar attached, and the sleeves set. Whatever the sequence, the lining ends up looking the same.

Here is a simple, accepted method for lining insertion.

Cut all lining pieces. Stitch any darts and press them flat toward the side seams. Fold the shoulder pleats along the designated lines and baste 1/4 inch from the fold.

With right sides together, stitch the front facings and the front lining sections (a). Press the seam allowances toward the lining. Construct the inside bound pocket (q.v.).

With right sides together, pin, then stitch the front facing/lining section to the edge of the garment front from the marking at the top of the lapel (where the collar will join it) to the bottom marking (b). Treat as an enclosed (encased) seam (q.v.). Turn the lining to the inside. Press the outer edges of the garment as sharply as the fabric can take it. Pin the lining to the garment front section at matching seams. Baste, leaving all outside edges free.

With right sides together, stitch all garment sections and press. (Do not include the front lining in the seams.) Prepare and attach the collar to the garment. Set and stitch the sleeves. Apply the sleeve heads

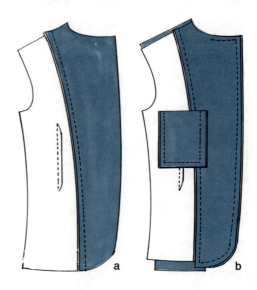

and the shoulder pads. Turn the facings to position and fasten. *See listings for each of these procedures.*

Continue with the lining. With right sides together, stitch all lining sections with the exception of the shoulder seams. Press. Lay a soft pleat at the neck edge of the center back and baste. Stay-stitch the neck edge. Ease-stitch the back shoulder edges. Turn under the seam allowances of neck and shoulder edges, clipping as necessary. Turn under the seam allowances at the vent (when there is one.) Pin and/or baste to position.

With wrong sides of garment and lining together, anchor the side or side-front seam allowances of the lining to those of the garment with long permanent basting stitches from the armhole to within several inches of the hem. Smooth and pin the lining in place at the armhole. Sew the armhole edges of garment and lining with permanent basting stitches in the seam allowance, close to the stitching. Start at the front shoulder and sew to within an inch or two of the back shoulder. Clip the seam allowances. Baste the front shoulder edges of the lining against the shoulder seams, smoothing them over the shoulder pads.

Lap and pin the turned-under edges of the lining back-shoulders and neck over the lining front-shoulders and garment neck edge. Slip-stitch the shoulder-neck-shoulder edges (a).

a

Stitch, press, and insert the sleeve lining by the same method as that for a tailored woman's garment (q.v.).

Set and turn up the lining hem allowance at the bottom of the garment and sleeve. Turn under the lining seam allowances at garment and sleeve vents when present. Slip-stitch lining in place. *See* LINING HEM.

For a partial lining (b), follow a similar procedure as far as necessary. Turn under a narrow hem across the back lining and machine-stitch. Keep it free-hanging.

b

LINING A TAILORED WOMAN'S GARMENT (HAND APPLICATION).

Construct the lining by machine and insert it by hand.

Cut, mark, and stitch the lining with the same care and precision as you did the fashion fabric. Be sure you have made the same corrections in the lining as in the garment.

Stitch all darts and seams with the exception of the shoulder seams (a). Press. Stitch the sleeve seams and press them open. Make two rows of gathering stitches across the sleeve cap. Draw them up to form a cap shape. Distribute the fullness evenly (b).

Lay a soft fold at the front shoulder and pin it to position. Fasten through all thicknesses with cross-stitches (c) or bar tacks *(See illustration on next page.)* (d). Lay a tenta-

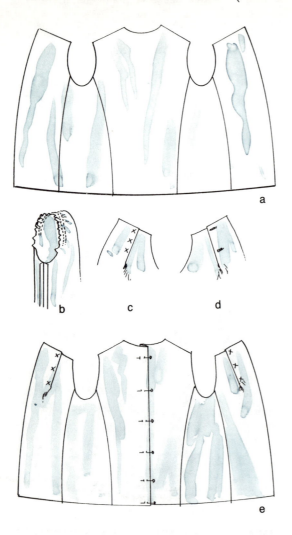

inches from the bottom and a coat lining free for about 6 inches from the bottom (a).

With permanent basting, stitch the lining firmly to the armhole seam allowance close to the seam. Start at the underarm and work toward the shoulder. Leave the back-armhole lining free for about 2 inches from the shoulder (b). Clip lining seam allowances at the underarm.

Turn under the seam allowances at the front edges of the lining (a). Pin in place over the front facings, raw edges matching. Slip-stitch lining to facing, leaving the bottom free for a few inches from the hemline. Attach the front lining to the back-shoulder seam allowance with permanent basting (b).

Clip the back neckline curve of the lin-

tive soft fold at the center back and pin to position (e).

Turn the garment inside out. Place it over a curved surface. A dress form is ideal; a tailor's ham is fine. Don't work on a flat surface or you will eliminate the ease so necessary to prevent drawing and pulling. By inserting the lining in a reverse curve, an extra bit of ease is added. Work from each front toward the center back. Do the same operation on each side before going on to the next.

With wrong sides of garment and lining together, match the open side seams. When there are no side seams, match the side-front or side-back seams instead. Join one seam allowance of each seam close to the stitching with loose permanent basting. Leave a jacket lining free for about 4

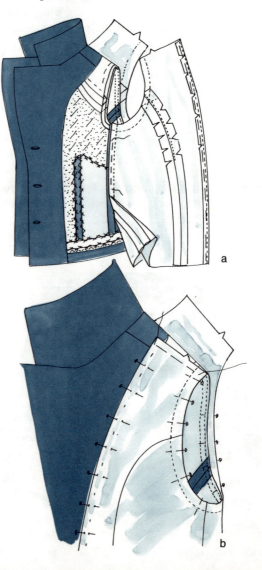

c

d

fold to meet the armhole seam. Match underarm, shoulder, and sleeve seams (d). Slip-stitch the sleeve lining to the garment lining. For a garment that is to get hard wear, tiny hemming stitches are preferable. Or use buttonhole twist or heavy-duty thread for sturdier hand stitches.

Alternate Method. Turn both sleeve and lining to the wrong side. Pin the lining seam allowance to the matching sleeve seam allowance (a). Fasten the seam allowances with permanent basting or running stitches to within 4 inches of the bottom. Slip the arm through the sleeve lining, grasp the bottom of the sleeve, and reverse the lining over the sleeve. Continue as for above sleeve lining (b).

When this much of the lining has been inserted, let the garment hang out for a while so that the lining settles before finishing the hem. Pin or baste the lining to the garment several inches above the hemline to hold it in place for finishing.

a

b

ing. Make any needed adjustments in the center-back pleat. The fold is directly on the center back; the pleat is on the right back. Fasten the pleat at the neck, waist, and lower edge with cross-stitches or bar tacks. Turn under the back-neckline and shoulder seam allowances of the lining and pin to position over the front lining at the shoulders and over the back neckline or facing, raw edges matching (c). Slip-stitch.

Slip the sleeve lining over the sleeve, wrong sides together. Clip the lining seam allowance on the underarm curve. Adjust the lining cap to fit the garment sleeve cap, distributing the ease. Turn under the lining seam allowance at the cap, bringing its

Jackets always have attached linings. (See LINING HEM: ATTACHED TO GARMENT.) Coat linings may be either attached like a jacket lining or free-hanging. (See LINING HEM: FREE-HANGING.)

LINING AT VENT. *See* VENT.

LINING CHOICES FOR TAILORED GARMENTS. Linings are like eyeglasses in the following respect: if they have to be, why not make them beautiful? Let them be seen and enjoyed. Add a splash of color, a dash of pattern, or a toasty-warm texture.

If the outer fabric is a solid color or has a solid-color effect, the choice is unlimited—colors that match, colors that blend, colors that contrast, prints, stripes, plaids, and weaves. If the outer fabric is elaborate in weave or has a printed surface, then the lining is best limited to a solid color.

If you are making a coat, consider the colors of the dresses or suits over which it will be worn. (Remember that one coat can't go over everything.) Choose a color for the lining that picks up the color of the outer fabric and yet blends with the clothing over which it will be worn.

A coat with lining and dress that match or a suit with lining and blouse that match can make an elegant ensemble out of what might otherwise be just another outfit.

Lining is best when of some soft fabric that facilitates slipping the garment on and off. It is usually lighter in weight than the outer fabric. Soft or lightweight satin, satin-backed crepe, crepe, soft taffeta or peau de soie, surah, China silk, soft cottons, and soft synthetics all make fine linings. When stiff, heavy, quilted, or fur linings are used, the sleeve lining should be made of some soft lining fabric.

With the perversity of all fashion, linings sometimes defy the rules. A silk coat with a wool lining can be useful as well as interesting. Wool with a contrasting wool lining makes a snug as well as beautiful coat.

A lining should be opaque, so that it really covers the inner construction. If the lining will show through a loosely woven outer fabric, choose one that matches in

color. Or back the fabric with an opaque underlining; this will leave you free to choose any contrasting or figured lining.

Whatever you do about a lining, don't be timid about it. Let it, too, make a fashion statement.

LINING-FACED WAISTBAND. When the waistband is made of heavy or bulky fabric, cut the underband (facing) of lining or other lightweight material.

With right sides of waistband and facing together, stitch the upper seam of the waistband. Turn and press. Proceed with the waistband construction (q.v.).

LINING: FREE-HANGING. Trim the lining 1 to 1½ inches below the finished hem (a). Turn up the lining to make a 2- to 2½-inch hem. This makes the lining 1 inch shorter than the garment.

The hem of the garment and the hem of the lining are each completed separately with any suitable edge finish. Close any remaining front or back edges (in coats or skirts with slits or vents, for example) with slip stitching. Attach the lining hem to the garment with 1-inch French tacks (q.v.) at all seams (b).

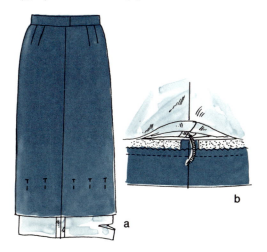

b

a

LINING HEM: ATTACHED TO GARMENT. Cut off any lining that shows below the finished hemline (a). Turn under

b

a

c

the lining seam allowance and pin it over the top of the hem, raw edges matching. Note the small tuck that provides the lengthwise ease (b). Slip-stitch the lining to the garment.

Smooth the lining down over the hem so the tuck ease forms a soft fold (c). Close any remaining front or back edges with slip stitching.

LINING PANTS. Pants are lined in the same way as a skirt (q.v.) with one exception. The hem at the bottom of each pant leg is attached to the garment rather than hanging free.

LINING PATTERN FOR TAILORED GARMENTS. Use the pattern for the lining that comes with the garment pattern. This does a good job of eliminating unnecessary details and stitching, converts shaping by darts into soft folds, and provides the necessary ease.

To Make a Lining When None Was Included in the Pattern: Start with the corrected pattern of the coat or jacket. Add to or cut away from the original pattern for the lining pattern. Should you wish to preserve the original pattern, trace the lining pattern onto fresh paper. Remember to transfer all the necessary pattern markings to the new pattern—grain lines, darts, notches, seam lines (if they will help).

Use the same number of sections for the lining as are in the garment. For instance, a separate underarm section as well as front and back (a) or several sections of a princess-style garment (b). Retain the original shaping by waistline darts in a fitted lining or lay the dart in a soft fold. In a garment with little or no waistline shaping, lay a soft fold at the shoulder. Be sure to add at the armhole the amount you've taken up in a fold.

Lining Front. Place the front facing over the front pattern. Trace the facing and remove it. To the facing line add 1¼ inches for a ⅝-inch overlap and a ⅝-inch turn-under. Use colored pencil for easy visibility (c). *(See illustration on next page.)*

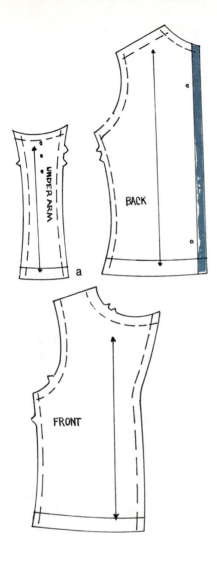

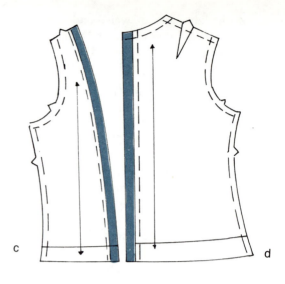

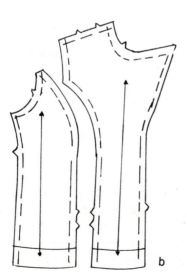

Lining Back. Place the back facing over the back pattern and trace it. Add 1¼ inches above the traced line for a ⅝-inch overlap and a ⅝-inch turn-under. Add a 1-inch strip of tissue to the center back for the back fold (d).

Lining Sleeve. Use the sleeve pattern.

Lining Hems. For an attached hem, trace or cut off the pattern at the hemline on garment and sleeve patterns. For a free-hanging lining, make it 1 inch shorter than the garment but add 2½ inches for a hem.

LINING RAGLAN- OR KIMONO-SLEEVE STYLES. Make the same adjustments on the lining as were made in the garment. Cut, mark, and stitch the entire lining together. Clip all curved seams. Press the seam allowances open. Turn the garment inside out.

With wrong sides of garment and lining together, match the side and underarm seams. Pin the seam allowances together. Fasten the seam allowances with permanent basting or running stitches close to the seams.

Fold under the seam allowances of all outside edges except the hem. Clip where necessary. Place the folded edges over the facings, raw edges matching. Slip-stitch lining to garment. Finish the hem as an attached or free-hanging hem (q.v.).

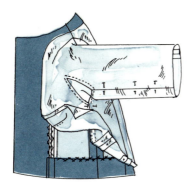

LINING STAY. Lining may be used as a stay to hold fullness in place and to prevent stretching or "bagging" of the outer fabric. It can be greatly aided in this by the character and grain of the lining material. Whenever possible, use fabric with little "give." Or cut the lining on crosswise rather than lengthwise grain, particularly in a skirt. Cutting the lining in this way utilizes the nonstretchability of the lengthwise straight of goods across the hips where it is needed most. It also makes it possible to use the selvage as the finished lower edge instead of making a hem.

LINK BUTTONS. Used on cuffs or where edges just meet on coats, vests, capes, and the like.

Use purchased or covered buttons. Determine the length needed between the buttonholes through which they are to pass. Join the buttons with heavy thread or buttonhole twist, carrying the strands back and forth through the buttons several times to the predetermined length. Work blanket stitches over the thread (a). Fasten securely. Or attach buttons to the ends of a length of narrow tubing (b).

LOCK STITCHES. Used to secure the beginning and ends of a line of stitching.

METHOD 1

Utilizes the reverse stitching action of the sewing machine. Lower the needle into the fabric about 1/2 inch from the end of the seam. Backstitch to the end of the fabric. Stitch forward directly over the previous stitching. Repeat the back-and-forth stitching at the end of the seam. *See* MACHINE BACKSTITCH.

METHOD 2

Utilizes the stitch-length mechanism. Set the stitch length to almost 0 (zero) so there will be practically no forward movement of stitching. Take 4 or 5 of these tiny stitches. Reset the stitch length for sewing the seam. End the seam with similar lock stitches.

LOOP-AND-BUTTON CLOSING. A decorative alternative to the buttonhole-and-button closing. It is particularly practical when cutting into fabric for a buttonhole is hazardous.

In a loop-and-button closing, both loops and buttons are stitched to the line of the closing. There is no overlap except that made by the loops themselves, but there is an underlap.

If the pattern is not planned for a loop-and-button closing, adjust it as follows. Cut the button side (underlap) as usual. On the loop side, mark the closing line. Add seam allowance. Trim away the rest of the extension. Make the facing match.

The button loops (q.v.) are inserted in the seam that joins facing to garment.

LOOPED SURFACE. A pile weave in which the yarn is looped over rods. When rods are removed, the loops remain.

Use a "With Nap" layout. If, in stitching, the loops get caught in the toes of the presser foot, wrap the toes with masking tape. *See* MACHINE STITCHING: GENERAL DIRECTIONS. In pressing, place the right side of the material against a strip of self-fabric or terry cloth. Steam from the wrong side. Apply the lightest touch of the iron. Pressure will flatten the raised surface.

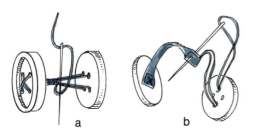

a   b

LOOP (TUBING) TURNER. A long, wire-like tool with a latch hook at one end and a loop at the other.

Slip the turner through the tubing to the opposite end. Pull it back until the latch hook grasps some of the fabric. With the hook side up, pull the turner through the tubing, reversing the fabric. Try to keep the tubing from twisting while it is being turned to the right side or the seam will spiral in the finished tubing.

MACHINE BACKSTITCHING (BACK-AND-FORTH STITCHING, LOCK STITCHING). A way of securing thread ends at the beginning and end of a seam by using the reverse mechanism of the sewing machine.

Lower the needle into the fabric about 1/2 inch from the end of the seam. Backstitch to the end of the fabric. Stitch forward directly over the previous stitching. When you come to the end of the seam, reverse the stitching.

Leave the needle completely down in the material before changing the direction of the stitching either forward or backward. The direction of the stitching is literally back (first) and forth (after).

Avoid backstitching beyond the edge of the fabric; this causes the material to be pulled into the throat-plate hole. It is not advisable to use such lock stitching at any point that requires precision stitching. For example, the point of a dart. It is practically impossible to get back on the stitching line accurately. Even if you could, the additional rows of stitching would stiffen the point.

If the fabric or the sewing thread tends to draw up along the line of stitching, do not backstitch at the end of the seam. Ease the thread through the fabric from the beginning of the seam to the end with finger pressing or with an iron.

MACHINE BAR TACK. Use a wide or medium-width zigzag stitch set at a very short stitch length. *See also* OVERHAND BAR TACK *and* BLANKET-STITCH BAR TACK.

MACHINE BASTING. If needle marks won't show and if the fabric is firm enough, you can save considerable time with machine basting.

Set the machine for the longest stitch. Loosen the tension somewhat so it will be easy to remove the basting. To remove, clip the top thread at frequent intervals and pull the bottom thread.

MACHINE BLINDSTITCH. *See* BLIND HEMMING STITCH.

MACHINE BLINDSTITCHED HEM. *See* BLINDSTITCHED HEM.

MACHINE BUTTONHOLE STITCH. This is a close zigzag stitch achieved either by a built-in mechanism on the machine or by a zigzag attachment.

With the built-in mechanism, the needle moves from side to side to form the zigzag stitch. With a zigzag attachment, the fabric is moved from side to side to form the stitch.

MACHINE OVERCAST STITCH. *See* OVERCASTING.

MACHINE OVEREDGE STITCHES. Present-day sewing machines offer a wide variety of stitches that are suitable for edge finishes. Some are built into the machine, others require the use of a cam.

The zigzag stitch is the basis for most of the overedge stitches. In some of the overedge or overlock stitches, the zigzag stitch is used in combination with a straight stitch. There are other automatic decorative patterns that can also be used as overedge finishes. Check your sewing machine to see what it is capable of doing in this respect.

MACHINE PADDING STITCHES. These go through all thicknesses. Because they are visible from the outside, they should be done through an underlayer only. Use either a straight stitch or a multistitch zigzag in a pattern that will best achieve the desired effect. *See listings under* PAD STITCHING.

MACHINE-ROLLED HEM. There are two ways of making a machine-rolled hem. The first requires the use of a hemmer (q.v.). The second can be done manually as follows.

Mark the hemline and trim the hem allowance to ½ inch. Turn under ¼ inch and press. Again turn under ¼ inch and press. Machine-stitch along the folded edge, keeping the grain lines of hem and garment aligned.

MACHINE STITCHING: GENERAL DIRECTIONS. Those of you who drive a car will recognize some of the same problems in handling your sewing machine: starting and stopping at a given spot, the relation of the pressure applied to the pedal (or knee control), and the speed, steering, maneuvering curves, turning corners, judging distances, hands and feet in position for coordinated action.

The operation of the sewing machine is really quite simple if you understand how its principal parts work and know how to thread your machine, regulate its tension, pressure, and stitch length. Keep the instruction book that comes with the sewing machine at hand.

Before settling yourself to the actual sewing, assemble and keep within reach all those tools you may need for the operation: a small pair of scissors or thread clips, a dressmaker's gauge, a blunt tool to push the cloth under the presser foot when necessary and for working out corners from the inside, a blunt needle or T pin for working out corners from the right side, pins, a hand needle and basting thread, extra thread for the garment you are sewing, and any other tools needed for a particular bit of sewing.

Seat yourself comfortably on a chair of proper height and in proper position, with light directed on the stitching area, foot in position to operate the pedal or knee control.

Raise the presser foot by lifting the lever. Raise the take-up lever to its highest point by turning the hand wheel toward you. Hold on to the upper thread so the machine does not come unthreaded. Place the needle and bobbin threads under the presser foot and diagonally toward the right back.

It is wise to make a test run of two layers of your cloth, using the needle, thread, and stitch length selected for the fabric. Start with 12 stitches per inch and adjust accordingly. You can also use the test seam or dart to test the pressing.

Place the fabric under the presser foot with the bulk of it to the left and the seam edge to the right. The space on the right is too small for large sections of a garment while stitching. Set the fabric so that the line of stitching will be directed toward you at a right angle.

Turn the hand wheel slowly until the needle is brought down into the fabric at the starting point. Lower the presser foot. Start the machine by turning the hand wheel with your right hand while applying pressure to the pedal or knee control. Hold the needle and bobbin threads taut for the first few stitches. Place your hands in position to guide the fabric, with one hand behind the presser foot and one forward. Keep your fingers away from all moving parts, particularly the needle.

Stitch slowly and evenly. Learn how much pressure is needed to produce the speed you want. Keep your eyes on the stitching. Use whatever guide you can to assure a correct seam: the throat-plate guidelines, a seam guide, the outer edge of the presser foot, any basting or marking. Learn to judge distances frequently come upon in sewing: ⅛, ¼, ⅜, ½, or ⅝ inch.

Slow down as you approach the end of the line of stitching and get ready to "brake" the machine. Stop the machine at the stopping point. Turn the hand wheel until the thread take-up lever is at its highest point so you will have enough thread when you begin to stitch again.

Raise the presser foot. Snip the thread ends with a small pair of scissors, thread clips, or the thread cutter on the machine. Leave an inch or two of the thread ends before cutting. Should you need to ease the thread through the seam, there will be enough extra thread to do so. Leave at least 2 inches of thread on the needle for the beginning of the next sewing.

Slip the fabric out from under the presser foot. Examine for accuracy of stitching. Make any necessary corrections. Proceed with the construction. *See also* SEAM STITCHING; DART STITCHED.

MACHINE-WORKED BUTTONHOLE.

Any zigzag sewing machine can make buttonholes with or without a built-in buttonhole mechanism or attachment.

There are several possibilities for kinds of thread, depending on the weight of the fabric and the degree of heaviness you wish for the buttonhole. You may use buttonhole twist for the upper thread and a regular size 50 thread for the bobbin; a double strand of mercerized thread for the upper thread and a single thread for the bobbin; single or double strands of silk thread for both upper and bobbin threads.

It is a good idea to do a bit of experimenting through the several layers of fabric, interfacing, and facing to arrive at the best possible combination of needle, thread, stitch width, and stitch length. The latter regulates the closeness of the stitches.

Should the one go-around produce a skimpy-looking buttonhole (it sometimes does), do a second stitching for a finer finish.

The *buttonhole attachment on one of the newer, more sophisticated sewing machines* is capable of automatically making a buttonhole of the correct length for the button to be used by placing the button at the back of the attachment as a guide.

When a buttonhole mechanism is built into the machine, each step in the making of the buttonhole is automatically controlled. Half the buttonhole is stitched forward, half backward, with bar tacks stitched at both ends. On the right side of the fabric, mark the location of the buttonhole, its beginning and its ending, with thread or tailor's chalk. Remove any thread as you

approach it so it won't be caught in the machine stitching. Set the machine as per the directions in the sewing machine instruction book.

When a buttonhole mechanism is not built in on a zigzag sewing machine, one must control the steps in the stitching manually.

Mark the position of the buttonhole, its beginning and its ending. Set the machine for zigzag stitching of the desired stitch width and stitch length.

Center the buttonhole position under the presser foot at one end of the buttonhole, placing the needle to the left side of the position line. Stitch forward slowly to a point several stitches beyond the end of the buttonhole so the bar tack will not subtract any of the size of the opening (a). End the stitching with the needle in the fabric. Raise the presser foot and pivot the fabric so it is in position to stitch forward again in the opposite direction for the second side of the buttonhole. Set the stitch width selector for the bar tack at a setting equal to the width of both rows of stitching. Take several wide zigzag stitches to form the tack. They will go over a few stitches on the first row of stitching (b). Reset the stitch width for the second row of stitching. Stitch the second side of the buttonhole, making it equal in length to the first. Once more reset the stitch width and stitch the second bar tack a few stitches beyond the buttonhole opening (c). *(See illustration on next page.)*

When making a buttonhole with a buttonholer on a straight-stitching machine, read carefully the instructions that come with the attachment, since each type differs somewhat in the method of operation. What all have in common is a cloth clamp that grips the fabric and moves it from side to side for a zigzag stitch, feeding it front to back for the length of the buttonhole. Dials control the stitch width and cutting space, which can be adjusted for the type of fabric. Templates can be selected for the style of buttonhole (straight, keyhole, eyelet) and its length.

Attach the buttonholer to the machine. Mark the position line of the buttonhole

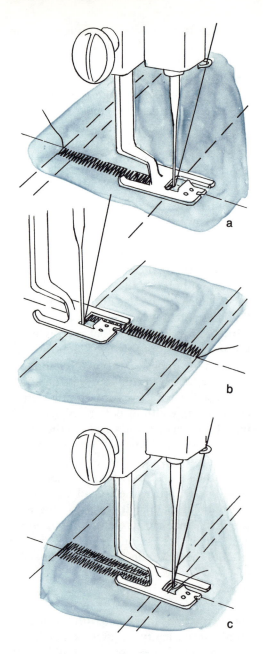

a

b

c

ing, and style details must be transferred from the pattern to the fabric. Mark everything you need to know! The more time you take to mark, the less work and guesswork when you come to join the sections of the garment.

Be Sure to Mark:

Assembly Details. The notches; special markings that show points or spots to be joined; the position of buttons, snaps, joinings, and so on.

Stitching Guides. Wrong-side construction markings.

Design Details. Right-side placement of buttonholes, pockets, tucks, pleats, topstitching, and so forth.

Wrong-Side Markings

These are for the big construction seams and darts. The darts should always be marked precisely. The seams may or may not be marked. Do mark them when seams require precision stitching. Don't mark them if fitting to your figure may create departures from the original seam line or if you can judge the seam allowance by eye. Many sewing machines have some measurements marked on the throat plate. If yours doesn't, you can make your own marking with masking tape or with a fine line of nail polish.

Wrong-side markings may be made with tailor's chalk, dressmaker's tracing (carbon) paper and a tracing wheel, or basting thread.

Tailor's chalk (q.v.) makes safe, quick, and easy markings. It leaves no permanent marks on the material. This feature is at once an asset and a drawback. You can't mark now and sew later: there may not be any markings left. If you plan to use tailor's chalk, mark as you sew.

Dressmaker's tracing (carbon) (q.v.) paper and a tracing wheel make excellent markings but must be used with caution. Marking with them doesn't take the time that thread

on the garment with chalk or basting thread. Place the garment under the cloth clamp. Align the buttonhole marking with the vertical lines of the cloth clamp at center front and back. Align the center line of the garment with the horizontal lines on both sides of the clamp for the starting point of the stitch. Stitch, following the directions in the instruction book.

MARKING METHODS. All of the markings that deal with the assembling, stitch-

markings do and this kind of marking lasts longer than chalk markings. Indeed some of it lasts forever, which is one of its drawbacks. There are a few others: the tracing wheel may bruise touchy fabrics and tear patterns. The carbon doesn't show on varicolored or textured material. While it is fairly impossible to see the markings on some woolens, they shine through brightly (and permanently) on white, light-colored, or sheer materials. Some brands and some colors of carbon *do* disappear in cleaning or pressing. Better test the tracing on a scrap of your material. Just be sure you know how the carbon will react on your fabric before proceeding. But, wherever you can, do use the dressmaker's tracing paper. It is an accurate, speedy guide for assembling and stitching a garment.

RIGHT-SIDE MARKINGS

Some markings are necessary on the right side of the garment while the work is in progress—the position of a pocket, a buttonhole, a button; the center front, a fold line for facing or a pleat, and the like.

Don't take chances with any marking that may mar the surface of the cloth. Safest is marking with thread of a contrasting color. Thread markings can be easily removed without leaving a trace when they have served their purpose. They are generally made *by hand. (See* THREAD TRACING; TAILOR'S TACKS; SIMPLIFIED TAILOR'S TACKS.) If you have many lines of marking to do (pleats, for instance), *machine basting* (q.v.) can be a great convenience. Tailor's tacks, too, can be made on some machines with the aid of a tailor tacking foot.

Different colors of basting thread can be used for the various markings. Don't use so many that you will confuse yourself when it's time to identify the markings.

NOTCHES

Those triangular or diamond shapes on the cutting line are a kind of marking used to match sections of a garment that are to be joined. *See separate listing.*

MATCHING FLORAL UNITS. *See* DESIGN UNITS.

MATCHING PLAIDS, STRIPES, CHECKS, GEOMETRIC REPEATS. *See* PLAIDS.

MATERNITY CLOTHES. Pregnancy used to be a period when a woman hid herself away, especially during the last, largish months. Today, pregnancy appears not to affect public appearances at all and many women retain their jobs right up to the end. The need for attractive maternity clothes that provide comfort as well as style becomes a must.

Any style that can accommodate the major growth areas will do, whether it is designed as a maternity garment or not. The major growth areas are the bust, waist, hips, front-waist and crotch lengths. In a period when loose-fitting and very loose-fitting designs are in vogue, one could get away with any in a range of standard sizes and styles. (A loose-fitting garment has 4 to 8 inches of ease above body measurements. A very loose-fitting garment has more than 8 inches of ease.) Barring that, choose a maternity pattern in your regular size (the size you wore before pregnancy).

Maternity patterns are presized for the ninth month of pregnancy and will accommodate a woman whether she is carrying high, low, or in between. Top, skirt, and dress hemlines are cut with a slight dip in front so that, when worn over the front bulge, the hemline will remain straight. (This may take some adjustment from time to time.) Waistbands of skirts and pants are located above the waistline and the fullest part of the abdomen so they won't slide down. The waistbands are adjustable via elastic or drawstring. (Elastic is cut to the maximum length, inserted in a casing, and stitched together at 1-inch intervals to be released as the size of the abdomen increases.)

Make any pattern corrections you would normally make except those in the major growth areas. These would be mainly length measurements; for instance, back waist length. Be sure that tops of any kind cover the maternity panel of pants or skirts.

Maternity stretch panels (commercially available) are used in some maternity patterns. This is a rectangle of very stretchable fabric, usually nylon, sewn into the garment at hip level and attached at the side seams. Such panels can be set into your regular-size pants or skirt as well as used in specially constructed clothing.

Face it! You really can't disguise or minimize that precious bulge. You may as well be bold about it with dramatic colors, textures, and styles. And don't count on wearing your maternity clothes after the baby is born as the books suggest. Because the time in which you wear them is relatively short, your wardrobe will undoubtedly be limited. You'll be pretty tired of the same daily dresses by the end of the ninth month. When you are a full-fledged mother, get into something fresh and new. Lend your maternity clothes to a friend or put them away for another pregnancy.

MEN'S TAILORING. *See* TAILORING FOR MEN.

METALLIC FABRICS. These gleaming, glistening, glittering fabrics are made from any of the standard fibers, which are generally used for the warp threads, and gold, silver, or copper filling yarns that form the pattern. How a particular metallic is handled depends on its fiber and texture. Common to all are the following considerations.

Because the fabric is so dazzling of itself, select simple patterns with few seams and darts. Avoid details like buttonholes or inset pockets that require slashes in the material.

A trial muslin is a must. You can't afford to make mistakes in the cutting and construction of such expensive material. Ripped-out stitching may leave holes and pressing leave permanent creases. Since many of these materials have very little or no give, allow sufficient ease for close-fitting gowns.

A "With Nap" layout is essential. The direction of light will affect the color, making it one color going up and another going down.

Avoid anything that will leave a permanent mark in a conspicuous place. Instead of pinning the grain line (usually right in the middle of the pattern section), weight it with dressmaker's weights, sewing equipment, anything heavy and safe.

Use silk or ball-point pins. Place them in the seam allowance closer to the cutting line than to the seam line. Mark carefully with silk thread and a fine needle. *Do not* use dressmaker's tracing paper and a tracing wheel.

Metallic fabrics have a tendency to ravel. Overcast all edges immediately after cutting. Work quickly.

Metallic threads are scratchy against the skin. Unless you enjoy being wounded, line the dress completely with a soft but closely woven lining material. If you leave the garment unlined, at least use silk fabric for all facings and be sure to bind all raw edges.

Machine Stitching.

Tension: Suitable for the weight of the fabric.

Pressure: Suitable for the weight of the fabric.

Stitch size: Medium, 12 to 14 stitches per inch.

Needle: Fine to medium, ball point. Make certain that the point has no burrs. If the fabric appears snagged despite a new or perfect needle, place strips of tissue paper over and under the seam line before stitching.

Thread: Suitable for the fiber of the fabric.

Hold the fabric taut while stitching to keep the two thicknesses feeding through the machine at the same rate. Stitch slowly.

Pressing. Metallic threads are permanently creased by pressing. Dampening may tarnish some metallics. Press very lightly with a warm iron over a dry press cloth. For raised metallics, pad the ironing board or press over a Turkish towel.

METRIC CONVERSION CHART. For measurements frequently used in dressmaking or tailoring.

Inches to Millimeters and Centimeters (Slightly Rounded for Convenience)

inches	mm		cm
1/8	3mm		
3/16	5mm		
1/4	6mm		
3/8	10mm	or	1cm
1/2	13mm	or	1.3cm
5/8	15mm	or	1.5cm
3/4	20mm	or	2cm
7/8	22mm	or	2.2cm
1	25mm	or	2.5cm

Approximate Conversion of Inches to Centimeters: Multiply number of inches by 2½

MITER. The diagonal joining of horizontal and vertical edges at a corner in such a way as to reduce the bulk of the joining. A miter may be folded or stitched in place.

There are two basic types of mitered corners: *outward* and *inward.* In an outward mitered corner, the mitered piece goes around the corner (a). In an inward mitered corner, the mitered piece lies within the corner (b).

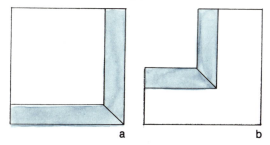

a   b

MITERED CONTINUOUS STRIP (Facing or Trimming).

Inward Corner. With right sides together, pin the facing (or trimming) to the garment, raw edges aligned along both sides of the corner. Pin the facing diagonally across the corner into a dart. Pin it tightly to itself (against the underlayer) (a). Remove the facing.

Stitch the facing along the diagonal line. Trim the excess fabric, leaving narrow seam allowances, tapering them at both ends (b). Press the seam allowances open over a point presser.

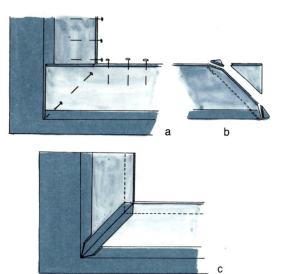

a   b

c

The miter has created a shaped facing. With right sides together, apply the mitered facing to the garment and treat in the same way as any other facing (q.v.) (c).

Outward Corner. With right sides together, pin the facing along one side to the point of the miter. Mark the point (a). Remove the facing. Reinforce the area with a row of small stay stitches. Clip the seam allowance at the point (b).

With right sides together, pin the facing to the garment along both sides, turning it at the clipped corner. Stitch the facing to the garment along the seam lines, pivoting at the corner (c).

Fold the excess material at the miter so it

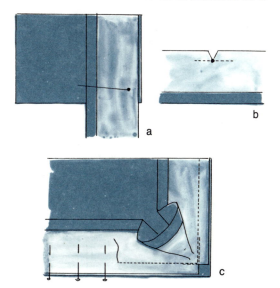

a

b

c

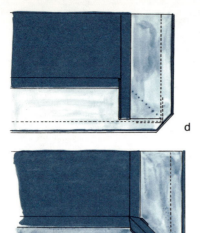

d

e

lies flat against the fabric (d). Press or pin, then stitch along the diagonal seam line that forms. Trim the seam allowances, tapering at the ends of the miter. Press them open over a point presser (e). Turn the facing to the inside. Press.

MITERED DOUBLE BANDING. The easiest and least bulky way to handle double banding is to miter it before applying it to the garment.

Cut the band to the desired length and double the width plus seam allowances. With right sides together, fold the band crosswise where the corner will be formed (a). Fold the doubled band lengthwise (b). You now have four thicknesses of cloth.

For an Outward Corner: Holding the band with the lengthwise fold at the right and the crosswise fold at the top, turn under the corner *toward the fold* to form a diagonal line (c).

For an Inward Corner: Holding the band with the lengthwise fold at the right and the crosswise fold at the top, fold over the corner *toward the raw edges* to form a diagonal line (d).

Press all diagonal lines sharply.

(If the fabric itself is too bulky to handle in this way, make a paper pattern by this method and cut the banding from it.)

Open out the band and mark along all diagonal lines (a) and (b). With right sides together, fold the band along the original crosswise fold. Stitch along the diagonal creases or markings, taking one stitch across the point to blunt it (c) and (d).

Cut away the excess fabric, leaving narrow seam allowances. For the outward corner, cut across the point to free it. For the inward corner, clip at the point to release it.

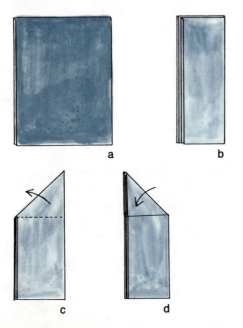

a

b

c

d

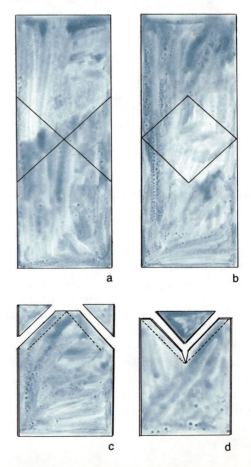

a

b

c

d

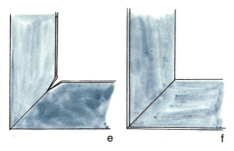

e   f

Press the seam allowances open over a point presser. Turn the banding to the right side, working out the corners carefully (e) and (f). Apply the band to the garment. *See* BANDING.

MITERED HEM. Mark the fold lines of the hem. Fold the corner up to the inside, bringing the lengthwise grain to the crosswise grain with the diagonal fold touching the point at which the fold lines of the hem meet (a). Press the diagonal fold into a sharp crease. This represents the stitching line for the miter (a).

Open out the corner. With right sides together, fold the lengthwise hem to meet the crosswise hem. Pin, then stitch the miter through the diagonal press lines, matching them (b). Trim away the excess fabric and press the seam open over a point presser. Taper the seam allowances at the point of the miter and at its outer edge (c). Turn the hem to the inside, working out the corner carefully.

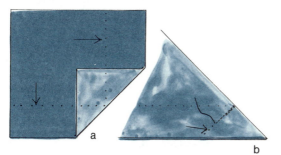

a   b

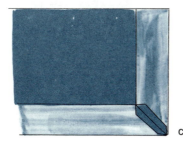

c

Here is another easy way to miter a corner in *light- or medium-weight material.*

Turn the hem (or seam allowances) to the outside along the fold lines, right sides together. Pinch the corner into a dart and pin (a). The pin is at the seam line. It must be tight against the underlayer. Stitch the seam line of the dart.

Trim the excess fabric and press the seam open over a point presser. Taper the seam allowances at the point of the miter and at its outer edge (b). Turn the mitered corner to the inside, gently working out the corner.

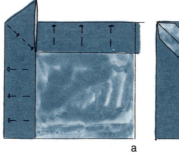

a   b

In *heavy fabric,* turn the hem (or seam allowance) to the inside, wrong sides together. Pinch the corner into a dart, keeping it tight against the underlayer. Trim the excess fabric that forms the dart diagonally across the corner (a). Stitch the raw edges securely in place with overhand stitches (b).

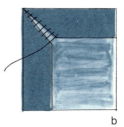

a   b

MITERED TRIM FOR A PLACKET OPENING. An interesting decorative detail when made of ribbon, braid, tape, embroidered or beaded edging.

The placket is constructed first. Mark the opening. Stay-stitch it on either side of the opening line and across its end. Slash through the center and diagonally to each corner (a). Turn a narrow seam allowance on the slashed edges to the *right* side of the fabric. Baste and press them flat (b). (The opening should be just large enough to take the zipper when used.) The seam allowances will be covered by the trim.

When a zipper is used, center it in the opening and edgestitch it in place before the trim is applied.

The miter may be pointed (c) or square (d). You will need two lengths of trim plus seam allowances for finishing the ends and an allowance for matching any design motifs in the trimming. In addition, you will need an allowance to form the miter equal to twice the width of the trim for the pointed miter and four times the width of the trim for the square end.

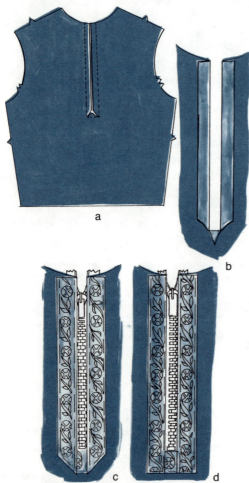

To Form the Pointed Miter: At the designated end of the trim, fold it to form a

45° triangle either over it (a) or under it (b). Fold it again, making an opposite 45° triangle either over it (c) or under it (d).

To Form a Square End: Form the pointed miter as directed above. Then fold the point either under the trim (e) or over it (f).

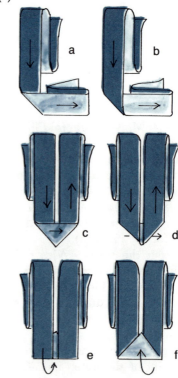

To Complete the Trimming: Baste the trim around the placket opening. Stitch it to position on all edges either by hand or by machine.

MOCK CASING. *See* CASINGS UTILIZING SEAM ALLOWANCES, NARROW HEMS, AND TUCKS.

MOCK SHIRT CUFF. An illusion of a cuff created by a tuck in a shirt sleeve.

On the pattern, draw a slash line for the tuck about 1 inch above and parallel to the sleeve hemline. Slash and spread the pattern 1/2 inch. Fill in the spread area with paper. Scotch-tape or pin it to the sleeve pattern. Correct the underarm seam lines (a).

Cut out the sleeve and mark the hemline. Turn under the hem along the marking and press. Make a line of thread tracing (q.v.) on the sleeve along the line made by the raw edge at the top of the hem.

From the right side, fold the sleeve along the guide basting. Make a ¼-inch tuck in from the fold, stitching through all thicknesses and enclosing the raw edge of the hem (b). Press the tuck up (c). Proceed with the shirt sleeve construction.

MOCK (SIMULATED) FRENCH SEAM.

This seam may be used in place of a French seam, particularly on curved edges.

With right sides of fabric together, make a plain seam. *Do not* press it open. Trim the seam allowances to ½ inch. Turn both seam allowances under (toward each other) ¼ inch and press. Edgestitch together close to the folds, thereby enclosing the raw edges. Press to one side.

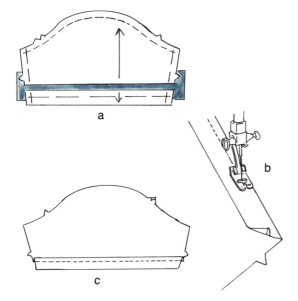

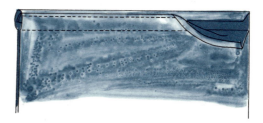

MOCK TURTLENECK COLLAR. One that
looks like a turtleneck collar but does not turn back on itself. It can be made of self-fabric cut on the bias (*See* BIAS-FOLD COLLARS) or of ribbed banding (q.v.).

NAPPED FABRIC: PRESSING. *See* PRESSING NAPPED FABRIC.

NAPPED FABRICS. Those whose projecting hairs or fibers are brushed after weaving to produce a soft, fuzzy, or downy surface that lies smoothly in one direction. Examples of short-nap fabrics: fleece, camel's hair, broadcloth. Examples of long-nap fabrics: shaggy cloth, fur fabric. Though their structure is different, short-pile fabrics like velvet and velveteen (q.q.v.) are considered and treated like napped fabrics.

Short-nap, long-nap, and short-pile fabrics—velvet (q.v.) is an exception—are cut with the nap going down, never crosswise. To avoid a patchwork of colors, place the pattern on the fabric in a directional ("With Nap") layout (q.v.). Should you make the sad discovery that the nap is running in the wrong way, stick with it. It is more important to be consistent than to switch direction in mid-cutting and have two different colors.

The direction of the nap is obvious in long-nap fabrics. It is the short-nap and short-pile fabrics about which there may be some question.

To determine the direction of the nap, place your fingertips lightly on the surface of the material. Jiggle them gently back and forth, riding the surface. When the surface feels smooth, the nap is running down. If there is resistance against the fingertips, the nap is running up. Mark the direction in which the nap moves with chalked arrows along the selvage, so that you will always be sure which way the nap is going. No need for uncertainty and for making the same decision over and over again.

NARROW HEM. Suitable for blouses, lingerie, and other lightweight garments.

Mark the hemline. Trim the hem allowance to 1/2 inch. Fold the edge under 1/4 inch and press. Fold the edge under 1/4 inch again and press. Either hem by hand along the hem edge or machine-stitch close to the upper fold.

NATURAL NECKLINE. One that curves around the base of the neck from the hollow between the collarbones in front to the back socket bone.

NATURAL NECKLINE PATTERN CORRECTIONS. *See* PATTERN CORRECTIONS for general information.

Neckline Too Large? Slip tissue under the pattern at the neckline and fasten with pins or Scotch tape. Draw new cutting and stitching lines in a raised position (a). Make a corresponding adjustment in a neck facing or a collar.

Neckline Too Tight? Draw new cutting and stitching lines in a lowered position (b). Make a corresponding adjustment in a facing or collar.

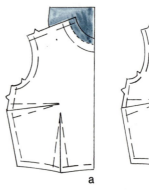 

a   b

If the garments you make slide back repeatedly, it may be because the *back neckline is too short.* Add length in the needed amount to the back shoulder seam at the neck only (a) or across the entire back shoulder seam (b).

If the shoulder seams in your garments are too far forward, so they are visible in front, the *back neckline is too long.* Take some length off the back shoulder seam in the needed amount at the neck only (c) or across the entire back shoulder seam (d).

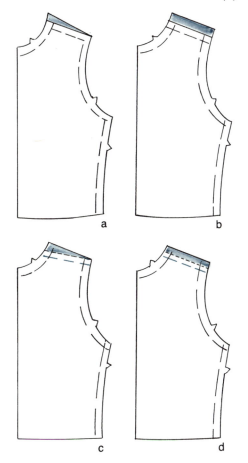

NECKLINE. From turtleneck to waistline plunge, it's a neckline! Whether it be round, square, jewel, oval, bateau, V-shaped, keyhole, scooped, asymmetric, high, low, in between, or any one of an endless number of variations, neckline shape is important. Sitting or standing, moving or at rest, your face and adjacent parts of the anatomy are the center of interest. An attractive or arresting neckline is very much part of the picture.

Anything higher than a "natural" neckline (q.v.), is called a raised neckline (q.v.). Anything lower is a dropped neckline (q.v.). A slightly dropped neckline creates the illusion of a slimmer neck. The "poor boy" turtleneck can be as flattering to the not quite so young as to the young. However low or however high, the neckline must lie smoothly against the body with no straining or gaping. In fit and construction it should be as perfect as one can make it.

NECKLINE: BIAS-BOUND FINISH. *See* BIAS BINDING.

NECKLINE: CORDED OR PIPED. *See* CORDED SEAM; CORDED SELF-FINISHED EDGE; PIPING.

NECKLINE FACING. The facing is generally cut in front and back sections, and joined at the shoulders. If the garment has been altered at the shoulders or neckline, make a similar correction in the facing. Either adjust the pattern (preferable) or adjust the facing itself by making the facing seams match garment seams (q.v.).

Stay-stitch the garment and facing necklines. Interface the garment neckline before applying the facing *or* interface the facing. *(See* INTERFACED FACING.)

With right sides together, join the garment at the shoulder seams; join the facing at the shoulder seams. Press all seam allowances open and trim. Free cross seams of bulk. Finish the outside edges of the facing (when necessary) in any way suitable for the fabric.

With right sides together, matching seams and centers, pin the facing to the garment, stretching as necessary. With the facing side up, stitch the two. Be sure to keep the seam an even distance from the raw edge (a).

If the neckline is square, reinforce the corners with short stitches for 1 inch on both sides of each corner (b). If the neckline is V, take one stitch across the point (c). Trim and grade all seam allowances, making those of the garment wider. Clip all curves, corners, or V (a,b,c).

Press the seam allowances open, a small section at a time, over the point presser for a straight seam, over the tailor's ham for a curved seam.

Turn the facing to the inside, rolling the joining seam to the underside too. Press.

To ensure that the facing will never slip into view, anchor it with topstitching (a) or understitching (q.q.v.) (b), by hand or by machine.

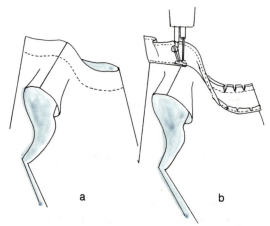

To fasten the outer edge of the facing to the garment, tack at all inner seams with a whipstitch, catch stitch or blindstitch to an underlining when there is one.

NECKLINE FACING PATTERN. Use the facing pattern provided in the pattern. If you would like to make your own, *see* FACING PATTERN FOR A SHAPED EDGE; FACING PATTERN FOR A STRAIGHT EDGE.

NECKLINE FINISHES. There are many ways of finishing a neckline, depending on the design and the fabric.

The most frequent, unobtrusive, unseen treatment is a facing. It may be shaped, straight, extended, bias. Such facings in no way detract from either the design of the garment or the fabric of which it is made. *See* FACING; COMBINATION NECK AND ARMHOLE FACING; NECKLINE FACING; FACING PATTERN FOR A SHAPED EDGE; FACING PATTERN FOR A STRAIGHT EDGE.

All other neckline finishes become part of the design of the garment. They are both functional and decorative. *See* BOUND EDGES; BOUND (PIPED) BUTTONHOLE PLACKET; CORDED SEAM; CORDED SELF-FINISHED EDGE; CROSSED-BAND NECKLINE FINISH; PLACKET; PLACKET BAND; PIPING; RIGHT-SIDE FACING; SHAPED (APPLIED) BAND NECKLINE FINISH; RIBBED BANDING. All of these have interesting possibilities as neckline finishes.

NECKLINE GAPES. A troublesome and frequent problem. Causes: It may be that the bust is fuller than that of the pattern. Since there is not enough width and length across the bust, the garment (therefore the neckline) cannot settle into its correct position. Or there may be too much length in the garment from the shoulders to the high point of the bust. This may be because the figure is hollow or pigeon-chested. Or the pattern size may be too big or too small.

Pattern Corrections for Gaping Neckline. For a full-busted figure, *see* BUST PATTERN CORRECTION FOR BUST WITH LARGE CUP. If the gaping neckline is not corrected by that adjustment, try this: Raise the waistline dart to bust-point height. Draw the new dart. Cut it out. Draw a slash line from the neckline to the new dart point (a).

Slash the pattern on the slash line and overlap the slashed edges at the neckline

in the amount you wish to shorten it (b). Correct the jog at the neckline. Draw a new, larger dart in the open area created by the adjustment. By this correction, the neckline has been shortened at the same time that more shaping has been provided.

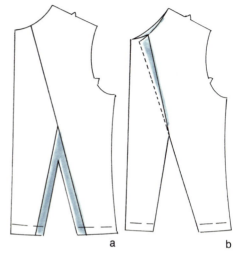

a   b

When there is *too much length* from the shoulders to the apex of the bust, shorten the pattern in one of the following ways.

Fold out the fullness in the pattern at the neckline in the needed amount and taper it to the armhole (a) *or* take a tuck across the entire chest if you wish to shorten the armholes as well as the neckline (b). Correct the neckline and armhole seams.

Sometimes a too tight armhole causes pulling, which makes the neckline gape at the point of distortion. Draw a slash line from neckline to armhole. Slash and

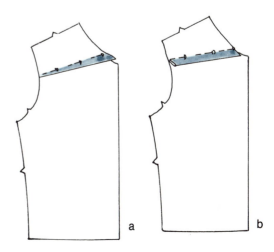

a   b

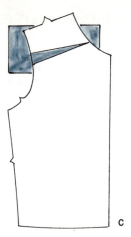

c

spread at the armhole to the amount needed to relieve the strain (c). Fill in the spread area with tissue.

Corrections in the Fitting. Unpin the shoulder seams. Starting at the center front and/or the center back, smooth the material over the body and up into the shoulder seams. Repin. Doing this may raise the neckline slightly but it can always be scooped out should you wish. The important thing is to have a neckline that hugs the body by removing the excess length at the neckline that causes the rippling or gaping.

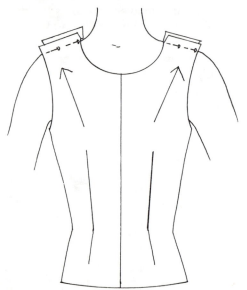

Sometimes, in correcting a gaping neckline as suggested, the front and back shoulder seams no longer match at the

neckline and armhole. Correct the neckline by trimming some of the seam allowance off the back neckline and using as much of the front seam allowance as possible to make a continuous line from center front to center back. Make a similar adjustment at the armhole where front and back armhole seams no longer meet.

Other Solutions. If consistent with the design, create neckline darts or gather the excess fullness.

Be sure to adjust facings or collar to fit the corrected neckline and facing or sleeve cap to fit the new armhole.

NEEDLES. Whether for hand or machine sewing, needles are designed for specific uses. They vary in type. They are graded from fine to coarse. Have an assortment on hand for your various stitching needs. *See* NEEDLE/THREAD/STITCH LENGTH GUIDE.

Types of Needles. Regular *sharp-pointed needles* (a) are the type most often used for all woven fabrics. *Ball-point needles* (b) are recommended for knit and stretch fabrics because their rounded points enter the fabric between the yarns rather than piercing them as sharp-pointed needles do. *Wedge-point (leather-point) needles* (c) have a specially designed cutting point that pierces rather than tears the skin of leather or leather-like fabrics. *See* NEEDLES FOR HAND SEWING *for each type.*

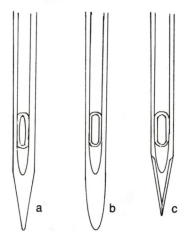

a   b   c

Care of Needles. Essential to perfect stitching is a perfect needle. Discard all bent, blunt, or damaged needles. The burr that often develops at needle point snags the material. Sticky or coated machine needles can cause skipped stitches. Out-of-set machine needles produce imperfect stitches or none at all.

Replace all problem needles with fresh, clean ones. To clean, work the needles through an emery cushion or wipe them with a cloth moistened with machine oil. Be sure to remove all traces of oil before using. The emery cushion is also used to file off burrs at needle point. The black paper package in which many needles are sold protects them from rust. Keep them there.

NEEDLES FOR HAND SEWING. Since the first primitive seamstress threaded her bone needle with a coarse sinew, there have been a multitude of hand needles devised for every conceivable purpose. No matter what needs sewing on—be it a bead, a mattress, a sail, a handkerchief, an upholstered sofa, a chiffon dress, a fur collar, or a hole in a sock—you can be sure there is a needle for it. Choose your needle according to the job you will be doing and the kind of thread you will be using. Choose those that are large enough to handle but small enough to avoid harming the fabric.

Needles for General Hand Sewing. Note that in these needles the smaller the number of the needle the longer and coarser it is. For dressmaking and tailoring the numbers 7 to 10 are best.

Sharps (sizes 1 to 12). Medium-length needles with small rounded eyes. They are suitable for almost all fabric weights.

Betweens (sizes 1 to 12). Shorter needles with small rounded eyes. Use them for work that requires fine stitches.

Both of the above are most easily obtainable of all needles but are hardest to thread because of their tiny eyes.

Milliner's needles (sizes 3/0 to 12). Long needles with small rounded eyes. These are useful for long basting stitches as well as millinery work.

Ball-points (sizes 5 to 10). Like sharps ex-

cept that the points are rounded. *See* NEEDLES: TYPES OF NEEDLES.

Calyx-eyes (sizes 4 to 8). Self-threading needles like sharps except that they have slits into the eyes into which the thread is slipped and pulled. They are used especially by those who find threading a needle difficult or for heavy threads like buttonhole twist or embroidery floss.

Needles for Heavy-Duty Sewing.
Sailmakers (sizes 14 to 17). For use on canvas and heavy leather. These needles have spearlike points (similar to the glover's needles) that extend part way up the shaft.

Curved needles (sizes 1½ to 3 inches). For use on upholstery or for any job where a straight needle would be difficult to use.

Needles For Specialized Sewing.
Cotton darners (sizes 1 to 19). Long-eyed needles designed for darning with cotton. They may also be used for basting.

Double longs (sizes 5/0 to 9). Longer than the cotton darners and able to span larger holes.

Yarn darners (sizes 14 to 18). The longest of the darning needles having large eyes, they are used for darning with heavy or multiple yarns.

Glover's needles (sizes 3/0 to 9). Short, round-eyed needles with wedge points. They are used on leather, leather-like fabrics, and fur.

NEEDLES FOR MACHINE SEWING. All-important to your stitching is the correct size, type, and insertion of the machine needle.

While the needles may be interchangeable, the size numbers of foreign and domestic needles differ.

Domestic		Foreign
# 9	fine	#60
#14	medium	#80
#19	heavy	100
	and sizes between	

To be sure of the correct size, read the specifications on the machine-needle package.

In general, the lower the number, the

finer the needle. In selecting the needle size, one must consider the weight and character of the fabric and thread used for sewing. Use the strongest fine thread available so you can use the finest needle possible for the material. The eye of the needle should be large enough to pass the thread through without fraying or breaking it. The needle blade should be fine enough to enter the fabric without marring it, yet heavy enough to pierce the fabric without being bent or broken. *See* NEEDLE/ THREAD/STITCH LENGTH GUIDE.

Ideally, the machine needle should be changed after stitching two or three garments, since it can become burred or bent from use. The former mars the fabric, the latter affects the stitching.

Twin and triple needles can be used on many sewing machines for decorative stitching. Consult your sewing machine instruction book for directions.

NEEDLE/THREAD/STITCH LENGTH GUIDE. The choice of needle, thread, and stitch length depend on the *fabric* weight, texture, structure, fiber content and the *function* of the stitching.

FABRIC
Weight—delicate, light, medium–light, medium, medium–heavy, heavy, very heavy.

Texture—soft, supple, pliable, to crisp, stiff, hard, firm; gauzy to heavy, dense, compact or bulky; flat, smooth or raised, blistered, looped, fuzzed.

Structure—woven, knit, felted, bonded, open mesh.

Fiber Content—cotton, silk, wool, flax, synthetic.

FUNCTION OF STITCHING
Temporary, permanent, decorative, stretch.

To meet this great range of fabric and function there is a choice of needles, threads, stitch lengths.

NEEDLES
Type—choose by fabric structure: sharp points for most sewing; ball-points for knits; wedge points for leather and leather-like fabrics.

Size—choose by the size of the fabric yarns: fine needles for fine yarns, medium-size needles for medium-size yarns, heavy needles for heavy yarns.

See NEEDLES FOR HAND SEWING; NEEDLES FOR MACHINE SEWING.

THREAD (q.v.)
Choose by fiber content of fabric (animal, vegetable, mineral, synthetic); the size of the fabric yarn (delicate to heavy); and fabric structure (woven, knit, and so on).

STITCH LENGTH
The most important consideration in the choice of stitch length is the weight and bulk of the fabric. In general, the heavier and/or bulkier the fabric, the larger the stitch; the lighter, the softer, the more delicate the fabric, the shorter the stitch. Also consider the *function of the stitching:* whether it is temporary, like basting, permanent, like a seam, stretch for stretch fabrics, decorative, like topstitching. *See listing for each.*

See also listings for particular fabrics or special uses: BEADED FABRIC; BUTTONS; BUTTONHOLE; FUR FABRIC; LEATHERLIKE FABRICS.

Before sewing any garment, make a test seam to determine the best combination of needle, thread, and stitch length. If the correct needles and threads are not available in your community, it is possible to obtain them from a mail-order supply company. These are advertised in the pattern magazines.

NET-BOUND EDGE FINISH. A lightweight inconspicuous finish for delicate fabrics. Cut a 1/2-inch strip of net for the binding. Fold it lengthwise not quite in half and press. Use the narrow side of the strip on top, the wider side on the underside of the seam allowance.

Slip the trimmed seam allowance of the garment into the fold of the net binding. From the upper side, stitch close to the raw edge of the net through all thicknesses, being sure to catch the net on the underside.

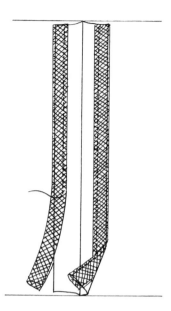

The latter are not cut individually but as groups. When you find a notch (or more than one) you will find its twin on another section of the garment. The two must be matched. This speeds up the assembling of a garment.

It is safest to cut the notches *out from the cutting line.* They may be cut into the seam allowance if the fabric won't ravel or if the seam allowance won't be needed for fitting.

A V-shaped notch may be *cut into the seam allowance* to eliminate bulk or rippling on a curved seam when it is pressed open, as in a princess-style garment.

To Cut a Notch into the Seam Allowance: Fold the material where the notch is indicated on the pattern (a). Snip diagonally across the corner (b). When the fabric is opened out, the complete notch will appear (c). When used for marking, the notch should be small.

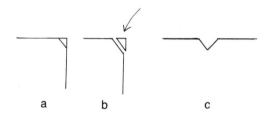

a   b   c

Other Ways of Marking the Notches. Make a short snip into the seam allowance. This may be harder to see but will do if you are in a hurry.

Make several loops of double thread of contrasting color. This is a good method for very heavy or varicolored fabrics or fabrics that ravel.

NOTIONS. The small articles or materials other than the fashion fabric or the interfacings that are used in the making of a garment—thread, zippers, closures, trims, elastic, and the like.

NYLON TAPE FASTENERS. There are two parts to the fastener: one tape with looped nap, the other with a hooked nap. The two lock like burrs when pressed together, un-

NONWOVEN INTERFACING. Made by fusing fibers with heat, this type of interfacing has no grain, can be cut in any direction, and won't ravel. It comes in light, medium, and heavy weights; in white, black, and some natural colors. It is both machine-washable and dry-cleanable.

Some nonwoven interfacings have an "all-bias" construction, with stretchability in every direction, making them suitable for some shaping. Some have durable-press finishes, making them useful for durable-press fabrics.

Choose a nonwoven interfacing that is compatible with the weight of the garment fabric and requires the same care and cleanability.

Nonwovens are fine for belled, bouffant, dramatic, or exaggerated style lines, and for stiff details like standing or shirt collars. They work well as reinforcement for small areas. But they do not have the ease, stretch, and shaping qualities of the woven interfacings, making them less desirable for tailoring and fine dressmaking.

NOTCHED COLLAR. For dressmaking method, *see* FLAT COLLAR. For tailoring, *see* TAILORED NOTCHED COLLAR.

NOTCHES. Triangular or diamond shapes on the cutting line of a pattern. They come singly or in twos or threes.

lock when pulled apart. It is a good closure for home decorating, upholstery, slipcovers, and the like. It is more limited for use in clothing because it produces a bulky closing.

These fasteners call for a lapped application. The seam allowance or facing edge should be wider than the tape. For extra strength, cut the underlap allowance double.

Place the hook tape on the underlap and stitch all around the edges through all layers of fabric. Position the loop tape on the overlap and stitch around all its edges through all layers of fabric.

For a neater but not as strong application, stitch the loop tape to the underside of the overlap around all its edges before turning the overlap to the underside. When in position, stitch along the open edge of the underlap only.

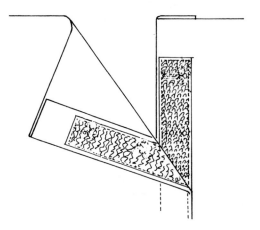

OFF-GRAIN PRINTED FABRIC. *See* FABRIC PRINTED OFF GRAIN.

OFF-GRAIN STITCHING. A useful method for easing a slight amount of fullness or for preventing the top layer of fabric from slipping forward. *See* EASE STITCHING.

OFF-SHOULDER NECKLINE. One cut low, just above the bustline, exposing the neck and upper arms. There is a semblance of a sleeve draped low on the upper arm.

The off-shoulder neckline is generally held within bounds with narrow elastic run through a casing stitched just inside the entire neckline or only over the arm. The elastic should fit tightly into the casing.

In styles in which this would not be a desirable effect, the dress is treated like a strapless one (q.v.) and requires a boned bodice or a boned lining.

ONE-PIECE COLLAR (OR CUFFS). This is a straight band collar with upper collar and undercollar (facing) cut all in one piece. Interfacing may be applied to the upper collar, the undercollar, or both. *See* COLLAR INTERFACING.

When the undercollar is interfaced, cut out the interfacing from the undercollar pattern to the fold line. Place it over the wrong side of the undercollar. Pin or baste it to position.

In *lightweight materials,* machine-stitch 3/4 inch in from the three outside edges. Trim the interfacing close to the stitching so none of it will be caught in the seam. To fasten the fourth edge along the fold, either machine-stitch 1/8 inch from the fold line or catch-stitch lightly along the fold line.

In *heavier materials,* trim away all seam allowances. Catch-stitch all edges of interfacing to collar.

When the upper collar is interfaced, use sheer or transparent materials so the joining seams will not be visible and soft or lightweight fabrics when a soft edge at the fold line is desirable.

Cut the interfacing from the upper collar pattern plus a seam allowance along the lengthwise fold. Place the interfacing over the wrong side of the upper collar and baste it to position. Tack the interfacing along the fold line (on the undercollar side) with long basting stitches, catching only a thread or two of the collar fabric. The remaining three edges are included in the construction seams, then trimmed close to the stitching (a).

In *lightweight or sheer materials,* both upper

collar and undercollar may be interfaced. Cut the interfacing from the collar facing pattern and apply it to the wrong side of the collar. Baste (invisibly) along the fold line (b).

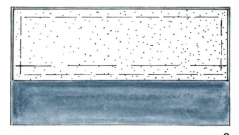

a

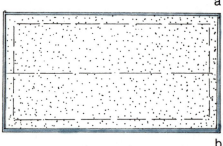

b

To Complete All Types of One-Piece Collars. With right sides together, fold the interfaced collar lengthwise along the fold line. Starting at the neck edge and tapering to nothing at the corners, set back the raw edge of the upper collar from the raw edges of the undercollar. This is done so that some of the collar seam allowance may be used for the extra length necessary to roll the joining seam to the underside. Across the ends, stitch a seam allowance in from the undercollar raw edges. Leave the neck edge open.

Press the seam allowances open, using the point presser to get into the corners of the collar. Trim the seam allowances and grade them. Snip diagonally across the corners to free them of bulk.

Turn the collar to the right side, carefully working out all corners with a blunt-edged instrument. Press all outside edges.

Attach the collar to the garment according to type—flat, rolled, or standing (q.q.v.).

OPEN DOUBLE LAYOUT. Used for fabrics that have nap, pile, or directional design. Open fabric to its full width, right side up.

Mark the direction of the fabric design or nap with chalked arrows along the selvage. Measure the amount of fabric needed for the complete one-way layout. (This calls for a trial layout.) Remove the pattern. Cut at the determined length along the crosswise straight of goods. Swing the fabric around so the nap or design of both layers are going in the same direction. (The arrows will indicate this.) Place the two thicknesses together, open full width, right sides inside. Replace the pattern on the double thicknesses for the final layout. *See also* CROSSWISE FOLD LAYOUT.

OPEN SINGLE LAYOUT. Sometimes pattern pieces are so wide that each section must be placed individually on the full width of the fabric. This is particularly true in the case of asymmetric and bias designs, which require a complete pattern section rather than the usual half pattern.

Open the fabric to its full width, right side up, single thickness. Place the pattern on the fabric with the printed side up—just as that section will appear in the finished garment.

ORGANZA. A sheer, crisp fabric. It is beautiful for dress or trimming. Because of its very light weight and crispness, it is also effective in the construction of a garment. As an underlining it adds lightweight support to many fabrics. Scraps of it can be used for covered snaps and for finishing the underside of bound buttonholes. It is also excellent as a facing or interfacing in sheer fabrics.

While silk organza makes a couture garment, the less expensive rayon (or other synthetic fiber) organza is more practical for inner construction purposes.

OUTLET (MEN'S TROUSERS). The extra fabric added at the waistline to the center back seam and at the top of the front inseam.

At the waistline, add 1 inch at the back crotch seam. Taper to the crotch point (a). This is a standard addition allowing for changes in weight and size at the waist and upper hip areas. Add a similar amount to the waistband.

For a more comfortable fit *at the inseam,* add 3/4 inch at the crotch point of the left or right front trouser leg. Taper toward the waist and toward the inseam 5 inches below the crotch point (b).

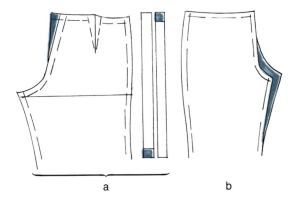

a   b

OVER-AND-OVER STITCH. This reinforcing stitch consists of two or more backstitches sewn one directly over the other.

OVERCASTING. A commonly used edge finish that can be done by hand or by machine.

By Hand. Work a series of loose, slanting stitches over either a single or double row of raw edges. Make them deep enough and close enough to prevent raveling. Keep the stitches even in depth and evenly spaced, "easy," not drawn up tight. Use a single thread (a).

By Machine. Set the sewing machine for an overedge zigzag stitch wide enough and close enough to protect the edge. How wide and how close depends on the fabric. Test (b).

If your sewing machine does not have an overedge capacity but does have a zigzag stitch, stitch near but not on the edge of the seam allowance. Trim close to the stitching (c).

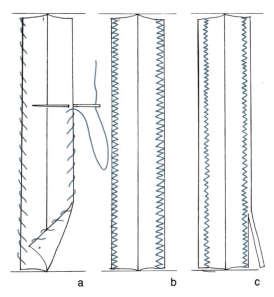

a   b   c

OVERCOAT BUTTON. To provide the necessary length for bridging the thickness of an overcoat overlap, it may be necessary to add a stem in addition to the metal shank of the button. *(See* BUTTON SHANK OR STEM.)

Secure the thread on the right side at the button placement. Place the forefinger between the button and the garment as a guide for the additional length. Take several stitches between the shank and the garment fabric (a). End with the thread just under the button. Wind it tightly around the stitches until you reach the garment (b). Fasten the thread on the underside.

If the button is subjected to great strain, as often happens in a heavy overcoat, the

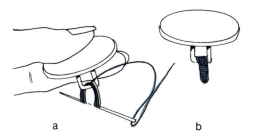

a   b

fabric at the base of the shank is apt to tear. To prevent this, a smaller button is used as a reinforcement on the underside of the garment directly under the overcoat button. *See* REINFORCING BUTTON.

OVEREDGE FINISH. If done *by hand,* work a series of overcast or blanket stitches (q.q.v.) over a turned-under edge. If done *by machine,* set it for one of the decorative overedge stitches.

OVEREDGE-STITCH SEAM. A very narrow (no more than 1/4 inch) seam used where minimum bulk and a degree of flexibility are required. Use a plain zigzag stitch or any decorative variation of it. This produces both seam and seam finish at the same time. Trim the seam allowances to the finished width before stitching or after. *See* DOUBLE-STITCHED SEAM; HAIR-LINE SEAM; ZIGZAG SEAM.

OVERHAND BAR TACK. Use a single matching thread. Fasten it on the underside and bring the needle through to the right side. Take several stitches directly over each other. Make them the length of the bar tack (a). Work closely spaced overhand stitches (q.v.) over them until completely covered (b). The stitches catch the fabric beneath.

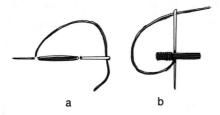

a   b

OVERHANDED TUCKS. A decorative trim taking very little material. Mark the tuck fold line. Fold and pin. Overhand with small even stitches.

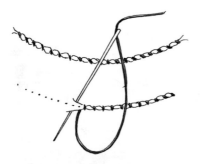

OVERHAND STITCH. Used whenever a strong, flat seam is desired, for instance, when working with lace or fur.

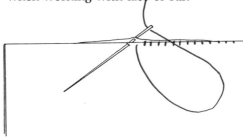

Use a fine needle and fine thread. With right sides together and edges aligned, pin or baste the two thicknesses together. Insert the needle at an angle but keep the stitches vertical, at right angles to the edge of the fabric, passing over and under the edges. The stitches are close, small, and even. Do not draw them up tightly. If you do, the seam will not lie flat when opened.

The stitch can also be worked on a flat surface as in the overhand bar tack (q.v.). When sewn in this manner, they resemble satin stitches.

OVERLAP BELT. A straight or shaped belt with sufficient overlap to take a fastening other than the usual buckle or tie. The fastening may be with buttons, snaps, hooks and eyes, a big pin, or some other decorative trim.

OVERLAP DART. *See* LAPPED DART.

OVERLAP SEAM. *See* LAPPED SEAM.

OVERLAP STITCHING. A method of securing the start and finish of a line of machine stitching where back-and-forth stitching might be imprecise or where tying the thread ends may not offer enough security.

Make the ending stitches directly over

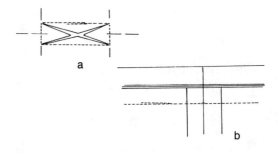

a

b

the beginning stitches for a short distance. Do not start and stop the stitching at a weak spot like a corner or a cross seam. Begin and end a little beyond (a and b).

OVERLOCK STITCH. A machine stitch consisting of several straight stitches and one overedge stitch. This combination both joins the seam and finishes the edge. This may be a stitch pattern on your machine or made with the use of an overlock foot. *See also* ZIGZAG STITCHING.

OVERTACKING. *See* OVER-AND-OVER STITCH.

PADDED EDGE. For use at hems, facings, or wherever a supersoft edge is in keeping with the fabric (satins, brocades, heavy silks) and the design.

Cut a 3-inch-wide strip of bias lamb's wool padding (q.v.) to fit the edge to be padded. (The strip may be slightly wider or narrower so all thicknesses are graded.)

Fold up 1 inch of the strip. Place the fold of the padding along the fold of the edge. Using matching thread, attach the padding to the garment with blindstitches, or to the interfacing or underlining, when present, with long, permanent basting stitches close to the fold. Catch-stitch the upper edge of the padding to interfacing or underlining *or* blindstitch it to the garment. Turn back the hem or facing and finish in an appropriate way.

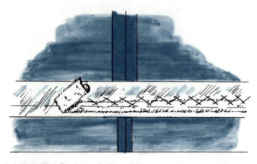

PADDING. Used for filling out or propping up all manner of curves and contours at shoulder, bust, or hips, for set-in, kimono, or raglan sleeves.

There are many commercially available standard pads. As with all standard items, these may be adjusted to individual needs —trimmed down, some stuffing removed or added. When unusual shaping is involved, appropriate padding can be made from the garment pattern.

For this purpose, there are many materials available by the sheet or yard—foam rubber, polyester filler, cotton felt, ozite, hair canvas, Pellon, crinoline, and the like. Anything is fair game if it can produce the shape you want. *See* INTERFACING; UNDERLINING MATERIALS; SHOULDER PADS.

PAD STITCHING. Used to permanently join an interfacing to an underlayer of fabric in a collar, lapel, cuffs. In traditional tailoring, it is also used to join the layers of the foundation. It adds firmness, some stiffness, and a degree of shaping to the pad-stitched area. To achieve all these purposes, pad stitching is generally done by hand. In a limited number of instances, it may be done by machine.

Pad stitching by hand is done like diagonal tacking (q.v.) except that the stitches are shorter and the needle picks up only one or two threads from the underside. (It is always on an undersurface so the stitches will never show.) Generally, hand pad stitches follow the grain of the fabric.

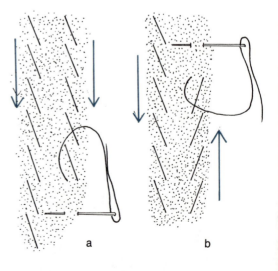

a   b

To form and control any shaping, make them 1/4 to 1/2 inch in length, in rows 1/4 to 1/2 inch apart. For just holding interfacing in place, make longer pad stitches in rows farther apart.

To make *parallel rows of pad stitches,* work each row in the same direction (a). For *chevron pad stitches,* work each row in the opposite direction from the preceding one. Keep alternating the rows; from top to bottom on one row, from bottom to top the next row, *without* turning the fabric (b). It does not matter whether the stitches are parallel or chevron. They function the same way. *See* PAD STITCHING: FOUNDATION FOR TAILORED MAN'S JACKET; PAD STITCHING: TAILORED COLLAR; PAD STITCHING: TAILORED LAPEL.

Pad stitching by machine may be done with straight or zigzag stitches. *(See* MACHINE PADDING STITCHES.) The fact that this produces visible stitches on the underlayer is not the real deterrent to its use. The chief argument against machine pad stitching is the inability to mold the garment section into its desired shape. Only hand pad stitching offers such control.

PAD STITCHING: FOUNDATION FOR TAILORED MAN'S JACKET. Considerable directional pad stitching is required to produce the firm foundation that supplies the subtle shaping of a traditional tailored man's jacket.

Assemble the several layers of the front interfacing and chest piece. *(See* INTERFACING FOR MAN'S JACKET *and* CHEST PIECE.) Join them with several lines of basting parallel to the roll line. Leave enough ease between bastings to pucker the canvas, but not so much that it can't be steam-pressed out in blocking (a).

Holding the foundation in wearing position, pad-stitch the chest piece and shoulder area from the roll line of the lapel to the armhole, except for the shoulder pad area. Pad-stitch in closely spaced, horizontal rows, easing the interfacing material and pulling up the thread tightly (b).

Locate the crest of the curve of the jacket below the chest piece and above any existing darts. Pad-stitch in vertical

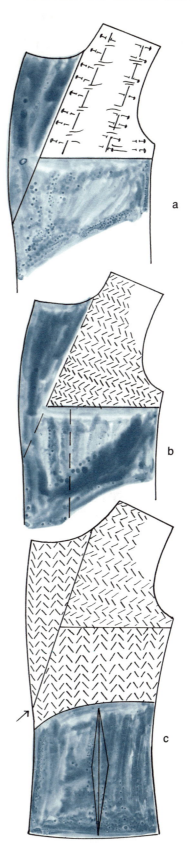

a

b

c

rows from the crest to the side seam, and from the crest to the jacket front just below the break of the lapel (c). Pad-stitch the lapel. *See* PAD STITCHING: TAILORED LAPEL.

When the pad stitching is completed, block the foundation over a tailor's ham or coat-and-jacket press board (q.v.).

PAD STITCHING: TAILORED COLLAR.

In a tailored collar, it is those hundreds of tiny hand stitches (plus the blocking) that give it shape. From the moment the collar interfacing is positioned on the undercollar, one must stop thinking of the two as flat lengths of cloth. Think of them in the round. After all, they are destined to fit *around* the neck.

Place the collar interfacing over the wrong side of the undercollar. Pin to position. Using matching thread, make a row of short, uneven horizontal basting stitches along the roll line. Catch only a thread or two of the undercollar fabric. When the entire row of stitching along the roll line is completed, tug the thread slightly until the collar begins to curve gently into a neck shape (a).

Fill the stand with parallel rows of similar uneven horizontal basting to the *neck seam line*. Tug the thread slightly at the end of each row (b) or fill the stand with short horizontal chevron pad stitching, drawing up the thread firmly (c).

Hold the collar over the hand in a neck shape while pad-stitching the fall. Starting at the center back and following the bias grain of the interfacing, pad-stitch the fall of the collar *from the roll line to the seam line* (d).

The smaller the stitches and the closer the rows, the stiffer the pad-stitched area becomes. Many sewers like to pad-stitch the stand heavily (1/4-inch stitches, rows 1/4 inch apart) and to pad-stitch the fall lightly (3/8- to 1/2-inch stitches, rows 3/8 to 1/2 inch apart). To ensure that the points of the collar (and lapel) lie flat against the body, the pad stitches may be made even smaller and the rows even closer together as they near the point.

Note: It is the way the collar is held while pad-stitching (in a curve) and the direction of the stitching that produce the collar contour. The horizontal stitching of the stand determines the neck shape; the bias pad stitching of the fall guarantees the easing around the shoulders.

PAD STITCHING: TAILORED LAPEL.

Holding the lapel over the hand in a wearing position (a), pad-stitch from the roll line to the seam line (b) or to the inner edge of tape when used (c).

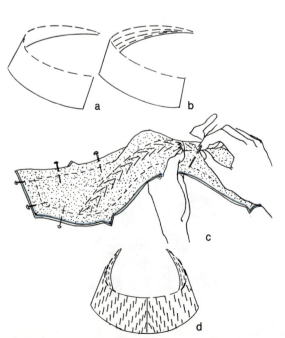

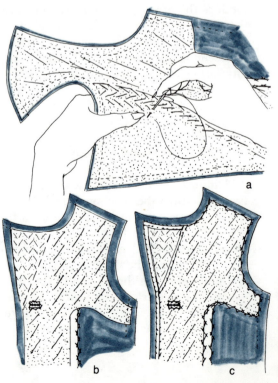

The stitches follow the grain of the interfacing and may be parallel or chevron. (*See* PAD STITCHING.) The size of the stitches and the space between the rows follow the same rules as for the undercollar. (*See* PAD STITCHING: TAILORED COLLAR.) If you have not already done so, trim away all interfacing seam allowances.

PANTS CONSTRUCTION. The construction of women's pants is no more difficult than making a simple dress. Anyone who can stitch a seam can make a pair of pants. *See* CROTCH SEAM; CROTCH REINFORCEMENT; WAISTBAND: BASIC METHOD; ZIPPERED CLOSINGS. *See also* PANTS PATTERN CORRECTIONS *and* FITTING PANTS.

PANTS FITTING. *See* FITTING PANTS.

PANTS PATTERN CORRECTIONS. Before tackling specific corrections *see* PATTERN CORRECTIONS for general directions.

ABDOMEN CORRECTIONS

Protruding Abdomen? Slash and spread the front crotch seam, taper to the side seam (a). If necessary, slash and spread vertically as well (b) and/or add to the inner leg seam (c).

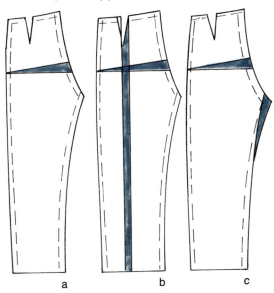

a   b   c

Flat Abdomen? Tuck the front crotch seam, taper to the side seam (a). If necessary, tuck vertically as well (b) and/or reduce the size of the darts.

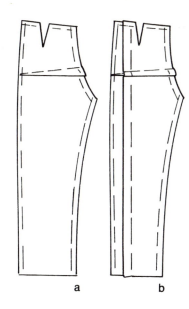

a   b

CROTCH CORRECTIONS

Crotch pattern changes are made first. Any crotch alterations may also affect the side seams, inseams, and waistline seams since these are interrelated.

The Crotch Position on the Pattern. Draw a line across the widest part of the crotch at right angles to the grain line (a).

Crotch Too Short? Slash the pattern and spread to the desired amount. Fill in the spread with tissue paper (b) and Scotch-tape to position.

Crotch Too Long? Tuck the pattern to the needed amount. Pin or Scotch-tape to position (c).

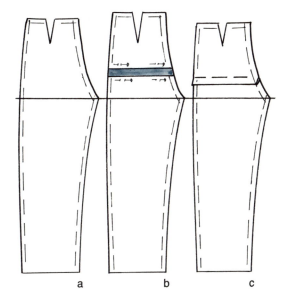

a   b   c

For other corrections that affect the crotch seam, see these listings under PANTS PATTERN CORRECTIONS: *Abdomen Corrections; Hip Corrections; Seat Corrections; Thigh Corrections; and Waist Corrections.*

HIP CORRECTIONS

Wide Hips? Add to the side seam and taper to the waist (a).

Narrow Hips? Take some off the side seam and taper to the waist (b).

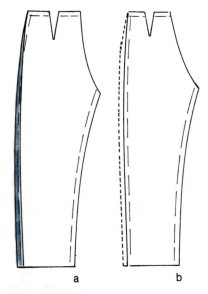

a   b

LENGTH CORRECTIONS.
These are made after the crotch changes.

Too Short? Slash and spread the pattern on the line indicated on the pattern (a).

Too Long? Tuck the pattern on the line indicated (b).

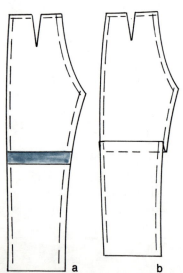

a   b

SEAT CORRECTIONS

Large Buttocks? Slash and spread on the back crotch seam, taper to the side seam (a). If necessary, add to the inner leg seam (b).

Flat Buttocks? Tuck the back crotch seam, taper to the side seam (c). If necessary, tuck vertically as well (d).

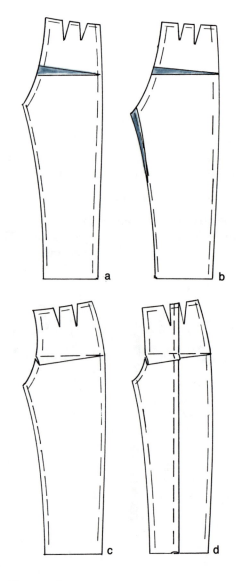

a   b

c   d

THIGH CORRECTIONS

Heavy Thigh? Add to the inseam (a).

Slender Thigh? Take some off the inseam (b).

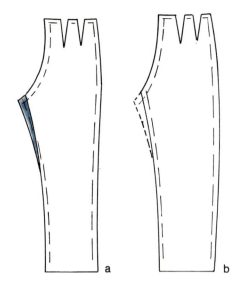

a
b

WAIST CORRECTIONS

Thick Waist? Add some to the waistline at the crotch and/or side seam. Taper to the crotch point and/or hips (a).

Slim Waist? Take some off the waistline at the crotch and/or side seams and taper to the crotch point and/or hips (b).

OR work with the existing darts, making them larger or smaller as necessary (c).

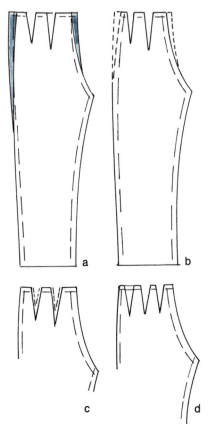

a
b

c
d

OR create darts where there are none (d). Darts can be used in this way for adding to or subtracting from the waistline measurement as well as for shaping.

WIDTH CORRECTIONS

There are at least four seam allowances on which you can make width changes—center front, center back (crotch seams), and both side seams. Divide what you need by 4 and make the correction on each seam. Remember that when you make a change on one seam line you must make a corresponding change on the seam line that will join it.

If this correction is not sufficient, draw a lengthwise slash line parallel to the grain line. For more width, slash, spread, and fill in the space with tissue paper to the needed amount. For less width, tuck the pants to the needed amount on the slash line.

PANTS PRESSING. *See* PRESSING PANTS.

PANTS SIZES. The trim fit of pants starts with the right size, generally selected by the waist measurement. Pants come in the same range of figure types as dresses. If the hips are much larger in proportion to the waist measurement than the standard size, select the size by the hip measurement.

If the pants that complete an outfit come with a jacket pattern, the size is determined by the size of the jacket. You may have to do a little altering to make the pants fit. (When you buy a pants pattern separately, you have more control.) Choose a size that comes closest to your lower-figure needs. Or, if you have a great disparity in sizes between top and bottom, buy two patterns—one for the top garment, the other for the pants. Alter your pattern in accordance with your personal measurements. *See* BODY MEASUREMENT CHART *and* PANTS PATTERN CORRECTIONS.

PARTIAL LENGTHWISE FOLD. One lengthwise fold made on the lengthwise grain.

Measure the widest part of the pattern piece(s) that need to be on a fold. Mark this measurement plus a bit more in from the selvage in a number of places sufficient to provide an accurate fold line. Use pins or a line of thread tracing (q.v.) for the marking. With right sides inside, fold the fabric along the marking. If the fabric has a visible stripe, fold and pin along it.

PARTIAL LINING FOR JACKET OR COAT.

This is often preferred to a fully lined garment because it is lighter in weight and cooler. The construction and insertion of a partial lining are basically the same as for a full lining (q.v.).

Cut the front lining to the underarm seam. Cut the back lining to cover the interfacing. Bring it down on the underarm seam to a point 3 inches below the armhole.

Finish the bottom edge of the back lining with a narrow machine-stitched hem. Join front and back linings at the underarm. Press the short seam allowances toward the front, and continue pressing the remainder of the unstitched front seam allowance toward the front. Insert the lining as usual. Slip-stitch the fold of the front-lining edge to the underarm seam. Bind or edgestitch all unlined parts of the garment that expose construction seams or unfinished edges.

PATCH POCKET.

There it is—out front—boldly exposed to view! By its very nature, the patch pocket becomes an integral part of the design of the garment. Its casualness belies its importance. Its size, shape, and positioning require careful consideration (perhaps experimentation). *See* POCKETS.

Mark the position of the pocket carefully on the right side of the garment with thread tracing (q.v.). If the garment has been altered in length or width, relocate the pocket. Sometimes, when the garment has fitted seams, the original pocket placement may not align exactly parallel to the center front, bottom edge, and side seams. Make the pocket edge closest to the center front parallel to it, even if the bottom and sides are thrown off slightly. If striped, plaid, or figured fabric is used, be sure to match pocket and garment.

Patch pockets may be lined, unlined, or self-lined. *(See listing for each.)* In the making of casual clothes—jeans, shirts, blouses, dresses, jackets, skirts, and the like—the patch pocket may be unlined or self-lined. In classic tailoring, the pocket is always lined. If loosely woven, limp, or lightweight garment fabric has necessitated an underlining, the pocket too should be underlined. Interface to prevent sagging if the fabric calls for it.

To ensure that pairs of pockets are the same size and shape, use a cardboard template (pattern) as a stitching guide.

CORNER REINFORCEMENT

A patch pocket attached to the garment with double topstitching will withstand considerable wear. Those patch pockets attached with a single row of machine topstitching or with slip stitching will need some reinforcement at the top corners to anchor them firmly to the garment.

For Machine-stitched Patch Pockets: Small, identical triangles (a), zigzag stitches (b), backstitches (c), or a patch of tape, fabric, or fusible interfacing placed on the wrong side of the garment (d).

For Slip-stitched Patch Pockets: Use cross-stitches, whipstitches (e), or bar tacks (f) on the underside. The latter may

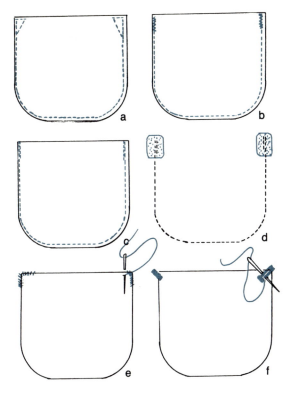

also be used on machine-stitched patch pockets.

ATTACHING THE POCKET TO THE GARMENT

Unlined pockets are machine-stitched to the garment for extra strength. *Lined pockets* are attached by slip-stitching from the right side, back- or whipstitching from the underside. When decorative topstitching is used, it is done *before* the pocket is slip-stitched to the garment; it is not used as *the* means of attaching the lined pocket to the garment.

Place the pocket in position on the garment. If the garment is unfitted, lay it on a flat surface. Allow a slight amount of ease to provide room for the hand to fit into in wearing. If the garment is fitted, place the pocket area over a curved pad to simulate the body curve. Position the pocket, allowing a slight amount of ease.

PATCH POCKET: LINED. Cut the pocket lining slightly smaller than the pocket so that the joining seam can be rolled to the underside.

When interfacing or underlining is used,

trim away all seam allowances and apply to the wrong side of the pocket with catch stitches (a).

Stitch the lining to the hem of the pocket, leaving a small opening at the center of the seam. Press the seam allowances open (b).

Fold the pocket along the fold line of the hem with right sides of pocket and lining together and raw edges matching. Ease the pocket to the lining and pin. Stitch around the remaining sides. Grade the seam allowances, free all corners of bulk, notch all curved edges (c). Press.

Turn the pocket to the right side through the opening at the hem. Carefully work out all corners with a blunt tool. Close the hem opening with slip stitching. Press the pocket, rolling the joining seam to the underside.

To Slip-stitch the Patch Pocket to the Garment: Reinforce the starting corner (a). Bring the needle up to the right side. Fold back the pocket against itself, making the fold slightly in from the finished edge of the pocket. Fold back the garment against itself (b). Slip the needle along the folds, alternating between the pocket and the garment (b). The lower stitch starts directly under the end of the upper stitch. Continue slip-stitching around the edge of

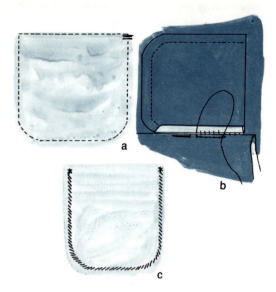

the pocket. Finish off by reinforcing the second corner.

If the pocket is to get hard wear, attach it to the garment with *backstitching or whipstitching* (c) on the underside. The stitches go through the garment and the underside of the pocket. Do not let them come through to the right side. Reinforce each corner.

PATCH POCKET: SELF-LINED. This pocket folds back on itself to form the lining. Cut the self-lined pocket double the size of the pocket. Make the underside a

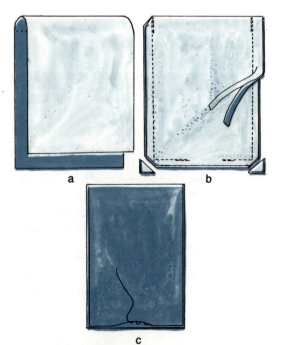

bit smaller on the outside edges. Keep the fold at the top edge (a). The pocket may be square or rounded; both have the same construction.

Fold the pocket in half, right sides together, raw edges matching. Stitch around the raw edges, leaving a small opening at the bottom edge (b). Press flat. Grade the seams. Free corners of bulk. Notch excess fabric on rounded pockets.

Turn the pocket to the right side through the opening at the bottom. Work out all corners and seams. Roll the joining seam to the underside. Close the opening with slip stitching (c). Press.

PATCH POCKET: UNLINED. Mark the fold line of the hem (a). Finish the hem edge in an appropriate manner (b). Turn the hem of the pocket to the outside (right side) along the fold line. Pin to position and stitch the raw edges together (c). Fasten the stitching securely at the hem edge.

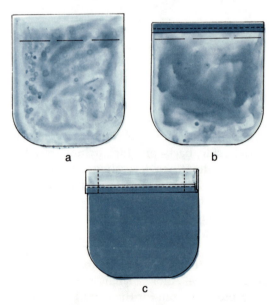

For Rounded Pockets: Continue as follows. Place a line of gathering stitches around the curve of the pocket about 1/4 inch away from the seam line.

Make a diagonal slash across each corner. Grade the hem seam allowances (a) and press them open over the point presser. Turn the hem to the inside, working out the corners carefully. Attach it to the pocket with machine stitching or slip stitching. Draw up the gathering stitches. Turn the seam allowances evenly to the wrong side. Trim the rippling seam allowance to about 3/8 inch (b). Notch sufficiently so the curve lies flat (c). Press.

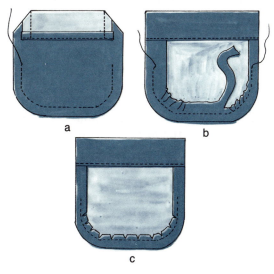

For Square Pockets: Continue as follows. Make a diagonal slash across each corner of the hem. Grade the seam allowances (a). Press them open over the point presser. Turn the hem to the inside, carefully working out the corners. Attach it to the pocket with machine stitching or slip stitching.

Miter (q.v.) the seam allowances of the remaining corners (b). Turn them to the inside, working them out carefully. Keep

the seam allowances even (c). Press the pocket.

Both Types. Place the pocket on the garment and pin to position. Attach with a single or double line of machine stitching. Use a regulation stitch size and matching or contrasting thread.

Make a *single line* of stitching close to and an even distance in from the edge (a). Begin the stitching at one corner and stitch to the opposite corner. Secure the corners.

Make a *double line* of stitching in the same way on a two-needle sewing machine (b). On a single-needle machine, start the stitching at the bottom (middle) of the pocket. Stitch to one end, pivot, stitch the first side and take a few stitches across the end (both to reinforce it and to place the needle in position for the second row of stitching). Stitch around the pocket to the other end; then stitch across the end and down the second side to the start of the stitching. Pull the thread ends through to the underside and tie them in a square knot. Follow the arrows in (c). Keep the rows of stitching an even distance from each other throughout. Take the same number of stitches across each end.

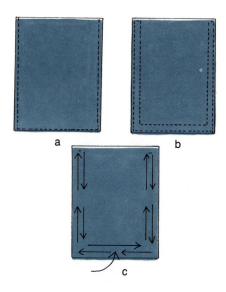

A very pretty patch pocket can be made by *topstitching in from the edge* (a and c). For this, a straight-sided pocket needs a much

a

b

c

d

deeper seam allowance (b) and a curved pocket needs a facing (d).

The topstitching can be used to attach the pocket to the garment, in which case it is done like the single-line-of-stitching pocket. The stitches may be as large as will make them interesting on the fabric while sewing the pocket on securely. Use matching or contrasting thread.

PATCH POCKET WITH SELF-FLAP. The flap is an extension of the pocket turned back against itself (a).

Cut the pocket-plus-flap as one piece. Cut a flap facing of pocket fabric either as an extension of the flap or as a separate piece. Make certain it is deep enough so its outer edge will be well hidden from view when the flap is turned to position. Mark the flap roll line (b). Finish the flap outer edge in a way appropriate for the fabric.

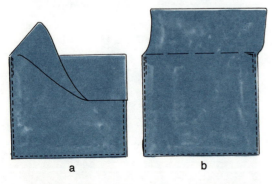

a

b

With right sides of flap and flap facing together, pin, then stitch them. Grade the seam allowances and press them open over the point presser. Free corners of bulk. Notch curved edges. Turn the flap to the right side and press.

Construct the pocket as for any other patch pocket, lined or unlined (q.q.v.). Attach the pocket to the garment, reinforcing the corners. Start and end the stitching (whether hand or machine) at the flap roll line, permitting the flap to hang free (b).

PATCH POCKET WITH SEPARATE FLAP. In this pocket a separate flap is attached to the garment above the opening of the patch pocket. It is turned and pressed down over the opening to conceal it.

Construct the flap (q.v.). Construct and attach the patch pocket to the garment (q.v.). Mark the seam line for the flap 5/8 inch above the top of the pocket.

Place the flap in position with the seam line of the flap over the seam line marking. Pin and stitch (a).

Trim the under seam allowance close to

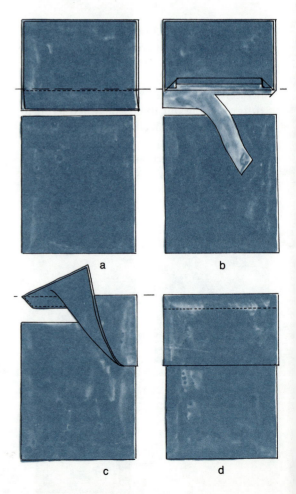

a

b

c

d

the stitching. Fold under the ends of the upper seam allowance diagonally. Turn under a narrow seam allowance on its long edge (b). If the pocket fabric does not ravel, the turn-under is unnecessary. Simply trim. Pin the upper seam allowance over the trimmed under seam allowance. Stitch around all edges (c). Secure the thread ends. Turn the flap to position and press. To hold it in place, slip-stitch it to the garment at the corners.

Alternate method: Skip the machine stitching in (c). Topstitch an even distance from the fold of the flap, enclosing the graded seam allowances (d).

PATTERN COPIED FROM A FAVORITE GARMENT.

It is possible to make a pattern from a favorite garment for which there is no commercial pattern available, reproducing the same style exactly.

The easiest way is to take the garment apart at its seams, darts, pleats, and other types of fullness. Use these cut-apart sections as a guide for your new paper pattern. If this is not possible, the garment can be copied in muslin as an intermediate step, then traced to heavy paper. If the garment is wrinkled or mussed, press it before starting.

Each section of the garment must be copied on the same grain as the finished garment to assure the same hang. Locate the lengthwise grain of the fabric in each part. In a cut-apart garment, run a line of basting along the grain line. In an intact garment, use pins instead; they are easier to detect when covered with muslin.

Run a line of pins or basting along all hemline folds or turnbacks (a facing that is an extension of the garment, for instance). Place thread marks on the sleeve at the shoulder and underarm seams, at the front and back armholes of sleeve and bodice at corresponding points where the overarm curve swings into an underarm curve. Mark the placement of buttonholes, buttons, pockets, points at which collars or cuffs join the garment. Mark any other design details with pins or basting.

When there are several sections in each front, back, sleeve, or other unit, make a separate pattern for each. Half a pattern is sufficient when both sides of the section are cut alike. Bias or asymmetric sections require a complete pattern. To make half a pattern, fold in half each part that is to be cut on a fold. Pin securely around all outside edges. For a complete pattern, mark the center line of the section with a row of pins or a line of basting. In cut-apart sections, identify each by pinning a piece of paper to it telling what each is (for instance, "skirt front," "bodice back," and so forth).

The Cut-Apart Garment. Lay each section on heavy wrapping paper and trace around all outside edges, all seams and darts, pleats, tucks, and other types of fullness. Trace hemlines and hem allowances, fold lines and widths of turned-under sections, the placement of all design details. Trace every part needed to copy the style exactly and all markings that will aid in assembling the garment. Trace the grain line.

Use a sharp-pronged tracing wheel that can go through the fabric to the wrapping paper. Or use dressmaker's tracing paper with the carbon side against the wrapping paper. Examine the tracings on the paper. Correct any wavering or indistinct lines. Use a ruler or yardstick for straight lines. Correct curved lines either freehand or with an appropriate drafting tool.

The Intact Garment. For a *half pattern,* cut a piece of muslin larger than the part to be copied. Straighten the lengthwise and crosswise grains. Place the straightened lengthwise edge on the right side of the garment along the fold and pin. Pin in any darts, tucks, pleats, or other fullness in the muslin to the same amount and in the same position as on the garment. Locate and place a row of pins on all seam lines and edges. Mark the position of buttonholes, buttons, plackets, pockets, collars, and any other design details with pins. Transfer all thread marks that will aid in assembling the garment. Mark the grain.

For a *complete pattern on straight grain,* cut a piece of muslin larger than the section to be copied. Straighten the lengthwise and crosswise grains. Draw a center line or draw a thread on a center line that corresponds to the center line of the section. Place the muslin over the section, matching center lines, and pin as for a half pattern. A sleeve roll or hand inserted in a sleeve makes it easier to work. Handle as for the half pattern.

For a *complete pattern on bias grain,* cut a piece of muslin on bias grain larger than the section to be copied. Mark its center line with a row of pins, basting, or chalk markings. Place the muslin over the garment, matching centers and grain lines. Place a row of pins along and through the center lines. Continue as for a half pattern.

Using pencil or tailor's chalk, mark all seam lines, darts, and so forth as pinned. When all markings are in place, remove the muslin. True the straight lines with a ruler or yardstick, the curved lines either freehand or with an appropriate drafting tool. Add seam and hem allowances. Transfer the corrected muslin to paper. Place an identifying mark on each pattern piece so you can tell what it is.

For All Types. It is wise to make a trial muslin from the completed paper pattern as a test for accuracy of reproduction and for fit. Make any necessary changes before cutting the new garment. Use the corrected paper pattern for cutting; it is more dependable than muslin.

PATTERN CORRECTIONS. The best place to start for fine fit is with the pattern. Working with your Body Measurement Chart (q.v.) and with the pattern measurements (q.v.), decide what in the pattern needs correcting and how much.

Very small changes—1/4 inch or less—can always be made in the seam allowances, particularly in the trial muslin. If

you have to make too many changes or consistent changes of 2 inches or more, get the next size pattern. There is a 2-inch difference between pattern sizes. If most of the pattern fits but some 2-inch changes are indicated, work with the pattern you have.

Pattern changes are very specific. Make them only *where* and *if* you need them. When there is to be more than one change, make each separately, one at a time. It is generally easier to make the lengthwise changes first, then the width adjustments.

Make all changes right on the pattern. Write notes to yourself, slash the pattern, spread, insert tissue, tuck or overlap, patch, pin, do anything that will make the change clear to you. When you have finished making the corrections, the pattern should be ready for use. The changes should be understandable when you pick up the pattern again later, without having to puzzle out or decode any of its cryptic messages.

When you make a change in one pattern piece, remember to make a corresponding change on all pieces that join it. For instance, if you lengthen the front, you must lengthen the front facing to match. If you change a neckline, you must also change the neckline facing and/or the collar and its facing. A change in a sleeve cap means a change in the armhole. And so on.

You will need some tools with which to make the changes: a ruler, yardstick, a tailor's square or 45° triangle, sharp-pointed pencils, Scotch tape, paper-cutting scissors, and tissue paper, shelf paper, or other unlined paper.

All changes in patterns are made at right angles to the grain, either vertical or horizontal. Use the 45° triangle or a tailor's square to determine the right angle.

In comparing pattern and body measurements, keep in mind that body width measurements are whole measurements while pattern measurements are only half (generally). Halve your personal width measurements to correspond to those of the pattern.

Also remember that you must add ease to your body measurements, while the pattern already includes all the ease necessary for the size and style. The pattern has shortened darts. *(See* DRESSMAKER DARTS.) Your measurements at bust and hips are at actual high points of the body.

SOME GENERAL RULES IN REGARD TO PATTERN CORRECTION.

The pattern may be altered on any outside seam line, any inside seam line, within the pattern section, or in all three places.

Length Changes on an Outside Seam. When a pattern has straight lines, it is easy enough to add or subtract at a hem or seam (a). When a pattern is shaped or styled, make the changes within the pattern to preserve the style line and details (b). Most patterns show where this change can be made.

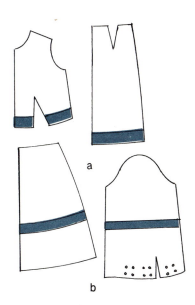

Such changes involve other considerations as well. For instance, in (a), the additional length increases the size of the bodice dart and decreases the front waist-line measurement. If a changed dart is also required, then the length adjustment does two things at once. But if it is not required, redraw the dart in the original amount and retain the original waistline measurement.

Width Changes on an Outside Seam. If the change is a relatively small one—say, up to the width of a seam allowance (5/8 inch)—it can be made at the center, at the side, or within the pattern. However, be mindful of the fact that a change at the center front or back will alter the neckline, waistline dart position, waistline, and hipline. A change at the side seam will alter the armhole, bustline, waistline, and hipline measurements. Remember to make a corresponding correction in any section that joins the key piece.

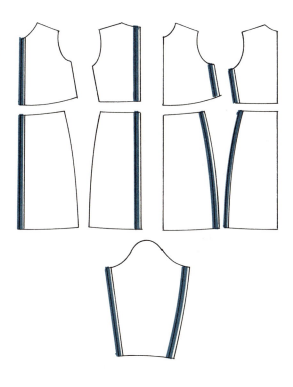

When the pattern change is more than the width of a seam allowance, it is advisable to make the adjustment in two or three places. This type of alteration makes the change gradual and preserves the proportions of the pattern.

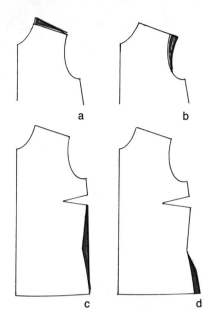

a　　　　　b

c　　　　　d

All of the above changes are *balanced* or *even* changes. It is possible to add width in *one place only:* at the neckline (a), at the shoulder (b), at the waistline (c), at the hipline (d).

Changes need not necessarily be made in pairs. For instance, you may add to the bodice-front side seam but not at the bodice-back side seam. You may add to the back sleeve seam but not to the front sleeve seam. Make changes only where needed.

Corrections may be different on each outside seam, though the two may be designed to be joined. For instance, you may need to add to the skirt-front side seam but subtract from the skirt-back side seam.

However, you must make corresponding changes in pattern sections that join where a change affects the joining. For instance, if you add to the bodice-back side seam, you must add to the back sleeve seam to provide a back sleeve cap that will fit the changes at the back armhole (a). If you narrow the bodice-front shoulder seam,

you must also narrow the bodice-back shoulder seam to match (b).

Length Changes Within the Pattern. Most patterns indicate a place where length changes can be made without distorting the shape of the pattern piece.

In the figure, the great divide is the waistline. It determines the proportion of bodice above to body below. The waistline of the pattern is designed to fit the waistline of the body. To preserve this waistline shaping of the pattern while providing for the proportions of the body, any changes in length must be made either above or below this line (a).

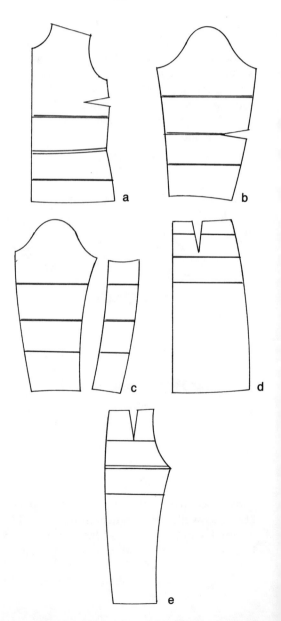

a　　　　　b

c　　　　　d

e

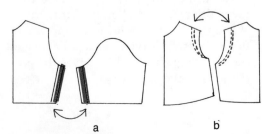

a　　　　　b

In the arm, the great divide is the elbow. It determines the proportion of upper arm to lower arm. The corresponding point on the pattern of a one-piece sleeve is the dart (b) or the elbow easing; in a two-piece sleeve, the fullest part of the curve of the sleeve seam (c). To preserve the sleeve shaping of the pattern while providing for the proportions of the arm, all sleeve changes must be made above or below the elbow.

The dividing line *in a skirt* is the hipline. Changes may be made above or below the hip (d).

In pants fitting, the divide is the line of the crotch. Make any length changes above or below the crotch line (e).

Width Changes Within the Pattern. A width change within the pattern has the merit of preserving the style line of the outside seam. Be sure to make a corresponding change on the seam that joins it.

Changes within the pattern are made on the principle of slash and spread or its reverse, slash and overlap or tuck. The changes may be equal (balanced) across the entire length or width or on one side only.

Balanced Pattern Corrections Within the Pattern. In this type of pattern change the spread or fullness is equal in width or length across the entire pattern.

When making *a change for more width,* draw a vertical slash line parallel to the grain line on the pattern (a). Draw a horizontal guideline at right angles to the grain line on the pattern and a similar one on the paper you plan to use for adding the width.

When making *a change for more length,* draw a horizontal slash line at right angles to the grain line on the pattern (b). Draw a vertical guideline parallel to the grain line on the pattern and a similar one on the paper you plan to use for adding the length.

These rules apply also to *bias-cut sections* of a garment: more width (c), more length (d).

For more width or length, slash the pattern

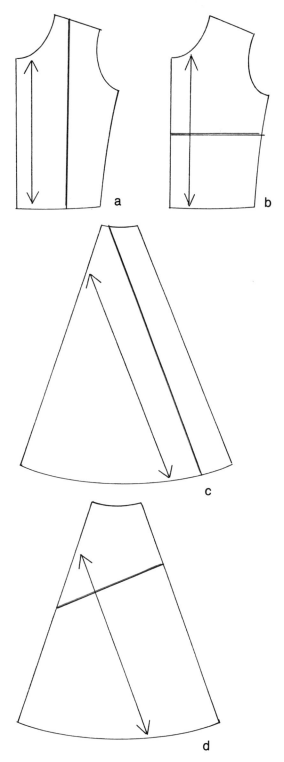

on the slash line clear through from one side of the pattern to the other. Using the guideline like a skewer, line up each pattern section on fresh paper, matching guidelines. Spread the sections to the desired amount and Scotch-tape or pin each section to the fresh paper. If more than two sections are involved in the change, it is a good idea to number them.

For less width or length, slash the pattern on the slash line and overlap the sections to the desired amount. Pin or Scotch-tape to position. Or tuck the pattern on the slash line. Remember that a tuck is equal to half the width of the desired change.

When changes in *both length and width* are involved, make the length changes first.

One-Side-Only Pattern Corrections Within the Pattern. In this type of pattern change, one edge remains constant while the other is spread or overlapped to the desired amount.

Draw a slash line from one side of the pattern to the other or from a dart point to the opposite side. Starting at the edge you wish to make full, slash the pattern on the slash line *to* the opposite edge or point but not through it. While maintaining the measurement of the unslashed edge, spread (for more length or width) (a) or overlap (for less length or width) (b) to the desired amount. Redraw the outside style line. (*See* PATTERN IRREGULARITIES RESULTING FROM PATTERN CHANGES. *See also* ABDOMEN, ARMHOLE, BACK, BUST, BUTTOCKS, CHEST, HIP, PANTS, PRINCESS-STYLE, SHOULDER, SKIRT, SET-IN SLEEVE, KIMONO SLEEVE, RAGLAN SLEEVE, WAIST PATTERN CORRECTIONS; NECKLINE GAPES.)

PATTERN IRREGULARITIES RESULTING FROM PATTERN CHANGES. As you have undoubtedly noticed, pattern changes often produce distortions: angularity where curves are necessary, jagged lines, no lines at all, and similar aberrations. Often the grain line is thrown off. All of these irregularities must be corrected to make the pattern usable.

Whenever an *undefined space* results from a slash and spread, new lines must be drawn to connect the ends of the broken line (a) or to continue the correction (b).

Whenever a *jagged line* results from a slash and spread (c) or overlap (d), a new

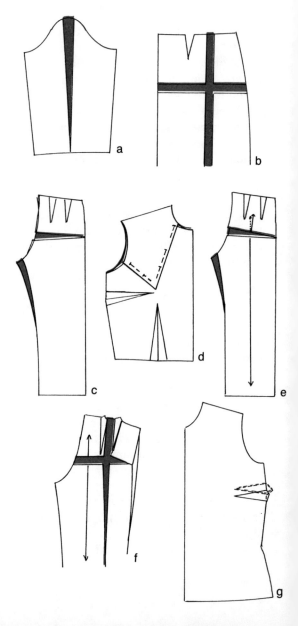

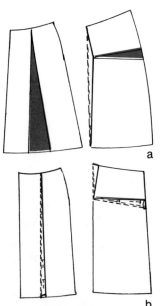

line must be drawn to correct the protruding pattern. The new line begins at the point where it originally began and goes to the point where it originally ended, cutting off all projecting edges. A *jagged grain line* can be corrected in the same way. If the grain line is thrown off close to one end, simply continue the grain line for most of the section (e).

When *angularity* results from a change where a curved line is required, correct it (f). When a *dart* is moved from its *original position,* that pointed little shape at the seam line and cutting line will need to be moved too (g). It represents the amount of material necessary to stitch the dart into the seam.

All seam lines meant to join each other must be made equal in length. This may mean adding to or subtracting from the length of any given seam, as necessary. Whether you add or subtract depends on which will provide the best fit.

PATTERN MEASUREMENTS. It is wise to adjust a pattern so it comes as close to one's figure requirements as measurements (and mathematics) can make it *before* cutting out the garment. After cutting is a little too late to make any major changes. To decide what changes are necessary, how much changing and where, one must measure the pattern and compare it with a set of body measurements (q.v.).

Measure the parts that make the whole. Assemble all parts of a pattern that make each completed front, back, and sleeve of a garment; all parts that make the front and back of skirts or pants. Set aside all applied pieces (like pockets) and one layer of double thicknesses (like facings).

Place the front and back patterns with center front and center back parallel to each other and waistlines of front and back in line with each other *(a, b,* and *c).* Place upper and under sleeves with grain lines parallel to each other and elbow positions in line with each other *(d).*

Using a tape measure, measure the part of the pattern that will appear on the surface of the finished garment.

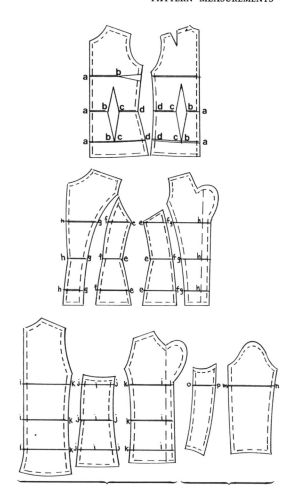

Measure from seam line to seam line. Do not include anything that will end up in a seam or dart. Use your tape measure like an adding machine.

Measure only to the line on which the garment will close. Do not include any section (like an extension) that overlaps a part of the garment already measured. For example: measure from the center front and back to the dart *(a* to *b),* from the dart to the side seam *(c* to *d)* at waist, bust, hips. Measure from seam line to seam line *(e* to *f),* from seam line to center front or back *(g* to *h)* at the bust, waist, hips. Measure from the underarm marking to the seam line *(i* to *j),* from the seam line to the center front or back *(k* to *l)* at bust, waist, hips. Measure from seam line to seam line across the upper sleeve *(m* to *n)* and from seam line to seam line across the under sleeve *(o* to *p).*

Pattern measurements are taken in the

same relative positions as are body measurements. The bust measurement is taken across the fullest part of both front and back about 1/2 inch above the point of a waistline dart and directly in line with an underarm dart. When there are shaping seams rather than darts, the measurement falls across the fullest part of the pattern.

The waist measurement is taken across the front and back as indicated by the waistline marking on a pattern or in line with the widest part of any waistline dart and/or the waistline indentation at the side seam.

In measuring the hips of the pattern, note how far below the waistline the fullest part of the pattern is.

Length Measurements. It is easy enough to determine the length of a garment when it has a natural neckline (q.v.). A problem in measurement develops when the style departs from this standard.

All garments designed to be worn over other articles of clothing are automatically dropped slightly from this line for ease. Many garments are dropped even more for design purposes. Sometimes an artist's drawing or an angled photograph on a pattern can be misleading. The pattern description on the back of the envelope merely notes that it is a dropped neckline but does not tell how much the drop is. So you can see how difficult this makes it to determine exactly the length from neck to waist or to hem. You can see, too, why a trial muslin (q.v.) could be of vital importance in this respect.

Measure the center back length of the pattern from neck to waist and from waist to hem from seam line to seam line (a). (The front pattern can be adjusted accordingly.)

Measure the length of the sleeve pattern from shoulder to elbow and from elbow to wrist (b). When the sleeve is less than full length, this presents the same problem in determining length as the dropped neckline. The trial muslin will help to determine a suitable length from elbow to wrist.

Measure the center front length of a

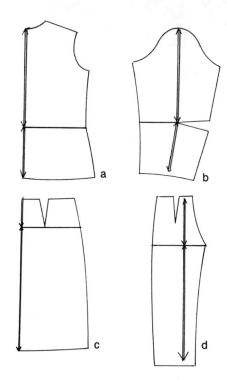

skirt pattern from waist to hipline and from hipline to hem (c).

Measure the center front length of pants from waist to crotch and from crotch to hem (d). Pants are drafted so that the center back curve is longer and deeper than the center front curve. This longer, deeper center back seam provides the length required to accommodate the buttocks when seated. This also makes the back of pants wider than the front.

Keep in mind that body width measurements are whole measurements while pattern width measurements are generally only half. Also remember that the pattern already includes all the necessary ease for the size and style while ease must be added to the body measurements for comparison.

PATTERN PREPARED FOR CUTTING. One might reasonably think that after all the adjustments are made for fit the pattern is ready for use. Not so. It must be further readied for cutting.

Select all the necessary pattern sections. Group them: those needed for the fashion fabric, those for the lining, those for the interfacing. Use each group as needed.

If the pattern is wrinkled, press it flat with a warm iron.

It is easier to cut sheer fabric through pattern tissue, but it is easier to cut woolens and other heavy fabrics beside the pattern tissue rather than through it. Cut off all unnecessary margins of tissue paper.

Elongate the grain lines to the entire length of the pattern section. *See* GRAIN MARKING ON PATTERN.

When a pattern piece needs to be used more than once or reversed, it is helpful to trace and cut out an extra one. This is a great advantage in a difficult layout or when a difference in length or width of pattern or fabric means departing from the suggested layout.

Determine the amount needed for seam allowances. On most commercial patterns seam allowances are generally 5/8 inch. Sheer fabrics need less since they are usually trimmed close to the stitching line. The same is true for many knit constructions. Heavier fabrics may need more, particularly if they have a tendency to ravel. In line with the present no-bulk theory of construction, seam allowances are trimmed back practically out of existence and hems are dispensed with almost entirely.

An extra seam allowance added to the placket on a dress, skirt, or pants will ensure an ample setting for a zipper.

In dealing with double thicknesses (collars, lapels, cuffs, welts, flaps, pockets, facings, and the like) there are the following considerations.

The seam that joins upper and lower thicknesses is rolled to the underside. *(See* FAVORING.) To accomplish this, an extra amount of material is added to the length and width of the upper layer. For instance, add to the outer edge of the upper collar, taper to the neck edge, but do not alter the edge that joins the garment. How much length and width one should add depends on the weight and texture of the fabric. One quarter inch makes 1/8-inch roll for

smooth, medium-weight material; 1/2 inch makes a 1/4-inch roll for heavier weights. For very heavy or textured fabrics, add even more allowance. For very lightweight and sheer fabrics add less—just enough to negotiate the turn. It is best to make a test turn to determine how much is needed.

An outside curve is longer than an inside curve. To accommodate this curve, the upper layer needs a little more length and/ or width. For instance, in a collar, the curve from neck seam to outside edge (a) and the curve from one end to the other (b).

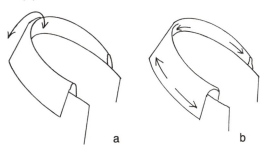

a   b

Add an amount sufficient to make the turns and taper to the ends. This amount is in addition to that already added for rolling the seam to the underside.

There are other places in the garment where one needs to make allowances for favoring the seam or for a turnback.

For a facing that becomes a lapel, add to the outer edge of what will eventually be the upper thickness, starting at the point where the lapel joins the collar and continuing to its break, at which point the favoring changes direction (a).

Below the break, it is the front edge of the garment that needs the allowance (b).

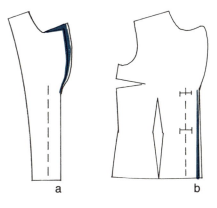

a   b

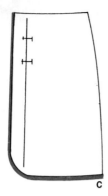

c

If the lower edge of the garment section is rounded, this extra seam allowance continues around the curve (c).

When there is no seam, there is no problem. For instance, an upper and under collar cut in one piece needs no allowance on the edge to be folded under but does need it along the ends (a).

When on this type of collar more length is needed from neck seam to outer edge, it is added to the neck edge (b)—an exception to the rule, since there is no other feasible edge.

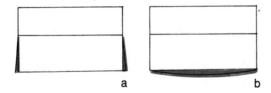

a   b

Why don't commercial patterns include these necessary adjustments? Sometimes they do. (It's a good idea to check your pattern before adding more.) Most often, they don't simply because the pattern company has no way of knowing the texture and weight of the material you will choose for your garment.

PATTERN SHADED, DOTTED, OR EX-TENDED IN LAYOUT CHART. When the layout chart shows a complete shaded pattern section it means the pattern must be placed with the printed side down. If two sections are cut at a time this makes no difference; you will end up with the two sections you need. Often, the first cutting of the pattern is with the printed side up, the second with the printed side

down like the sleeves in the illustration. This layout produces a pair of pattern sections (a).

When the layout chart shows a complete pattern, half of which is shaded, it means the pattern is cut on a fold in that space (b). Either trace, cut out, and add the second half of the pattern for a complete pattern. Or, after the rest of the pattern pieces have been cut out, refold the fabric on grain. Place the half pattern on the fold of fabric.

A dotted-line pattern means the pattern is cut single a second time. A duplicate pattern is a great convenience when the second cutting is the reverse of the first (c).

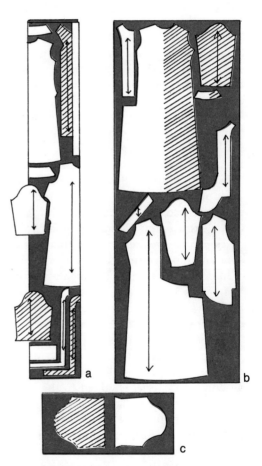

a   b

c

When a pattern piece is shown extending beyond a folded edge (a), it means this piece must be cut in that space after all the other pieces have been cut and the remainder of the cloth is opened out.

Rather than reestablishing the straight grain in this cut-away piece (you may not have enough material left were you to pull threads to straighten the fabric again), establish a grain line in the space parallel to the selvage *before* you begin your cutting. On a wrong-side layout use tailor's chalk. On a right-side layout use pins or basting thread.

PATTERN SIGNS AND SYMBOLS. A pattern contains certain signs and symbols that make cutting accurate and assembling a garment easier. Commercial patterns leave very little to chance or misinterpretation. They use not only signs and symbols but printed directions as well. Even were you to lose that fateful sheet of pattern directions, you could still put your garment together with all the information you will find on the pattern itself.

Every pattern includes a diagram showing all the pattern pieces and their symbols. The pieces are placed in the position in which they will be worn—that is, neck to hem. (It is always vital to know which end of the pattern is up.) Place your pattern in a similar position. Be guided by the shape of the pattern, the position of the printing on it, and the notches.

Some of the markings are for identification only: the name of the pattern company, the number of the pattern, the name of the pattern piece. If no pattern piece name is printed on the pattern, it will have another kind of identification, either a letter—A,B,C,D—or a number—1,2,3,4. In that event, you must consult the pattern diagram on the instruction sheet to find out what the letter or number stands for. Often the pattern will have a letter or number in addition to the printed name.

Some of the markings show how the pattern is to be laid on the fabric and cut out: the fold of fabric, the grain line, the cutting line, the number of times the same pattern piece is to be used.

The symbol for a fold of fabric is two medium-sized perforations or two medium-sized circles ($\begin{smallmatrix} o \\ o \end{smallmatrix}$) placed at the center of the fold line. Or a direction may appear along the fold line: "Place on fold of fabric," or simply, "Fold of fabric."

The heavy outside line is the cutting line. *(See PATTERN PREPARED FOR CUTTING.)* Often a scissors symbol will indicate the direction of the cutting.

Each pattern piece, no matter how small or how large, will indicate the direction for placement of the grain. In most patterns, this is indicated by a long line with an arrow at each end. Occasionally the grain is indicated along one edge of the pattern by the printed direction, "Place this edge on the straight of goods." Some patterns use the symbol of two large perforations.

Some of the markings show how the garment is assembled: the notches (q.v.), special markings which show points or spots that need to be joined. You will have to consult the step-by-step directions for their special meaning in a particular pattern.

Some of the markings will tell how the garment is to be stitched: the seam line, the darts, the directions of the stitching.

In from the cutting line you will find the seam line. This is the line that, matched to a corresponding line, is stitched to produce the garment. It may appear as a light line, a broken line, or a line of perforations. Often an arrow or a presser-foot symbol indicates the direction of the stitching.

The space between the seam line and cutting line is the seam allowance. In most patterns and in most places on the pattern the seam allowance is 5/8 inch. However, there are some patterns and some places on them that call for less. Using a gauge, spot-check the amount of seam allowance in the pattern.

The long triangular or diamond-shaped markings on the pattern indicate darts. These, when stitched, give the garment its shape.

The solid line through the middle of a dart is a fold line. Since all darts must be folded before they can be pinned, basted, and stitched, this is a useful marking. If the pattern doesn't have a fold line you can easily put one in. Draw a line through the center of the dart from the dart point to the base. The little jog at the end of a dart provides enough material to stitch the dart into the seam.

Since there must be some way of getting into a garment, the pattern provides some form of closing. The easiest to handle is a zippered closing. Examine your pattern for a seam that says "Leave open above notch" or "Stitch to O." The part of the seam that is left open will be the place where the zipper is inserted.

Some markings tell where is a good place to alter a pattern for better fit or where it may be lengthened or shortened. (See PATTERN CORRECTIONS.)

In complex patterns you will find markings for the many style and construction details: center front, buttonhole placement and buttons, extension folds, dart tucks, pleats, gathers, topstitching, and so on. The symbols for all these are made up of solid or broken lines, printed directions, perforations, arrows, notches. To understand them, you must "read" them in conjunction with the step-by-step directions.

The first thing to do whenever you open out a pattern is to "read" it for all the information (and there is considerable) represented by the symbols.

Each pattern company strives to be different in some way from its competitors. You may develop a preference for a certain make of pattern for its easy-to-follow markings and instructions as well as for its styles.

PATTERN SIZES: CHILDREN. Children's sizes are designated according to the size and physical development of the average child at a certain age. However, since children develop at different rates, make the selection according to the measurements rather than the age group of the child. See BODY MEASUREMENT CHART: CHILDREN.

For Boys and Girls
Babies' sizes are for infants who do not yet walk. There is a diaper allowance. Patterns are selected by height, weight, and age—newborn (1 to 3 months) and 6 months.

Toddlers' sizes are for the stage between

baby and child. A diaper allowance is included. The pattern is selected by chest and waist measurements and the finished length of the garment. The sizes are 1/2 to 4.

Children's sizes are for children taller than toddlers but having the same breast and waist measurements. Sizes 1 to 6X.

Girls' sizes are for figures that have not yet begun to mature. Size is selected by breast, waist, hip, back waist, length and approximate heights. Sizes 7 to 14.

Chubbie sizes are for girls whose weight is above average for age and height. Size is selected by breast, waist, hip, back waist length, and approximate height. Sizes 8½ C to 14½ C.

Boys' sizes are designed for growing boys with young build: height 4' to 4'10". Size is selected by chest, waist, hip (seated), and neckband measurement. Sizes 7 to 12.

Choose sizes that fit with as few alterations as possible. While the measurements are smaller, the proportionate amount of ease is greater than in grown-ups' clothes. For comfort, children's clothes must be roomy, particularly at the armholes and crotch. All-in-one garments such as snowsuits, creepers, or pajamas need a low crotch to provide ample room for sitting (particularly if there are diapers beneath). Necklines should have plenty of ease. Hems should be generous.

PATTERN SIZES: MEN AND TEEN BOYS.
Teen Boys' sizes are designed for an adolescent figure, smaller in the shoulders and narrower in the hips than a man's. Height from 5'1" to 5'8".

Men's sizes are for adult males with average, fully matured build and average height—about 5'10".

Take and record body measurements. (See BODY MEASUREMENT CHART.) Consult the Standard Measurement Chart in the pattern catalog. Study it until you locate a set of measurements closest to body measurements at chest, waist, hip, neckband, shirt sleeve. Purchase collared shirt patterns by the neck size, chest size, or small, medium, large.

Jacket and coat sizes are selected by

chest size. All the necessary allowances are built into the pattern. If pants or jacket are part of a suit, choose the size by the chest measurement and alter the pants to fit. (See PANTS PATTERN CORRECTIONS.) If there is a wide discrepancy in measurements between jacket and pants or too many crotch corrections, buy two patterns—one for the jacket, the other for the trousers.

If a set of personal measurements falls between two sizes, consider the build of the man or teen boy. If slender or small-boned, choose the smaller size. If husky or large-boned, choose the larger size.

PATTERN SIZES: WOMEN'S, MISSES', TEENS. To guarantee that your clothes will really fit, know your figure type as well as your personal measurements for choosing your pattern size. (See FIGURE TYPES and BODY MEASUREMENT CHART.)

Study the Standard Measurement Chart found in the pattern catalog until you locate a set of measurements most nearly like your own. If you are a rarity, you may match all four measurements (bust, waist, hips, back waist length) needed to determine your figure type and the size of all garments except pants. If you are lucky, perhaps you will match three of the four. If you are a borderline size, that is, somewhere between two sizes, choose the smaller one and grade it up.

It is generally more advisable to make a pattern larger than smaller. Should the discrepancy between bodice and skirt measurements be very great—say, a difference of more than one size—it may be better to buy two patterns, one for the top and one for your bottom, altering both so they merge at the waistline. This would be particularly desirable if the design had considerable or intricate detail.

Since the bodice is the most difficult to fit, size is usually determined by bust measurement. You should know, however, that patterns are generally designed for a B cup. If the pattern fits everywhere except over the bust, buy the pattern that fits most measurements and make the pattern adjustment for an A, C, D, or DD cup

rather than going to another size. See BUST PATTERN CORRECTIONS.

Take into account your shoulder width. If you are broad-shouldered or square-shouldered, use the size pattern indicated. If you are narrow-shouldered, you may be able to get away with a smaller size.

Skirt sizes are determined by waist measurement. Pants sizes are generally determined by hip measurement.

The style of the garment may also be a determining factor in the choice of size. If the design has much fullness, you may be able to wear a smaller size—that is, if you are willing to settle for less fullness than the designer intended. If a design calls for a close fit, you may need a larger size in that particular pattern.

Buy the same size pattern for a jacket, coat, suit, or any garment designed to be worn over another that you would for a dress. All the necessary allowances are built right into the pattern.

In maternity clothes (q.v.), buy the same size as you did before pregnancy.

Having taken such trouble to determine it, insist on the correct pattern size. If your size is not in stock, order it. To settle for another size in the hope of grading it to your size is to invite trouble.

There are many theories and tricks about selecting the correct pattern size. In the end, the sewer herself must decide the size that suits her best with the least amount of adjustment. Success can only come from experimentation.

PETER PAN COLLAR. A turned-down two-piece collar with rounded ends that meet at center front and center back. From the standpoint of construction, it is considered a flat collar (q.v.).

PICKSTITCH. Any of the back stitches worked through only the upper of two or more layers. It can be used decoratively for topstitching or for hand understitching.

PICOT EDGE FINISH. A series of tiny loops forming an edge finish on laces, for instance. Or the picot edge may take the form of tiny points produced by cutting through the center of machine hem-stitching. The latter is used as a finish on sheer fabrics.

PIECING FABRIC. Adding a piece to the length or width of fabric to accommodate the width of a garment section or pattern. The piecing must look like an extension of the fabric. The added piece must be cut on the same grain. If there is a decorative weave or print, it is desirable that the motifs match. The piecing must be placed in such position that it will be lost in the folds of a full section or in the depths of a pleat or tuck where it will not show.

PILE FABRICS. Fabrics woven or knitted to produce a variety of interesting nap effects. The knit-back piles are more flexible and easier to handle than the woven-back piles, which tend to be stiff and hard to ease.

All pile fabrics have directional surfaces and are often referred to as napped fabrics (q.v.). Use a "With Nap" yardage, a "With Nap" directional layout, and listings for specific nap or pile fabrics.

Don't leave pile fabrics folded. Roll them or, better yet, hang them up for storage. Choice of pattern depends on whether the pile is short or deep, sparse or dense. Try to visualize the garment with the bulk of the pile. Choose styles with as few seams as possible. Design lines and shaping seams are extra work that won't even show. Avoid buttonholes; plan another type of closure. A trial muslin is a must. It is difficult to make changes, once stitched. Ripping and restitching may damage the fabric.

PILE FABRICS: PRESSING. *See* PRESSING PILE FABRICS.

PILE FABRICS: STITCHING. The sewing machine is set for flat fabrics. When two layers of pile fabric are fed into it, stitching problems may develop. The piles may lock, the upper layer may tend to creep forward. To avoid this, try one of the following.

Instead of basting all sections together before stitching, hand-backstitch. It holds the layers together firmly. Machine-stitch over the backstitches.

Loosen the tension slightly and reduce the pressure on the presser foot. Raising the presser bar will provide room for the depth of the piles.

To keep the piles from locking, keep the layers separated until they are fed into the machine.

An even-feed either built into your sewing machine or added as an attachment is helpful in letting the fabric "ride" through the machine. *See also* VELVET; FUR FABRIC.

PILE LINING. A fashionable way to add warmth to a garment. It doubles as a lining-interlining and contains features of both. The pattern is like the one for the interlining (q.v.). The construction and insertion are like that of the lining (q.v.) except for the outside edges. Avoid turn-unders and double thicknesses. Obviously, it is important to reduce the bulk of such linings wherever possible.

Choose a style that has enough fullness to accommodate the bulkiness. Eliminate the center back pleat of the lining pattern. Convert the front shoulder dart tuck into a dart. Trim away all but 1/4 inch on all outside edges for a slight overlap at facings and hem. Finish with seam binding. Attach the binding to the garment. Make the sleeves of an easy-to-get-into silky material.

PIN FITTING. Before any stitching is done, it is wise to make sure that the darts and seams are in the right places. For this first fitting, pin-fit the shell of the garment only. Do not include set-in sleeves, collars, or facings or any other double thicknesses of material.

Do all fitting from the right side. Right-side adjustments are transferred to the wrong side with tailor's chalk, pencil, or basting thread. These marks become the new stitching lines. Be sure to make similar adjustments in everything that goes underneath the outer fabric—the interfacing, underlining, lining, and interlining when used.

You'll get a better idea of how the completed garment will look if the darts and seams are pinned on the wrong side. However, it is easier to make the needed changes if the pins are on the right side. Perhaps some of each?

Try on the garment. Pin it on the closing line. When shoulder pads are to be used, set them in place. If necessary for a better judgment of fit, slip the pinned or basted interfacing or underlining into position.

Check the position of the darts and shaping seams. Check the ease and fullness. Keep in mind that the garment will look quite different after pressing, blocking, and the addition of the completed interfacing or underlining. This fitting is not so much for appearance as for size and shaping.

Determine the exact location of the buttonholes, especially if there have been pattern corrections. Decide the best placement of the pockets. (When the design depends on a particular location for the pocket, you may not have much choice about placement.) Check the neckline for style and comfort. Turn up a tentative hem so you can better judge proportion and length. Follow all the rules for fitting with the grain.

Better to make all necessary changes in the pin fitting than after the seams are stitched.

PINKED EDGE FINISH. A pretty finish, but only marginally effective in preventing raveling. Use only on closely woven fabric.

Using pinking shears (q.v.), cut along the edge of the seam allowance. In lightweight or crisp materials, both seam allowances may be pinked at the same time before being pressed open. The seam allowances of heavier fabric should be pinked one edge at a time. *See* PINKED HEM.

PINKED HEM. A quick finish for materials that don't ravel. Simply pink the edge of the hem.

For a *stitched and pinked edge,* make a line of machine stitching 1/4 inch in from the hem edge. Trim the edge above the stitching

with pinking shears. This is a good finish for knits.

Fasten either type of hem to the garment with a blind hemming stitch (q.v.) or a blind catch stitch (q.v.); the latter is preferable for heavy fabrics.

PINKING SHEARS. These come in 5½- to 10½-inch lengths, with the 7½-inch shears most generally used. The blades are not easily sharpened, so cut with caution; the manufacturers of these shears offer a sharpening service.

Pinking produces a decorative edge finish where it can be used. *(See* PINKED EDGE FINISH *and* PINKED HEM.) Don't use pinking shears for cutting out a pattern. They do not give a true cutting line, make it too difficult to judge seam allowances when sewing, and make cutting through pattern and double thicknesses of cloth too hard.

To use, take a long stroke. Start a new stroke at the end of or overlapping the last saw-toothed cut so the pinking is continuous.

PINNING PATTERN TO FABRIC. When you are satisfied with the trial layout (q.v.) of the pattern on the fabric, go back and pin for the actual cutting.

Start at one end of the fabric and place (or check) each pattern piece on it, following its position on the layout chart. As the pattern is pinned, fold the completed end and pull up more cloth. Repeat the procedure until the entire layout is pinned.

First pin the grain line (straight of goods) parallel to the selvage in a number of places for the entire length of the pattern piece. When the grain line is set, smooth the pattern toward the outer edges and pin the rest.

Keep the pattern and fabric as flat as possible, trying not to raise them from the cutting surface any more than is necessary. The pins are placed whichever way will best do this: either parallel to the seam line or at right angles to it. Use one hand as an anchor and the other to pin. Keep smoothing the fabric as you go along.

The pins must go through the pattern and both thicknesses of cloth. Use pins large enough to do so. Place them 2 to 3 inches apart or as close as necessary to provide a true cutting edge. Curves require more pins than straight lines.

Use fine silk pins or fine needles used as pins on fabrics that bruise easily.

When additional seam or hem allowances are needed, mark them with tailor's chalk.

When you have finished the pinning, check the layout with the one on the layout chart. Check off each section to make sure you have them all. Double-check pattern sections that need to be reversed, such as sleeves. Double-check the matching of stripes, checks, plaids, or other motifs. This is the last chance to catch any errors before cutting. Cutting is so final!

Remove the pins from the grain line. There's no need for them any longer. The prolonged presence of pins may leave holes in the fabric.

PINS. There is a type and length of pin for every purpose. They are made of steel, brass, or stainless steel. The stainless steel pins provide the best results since they do not rust. The nickel plating on the brass or steel pins sometimes leaves marks on the fabric.

There are three types of pin heads: flat, color ball (glass or plastic), and T. The flat are the usual type. The color ball is easier to see.

Standard straight, sharp-pointed pins range in size from 3/8 to 2 inches. The standard pin length for dressmaking is No. 17, which is 1 1/16 inches long. It is called a seamstress pin and is good for light- to medium-weight fabrics. No. 16 (a 1-inch pin), while designed for delicate fabrics, is in reality a good all-around pin. For heavier materials, use the larger sizes, Nos. 17, 20, and up. For very heavy or loosely woven materials, use T pins (upholsterer's pins). They won't slip through the fabric. For finer materials, use the smaller sizes, Nos. 14, 12, or silk pins.

Straight pins are available in box packings of 1/4, 1/2, 1 lb., and 5 lbs.

Color-ball pins come in sizes Nos. 16, 17,

20 in white, black, red, blue, yellow, and assorted colors.

Ball-point pins are designed to slip between the threads of knitted fabric rather than piercing them as sharp-pointed pins may.

Discard all old, bent, rusted, coarse pins or those with burrs. Your new garment deserves sharp, new pins appropriate for the fabric.

PIN TACK. Several machine stitches made in the same place. *See* LOCK STITCHES.

PIN TUCKS. Very narrow, spaced tucks, the size of a pin, several threads of fabric, or no more than 1/16 inch wide.

If done by hand, use very tiny running stitches. An edgestitcher or pin tuck foot simplifies the machine stitching of pin tucks. *See* TUCKS.

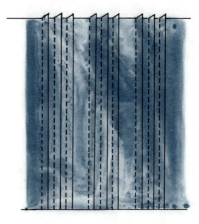

PIPED BUTTONHOLE PLACKET. *See* BOUND (PIPED) BUTTONHOLE PLACKET.

PIPING. A decorative narrow bias fold of fabric or braid included in a seam and showing on the right side. It is made with a filler in the same way as cording.

Piping can be purchased or self-made. The former is limited in color and fabric while the latter can be anything you want —solid color, striped, patterned, cotton, silk, wool. Piping can be stitched into any seam or along any edge. *See listings under* CORDING.

PLACKET. A finished opening in fitted or semifitted styles for convenience in putting them on. There are a number of finishes suitable for a placket opening, depending on the type of garment, the design, the fabric, the location of the opening, and the kind and amount of wear it is to get. Plackets may be made in the opening left in a seam, added to a seam, or in a slash in the garment.

A placket in a seam makes a neat, flat finish and is quite secure; for example, a zippered placket. When a zipper is not available or is inappropriate for very delicate or very heavy fabric, the placket may be closed with snaps, hooks and eyes, or loops and buttons instead. Such plackets may require the creation of an overlap or underlap at the opening. *See* DRESS PLACKET; LOOP-AND-BUTTON CLOSING.

A placket added to a seam is strong as well as decorative. An example would be a sleeve vent with self-facing, typical of suit jackets or tailored coats.

A placket set in a slash is often used where there is no convenient seam to use for the purpose. The finish can be unobtrusive, as in a faced placket or continuous-bound placket. It can be decorative, as in a tailored placket or bound (piped) buttonhole placket. *See listing for each.*

When a placket is meant to be inconspicuous, keep it flat, neat, without bulges or puckers, and with sufficient overlap so it doesn't gap. When the placket is meant to be decorative, be very precise in the stitching.

PLACKET BAND. A type of finished garment opening. It may be a straight placket band (a), a combination neckline-and-placket band (b), or a tailored (French or shirt) placket band (c).

In essence, the construction of the placket band is the same whether it be as simple as the straight placket band or as complicated as the tailored placket. It is this: a band with its facing, generally cut as one piece, is attached to each side of a placket opening in such a way that one band overlaps the other for the closing. *See* SHAPED (APPLIED) BAND NECKLINE FINISH; STRAIGHT PLACKET BAND; TAILORED *(French)* PLACKET.

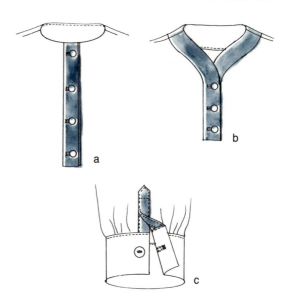

PLAIDS. Designs of printed or woven color bars and stripes crossing each other at right angles to form varied squares or rectangles. One four-sided area in which the color bars form a complete design unit is called a repeat. The repeats may be even or uneven. *See* PLAIDS: TEST FOR EVENNESS OR UNEVENNESS.

Not all styles are suitable for plaids. See the back of the pattern envelope. If it says "Not Suitable for Plaids," it means that the darts and seams cannot be properly matched. Avoid complicated patterns that require much matching and don't show their style lines for all your effort. Choose a design with either vertical or horizontal darts that can be balanced on the straight lines of the fabric design. Avoid diagonal or curved style lines.

You will need extra yardage depending on the size and direction of the repeats and how many seams have to be matched. *See* PLAIDS: LAYOUT; MATCHING; PLACEMENT OF DOMINANT LINES OR COLOR BARS ON THE FIGURE.

PLAIDS: BIAS CUT. For bias plaid designs, choose a pattern with a center seam or opening and even plaids so the two sets of stripes or bars meet at identical angles when the sections are joined (a).

If your pattern is not planned for a bias cut, establish a bias grain line by drawing a line at a 45° angle to the vertical grain

a

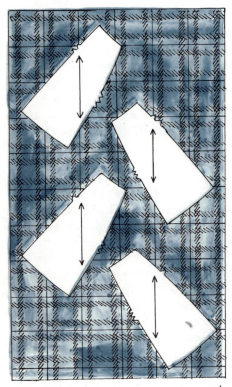

b

line. Make all seam allowances 1 inch. *See* BIAS FITTING.

For accuracy, each section should be cut individually on a single layer of fabric, right side up. If your pattern doesn't provide a right and left side, trace and cut out a second section. Reverse it to make a complete front or back (b).

Match all joining seams perfectly. *See* PLAIDS: SEAMS.

PLAIDS: HEMLINES. Most hemlines are slightly curved to follow the natural curve (circumference) of the body. In plaids (or stripes) it is often better to sacrifice the truth of such a setting for an optical illusion. Notice how the straight line of the fabric makes the hem look even (a). Were you to follow the curve-of-the-body setting, the hem would look uneven (b).

Wherever possible, set the hipline and hemline of a skirt on a straight line, dominant bar, or color, parallel to the floor. Then fit the waist-to-hip area, adjusting the length as necessary. This is the reverse of the usual procedure. In the same way, set the hemline of a jacket or coat in a straight line, dominant bar, or color, parallel to the floor. Fit the bosom-to-shoulder area, adjusting the length as necessary.

Where a curve must be maintained as in an A-line skirt or a slightly flared jacket or coat, set the hemline on the least noticeable color between bars or stripes so you will not call attention to the off-the-straight line (c).

a

b

c

PLAIDS: LAYOUT. The layout depends on whether the plaid is even (balanced) or uneven (unbalanced). *(See* PLAIDS: TEST FOR EVENNESS OR UNEVENNESS.) It is important to determine which type the plaid is.

When the plaid has an up-and-down movement, place all pattern pieces going in the same direction "With Nap." When the movement is right and left, you have a choice. The bars and stripes may move around the body, all heading in the same direction (a), or they may be arranged in a mirror image (b), one side the reverse of the other.

To have plaids and stripes *move around the body* in the same direction, choose the bar or stripe you want for the center, *fold the material lengthwise,* and place the pattern in a directional layout (c).

To achieve a *mirror image, fold the material crosswise,* matching bars or stripes. Place the center line on the exact center of a vertical stripe (d).

When the movement of a plaid is both up and down and right and left (unbalanced) (a), the layout must be directional. The plaids may move around the body or be arranged in a mirror image.

If the fabric is reversible, the crosswise imbalance can be balanced by using the following layout.

On a single thickness of the fabric cut two identical pieces, using the same pattern going in the same direction on similar lengthwise and crosswise plaids (b). Use the reverse side of one as the right side. (This method is workable in diagonal materials, too.)

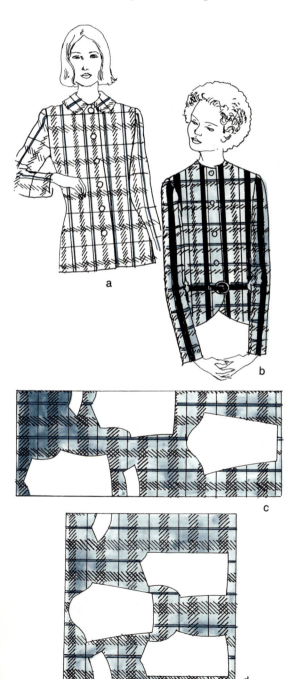

a

b

c

d

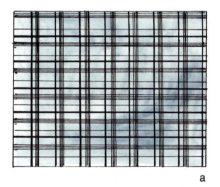

a

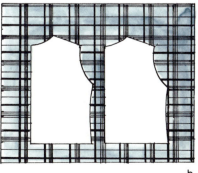

b

PLAIDS: MATCHING. Whether printed, woven, or knit, all plaids (also stripes and blocks) must be matched. The matching is not only horizontal at the construction seams but vertical as well.

The plaids or stripes on the pants begin where the jacket leaves off. The vertical line of the block follows from shoulder to ankle. Note how the patch pocket and flap have been so carefully positioned that they continue the fabric design both horizontally and vertically (a).

In a two-piece ensemble, the matching must be both top to toe and under and over as well (b).

Sometimes, in an effort to dodge the intricate matching, part of a garment is cut on the bias. The collar and sleeve band of this design have been so cut (c). The bias cut, with its change of direction of stripes, also contributes to the design interest.

All dominant lines must be so placed that the finished look is one of continuous plaids with no break between parts of the ensemble. The garment should close with the crosswise dominant lines matching. Plaids are closed over each other so that a complete plaid (usually dominant) is directly on center.

Every part of a garment that joins or overlaps another part must match or complete the unit. This rule applies to the major sections and to the smaller parts.

The center back of a collar should match the center back of the garment. The undercollar should match the upper collar if they are cut on the same grain. The facings must match the edges to be faced; the pockets, buttonholes, and belts must match the areas in which they are located.

Crosswise lines must match at side and shaping seams, center front and back, sleeve seams, and lapels.

Dart legs should be centered and match.

In set-in sleeves the heaviest crosswise lines should match the heaviest crosswise lines of the garment. In kimono sleeves, the dominant lines must match at the seams that join front to back. In raglan sleeves, the dominant lines of sleeves must match those of the garment back and front.

It is wise to let a set-in sleeve pattern and collar pattern, pinned and *un*cut, each rest in the area in which it is tentatively located. Leave sufficient room around it so the pattern can be moved for exact matching after the shoulder seams and the undercollar have been fitted.

It is easier to match plaids and stripes when the right side of the fabric is up. Fold the fabric for the layout in either the lengthwise or crosswise fold. Line up the stripes and color bars. Pin or baste them every few inches to ensure that the underlayer is cut on the same plaid as the upper layer.

The *key pattern piece* is the front. Place it

first on the fabric. Note the position of the notches in relation to the fabric design. Be mindful of the fact that it is the *stitching lines that must be matched,* not the cutting lines. For this reason, it is very important to make all fitting adjustments in a trial muslin (q.v.). If you must fit after cutting, you may displace all your careful matching.

Next, place the section that joins the front on similar lines or bars of the fabric. Continue in this way until every piece has been correctly placed to match those it must join.

Sometimes it is impossible to make every pair of seam lines match. For instance, you may be able to match the front sleeve cap to the front armhole but this may not necessarily make the back sleeve cap and back armhole match. The bodice side seams may match but the shoulder seams may not. Darts always interrupt the matching so that the underarm sleeve seams can match only to the elbow either from the wrist up or from the shoulder down but not both. What to do? *Make those seams match that will be most prominent* and hope for the best from the rest.

PLAIDS: PLACEMENT OF DOMINANT LINES OR COLOR BARS ON THE FIGURE.

Where you place the dominant lines and color bars of your plaid will affect the design of the garment and how it looks on you. Place them where they will be most flattering.

Drape the fabric over your figure and study the effect in a mirror. Note what happens when you place the lines or bars at the center front and back with plaids and stripes evenly balanced on either side (a). (This is the placement of plaids on a jacket or coat. They close at center of dominant overlapping plaids.)

Or place the dominant vertical stripe or color bar toward the side seams, equally spaced from the center (b).

Place a similar stripe or color bar at the center of a sleeve.

If you have a heavier-than-standard figure, avoid placing dominant crosswise color bars or stripes at bustline, waistline, or hipline. They will accentuate your size.

Where possible, place a dominant line or color bar at the hemline of a straight-hanging garment. *See* PLAIDS: HEMLINES.

Often, for design interest, the dominant lines or bars are used vertically in one part of a garment and horizontally or bias in another (c).

PLAIDS: SEAMS. The perfect joining of plaid seams can be accomplished from the right or wrong side.

From the Right Side. Turn under the seam allowance of one side. Lap the folded edge over the seam line of the second side, matching all bars and stripes. Pin and slip-baste (a). Machine-stitch on the wrong side.

From the Wrong Side. Place the corresponding bars and stripes of both thicknesses of fabric together. Pin at right angles to the seam and carefully stitch over the pins (b).

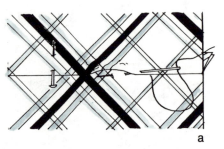

a

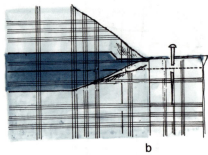

b

Combination Method. It is true that you can see the matching better from the right side but that is no guarantee that the precision matching can be retained when stitched on the wrong side. Often the pressure of the presser foot displaces it. Pinning the crossbars is a surer way; stitching cannot dislodge the pins. Try a combination of both methods.

Bias Seams. Use the combination method of matching the plaids. Stabilize

the bias seam by placing a strip of tissue paper under the seam for stitching. Strip away the tissue after the seam is completed.

PLAIDS: TEST FOR EVENNESS OR UNEVENNESS. Plaids are designed with an even (balanced) or uneven (unbalanced) placement of lines, bars, and colors. To complicate matters, the plaids may be square or rectangular. The former are easier to work with than the latter. Before you can decide how to use them, you must determine which type your plaid is. There are two ways you can test. Choose whichever is easier for you.

a

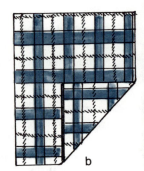
b

METHOD 1. FOLD THE FABRIC
Fold the fabric diagonally through the center of any repeat. In an even plaid, the spaces and colors match both lengthwise and crosswise (a). In an uneven plaid, the spaces and colors mismatch in one or both directions (b).

METHOD 2. "READ" THE DESIGN
Does the fabric have an up-and-down effect? Find the center or dominant horizontal line, bar, or color. "Read" the lines above and below this. If they are the same (a), the plaid is balanced or even. If they are different (b), the plaid or stripe is unbalanced or uneven.

Does the fabric have a right-and-left effect? Find the dominant vertical line or bar or color. Read the lines, bars, or colors to the right and left of this. If they are the same on both sides, the plaid is balanced or even (c). If they are different, the plaid

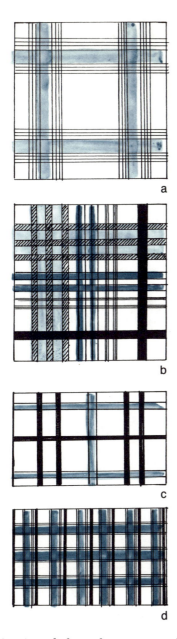

a

b

c

d

Straight Seam. With right sides of material together, stitch the seam on the stitching line, keeping it an even distance from the cut edge for the entire length of the seam. Generally a straight stitch is used. For stretchy fabrics, a very narrow zigzag or stretch stitch may be used. Lock the stitches at the start of the stitching but not at the end. Ease the thread through the length of stitching with thumb or forefinger or by pressing.

Press the seam allowances open. The edges of the seam allowances may be finished in any manner appropriate for the fabric. (See EDGE FINISHES.)

Curved Seam. This calls for very careful guidance so the seam will be an even distance from the cut edge for the entire length of the curve. Use any gauge or measuring device that will help. A separate seam gauge or guide works well. Position it at an angle for a uniform seam edge.

Use a shorter stitch for the curved seam than one would normally use for a straight seam. Stitch slowly. Lock the stitches at the start of the stitching but not at the end. Ease the thread through the length of stitching with thumb and forefinger or by pressing. The clipping and notching of this seam are important for a flat finish. See CURVED PLAIN SEAM.

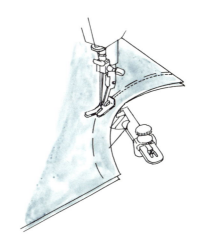

or stripe is unbalanced or uneven (b and d).

It is very possible to get fabrics in which the lines, bars, or colors are even in one direction and uneven in another, or even in both directions, or uneven in both directions.

PLAIDS: ZIPPER IN. See ZIPPER IN PLAID, STRIPED OR CHECKED MATERIAL.

PLAIN SEAM. The one most frequently used in dressmaking and tailoring. The seam may be straight or curved.

PLAIN-STITCH TACK. This is like a blind hemming stitch (q.v.) except that the stitches are farther apart, about 1/2 to 1 inch. It is used for tacking together two sections of a garment.

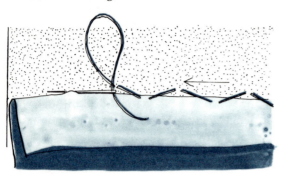

PLATE COVER FOR IRON. A cloth cover that can be slipped over the plate of the iron and used in lieu of a press cloth (it makes it easier to see what you are doing). Commercially available or make one yourself.

To make the cover, place the iron over the cloth to be used. This may be either cotton or wool. Perhaps you will want one of each. (*See* PRESSING WOOL.) Trace around the iron. Extend the outline sufficiently beyond the tracing to bring the slipcover up on the iron and allow for a casing. Use elastic, a shoelace, or string through the casing to draw up the cover to fit the iron.

PLEATED SKIRT FITTING. Despite its fullness, which one might think would cover a multitude of sins, a pleated skirt requires the same careful fitting as a slim, fitted skirt.

Begin with the pattern. Form the pleats on the pattern and pin them into position. Measure the pattern for length and width at the waist and hips. Compare the measurements with your own. Make the necessary overall width and length changes. Length changes are comparatively simple. It is the width adjustments that call for more doing.

In a garment with a single pleat or a cluster of pleats, make the adjustments in the unpleated sections; leave the pleats alone. In a skirt with all-around pleats, the width alterations must be divided and applied equally to each of the pleats. This will mean changing the fold and placement lines for the marking. If you are us-

ing striped or plaid material, make your alterations conform to their lines even if this means adding or subtracting a pleat. *See* PLEATS IN STRIPED OR PLAID MATERIAL WITHOUT A PATTERN.

Cut the fabric from the adjusted pattern. Form the pleats in the fabric, following the fold and placement lines. Baste the pleats in position. Don't depend on open pleats to provide the necessary waist or hip width. They don't look pretty that way. Besides, the grain should fall in a straight line. Pin the pleated skirt to a temporary waistband of grosgrain ribbon for support and correct hang.

When there is shaping from hips to waist, lay in the pleats to fit at the hips. *All fitting starts at the hips.* Slightly overlap each pleat from waist to hips. Keep the top fold on straight grain.

Try on the garment. Knife, box, or inverted pleats hang straight from the hips on straight grain (stripe or plaid) at right angles to the floor. The horizontal grain (stripe or plaid) is parallel to the floor. The shaping of skirts from waist to hips may throw off the grain slightly in this area. Determine where and how much change is needed, if any. Remove the garment and

a   b

release the basting. Keep in mind that even a small amount on each pleat will add up quickly to a much larger amount. Refold the pleats in the new position, baste, and fit once more.

If pleats overlap below the hips (a), refit them above the hips until they hang straight. Or release the side seams and raise the skirt until the hem is even and pleats hang straight.

If pleats spread open below the hips (b), raise the waist at the center until the pleats hang straight and the hem is even. Lower the waistline accordingly. Or release the side seams until the pleats hang straight and refit the seams.

PLEATS. A way of adding controlled fullness, providing grace of movement and design interest as well. They are folds of fabric, usually lengthwise, made by doubling the material on itself. This forms a section of three thicknesses—the pleat (the part that appears on the surface), the underfold (turn-under), and the underlay (return). The three thicknesses are stitched as one along the side that will be attached to another section of the garment. The pleats may either hang free for their entire length or be stitched part way. They may be made singly, in clusters, or in a series. They may be even, uneven, pressed or unpressed, stitched or unstitched, shallow or deep.

A standard pleat requires three times its width. For fuller pleats, make the underfold and underlay deeper than the pleat itself. For less fullness, make the underfold and underlay shallower than the pleat itself. Heavy fabrics require deep pleats (the effect is very bulky, of course). Sheer fabrics may have shallow pleats. Most light- to medium-weight fabrics in almost any fiber can be pleated in some way. Heavy cloth is more difficult.

Some fabrics lend themselves better to one type of pleating than another. Sharp pleats require firm, closely woven fabrics. Unpressed pleats can be done in any fabric but are best in soft fabrics. Knitted fabrics and crease-resistant finishes on fabrics

make pleating difficult. Soft fabrics and wash-and-wear fabrics (except of the permanent-press type) obviously won't hold pleats. In fact, any laundering or dry cleaning will remove pleats. When dry-cleaned commercially, the pleats are set in the pressing. Professional pleaters add a permanent finish to pleats. Some (knife, accordion, sunburst, or crystal pleats) are best done by commercial pleaters.

To ensure that pleats stay in and/or to crisp soft edges, edgestitch both front and back folds of the pleats. Topstitching from waist to hips is often used for a fitted effect.

It is easier to crease, press, or stitch a pleat if it is cut on the lengthwise grain and if its fullness is balanced top and bottom. Pleats cut on the crosswise grain tend to stand out more stiffly. (This would have to be the case with most border prints.) Part of a flared pleat is always cut off grain. For this reason, a flared pleat is generally a soft fold of fabric. (The exception is the sunburst pleat.) To prevent stretching at the folded edge of off-grain pleats, tape the back edges.

Another method for dealing with flared pleats is to cut each pleat separately on straight grain (a). By stitching the sections together one can achieve great circularity without throwing off the grain too much in each pleat (b). You can see how helpful this would be not only for the hang of the pleats but in using striped, plaid, or checked fabric.

When pleats are not made with a separate underlay, they are made in one long piece. If a sufficiently long or wide continuous piece is not available, several pieces may be joined for the necessary length. *(See* PIECING FABRIC.) Any seaming for additional

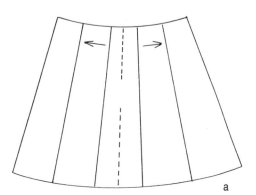

a

b

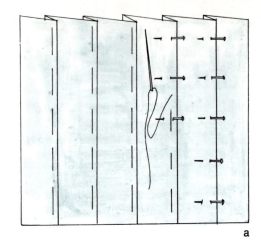

a

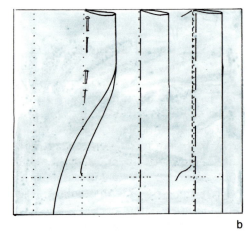

b

length or width or for joining sections is always concealed in the depth of the pleat.

PLEATS: FORMING AND STITCHING.

Pleats may be formed and stitched on either the right or wrong side of the garment, depending on the design and type of pleat. When pleats are to be formed on the right side, the markings must show on the right side. Pleats that are stitched on the inside (for instance, a fitted waist-to-hip area or a pleat with a separate underlay) are marked on the wrong side.

To Form Pleats on the Right Side: Fold the fabric along the fold line of the pleat and bring it to the placement line. Pin through all thicknesses at right angles to the pleat. Baste each pleat close to the fold (a).

To Form Pleats on the Wrong Side: Bring the marked stitching lines together. Pin and baste or stitch (b).

Baste all pleats in place along the edge to be attached to another section of the garment. To prevent the folds from being pulled out of position by machine stitching, anchor each one with several over-and-over stitches or pin in place. Machine-stitch carefully over the pin.

Pleats may also be formed by pressing to position. Place the fabric to be pleated on an ironing board.

Bring the pleat markings together. Pin at top, bottom, and at sufficient intervals between, at right angles to the fold. Press lightly, removing the pins as you reach the area to be pressed. Replace them when the pressing is done. In a skirt this pressing is done to within 6 inches of the lower edge. When the hem is set and stitched, fold the pleats once more to position and complete the pressing. Baste the pleats firmly to position—down each pleat and across the edge to be joined with another section.

PLEATS: HEM TREATMENT. The hem
treatment depends on many factors: the

type of pleat, whether the construction seams are stitched before or after the pleats are formed, whether the seam within the hem is at a flat part or at the backfold of a pleat, and whether the pleats are pressed or unpressed.

Hemming before the pleats are formed is easier when the pleats are all-around and straight or when the top of the pleats doesn't require much fitting. *Hemming after the pleats are formed* is the usual way when there is only a single pleat, a cluster of pleats, when the pleat has a separate underlay, unpressed pleats, or when the pleats on an all-around garment are seamed or fitted at the top.

WHEN A CONSTRUCTION SEAM ENTERS A HEM AT THE FLAT PART OF A PLEAT

Before the Hem Is Done. Stitch the seam, press it open, and trim the seam allowances in the hem area to half width (a). Edge-finish the hem and turn it up to position, matching seam lines (b). Fasten the hem to the garment in a manner suitable for the fabric.

After the Hem Is Done. Mark and turn up the hem on each section of the pleat. Make sure the length of both open edges are equal in length. Edge-finish the hem and fasten it to the garment in a manner appropriate for the fabric. Stitch the con-

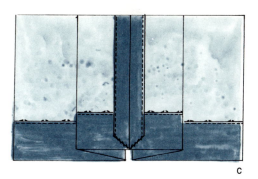

struction seam and press it open. Trim the ends of the seam allowances diagonally and whipstitch them flat to the hem (c).

WHEN A CONSTRUCTION SEAM ENTERS THE HEM AT A BACKFOLD OF A PLEAT

Before the Hem Is Done. Stitch the seam. Clip the seam allowances at the top of the hem. Trim the seam allowances in the hem area to half width. Press the seam allowances in the hem area open and to one side above the hem (a). Turn up the hem. Edge-finish it. Fasten the hem to the garment in a manner suitable for the fabric. To keep a sharp crease at the backfold, edgestitch the hem close to the fold from the hemline to the clip at the top of the hem (b).

After the Hem Is Done. Mark and turn up the hem in each section. Make sure both open edges are equal in length. Edge-finish the hem and fasten it to the garment in a manner appropriate for the fabric. Stitch the construction seam (c). Press it to

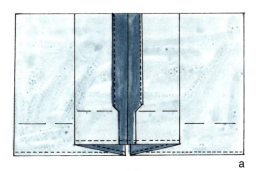

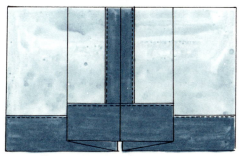

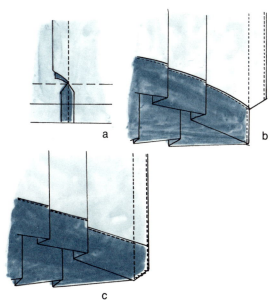

one side. Trim the ends of the seam allowances diagonally. Whipstitch them together in the hem area.

PLEATS IN STRIPED OR PLAID MATERIAL WITHOUT A PATTERN. When pattern markings do not coincide with or effectively utilize the design of the striped or plaid material, pleat the fabric without a pattern. Let the fabric be your guide as to how the pleats should be formed. Make the pleats deep enough to provide the proper swing but not so deep as to be bulky.

Decide on the type and number of pleats you wish. Decide on the dominant color and tonality you wish to feature. You will get entirely different effects by how you fold the material into pleats. Decide the length and which dominant color you wish for the lower edge. Add allowances for hems, seams, and matching of stripes or plaids.

Estimate the number of lengths required, keeping in mind the length plus matching. Remember that several inches will be taken up by the folding of the fabric and the inevitable small inaccuracies of making the pleats meet.

How much material you will need depends on the length of the garment, your width, the width of the material, the depth and number of pleats, the number of lengths required, and the matching of the plaids or stripes.

PLEATS: LINING. Generally lining is unnecessary in a pleated garment. When used in a skirt, the lining should be unpleated but should not impede the movement of the pleats. An A-line skirt lining would do. Other possibilities are a full-length slim lining with long enough slits to permit movement, or a half lining—one that extends a little below the fullest part of the hips and buttocks. Use any appropriate pattern in your collection.

PLEATS: MARKING. Successful pleats depend on accurately transferring the pattern pleat markings to the fabric. Pairs of markings are necessary for each pleat—one line for the fold of the pleat (fold line),

the other for the line to which the fold is brought (placement line). In commercial patterns the term "roll line" is used for pleats that will form soft folds; the term "fold line" is used for crisp or edgestitched pleats.

When no pattern is used, make your own markings. Use a ruler or gauge for accurate measurements.

When pleats are to be stitched on the wrong side, the most accurate marking is done with dressmaker's tracing (carbon) paper (q.v.). For right-side pleating, mark all pleat lines with thread tracing or simplified tailor's tacks (q.v.). Or transfer wrong-side carbon markings to the right side with thread tracing.

To differentiate fold lines and placement lines, use a different color thread for each.

PLEATS: PREPARING FABRIC FOR COMMERCIAL PLEATING. For a skirt that is pleated all around, commercial pleating, when available, is a great time-saver.

Determine the length of the section to be pleated. Add a hem and seam allowances. Estimate the width measurement when completed plus ease (2 inches for a plain skirt). Allow a bit extra (an inch or two) that is taken up by the folding of the fabric. Three times the width plus these extras is the amount generally required for a knife-pleated skirt.

Stitch and press all seams but one so the fabric can be handled flat during the machine pleating. Turn up and sew the hem. The fabric is now ready for commercial pleating.

PLEATS: PRESSING. Correct pressing of pleats is an important element in their appearance. *See* PRESSING PLEATS.

PLEAT STAY. When one or both layers of the underside of a pleat have been trimmed away to remove the bulk, a stay of some kind is needed to hold the upper edge of the pleat in place.

A separate stay is needed for support when the entire top part of the underfold has been trimmed away, leaving only seam allowances. Turn and baste the remainder

of the pleat and the trimmed seam allowances in the direction in which the pleat
will be worn (a).

Cut a stay of lining material. Make it as
wide as the garment section and as deep as
is necessary to bring the finished edge of
the stay to the seam line at the top of the
pleats. Turn and edgestitch the lower edge
of the stay. Pin (b), then baste the stay on
the underside of the garment around all
outside edges. Slip-stitch the finished
lower edge of the stay to the tops of the
pleats along the seam lines.

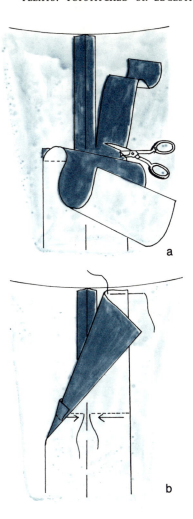

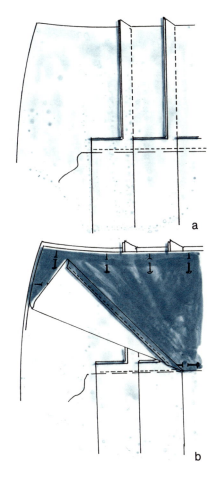

A **self-stay** remains when only one
layer of the pleat has been trimmed (a).

Baste the top of the remaining single
layer of fabric across the upper edge of the
garment section for a support (b).

Both Types. Include the basted edges in
the seams of the garment.

**PLEATS: TOPSTITCHED OR EDGE-
STITCHED.** Decorative ways of holding
pleats in place.

Topstitching is done through all thicknesses of the pleat. Pin-mark the position
of the start of the topstitching. With right
side up, stitch an even distance from the
fold or seam, from the pin mark to the top
of the pleat. Bring the starting thread ends
through to the underside and tie.

To topstitch inverted pleats, start at the
seam line, take several stitches across the
pleat, pivot, then stitch to the top of the
pleat. Do the same on the other side (a).
Bring the starting thread ends through to
the underside and tie.

Edgestitching not only maintains the
folds of the pleat, it provides a sharp
crease at one edge. *(See illustrations on next*

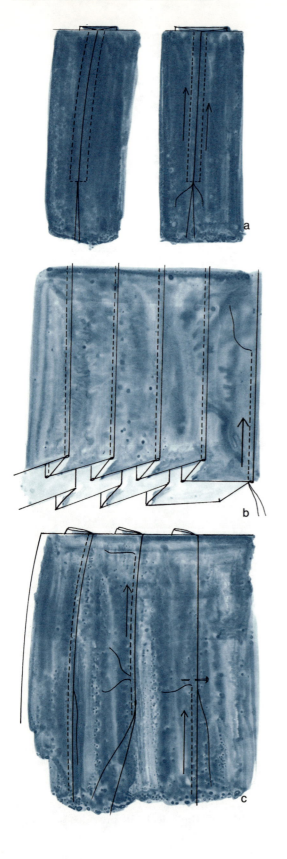

page.) It is done after the hem is completed. Stitch as close to the fold as possible. Stitch from the bottom edge up. Bring the thread ends through to the underside and tie (b). If desired, stitch the inside folds on the wrong side.

To Both Topstitch and Edgestitch: Pin-mark the point at which the topstitching ends and the edgestitching begins. Edgestitch the fold of the pleat from the bottom to the pin mark. Begin the topstitching from the pin mark to the top of the pleat through all thicknesses. The topstitching begins precisely at the point where the edgestitching ends. Bring all thread ends through to the underside and tie (c).

PLEATS: TO REMOVE BULK IN A FITTED AREA. Trim away one (a) or both (b) layers of the pleat. Leave seam allowances along the seam line.

When only one layer of the pleat is

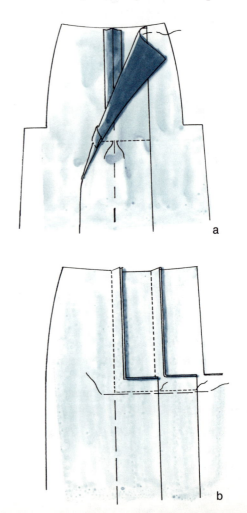

trimmed, the remaining layer acts as a self-stay. Baste the pleat across the upper edge for support. *See* PLEAT STAY.

When both layers of the pleat are trimmed, a stay lining will be needed to support the upper edge of the pleat. *See* PLEAT STAY.

PLEATS: UNDERLINING. Not recommended for multiple-pleated garments. It is too difficult to keep the two layers in precise position for pleating. However, should it be necessary to underline a garment with some pleats, carefully position the underlining, tack it to the pleat lines, and edgestitch the folds.

PLEATS: UNPRESSED. Almost any fabric is suitable for unpressed pleats but soft fabric that will fall in graceful folds is best.

Mark and form these pleats like others. Steam them, holding the iron 2 to 3 inches above the fabric. Let the pleats dry in place, then baste them to position. Allow them to hang out in this way for at least twenty-four hours to "train" them in position. Remove the basting when the garment is completed.

PLEATS: ZIPPER IN. *See* ZIPPER IN PLEATED GARMENT.

PLEAT TYPES.

Accordion. Narrow pleats of uniform width that overlap one another when closed and stand out when worn. They resemble the bellows of an accordion. The front folds stand away from the body. They are best produced by a professional pleater.

Box. Formed of two side pleats whose folds turn in opposite directions on the right side and meet at the center on the wrong side. A flared box pleat is one to which additional fullness has been added at the hem.

Cartridge. Rounded pleats in a series, standing away from the garment, resembling a cartridge belt. *See individual listing.*

Inverted. Formed of two side pleats whose folds meet on the right side. It is the reverse of a box pleat.

Kick. A side or inverted pleat used near the hemline of a narrow skirt to provide walking room. Because the pleat exists only where the action is needed, there is no extra material from the pleat to the waist. Because it lacks such a stay, the pleat must be anchored with topstitching. Use it when visible stitching is consistent with the design of the skirt.

Kilt. Large vertical side pleats, each one overlapping half the next one in a one-way series, as in a Scotch kilt.

Knife. Crisply pressed, even side pleats of any size, folded so they all go in one direction.

Side. A vertical fold in either direction.

Simulated. A line pressed or stitched to imitate a pleat but not constructed like one.

Sunburst. Accordion-like pleats that are narrow at the top and wider at the bottom, producing a flare.

Umbrella. Flared seams or lines pressed or stitched close to the edge to suggest the rib lines of an umbrella.

Unpressed. Folds of fabric forming pleats that hang free. They are neither pressed nor stitched. *See* PLEATS: UNPRESSED.

PLEAT: WITH SEPARATE UNDERLAY. This type of pleat is generally a single pleat, constructed on the inside of the garment.

Bring the fold lines of the pleat extensions together and pin or baste. If these are to be stitched part way, do this step now and remove the basting in the stitched

a

b

area. Open out the pleat extensions (a) and press along the fold lines.

Place the underlay against the pleat extensions, right sides together and seam lines matching. Pin and/or baste. Stitch each side of the pleat underlay to the pleat extension, leaving 6 to 8 inches unstitched at the hem edge. Press the seam flat as stitched, then press the seam allowances to one side away from the underlay. Baste both underlay and extensions in place across the top edge (b).

When the rest of the garment has been completed, turn up and finish the hem. *See* PLEATS: HEM TREATMENT.

POCKET. From the standpoint of design, there are no limits to size, shape, or placement of pockets in women's clothing. They appear in baffling sizes and in highly improbable places. However well or little they may function as pockets, there's no denying they add dash to a design. Pockets in men's clothing are more functional. *(See* POCKETS: MEN'S TAILORING.)

Even if your pattern doesn't have pockets, you can add them. Or you can substitute one type of pocket for another if it is consistent with the design. Many garments are so simply cut that they offer considerable leeway in the choice of pocket design. In fact, pockets become the chief design detail.

There are pockets applied to the surface like the *patch pocket.* Also applied to the surface are the *fake flaps or welts* that simulate pockets.

There are pockets stitched into a construction seam like the *in-seam pocket* or into a style line like the *front hip (frontier) pocket.*

There are pockets set into a slash of the material like the *bound pocket* and the *single-welt pocket.*

There are pockets that have elements of all these constructions—part applied, part set in a seam or slash like the *welt* or *flap pocket. See the listing for each of these pocket types.*

POCKETING (SILESIA). A firmly woven, lightweight fabric of cotton or a blend of cotton and synthetic fibers that is used in men's tailoring, largely for pockets but also for the zipper fly stay, the fly shield lining, and the waistband facing in men's trousers.

POCKETS: DESIGN YOUR OWN. Experiment with paper cutouts or scraps of fabric until you get the right size, shape, placement, and number of pockets you like. Just remember to keep the lines of the pocket in harmony with the lines of the garment design.

Trace the chosen pocket on fresh paper. Add seam allowances and a hem where necessary. Decide whether you want the pocket on straight grain, cross grain, or bias, and whether it is to be lined or not. If lined, trace the amount of lining from the pocket pattern. Consider a trimming of braid, ribbon, or topstitching. Let yourself go!

When a pocket is meant to be used, rather than just to be decorative, it should be in such a place and of such a size that one can get a hand into it easily and deep enough to let the hand settle comfortably.

The general rule for practical pockets is as follows.

For Horizontal and Diagonal Openings: Make them as wide as the fullest part of your hand plus 1 inch for ease.

Pockets—Practical or Just Plain Pretty

For Vertical Openings: Make them as wide as the fullest part of the hand plus 2 inches to accommodate the double motion the hand must make to get into the pocket —forward and down.

Do place pockets within easy reach. Change the position of a pocket on a pattern if need be. (Often, coat pockets are placed so low on the garment that one must assume an apelike posture in order to reach them.)

POCKET SET IN A SLASH. Carefully mark the slash line. Reinforce it with a strip of lightweight interfacing or iron-on material applied to the underside. Make the reinforcement 2 inches longer than the pocket, 1 inch on either side.

The pocket is composed of two parts. One part is seen from the outside as a binding, a welt, or a flap. The other part is a pouch, the pocket proper, which is attached to the underside. The under pocket is just that much longer than the upper pocket to compensate for the depth of the opening. Both are as wide as the opening plus a seam allowance on either side. If you really intend to use the opening as a pocket, make it deep enough to get your hand into it comfortably. *See* POCKETS: DE-SIGN YOUR OWN.

POCKETS: MEN'S TAILORING. While basically the same as in women's clothing, because of their considerable use pockets in men's clothing are made of sturdier stuff and are of sturdier construction. Pocketing (silesia) (q.v.) is the material generally used. In trousers, the pockets extend to the waist seam. Pocket sections are joined in a French seam or are double-stitched. Topstitching in a groove formed by stitching is frequent. Bar tacks at open ends are used for reinforcement.

In addition to the standard pockets— bound, patch, welt, flap—the following are particularly associated with men's tailoring: back hip pocket, breast pocket, change (watch or ticket) pocket, front hip (frontier) pocket, inside bound pocket, and the pocket tab. *See listing for each.*

POCKETS: PRESSING. Use the pressing technique deemed best for the fabric. *In construction,* observe all the rules for pressing an enclosed seam and for the finished flap, welt, binding, or patch. In the *completed garment,* prevent an imprint of a flap, welt, binding, or patch pocket. *See* PRESSING: PRE-VENT IMPRINTS.

POCKET TAB. A decorative way of securing an opening in a pocket. The tab is attached after a bound pocket has been completed on the right side and before the pocket sections are joined on the underside.

Construct the tab *(see* FLAP*).* Work a buttonhole in it by hand or by machine.

On the inside of the garment, center and pin (or baste) the tab to the seam allowance of the upper welt (binding) (a). Test the closure of the tab by pushing it through the pocket opening. Make certain there is sufficient length for easy buttoning. Bring the tab back to the underside.

Stitch through all layers of tab and seam allowance close to the previous line of stitching on the binding. The stitching does *not* come through to the right side. Make a second row of stitching close to the first. Trim the excess fabric (b).

Slip the tab through the opening of the pocket and mark the position for the button. Sew on the button (c). Complete the pocket on the underside.

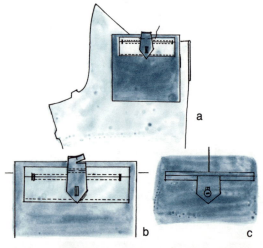

POINT PRESSER (EDGE AND POINT PRESSER). A wooden pressing tool (a), great for getting into and for pressing the

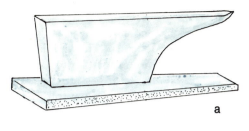

a

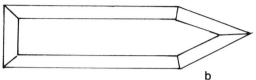

b

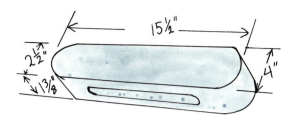

points of collars, cuffs, lapels, welts, flaps, and the like. It is also used to prevent seam imprints on the right side of the fabric when seams are pressed open over its long surface. This is because the iron doesn't hit the edges of the seam allowances.

A *hand-held point presser* (b) is a convenient tool for maneuvering more easily into small areas. Since none are commercially available, you will have to make your own.

Cut a stick of 1/2-inch nonresinous wood, 6 inches long by 1 inch wide. Square off one end and point the other. Bevel the entire outline on both sides. Sand till smooth.

POINT PRESSER AND POUNDING BLOCK. This wooden pressing tool combines the features of the point presser (q.v.) and the pounding block (q.v.). It is a little more cumbersome to use than the individual pieces of equipment.

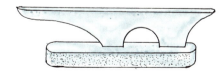

POUNDING BLOCK (SPANKER, CLAP-PER). A pressing tool used for pounding seams flat and edges crisp in firmly woven, hard-surfaced woolens. It is a heavy block of nonresinous hardwood sanded smooth so that it will not snag any fabric. It is generally used in conjunction with a press block (q.v.). *See also* PRESSING WORSTED, HARD-SURFACED OR FIRMLY WOVEN WOOLENS.

POWER NET. A figure-control lingerie fabric containing spandex yarns. *(See also* STRETCH FABRICS.) Most girdles and many bra backs are made of power net.

In general, power net is treated in much the same way as other stretch fabrics. *Stretch stitches are a must.* Use either a straight stretch stitch, a narrow zigzag stitch, any of the overedge stretch stitches, or the multistitch zigzag. Use nylon or spun polyester thread and a ball-point needle.

Two types of seams are effective: the plain seam or the overlap seam. *(See* STRETCH SEAMS.) Seam finishes are not necessary since power net doesn't ravel.

POWER NET GIRDLE. Cut and stitch by plain or overlap seams. *See* STRETCH SEAMS.

When *figure-control panels* are used in areas that need firm control, pin the panel in place on the underside. Stitch near the panel edge from the right side, using the featherstitch, the multistitch zigzag or any of the decorative stretch stitches.

Crotch and leg seams consist of two layers of nylon tricot and one layer of power net with 1/4-inch seam allowances. Stitch through all three with an overedge stretch stitch.

For *leg finishes,* use stretch lace or soft-back elastic. When stretch lace is used, join the ends of the leg band with a stretch overedge stitch. Topstitch the seam from the outside. Overlap and pin the lace on the bottom edge of the leg. Don't stretch or ease either edge. They should be equal in length. Topstitch the lace near the edge, using a zigzag stitch, featherstitch, or multistitch zigzag. When a soft-back elastic finish is desired, treat in the same way as the waistline finish below.

For a *waistline finish,* use a wide or narrow width of soft-back elastic. Overlap the elastic with the soft side up on the right side of waistline seam allowance. Place the top edge of the elastic slightly below the seam line into the seam allowance. Do not stretch or ease either girdle or elastic. They should be of equal length. Stitch with a narrow zigzag stitch close to the top edge of the elastic. Turn the elastic to the inside of the garment with the joining seam rolled to the underside. Topstitch the bottom edge of the elastic with a decorative stretch stitch going through both elastic and girdle. *See* ELASTIC DECORATIVE WAIST-BAND; ELASTIC EDGING FOR LINGERIE.

PRESHAPING TAPE, RIBBON, OR BIAS BINDING.

When a straight length of tape, ribbon, or bias strip is to be stitched to a curved seam line, its application is made easier and more accurate if it is swirled into shape first. There are several ways in which this can be done but each method calls for dampening the tape, ribbon, or bias strip.

METHOD 1

Place the dampened tape, ribbon, or binding over the garment pattern with the outer edge along the curved seam line. Set the iron on STEAM and swirl slowly into shape. Use one hand to do the swirling into a curve while the other guides the iron (a). The side of the iron is parallel to the edge of the strip. Push the iron from outer or longer edge to the inner or shorter edge, easing in the fullness while shaping (b).

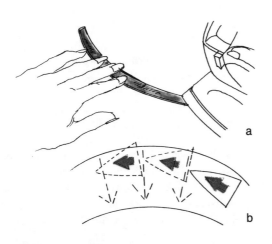

a

b

METHOD 2

Use the garment itself rather than the pattern as a guide for the shape. Place the length of tape, ribbon, or binding on the ironing board beside the seam line and parallel to it. This avoids a wet imprint on the fabric. Proceed as above.

METHOD 3

Use neither pattern nor garment but approximate the curve of the seam line on the ironing board. True up the shape when applying the tape, ribbon, or binding to the garment. Steam-press it after it is applied.

PRESHRINKING FABRIC.

It's a heart-breaking experience to get a suit or dress back from the cleaner's or laundry and find it a size too small for you. To prevent such disasters, fabrics are generally treated in some way, either at the factory or by you.

Treating Woolens. Those treated at the factory are marked "Ready to Sew," "Sponged," "Ready for the needle," or in some similar way. If the material is not so marked, it is wise to have it sponged by a professional service or to do it yourself. If you have any doubts at all about whether the fabric has been factory-sponged, you had better do it or have it done.

Steam pressing is not enough to do the trick. Cleaning before cutting is a good possibility, though reluctance to do this is very understandable. Sponging (q.v.) is best.

Treating Silks. All one can do with silk material is to dry-clean it. It should not be subjected to water or moisture. It is not that silk can't take water but that water spots silk and may affect the dyes.

Treating Cottons or Linens. Shrink-resistant finishes added to cottons and linens reduce shrinking to a minimum. However, even the slightest shrinkage may affect the fit, particularly if it is a close one. It is wise to treat these fabrics, too, before cutting.

Cottons and linens may be sponged in the same way as woolens, they may be dry-cleaned before cutting, or they may be laundered and dried by the same method that will be used for the garment. Follow the fabric care directions suggested for the material. (The use of a fabric softener in the water helps preserve the finish and makes the fabric easier to iron.) Unlike wool, these fabrics may be pressed when almost dry.

Treating Synthetics. All synthetic materials should be rinsed or soaked in cold water before cutting. Observe the care directions suggested for the material.

PRESHRINKING UNDERSTRUCTURE MATERIALS.

Everything that goes inside a garment (with the exception of silk linings) should be preshrunk.

Interfacings, unless labeled preshrunk, should be preshrunk. Set the material in a basin of hot water and let stand until it cools. Allow it to dry naturally. Press only when dry.

Interlinings of lamb's wool are sponged like wool.

Underlinings should be rinsed or soaked in cold water and pressed when dry.

Cotton tape can be immersed in water and left there until it has thoroughly absorbed the moisture. Allow it to dry naturally. It can be pressed to shape when used.

Some schools of thought would have you preshrink the zipper and even wrap thread in a damp cloth for several hours. Perhaps you think this is overdoing the safety bit, but it emphasizes the point.

PRESS BLOCK.

Used in conjunction with a pounding block for pressing firmly woven, hard-surfaced woolens. Like it, the press block is smooth and of nonresinous hardwood. A new, clean cheese board, bread board, or chopping block will do. An extra pounding block to be used as a press block is a wonderful convenience for pressing sleeve seams in fabric that needs pounding. *See* PRESSING WORSTED, HARD-SURFACED, OR FIRMLY WOVEN WOOLENS.

PRESS CLOTHS.

In pressing (as distinct from ironing), the iron should never come in direct contact with the fabric. A press cloth is always placed between the cloth and the iron. Since only a small area of the garment is pressed at a time, the press cloths can be fairly short, narrow strips—4 to 6 inches wide by 8 to 10 inches long. Buy or make them of unsized muslin, drill, linen, or double thicknesses of cheesecloth. Wash them thoroughly to make sure that all sizing and lint have been removed. Old, worn sheets, pillowcases, dish towels, and napkins, though unprofessional, are effective for this purpose. To protect woolen surfaces, make the press cloth of wool. To protect the surface of napped, nubby, or any other raised surfaces, use strips of self-fabric or terry cloth. For very heavy fabrics, use drill or a chemically treated commercial press cloth.

In lieu of a press cloth, try a slipcover or a plate cover (q.v.) for the iron. The former can be made, the latter bought. The advantage of a cover is that you can more readily see where you are pressing.

Press cloths are used so pervasively throughout the pressing process that directions for use appear in all discussions of pressing.

PRESSING.

Press or iron—which?

To get wrinkles out of a handkerchief you push the iron along. That's ironing, a gliding motion. *(See* IRONING TECHNIQUES.) Pressing is an up-and-down motion. Lower the iron, press, lift, and move on to a new section of the fabric. Then lower, press, lift.

Because of the long stroke, ironing is always done on a flat surface. Because it involves only a small area, pressing can be done on a shaped pad, small though that may be, as well as on a flat surface. Because of the careful up-and-down motion there is little or no movement forward of the iron on the fabric and nothing gets pushed out of shape. Save the ironing for smooth-surfaced flat work. For shaped garments (which is most of them), press on a shaped pad.

There is this, too: while fabrics that can be laundered (cottons, linens, synthetics) are ironed smooth, even well-made garments of these fibers are better off pressed because of their construction. Garments that require dry cleaning because of either their fibers, their textures, or their inner construction, are pressed. Since fine dressmaking and tailoring have all these characteristics, they are always pressed. Indeed, in tailoring pressing is raised to a fine art; it is crucial in obtaining those crisp edges, flat seams, and that subtly blocked-to-shape sculptured form.

Whatever the fabric, and whether it's dressmaking or tailoring, your garment will look so much better if you:

—press every dart and seam open (when desirable) before stitching it to a cross seam.

—press each section of a garment before stitching it to another.

—press open every enclosed seam before turning the facing back to the underside (collars, cuffs, welts, flaps, lapels, closings, and so on).

—block over appropriate press pads all darts and shaping seams, as well as all straight pieces destined to fit curved areas. This applies to tailored collars, lapels, sleeve caps, and so forth.

—press and shape each unit of work separately in outer fabric, interfacing, underlining, interlining, and lining before applying it to another or before joining back to front at the shoulders and side seams.

And it's so much easier:

—to topstitch an edge when it has been pressed flat first.

—to insert a zipper when the seam allowance is pressed back first.

—to achieve a smooth and flat hem if the fullness at the raw edge is ease-pressed before finishing and attaching.

—to set a sleeve when the cap has been blocked first.

—to stitch a lapped seam when the seam allowance has been turned under and pressed back first.

While each garment presents an individual pressing problem, there are some general rules that apply to all.

Since you must press as you sew, set up your pressing equipment along with your sewing equipment. Place a chair or table close to the ironing board to support any fabric that may otherwise trail on the floor.

Don't press darts, seams, folds, pleats, or anything else unless you are absolutely sure they are exactly where you want them. It is often impossible to press out the sharp crease produced by the pressing.

Pressing is directional. Press all woven fabrics with the grain: off-grain pressing pushes material out of shape or stretches it. Press all knit fabrics with the lengthwise rib: pressing across the ribs stretches the fabric. Press all napped fabrics with the nap.

Don't begin your pressing until you are sure how your fabric will react to heat, moisture, and pressure. Experiment with a test seam or dart to determine the best heat setting on the iron, the correct amount of moisture, the best method for flattening seams and edges, some way in which the surface texture can be preserved, and how to prevent seam imprints or iron marks. Avoid overdampening and overpressing.

You may do your ironing on the right side, but for pressing the wrong side is the correct side. If the right side must be pressed, protect it with a suitable press cloth. Direct contact with the iron is a sure way to produce a shine.

Don't press over pins or bastings: both leave marks. If basting is absolutely necessary, use silk thread, which is less apt to leave marks.

In double thicknesses of fabric (facings, hems, and so on) press the underside first, then the upper (using a press cloth).

With seam allowances closed, press the seams along the stitching line in the same direction as stitched. This distributes the thread evenly along the seam and blends it into the fabric. Then press the seam allowances open.

Keep trimming scissors handy. Clip or notch where needed to make a seam or dart lie flat. Slash and grade to reduce bulk.

When seam allowances are pressed in

one direction, press in the direction that produces the least bulk.

Hang up each pressed section as soon as the pressing is complete. If you must store your work in progress, don't fold any more than necessary or fold over tissue paper as if for packing.

Settle for the best results you can get. Don't attempt the impossible for the fabric. Quit while you're ahead.

PRESSING BLENDS OF FIBERS. Set the temperature for the fiber requiring the lowest degree of heat. Press on the wrong side, using a press cloth.

PRESSING: BLOCKING A "NO-DART, NO-SEAM" GARMENT. Place the garment on an appropriate curve of the tailor's ham (q.v.), wrong side up. Press to shape. Start at the center front (or back) and press toward the outer edges—neck, shoulders, armholes, underarm, bust, waist, hips. When dry, reverse to the right side.

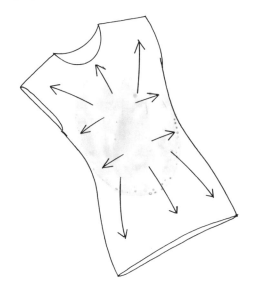

PRESSING: BLOCKING A SLEEVE CAP. *See* SET-IN SLEEVE CAP EASE BLOCKED.

PRESSING: BLOCKING A TAILORED GARMENT. Contour pressing (blocking) is the means of creating shape in any flat surface: a collar, lapel, sleeve cap, or even a "no-shape" garment—that is, one without darts or shaping seams.

However flat they may look on the cutting board, with or without darts or shaping seams, clothes will eventually take on some of the shape of the wearer: witness your favorite sweaters. That's because the body's 98° temperature does a bit of blocking on its own. While this is sufficient for some no-shape clothes, for classic tailoring one can't rely on nature alone to do the garment shaping. Here not only the outer fabric but the individual layers of supporting material must be blocked separately before they can be put together.

All areas of a garment that go over and around some part of the body (which is just about everywhere) are blocked over an appropriately rounded press pad. It really doesn't make sense to press curves on a flat ironing board. You find yourself pressing out of a garment all the shape you painstakingly stitched into it.

The seams and darts of worsted and other hard-surfaced fabrics may be pressed open first with the press board and pounding block, then shaped and blocked over a curved press pad. The darts and seams of softer fabrics may be both pressed and shaped at the same time.

PRESSING: BLOCKING THE UNDERSTRUCTURE. Interfacing, underlining, and interlining materials are blocked to shape in the same way as the outer fabric except that pressing may be done with a steam iron directly on the material without a press cloth.

PRESSING BOUND BUTTONHOLES AND BOUND POCKETS. To prevent the imprint of the bindings on the right side of the garment, insert wrapping-paper strips under the edges of the binding. Use the pressing technique best suited for the fabric. Carefully press the area between the buttonholes and around the pocket.

PRESSING CREPE WEAVES. Crepe weaves tend to shrivel when damp and stretch with pressure. Place a press pad under the crepe and a press cloth over the fabric to retain the crinkle. Use the heat setting required by the fiber. Press lightly.

PRESSING CUFFS. *See* PRESSING FACED SECTIONS.

PRESSING CURVED SEAMS. All curved seams should be pressed over an appropriate curve of the tailor's ham (q.v.).

Place the right side of the garment over the tailor's ham. This temporarily produces a reverse curve. When the pressed garment is returned to its right-side-out position, it will assume its correct contour.

Insert folded strips of wrapping paper under the seam allowances to prevent seam imprint. When necessary, cover with a dry or dampened press cloth. Press with the lengthwise grain or nap.

When a dampened press cloth has been used, lift it and allow the steam to escape. Remove the wrapping-paper strips. Allow the garment to dry naturally on the tailor's ham. If you remove it while the garment is still damp, you may lose the shaping.

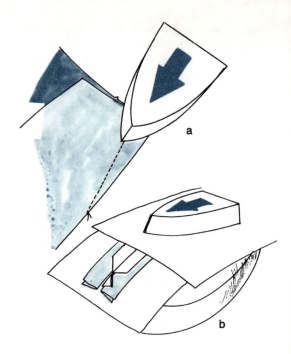

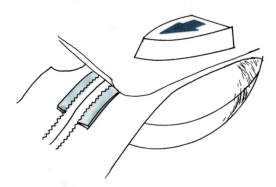

PRESSING DARTS. The first step in pressing a dart is always to extend it and press it flat as stitched from the wide end to the point, being careful not to press a crease in the fabric beyond it (a).

To press a dart over the tailor's ham (b), place the opened dart over a corresponding curve of the ham. When necessary, slip wrapping-paper strips under the seam allowances to prevent seam imprints. Cover with a dampened press cloth.

Start the pressing at the wide end and press to the dart point. Use a slight rotary motion to smooth out the dart point. Try for a perfect blend. It is often necessary to pull fabric taut while trying to achieve this. Round out the area adjacent to the dart.

Narrow Darts and Darts in Lightweight Fabric. Place the right side of the garment over the tailor's ham and press the dart in the direction it will assume in the finished garment: horizontal darts are pressed down; vertical darts are pressed toward the center.

Wide Darts and Darts in Medium-to-Heavy Soft Fabrics. Trim and slash the dart. Over the tailor's ham, press it open where slashed and to one side where unslashed.

Darts in Worsted and Other Hard-Surfaced Fabrics. Press open first with the pounding block and press board (*see* PRESSING WORSTED, HARD-SURFACED, OR FIRMLY WOVEN WOOLENS), then press to shape over the tailor's ham.

Double-Pointed Waistline Dart. Clip the dart at the waistline. Press the dart above and below the clip as if it were a standard dart.

Darts in Interfacing, Underlining, or Interlining. Press and block to shape over the tailor's ham. The pressing may be done with the steam iron directly on the material without a press cloth.

PRESSING DEEP FLEECE, DEEP FURRY NAPS, AND DEEP RAISED SURFACES.

See PRESSING FUR FABRIC; PRESSING NAPPED FABRICS; PRESSING PILE FABRICS; PRESSING RAISED-SURFACE FABRICS.

PRESSING: DIRECTION IN WHICH TO PRESS SEAM ALLOWANCES AND DARTS.

The safest rule to follow is to press in the direction that produces the least bulk.

Uncut Darts. Unless otherwise noted in the pattern, press as follows: horizontal darts, down; elbow darts, down; vertical darts, toward the center. When an uncut dart in the lining falls directly over an uncut dart of the outer fabric, press one vertical dart toward the center and the other toward the side; press one horizontal dart up and the other down.

Yoke Seam Allowances. Generally pressed away from gathers or other types of fullness. When there is no fullness, press them up.

Armhole Seam Allowances. In a set-in sleeve, they are generally pressed into the sleeve, adding to the roundness of the cap. When decorative welt stitching is used around the armhole, the seam allowance is pressed toward the garment. A sleeve set on a dropped shoulder has its seam allowances pressed open to eliminate bulk at the seam line. The same is true of a raglan sleeve.

Waistline Seam Allowances. In a dress they may be pressed either toward the bodice, toward the skirt, or opened flat—whichever direction produces the least bulk. Clip the seam allowances where necessary to make them lie flat. In a skirt or pants, the seam allowances are pressed into the waistband.

Pleat Seam Allowances. Generally pressed together at the back of a pleat. When a hem is involved, clip the seam allowance at the top of the hem. Press it open below the clip (in the hem area) and to one side above it.

PRESSING EQUIPMENT.

To meet all the contingencies of design, shape, and fabric, a variety of pressing equipment is essential for fine dressmaking and tailoring. In fact, a large proportion of all sewing equipment is used for pressing.

Some of the equipment will be familiar to you and is undoubtedly part of your household pressing equipment. Whatever new tools are needed can be purchased at a tailor's or dressmaker's supply store, a department store, or one of the numerous chain stores or mail-order houses. Some of the tools can be made by you or any willing friend or relative to the dimensions provided in the illustrations. *See* EDGE AND POINT PRESSER; POUNDING BLOCK; PRESS BLOCK; SEAM ROLL; SLEEVE BOARD.

Blocking the contours that have been so painstakingly fitted and stitched into the garment is an extremely important part of dressmaking and tailoring. To accomplish this, a great variety of press pads or cushions that fit practically every curve of the body have been devised. You really don't need all of them, nice as they are to have. Where there is a duplication of function, choose the press pad easiest for you to come by or to use. *See* COLLAR PRESS PADS; PRESSING PAD; PRESS MITT; SLEEVE PRESS PAD; SLEEVE ROLL; TAILOR'S PRESS BOARD; TAILOR'S HAM.

Additional Equipment for Men's Tailoring. While the tailor's ham is an excellent all-around shaping pad for women's clothing, the larger, more subtle shaping of men's coats and jackets calls for a larger, more subtly curved press pad. *See* COAT-AND-JACKET PRESS BOARD.

Easier to use than the standard point presser in some instances when pressing points of collars, lapels, ties, and the like is a hand-held point presser (q.v.).

Why Wood? Most woolen fabric requires more steam than that produced by an ordinary steam iron. This added moisture becomes a problem on the usual well-padded ironing board, which tends to reflect moisture rather than absorb it. Wood, on the other hand, absorbs moisture quickly and effectively. This shorter, natural drying time is important in the pressing and shaping of wool.

PRESSING FACED SECTIONS.

After the seam allowances have been trimmed and graded, clipped and/or notched, first press the seam in the direction of the stitching, then press the seam allowances open. Use the heat and moisture required for the fabric.

For collars, cuffs, welts, flaps, and the like, press straight seams open over the point presser, slipping its point into the corner of the double thickness. Press open curved seams, a small section at a time, over a curve of the tailor's ham or tailor's press board.

Turn the facing, right side out, to the underside, working out the corners carefully and easing the seam toward the underside so it will not show from the right side. Press from the underside, protecting the fabric as necessary.

Press before basting the edges to avoid leaving an imprint of the thread on the fabric. If you must baste before pressing, use silk thread, which is less likely to leave an imprint.

PRESSING: FINAL PRESSING OF TAILORED GARMENTS.

If the garment has been carefully and properly pressed during construction it should not need much of a pressing now. One final hand pressing is advisable, however, before inserting the lining; this is your last chance to get at any part of the inside of the garment before it is covered by the lining. Of course, if it is an unlined garment, you will want to make sure that the exposed underside looks beautiful.

Remove all basting and tailor's tacks and any stray threads or other matter picked up while in construction. Press both inside and outside of the garment, using the technique best suited to the fabric. Use the steam iron and press cloths. Be very careful to maintain the shaping of the garment. Use the same press pads as were used for the construction pressing.

Before the Lining Is Inserted. This is the order in which the garment is pressed. *On the underside,* press flat the outer edges of the collar, lapels, facings, hems. Press the facing first, making sure that any joining seam is rolled to the underside. *On the inside,* press one front, starting at the lower edge, and press as far as the shoulder area but do not press the shoulder area. Press the other front and the back in the same way. Be sure to insert folded strips of wrapping paper in any seam allowances, pockets, or welts to avoid imprints.

Place one shoulder area over the tailor's ham or over the narrow end of the ironing board. Press the front, then the back. Do the same on the other shoulder.

Slip the sleeve over the sleeve board, sleeve roll, or sleeve pad and press. Start at the underarm and rotate until you have pressed the entire sleeve except the cap. Press the sleeve cap over a suitable press pad. Take special care not to flatten it.

On the right side, lightly steam-press the body of the garment in the same order as the underside. Steam-press the sleeve and cap. Protect the surface with a press cloth.

Press the collar and lapels. Place a folded strip of wrapping paper between the collar, lapels, and garment to prevent an imprint. Press the collar from the outer edge to the roll line over a suitable press pad. Make sure that the lower edge of the collar covers the neckline seam by at least 1/2 inch. "Press" a soft roll or a sharp crease into the collar (both are acceptable) and continue for several inches down on the lapel.

With the facing up, place the lapel and front edge over the ham and steam-press. Be careful not to press out the roll line.

Place the newly pressed garment on a dress form or stuff the shoulders, sleeve cap, collar, and bust or chest area with tissue paper and place on a sturdy hanger. Pin the garment closed. Allow it to settle and dry thoroughly for a few hours before inserting the lining.

If the garment is unlined, your pressing chores are over. When a lining is involved, proceed as follows.

Before inserting the lining in the garment, press open all its seams, following the general directions for pressing of the lining fiber.

After the Lining Has Been Attached to the Garment. Place the garment over the ironing board, lining side up. Use a moderately warm, dry iron and a dry press cloth to prevent scorching and shine.

Press one front and back from the lower edge to the shoulder area. Press the other front and back to the shoulder area. Press so that a soft fold of the lining covers the stitching line all along the facings and hem. Press a sharp pleat at the center back.

Place the shoulder area, lining side up, over a suitable press pad or the narrow end of the ironing board. Press the front lining, then the back lining. Repeat the procedure for the other shoulder area.

With the lining side up, slip the sleeve over a sleeve board or sleeve roll with the cap over the broad end. Press a soft fold along the hem edge. Press the sleeve upward toward the cap. Press the cap carefully.

Turn the garment to the right side and hang up.

PRESSING FUR FABRIC. Fur fabric requires very little or no pressing. Finger pressing does for most. Should you choose to press lightly, press on the wrong side, using a cool, dry iron. Press over a needle board (best of all), a strip of self-fabric, or a Turkish towel. Brush up the nap after pressing.

You may use a steam iron for flattening edges. Hold it a few inches *above* the fur, merely steaming it. Pound the edge with a mallet or the tip of your pounding block. Should you be tempted to use this technique, better test your "fur" first. Steam will mat some piles and, of course, the pounding will flatten the fluff. In many cases a gentle patting with the press mitt is sufficient.

PRESSING GATHERS. Press with lengthwise (vertical) strokes on the wrong side, working the tip of the iron into the gathers. *(See illustration top of next column.)*

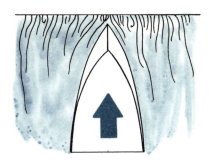

PRESSING: HEAT SETTING. Use the heat setting suitable for the fiber, as marked on the iron.

High heat for the vegetable fibers—cotton, linen. (The vegetables can take it.)

Moderate heat for the animal fibers—silk, wool. (The only kind of heat an animal can take—moderate.)

Low heat for all synthetics. (Heat melts the chemicals of which synthetics are made.)

In combinations of fibers, use the heat setting for the most delicate fiber present. For instance, handle polyester and cotton as if it were all polyester.

There is this, too: holding the iron on one spot for any length of time intensifies the heat. For slow work, reduce the heat.

A moist press cloth tends to reduce the heat. When used on some fabrics, it may be necessary to increase the heat setting.

PRESSING HEMS. The depth of a hem should be only as much as will lie flat when the fullness is steamed out. Press all inside seam allowances open before marking and turning up the hem. Grade the hem seam allowances.

Straight Hems. When the hem is turned up, press it with short strokes from the lower edge up, removing any bastings as you do a small section at a time. (Pressing parallel to the fold of the hem stretches its edge.)

For a very sharp hem edge in fabric that can take it, "spank" with the pounding block. For a soft edge, steam the fabric, holding the iron 2 to 3 inches above it.

To shrink out the hem without shrinking the fabric beneath, as well as to prevent a hem imprint, insert a wrapping-pa-

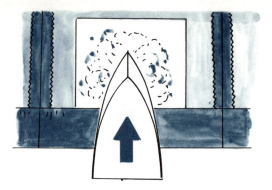

per strip as a shield between the hem and the garment. Press. Rebaste or pin the hem to position when dry.

Circular Hems. When there is too much fullness at the upper edge of the turned-up hem, run a line of gathering at the hem edge. Pull up the thread until the hem fits the garment. Distribute the fullness as evenly as possible, keeping the same grain in as many places as possible. Proceed as for straight hems.

PRESSING: MOISTURE NEEDED. Most fabrics press better with some degree of moisture. Whether you apply it by hand, by eye dropper, or by press cloth, or whether you sprinkle, spray, sponge, or steam it depends on the fabric.

Dampened cottons and linens are ironed until they are dry. They wrinkle and muss when limp.

Woolens, however, must never be pressed until dry. Allow them to dry naturally. Handle them very carefully while damp, since they are easily manipulated out of shape.

No moisture should be used for silks and synthetics; press them while dry.

PRESSING NAPPED FABRICS. A press cloth of self-fabric is about as good a protection as one can get for any napped or otherwise raised surface. When the raised surface of the fashion fabric is pressed against the raised surface of the self-fabric strip, the naps interlock, thereby preserving each other. Moreover, naps so pressed tend to adhere. As the two layers of fabric are separated, the naps are lifted.

In the event that you don't have enough

self-fabric for a press cloth, use a strip of terry cloth or any other raised-surface material.

When the right side of a fabric is turned to the wrong side for a hem or facing, that, too, needs protection. (One never knows when one may be needing the underlayer for an upper layer.) Use a self-fabric press cloth both under and over the two thicknesses for double protection.

Assemble the needed equipment: the ironing board and iron, press mitt, small bowl of water, folded strips of wrapping paper, standard and self-fabric press cloths.

Place the self-fabric press cloth on the ironing board with its raised surface up. Place the right side of the garment against it. Open the seam allowances with finger pressing. Slip the strips of wrapping paper under them. Cover any turned-back fabric with a second self-fabric press cloth. Dampen the standard press cloth and place it over the area.

Lower the dry iron (set at a moderate heat) onto the damp press cloth. Press lightly and briefly. Whisk off the press cloths with one hand and, with the other hand slipped into the press mitt, pat gently.

If, by chance, you have flattened the surface of the fabric, brush it up while damp to restore it.

Don't attempt the impossible with napped or raised-surface fabrics. They can never be pressed as flat as worsted—nor should they be. That would destroy their very special quality.

PRESSING PAD. You can make your own pad for the special pressing of monograms, lace, zipper, corded buttonholes, sequinned or beaded fabrics, and any other napped, embroidered, or similar surfaces. It prevents flattening of the decoration.

Cut three or four thicknesses of white or natural-color wool interlining about 20 inches long by 24 inches wide. Place them one over the other and stitch them to a drill backing of the same size. Use with the wool interlining up.

PRESSING PANTS. *In construction,* press all seams and darts, using the technique best suited to the fabric.

On completion, turn the pants to the right side. Fold each leg in half lengthwise, matching the inseam and side seam at the crotch and hem edges.

Press the back crease. In men's trousers or narrow women's pants, pull the calf area outward in a slight curve and press. Pants so pressed fall gracefully over the calf.

Press the front creases to about 6 inches from the waist. Shrink out the ripples caused by the outward pull at the calf (when this is done). Press the back creases even with the crotch.

In flared-leg pants, press the areas above and below the knee separately.

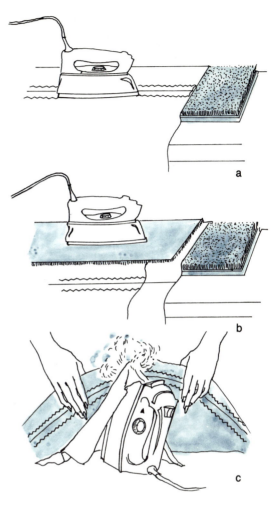

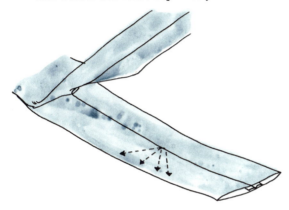

PRESSING PILE FABRICS. There are two methods of "pressing" such a fabric to preserve the pile.

METHOD 1

Place the pile of the fabric against the needles of a needle board. Steam-press the wrong side, using very little pressure (a). Let the steam do the work. Press over the center of the needle board: pressing too close to the edge will leave an imprint. Press with the nap. If a needle board is not available, use a strip of self-fabric or any other raised surface like terry cloth.

When pile fabric is turned back to the wrong side in seam allowances, hems, facing, they, too, need protection. Use a top needle board or a second strip of self-fabric (b).

METHOD 2

Stand a hot, dry iron on end. Cover it with a damp cloth. This creates steam. Draw the wrong side of the pile fabric against the steaming iron (c). Handle lightly to prevent finger marks. If necessary, these can be steamed out and brushed up.

Both methods work well. Hang the garment on a hanger or dress form while drying.

PRESSING PLEATS. To achieve sharp pleats, each side of both upper and under folds should be pressed thoroughly.

Sometimes it is easier to *press each fold separately.* Place the fold of the pleat near the edge of the ironing board and press, using the pressing technique deemed best for the fabric.

Often pleats are *pressed in a series.* Insert wrapping-paper strips between pleats to prevent imprints. Pin the top and bottom of the pleats in place on the ironing board over a damp press cloth. Pin along the sides of the fabric so that its weight will not pull the pleats out of place. Remove the pins as you reach the area to be pressed. Replace them after pressing. Place a dampened press cloth over the pleats. (In this way both the underside and the right side are against damp press cloths.) Press with the grain, using lengthwise strokes in the direction of the pleats. When the right side is completed, turn to the underside and repeat the procedure.

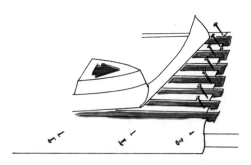

Unpressed Pleats. Lay in soft folds on the ironing board. Steam, holding the iron 2 to 3 inches above the fabric. Allow the pleats to dry in place.

PRESSING: PRESSURE—HOW MUCH? Pressure may be anything from a loving pat to the 1600 pounds per square inch applied to the edge of a man's coat in a clothing factory.

For some fabrics, the pressure of the iron is sufficient. Others are pressed, then patted with a press mitt. Heavy or firmly woven woolens are beaten and pounded with a pounding block (the home sewer's answer to the pressure exerted by the factory pressing machines).

PRESSING: PREVENT IMPRINTS. A garment needs to be protected from itself—from its seam allowances, pockets, welts, flaps, hems, pleats, lapels, collar, cuffs, bound buttonholes, darts—indeed, from any applied, folded-over, or more-than-single thickness. The damage comes in

pressing when the outlines of these details are imprinted on the garment, unless they are prevented from doing so.

The simplest and best protection is a strip of *brown wrapping paper* to cushion the pressure. The strip may be of any convenient length—as short as 3 to 4 inches to as long as 8 to 10 inches. This will depend on the length of the area in which you are working. The strip should be wide enough to fold in half or in thirds lengthwise plus enough to extend beyond the edge that may leave the imprint.

If, inadvertently, an imprint has been made, lift the offending thickness and press out the mark.

Caution: Do not use any paper (white or color) to which chemicals or dyes have been applied. They will come off on the fabric.

The point presser (q.v.) may also be used to prevent a seam imprint.

PRESSING RAISED-SURFACE FABRICS. One certainly wouldn't want to flatten a raised surface that is *the* attraction of the fabric. Such fabrics need protection.

Nubbed, Slubbed, Looped, Ribbed Fabrics. Place the right side of the material against the raised surface of a strip of self-fabric or terry cloth. Steam from the wrong side. Use a light touch. Let the steam do the work.

Crinkled, Blistered, Puckered, Embossed, or Other Novelty Surfaces. Finger-press seams and darts. Press very lightly, if at all, over a softly padded surface. For many such fabrics it is preferable to hold the steam iron an inch or two above the surface and allow the steam to play over it.

Don't try for a sharp press. It is not in the nature of these fabrics to respond so. You'll ruin them if you persist. Quit while you're ahead with a reasonably flattened dart or seam.

PRESSING: RIGHT-SIDE TOUCH-UP FOR A TAILORED GARMENT. When a tailored garment is completely finished, you may want to give it a right-side touch-up. This is a very light pressing over a press cloth.

A good way to simulate the kind of steam pressing currently done in cleaning and tailoring establishments is to steam the garment on a dress form. Use any steaming device (there are several on the market) or the steam iron. Allow the garment to dry thoroughly on the dress form or hanger before wearing.

PRESSING SHIRRING AND SMOCKING.

Place the shirred or smocked area on the ironing board, right side up. Steam the fabric, holding the iron 1 to 2 inches above it and moving slowly over the area. This preserves the raised effect. Do not touch the surface with the iron, however lightly: let the steam do the work.

Should you wish, you may press below the shirring or smocking on the wrong side. Work the tip of the iron into the gathers with lengthwise strokes.

PRESSING SKIRTS.
Use the pressing technique best suited to the fabric. If the skirt has a free-hanging lining, press each separately. Slip the skirt over the ironing board, wrong side up. Press from the hem up.

Slip the tailor's ham under the hip area and press all darts and curved seams. Press the placket with the zipper closed. Press the waistband. Press the skirt with the lengthwise grain, the iron parallel to the seam lines of the skirt and waistband.

PRESSING TAILORED COLLAR. *See* TAILORED COLLAR: PRESSING AND BLOCKING.

PRESSING TAILORED LAPEL. *See* TAILORED LAPEL: PRESSING.

PRESSING TUCKS.
Use the heat setting on the iron and the degree of moisture required by the fabric.

Press tucks in the same position and direction as stitched. If the tucks appear on the right side of the garment, press them in the direction of the garment design. If they appear on the wrong side, press all lengthwise tucks toward the center; all horizontal tucks, down.

PRESSING ULTRASUEDE. *See* ULTRASUEDE: PRESSING.

PRESSING WELTS AND FLAPS.
Press in construction like a flap (q.v.). For a right-side touch-up on the finished garment, insert wrapping paper under the welt or flap to prevent an imprint.

PRESSING WOOL.

Heat: Wool takes a moderate setting on the iron. Excessive heat directly applied causes the overlapping scales of the wool fiber to lock, reducing its flexibility and producing a shine. It also damages the fibers and makes them feel harsh.

Moisture: Wool is pressed and shaped with moist heat. The degree of moisture and heat varies with the kind of wool. Some require little and some more. The use of the steam iron for pressing is limited to fabrics that respond to a short, light steaming. Most woolens for tailoring require the kind and amount of steam produced when a moderately hot, dry iron is pressed against a damp press cloth.

Though water cannot hurt wool (imagine sheep that weren't waterproof!), it is the press cloth rather than the wool that is dampened. The cloth should be damp, not wet. Wetness plus heat can shrink or mat wool. Furthermore, the cloth must be uniformly damp so that no part of the fabric will be subjected to more moisture than any other, hence shrinking or matting one part and not another.

A press cloth may be dampened by one of the following methods. Dip about one third of the cloth in water and wring it out. Roll or fold the rest of it around the damp third until the entire cloth is uniformly damp. Or rub a wet sponge or dampening cloth over the press cloth until it is moist (a). The advantage of this method over the first is that the press cloth is less likely to get too wet.

Place the damp press cloth against the wrong side of the garment. Apply the dry iron to it with a lower-and-lift motion. Press lightly until the moisture changes to steam, then apply more pressure. From

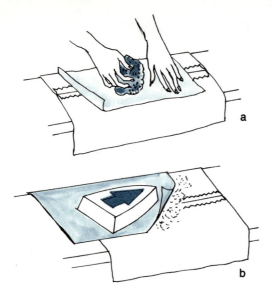

a

b

time to time allow the steam to escape by raising the press cloth (b). Stop pressing while the fabric is still steaming.

The use of a dampened press cloth both above and below the fabric creates steam that penetrates it. The upper steaming flattens where necessary, the lower steaming freshens and restores the wool. Wrinkles, creases, and folds in the fabric are better smoothed out by this treatment.

Allow wool to dry naturally. Hang the garment on a dress form or a tissue-paper-padded hanger so it will not lose its shaping.

Pressure: For lightweight woolens, the pressure of the iron is sufficient. For hard-surfaced woolens and worsteds, use the pounding block and press board to achieve a clean, crisp, flat look. *See* PRESSING WORSTED, HARD-SURFACED, OR FIRMLY WOVEN WOOLENS.

Protection: Whatever the degree of heat, the iron should never be brought into direct contact with wool fabric, on either the right or the wrong side. Use a press cloth for protection. A slipcover or protective plate cover is a convenient substitute for a press cloth. All raised and novelty surfaces need particular protection. *See* PRESSING RAISED-SURFACE FABRICS.

PRESSING WORSTED, HARD-SURFACED, OR FIRMLY WOVEN

WOOLENS. Assemble all the equipment you will need: the iron and ironing board, the press board and pounding block, a press cloth and a small bowl of water, plus two folded strips of wrapping paper. Place everything within easy reach, for this is a very quick operation.

Place the press board on the ironing board or on a sturdy table. Place the right side of the garment against the press board. The wrong side is up for pressing. Open the seam allowances with finger pressing. Slip the strips of wrapping paper under them. Dampen the press cloth. (*See* PRESSING WOOL.) Place the damp press cloth over the opened seam.

Use a dry iron set on WOOL. Press it onto the damp press cloth. Keep the iron on just long enough to create a good head of steam. Lift the iron and set it aside. Then quickly whisk the press cloth off with one hand while the fabric is still steaming. Almost simultaneously, slap the pounding block on the seam with the other hand. Bring it down with considerable force. Let the pounding block rest there a minute before removing it. Presto! Your magically flattened seam. One forceful blow should work. If the fabric proves stubborn (some are hard to flatten) or you enjoy the pounding, repeat the performance.

Are you curious to know why and how this works? The pounding block forces the steam into the porous surface of the press board, which obligingly absorbs it, drying the fabric naturally in the process. The seam is held in place by the pounding block just long enough to train it flat while it is drying. This is why so much of the pressing equipment is of wood—press boards, pounding block, shaping blocks, and point presser. The rest—the assorted seam rolls, press pads, and tailor's ham—are best when stuffed with hardwood sawdust.

Move on to the next section and repeat the operation.

This pounding method of pressing may also be effective on heavy or firmly woven cottons or raw silks.

Whenever the fabric can take it, use the

press board and pounding block to achieve the very flattest seams and the sharpest edges. This is particularly desirable in lapels, the front closing, facings, hems, pleats, cuffs, collars, welts, pockets, belts, buttonholes—just about anywhere on the garment where a thin, crisp edge is called for.

PRESSING ZIPPERED AREA. This is best pressed before the zipper application. If pressing is necessary after the zipper has been installed, place the right side down over a heavy press cloth or Turkish towel. Press with the tip of the iron *beside* the metal or plastic. Use wrapping-paper strips as a cushion under the placket lap to prevent an imprint.

PRESS MITT. A press pad shaped like a mitt, a "handy" piece of equipment for getting into and under hard-to-reach places. It is also good for shaping small areas (like a sleeve cap) and for patting flat those materials one dare not pound with the block. It can also be slipped over the narrow end of the sleeve board for shaping. It is available commercially or you can make your own to the dimensions given in the accompanying illustration. *See* PRESSING NAPPED FABRICS; PRESSING PILE FABRICS; PRESSING RAISED-SURFACE FABRICS.

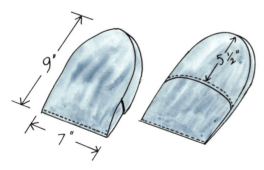

PRICK STITCH. A delicate but strong stitch made like a half backstitch (q.v.) except that the surface stitch is a tiny one.

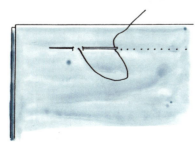

PRINCESS SEAM. Designed to fit the contour of the body, the seam goes in and out with the curves. *See* PRINCESS STYLE.

Stay-stitch both curved edges in the seam allowances 1/8 inch from the seam line. To facilitate the alignment of seam lines, clip the seam allowances of the center panel between the notches that indicate the deepest part of the curved seam (a).

With right sides together and the clipped edges uppermost, match and pin the seam lines, spreading the clipped edges to fit the side sections (b). Make additional clips if necessary. Stitch the two edges together in a plain seam. Notch the seam allowances of the side sections, keeping the notches between the clips to reduce the strain on the stitching (c).

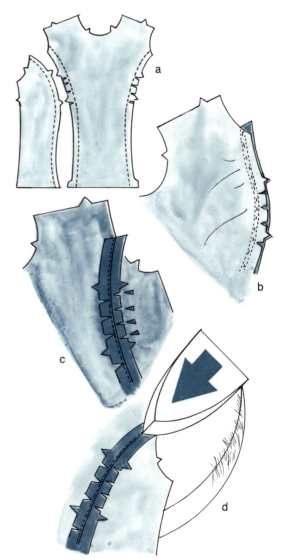

First press the seam flat, then open over a curve of the tailor's ham (d). *See also* CURVED PLAIN SEAM.

PRINCESS STYLE. A garment in which the shaping is done by lengthwise seams following the body contours. The princess line may start at the shoulder (a) or at the armhole (b). Such styles may extend to the waist, to the hips, or to short or long dress length.

The front and back are each cut in three sections—a center panel and two side sections. When put together, it is possible to fit shoulders, chest, bust, waist, and hips

in one style line. The back is similarly fitted. It's great shaping but it must follow the curves of the body perfectly.

Do not cut into the fashion fabric unless you are very sure of the fit. It is practically impossible to do much after the fabric is cut because of the complex in-and-out shaping of the pattern pieces. Make all the necessary adjustments for length, width, and shaping in the pattern. *(See* PRINCESS-STYLE PATTERN CORRECTIONS.*)* Better yet, make very sure of correct fit by testing the adjusted pattern in muslin or a similar test fabric.

Construction of princess-style garments also calls for very careful stitching, clipping, notching, and pressing over a tailor's ham. *See* CURVED PLAIN SEAM *and* PRINCESS SEAM.

PRINCESS-STYLE PATTERN CORRECTIONS. Before making any pattern changes *see* PATTERN CORRECTIONS for general information.

Because the princess style is a way in which a designer can incorporate shape and style in one seam line, it is a frequent form of styling. Because there are so many places where one can make a needed adjustment without detracting from the style lines, it is a favorite choice of many sewers.

In working with princess-style patterns, remember that you have four seams in addition to the usual two side seams. A total amount of width correction can be divided by 6 to determine how much to add or subtract at each seam. In this way, a very small correction on each seam can make a big difference.

BUST CORRECTIONS

High Bust. To bring the most curved portion of the pattern to the position nec-

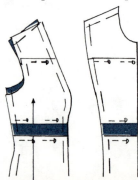

essary for a high bust, tuck the front and side front pattern sections above the armhole notch in the needed amount.

To preserve the bodice length, slash the pattern below the bust line but above the waistline. Spread it to the total amount of the tuck. Fill in the spread area with tissue paper. Fasten with pins or Scotch tape. Redraw the armhole, using the original armhole shape of the pattern.

Low Bust. To bring the most curved position of the pattern to the position necessary for a low bust, reverse the above procedure by slashing the front and side front pattern sections in a line just above the armhole notch. Spread to the needed amount. Fill in the spread with tissue paper. Fasten with pins or Scotch tape.

To preserve the bodice length, tuck the pattern below the bust line but above the waistline in the amount of the spread. Redraw the armhole, using the original armhole shape of the pattern.

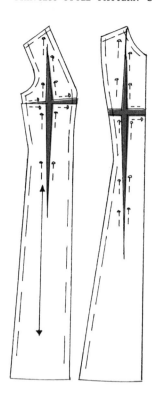

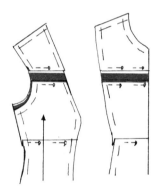

Bust with Large Cup. Draw vertical slash lines on the front and side front sections. Draw horizontal slash lines on the front and side front sections at the bust line.

Spread the front pattern vertically at the bust line and taper to nothing at the neck and at about the thigh. Spread the side front section vertically at the bust line, taper to nothing at the shoulder and at mid-thigh.

Spread the front section horizontally equally across the bust line. Spread the side front section at the bust line in the same amount as at the style line and taper to nothing at the side seams.

Insert paper in all spread areas. Redraw the seam lines.

Bust with Small Cup. Reverse the procedure for *Bust With Large Cup,* tucking instead of slashing and spreading.

BACK CORRECTIONS

Erect Back. Remove some of the excess length by dropping the neckline of both back and side back sections. If necessary, flatten the princess seam.

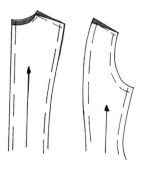

Rounded Back. Draw horizontal slash lines across the back and side back sections several inches below the neckline.

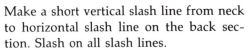

Make a short vertical slash line from neck to horizontal slash line on the back section. Slash on all slash lines.

On the back section, spread from the center back to the short vertical slash line in an even amount; from the short vertical slash line to the style line in a slightly tapered amount.

On the side back section, spread from the style line in the same amount as the back section, taper to nothing at the armhole. Insert paper in all spread areas. Pin or Scotch-tape.

Create a dart in the spread space at the neck of the back section. Redraw all seam lines.

CHEST CORRECTIONS

Hollow Chest. Remove some of the excess length at the shoulder seams of front and side front sections.

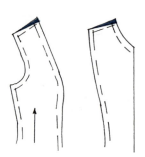

Pigeon Chest. Draw an L-shaped slash line from shoulder to armhole in the side front section. Slash and spread to the needed amount. Fill in the spread area with tissue paper and fasten with pins or Scotch tape. Redraw the underarm curve of the armhole, continuing the amount

added at the upper armhole. Correct the side seam, adding the necessary amount at the armhole and tapering to nothing at the side seam. Redraw the shoulder seam.

HIP CORRECTIONS

Large Hips. For a slight increase (2 inches or less), add to the side seams of the side front and side back sections (a).

For a large increase (more than 2 inches), apportion the increase over all seams (b). Carry the correction to the hemline.

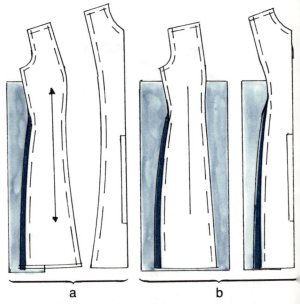

a   b

Slight Hips. For a slight decrease (1 inch or less) or a large one (1 to 2 inches), reverse the correction procedure for *Large Hips* by taking a bit off seams instead of adding to them.

LENGTH CORRECTIONS

To Lengthen the Bodice: Draw horizontal slash lines above the waist in all pattern sections. Slash and spread; fill in all spread areas with tissue paper. Fasten with pins or Scotch tape.

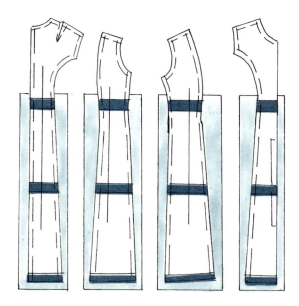

To Lengthen the Skirt: Draw horizontal slash lines below the waist in all pattern sections. Slash and spread; fill in all spread areas with tissue paper. Fasten.

This correction will retain the original hemline fullness. If you wish to add fullness in proportion to the length, add length at the hemline.

For Overall Length: Make pattern corrections above and below the waist as well as at the hemline.

To Shorten the Bodice, Skirt, or Overall Length: Reverse the lengthening process by tucking in the same places instead of slashing and spreading.

WAIST CORRECTIONS

Large Waist. For a slight increase at the waist, add the needed amount to the side seams of the side front and side back sections (a).

For a large increase, apportion the needed amount over all seams (b).

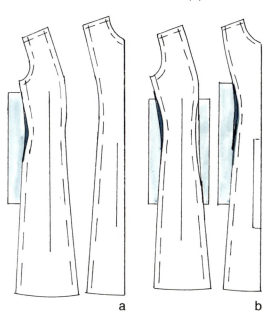

a   b

Small Waist. For a slight or large decrease, reverse the process above, taking off a bit instead of adding it.

PROFESSIONAL WAISTBANDING. A commercially available, flexible, woven synthetic, in widths from 3/4 inch to 2 inches. Purchase the exact width desired for the finished waistband. Do not cut it narrower; this removes its finished edges. You will need the exact waistline length without seam allowances. *See* WAISTBAND WITH PROFESSIONAL WAISTBANDING.

PUFFED SLEEVE. One gathered across the cap and sometimes at the hem too. If the fabric is not stiff enough to sustain the puff, it must be stiffened in some way *(see* LEG-OF-MUTTON SLEEVE) or bolstered with a shoulder pad *(see* PUFF SHOULDER PAD).

PUFF SHOULDER PADS. Commercially available shoulder pads designed especially for puffed sleeve caps. Insert the pad in the sleeve so it props up the puff. Stitch it to the armhole seam, lining up the notch on its straight edge with the shoulder seam.

R

RAGLAN SLEEVE. Its comfort and comparatively easy construction make the raglan sleeve a great favorite in all its design variations. In coats and jackets, it is roomy enough to wear over other garments. In hard-to-ease fabrics there is none of the struggle of a set-in sleeve. It is a natural choice for a double-faced fabric or reversible garment, for there is none of the bulk or bother there is with set-in sleeves.

In the raglan sleeve, part of the front and back of the garment are cut in one with the sleeve. The sleeve is joined to the garment in a style line that extends from neckline to underarm.

RAGLAN-SLEEVE FITTING. The raglan sleeve may be cut in one piece and shaped on the seams that join it at front and back or at the shoulder by a slightly curved shoulder dart, or cut in two pieces—a front and a back—joined by a seam shaped over the shoulder that continues throughout the length of the sleeve.

Whether by seam or by dart, the shaping must conform to the shoulder shape of the wearer. This calls for a very careful trial fitting, which could mean moving the shoulder dart or seam forward or backward to make the deepest part of the curve fall over the edge of the shoulder.

The same rules apply to the fitting of the shoulder of a raglan sleeve as for fitting any other shoulder. (*See* SHOULDER SEAM.) The correctly established seam line is carried down the full length of the sleeve. If the shoulder is fitted by a dart, it must be placed in the same relative position as a shoulder seam.

Caution: Don't overfit the shoulder curve. Allow enough ease for comfortable movement.

Raglan Sleeves

RAGLAN-SLEEVE PATTERN CORRECTIONS.

Like other sleeve types, the raglan sleeve pattern can be corrected to fit the figure. Before making any changes, *see Pattern Corrections* for general information. The following illustrations show raglan sleeve corrections when there is a shoulder dart. When there is no shoulder dart, carry the slash line for the correction down and/or across the sleeve pattern from seam to seam.

ARM CORRECTIONS

Large Arm. Draw a vertical slash line on the pattern from the point of the shoulder dart to the wrist and a horizontal slash line across the sleeve pattern from underarm to underarm. Slash both lines.

Spread the vertical slash line to the desired width where it crosses the horizontal slash line. Taper to the dart point and to the wrist. Overlap the horizontal slash line at the spread, tapering to the sleeve seam in an amount sufficient to keep the pattern flat. Insert pattern paper in the spread area and Scotch-tape to position. Redraw the dart as it was originally.

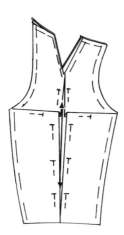

Large Upper Arm. Draw a vertical slash line on the pattern from dart point to wrist. Slash and spread the pattern at the dart point and taper to nothing at the wrist. Insert pattern paper in the spread area and Scotch-tape to position. Redraw the larger shoulder dart in the open space.

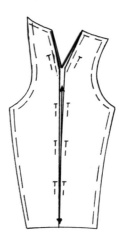

Thin Arm. Remove excess fullness by tucking the pattern down the center to the needed amount. Redraw the smaller dart.

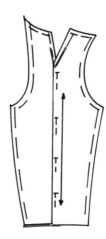

Thick Elbow (More Elbow Room Needed). Draw an L-shaped slash line on the pattern down the center of the raglan sleeve from the dart point to the elbow position.

Slash and spread at the elbow to the desired amount and taper to nothing at the

dart point. Insert paper in the spread area and Scotch-tape to position. Redraw the back sleeve seam, correcting it from elbow to wrist.

BACK CORRECTIONS

Erect Back. Remove some of the length by dropping the neckline on the back and sleeve patterns.

Take some off the back shoulder dart of the raglan sleeve.

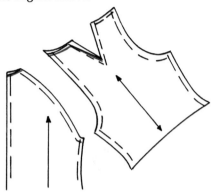

Rounded Back. Draw a horizontal slash line across the back pattern section 2 to 3 inches below the neckline. Slash and spread to the necessary amount.

Draw a slash line on the back part of the raglan sleeve from the shoulder dart to the style line. Slash and spread at the style line in the same amount as at the back section. Taper to nothing at the dart.

Insert pattern paper in the spread areas and Scotch-tape to position. Redraw the seam lines, curving them slightly.

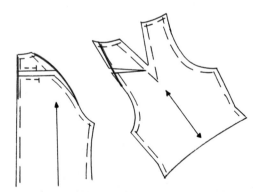

Large Back or Prominent Shoulder Blades. Draw an L-shaped slash line on the garment back pattern from the raglan style line to the side seam. Slash and spread along the vertical part of the slash line. Insert paper and Scotch-tape to position. Correct the raglan style line and the side seam.

Draw a slash line at the back of the raglan sleeve from the raglan style line to the dart. Slash and spread at the style line in an amount equal to the spread at the back section. Taper to nothing at the dart. Insert pattern paper in the spread area and Scotch-tape to position. Redraw the raglan style line.

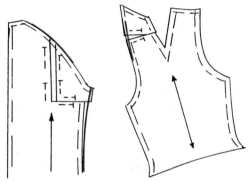

BUST CORRECTIONS

Bust with Large Cup. Draw a vertical slash line on the front pattern from the raglan style line to the hem. Draw a horizontal slash line across the pattern at the bust line from the side seam to the center front.

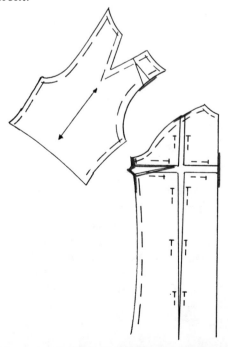

Spread vertically to the amount needed at the bust line. Taper slightly to the style line and to nothing at the hem. Spread horizontally equally across the pattern from the side seam to the vertical spread and to the center front. Insert paper in the spread areas and Scotch-tape. Create a dart at the bust line in the spread space. Correct the center front, the style line, and the side seam.

On the raglan sleeve, draw a slash line at the sleeve front from the shoulder dart to the style line. Slash and spread in the same amount at the sleeve style line as at the front style line. Taper to nothing at the dart. Insert paper in the spread area and Scotch-tape. Correct the sleeve style line.

Bust with Small Cup. Tuck the front pattern vertically in the needed amount, starting at the style line and tapering to nothing at the hem. To remove sag, tuck the front pattern horizontally across the front at the bust line from the side seam to the center front. Pin or Scotch-tape in place.

Tuck the raglan sleeve front in the same amount at its style line as at the front style line. Taper to nothing at the shoulder dart. Pin or Scotch-tape to position.

Redraw the seam lines of shoulder dart, style lines of sleeve and front, and side seam.

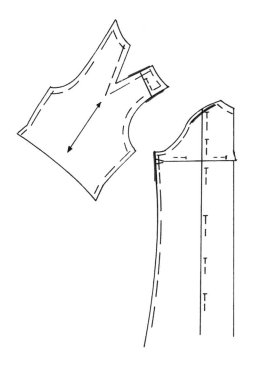

CHEST CORRECTIONS

Hollow Chest. Remove some of the length by dropping the neckline on the sleeve and front patterns. Make a slightly larger dart.

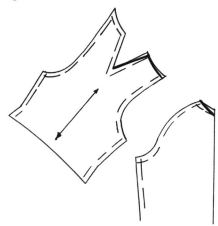

Pigeon Chest. Draw an L-shaped slash line into the front pattern from and to the raglan style line. Slash and spread to the needed amount vertically and horizontally. Fill in the spread area with paper and Scotch-tape to position.

Draw a slash line on the raglan sleeve front from the style line to the shoulder dart. Slash and spread the style line in the same amount as at the front style line. Taper to nothing at the dart. Insert paper in the spread areas and Scotch-tape in place.

Correct the style line of front, sleeve, and shoulder dart.

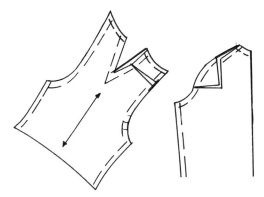

SHOULDER CORRECTIONS

Broad Shoulders. Draw L-shaped slash lines on front and back patterns, from and to the raglan style lines. Slash and spread to the needed amount vertically and horizontally. Insert paper in the spread area and Scotch-tape in place.

Slash the front and back raglan sleeve from the shoulder dart to the style lines. Spread in the needed amount at the dart, taper slightly at the style lines in amounts to match those of front and back. Pin or Scotch-tape in place.

Correct and redraw the new longer dart and all style lines.

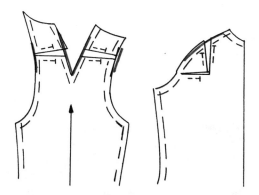

Narrow Shoulders. Draw L-shaped slash lines into the front and back patterns from and to the raglan style lines. Slash and overlap to the needed amount vertically and horizontally. Pin or Scotch-tape in place.

Tuck the raglan sleeve from shoulder dart to style lines as needed at the dart, tapering to the style lines in amounts to match those of front and back. Pin or Scotch-tape in place.

Correct and redraw the new shorter dart and all style lines.

Square Shoulders. Make a shorter dart at the shoulder. If this adjustment is not sufficient, make a square shoulder pattern correction (q.v.).

Sloping Shoulders. Make a deeper, longer dart at the shoulder. If this adjustment is not sufficient, make a sloping shoulder pattern correction (q.v.).

RAGLAN SLEEVE: SETTING AND STITCHING. With right sides together, stitch the shoulder dart of the one-piece raglan sleeve, taking special care that the dart point blends into the fabric in a soft curve rather than jutting out in a straight line. Slash the dart as far as possible. Clip across the dart where unslashed (a). Or stitch the shoulder seam from neck to hem of a two-piece raglan sleeve. Notch the seam allowances along the deep shoulder curve (b).

Pin and stitch the underarm seam. Press all seams flat first, then open. Press the unslashed end of the shoulder dart to one side. Press the curved shoulder of seam or dart over the tailor's ham or similar curved pad.

Set the sleeve into the armhole, matching notches, markings, and underarm

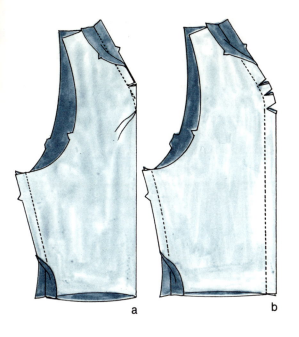

a   b

seams of garment and sleeve. Pin and
baste, working with the sleeve uppermost.

RAINCOATS. Time was when a raincoat
was something one always had to buy.
Now, with all the bright new waterproofed fabrics and the new methods by
which any good cleaning service can waterproof many fabrics, making one's own
raingear is a breeze.

Make a raincoat of vinyl, of rain-resis-
tant lacquered cotton, of waterproofed
silk, of plastic-finished wool, of water-re-
sistant lush velveteen, of unlikely upholstery or drapery. Even the tough fabrics
such as canvas, duck, and the like make
wonderful raincoats. Just to be sure,
choose a color-fast cloth. (It would be aw-
ful to leave little pools of color behind you
on the first wet day.)

Any coat pattern that doesn't have too
many seams, darts, or dressmaking details
will do. Choose an easy, roomy style that
will fit over all the layers one is apt to
wear on a rainy day. Deep armhole, raglan
or kimono sleeves are best. Consider making a matching hood or hat. And why not
a rain suit or rain cape to add to your collection of rain-chasers?

Suit the style and design to your taste.
Suit the tailoring to your fabric. And,

when you have finished all that, pray for a
rainy day.

RAYON. A synthetic fiber.

Advantages: Soft, comfortable, absorbent, good affinity for dyes, generally colorfast.

Disadvantages: Relatively weak (even
weaker when wet), holds in body heat,
wrinkles, shrinks, stretches unless treated,
low resistance to mildew, weakened by
prolonged exposure to light.

Care: Rayon usually needs dry cleaning.
It may be hand- or machine-washed in
warm water. Use a gentle machine cycle
and tumble-dry.

Pressing rayon presents problems. It has
a tendency to shine where an iron touches
it or sizing may stick to the iron, leaving
brown streaks. It is very sensitive to heat;
the fabric may be injured or scorched by a
too warm iron. Many rayons shrink with
moisture yet require it for flattening
seams. Steam discolors some rayons; others water-spot.

To overcome these hazards, press lightly
while damp on the wrong side with a cool
to moderate iron, or over a very slightly
dampened press cloth or several layers of
tissue paper between fabric and press
cloth.

REINFORCE A CORNER. Use stay stitching
or a patch of seam binding, organza, or
iron-on material.

With Stay Stitching: Make a double
row of tiny machine stitches for about an
inch on each side of the corner. Clip diagonally to the corner close to the line of
stitching.

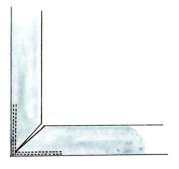

With a Patch of Seam Binding, Organza, or Iron-on: *See* REINFORCE A SLASH LINE: *Method 2.*

REINFORCE A SLASH LINE. Use either of the following methods for gussets, sleeve openings, or wherever slash lines are involved.

METHOD 1

Stay-stitch both sides of the slash, tapering toward the point of the slash. Use small stitches—15 to 20 per inch. Take one stitch across the point to provide the space for turning (a). Clip the point to the stitching.

METHOD 2

Place a patch of seam binding or organza on the right side of the material over the point of the slash and stitch both sides of the point as if for stay stitching (b). Clip to the point and pull the patch through to the wrong side like a facing. Press carefully.

Place a patch of iron-on material over the point on the wrong side of the fabric. Press (c). Clip to the point.

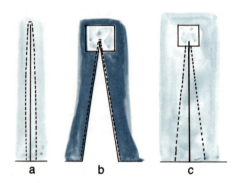

a b c

REINFORCED SLASH BUTTONHOLE. A type of buttonhole that can be used only on fabrics that won't ravel, such as felt, leather, Ultrasuede.

Mark the position of the opening of the buttonhole on the garment. Remove 1/8 inch of interfacing around the marking to keep it from showing in the completed buttonhole. Stitch a rectangle around and close to the opening line. Slash the buttonhole on the opening line.

REINFORCING BUTTON. When a button is subjected to great strain, as in a heavy overcoat, the fabric at the base of the shank is apt to tear. To prevent this, a smaller button is used as a reinforcement.

Attach the reinforcing button to the underside of the garment directly under the garment button. Both buttons are stitched in one operation. (Obviously, the buttons should have the same number of holes.) On the last stitch, bring the needle through the top button only. Complete the shank (q.v.). Anchor the ends in the fabric at the base of the button with tiny back stitches.

In lightweight or delicate fabrics, a doubled square of fabric or seam binding may be used in place of a reinforcing button.

RELEASED TUCK. One that is stitched only part way, releasing its fullness at one or both ends, depending on where it is located on the garment. For instance, a waistline released tuck in a garment with a waistline seam has its lower end included in that seam while releasing its fullness at its upper end (a). A waistline released tuck in a garment without a waistline seam releases its fullness at both ends (b). In both instances, the tuck is stitched as a tuck an even distance from the fold. (Where there is shaping with released fullness, the tuck is called a dart tuck [q.v.].)

The released tucks may be stitched on the outside or inside of the garment, depending on its design. Sometimes they are stitched across the top and bottom of the tuck. If the tuck is stitched on the right side, it is stronger and more attractive if stitched by the method used for the continuous-thread dart (q.v.); there are no thread knots or backstitching to show.

When one end of the released tuck is to be included in a seam, begin the stitching at the other end. Secure the tuck with

a b

backstitching at the seam edge. If the tuck is stitched on the wrong side, both ends may be secured with backstitching.

Do not press the released fullness flat or you will lose the main feature of this tuck —soft fullness. *See* TUCKS.

RELINING A COAT OR JACKET. Replacing a worn lining or exchanging a dull lining for a more attractive one can give new life to an old garment.

In relining a coat or jacket, give yourself all the help you can get from the old lining. It is its own best guide. Using contrasting thread, mark the sleeve setting at the shoulder, the underarm, and where notches would ordinarily be placed—at those points, both front and back, where the overarm curve swings into the underarm curve. Make a thread loop on the sleeve and directly opposite on the lining. Make similar pairs of markings on the lining and back neck facing or collar, on the lining and hem, on the lining and front facing, and somewhere on the underarm seam of the sleeve. The seam lines will be indicated by the remaining needle holes or press-creases when the lining is ripped apart.

Carefully remove the lining. Rip the sections apart at the seams. If there are any darts, rip them open. Remove the stitches that hold folds (for instance, at center back) and open out the folds. Press each section. Mark the seam lines with chalk. Add seam allowance. Trim away any excess material.

Check the shapes of the lining sections to see if both fronts, both backs, and both sleeves are identical. If great discrepancies in shape are due to the precise fitting of left and right, then cut each new section individually. Slight discrepancies that show up in the comparison should be balanced out. They are generally insignificant, likely to be slight errors in the insertion or stitching of the lining.

Determine the grain of each section by following or pulling a thread. Mark the grain with tailor's chalk or thread as a guide for placement on the new lining material.

It is not the old lining one uses for cutting out the new lining, it's a paper pattern. Lining material can too easily be forced out of shape or off grain in an effort to make it fit the new fabric. You can't play tricks with a paper pattern. Since it won't budge, the cutting is accurate.

Place the corrected lining over a sheet of paper. Trace around all outside edges. Trace darts and fold lines for pleats. Trace the grain line. Trace the pairs of thread markings. Use the new pattern to estimate the yardage needed for the new lining.

Cut out the new lining. Stitch, press, and insert it. *See* LINING A TAILORED GARMENT.

REPEATS. In every fabric where there is a design either as an integral part of its structure (weaving or knitting) or superimposed by printing, there is a place where the design motif or unit starts all over again. This is known as a repeat. Units are arranged in a planned, formal, regular pattern.

Textile designers strive to disguise the point at which each repeat begins and ends so the flow of the design is continuous and the mechanical structure or layout of the design is indiscernible. So clever and so ingenious are they at this that frequently it is difficult to determine the be-

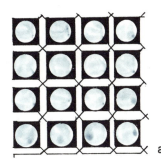

a

b

ginning and ending of the repeat. But determine it you must.

To preserve the continuity of the fabric design, the repeats must be matched in your garment. The only exception to this would be a fabric of very small motifs in an overall coverage in which the disturbance caused by the darts and seams is minimal.

Each repeat is made up of a motif (or motifs) which may be nondirectional (a) or directional (b).

If the design of your fabric is nondirectional, it makes no difference how you hold it. The design is the same all the way around. Your pattern can be placed in any direction. If, however, your fabric is directional, the movement of the motifs is all in one direction. All pattern pieces must be placed going in the same direction.

When buying your fabric, find the repeats. (Stripes and plaids as well as florals and geometrics have repeats.) Study your pattern for the number of sections that must match as they join. Note the direction of the motifs. Determine the amount of yardage, depending on the size of the repeats, the direction of the motifs, and the number of sections that need matching. *See* DIRECTIONAL LAYOUT; DESIGN UNITS; MATCHING PLAIDS, STRIPES, CHECKS, GEOMETRIC REPEATS.

REVERSED SEAM. One used when facing or hem is turned to the right side for decorative effect. It provides a finished seam at the garment edge.

Mark the point on the seam line at which the seam will be reversed. From the garment's edge, make it equal to the width of a facing or twice the width of a hem.

With right sides together, stitch the garment seam a few stitches beyond the marking into the area designated for facing or hem. Clip the seam allowances at the end of the stitching to the seam (a). Press the seam allowances open.

Turn the garment to the right side. Reverse the seam allowances to the right side. *With wrong sides together,* stitch them (b). Grade the seam allowances and press them open.

a   b

Apply the facing. *See* RIGHT-SIDE FACING. Finish the hem. *See* RIGHT-SIDE HEM.

REVERSIBLE GARMENT. One that can be worn with either side out. There are two types of reversibles: those made of fabric whose layers are joined by weaving or bonding (double-faced fabric) and those that you can join by putting together two separate fabrics. The problems of pattern selection are the same for both types. For construction of each type, *see* DOUBLE-FACED FABRIC *and* TWO-FABRICS REVERSIBLE.

RIBBED BANDING INSET. *See* INSET WAISTBAND.

RIBBED BANDING (RIBBING). A rib-knit banding used for close fit as well as decorative effect. Ribbing is used for band collars like the crew, mock turtleneck, or turtleneck; for the lower edge of sleeves, shirts, jackets, pants, and the like. This stretchy knit strip is available by the yard or prepackaged. It comes in several widths with both long edges finished or with one long raw edge. The raw edge is attached to the garment. (When both long edges are finished, either can be attached to the garment.)

When used as a slipover, the ribbing should be stretchy enough to go over the part of the body involved—head, hand, foot, and so on. It should also have the ability to recover (return to its original measurement after having been stretched). It is generally cut several inches shorter than the edge to which it is to be attached. Test the ribbing for a comfortable or snug fit. Cut the desired length plus seam allowances at each end. Stitch the ends together with an overedge seam or a double-stitched seam. Trim the excess. Press toward one side.

When ribbing is to be used with some kind of closing (zipper, buttons), cut it slightly shorter than the garment edge to which it is to be attached. Leave the ends open and edge-finish them.

For both types, section the banding and the garment edge it is to fit into four or more equal parts, depending on the length of the ribbing. Mark with pins.

With right sides together, match the edges and pin markings. Stretch the banding to fit the garment edge and pin at intervals between to keep the band stretched (a). With the band side up, stitch the banding to the garment (b). Use an overedge seam or a double-stitched seam.

Hold the steam iron above the seam, al-

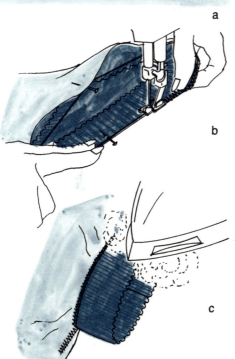

a

b

c

lowing the steam to return the ribbing to its original measurement (c). Press the seam allowances toward the garment. Let the banding dry before further handling.

RIBBINGS. Narrow to wide knitted, stretchy, decorative bands. *See* RIBBED BANDING.

RIBBON-FACED WAISTBAND. An excellent way to handle waistbands of heavy or bulky materials or those that need to be stayed because of stretchability.

Cut the upper waistband of the fashion fabric plus seam allowances. Cut a similar length of preshrunk grosgrain ribbon of the same width the finished waistband is to be.

Overlap and pin the ribbon on the right side of the fashion fabric waistband so one edge is about 1/4 inch from the seam line (into the seam allowance). This will provide an allowance for rolling the seam to the underside. Stitch close to the edge of the ribbon.

Attach the waistband to the skirt waistline seam (*see* WAISTBAND: BASIC METHOD).

RIBBON-FACED WAISTLINE. A relief from the monotony of miles and miles of self-fabric waistbands encountered during a lifetime. Ribbon facing does an inside job of holding a skirt or pants in place while retaining its anonymity.

Use a length of 1- to 1½-inch preshrunk grosgrain ribbon. Cut it to the waistline measurement plus ease plus two seam allowances. Turn under the seam allowances at each end and stitch (a). Swirl the grosgrain ribbon into a slight curve with the steam iron. The waistband will fit better if contoured. (*See* PRESHAPING TAPE, RIBBON, *or* BIAS BINDING.)

With right sides up, overlap and pin the ribbon on the skirt at least 1/4 inch above the waistline seam line into the seam al-

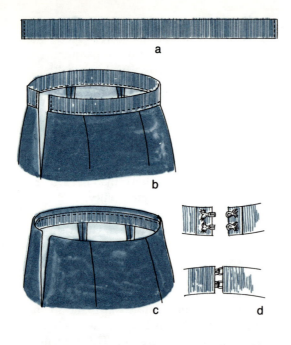

a

b

c

d

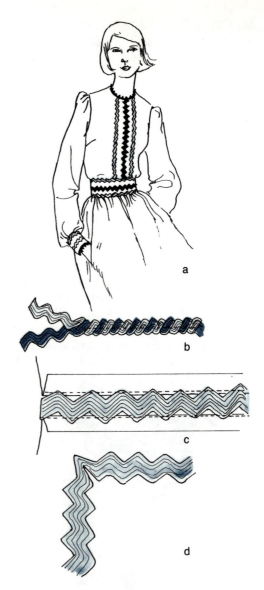

a

b

c

d

lowance. This will provide an allowance for rolling the seam to the underside. In heavier fabrics, you may need more than 1/4 inch. Use your judgment. Stitch (b).

Trim and clip the seam allowance under the ribbon for a flat and easy turning. Turn the waistband to the inside of the skirt or pants, rolling the seam to the underside. Press to position (c). Tack the band securely to all seams and darts on the underside.

Optional: You may topstitch the band to position if it is consistent with the design of the garment.

Sew hooks and eyes to the ends of the band for fastening (d).

RICKRACK BRAID. A very flexible saw-toothed-edged braid generally made of cotton. It comes in a range of sizes and colors and is particularly effective when used in such combinations (a). Two lengths intertwined form an interesting banding (b). Insertions of rickrack make an unusual trim (c). (Apply in the same way as lace insertions [q.v.].) Since it is so flexible, it can be used for all kinds of shapes. For a squared effect, arrange the braid so there is a point at the corner (d).

When used full width, machine-stitch down the center of the braid. When ap-

plied by hand, attach with tiny stitches at each point.

RIGHT-SIDE FACING. Why hide a facing on the underside of the garment when it can become an attractive feature on the outside? Perhaps it has an unusual shape (a) or is of a contrasting color (b) or a different texture (c).

About the easiest and most effective way to cope with a decorative top facing is to face the facing first and then attach it. There are two bonuses to this method. The facing edge is finished before being attached to the garment. (It's so much less

bulky this way.) The facing's facing functions as an interfacing.

Treat all garment seams that enter the facing area as reversed seams (q.v.).

In attaching the facing to the outside of the garment, some of the operations are the reverse of those used for applying it to the inside. Since the facing must fit the outside measurement of the garment, make it slightly larger than the area it is to face. Add at the shoulders or slash and spread the facing pattern in several places to enlarge it gradually.

Cut out the decorative facing. Cut its facing of a lightweight interfacing material in a matching color, if possible. Make the interfacing just a bit smaller than the facing.

With right sides together, join the facing and its interfacing on all outside edges (a). Leave the edge that joins the garment open. Press the seam allowances open. Trim and grade them. Clip or notch the edges as necessary.

Turn the facing to the right side. Press the edges flat, being careful to roll the

joining seam to the underside. Baste to position. Place the right side of the facing against the wrong side of the garment (b). Match raw edges, center, seams. Stretch the garment to match the facing. Pin to position.

With the garment side up, stitch the decorative facing to the garment an even distance from the raw edges. Trim and grade the seam allowances. Notch or clip as necessary. Turn the facing to the right side of the garment, being careful to roll the joining seam to the underside. Pin and/or baste to position. Topstitch (c) if consistent with the design or slip-stitch the outer edges to the garment.

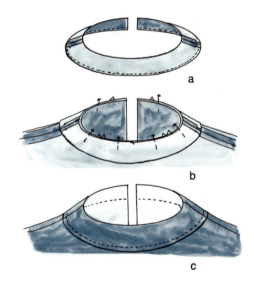

RIGHT-SIDE HEM. This forms a decorative band at the lower edge of a skirt, sleeve, overblouse, jacket, and the like.

Set the hemline before finishing the garment seams that enter the hem. Measure and mark the hem. Mark a point on the garment seam to indicate the top of the hem below which the seam is reversed. This should allow enough depth for the hem edge finish. Make the reversed seam (q.v.).

Turn the hem to the right side, pin and/or baste to position. Turn under the hem edge and press. Topstitch (if consistent with the design of the garment) or slip-stitch the hem edge to the garment.

RIGHT-SIDE MARKINGS. Some markings are necessary on the right side of the garment while the work is in progress: the position of a pocket, a buttonhole, or a button; the center front or the fold line of a facing or pleat. Any detail of trimming or construction that must be done from the right side must be so marked.

The safest right-side marking is basting thread of a contrasting color. *See* MARKING METHODS.

RING COLLAR. A rectangular band the exact length of the garment neckline. It stands away from the neck at its upper edge because the neck measurement at this position is less than at its base. For construction, *see* STANDING COLLAR.

ROLLED COLLAR: ROLL LINE ESTABLISHED. Lap the undercollar over the garment with neck seam lines matching. Pin. Try on the garment, rolling the collar to position. Pin the front closed. Pin along the roll line. Remove the garment and unpin the collar. Baste along the roll line through all thicknesses (a). If the fabric can take it, steam the collar into shape over the tailor's ham and let it dry in position (b).

ROLLED DRESSMAKER COLLAR. This is a molded collar with a pronounced roll. The roll line divides the collar into a stand and fall *(see* FALL OF COLLAR) (a).

Generally the undercollar and interfacing are cut on the bias from the same pattern. It is the bias-interfaced undercollar that provides the excellent fit and control. The upper collar (cut on vertical or cross grain) functions mainly as decoration. When the design is a standaway rolled collar (b), the entire collar is cut on the bias, frequently in one piece. In this collar, because of the bias, both undercollar and upper collar are molded and carefully shaped to carry out the lines of the design.

The dressmaker notched collar (c) and the shawl collar (q.v.) (d) are classified as rolled collars. While this notched collar may appear complicated, it is in fact simply a rolled collar with extensions added for the lapels and is constructed like any other rolled collar. However, if the fabric is heavy, bulky, or difficult to handle, best results are obtained by using a tailoring instead of a dressmaking technique for the construction. *See* TAILORED NOTCHED COLLAR.

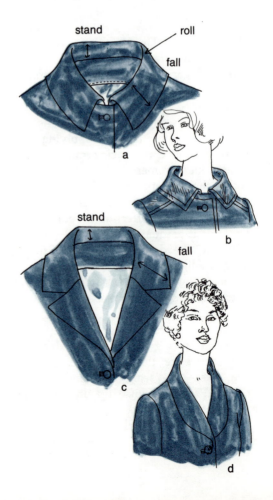

Cut out the upper collar and undercollar. Remember to make the upper collar just a bit larger so that the joining seam may be rolled to the underside. Cut out the interfacing.

In lightweight fabric and interfacing, trim off the corners of the interfacing to about 1/4 inch beyond the seam lines (a). Eliminating the interfacing from the corners prevents bulk when the collar is turned to the right side. Apply the interfacing to the wrong side of the undercollar. Baste. This interfacing is included in the seam that joins upper collar and undercollar, then trimmed close to the stitching.

In medium-weight fabric, trim away all seam allowances of the interfacing. Apply it to the wrong side of the undercollar and catch-stitch around all edges (b).

In a one-piece collar, apply the interfacing to the undercollar section. Catch-stitch along the roll line (c).

How you handle the collar from this point on depends on the weight of the material and the type of application.

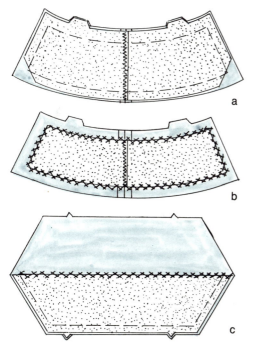

METHOD 1. SUITABLE FOR LIGHTWEIGHT FABRICS

With right sides together, pin and/or baste the interfaced undercollar to the neck edge of the garment, matching backs, shoulder seam markings, and points at which the collar joins the front neckline or lapel. Clip the garment at the shoulders and wherever else necessary for a smooth joining. Stitch the undercollar to the garment (a).

If there is a back facing, stitch it to the front facing at the shoulders (b). Press the seam allowances open. Pin the upper collar to the facing neck edge, matching markings, center backs, and points at which the collar joins the facing at the front. Clip the facing where necessary. Baste. Stitch the upper collar to the facings (c). Press all seam allowances open, then trim.

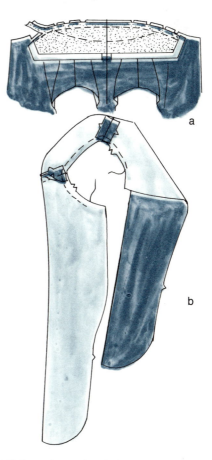

If there is no back facing, fold back the shoulder seam allowances of the front facings. Baste, press. Pin, baste, and stitch the upper collar to the neck edges of the front facings from the shoulders to the point at which the collar joins the front facings.

Clip the upper collar seam allowances to the seam lines at both shoulders. In ravelly fabrics, reinforce this point with small machine stitches. Clip, trim, and press open the seam allowances. Turn under the free edge of the upper collar seam allowance at the neck edge, clipping as necessary. Baste close to the fold (d). Press the seam allowance toward the collar.

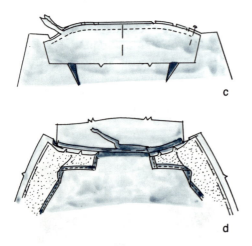

Both Types. With right sides together, pin the upper-collar-and-facing to the undercollar-and-garment. Stitch the front opening and lapel edges, stretching the garment to fit the slightly larger opening-and-lapel edges. Stitch the collar sections together, stretching the undercollar to fit the slightly larger upper collar (a).

Trim and grade all seam allowances, making the upper ones the wider of the two. Free corners of bulk (b). Press all seams open. Use the point presser for the corners.

Turn the collar to the right side. Carefully work out the corners by pushing gently from the inside. Press all outside edges, rolling the seam to the underside. If the collar is not to be topstitched, understitch it by hand or by machine to within 1 inch of each end, fastening the upper wide seam allowance to the undercollar through all thicknesses and enclosing the narrower undercollar seam allowance (c). Hold the outer edges in place with straight or diagonal basting. Establish the roll line *(see* ROLLED COLLAR: ROLL LINE ESTABLISHED).

When there is a back facing, lift it and tack the seam allowances of collar and garment together loosely by hand (d). Turn the facing down.

When there is no back facing, turn the garment neck-edge seam allowances into the collar. Slip-stitch the basted edges of the upper collar and front facing to the neck and shoulder seams (e).

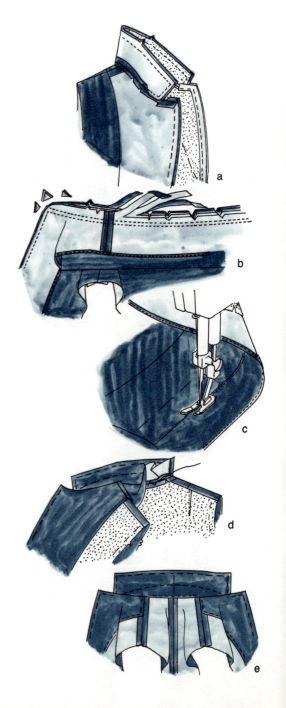

METHOD 2. SUITABLE FOR MEDIUM-WEIGHT FABRICS

With right sides together, join the upper collar and the interfaced undercollar around all outside edges (leaving the neck edge free). Leave 5/8-inch neck-edge seam allowances open at both ends (a). Trim and grade the seam allowances. Press them open over a point presser. Clip or notch them as necessary. Free corners of bulk.

Turn the collar to the right side. Work out the corners carefully. Press so the joining seam is rolled to the underside. Hold the outer edges in place with edge or diagonal basting. Establish the roll line (see ROLLED COLLAR) and baste through all layers along it.

Pin, baste, then stitch the neck edge of the undercollar to the neck edge of the garment (b). Pin, baste, then stitch the neck edge of the upper collar to the neck edge of the facing (c). Stitch the front facing to the garment extension at the opening edge and lapel (if there is one) (d).

Clip, trim, and grade all seam allowances. Free all corners of bulk. Press the seam allowances open over the point presser. Turn the facing to the inside.

When there is a back facing, allow the collar to fall into position. Because of the roll, it is likely that the seam allowances will not be one directly over the other. Lightly tack the two (a).

When there is no back facing, press the garment seam allowances into the collar. Turn under the upper collar neck-edge seam allowance and baste. Slip-stitch the basted edges of upper collar and front facing to the neck and shoulder seams (b).

a

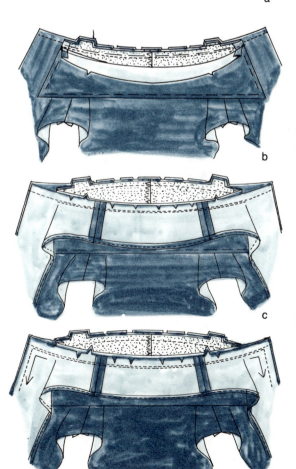

b

c

d

a

b

ROLLED HEM. For an elegant hem in a soft fabric, make a hand-rolled hem (q.v.). If

Ruffles Add a Romantic Touch

you prefer machine stitching to the time-consuming hand stitching, *see* MACHINE-ROLLED HEM.

RUCHING. A pleated or gathered strip of silk, net, ribbon, crepe, chiffon, lace, or other lightweight fabric. It is used as a trimming, usually at the neck and/or wrist, but it can also be used in rows.

RUFFLE. It's easy enough to make a ruffle. You don't need a pattern. It can be any width and have any fullness. It can be straight or circular, gathered or pleated, on straight grain or bias, a single layer, double layer, or layer on layer.

Ruffles fall into two main types: straight or circular. In a straight ruffle, the fullness is created by gathering or pleating a strip of fabric both of whose edges are the same length (a). In the circular ruffle, fullness is created when the inner curve of the cut-out circle is straightened (b).

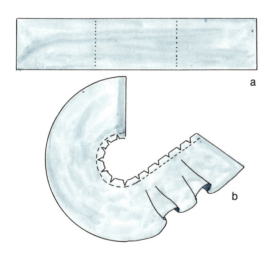

Where a ruffle is placed, the type of ruffle it is, the character of the fabric of which it is made, all determine how much fabric will be needed.

Straight or circular ruffles may be single or double (faced) layers. If piecing is necessary to produce the appropriate length of a straight ruffle, keep the strips on the same grain and be sure to match any motifs in the design of the fabric. To avoid piecing, cut a long strip along the selvage instead of crosswise (if there is no directional movement of weave or printed surface of the fabric).

The length of each piece of circular ruffle is the circumference of the inner circle. If piecing is necessary, cut as many circles as are needed to produce the desired length.

For a straight, gathered ruffle, you will need a strip of fabric two to three times longer than the finished ruffle or the edge it is to join. Soft or sheer fabrics look better with more fullness; stiff fabrics look better with less fullness. Deep ruffles need more fullness than narrow ones. Inward corners require less fullness, outward corners more fullness than the rest of the ruffle. Whatever the gathered ruffle, be generous; don't let it look skimpy. Add seam and hem allowances. *(See illustration on page 384.)*

The amount of material necessary *for a circular ruffle* will depend on the desired size of the circle.

RUFFLE: CIRCULAR. This ruffle produces fullness with a minimum of bulk. It is effective when made of soft or sheer fabric or of a fabric that falls in graceful folds. It is cut from a circle of cloth. The outer edge remains free while the inner edge is attached to the garment.

To make a pattern for a circular ruffle, draw two concentric circles on paper. The distance between the two equals the desired width of the ruffle. If only one length is needed, make the circumference of the inner circle the desired length. (Remember that the circumference is equal to approximately three times the diameter of the circle.) Add seam allowance to each circle. The exact location and maintenance of the grain line is important so the ruffle falls and drapes correctly.

If more than one circle is needed for the necessary length, apportion the amount over each inner circle. It will facilitate the cutting to make or trace the patterns for as many circles as are needed.

Draw a slash line on straight grain of the fabric for ends or for piecing. Place the pattern on the fabric. Pin and cut, first along the outer circle, then cut the slash line, and lastly cut out the inner circle.

Stay-stitch the inner circle just inside the seam line in the seam allowance. Clip the seam allowance at frequent intervals. Start with 1/2-inch intervals (a). If the ruffle doesn't straighten out when stretched, clip more frequently. If more than one circle is needed, join them on straight ends. Press the seam allowances open.

Finish the outer edge of a *single-layer* circular ruffle with a narrow rolled hem, ei-

ther by hand or by machine (q.v.) (b) or with decorative stitching.

For a *self-faced* circular ruffle, cut twice the number of circles needed for the desired length. For a contrasting fabric, cut an equal number of circles. With right sides together, stitch ruffle and facing along the outer edge. Trim the seam allowance close to the stitching or leave a narrow seam allowance notched at frequent intervals to prevent rippling when turned. Turn the facing to the right side and press along the edges. Baste the inner edges together (c).

To attach the circular ruffle to the garment, pin the inner edge of the ruffle to the stay-stitched edge of the garment. If a single-layer ruffle, place the wrong side of the ruffle against the right side of the garment. If a faced ruffle, place the underside of the ruffle against the right side of the garment. Align the raw edges and fit the ruffle smoothly on the seam line. Baste through all layers (a). This edge is included in the garment seam. For a finish, use a facing (q.v.) (b) or a bias binding (q.v.). If two sections of a garment are being joined, sandwich the ruffle between them (c).

When a facing has been attached, turn the ruffle away from the garment. Press the seam of the facing with the tip of the iron but *do not* press the ruffle. Understitch the facing to the seam allowances. Turn facing and ruffle to finished positions (d). Fasten the facing on the underside.

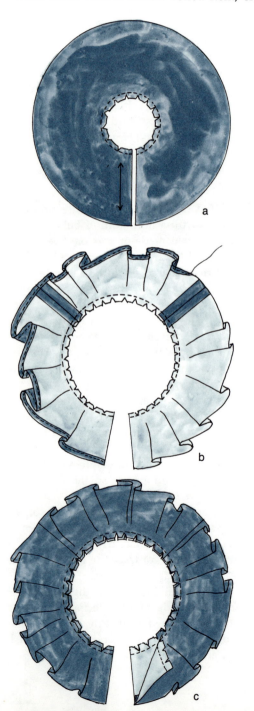

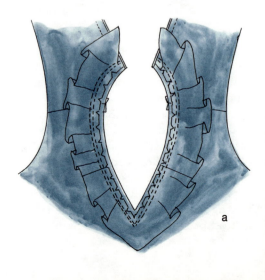

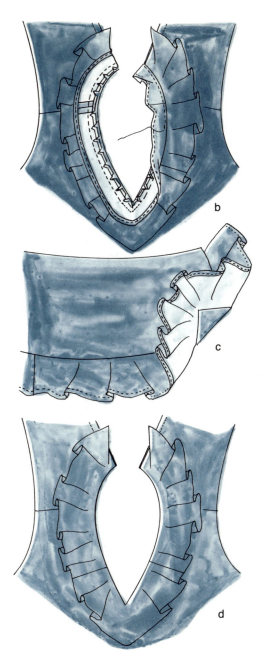

off center for the ruffle with a heading. Try for a pleasing proportion between the top and bottom of the latter ruffle.

Lay in the pleats of a pleated ruffle and baste across the top. Draw up the gathering of a gathered ruffle to match the edge to which it is to be attached.

For a Self-faced Double Ruffle: Cut the rectangular strip of cloth twice the desired width of the ruffle. Fold the fabric with wrong sides together so the edges meet at center (a) or off center (b). Pin.

Make two rows of gathering above and below the cut edges (a and b). Gather up the ruffle to the desired fullness and pin to position on the garment. If the ruffle is to be pleated, baste along the cut edges and lay in the pleats as planned.

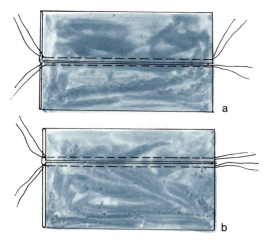

To attach a double or headed ruffle to an unfinished edge, place the ruffle along the edge to be joined upside down. Wrong

RUFFLE: DOUBLE. A variation of the straight, gathered ruffle (q.v.). The double ruffle has two free edges with gathering either in the center or off center. The latter is known as a *ruffle with a heading.*

For a Single-Layer Double Ruffle: Cut a rectangular strip of fabric to the desired width plus ¾ inch for two ⅜-inch hems by the desired length. Gather or pleat through the center for the double ruffle or

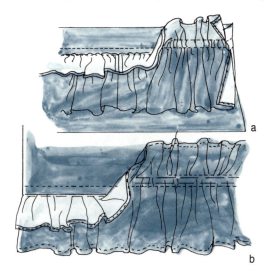

sides of ruffle and garment are together. Match the bottom row of gathers to the seam line of the garment. With the ruffle on top, baste beside the seam line, distributing the gathers evenly. Stitch, adjusting the gathers (a). Place and stitch a pleated ruffle in the same way.

Trim the garment seam allowance to ¼ inch. Turn the ruffle to position on the right side of the garment, enclosing it. Baste. Topstitch along the top row of gathering or basting stitches (b). Remove all bastings.

To attach a double or headed ruffle to a finished edge, place and pin the wrong side of the ruffle to the right side of the garment. Baste. With the ruffle on top, topstitch twice, stitching close to each row of gathering or basting stitches. Remove all bastings.

If the ruffle is *at a location within the garment,* mark the placement of the ruffle on the right side of the garment.

Center the ruffle over the marking and pin. Baste. With the ruffle on top, topstitch it to the garment along both rows of gathering or basting stitches (a). Such ruffles are almost always included in a cross seam (b).

RUFFLE: ENDS FINISHED. There are several ways in which the ends of ruffles may be handled.

The ends may be *tapered into the garment seam lines.* This is a pretty method, particularly if the ruffle does not continue for the full length of the seam. Place the ruffle along the edge, seam lines matching. Draw up the end of the ruffle until its outer edge crosses the seam line at the point where the ruffle will end (a). Place a facing or another section of garment over the ruffle, right sides together, and stitch the seam, enclosing the ruffle and its tapered end.

When the ends are free-hanging, *make a rolled hem* at each edge and slip-stitch it (b).

The ends of the ruffle may be *sewn into a cross seam* (c). Make certain that the cross seams match on both edges. With right sides together, stitch the seam. Press the seam allowances open. Trim or fold under

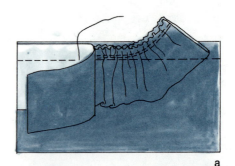

a

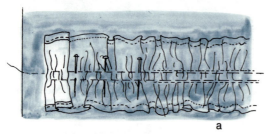

a

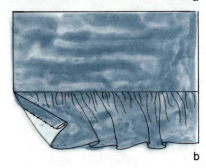

b

b

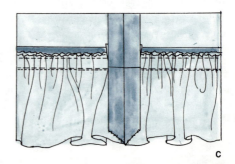

c

the seam allowances diagonally at the bottom edge and tack or slip-stitch them.

The *ends* of the ruffle *may be joined* before it is attached to the garment.

RUFFLE ON LINGERIE EDGE. With right sides together, pin the ruffle to the garment. Keep the edges aligned. Stitch with the ruffle on top. Trim the seam allowances to 1/4 inch. Overcast the edges by hand or by machine, using any of the overedge stitches. Use a medium stitch width and a short stitch setting.

RUFFLE: STRAIGHT, GATHERED. This ruffle has one free edge and one gathered or pleated edge that is attached to the garment.

For a Single-Layer Straight Ruffle: Cut to the desired length and width; edge-finish its free edge.

For a Self-faced Ruffle: Cut the strips twice as wide as the finished ruffle plus 1 1/4 inches for two 5/8-inch seam allowances by the desired length. Fold the single layer back on itself, wrong sides together. Baste across the top.

For a Faced Ruffle: Cut two lengths of fabric of the desired width of the ruffle plus 1 1/4 inches for two 5/8-inch seam allowances at top and bottom by the predetermined length. Join the lengths along one lengthwise edge, right sides together. Press the seam allowances open; grade them. Turn the ruffle to the right side. Press along the turned edge. Gather (or pleat) the raw edges. A very attractive effect can be achieved if the facing is of another color.

All Types. Section the length of ruffle and the edge to which it is to be joined into halves, quarters, eighths. Mark with pins, notches, or thread. Gather the ruffle by hand or by machine. For a long ruffle, gather in sections. It is easier to pull up the shorter lengths for even spacing without the risk of breaking the thread. If you machine-gather the entire length, pull up the gathering thread in sections.

Pin the gathered edge of the ruffle to the garment edge, matching markings (a). Draw up the gathering until the ruffle equals the garment edge. Fasten the threads at each end. Distribute the fullness evenly between the markings (b). Stitch. *See* JOINING GATHERED EDGE TO STRAIGHT EDGE and JOINING GATHERED EDGE TO GATHERED EDGE.

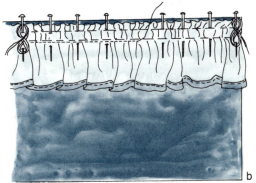

Ruffle with Self-finish (for straight edge only). When the ruffle has been stitched to the edge, trim the ruffle seam allowance to 1/8 inch. Fold the untrimmed seam allowance over twice so the trimmed edge will be enclosed. Place the second fold on the seam line. Pin. Topstitch along the edge through the seam allowances only (a).

Turn and press the finished seam allowance toward the garment and slip-stitch it (b) or hem it (c). *(See illustration on next page.)*

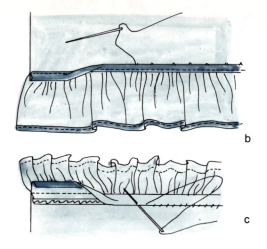

b

c

Ruffle with Bias Binding Finish (for straight or curved edge). Fold the ruffle toward the garment.

Place a length of 1½-inch bias binding over the wrong side of the ruffle with raw edges aligned. Stitch through all thicknesses on the seam line (a). Trim and grade the seam allowances, eliminating as much bulk as possible. Turn the ruffle to position and bias binding toward the garment. Turn under the raw edge of the binding and slip-stitch it through the fold to the garment (b). Press flat.

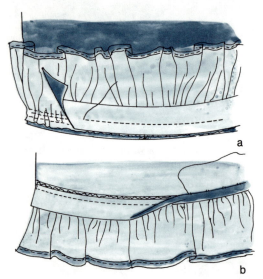

a

b

Ruffle with Facing for a Finish. With right sides together, stitch the ruffle to the garment edge. Press and grade the seam allowances, remembering that the facing seam allowance is yet to come. With right sides together, pin the facing to the garment edge with the ruffle between them. Stitch beside the previous line of stitching so no stitching is visible when the facing is turned to the underside. This would be the way a ruffle is inserted between a collar, cuff, or sleeve band and its facing.

RUFFLE: STRAIGHT, PLEATED. This offers more controlled fullness than the bouncy gathered ruffle. Generally used are knife or box pleats.

Cut the strip to the desired length and width. If pleated by hand, transfer the pattern pleat markings. If no pattern is used, make your own markings. Lay in the pleats. (See PLEATS: FORMING AND STITCHING.) Pleating may also be made with the aid of a ruffler or it can be done commercially.

Gathered Ruffle

SADDLE SLEEVE. *See* STRAP SLEEVE.

SADDLE STITCH. Used for hand top-stitching. It is an even basting stitch, 1/4 to 1/2 inch long, the same on the right side and underside. Use buttonhole twist, embroidery floss, or yarn.

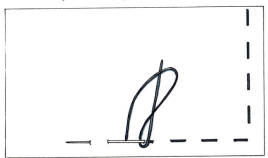

SASH. An ornamental band, scarf, strip, or belt worn around the waist and fastened with a loop, knot, or bow. Bias-cut fabric sashes drape well and ends fall in graceful folds. If bias is not available, cut the sash on the lengthwise grain.

The finest finish for a single thickness of sash is a hand-rolled hem (q.v.) though a machine-rolled hem (q.v.) is acceptable. Sashes of double thicknesses can be made like a tie belt (q.v.).

SATIN FABRIC. Don't attempt to work with this fabric unless you have a sure hand in sewing and an accurate eye for fitting. You get no second chances if anything goes wrong. Ripped-out stitching leaves holes and pressing leaves permanent creases. Because of the minimal interlacing of warp and filler yarns, they *float* on the surface of the fabric, making it lustrous but easily bruised.

Light plays tricks on the directional weave of satin, making it have one color and sheen going up, another down. For uniform color, place all pattern pieces in a directional layout (q.v.).

Avoid anything that will leave a permanent mark in a conspicuous place. Instead of pinning the grain line (usually right in the middle of a pattern section), anchor it with dressmaker's weights. Use silk pins, placing them in the seam allowance closer to the cutting line than to the seam line. Mark carefully with silk thread and a fine needle. *Do not* use dressmaker's carbon paper and the tracing wheel.

MACHINE STITCHING

Tension: Suitable for the weight of the fabric.

Pressure: Suitable for the weight of the fabric.

Stitch size: Medium, 12 to 14 stitches per inch.

Needle: Fine to medium; make certain that the point is sharp to avoid snagging the floats.

Thread: Suitable for the fiber of the fabric.

Hold the fabric taut while stitching to keep the two thicknesses feeding through the machine at the same rate. Stitch slowly.

Press very lightly. Don't try for ultraflat seams or sharp edges. A soft edge is the one called for. *(See* PADDED EDGE.) Satins are very touchy. Steam and moisture destroy the luster and leave an imprint of the iron. Press on the wrong side with a dry iron. Do protect the fabric with a dry press cloth, particularly if steam must be used to flatten the seams.

SATIN STITCH. Used for eyelets, scallops, embroidery. It may be made by hand or by machine.

BY HAND

Work the satin stitch in a series of parallel, very close backstitches to produce a smooth, satinlike surface (a). The stitches may be made with or without padding. The padding consists of lines of small running stitches with most of the thread on the surface down the center of the motif (b) or throughout, depending on the desired effect.

BY MACHINE

The machine satin stitch is a zigzag stitch worked closely to produce the smooth, satinlike surface. Set the stitch length for the desired density of the stitch. Set the stitch width for that of your choice. Adjust the tension. The wider the stitch, the lighter the tension. The regulation zigzag foot may be used, but a special-purpose or Embroidery Foot is recommended, particularly when padding the stitches.

SAW-TOOTH EDGE TRIMMING. A series of overlapping triangles of folded cloth which create an effect as interesting in a dainty sheer fabric as in a bold stiff one.

To make the pattern for the trim, draw a square. Draw diagonal lines from corner to corner. The size of each finished triangle that makes the saw-tooth edge will be equal to one of the triangles in the square (a). You may have to do some experimenting to get the right size.

Cut squares of fabric (self- or contrasting) from the paper pattern. Fold each square diagonally into a triangle (b). Fold the triangle in half so all raw edges except the base are concealed (c).

Rule a paper guide for the position of each triangle. Place each triangle on the paper guide with its point in position on the top line. Overlap slightly the lower left point of one triangle on the lower right point of the preceding one (d). Stitch the triangles to the paper guide. Strip the paper away. Attach the trimming to the garment edge like piping (q.v.) (e).

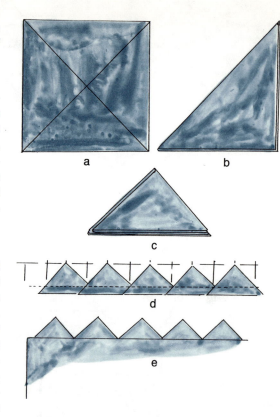

a

b

c

d

e

SCALLOPED EDGE FINISH. Similar to a pinked edge except that this finish is made with scalloping shears.

SCALLOPED TUCKS. May be worked as plain, faced tucks or have their edges embroidered. Allow sufficient width of fabric for the tucks. For faced scallops, include a narrow seam allowance.

Faced Scalloped Tucks. With right sides together, crease or press the fold line of the tuck. Trace the scallops on the wrong side so the highest points of the arcs are in from the folded edge a width equal to that of the narrow seam allowance. Work like faced scallops (see SCALLOPS: FACED). Turn to the right side and press.

To form the tucks, stitch in a straight line an even distance in from the outermost edge of the scallops (a).

Embroidered Scalloped Tucks. With wrong sides together, crease or press the fold line of the tuck. Trace the scallops on the right side so the highest points of the arcs touch the fold line. To form the tucks,

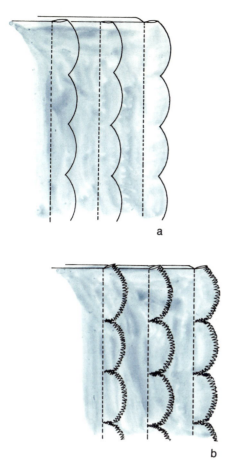

a

b

stitch in a straight line an even distance in from the outermost edge of the scallops. Work hand- or machine-embroidered; scallops along the edge (b). *See* SCALLOPS: HAND-EMBROIDERED: SCALLOPS: MACHINE-EMBROIDERED.)

SCALLOPS. A series of curves (arcs) joined to form a decorative edge. Since scallops must be accurate, a pattern or guide is essential. Often the pattern you are using for your garment will include a pattern for the scalloped edge. Either trace the scalloped seam line on the fabric or use the pattern tissue itself as a guide for the stitching. If the pattern does not include a scallop guide, make your own. Trace the scallops on stiff paper or cardboard. Cut them out. Trace around them.

Scallops may be any length or depth, depending on the design and the length of the area to be scalloped. Generally, the height of the scallop is about $1/3$ of the width at its base. Use a scalloped ruler, a coin, a compass, or any suitable arc for tracing. Add a narrow seam allowance.

SCALLOPS: FACED. To prevent stretching the scalloped line when stitching, it is wise to cut the edge of the garment and facing on straight grain. Make the facing as deep as necessary. Baste it in position. If a lightweight interfacing is used, cut it from the facing pattern and baste it to the underside of the garment before applying the facing. *Do not cut out the scallops.*

Mark the scallops. Stitch around them, taking one stitch across each point. Leave the needle in the material at the corner when lifting the presser foot to start the next scallop. Stitch slowly and carefully. Use small reinforcement stitches (15 to 20 per inch), a slightly loosened tension, and slightly lighter than regular pressure to prevent puckering. Cut around the scallops, leaving a narrow seam allowance. Carefully clip the seam allowance into each point, taking care not to cut the stitching. Trim any interfacing close to the stitching. Grade the seam allowances. Notch the curves to prevent bulk when the scallop is turned to the right side (a).

Turn the scallops to the right side, working out the edges with a blunt needle until they are smooth. Baste close to the edge and press (b). Edge-finish the facing.

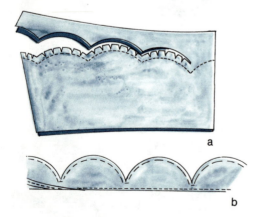

a

b

SCALLOPS: HAND-EMBROIDERED.

On a Single Thickness of Fabric. Trace the scallops on the right side of the fabric 1/8 inch from the edge of the fabric, using a stencil or transfer paper. To provide the needed firmness that helps retain the shape of the scallops while working, spray the edge with spray starch or sizing *or* back the edge with a strip of crisp lawn or organdy. *Optional:* Pad the scallops with horizontal running stitches, using a darning or pearl cotton (a).

Using embroidery floss, work either single-purl buttonhole stitches (b) or blanket stitches (c) around the scallops. Keep the stitches close so they touch, uniform and even in tension, and at right angles to the outer edge at all points.

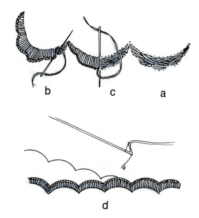

b   c   a

d

Press on the wrong side over a padded ironing board or pressing pad (q.v.). Carefully trim the surplus fabric close to the edge of the scallops, being careful not to cut the embroidery floss (d).

Should you desire to reinforce the edge, work tiny overhand or single-purl buttonhole stitches *over* the purling, taking one stitch in each purl.

Alternative Method. Cut out the scallops after the pad stitching. Overcast or stay-stitch the edges to firm them and keep the fabric from raveling. Work the buttonhole or blanket stitches around the scallops, keeping the purls directly on the edge. This calls for very careful handling so the scallops are not stretched out of shape.

Faced Sections. Baste lightweight interfacing to the wrong side of the garment or garment section. With wrong sides of interfaced garment and facing together,

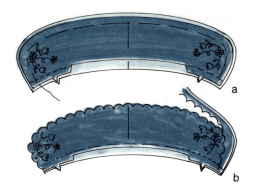

a

b

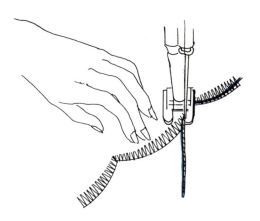

baste through all thicknesses (a). Trace and embroider the scallops. Trim any excess fabric (b).

SCALLOPS: MACHINE-EMBROIDERED.

Small, decorative scalloped edges may be made on many sewing machines that have built-in scallop patterns. Larger scallops may be made with satin stitches following traced scallops with either zigzag stitching or with free-motion embroidery stitching.

By Automatic Pattern. Back the fabric with not too soft paper or spray the edge with spray starch or sizing. Use the embroidery or zigzag foot, embroidery thread, and a zigzag stitch set almost to 0. Set the selector for the scallop pattern. Work scallops along the edge, starting at the beginning of a scallop unit and ending at the end of a scallop unit. Trim excess material around the scallops. Tear away paper when used.

Satin-Stitch Embroidered Scallops. Trace scallops on the right side of the fabric. Mark the corners with tailor's chalk to the depth of the stitch. Back the edge with a strip of crisp lawn, organdy, or paper (to be torn away when work is completed).

Note: The machine feeds in a straight line, so you must guide both scallops and cord for scallop shaping. Two runs are necessary to complete the scallops.

First run: Set the desired stitch width. Set the stitch length to almost 0. Sew satin stitches around the scallops to the marked corner, ending with the needle at the left of the marking. Raise the foot, turn the work, turn the zigzag setting to 0. Lower the foot. As you continue to sew the cor-

ner in the new direction, gradually adjust the bight size until it reaches the desired width. Sew slowly. Carefully trim away any organdy or lawn. Cut around the scallops.

Second run: Set the machine for a slightly narrower and slightly longer stitch. Oversew the edge with the satin stitch over a pearl cord padding along the edge of the stitching.

Free-Motion Scallop Stitching. Trace the scallops on the right side of the fabric. Remove the presser foot. Make the feed inoperative. (See instruction book for your machine.) Movement is controlled by means of an embroidery hoop. Set the machine for medium to wide satin stitches and a lighter tension.

Allow a 1-inch seam allowance along the scallops. Machine-baste a strip of fabric along the edge to enlarge it sufficiently to fit in the embroidery hoop. Back this with crisp lawn or organdy, slightly wider

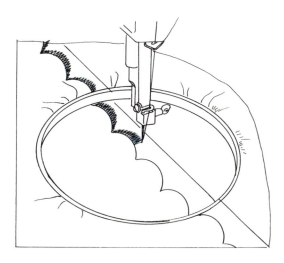

than the hoop. Center the work in the embroidery hoop and position it under the needle with the fabric flat against the bed of the machine. Work satin stitches around the scallops, maintaining a slow, even speed. Shaping of the scallops is accomplished by moving the hoop to the right and left in such a way that on its left swing the needle follows the scallop marking. This produces a narrow stitch at the point between the scallops and a wide stitch at the highest point of its arc. Remove the work from the hoop. Trim away the excess material around the scallops.

Optional: Scallops can be corded by inserting a pearl thread (cord) through the eyelet of the embroidery foot. Work over the edge of the scallop with narrow, closely spaced satin stitches.

SEAM. A line of stitching that holds two (sometimes more) pieces of fabric together permanently. It is *the* basic structural element of a garment. It must be done so that it lasts the life of the garment. *See* SEAM STITCHING.

Pin at the beginning and end of the seam line, at all notches, and a sufficient number

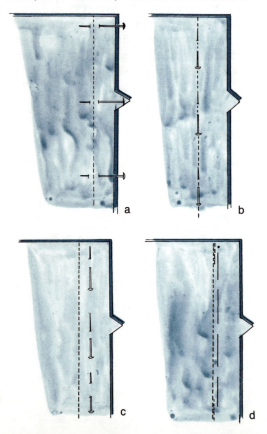

a   b

c   d

of places between. Pins may be placed at right angles to the seam line (a) or lengthwise—points facing the top of the seam (b). Fabrics that bruise easily are pinned in the seam allowance rather than on the stitching line (c).

In stitching, it is generally best to remove the pins just before the presser foot reaches them. The exception is the stitching of cross (intersecting) seams, plaids, stripes, checked fabrics (q.q.v.).

Baste just inside the seam line (d), never directly on it. Machine stitching directly over basting makes it impossible to remove the basting thread when stitching is completed.

SEAM ALLOWANCE. The amount of fabric between the stitching line and the cutting line. In most commercial patterns and in most places on a pattern, the standard seam allowance is 5/8 inch.

Less than this amount may be used when working with nonravelly sheer fabrics, knits, stretch fabrics, any garment sections to be joined with overedge stitching, or where the seam allowances are to be trimmed sharply after stitching.

More than this amount may be used when working with bias-cut, heavy, or ravelly fabrics or where topstitching is to be done. If you are uncertain about fit, it is wise to allow more than the standard seam allowance.

SEAM BINDING. A narrow strip of ribbon-like woven tape used as an edge finish or as a stay. A lace tape seam binding has stretch and can be used wherever that seems appropriate.

As an edge finish, it is probably the one most associated with hems, though it is not necessarily the best or most appropriate. Use it for loosely woven fabrics that tend to ravel and for machine-washable garments.

Binding can be applied either full width or in a lengthwise fold. It can be preshaped to fit a slightly curved edge *(see* PRESHAPING: BIAS BINDING*)*. Lace seam binding is used full width.

FULL-WIDTH APPLICATION

By Overlap Seam: Overlap one edge of the binding on the fabric edge and top-stitch close to the edge (a). This is the method generally used on ready-to-wear clothing. It produces a flat finish but in the hands of less than skilled machine operators comes off as a line of wavering machine stitching.

By Inside Seam: With right sides together and raw edges matching, machine-stitch 1/8 inch from the edges. Turn the binding to conceal the inside seam and press it to position (b). Attach upper edge to garment. This makes a much neater and stronger finish without the hazards of the overlap-topstitch method.

LENGTHWISE-FOLD APPLICATION

Fold the binding lengthwise with the bottom half slightly wider than the top to make sure the loose under edge is caught in the machine stitching. Press. Enclose the raw edge of the fabric with the binding. Pin or baste to position. Topstitch close to the edge (c). This application may also be accomplished with the use of the binder.

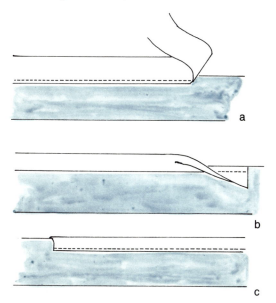

SEAM BINDING USED AS A STAY. *See* STAY; TAPED SEAM; KIMONO SLEEVE WITHOUT A GUSSET, METHODS 1 AND 2.

SEAM ELIMINATED. Two pattern sections may be joined as one, thereby eliminating the joining seam, IF the grain of the fabric can be preserved, the seam is not a shaping seam, the fabric is wide enough and long enough to accommodate the enlarged pattern.

To join sections, overlap the pattern seam lines and tape. Note that this can be done to join a facing to a garment so the two are cut as one (a). A yoke can be joined to a lower section to make a complete front or back (b). An undercollar can be cut in one piece on the bias instead of two sections joined by a center back seam (c).

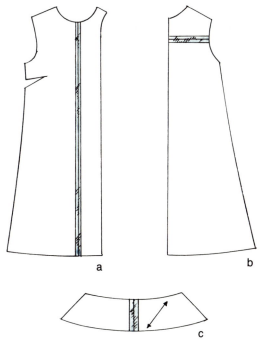

A two-piece straight back can be cut in one piece by cutting off the seam allowance and placing the center back seam line on a fold of fabric (a).

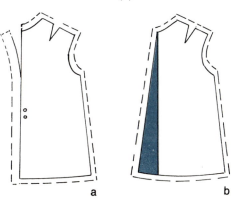

Flare can be removed (b) so the resulting straight edge can be placed on a fold.

To eliminate a seam is to eliminate a matching problem in a plaid or stripe or extra work in a pile fabric when the seam won't even be visible when finished. The reason for preserving any seam is to shape the garment or to preserve its style lines.

SEAM FINISHES. *See* EDGE FINISHES.

SEAM GUIDELINES. Markings etched on the throat plate of the sewing machine. Starting at 3/8 inch from the needle, they progress at 1/8-inch intervals to 3/4 inch. They are used for keeping seams an even distance from the cut edge.

SEAM PLACKET. *See* PLACKET.

SEAM POCKET. *See* IN-SEAM POCKET.

SEAM ROLL. A long, tubular, firmly packed pressing cushion rounded at each end, sometimes tapered at one end. It is used for pressing long seams in narrow areas—sleeves, for instance. It is easier to manipulate than a sleeve board. Buy or make the sleeve roll with the same materials as those used for the tailor's ham (q.v.).

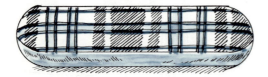

SEAMS AND DARTS IN UNLINED GARMENTS. *See* UNLINED GARMENT: SEAMS AND DARTS.

SEAM STITCHING. For stitching a particular fabric or for a special stitching technique, see the listing for the fabric or situation. *See also* MACHINE STITCHING.

Compare the pattern seam lengths of the sections to be joined. If they are equal, you must stitch so they remain so. If one length is really meant to be longer than the other, the extra amount may be eased in.

Adjust your sewing machine to the fabric for stitch length, tension, and pressure. Use appropriate thread and needle.

Whenever possible, lock the stitches at the beginning of each seam with back-

and-forth stitching. Where lock stitching is inadvisable (as at a point of precision), pull the thread ends through to one side and tie in a square knot. Leave the end of the stitching unsecured so the thread, when pressed, can be eased through the fabric for an unpuckered seam.

Seam stitching is directional to preserve the grain, the length, and the shape of the garment section. *See* DIRECTIONAL STITCHING *and* STAY STITCHING.

Be sure to stitch the full seam allowance —either that planned in the pattern or that determined by your fitting. A fraction of an inch may not seem much to you but a little arithmetic will quickly disclose that a tiny bit on each of several seams could be adding enough to grade the garment up or down to the next size.

Stitch the seam slowly. Speed stitching is of no particular value to home sewers. There are not so many yards of machine stitching in any garment that the time saved is worth the risk of faulty stitching. However, if you are stitching yards and yards of draperies, stitch as fast as you can accurately.

If you need to go back over a line of stitching to correct it, be sure to remove the first stitching. Every added row of machine stitching makes the area that much stiffer.

To prevent lightweight fabrics from getting sucked into the hole on the throat plate, position the fabric and lower the needle 1/2 inch from the end of the seam before lowering the presser foot. Grasp the ends of the thread and hold them taut as you slowly take the first few stitches.

SEAMS WITH FULLNESS. Often designs call for some fullness on one of the two layers that form the seam.

With Slight Fullness (for instance, back shoulder seam into front shoulder seam). Working with the longer side up, pin at right angles to the seam at each end of the two layers, at any notches, and at intervals between (a). Ease the fullness between the pins, distributing it evenly. With the shorter length on top, machine-

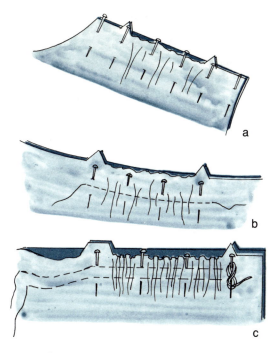

a

b

c

stitch, removing the pins as you come to them and stretching the top layer to match the longer underlayer. *See also* EASE STITCH-ING.

With Moderate Fullness. Make one row of machine or hand gathering in the seam allowance just beside the seam line of the longer length. Pin at ends, at notches, at intervals between, distributing the fullness (b). With the longer length on top, machine-stitch, adjusting the fullness further as needed. *See* JOINING GATHERED EDGE TO STRAIGHT EDGE.

With Considerable Fullness (as at front bodice below a yoke). Follow the procedure for seams with moderate fullness except that two rows of gathering are required (c). *See* JOINING GATHERED EDGE TO GATHERED EDGE *and* JOINING GATHERED EDGE TO STRAIGHT EDGE.

SEAM TYPES. The type of seam used for any particular garment or any special part of it depends on the fabric, the style, and whether or not the seam will be exposed. The range is great. Following is a list of the seams included in this volume: ABUTTED SEAM, BIAS SEAMS; CATCH-STITCHED SEAM; CORDED SEAM; CORNERED SEAM; CROSS (INTER-

SECTING) SEAMS; CURVED LAPPED SEAM; CURVED OPPOSING SEAM LINES; CURVED PLAIN SEAM; CURVED SEAM LINE STITCHED TO A STRAIGHT SEAM LINE; DOUBLE-STITCHED SEAM; DOUBLE-STITCHED WELT SEAM; DOUBLE TOPSTITCHED SEAM; ENCLOSED (ENCASED) SEAM; FAGOTED SEAM; FLAT FELL SEAM; FRENCH SEAM; HAIRLINE SEAM; JOINING CROSS SEAMS; LAPPED (OVER-LAP) SEAM; LINGERIE SEAM; MOCK (SIMULATED) FRENCH SEAM; OVEREDGE-STITCH SEAM; PLAIN SEAM; PRINCESS SEAM; for seams in special fabrics, *see listing* under fabric type; for seams in unlike fabrics, *see* JOINING KNIT TO WOVEN FABRIC; JOINING PILE OR NAP TO SMOOTH UNNAPPED FABRIC; SEAMS WITH FULLNESS *(see also* JOINING GATHERED EDGE TO STRAIGHT EDGE; JOINING GATHERED EDGE TO GATHERED EDGE); SELF-BOUND SEAM; SELF-ENCLOSED SEAM; SHOULDER SEAM; SLOT SEAM; TAPED SEAM; TUCKED SEAM; WELT SEAM; ZIGZAG SEAM.

SECOND FITTING. *(See Fittings—How Many? under* FITTING) The second fitting locates the position of the outline seams (q.v.). It is also a time to refine and perfect the fitting of the interfaced and underlined sections. Often the addition of the understructure does make a difference in the ease and fit.

Using your fitted trial muslin as a guide, tentatively pin the shoulders and side (or underarm) seams on the right side of the garment. (Remember that all fitting is done from the right side.)

If the garment is to be worn over another, try it on that way. When shoulder pads are to be used, slip them into position. Pin the garment closed from the top button to the bottom, matching the center or closing markings.

Perfect the fit. *(See* FITTING.) Remove the garment. Transfer the right-side fitting to the wrong side for stitching.

SELF-BOUND SEAM. This seam works best on lightweight fabric that does not ravel easily.

With right sides together, make a plain seam (q.v.). Trim one seam allowance to 1/8 or 1/4 inch (depending on the fabric). Turn under the edge of the other seam allowance a similar amount and press (a). Turn and press again, bringing the folded

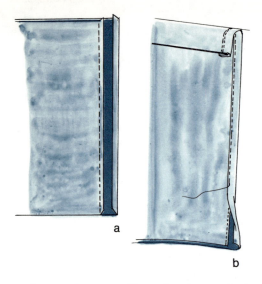

a

b

edge to the seam line, thereby enclosing the trimmed edge. Slip-stitch or machine-stitch (b) over the seam.

SELF-CASING (FOLD-DOWN CASING).

See CASING before proceeding. This is an excellent way of handling pull-on pants and skirts; the lower edge of a blouse, jacket, sleeve; the waistline edge of lingerie, pajamas, and the like. It is very easy to do along any straight or slightly curved edge.

Turn under a 1/4-inch seam allowance for a finished edge and press. Turn the casing to the inside to the desired depth and pin. Machine-stitch the lower edge close

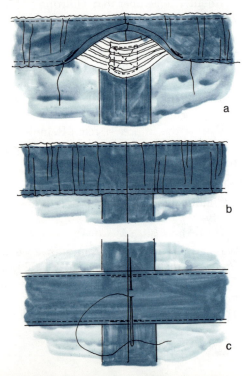

a

b

c

to the fold, leaving an opening large enough to take the elastic or drawstring. Thread through the casing. Join the ends of elastic with several rows of zigzag stitching or stitch a square and corner to corner, diagonally (a). Pull the joined ends inside the casing. Close the opening by edge-stitching (b). Take care not to catch the elastic in the stitching. When an opening has been left in a construction seam, close it with slip stitching (c).

SELF-ENCLOSED SEAM. One in which the seam allowances are so worked that there are no exposed raw edges. Examples are the French seam, the mock (simulated) French seam, the flat fell seam, and the self-bound seam. *See listing for each.*

Being strong and protected, such seam finishes are particularly suitable for visible seams in sheer fabrics, unlined garments, and garments that get much wear or much laundering.

SELF-WELT OR STAND POCKET. *See* SINGLE-WELT POCKET.

SELVAGE. The lengthwise self-finished edge of woven fabric worked so that it won't ravel. It is the true vertical grain of the fabric and generally needs no further treatment. The exception would be a puckered selvage, in which case, clip every few inches to release the strain but do not cut the selvage away. If you do, you will have to re-establish the vertical grain for the correct placement of all pattern pieces.

Generally, the selvage is smoother on the right side than on the wrong. In some fabrics, it appears as a border woven of different or heavier threads or in a different weave, often attractive enough to use as a trimming or as a finished edge in a garment.

SELVAGE WAISTBAND. A good way to eliminate the bulk that forms at the waistline when the many seam allowances of waistband and garment are turned in the same direction. Use a selvage for the lower edge of the waistband facing.

Lay the pattern for the waistband so the seam line of the inner edge of the facing is

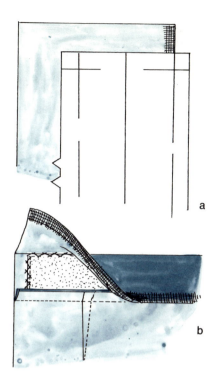

Separating Zippers

even with the selvage (a). Since this is a finished edge, it need not be turned under when the waistband is turned to the inside. Sew this edge to the waist seam line (b).

SEPARATING ZIPPER. A favorite form of closing for casual jackets. Separating zippers come in several weights, in both nylon and metal. They may be inserted so the zipper teeth are exposed (a) or hidden (b and c). When the garment closing is faced, the zipper is sandwiched between the outer fabric and the facing.

The installation of this zipper can be that of the exposed zipper (a), a centered (slot-seam) (b) or lapped (regulation) (c) construction. *See listing for each type.*

SEQUINED FABRIC. By-the-yard glitter. Such fabrics are handled in the same way as beaded fabric (q.v.).

SET-IN SLEEVE. This classic and popular sleeve style is a little more difficult to handle in sewing than one cut all in one with or as part of the bodice. However, it has certain built-in advantages. The sleeve fol-lows the natural "hang" of the arm while retaining freedom of movement—all this without bulk or underarm wrinkling.

Sleeves come in pairs. Lay the bodice front, bodice back, and sleeve side by side on a flat surface. Place the front of the sleeve toward the front bodice, the back of the sleeve toward the back bodice.

That portion of the sleeve above the horizontal line in the illustration is the *sleeve cap.* The vertical broken line separates the cap into front and back. The front cap is drafted to fit the front armhole, the back cap to fit the back armhole. Note that the division produces a deeper curve on the front armhole than the back.

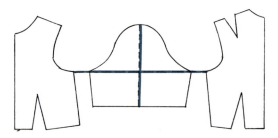

Fronts and backs are not reversible. There is a right sleeve and a left sleeve, therefore a right sleeve front and a left sleeve front, a right sleeve back and a left sleeve back. The notches on the pattern tell which is which. In setting the sleeve into the armhole, you must make very sure that you match the right front sleeve with the right front armhole and the left front sleeve with the left front armhole. Reverse the sleeves and they won't fit!

If you are ever in doubt as to which is front and which is back of a fitted sleeve, fold the sleeve in half lengthwise. The front cap is always the deeper curve (a). In a below-elbow-length sleeve, there is an-

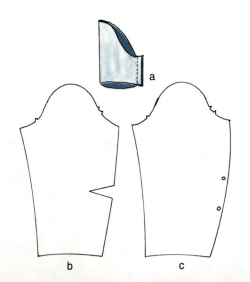

other way to tell front from back. The elbow darts (b), gathers or easing (c) are always in back.

The armhole and sleeve cap are also divided into *overarm and underarm.*

Notches are placed at those points where the seam lines that arch over the shoulders swing into underarm curves. Change of direction occurs at the points where arm and body meet, both front and back.

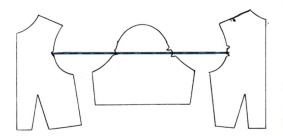

The *underarm curves* of both sleeve cap and armhole are identical, therefore easy to match when setting the sleeve. In a fitted misses' dress, the armhole generally drops 1¹/₂ inches below the arm. This provides comfort in wearing and room for movement. Many great couturiers set the sleeve higher on the underarm than this. They hold that a high setting provides greater ease of movement (no unsightly pulling up of garment when the arm is raised) and greater trimness to the garment.

Sleeveless dresses, too, are generally built up under the arm. Since there is no sleeve to restrict the motion in any way, the underarm curve can be brought up as high as is comfortable. In patterns that show the style with and without sleeves, note the two underarm stitching lines. Choose the upper seam line for the sleeveless version.

The *overarm curves* of sleeve and armhole, unlike the underarm, do not match in length and shape. The sleeve cap is slightly longer than the armhole and has a different curve. This difference in length and shape represents the ease (q.v.).

SET-IN SLEEVE CAP EASE. Ease is a must —as necessary in a sleeve as it is in a bodice or skirt and for the same reasons: comfort and ease of movement. It is a very great temptation to eliminate the ease in order to make the sleeve setting easier. But sleeve ease must be retained or the sleeve will not fit well or feel comfortable. Since this part of the cap is on a near bias angle, most fabrics can be eased into the armhole fairly readily.

In a fitted dress sleeve, the minimum ease is 1 to 1½ inches. In fitted jacket and coat sleeves, the minimum ease is 1½ to 2 inches. How can you tell if the amount is right? By comparison to sleeve cap with the armhole.

How to Compare the Sleeve Cap with the Armhole. Start at the front underarm seam and match the sleeve underarm curve with the armhole underarm curve (a). Using a pin for a pivot, continue to match a tiny section at a time (about ⅛ inch) of sleeve and armhole from underarm to shoulder. Mark the point where the garment shoulder appears on the sleeve cap. Do the same for the back. The leftover space between the two marks is the ease (b). Place the shoulder notch of the sleeve cap at the center of the space dividing the ease equally front and back (c).

Note: The notch should be at the crest of the curve. If it isn't (as a result of shoulder fitting), redraw the curve so that it will be (d). This will assure that the back sleeve cap will fit the back armhole and the front sleeve cap the front armhole.

If the comparison of sleeve cap and armhole reveals too much ease or too little ease, make the necessary adjustment. *(See below.)* The only way to tell if the correction yields the right amount of ease is to test the sleeve cap in the armhole.

If in fitting the shoulder and underarm seams the shape and/or size of the armhole has been changed, it is necessary to re-establish it. *See* SET-IN SLEEVE: PREPARING THE ARMHOLE FOR THE SLEEVE SETTING.

Too Little Ease. Not often does it happen that one has too little ease in a sleeve. The usual complaint is that there is too much.

Too little ease may result if you've used a set-in sleeve from one pattern to fit the armhole of another. If that is the case, either the armhole or the sleeve cap should be recut so the two fit.

Unfortunately, one usually discovers this only when the sleeve is being set. The following rescue operation may help. Refit any seams that enter the armhole, taking larger seam allowances to reduce the size of the armholes. Use as much of the sleeve cap seam allowance as possible to add length and width to the sleeve cap. Taper to the original underarm seam line.

If you can anticipate this problem, make the necessary pattern correction.

On the pattern, draw a line across the cap of the sleeve. Draw another line at right angles to this, extending it to the shoulder marking (a). Slash both lines and spread at the cap (b). Insert paper and pin or Scotch-tape. The added length and width provide the additional ease. Redraw the sleeve cap. Test the amount of ease. *See* HOW TO COMPARE THE SLEEVE CAP WITH THE ARMHOLE, *above.*

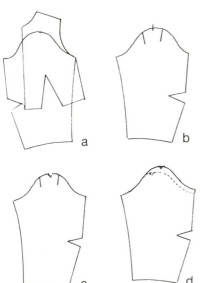

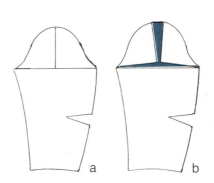

Too Much Ease. The standard amount of sleeve cap ease contained in patterns is no problem in most fabrics. However, in stiff and firmly woven materials, this amount may be too difficult to ease into the armhole designed for the sleeve.

Ease can be removed in one of two ways, depending on the build of the arm. Method 1 lowers and flattens the sleeve cap, retaining its width. Method 2 retains the height of the sleeve cap but narrows it on both sides.

METHOD 1

Draw a slash line across the cap of the sleeve. Draw a line at right angles to this, extending it to the shoulder mark (a). Slash both lines. Overlap a small amount at the cap (b). Note that there will also be some overlapping at the horizontal slash line. Redraw the cap.

METHOD 2

Draw a new stitching line on the sleeve pattern, starting at the top of the cap, continuing *in from* the original overarm curves at both sides and blending into the underarm curves at the notches (c). Start by removing a small amount. Repeat as deemed necessary by testing.

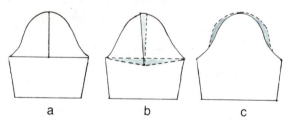

a   b   c

SET-IN SLEEVE CAP EASE BLOCKED. In a well-set tailored sleeve, the ease appears as a nicely rounded cap. In woolen fabrics, the material of the classic tailored garment, the ease is shrunk out and the cap blocked into its rounded shape before setting it. For one thing, it is much easier to do the shaping before setting the sleeve than after. With the cap ease disposed of, the seam line of the sleeve now closely matches the seam line of the armhole in length.

The following methods are recommended for wool and any other flexible fabric that can take steam. For a press pad, use any of these: the narrow end of the tailor's ham, the broad end of a sleeve board or sleeve pad, the press mitt, or any other similarly shaped pad or board.

METHOD 1. (THE MOST USUAL)

With wrong side up, slip the sleeve over a suitable press pad or board and press the seam allowances open in the technique best suited for the fabric.

Draw up the gathering at the sleeve cap into a cap shape. Distribute the fullness evenly. Slip the sleeve over the press pad, wrong side up. Fit the cap over the pad or board.

Shrink out the ease in the cap with the point of the steam iron (a). Don't worry about shrinking out too much. One can always spread the sleeve cap to fit the armhole. It is unnecessary to shrink out all the rippling of the seam allowance at the cut edge, but the ease should be removed at the seam line.

Block a softly rounded cap 3/8 to 1/2 inch into the sleeve. When dry, gently turn the blocked cap to the right side. You should be able to hold the cap with your hooked fingers (b).

METHOD 2

Leave the sleeve seam unstitched. Gather across the cap and draw up the gathers into a cap shape. Distribute the fullness evenly. Place the sleeve cap, wrong side up, over the tailor's ham. Shrink out the fullness with the point of the steam iron (c). Reverse the curve to the right side. Stitch the sleeve seam and press it open.

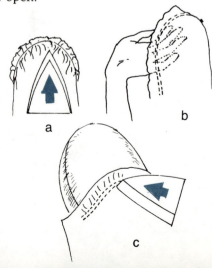

a

b

c

SET-IN SLEEVE: FITTING. Any fitting faults that extend to the armhole will become much more obvious when the sleeves are set. Sometimes what appear to be sleeve fitting problems are in reality fitting problems of the body of the garment.

It is very important that the shoulder fitting be accurate. The sleeve hangs from the shoulder and setting starts at the shoulder. *(See* SHOULDER SEAM.)

Sufficient ease across the chest and back will avoid pulling and straining across the cap and/or the chest or back. Back ease is particularly necessary for the forward movement of the arms. See that the armhole is neither too loose nor too tight. *See the appropriate pattern corrections for armhole, chest, and back. See also* SET-IN SLEEVE FITTING: *Common Problems.*

Pin and baste the sleeve seam. Gather the sleeve cap. (In tailoring, block it.) Pin it tentatively into the armhole, easing as necessary. Match the shoulder marking and underarm seam or marking. *(See* SET-IN SLEEVE: SETTING.)

Try on the garment. Facing a mirror, examine the fit of the sleeve. Turn so that you can see the entire sleeve setting. The sleeve should hang evenly, smoothly, and gracefully, conforming to the natural curve of the arm from shoulder to lower edge. The sleeve cap must be neither too loose nor too tight. There should be sufficient room at the elbow for the bend of the arm. The elbow shaping should be *at* the elbow.

To hang properly, the sleeve must be balanced from front to back. Variations in build and posture may make it necessary to shift the top point of the sleeve to the front or back.

The vertical grain (as well as all vertical lines, stripes, plaids) should be at right angles to the floor, the horizontal grain parallel to the floor. *See* GRAIN—CLUE TO GOOD FIT.

Note any adjustments that need to be made in the sleeve. Remove the garment. Make the necessary changes and try it on again. Examine the fit of the sleeve once more. Unless someone sets the sleeve for you (preferable, if you can manage it), you may have to repeat this procedure until you are satisfied with the setting and feel of the sleeve.

SET-IN SLEEVE FITTING: COMMON PROBLEMS.

Wrinkling, Pulling, Straining, Binding. This may be due to insufficient width across the sleeve cap, across the chest or back. Unpin the sleeve. Use some of the seam allowances of the armhole and sleeve cap for more width. Use the underarm seam, too, when necessary. *See* SET-IN SLEEVE: PATTERN CORRECTION FOR HEAVY ARM. *See also* EASE.

Too Tight Armhole. Drop the armhole. Add width at both the armhole and sleeve cap by using some of the seam allowances. Use some of the underarm seam allowances of sleeve and side seam. *See* ARMHOLE PATTERN CORRECTIONS. *See also* EASE.

Short Sleeve Pokes Out at Hem. This is due to insufficient length at the sleeve cap. Release the armhole seam. Reset the sleeve, using the horizontal grain as a guide. Use as much sleeve cap seam allowance as you can salvage. *See* SET-IN SLEEVE: PATTERN CORRECTION FOR TOO SHORT CAP.

Skimpy Sleeve Cap. To correct this, add length to the sleeve cap. *See pattern correction immediately preceding.*

Sleeve Cap Wrinkles Across the Top of the Sleeve. This indicates too much length in the sleeve cap. *See* SET-IN SLEEVE: PATTERN CORRECTION FOR TOO LONG CAP. Recut the cap of the sleeve from the corrected pattern.

SET-IN SLEEVE: PATTERN CORRECTIONS. The set-in sleeve, with just the right amount of ease, must fit into the armhole precisely. Any sleeve changes that affect the sleeve cap require corresponding changes in the armhole seam. *See* ARMHOLE PATTERN CORRECTIONS *and Cap Corrections immediately following.*

CAP CORRECTIONS

Too Long Cap. Make a tuck across the sleeve cap. Correct the seam line for shoulder to underarm. Slice off the jog (a).

Too Short Cap. Draw a slash line across the sleeve cap. Slash and spread to the needed amount. Fill in the spread with paper. Correct the seam line (b).

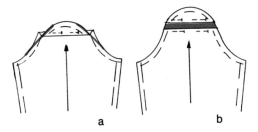

a   b

Ease Corrections. *See* SET-IN SLEEVE CAP EASE.

ARM CORRECTIONS

Heavy Arm. Draw an inverted L-shaped slash line on each side of the sleeve, starting at the underarm and ending at the lower edge of the sleeve. Slash and spread the pattern, adding one half the needed amount on each side at the underarm and tapering to the lower edge (a). Insert tissue and pin or Scotch-tape to position.

To make a corresponding correction in the armhole seam, draw a slash line from the underarm to the waistline on front and back bodices. Slash and spread in the same amount as that added at each side of the sleeve (b).

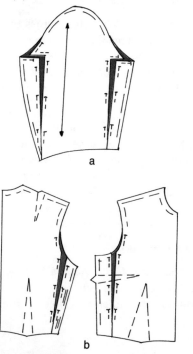

a

b

Heavy Upper Arm. Draw a slash line along the lengthwise grain and across the underarm. Slash and spread the pattern at the underarm position in the amount needed. Fold a dart on each side of the sleeve until the edges of the cap touch and the pattern lies flat. Taper the spread toward the lower edge of the sleeve (a). Fill in the spread area with tissue paper and pin or Scotch-tape to position.

Lower the armhole of the bodice at the underarm in an amount equal to that of the adjusted sleeve (b). Redraw the sleeve cap as it was originally (a). Draw a new grain line parallel to the new center line of the sleeve.

Alternate Method. Slash the sleeve from shoulder to lower edge. Spread at the cap to the necessary amount, tapering to the lower edge (c). Insert paper in the spread area and pin or Scotch-tape. Adjust the armhole as above.

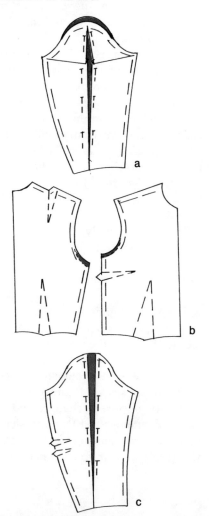

a

b

c

Muscular Arm. This correction is the same as for the heavy arm but at the front only.

Slim Arm. Tuck the sleeve pattern down the center from the top of the cap, tapering to nothing at the wrist (a). If only the upper arm part of the pattern is too big, taper the tuck to nothing at the elbow (b). Make the tuck half the desired amount of the change.

Since the tuck removes some of the ease in the sleeve cap, a corresponding change is made on the bodice pattern at the armhole by raising the underarm curve (c).

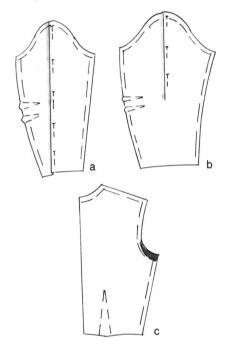

Correct the grain line by making it parallel to the new center line of the sleeve. Correct the sleeve cap.

Narrow Wrist. Draw a slash line on the sleeve pattern from sleeve cap to wrist. Slash and overlap the pattern in the

needed amount at the wrist, tapering to nothing at the cap. Pin or Scotch-tape. Correct the wrist seam. Draw a new grain line parallel to the new center line of the sleeve.

Wide Wrist. Reverse the procedure for narrow wrist, slashing and spreading instead of overlapping.

Thick Elbow. (More elbow room needed). Draw an L-shaped slash line down the center of the sleeve pattern to the elbow and through the elbow dart or darts. Slash and spread to the needed amount, tapering to the sleeve cap. Insert paper in the spread area and pin or Scotch-tape. Correct the sleeve seam below the slash. Make the dart (or darts) larger to absorb the amount of the increase. Draw a new grain line parallel to the new center line of the sleeve.

Thin Elbow (Less elbow room needed). Reverse the procedure for thick elbow, overlapping instead of spreading. *(See illustration on page 402.)*

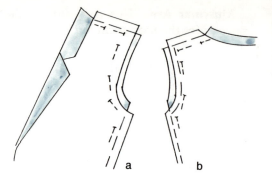

SET-IN SLEEVE: PREPARING THE ARM-HOLE FOR THE SLEEVE SETTING. The

sleeve cap in the pattern is meant to fit not just any armhole but *the* armhole of the pattern. However, it may be that, in the fitting of shoulder and underarm seams, the shape and size of the original armhole have been changed. If so, it is necessary to reestablish the armhole before the sleeve can be set. The easiest way to do this is to use the unaltered pattern as a guide for re-cutting the armhole.

To do so, one must first establish the point on the shoulder where the sleeve is to be set. It's ideal to have someone determine this for you but you can do it yourself if you must. Try on the garment and pin it closed. If shoulder pads are necessary for the style, pin them in place. Slip the sleeve over your arm, bringing the cap to the shoulder point. Using a safety pin, mark the position on the shoulder seam where the sleeve cap joins it. This gives you the shoulder point. Remove the garment. Should it be necessary, pin together as many sections of the original pattern as will produce the complete, unaltered front and back armholes.

Set the armhole seam of the pattern at the newly established shoulder point. Pin the shoulder seam of the pattern front on the shoulder seam of the garment front. Pin the side seam of the pattern on the side seam of the garment, letting the underarm of the pattern fall as much below the armhole of the garment as is necessary to make the pattern lie flat (a).

Repeat the procedure for the back (b). The back shoulder seam must match the front shoulder seam. The back side seam must match the front side seam.

Using the pattern in this new position, cut out the armhole. The shaded areas in the illustration represent the fitted armhole that needs changing. The unshaded part of the illustration shows the change that has been made.

The shoulder marking on the sleeve cap should be at the crest of the sleeve cap curve. For instance, if, in fitting, the shoulder seam has been brought forward, then the crest of the cap curve and the shoulder marking should be brought forward a corresponding amount. Redraw the sleeve cap, making the needed adjustment.

Another way to correct the armhole is to use the sleeve itself as a pattern. *See* SET-IN SLEEVE: SETTING.

To preserve the shape of the armhole, stay-stitch it or stay it with tape or with chain stitches. *See* ARMHOLE STAY. In some garments, it is wise to ease the underarm curves before setting. *See* ARMHOLE EASE.

SET-IN SLEEVE: SETTING. A well-set

sleeve should have a continuously smooth line across the cap with no puckering or puffing along the seam line.

In setting the sleeve, start at the shoulder and work down! This is the reverse of the generally accepted procedure but it works like magic. When you start the setting at the underarm and work your way up the sleeve cap, you may end up with a handful of fabric at the shoulder that has no place to go except into a leg-of-mutton puff. Whereas, if you start at the sleeve cap and work down, such slight adjustments as still need to be made can be done at the underarm, where there is some room for a change.

Stitch and press the sleeve seam. Gather across the sleeve cap and, when possible, block it so it cups over your hooked fingers (a). *See* SET-IN SLEEVE CAP EASE BLOCKED.

An ideal method for setting a sleeve is to have someone do it for you from the right side. Or do it yourself over a dress form. Turn under the seam allowance of the gathered cap. Overlap it on the armhole, distributing the fullness. Pin to position. Slip-baste the cap to the bodice.

If such fitting is not available to you, try the following method. With right sides together, insert the sleeve into the armhole. Work on the wrong side with the sleeve up. Hold the sleeve in the outside curve it will assume when worn. Match the shoulder seam of the bodice with the shoulder marking of the sleeve cap. Working down on each side, distribute the fullness evenly across the cap down to the notches. Some experts suggest no ease for 1/2 inch on either side of the shoulder marking. Place the pins at right angles to the seam line (b). Use your fingertips or the point of a pin or needle for separating and distributing the gathers.

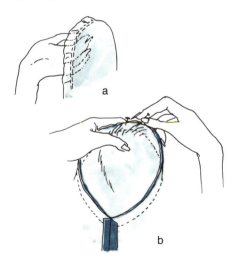

Pin the underarm into the armhole, matching the underarm seams or markings of both sleeve and garment.

In hard-to-ease fabrics (rigid, firmly woven, or stiff), distribute the fullness so the cap drops slightly at the underarm of the garment. The drop may be as much as a seam allowance but no more. Using the underarm of the sleeve as a pattern, cut away the garment to match the sleeve. This is also a good method to use when an adjustment in fitting has altered or reduced the size of the armhole.

In setting the sleeve by this method, there is often the great temptation to eliminate a good deal of the ease at the cap. Don't! Ease is a must for comfort and movement.

Baste the sleeve into the armhole. Try on the garment. Check the fitting. (*See* SET-IN SLEEVE: FITTING.) Make the needed changes. Rebaste.

Where a precise matching of stripes, plaids, checks, or motifs is called for, pin carefully as a preparation for the stitching. Pins hold more securely than basting alone.

SET-IN SLEEVE: STITCHING. Work with the sleeve side up so you can control the ease.

Sure Sewers. Starting at one notch, stitch around the sleeve until you return to the starting point *but do not stop.* Continue the stitching until you get to the opposite notch (a). This reinforces the underarm, a stress area.

Unsure Sewers. Start the stitching at the underarm seam and stitch until you return to the starting point. Secure the stitching. Examine the stitching line from the bodice side. If the stitching is somewhat wavering, make a second row of stitching very close to the first, correcting it where needed as you sew (b). This time, work with the bodice side up so you can see what needs correction. This method

ensures stitching perfection as well as underarm reinforcement. Remove any incorrect stitching.

The sleeve is meant to fit at the armhole seam and not at the cut edge, which is shorter. So clip the seam allowances at the notches almost to the stitching. Clip the underarm seam allowances every half inch (a). If you skip the clipping, your sleeve will be too tight on the underarm.

Alternative Method. Since you have two rows of stitching for strength on the underarm, you can safely trim the seam allowances close to the underarm seam. Press the remaining seam allowances into the cap of the sleeve where they serve as a tiny prop for the cap (b).

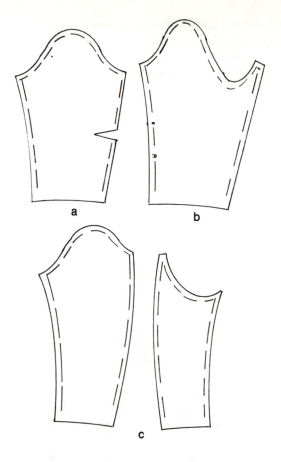

a   b

c

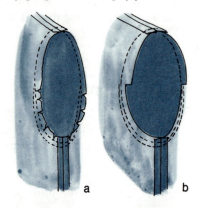

a   b

If necessary, edge-finish the raw edges with hand or machine overcasting. Or trim all seam allowances to 1/4 inch and cover the raw edges with bias binding.

SET-IN SLEEVE TYPES. While the cap may be the same, the sleeve itself may be cut in one or two pieces. On rare occasions, more.

The one-piece sleeve, shaped at the elbow with darts or gathers, is the one most frequently used for dresses, blouses, dressmaker-type jackets and coats. Usually the sleeve seam is an underarm one (a). Sometimes the underarm section is cut in one with the upper arm section and the sleeve is seamed at the back (b).

The two-piece sleeve is the one usually found in tailored garments. Instead of darts or gathers, its shaping is in its seams,

providing a more natural arm shape than the one-piece sleeve (c).

From the standpoint of design, the two-piece sleeve offers more opportunity for style features—for instance, a buttoned vent (a), a shaped opening (b), flare added

a   b

to one section (c). Or the design lines of the rest of the garment may be carried into the division of the sleeve; continuing the shoulder line into the sleeve (d) would be one such example.

SEW-THROUGH BUTTON. One that requires a thread shank to make it sit smoothly on the surface of the buttoned garment. The button may be sewn on by hand (a safer and more secure method) or by machine (if you have the kind that can perform this operation).

By Hand. In the two-hole button there is no choice but to sew through both holes to form a bar (a). In the four-hole button there are other possibilities. In tailored clothes, the thread is so worked as to form parallel bars (b) or a cross (c). In other types of garments, in addition to these two patterns, the buttons may be sewn decora-

tively to form a square (d) or a leaf or feather shape (e).

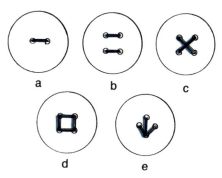

Use a not too long *single* thread (double threads tend to pull up unevenly) of buttonhole twist, heavy-duty thread, a waxed buttonhole thread, or mercerized thread that has been drawn through beeswax. Use a needle long enough to go easily through the several thicknesses of button and fabric and of a thickness that will pass easily through the holes of the button.

Fasten the thread with several tiny backstitches on the right side at the position indicated for the button. Place a matchstick, toothpick, darning needle, or any similar object over the button (a). All sewing is done over the object to provide enough thread for the stem. This is also an easy way to keep all the stitches equal in length. The length of the stem will determine what you use for your prop. Make the stem as long as the several layers of fabric are thick plus a tiny bit for ease.

Another way to provide enough thread for the stem is to hold the garment over the forefinger. Pinch the bottom of the button against the forefinger with your thumb so that the top of the button stands away from the fabric in the amount you wish for the stem. If you wish you may, in addition, use a pin or toothpick in position over the button (b). Bring the needle up through one hole and down through a second. Catch a little of the fabric (and interfacing when present) at the base of the button but do not go through to the facing. Bring the needle up through a third hole and down through a fourth (when there is a third and fourth). Repeat about four times.

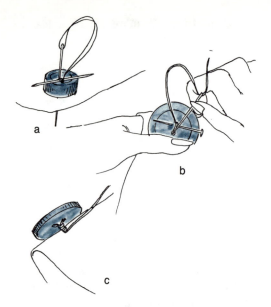

Remove any prop that has been used, raise the button to the top of the stitches. Wind the thread around the stitches to form the stem (c). Start the winding right under the button and end it near the fabric where it can be anchored with several tiny backstitches.

Large-hole sew-through buttons may be attached to the garment with ribbon, braid, yarn, cord, or strips of self-fabric.

Cut the material to the proper length for a loop. Thread the loop through the holes of the button. Stitch the ends of the loop together and fasten it to the garment.

By Machine. Any zigzag sewing machine can be used to sew on sew-through buttons but they may differ somewhat in the mechanism by which this can be done. Consult your sewing machine instruction book for directions. A special presser foot allows a wider gap with a clearer view (a).

Make whatever settings or adjustments are necessary on your machine. Slide the garment under the presser foot. Place a button on the predetermined location. Adjust the zigzag width to the distance be-

tween the holes (b). Sew on the button. It may be necessary to do a little experimenting to get this just right.

Less stitches are needed for lightweight materials. Four-hole buttons require two separate stitchings, one for each pair of holes. Finish by raising the presser foot. Sew several lock stitches (q.v.) in place. If a shank is required, place a darning needle (or other heavy needle) on the button and sew over it (c). (There is a type of presser foot that has a groove into which one may slide a needle.) The stitches pass over the needle to form the shank. The thicker the needle, the longer the shank. Heavy fabrics and longer shanks take a few more stitches.

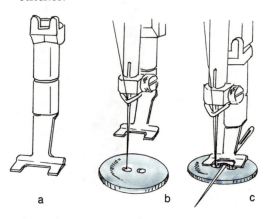

SHANK BUTTON. One with either a wire shank or a tunnel (self-) shank. *See listing for each.*

The shank button is attached to the garment by sewing through the shank, taking enough stitches to fasten it securely. The shank of the button is always aligned with the direction of the buttonhole to prevent it from spreading the buttonhole open. In a heavy overcoat, it may be necessary to add a thread stem to the metal shank to create the necessary length for a proper closing. *See* OVERCOAT BUTTON.

SHAPED (APPLIED) BAND NECKLINE FINISH. Stay-stitch the neck and outer edges of the band (a). Stay-stitch the neck edge of the facing and the top edge of the garment (b and c). Reinforce the corners of a square neckline and clip into them.

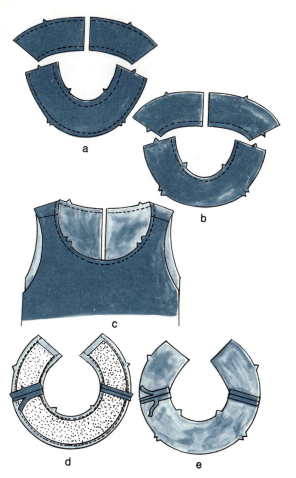

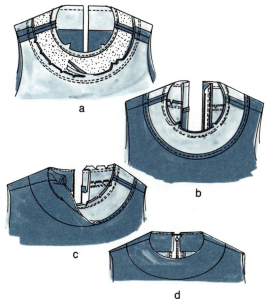

edge (b). Stitch, then remove the basting, grade and clip the seam allowances. Press the seam allowances open first, then toward the facing. With the right side up, understitch the facing to the seam allowances through all thicknesses (c).

Turn the facing to the inside, rolling the neckline seam to the underside. When there is a zipper, turn in the ends of the facing diagonally to clear the zipper teeth. Turn under and press the seam allowance of the facing at its outer edge. Notch the seam allowance to fit. Pin in place, then slip-stitch the facing to the band along the band seam line and to the zipper tape (d).

If the fabric you are working with is a knit, it will make a less bulky facing finish to allow the unnotched outer edges to extend below the seam line with no turn-under. Attach the facing seam allowance with permanent running or blind catch stitches along the band seam line.

SHAPED CASING. A decorative method of holding circular gathering or shirring in place. Plan this detail on the flat pattern or on a flat section of the garment.

Mark the position line for the casing on the wrong side of the garment. Cut the casing of a lightweight material on the same grain as that of the garment. Do

Cut the interfacing from the interfacing or band pattern. Apply the interfacing to the wrong side of the band sections, front and back. If the interfacing is lightweight, it may be included in the band seams, then trimmed close to the seam line. If the interfacing is medium to heavy weight, trim away the seam allowances and apply to the band with catch stitches along the seam line.

Join the front and back bands at the shoulders. Join the front and back facings at the shoulders. Press the seam allowances open, then trim them (d and e).

With right sides together, pin and/or baste the interfaced band to the garment. Stitch, remove the basting. Trim, grade, and notch the seam allowances (a). Press the seam flat toward the band. Insert the zipper when there is one.

With right sides together, pin and/or baste the facing to the band along the neck

whatever piecing is necessary. Turn under
1/4-inch seam allowances on the long
edges and press. This is easier and more
accurate if done over a firm paper pattern
of the finished casing (a).

Pin and/or baste the casing in place on
the underside of the garment. Stitch along
both long edges close to the folds. Thread
with drawstring and draw up. Adjust the
gathers (b).

SHAPING SEAMS. When a design line falls
across a high point of the body (bust,
shoulder blades, hips, buttocks, abdomen),
the shaping may be concealed in the seam
that joins sections of a garment. In patternmaking, this is called a *control seam*. Designers are partial to this method of shaping, for they can control fit and style at the
same time.

For instance: shaping from neck to bust
and bust to waist can be hidden in interesting design lines accented by a contrasting trim (a). A yoke seam, passing over the
apex of the bust, does the shaping as well

as providing an interesting division of textured fabric and plain (b). Bust, waist, and
hip shaping are absorbed in a princess-line
style. A seam such as this provides excellent opportunities for trimming as well as
fitting (c).

Not all seams in a garment are shaping
seams. Some are merely style lines (d). It is
important to distinguish which seam line
carries the burden of the shaping (the upper seam) and which repeats the line for
design purposes (the lower seam).

**How to Tell a Shaping Seam from a
Style Line.** Place the adjoining pattern

sections side by side with the grain lines parallel to each other. You can see immediately when there is a dartlike shaping in the seam (a). If there is, the seam can be used for fitting. When the lines are exactly alike as the closest-to-center seam in (b), they cannot.

While a shaping seam fits best when it falls across a high point of the body, the design of a garment is often improved when the shaping seams are moved slightly (no more than 1 inch) to either side. If they are moved more than this, the seams lose their power to shape to the degree that they are so moved. They must then be assisted by other seams and/or darts (c).

SHARPLY INDENTED SEAM. (As at a waistline.) Reinforce the area with a second row of machine stitching close to the first. To prevent strain on the seam, clip the seam allowances diagonally rather than at right angles to the seam line. *See* CURVED PLAIN SEAM.

SHAWL COLLAR. A variety of rolled dressmaker collar (q.v.) whose upper collar and front facing are cut as one piece. Right and left collars are joined by a seam at center back. No seaming is visible from the front. The style line is usually an unbroken line from center back to front break (a), though it may be cut to simulate a notched collar (b) or be scalloped for a fancier effect (c).

There are two types of shawl collar construction. In one type, the undercollar is cut in one piece with the garment. Because it produces a soft collar, it is used for *dressmaker styles. (See Method 1.)* In the other type, the undercollar is cut as a separate section, its size and shape determined by the designer. Because it is a separate section, it offers the same opportunity for shaping and fitting as the tailored notched collar (q.v.). Since this construction produces a crisper collar, it is the one used for *tailored garments,* though it could also be used for dressmaker styles. *(See Method 2.)*

BOTH TYPES

Stitch and press open all seams and darts that enter the garment neckline.

METHOD 1. UNDERCOLLAR CUT IN ONE WITH THE GARMENT (a)

Cut the interfacing from the one-piece upper collar/front facing pattern. Apply it to the wrong side of the garment front/undercollar unit. Join the undercollar sections at the center back and press the seam allowances open. Join the upper collar/front facings at the center back and press the seam allowances open.

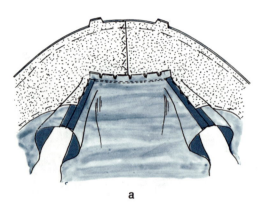

a

METHOD 2. UNDERCOLLAR CUT AS A SEPARATE SECTION (b).

Cut and apply the front interfacings to the garment fronts. Cut and apply the separate undercollar interfacing to the wrong side of the undercollar. Pad-stitch undercollar and lapels if desired. *See* TAILORED COLLAR; TAILORED SHAWL COLLAR.

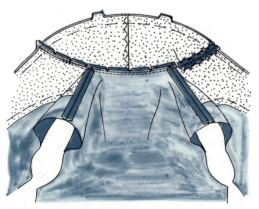

b

With the right sides together, baste the collar/facing unit to the garment/undercollar unit, stretching the undercollar to fit. Start the stitching at the center back and continue to the bottom edge (c). The directional stitching of the long seams preserves the grain and shape of the collar.

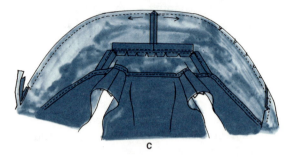

c

Clip the seam allowances at the break of the collar. Grade the seam allowances, making those of the garment wider than the facing. Clip and notch the seam allowances where necessary; press them open.

Turn the collar to the right side. Press so that the joining seam is rolled to the underside of the collar above the break and to the underside of the garment below it. Understitch (q.v.) in this position by hand or by machine, from the center back to the break and from the break to the bottom of the garment. Or, if appropriate for the design, topstitch *(see* TOPSTITCHING) an even distance from the finished edge.

With the collar turned to the right side, establish its roll line and baste along it. Let the stand of the collar fall into place. Pin through all layers of the stand. Lift the back neck facing and lightly tack the seam

allowances of the collar and garment at the neck edge, allowing some play to the stitches so as not to restrain the roll of the collar. Tack the edges of the facing to the shoulder seams.

SHEER FABRICS. What you don't see is often more intriguing than what you do see. Hence the universal popularity of the see-through fabrics—the chiffons and voiles, the organdies and organzas, the gauzy nets and laces.

For sheer pleasure, let the fabric float free, independent of an understructure (a). Make a separate slip or underdress. This not only provides a certain discreet opaqueness, it also presents an opportunity to play with the color of a gown. For instance: intensify a pale pink color by using a deeper, brighter pink under it. Soften

a taupe color by using a pale beige under it. Green a yellow by placing a blue under it, producing a lovely shimmer as well. Give dramatic impact to black lace by placing red or vivid green under it.

To create a firmer, opaque fabric of the filmy see-through variety, underline it. Underline the entire dress (b). Or underline part of it while unlined sections veil the body or underdress (c).

See-through to you is the whole point of sheer fabrics. You certainly do not want to divert that attention to the inner workings of the construction.

Choose styles with unbroken lines, few seams, and few darts. Small darts are better than large ones. No darts are best of all. Avoid designs with visible constructions: no bound buttonholes and no inset pockets. If pockets there must be, strategically placed patch pockets are preferable (d).

Fragile fabrics require delicate handling. The crisp sheers (organdy) are somewhat easier to work with than the soft ones (like chiffon). The latter have a tendency to slip away in cutting and sewing.

Cutting. To prevent slipping, cover the cutting surface with a sheet of tissue paper *(the* great stabilizer of all elusive and unmanageable fabrics). Sandwich the fabric between the tissue-paper table cover and the tissue-paper pattern. Place silk pins in the seam allowances so they won't injure the fabric. If pins will not mar the fabric, use two rows of sharp pins placed close together, one row on either side of the cutting line. Cut through all layers of paper and cloth with sharp scissors.

Marking. There are several possibilities for marking. Either mark the fabric itself with tailor's tacks or thread tracing (q.v.), or mark an underlayer instead.

The underlayer could be the underlining, marked with tailor's chalk or even dressmaker's carbon paper if that will not show through. The underlayer could also be tissue paper cut from the pattern, marked, applied to the fabric, and torn away when the stitching is completed.

In the case of double- or triple-layered sheers, cut each separately. Mark the bottom layer only. Place the identical sections one over the other, all right sides up. Match the grain lines, the centers, the raw edges. Baste through the center of each garment section. Smooth toward the outer edges and baste. In large areas, smooth and baste every 6 to 8 inches until the edge is reached.

Stitching. Use very fine machine needles (size 9), sharp-pointed to prevent snagging. Use fine thread of the same fiber as the fabric. Short stitches—15 to 18 per inch—are suggested. If you are stitching with cotton thread, use a medium tension and a light to medium pressure. If you are using silk thread, lessen the tension somewhat. Use a light pressure for soft sheers and a light to medium pressure for crisp sheers. Strips of tissue paper placed under the fabric make stitching easier. Tear the paper away when the stitching is completed.

Use a fine hand needle for hand finishing.

Seams and Seam Finishes. French seams (q.v.) are classic for this type of construction. A double row of stitching trimmed close to the line of stitching is also acceptable. The second row of stitching could be one of the overedge stitches. For sheer cottons, an edgestitched finish *(see* EDGE FINISHES) is appropriate. Bound edges (q.v.) of seam allowances make organdies, nets, and other scratchy sheers feel more comfortable. A self-bound seam (q.v.) produces an excellent finish.

Zippered Closing. Use the very thinnest and sheerest of zippers. If necessary, trim away some of the zipper tape and overcast the raw edges to prevent raveling.

Zippers are best installed by hand, using a prick stitch (q.v.). Covered snaps and hooks and eyes (q.q.v.) prevent the glint of metal, which can be a jarring note in an otherwise concealed construction.

When buttonholes are necessary in sheers, they are machine-made or worked by hand, the latter a couture touch.

Hems. Allow skirts to hang out at least twenty-four hours before setting. Circles of chiffon will continue to dip outrageously even after careful setting. There is little one can do about it except to correct the dip from time to time.

There are several ways in which the hem may be handled. *See* TURNED AND TOP-STITCHED HEM EDGE, HAND-ROLLED HEM *and* DOUBLE-FOLD HEM. The first two of these are fine edges for scarfs, bows, ruffles, flounces, or sashes in sheer fabrics. In soft sheers that tend to stretch, rolled hems are advisable.

Pressing. Follow the heat and moisture settings listed on your iron for the individual fibers. Take care to use appropriate pressure and protection. If the sheer has a crepe construction (this is true of chiffon), observe all the rules for pressing crepe (q.v.).

SHELL-STITCHED (SCALLOPED) EDGE.

A delicate edging consisting of a series of tiny scallops along a turned edge. The stitching may be done by hand or by machine. This edging is suitable for hems or tucks on lingerie, lingerie blouses, nightgowns, babies' dresses, and other garments of very lightweight or sheer material.

Hand-Stitched Shell Edge (a). Staystitch the edge and trim it close to the stitching. Fold under twice as for a narrow hem. Lightly mark the size and spacing of each shell or scallop (generally 1/4 to 3/8 inch apart). Anchor the thread at one end and slide the needle through the lower fold to the first marking. Take two overhanding stitches over the hem, drawing them up tightly to form the shell. Slip the needle through the lower fold once again and bring it up for the next stitch. Repeat across the entire edge.

Machine-Stitched Shell Edge (b). Fold under 3/8 inch along the edge to be shell-stitched. Set the machine for the blind-stitch and set the fabric in place with the folded edge to the left. Stitch on the right side about 1/4 inch from the fold. The zigzag stitches of the blind stitch reach over the folded edge at intervals. They should draw up the edge to form the scallops.

Make a test run to determine the correct tension, stitch length, stitch width, and proper drawing up of the zigzag stitch.

SHELL TUCKS. These tucks may be done by hand or by machine but look best when hand-stitched.

Hand-Stitched Shell Tucks. Form 1/8-inch to 1/4-inch tucks. Pin or baste to position. Sew the tuck with running stitches

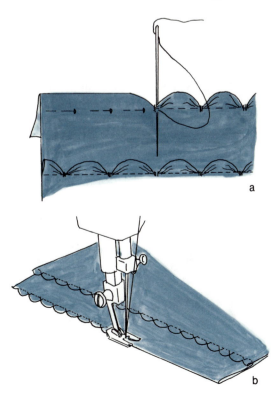

a

b

but, at marked even intervals about twice the depth of the tuck, make one to three overhand stitches (one directly over the other) (a). Draw up the overhand stitches tightly to form the shell or scallop.

Machine-Stitched Shell Tucks. Mark the position of each tuck. Set the sewing machine for the blindstitch. Work like the machine-stitched shell edge (b). *See* SHELL-STITCHED (SCALLOPED) EDGE.

SHIRRED BANDING. *See* ELASTIC DECORATIVE WAISTBAND.

SHIRRING. Multiple rows of gathering worked either by hand or by machine for decorative effect. Use soft or lightweight fabric. Crisp fabrics can be readied for shirring by steam-pressing to soften the finish. Stitch while damp.

For best effects, gather on bias or crosswise grain. Stitching must be in very accurate, straight rows, equidistant from each other. Mark with chalk pencil, thread tracing (q.v.), drawing out a single thread or creasing across the length to be shirred. When shirring by machine, only the first row need be marked. Subsequent rows may be gauged by the edge of the gathering foot.

Thread ends are fastened in a square knot. When not included in a seam, fold fabric on the wrong side and stitch narrow pin tucks over the knotted ends.

To prevent strain on shirring, stay it with a strip of self-fabric or lining material placed over the wrong side of the shirred area. Cut the strip wide enough to fit across the length and 1/2 inch deeper than the rows of shirring. Turn under the raw edge and hem or slip-stitch with small stitches across the top and bottom. When shirring is to be included in a seam, baste the stay in position for machine stitching.

Shirring by Hand. Make parallel rows of gathering to the desired depth. *See* GATHERING BY HAND.

Shirring by Machine. Make parallel rows of gathering to the desired depth. *See* GATHERING BY MACHINE.

When *shirring an entire section,* it is often easier to shirr the fabric first before cutting it out.

For interesting variations of shirring, *see* CORDED SHIRRING; ELASTICIZED GATHERING; ELASTICIZED SHIRRING; SHIRRING WITH SELF-FACING; WAFFLE SHIRRING.

For pressing directions, *see* PRESSING SHIRRING AND SMOCKING.

SHIRRING WITH ELASTIC THREAD. *See* ELASTICIZED GATHERING; ELASTICIZED SHIRRING.

SHIRRING WITH SELF-FACING. Self-fabric forms a casing through which is drawn string, thread, or elastic.

METHOD 1

Allow sufficient material in seam allowances to form facings on both sides. Stitch a plain seam and press it open. Stitch on both sides of the seam to form casings. Draw a length of string, thread, or elastic through each casing to the desired fullness. Adjust the shirring (a). Tie ends or overlap and stitch as directed below.

METHOD 2

Add a facing to the edge to be shirred. Stitch the garment seam up to the fold line

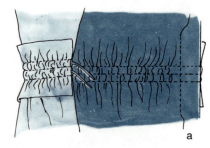

a

b

of the facing. Press the seam allowances open, continuing along the unstitched portion of the facing. Trim all seam allowances in the casing area to 1/8 to 1/4 inch and/or catch-stitch the seam allowances to the outer fabric. Doing so will facilitate the threading of the elastic, which otherwise would get trapped by the seam allowance.

Edge-finish the facing. Turn it to the inside along the fold line. Press the fold. Make several rows of stitching an even distance from the fold line and from each other to form the casings.

Cut strips of elastic to the desired length plus 1/2 inch for an overlap. Thread through the casings. Overlap the ends and stitch securely. Pull the joined ends inside the casing (b). Close the opening of the casings by slip-stitching the ends. Adjust the shirring.

SHIRT BUTTONHOLE. Because most shirts are washable, the characteristic shirt buttonhole is machine-worked (q.v.). This is also suitable for a shirt jacket.

The buttonholes are made vertically along the shirt front or band (when present) except for the top buttonhole on the collar band, which is horizontal.

SHIRT COLLAR. This is the characteristic collar of a man's shirt or its feminine counterpart, the shirtwaist. It may be made with a self-band and cut in one piece. (See SHIRT COLLAR WITH SELF-BAND.) Or it may be made in two pieces with a separate band. (See SHIRT COLLAR WITH SEPARATE BAND.)

Each section of the shirt collar is faced. In a two-piece collar, the band is always interfaced to provide the necessary stiffness to make the collar really stand. The separate collar may or may not be interfaced, though it usually is. In a one-piece collar with self-band, both collar and band are interfaced. (See COLLAR INTERFACING.) Whether one- or two-piece, the band is applied to the garment like a standing collar (q.v.).

The band closes with a horizontal buttonhole and button. If the buttonhole is a hand- or machine-made one, work it after the collar has been attached to the garment. If the buttonhole is a bound one (as in some women's shirt collars), make it on the interfaced band before it is joined to the collar and/or the garment.

SHIRT COLLAR STAY. An optional but effective way of firming the points of the shirt collar. A plastic stay is inserted through a buttonhole in the undercollar into a pocket formed between the undercollar and the interfacing.

The stay should be long enough to reach diagonally from the collar roll to within 3/8 inch of the finished point (or to slightly above topstitching when present). Allow for the upper end of the stay to protrude a bit for easy handling.

On the right side of the undercollar, mark the position for the buttonhole placement and the pocket. Pin-mark a diagonal line from what will be the point of the collar to a point equal to the finished length of the pocket. Make it equidistant from the collar edges. With a chalk pencil, mark the line for the buttonhole, centered over the diagonal line and at right angles to it. Make it slightly wider than the stay. Place the stay, centered over the diagonal line. Lightly mark a line on each side of it for the stitching lines of the pocket (a).

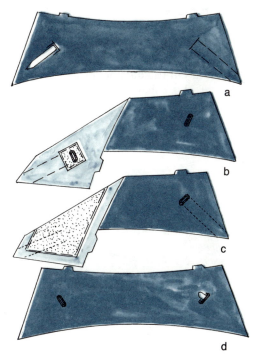

a

b

c

d

Reinforce the buttonhole area with a square of self-fabric or fusible web placed on the wrong side of the undercollar. Make the buttonhole by hand or by machine (b).

Baste the interfacing to the wrong side of the undercollar. *Note:* Do not use fusible interfacing. It does not permit the formation of the pocket. To form the pocket for the stay, stitch along the parallel lines through the undercollar and the interfacing (c).

Complete the collar construction. Slip the pointed end of the stay into the pocket (d). It can be easily removed for laundering.

SHIRT COLLAR WITH SELF-BAND (Cut All in One Piece). Interface the entire collar (a). With right sides together, pin and/or baste, then stitch the upper collar and undercollar on all but the neck edge. Trim and grade the seam allowances. Clip and notch as necessary. Slash diagonally across the corners. Clip to the stitching at the front corners (b).

Turn the collar to the right side and press. Treat as an enclosed (encased) seam (q.v.). Establish the roll line (*see* ROLLED COLLAR: ROLL LINE ESTABLISHED).

To attach the collar to the garment, place the right side of the collar neck edge against the wrong side of the garment neckline. Pin and/or baste, then stitch. Press the seam. Trim, grade, clip, and notch as necessary and press toward the stand (c). On the outside, bring the folded edge of the collar facing over the neck seam. Pin and/or baste. Slip-stitch or top-stitch through all thicknesses (d). *Optional:* Carry the topstitching around all edges of the collar (e).

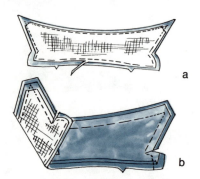

SHIRT COLLAR WITH SEPARATE BAND
(Cut in Two Pieces).

Prepare the Collar. Interface the upper collar or undercollar as the fabric requires (a). *(See* COLLAR INTERFACING.) With right sides together, pin and/or baste, then stitch the upper collar to the undercollar on all edges but those that will join the band (b). Trim and grade the seam allowances. Clip and notch as necessary. Slash diagonally across the corners.

Turn the collar to the right side and press. Treat as an enclosed seam (q.v.). Baste the open edge closed. If topstitching is called for, do it now (c).

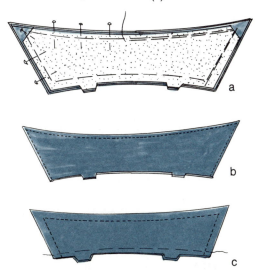

Prepare the Band. Interface the band or band facing (a). Make the interfacing as stiff as the design and the fabric require.

Turn under the neck seam allowance of the band facing to the wrong side. Baste it close to the fold. Trim the seam allowance to half width and press (b).

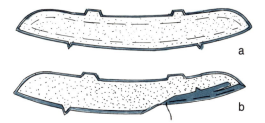

Attach Band to Collar. With right sides of undercollar and band together, match, pin, and baste the lower edge of the collar to the upper edge of the band. Note that the band extends beyond the ends of the collar. See that the extensions are even (a).

With right side of upper collar and band facing together, match, pin and/or baste the facing to the band with the collar sandwiched between them. Stitch the ends and upper edges of both band and facing through all thicknesses (b).

Trim, grade, clip, and notch the seam allowances as necessary. Turn the band and facing to the right side and press (c).

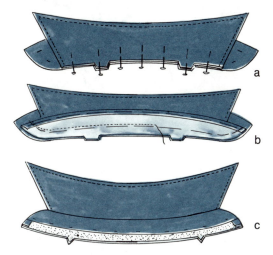

Attach Collar to Garment. Use the same method as for the standing collar (q.v.) or the shirt collar with self-band (q.v.). *Optional:* Topstitch the band. Start and end the topstitching on the upper edge of the band at the center back. Pull the thread ends through to the underside and tie in a square knot.

This type of construction can also be used to great advantage in deep coat collars of heavy material. The separate band avoids the excess fullness or rippling that tends to form at the inner neckline of bulky rolled collars. With exaggerated style lines, the collar with separate band can be effective from the standpoint of design.

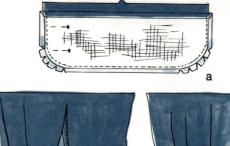

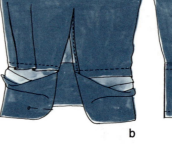

b   c

SHIRT CUFF. A crisp, neat, tailored finish for a shirt sleeve. Prepare the bottom of the sleeve (pleated or gathered) and the tailored placket (q.v.). Prepare the cuff (q.v.) (a). Use a crisp interfacing, either woven, nonwoven, or fusible. *See* CUFF IN-TERFACING.

Remember that cuffs come in pairs—a right and a left. Mark the buttonhole placement on the right side of each cuff. Fold the upper seam allowance of the interfaced cuff to the wrong side and press. Trim the seam allowance to half width. Baste close to the fold.

Pin the right side of the cuff facing to the wrong side of the sleeve. Match all markings. Stitch the cuff facing to the sleeve slowly, taking care that the pleats or gathers stay in position. Grade the seam allowances and press them toward the cuff (b). On the right side, pin and/or baste the folded edge of the cuff over the seam. Edgestitch along the basted edge. For the cuff finish, either continue the edgestitching around the cuff or topstitch (c).

Should you not wish edgestitching or topstitching, reverse the procedure for attaching the cuff. With right sides together, pin and/or baste the interfaced cuff to the sleeve. Stitch. Grade the seam allowances and press them toward the cuff. On the wrong side, turn under the seam allowance of the facing and bring its folded edge to the seam. Pin and/or baste. Slip-stitch the facing to the seam.

Remove all bastings. Press the cuffs. Make hand- or machine-worked buttonholes (q.v.).

SHIRT HEM. A shirt hem that will be *tucked in* is narrow and machine-stitched. Fold a narrow hem twice. Stitch close to the folded edge. Make a second row of stitching 1/8 inch from the first. The firmness provided by this hem keeps the edge from rolling up.

A hem on a shirt to be *worn over pants or skirt* is wider. Turn under the raw edge and edgestitch. Turn up the hem and blind-stitch it by hand or by machine. If consistent with the design of the shirt, topstitch it. *Short shirt-sleeve hems* are made in the same way. *See also* MOCK SHIRT CUFF.

SHIRT PLACKET. *See* TAILORED PLACKET.

SHIRT SEAM. The traditional shirt seam is a flat-fell seam (q.v.), so there are no exposed edges. Unlike other flat fell seams, these are made on the wrong side. Only one row of stitching is visible from the right side.

The direction of the fell is important. On the armhole seam, the fell is away from the sleeve. On the shoulder seam, the fell is toward the front. On the sleeve-and-side seam, the fell is toward the back.

SHIRT SLEEVE. Because there is only a slight amount of ease in the shirt-sleeve

cap, it is easy to set and stitch the shirt sleeve *before* the underarm seam of either sleeve or shirt is sewed.

Make the shirt-sleeve placket. *(See* TAILORED PLACKET.)

With right sides together, match, pin, and/or baste the sleeve cap into the armhole, easing as necessary. Stitch with the sleeve side up. Flat fell seams (q.v.) are the usual construction (a). *See* SHIRT SEAM.

With right sides together, stitch the underarm of shirt and sleeve in one continuous seam from the bottom of the shirt to the bottom of the sleeve (b). This, too, is a flat-fell seam.

Construct the shirt cuff (q.v.) and apply it to the sleeve.

SHIRT YOKE. The classic shirt yoke is a faced one constructed so all seams are enclosed. There are several methods of accomplishing this but all start the same way.

Cut the yoke and facing of self-fabric. With right sides together, baste the yoke to the shirt back at its upper seam line. With right side of the yoke facing to the

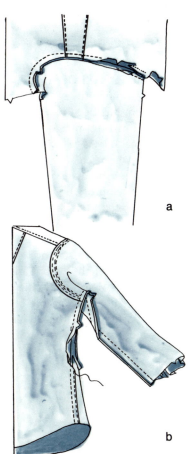

a

b

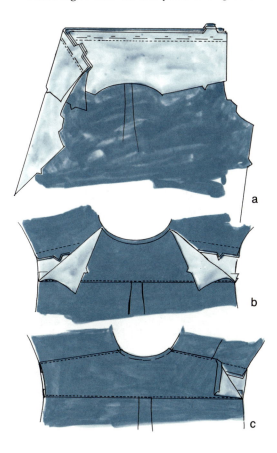

a

b

c

wrong side of the back, baste it at the yoke seam. (The shirt is now between the yoke and yoke facing.) Machine-stitch through all thicknesses—yoke, shirt back, yoke facing (a). Grade all seam allowances, leaving those of the yoke widest. Press them toward the yoke. Turn the yoke and facing to wearing position and press.

If Topstitching Is Desired: After the yoke and facing have been turned to position, topstitch them close to the fold of the yoke seam.

Pin and/or baste the right side of each front yoke facing to the wrong side of each shirt front at the shoulder seams. Stitch and grade the seam allowances. Press them toward the yoke (b). Trim and turn under the yoke shoulder seam allowances. Press. Bring the folded edges of the yokes over the front shoulder seams. Pin and/or baste. Topstitch close to the fold through all thicknesses (c). Baste the neck and armhole edges of yoke and yoke facing together.

If Topstitching Is Not Desired: There are two ways of handling the front shoulder seams—by hand or by machine stitching.

METHOD 1. BY HAND STITCHING

With the right sides of each yoke and corresponding shirt front together, pin and/or baste, then stitch each front shoulder seam. Grade the seam allowances and press them toward the yoke. Turn under the front seam allowance of each yoke facing. Bring the fold to the shoulder seam line and slip-stitch.

METHOD 2. BY MACHINE STITCHING

Pin or baste the right side of each yoke

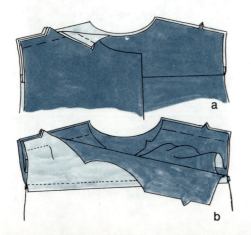

facing to the wrong side of its corresponding shirt front at the shoulder seam (a). With right sides of yoke and yoke facing toward each other and the shirt between them (b), reach up under the yoke, grasp the seam, and pull it through the neck opening. Pin and/or baste the seam, then stitch through all thicknesses. Grade the seam allowances. Pull the finished seam back through the neck opening to its correct position and press. Baste the yoke and yoke facing together at neck and armhole. *See also* WESTERN SHIRT YOKE.

SHOESTRING STRAPS. Very narrow cord, ribbon, or tubing used as shoulder straps on an otherwise strapless dress. They really don't hold much but one's interest.

Insert them in position between the garment and its facing. Include in the seam that joins them.

SHORTEN A DART. *See* DART SHORTENED.

SHORTEN A PATTERN. *See* PATTERN CORRECTIONS.

SHORTEN A SKIRT. *See* HEM RESETTING *and* ALTERING A GARMENT.

SHORTS. For women, *see* PANTS LISTINGS. For men, *see* TROUSER LISTINGS.

SHOULDER-PAD ALLOWANCE. When a design calls for shoulder pads, an allowance for them has been made. Check your pattern. All fitting must be done with them in place. *Should you wish to use shoulder pads when they are not called for,* allowances for them must then be made on the shoulder and armhole seam of the pattern.

Raise and extend the shoulder seam half the thickness of the pad at both front and back. If the shoulder pad is 1/2 inch thick, for instance, then raise and extend the shoulder seam 1/4 inch in front and 1/4 inch in back. The new shoulder line tapers to the neckline; the new armhole blends into the original armhole at the underarm (a).

A corresponding adjustment needs to be made on the sleeve cap. Draw a slash line across the cap from underarm to underarm. Draw a slash line at right angles to this line extending to the top of the cap

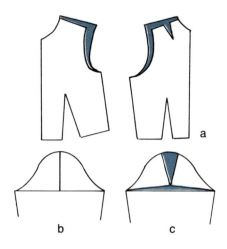

b   c

(b). Slash these lines. Raise the cap to the amount of the thickness of the pad (c). This spreads the top of the cap in just the right amount to accommodate the raised and extended shoulder. Locate a new shoulder marking at the center of the spread.

SHOULDER-PAD ALLOWANCE REMOVED. If you wish to dispense with shoulder pads in a design that calls for them, reverse the procedure for adding shoulder-pad allowance (q.v.). Overlap the slashed lines.

SHOULDER-PAD POCKET. This is the smallest of the graded layers of a chest piece (q.v.), used in men's tailoring. It is attached along its inside curved edge while the shoulder and armhole are left open. One third of the shoulder pad is inserted in it.

SHOULDER PADS. Shoulder pads come in as many sizes, shapes, thicknesses, widths, lengths, and kinds of material as will sustain the design of the shoulder area or will control the fit and appearance at the shoulders. With padding, fabric falls from the shoulders without collapsing in the hollow just below the front shoulder or jutting out over the shoulder blades.

While literally hundreds of varieties of shoulder pads are manufactured to designers' specifications for the ready-to-wear industry, only a few types are commercially available to home sewers, for whom the problem of shoulder support is equally important. What is available is often inadequate. However, using your pattern as a basis, you can make your own individualized pads with a little stiffening, a little stuffing, and, in unlined garments, a covering fabric.

For set-in sleeves there are two types of easily made shoulder pads: shoulder-shape pads (q.v.) (a) and square-front shoulder pads (q.v.) (b). Shoulder pads for dropped-shoulder, kimono, or raglan sleeves (q.v.) (c) are shaped to cup the shoulder.

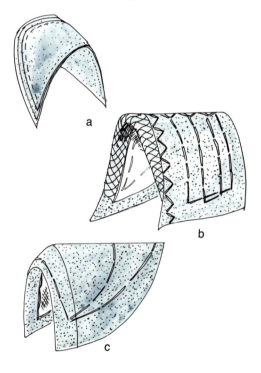

a

b

c

Whether light-, medium-, or heavyweight and whether for dressmaking or tailoring projects, pads follow the same general shapes and principles. Those for dresses and blouses generally tend to be thinner and smaller than those used for jackets and coats.

These materials may be used *for stiffening:* hair canvas or any other canvas, Pellon, crinoline, or any other sufficiently stiff foundation fabric.

The materials used *for padding* are flannel, felting, cotton wadding, quilting cotton, foam rubber, polyester fiber, or any other similar materials.

Covering fabric may be a lightweight silk or silky material or self-fabric if not too heavy.

Exaggerated shoulder styles come and go in fashion. While retaining the same basic shape as light- or medium-weight ones, such pads can be heavily built up. Commercial pads can be altered to your preference by adding or removing some of the stuffing or by trimming the inner (neck) edge. *See also* SHOULDER-PAD ALLOWANCE; SHOULDER-PAD POCKET; SHOULDER REINFORCEMENT; PUFF SHOULDER PADS; SLEEVE CAP SUPPORTS.

To make your own shoulder pads, use the adjusted garment pattern as the basis for the shoulder pad pattern. If it is in several sections, pin together all those that make the front shoulder and armhole area and those that make the back shoulder and armhole area. *See* SHOULDER-SHAPE PADS; SHOULDER PADS FOR DROPPED-SHOULDER, KIMONO, OR RAGLAN SLEEVES.

SHOULDER PADS FOR DROPPED-SHOULDER, KIMONO, OR RAGLAN SLEEVES.

Your chances for getting away without shoulder pads are best in dropped-shoulder, kimono-, or raglan-sleeve styles. The soft, natural shoulder lines are part of the charm of these designs. If padding is used to define the shoulder, the pads (molded and rounded) should cup it. *See* SHOULDER PADS *(c)* for an example of such a commercial pad. Directions for making your own follow.

a-b equals the shoulder length.
a-c equals half the front armhole.
a-d equals half the back armhole.
a-e equals the desired depth of the pad over the shoulder.

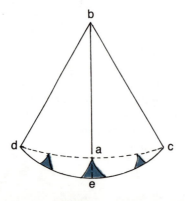

Shape the pads with slightly curved darts.

Using this pattern, cut the pads of shaping material. *(See* SHOULDER PADS.) Slash one dart leg of each dart and overlap on the other. Fit the pads carefully to your shoulder. Pin and stitch the darts. Trim away the excess material. Stuff with any of the padding materials to the desired thickness. Pad-stitch to hold all thicknesses in place.

To Set and Sew the Pads. Try on the garment and slip one shoulder pad into position, cupping the shoulder (a). Pin the pad in place from the outside along the shoulder seam. Remove the garment. Measure carefully the distance from the neck to the shoulder-point setting.

On the inside, set the second shoulder pad in exactly the same position on the other shoulder. The shoulders must balance.

Working on the inside, slip the neck end of the shoulder pad under the neck facing. Using a single matching thread, fasten the shoulder pad securely to the shoulder seam with stab stitches (q.v.) or blind-stitches (q.v.) (b).

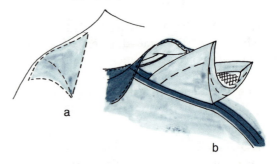

Turn both garment and pad to wearing position. On the outside, pin the ends of the pad to the garment. Turn once more to the underside. Fasten the tips of the shoulder pads in place with swing tacks (q.v.), or catch-stitch the entire front and back edges of the pad to the front and back interfacings.

Bring the facing down over the pad. Pin and catch-stitch it to the shoulder pad.

SHOULDER PATTERN CORRECTIONS.

Because clothes hang from the shoulders, their correct fit establishes the lines and shaping of the rest of the garment. Attention to fit is important also because this is the area that is seen first and that remains in view whether the wearer is sitting or standing.

Broad Shoulders. On the front and back patterns, draw L-shaped slash lines from mid-shoulder to the notches on the armhole. Slash and spread the pattern at the shoulder to the needed amount. Insert paper in the spread area and pin or Scotch-tape to position. Correct the shoulder line.

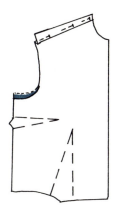

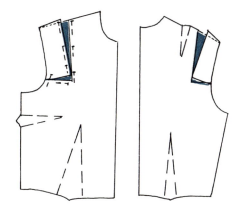

Narrow Shoulders. Reverse the procedure for broad shoulders, slashing and overlapping instead of slashing and spreading.

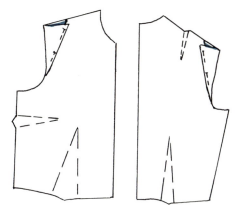

Round Shoulders. *See* BACK PATTERN CORRECTIONS.

Sloping Shoulders. On the front and back patterns, draw slash lines from neck to armhole edges. Slash and overlap the pattern at the armhole edges to the needed

amount. Pin or Scotch-tape to position. Redraw the armhole, lowering it at the underarms in an amount equal to that taken off by the correction. Correct the armhole seam line.

Square Shoulders. Reverse the procedure for round shoulders, slashing and spreading instead of slashing and overlapping. Raise the armhole as necessary rather than lowering it.

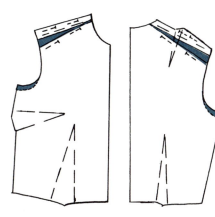

SHOULDER REINFORCEMENT. If you don't like shoulder padding, try this version of the chest piece (q.v.) to firm up and fill out hollows at the armhole edge of front and back.

Using the interfacing pattern as a guide, make a pattern for the shoulder reinforcement. Make it the width of the shoulder less ½ inch at the neck and minus all seam allowances. Follow the shape of the armhole at one edge, continuing down the side seam for a short distance. Draw a curve from shoulder to underarm at the other edge. Mark the same grain as the interfacing pattern (a).

Cut a layer of hair canvas from this pattern. Superimpose it on the front and/or back interfacing, setting it into position on the seam lines. Join the two with long running stitches on all edges and diagonal basting to hold the rest (b).

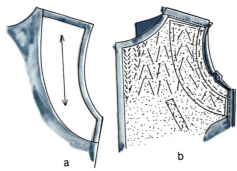

a   b

If more padding is needed or desired, *see* CHEST PIECE construction.

SHOULDER SEAM. This lies along the crest of the shoulder just *slightly* forward of the trapezius muscle from the base of the neck to the shoulder socket. This slightly forward position of the shoulder seam hangs the garment securely from the shoulder. It is perhaps the most difficult seam to position correctly. It requires a sensitivity to placement and a good eye. It must be just right—not so far forward that it looks like a yoke and not so far backward that the garment keeps sliding back.

SHOULDER-SHAPE PADS (For Set-in Sleeves). Carefully fit the shoulder seam. Transfer any corrections to the pattern. Pin together any darts or seams in the pattern that complete the front and back shoulder areas. Overlap the shoulder seams and pin.

Draw the shape of the pad on the pattern. The armhole curve extends from front notch to back notch, 3/8 to 1/2 inch out from the armhole seam at the shoulder line. The widest point of the shoulder curve is 1 inch from the neckline at the shoulder line. This becomes the basic pattern (a).

Using the basic pattern, cut a number of graduated layers of interfacing or padding

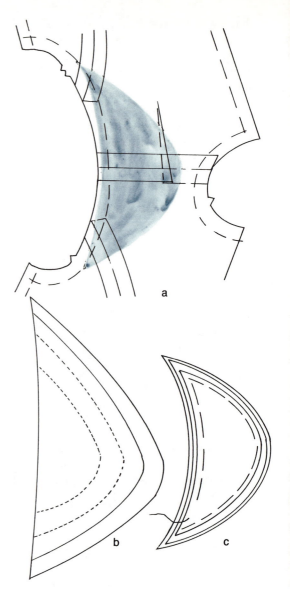

a

b   c

material (b). Stitch the layers together with long, permanent basting stitches (c). Steam the pad in a shoulder curve to fit easily into the garment.

To Set and Sew the Pads. Try on the garment. Slip the shoulder pad into the most becoming or effective position. Generally, this means extending the pad 3/8 to 1/2 inch out from the armhole seam into the sleeve cap. Pin the shoulder line from armhole to neck. Pin the ends of the pad at front and back (a).

Remove the garment. Turn it to the wrong side. Flip up the facing. With permanent basting stitches, fasten the pad to the armhole seam allowance, close to the seam line. Make a swing tack (q.v.) or catch-stitch at the shoulder end of the pad (b).

Bring the facing down over the pad and

catch-stitch its edge to the shoulder pad (c).

SIDE SEAM. In profile, the side seam appears as a continuation of the shoulder seam (a).

It starts at the underarm, about ½ inch (on average) back of the middle of the total armhole (b), and continues in a plumb line to the floor. In doing so, the side seam divides the circumferences so that front is larger than back—a variable amount at the bust, depending on the figure; about ½ inch at the waist; and 1 inch at the hips.

One good way to test for the correct position of the side seam: allow the arms to hang naturally at the sides. The middle fingers should touch the side seams of the skirt.

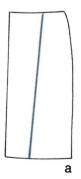
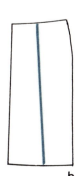
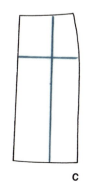

If the side seam swings forward at the hem (a) or backward (b), reset the seam in the following way. Release the side seams. Let the fabric hang out naturally. Check the grain and the darts. Repin the skirt so the side seams hang straight, at right angles to the floor (c).

SILK. Always a prized fabric, the early mystery and difficulty surrounding its production and the limited supply available (even today) have made silk a prestige cloth. Beautiful in luster and soft to the touch, it always gives a feeling of luxury.

Silk comes from the cocoon of the silkworm in long filaments. Though delicate in appearance and often woven into fragile fabrics, the fiber itself is very strong. There are four kinds of silk fiber.

Cultivated silk comes from domesticated silkworms. The filaments are fine and even in size. Crepe, satin, peau de soie, chiffon, and other dress silks are made of cultivated silk.

Wild, tussah, or raw silks come from wild silkworms. The fibers are coarse, nonuniform, and dry to the touch. They come in both light and heavy weights. They may have some sheen but are usually dull. There is a randomness about the fibers that makes fabric of very interesting texture. These silks require a rather sophisticated taste but do make handsome dresses, suits, and coats.

Doupioni silk is the silk from cocoons that have grown together. As a result the fibers are joined at irregular intervals, making uneven nubs. These fibers are used for quality shantung and other slubbed fabrics.

Waste silk is the tangled mass of silk called noils, taken from the outside of the cocoons or from damaged cocoons. Noils are fuzzy and dull. Spun silk is made from waste silk. Its irregular slubs, somewhat similar to doupioni, make it usable for less expensive shantung and other rough-textured silks.

Silk requires labeling. If the silk contains no fiber other than silk it may be labeled "pure dye," "pure dye silk," "silk," "all silk," or "pure silk." When the fabric contains any metallic weighting, any loading or adulterating materials, it must be labeled accordingly and the percentage noted.

Silk has excellent draping qualities. It is naturally resilient. It takes dye well; this, coupled with its natural luster, makes the color of silk a joy to behold. Many silks are colorfast but some are subject to fading. White silks tend to yellow with age. (This goes for white silk thread, too.)

Silk requires care in pinning, cutting, stitching, and pressing. But, despite the hazards of construction, its beauty is such that it makes the effort worth while.

SILK CARE. Although silk fiber itself is washable, most silk fabrics retain their original appearance best when dry-cleaned. Silk is damaged by heat. Avoid prolonged exposure to sunlight, which weakens it.

Dry-clean bright and dark-colored silks, iridescents, and prints that may run. Also dry-clean fragile fabrics like chiffon, satin, and crepe, which will lose its crepe finish in washing. Dry-clean all structured garments.

Some silks are hand-washable and are so labeled. In fact, the natural gumlike coating on silk fiber is refreshed by careful hand washing.

To hand-wash silk, use cool water and mild soap flakes (not detergent). Rinse thoroughly in cool water. Roll in a towel to remove excess moisture and set in the refrigerator for at least an hour before pressing. Iron it dry on the wrong side while still damp at a moderately low temperature setting.

To keep washable silks white, occasionally put a drop or two of ammonia and hydrogen peroxide into the sudsy wash water. *To remove yellowing from pale-colored silks,* add 3 tablespoons of white vinegar to a basin of cool water.

Water spots and surface shines: On dry-cleanable garments, remove by dry-cleaning; on washable garments, hand-wash as directed above.

Stains on both washable and dry-cleanable silks can be removed by dry-cleaning. Perspiration and deodorant stains are not removable.

SILK—SEWING TECHNIQUES. These depend on the particular type and weight of the silk. Keep the following guidelines in mind for all silks.

General Rules for Sewing Silk

Silk pins: Placed in seam allowances and within darts to avoid bruising fabric.

Needles: From fine to medium depending on the weight of the fabric.

Thread: Silk, to match the fiber of the fabric.

Marking: Tailor's chalk (not the waxy kind that will cause stains when pressed).

Tension: Loose, well balanced, depending on the weight and texture of the fabric.

Pressure: Light.

Stitches: For fine fabrics 10 to 12 per inch; for heavy fabrics 8 to 10 per inch.

Interfacings: Lighter in weight than the fabric. Do not use fusibles.

Linings and underlinings: China silk or silk broadcloth for silk suitings. In medium to lightweight garments, use self-fabric, organdy, organza, or similar lightweight fabric or a lightweight commercial interfacing or underlining material.

Seam finishes: Suited to the fabric. *See* EDGE FINISHES.

Zippers: On lightweight silks, use hand-applied nylon coil zippers. Do not use invisible zippers; they are too rigid.

SIMPLIFIED TAILOR'S TACKS. Clipped lines of uneven basting that leave tuft markings. They hold better through a single layer of fabric but with care they can also work on double layers. This is useful marking for a fold line, a center line, or any other line that must appear on the right side of the garment in construction.

Using a double thread of contrasting color, take small stitches through pattern and fabric along the line to be marked. Leave 1-inch loops of thread (or slack thread) placed 2 to 3 inches apart between the stitches.

For Double Layers: Open the layers of fabric carefully and cut the thread be-

tween, leaving small tufts. Clip the stitches that appear on the surface of the pattern to release them.

For Single Layers: Clip the threads between the stitches.

For Both Types: Carefully remove the pattern so as not to pull out the tufts. It is wise to replace them immediately with a line of thread tracing (q.v.) on the right side. Remove the tufts. *See also* MARKING METHODS.

SINGLE-LAYER COLLAR. A lightweight, bulkless collar, made without facing or interfacing. Because of its flat, smooth fit, it is ideal for wearing under an outer garment.

The outer edges of the collar can be bound with bias self- or contrasting fabric. A wide seam allowance the raw edges of which are bound or overcast can be mitered at the corners, turned to the underside, and secured with blindstitching. In nonravelly fabrics a simple turned-under and topstitched finish works well.

The collar is attached to the garment by a hand-felled seam. Place the right side of the collar against the wrong side of the garment. Pin, baste, then stitch. Trim the collar seam allowance to a scant 1/4 inch (adjust this amount to the thickness of the fabric). Press the seam allowance toward the collar. Turn under the garment seam allowance to cover the trimmed raw edges of the collar. Pin and/or baste to position. Hem or slip-stitch.

SINGLE-POINTED DART. Transfer the pattern markings to the wrong side of the fabric, using a marking method suitable for it.

With right sides inside and stitching lines matching, pin the dart. Place the fabric in the machine with the wide end of the dart at the top. The stitching line (rather than the fold line) and the dart point are directed toward your body at a right angle.

Begin with back-and-forth lock stitching and stitch from wide end to dart point. Keep the last two or three stitches practically parallel (a thread's width) to the fold (a). Cut the thread, leaving ends of several inches. Tie the cut ends in a square knot (b). Lock stitching may be used at the wide end of a dart but *never* at the dart point. It is practically impossible to get back on the stitching line accurately. Besides, the additional stitching stiffens the point, which should blend smoothly into the material.

When knotting the thread at the dart point detracts from the appearance of the garment (sheer material or right-side decorative darts), use a continuous-thread dart (q.v.).

On the wrong side, this dart will look like a triangle; on the right side like a partial or incomplete seam.

Place the garment over the tailor's ham with the dart up. First press the dart over the ham in the direction of the stitching, then in the direction the dart will take in the finished garment (c). When necessary, slash the dart open and press. *See* DARTS: TRIMMING *and* PRESSING DARTS.

SINGLE-WELT POCKET (SELF-WELT OR STAND POCKET). This is the type often used for the back hip pocket in men's tailoring. The single welt is formed within a faced opening (a).

With basting thread, mark the position for the pocket opening—a rectangle equal to the width and length of the finished welt. Reinforce the underside of the opening with a lightweight interfacing or fusible.

Cut the welt of garment fabric equal to twice its width by its length-plus-seam-allowances. Interface it to the fold line or fuse it in half lengthwise with fusible web. Fold it in half lengthwise, right side out, and baste.

Place the welt in position on the right side of the garment with its seam line on the lower stitching line of the pocket marking. Stitch it from one end of the

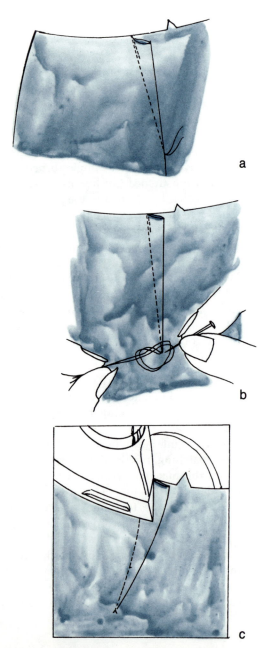

a

b

c

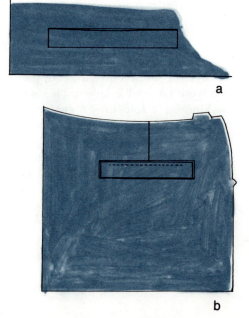

a

b

opening to the other. Secure the thread ends (b).

Cut the pocket of pocketing (q.v.) or lining material in a single piece equal to twice the depth of the pocket plus the depth of the pocket opening. If this is to be a back hip pocket in men's trousers, add an amount equal to the distance between the top of the pocket opening and the waistline seam. Make the pocket 1 inch wider than the opening. Add generous seam allowances on all sides.

Cut a pocket facing of garment fabric equal to the length and width of the pocket opening plus generous seam allowances on all sides. Turn under 1/4 inch of the lower edge and press. Place the facing in position on the under pocket section, with both right sides up. Stitch it in place. Turn 1/4 inch of both long edges of the pocket to the right side. Press and machine-stitch them close to the fold (a).

With right sides together, pin the unfaced end of the pocket over the welt, centering it, and baste. It's easier to do the stitching of the opening from the underside where you can see the marked stitching lines clearly. Stitch directly over the previous line of stitching that attached welt to garment. Stitch along the marked upper stitching line. *Do not* stitch across the ends.

First from the garment side and then from the pocket side, slash through the center of the stitching and diagonally to the corners but do not cut into the welt (b).

Carefully turn the pocket and welt to the inside through the opening. Press the four sides of the rectangular opening so they are flat and all corners are sharp. Bring the top of the welt to the top of the opening and fasten it in place with diagonal basting (c). Fold back the garment upon itself at each end of the welt, exposing the clipped triangles. Stitch each triangle to a welt end close to the fold (d).

Fold the pocket along the fold line, bringing the free edge to the top of the upper pocket with the facing directly behind the opening. Pin, then baste. In men's trousers, the free edge will extend to the waistline but do not baste it yet. Pin the sides of the pocket together with the folded edges aligned. Stitch close to the folds. Stitch again 3/8 inch in from the folded edges. Include the triangles and welts in the seams (a).

Fold back the garment against itself along the upper edge of the opening, exposing the slashed edges and the pocket. Pin, then stitch through all thicknesses

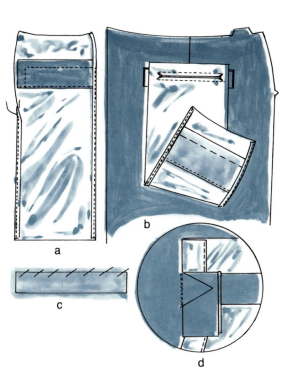

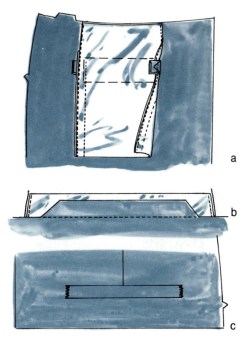

over the previous line of stitching (b). Turn up the garment. In men's trousers, baste the upper edge of the pocket to the waistline.

Optional: Bar-tack (q.v.) the ends of the pocket to reinforce them (c).

SKIPPED STITCHES. The most common cause of skipped stitches is the needle. Check it first. Make sure it is the right type and size for the fabric being sewn, that it has been inserted correctly, and that it is pushed all the way up into the clamp. Discard any blunt or bent needles. If the needle has accumulated lint or dirt, clean it or change it.

Skipped stitches frequently occur when stitching fabrics to which solutions have been applied to impart special finishes or when the fibers of the fabrics are themselves of chemical origin (synthetics). It is the heat generated by the friction of the needle penetrating such fabric at a fast and constant speed which causes some of the remains of the chemical in the fabric to rub off on the needle, thereby coating it. If you are sewing a synthetic or treated fabric, it is wise to wash it to remove any excess chemical that may remain on the surface.

To remove the coating from the needle, work it through an emery cushion or wipe it with a cloth moistened with machine oil. Be sure to remove all traces of the oil before stitching.

There is this too: closely constructed fabrics of nylon or polyester fibers or those with heat-set or fused surfaces tend to resist the needle's penetration, also causing stitches to skip. In some instances the fabric clings to the needle, choking off the supply of thread. To correct such skipping, use finer needle and finer thread.

Other causes of skipped stitches: incorrect or insufficient pressure, the wrong throat plate, stitching at an uneven speed or pulling the fabric too hard so a stitch can't form.

SKIRT LENGTHS. It's amazing how many skirt lengths one can live through in a lifetime. Up as far as one can go respectably,

down as far as one can go comfortably, and all the pinpoint gradations between.

Here are the principle designations of skirt lengths. When new ones arrive on the fashion scene, they will undoubtedly be defined in relation to these lengths.

Knee length refers to mid-knee.

Above-knee lengths: Short is just above the knee. *Mini* is mid-thigh. *Micro-mini* is thigh-high.

Below-knee lengths: Above calf is just below the knee. *Mid-calf* is half-way between knee and ankle. *Midi* is between mid-calf and ankle. *Ballerina* is above-ankle length. *Maxi or Ankle* is even with the ankle bone. *Evening length* is one inch above the floor. *Floor length* touches the floor.

SKIRT PATTERN CORRECTIONS. *See* ABDOMEN PATTERN CORRECTIONS; BUTTOCKS PATTERN CORRECTIONS; "HIKING UP"; HIP PATTERN CORRECTIONS; SKIRT PATTERN LENGTHENED OR SHORTENED; WAIST PATTERN CORRECTIONS.

SKIRT PATTERN LENGTHENED OR SHORTENED. A straight skirt with no design detail at the hem may be lengthened or shortened at the hem (a). One with design detail at the hem should be lengthened or shortened at the place indicated on the pattern to preserve its style line (b).

To preserve the sweep at the hem of a flared skirt, shorten or lengthen at the place indicated on the pattern (c) or at

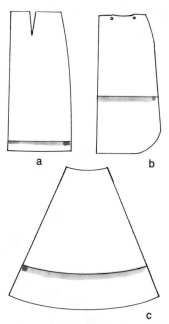

a   b

c

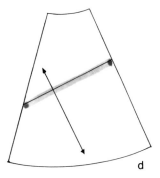

d

right angles to the grain line in bias-cut flared skirts (d). To shorten at the hem reduces the fullness. To lengthen at the hem increases it. If either of the last two is desired, alter the pattern at the hem.

SKIRT PATTERN SIZES. Skirts are generally selected by the waist measurement. Hip-hugger skirts are selected by the hip measurement. If hips are much larger in proportion to waist than the standard size, select the pattern size by hip measurement.

If a dress pattern selected by bust measurement has a smaller skirt than is needed, add the necessary amount. *See* PATTERN CORRECTIONS *for width and length.* Should the skirt pattern be an intricate one, it would be better to buy a second pattern of a larger size to fit the lower part of the body. This would also be true for a suit pattern.

SKIRT PRESSING. *See* PRESSING SKIRTS.

SLACKS. For women, *see* PANTS *listings.* For men, *see* TROUSER *listings.*

SLANT HEMMING STITCH. A small diagonal stitch that goes through two thicknesses of fabric, one of which is usually a hem edge. Both needle and stitch are slanted. Work from right to left. Left-handed sewers: reverse the direction.

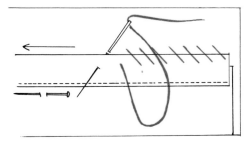

Version 1. Lift *one* thread of the outer fabric and bring the needle up through the edge of the hem.

Version 2. Take a stitch through both outer fabric and hem edge in one motion. The stitches are visible on both right and wrong sides of the fabric. This is the fastest, strongest, but most conspicuous of the hemming stitches. Better use it when it can be concealed or when visibility is not a factor.

SLASHED NECKLINE OPENING. For garments in which both center front and back are cut on a fold of fabric. If this is the only opening by which you can get into the garment, make sure it is large enough for the head to slide through.

Cut out the garment but do not cut the opening. That is cut after the slit is faced. Mark the position of the opening with thread tracing (q.v.).

A slashed neckline requires an interfacing to keep the opening from drooping. If the pattern doesn't include one, make your own from the facing pattern. Trim away all seam allowances (including the opening edges) of the interfacing. Apply it to the underside of the front and/or back bodices before they are joined. Catch-stitch the interfacing to the garment at all seam lines (a). *(See illustration on page 432.)*

Stitch the front and back bodices at the shoulders and press the seam allowances open. Stitch the front and back facings at the shoulders and press the seam allowances open. Finish the outer edge of the facing as desired.

With right sides together, pin the facing to the garment, matching neckline, shoulders, and thread tracing at the opening. Baste at the neck and opening edges. Stitch the opening, changing to smaller stitches (15 to 20 per inch) for 2 inches on either side of the point of the opening. Taper to the end of the slash. Take one stitch across the point. Stitch the remainder of the opening and the neck edge. Slash the opening to the point, being careful not to cut through the stitching. Trim, grade, clip, and notch the seam allowances as necessary (b).

Turn the facing to the underside, rolling the joining seam to the inside. Press to position. Understitch the facing to the seam allowances and tack it at the shoulders or to any underlining if present (c).

SLEEVE BOARD. A piece of pressing equipment that may be placed on the regular ironing board or on a table top. It is designed for pressing long seams in tubular constructions too narrow to fit over the regular ironing board, such as sleeve or shoulder seams. It can also be used for pressing small areas and fine details. The sleeve cap can be blocked on its broad, rounded end. *See also* PRESSING EQUIPMENT.

SLEEVE CAP SUPPORTS. In periods when exaggerated shoulders are in fashion, the drama extends to the sleeve caps, which are so designed as to add bulk and width.

While such sleeves are best made of material firm enough to sustain their shape, puffs and extensions often require additional support. This may be provided by

an underlining and/or a variety of pads, rolls, and ruffles—any sort of prop that will bolster the design of the sleeve cap. Some of these are commercially available. *(See* PUFF SHOULDER PADS.) Often a garment pattern will include a pattern for the necessary support. Or you can make your own to fit your particular sleeve.

Start with the pattern for the sleeve cap. Cut a sleeve cap underlining to its exact size and shape (a). Include in it all darts (b), gathers (c), and seams. Or add gathered (d) or pleated (e) ruffles at the sleeve cap for a puffed sleeve. For extended shoulder styles, make a crescent-shaped pad and attach it to the armhole seam (f).

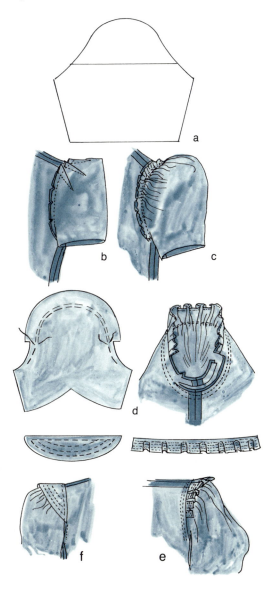

Use any suitable fabric, interfacing, or padding. *See* INTERFACINGS, UNDERLININGS, SHOULDER PADS for suggested materials and techniques.

SLEEVE CAP UNDERLINING. Used to prevent collapse of the cap or to sustain the lines of the sleeve design.

For a tailored sleeve, use the upper portion of the sleeve cap pattern to cut the underlining. Use lamb's wool padding (q.v.) (best for the purpose) or any other similar soft fabric (self-fabric, flannel, muslin, polyester fleece). The underlining may be applied before or after the sleeve has been stitched into the armhole.

Before: Place the underlining in position on the underside of the sleeve cap; baste. Include the underlining in the sleeve seams. Trim its seam allowance close to the stitching.

After: Trim the seam allowances of the underlining. Insert it in the sleeve and position it on the underside of the sleeve cap. Fasten it to the armhole seam with catch stitches or whipstitches.

For puffed or extended sleeve caps *(see* SLEEVE CAP SUPPORTS), cut the underlining from the sleeve pattern, using as much of it as necessary to sustain the lines of the design. Use any stiff fabric. Apply the underlining to the underside of the sleeve cap; baste. Include it in all darts, gathers, seams. Trim the seam allowance of the underlining close to the armhole seam.

SLEEVE FINISHES. How a sleeve is finished depends on the design of the garment. Changing a sleeve finish, like changing a neckline finish, changes the style of the garment.

The following are possibilities for sleeve finishes. *See* HEM *and listings suggested under it;* SLEEVE PLACKET *and listings under it. See also* BAND CUFF; BIAS BINDING; CASING UTILIZING SEAM ALLOWANCES, NARROW HEMS *(and so on);* CORDING; CUFF; PIPING; RIBBED BANDING; SLEEVE VENT WITH SELF-FACING.

Try on the garment with the sleeves basted into the armholes. With arms bent, determine the length of the sleeves. Determine the circumference at the bottom of the sleeve. If there is no closing in a long sleeve, there must be an opening big enough for the hand to pass through. A sleeve with a closing can have a smaller opening but be sure to allow a bit of ease when the sleeve is fastened.

When a sleeve has a hem for a finish, it can be done after the sleeve is set and stitched. When a sleeve has some style detail at the bottom, remove the basted sleeve from the garment. It is much easier to handle the sleeve alone rather than sleeve-plus-rest-of-garment.

When there is a placket, make sure that right and left sleeves open properly in opposite directions. Use all your sewing expertise in matching, stitching, trimming, pressing, interfacing for a trim and fitting end to your sleeve.

SLEEVE HEAD. A prop for the sleeve cap that provides a soft, rounded appearance. Sleeve heads are commercially available by the yard, but they can easily be made with any appropriate fabric.

Cut a bias strip of lamb's wool padding (q.v.). (Self-fabric, flannel, muslin, or any other similar soft fabric will also do.) Make the strip 5 to 8 inches long by 3 inches wide.

For a *light padding,* make a 1-inch lengthwise fold (a). For *more thickness,* fold the strip into thirds lengthwise (b).

Place the sleeve head into the sleeve cap with a folded edge along the armhole seam —half to the front, half to the back. In the one-fold sleeve head, place the wider portion against the sleeve (c). Fasten the fold

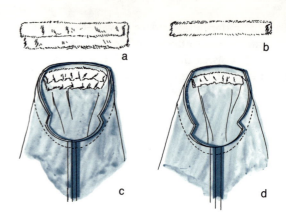

of the head to the armhole seam with slip stitches or whipstitches (d).

SLEEVE LENGTHS. Pattern reference to sleeve length assumes the sleeve will reach to the following points on your arm.

Cap: A very short sleeve extending from the shoulder like a kimono sleeve.

Short: As short as the season, the fashion, and the beauty of your arm permit.

Above-Elbow: As the name implies—just above the elbow.

Three-quarter: Halfway between elbow and wrist bone.

Seven-eighths: Halfway between the three-quarter and the long sleeve.

Wrist Length: Just grazes the wrist at the wrist bone.

Long: Ends 1 inch below the wrist bone.

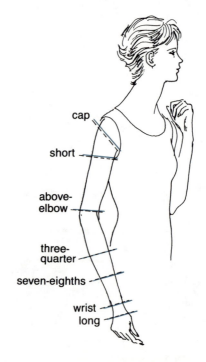

In a coat, long is just above the first thumb joint.

There are so many gradations of lengths between these designations, you should feel free to choose one that is becoming to you within the category dictated by the design of the garment.

SLEEVELESS STYLES. A sleeveless style is not just one with sleeves left out. It has a design of its own. While a garment with sleeves needs an armhole large enough to provide ease of movement, the sleeveless style has no such problem. Nothing hampers its movement. It can afford to be built up closer to the arm. This is the construction of the familiar sleeveless design (a).

The armhole may be finished in any of the ways suggested for a neckline—faced, corded, bound, piped, banded, and so on. *See* NECKLINE FINISHES.

When the garment is collarless as well as sleeveless, the facing is generally cut in one piece. *See* COMBINATION NECK AND ARM-HOLE FACING.

"Sleeveless" need not end at the armhole. It also describes a whole crop of more décolleté garments of intricate design (b and c). Since the construction of these depends on the particular design of the garment, one must follow the pattern directions carefully.

SLEEVE LOOP-AND-BUTTON CLOSING. A couture touch for a long, fitted sleeve. The loops may be of thread or of fabric tubing (q.v.).

With Thread Loops. Finish the hem and the opening edges of the closing as for the sleeve snap closing (q.v.). Align the buttons on the underlap with the edge of the overlap. Space them evenly. Sew them on. Make the thread loops (q.v.) to go around them (a).

With Fabric Loops. Finish the hem and the back opening edge of the closing as for the sleeve snap closing (q.v.). Make, position, and machine-baste the button loops (q.v.) along the seam line of the front edge of the closing (b). Place the facing or a strip of ribbon seam binding on the right side over the loop ends along the seam line and stitch close to it. Turn the binding or facing to the inside along the seam line and pin (c). Turn under top and bottom ends of the binding and slip-stitch entire binding. Align the buttons on the un-

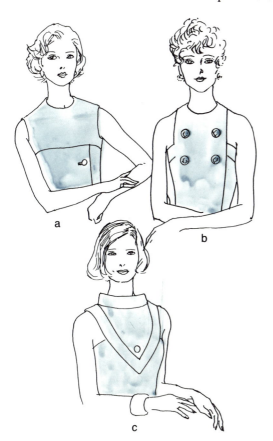

a

b

c

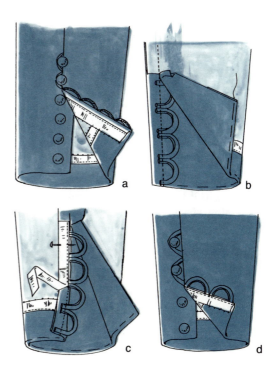

a

b

c

d

derlap with the edge of the overlap. Sew on the buttons (d).

SLEEVE PLACKET. When a sleeve is designed to fit close to the arm or wrist at its hem, some opening (placket) must be provided for easy access. Since all sleeve plackets work equally well, you may substitute one of your choosing for the one on your pattern. Select a type consistent with the design of the garment, the kind and amount of wear it is to get, the character of the fabric, your degree of skill, and the time at your disposal.

Remember that sleeves come in pairs, so that right and left sleeves will open in opposite directions. Except for those incorporated in a seam, the openings are located toward the back of the sleeve in a line with the little finger.

The easiest sleeve plackets to construct are those that utilize a seam or dart of the sleeve for the opening. *See* IN-A-DART SLEEVE PLACKET; IN-SEAM SLEEVE PLACKET; LAPPED SLEEVE CLOSING WITH A ROLLED HEM.

Simple to construct are the ZIPPERED CLOSING; the FACED PLACKET; and the CONTINUOUS BOUND PLACKET.

These take a little more doing: SLEEVE SNAP CLOSING; SLEEVE LOOP–AND–BUTTON CLOSING.

The most difficult to construct is the TAILORED PLACKET often used on shirts and shirtwaists.

SLEEVE PRESS PAD. A very useful pad for pressing sleeve seams open and for blocking the sleeve cap. It is a long, flat, heavily padded tailor's cushion just wide enough to be inserted into a finished sleeve. It has one rounded end that can be slipped under the sleeve cap. *See* SET-IN SLEEVE CAP EASE BLOCKED.

SLEEVE ROLL. A long stuffed roll used for pressing sleeve seams (or any other long seam in a tubular construction).

SLEEVE SHORTENED. *(See* SLEEVE LENGTHS.)

To Above-Elbow Length. Measure down an equal distance from the base of the sleeve cap on both underarm seams.

To Below-Elbow Length. Measure up an equal distance from the wrist at both underarm seams.

Both Types. Draw the lower line of the sleeve. This may be a straight line (a) or a slightly curved line (b). If the lower line is straight, an extended facing may be turned up as a hem (c). *(See* FACING PATTERN FOR A STRAIGHT EDGE.) If the lower line is curved, a separate facing must be provided (d). *(See* FACING PATTERN FOR A SHAPED EDGE.)

Note: The standard long, fitted sleeve contains at least 2 inches of ease at the biceps. This may make the short sleeve derived from it too wide to be pretty. Reduce a bit of the width at the hemline on the underarm seams. The broken lines in illustration (e) are the original pattern; the solid lines, the adjusted pattern.

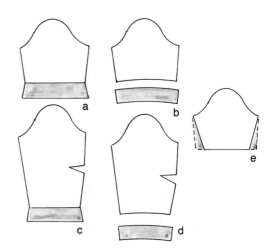

SLEEVE SNAP CLOSING. An easy closing for a long, fitted sleeve.

Stitch the sleeve seam above the marking for the sleeve opening. Clip the back seam allowance 1/2 inch above the end of the stitching. Press the seam open above the clip. Continue pressing the front edge to the inside along the seam line.

Turn up the sleeve hem and baste it close to the fold. Finish its raw edges with strips of ribbon seam binding and hem. Finish the raw edges of the opening seam allowances with seam binding. Allow 1/4 inch for a turn-under at each end (a).

Turn the front edge to the inside along the pressed seam line. Turn under the binding on the back edge and press. Turn under the binding on the upper and lower edges. Slip-stitch the lower ends and the long edges of the seam binding to the sleeve (b).

On the *inside,* lap the back edge of the opening over the front matching seam lines. Slip-stitch the upper turned-under edges in place.

From the *outside,* and with the closing in position, locate the placement of the balls and sockets of the snaps. Sew them in place (c). *See* SNAPS.

these types. The construction of a sleeve will depend on its basic type as well as its style.

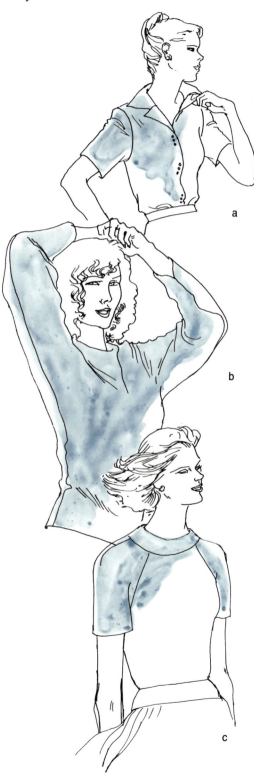

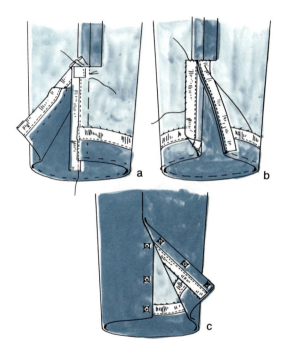

SLEEVE TYPES. There is enough variety in sleeve styles to suit every taste, every fabric, every function, and every mood. The range may be great but essentially there are three basic sleeve types: the set-in sleeve, which is stitched into an armhole (a), sleeves cut all in one with the bodice, like the kimono sleeve (b), and those sleeves for which only part of the bodice is cut in one with the sleeve, like the raglan (c).

There are many variations of each of

SLEEVE VENT WITH SELF-FACING. An opening in a vertical seam.

Before stitching the sleeve seam, interface the opening and the hem with a one-piece bias strip (a). Miter the corners (b).

Stitch the sleeve seam to the end of the opening. Turn the self-facing and hem to the inside along the fold lines. Press. Baste close to the folds. Finish the raw edges and blindstitch them to the sleeve. Reinforce the end of the slit with a bar tack (q.v.) on the inside (c).

c

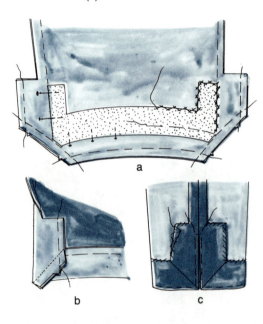

a

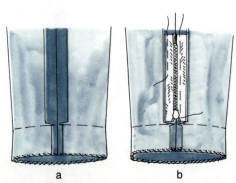

b   c

SLEEVE ZIPPER CLOSING. A sturdy placket treatment for garments that get considerable wear or for very closely fitted sleeves in opaque fabric. Use a regular neckline zipper for the former and a fine neckline zipper for the latter.

Stitch the sleeve seam above the placket opening. Baste the opening. Clip the seam allowance at the hemline. Grade the seam allowances in the hem area. Press them open to the hem edge. Finish the hem edge (a).

Insert the zipper in a centered application (*see* CENTERED [SLOT-SEAM] ZIPPER) (b). Turn up the hem. Turn in its ends diagonally to clear the zipper teeth and slipstitch. Blindstitch the hem in place (c).

SLIP BASTING (ALTERATION BASTING). Used for precise matching of stripes, plaids, motifs, cross seams, and the like; for transferring right-side fitting information to the wrong side as a guide for machine stitching; and for temporary positioning of seams.

Work from the right side. Turn under the seam allowance of one edge. Overlap the folded edge on the seam line of the lower single layer. Pin. Slip the needle along the upper fold, bringing it out a stitch ahead from the point of entry. Take a similar stitch through the lower layer, starting the new stitch directly under the ending of the first. Repeat, alternating stitches between the two layers of cloth. The stitches are invisible from the right side but form a line of thread tracing on the underside. *See also* SLIP STITCH.

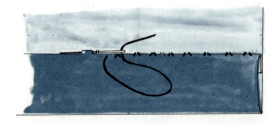

SLIP STITCH. A very small slip-basting stitch (q.v.), but unlike slip basting, which is a temporary stitch, the slip stitch is a

a   b

permanent one. The stitches, while worked from the right side, are invisible from it. They slip alternately from right to left between one layer of fabric and another.

An *even slip stitch* is used to join two folded edges of fabric. *An uneven slip stitch,* like a slip-basting stitch, joins one folded edge to a flat surface; for instance, hems, linings, applied bands, pockets, or other decorative features. The stronger of the two is the even slip stitch. For that reason it is used wherever a strong joining is required; for instance, in the hand application of a pocket or the gorge line of a tailored collar. It is also a good method for mending or hand-stitching a seam from the right side.

Even Slip Stitch. Fasten the thread on the underside and bring the needle to the right side through the fold of one edge. Directly under the end of the first stitch, slip the needle through the fold of the opposite edge. Continue weaving from one folded edge to the other. All stitches are even in size. When the thread is drawn up, a row of close, tiny stitches appears on the wrong side.

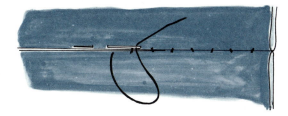

Uneven Slip Stitch. Fasten the thread on the underside. Bring the needle to the right side through the folded edge. Directly above (or below) the ending of the first stitch, take a small stitch in the garment fabric, lifting only a thread or two. Directly opposite this tiny stitch, slip the needle through the fold for about 1/4 inch and repeat the stitch, alternating between the fold and the flat surface.

SLIT SKIRT. A slit in a skirt provides ease of movement. The slit may be located in any convenient construction seam—front, side,

or back. Slits may be as high or as low as you would like—or dare.

To Construct the Slit: Stitch the skirt seam to the marking at the end of the opening (a). Press the seam allowances open. Reinforce the end of the slit on the underside with a bar tack (q.v.) or a strip of folded, preshrunk straight seam binding placed across the seam and stitched to the seam allowances (b).

The usual (most effective, prettiest) finish for a slit is self-facing. Most patterns provide for this. You can add self-facing to any seam you plan to use for a slit. If you must (though it's a rather skimpy finish),

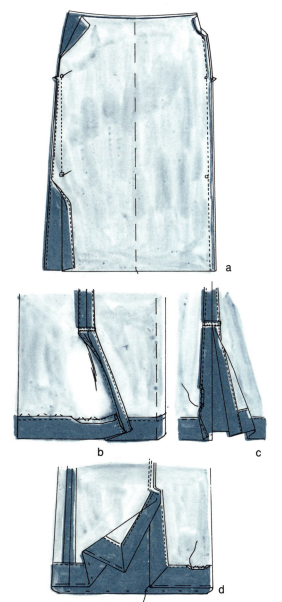

use the seam allowance in place of a facing.

Open out the facings on both sides of the slit. Turn up the hem of the skirt and baste it to position. Finish all raw edges of hem and facing as appropriate for the fabric. Fasten the hem edge to the skirt with any flat or blind hemming stitches.

Turn back the self-facings (or seam allowances) along the fold lines and baste. Either blindstitch the outer edges of the self-facings down to the fold of the hem and slip-stitch across it (c) or miter (q.v.) the corner of hem and facing (d). Fasten the rest of the facing and hem with blindstitches.

It is practically impossible to wear a slip under a slit skirt without its showing, even one with a slit in it. The best thing to do is to line or underline the skirt and dispense with the necessity for a slip.

A more subtle way to provide the same type of free movement in a slim skirt is a *vent* opening (q.v.).

SLOT SEAM. Can be used as a decorative feature for an otherwise simple design, particularly if the underlay is a contrasting color. It is a beautiful method for joining the sections of suede skins when they are used for dresses, jackets, and coats.

Turn under the edges of the fabric along the seam lines and press to position. Cut a 1½-inch-wide strip of self- or contrasting

fabric for an underlay. Mark the center of the underlay with a line of basting.

Position the turned-under edges on the right side of the underlay, bringing the folds to meet at the center marking. Pin and/or baste to position. Topstitch an equal distance from the folded edges.

SLOT-SEAM ZIPPER INSTALLATION. *See* CENTERED (SLOT-SEAM) ZIPPER.

SNAPS. Snaps come in sizes from small (4/0 to 1) to large (2 to 4), in nickel or black enamel-coated metal and in see-through clear nylon. Available also are ready-made covered, heavy-duty snaps for use where metal snaps would create a jarring note. For a perfect color match, make your own covers for any size snaps. *(See* COVERED SNAPS.) Easily and quickly applied without sewing are no-sew snaps, whose socket and ball fasteners are held in place by pronged rings.

The application of snaps depends on their use at overlapping or abutted edges. *See* SNAPS FOR OVERLAPPING EDGES; EXTENDED SNAP; HANGING SNAP.

SNAPS FOR OVERLAPPING EDGES. Sew the ball on the underside of the overlap far enough in from the edge so it won't show. Use several overhand (whipping) stitches through each of the small holes at the edge. Carry the thread under the snap from hole to hole. Make sure that the stitches do not come through to the outside. They should never show.

Press the ball against the opposite edge to locate the exact position of the center of the socket. Mark with chalk or a pin. On some fabrics, chalking the ball and pressing it against the opposite side works well. Center the socket over the marking and sew with overhand stitches through the small holes at the edge.

SNAP TAPE. A fast method of applying multiple snaps. It consists of a length of cotton or tricot tape to which are attached regular or no-sew snaps. Snap tape is sold by the yard or in precut lengths.

Snap tape requires a lapped application. Both garment edges (facings, hems, or seam allowances) should be wider than the tapes. For a stronger underlap, cut the allowance a double width. Fold it under to create a double thickness.

For a Strong Application: Turn the facing, hem, or seam allowance of the overlap to the underside. Place the ball tape over it, aligning the position of the balls and sockets. Stitch around all edges through all layers, using the zipper foot to avoid hitting the snaps.

For a Less Conspicuous Application: Place the ball tape over the right side of the overlap and stitch around all edges *before* folding the underlap to the underside. Stitch along the free edge through all layers.

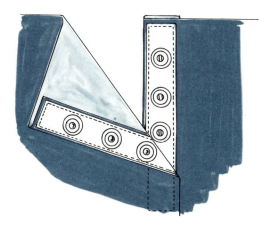

groove with tiny invisible hand stitches or by machine, using the zipper foot. Press over a soft pad.

For a raised effect, hem or machine-stitch one edge of the braid. To preserve the raised edge, press by passing the wrong side of the material over an iron.

SOUTACHE BRAID. A loosely woven, round, flexible braid used to follow design lines with tracery for a decorative trim. It comes in 1/8-inch width in a range of colors.

Mark the design in chalk, thread, or by hot transfer paper. Pin the soutache in place. Curve it as necessary. Ease it around corners; it cannot make a sharp corner. If the ends are not included in a seam, punch a tiny hole with an embroidery stiletto at the beginning and end of the braiding. Push the braid through the hole to the underside and fasten it with tiny invisible stitches. Sew the soutache in its center

SPACED TUCKS. A series of tucks with predetermined spaces between them. *See also* TUCKS.

SPAGHETTI STRAPS. *See* SHOESTRING STRAPS.

SPANDEX. A synthetic fiber used to produce stretchable, flexible, supple, lightweight fabrics. It is used extensively in foundation garments, swimwear, ski pants, and other active sportswear as well as for elastic banding. When combined with yarns of other fibers, spandex yarns impart stretch and recovery to any knit fabric.

Advantages: Strong, durable, lightweight, great elasticity.

Disadvantages: Nonabsorbent, may yellow.

Care: Wash gently by hand or in washing machine, using warm water. Rinse well and drip-dry or tumble-dry at a cool setting. Don't overdry. Iron at a low temperature. See hang tag for special laundering instructions.

Construction: Standard fabrics are cut and stitched like other stretch fabrics (q.v.). They require stretch stitches (q.v.).

The surface appearance of spandex depends on the direction from which the fabric is viewed—shiny one way, dull another. Decide which way you would like to use the fabric and use a directional layout (q.v.). Whether you cut on the crosswise or lengthwise grain, be consistent throughout.

SPLICED HEM. Extremely or intricately curved hems in fabrics that won't ravel or heavy woolens that resist easing can be spliced.

Cut narrow wedges at evenly spaced intervals, several inches apart. Make the cuts just wide enough to ensure that the upper edge of the hem lies smoothly against the garment. Do not make them any deeper than 1 inch from the fold (a). (In many instances, a lining will be brought to this length and will cover the cut.)

Bring the cut edges together with a line of machine stitching 1/4 inch from the raw edge of the hem. Darn the slashes with yarn drawn from the weave of the fabric or close the slashes with a flat catch stitch (b) in matching thread.

SPONGING. *(See* PRESHRINKING FABRIC.) Sponging is a *partial shrinking* by absorption of moisture.

Unless sponged at the factory, woolens should be sponged before cutting, either by you or by a sponging service. Steam pressing is not sufficient. A very good job of sponging can be done at home if you follow the directions below.

Straighten the grain of the fabric on both cut edges. Fold the material in half lengthwise with the right sides together. Pin or baste together both straightened edges and both selvages.

Make a sponging cloth at least 40 inches wide to accommodate the width of the folded fabric and long enough to cover it all. Old sheets will do, or a length of washable cotton bought just for this purpose. (Make sure all sizing and lint are removed before using it.)

Wet one third of the sponging cloth. Starting at the wet end, roll the entire length. Let it rest until the cloth is damp (not wet), as if for ironing. Spread out the sponging cloth on a large, flat surface. Place the fabric on the cloth in a perfect rectangle. Smooth out any wrinkles so that the material is absolutely flat (a).

Fold all ends of the sponging cloth over the fabric. Roll the entire length of fabric and sponging cloth (b), or fold loosely into sections from both ends to meet at the center (c). Cover the roll or folds completely with a Turkish towel, brown paper, or, best of all, a plastic bag. The plastic bags in which clothes are returned from the cleaner's are fine for this purpose.

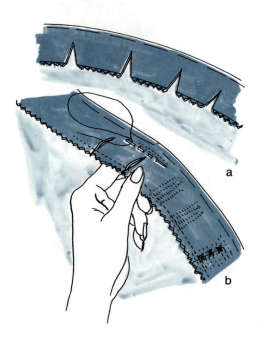

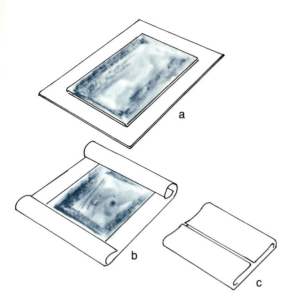

Covering in this way prevents the outer layers from drying while the inner layers remain damp, which would cause an uneven absorption of moisture.

Let stand for several hours. Most tailoring experts say three to four hours are sufficient. The Wool Bureau, Inc., recommends six to eight hours for light woolens, longer for heavier ones. Perhaps the tailoring experts are afraid that amateurs may overshrink or mat the fabric. By all means avoid overshrinking.

When the moisture has been absorbed, unroll the wool. Lay it out flat to dry. Smooth out any wrinkles. Make certain the grain is correct. If you don't have a large enough flat surface for drying, hang the wool over a door or shower rod well padded with Turkish towels. Turn the wool once during the drying process as if you were drying a sweater. Wool should dry naturally. Pressing fabric dry may make it stiff or push it off grain.

If it is necessary to remove any wrinkling after the wool is dry, press it on the wrong side, using a press cloth. Press with the grain. Press to within 1 inch of the center fold. Do not press the fold. Open the fabric and press the center section. *See* PRESSING WOOL.

One of the nice things about having the

factory or a professional service do the sponging for you is that it comes back in such a beautifully finished state.

SPORT-SHIRT SLEEVE. *See* SHIRT SLEEVE.

SQUARE-FRONT SHOULDER PADS (For Set-in Sleeves). *See* SHOULDER PADS.

Draw the shape of the shoulder pad on the front and back patterns. Come down the armhole to the notches at front and back. Square off the front; taper the back. Make the shoulder length of the pad equal to the shoulder measurement from neckline to armhole minus 1 inch (a).

Trace the front and back shoulder pad patterns on paper. Cut them out of hair canvas on the straight grain. Join front and back canvases by overlapping at the shoulder seams. Stitch. Trim away the seam allowances close to the stitching (b).

Cut a strip of bias muslin 9 inches long by 2½ inches wide. Fold it in half lengthwise. Insert a layer (or layers) of padding. Make diagonal rows of machine stitching to hold the padding in place (c). Stitch the padded muslin strip to the underside of the hair canvas, extending it about ⅜ to ½ inch at the shoulder/armhole edge and tapering to nothing at each end.

To the hair canvas, add layers of pad-

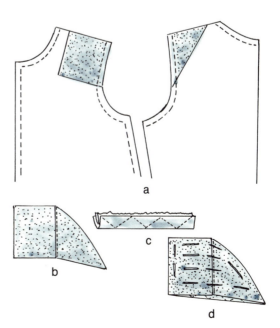

ding cut to shape. (This is your great chance to get a shoulder pad just to your liking—not too thick, not too thin.) The thickest part of the pad should be at the armhole edge of the shoulder. Taper the thickness toward the neck and toward the ends. Quilt the pad with rows of hand or machine stitching to hold all the stuffing in place (d).

An even lighter pad may be made by substituting a layer of felt or flannelette for the padding. A very satisfactory pad may be made of the hair canvas and several graded layers of Pellon.

To Set and Sew the Pads

Turn the garment inside out. Place the pad so that the shoulder line of the pad matches the shoulder seam of the garment and the edge of the pad extends 3/8 to 1/2 inch into the sleeve cap (a). Remember that the square part of the pad is in front.

From the Outside: "Pinch" the pad, holding it firmly in place with one hand. Reverse the garment to its normal wearing position. Slip the shoulder pad under the neck facing. While holding the pad in position, pin it securely at the armhole and at the neck (b).

Slip your hand under the pad. Smooth the material down from the shoulder. Locate the point at which the tip of the shoulder pad meets the front armhole seam. Pin (c). Do the same for the back (d). (If you are using a commercial pad, don't force this. Let the tips of the pad go where they want to go even if this means that

they go off the armhole seam somewhat. If you force the position of the pad tips on the armhole seam, you will create a bulge in the shoulder area.)

Anchor the pads in either of the following ways. For both methods, fasten the end of a matching single thread on the underside at the point where the shoulder pad meets the armhole seam at front or back. Use over-and-over stitches.

Method 1. For Thick Pads

Bring the needle up to the right side directly into the armhole seam. Working from the right side, fasten the pad to the garment along the armhole seam with stab stitches (q.v.). Take a tiny stitch on the surface directly into the armhole seam straight through the garment and shoulder pad. Bring the needle up through all thicknesses into the armhole seam for the next stitch, about 1/2 inch away. Do only one stitch at a time. Repeat until you reach the other end of the pad. Keep the stitches relaxed, not tight. Fasten on the underside with over-and-over stitches.

Method 2. For Medium- or Light-weight Shoulder Pads

Working on the underside, sew the pads to the seam allowances close to the armhole seam with permanent basting stitches or blindstitches.

For Both Methods. Fasten all loose, unattached points of the shoulder pad at front, back, and neck to the interfacing with swing tacks (q.v.).

STAB STITCH. Used chiefly by tailors through heavy layers of cloth. Only one stitch at a time can be done.

The needle enters (stabs) the fabric at a right angle. Both needle and thread are drawn through the cloth completely before the next stitch is taken.

STANDARD ZIPPER CONVERTED TO AN UNDERARM DRESS ZIPPER. Whipstitch the edges of the tapes together 1/4 inch above the top stop (a) and/or place a metal eye across the edges above the whip stitches (b). Fasten securely to the tapes. Zipper installation is usually by

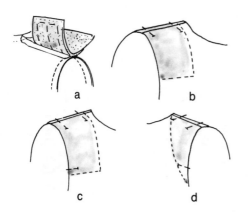

a   b

c   d

the lapped method. *See* LAPPED (REGULATION) ZIPPER APPLICATION; UNDERARM DRESS ZIPPER.

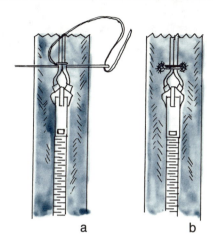

a   b

STANDING COLLAR. There are two types of standing collar—those stiffened to stand like a band and those soft enough to fold over like the turtleneck or roll-over collar.

A *stiff standing collar* can be either rectangular or curved in design. Because of its straight shape and equal length at upper and lower edges, the rectangular collar stands away from the neck as in a ring collar. Because a curved standing collar has a smaller measurement at its upper edge, it can fit closer to the neck like a Chinese collar (q.v.). Both types are generally cut on straight grain, though curved collars are sometimes cut on the bias.

The *soft standing collar* is generally rectangular in shape and cut on the bias for an easy fit around the neck. *See* BIAS FOLD COLLARS; BIAS FUNNEL COLLAR; BIAS TURNOVER COLLAR.

A rectangular collar can be cut so collar and facing are in one piece or in two pieces —a separate collar and facing. The curved standing collar must, of necessity, be cut in two pieces.

STANDING COLLAR: INTERFACING. There are several ways to make a standing collar really stand. Generally only the collar is interfaced. Sometimes both collar and facing are interfaced. Which you choose to do depends on the weight of the fabric. *(See* COLLAR INTERFACING.) The accom-

panying illustrations show a rectangular collar. The same would be true for a curved collar.

The Iron-on Method. Using the collar pattern minus its seam allowances, cut the interfacing from some fusible material. Place it in position on the wrong side of the collar and press it on (a).

The Stiff Interfacing Method. Cut a length of stiff interfacing material from the collar pattern minus its seam allowances. Place in position on the wrong side of the collar and lightly catch-stitch around all edges (b).

The Stiffened Interfacing Method. Cut a length of interfacing material, either single or double thickness, from the collar pattern minus seam allowances. Make rows of machine stitching until the interfacing is the desired degree of stiffness. Catch-stitch all edges (c). The smaller the stiffening stitches and the closer the rows, the stiffer the interfacing will be (d). Place

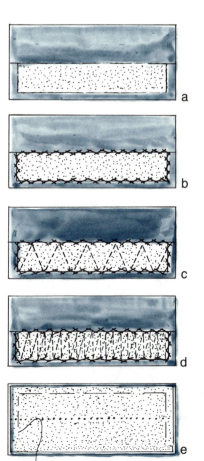

a

b

c

d

e

the interfacing in position on the wrong side of the collar.

Both Collar and Facing Interfaced. Cut the interfacing for both collar and facing in one piece for a rectangular collar, in two pieces for a curved collar. Trim away the seam allowances. Remember that the interfacing will be twice as stiff when the collar and its facing are joined. Place the interfacing in position on the underside of the collar and facing. Lightly catch-stitch around all edges. Lightly tack interfacing to collar along foldline of a one-piece collar.

In a *roll-over collar,* it is often desirable to tack the interfacing lightly to the facing close to the roll line of the collar.

In *lightweight, washable materials* interfaced with lightweight, washable interfacing material, it is not necessary to trim away the seam allowances before applying the interfacing to the collar. They may be included in the seam (e), then trimmed close to it.

STANDING COLLAR STITCHED TO THE GARMENT. Complete the collar. *(See* ONE-PIECE COLLAR, TWO-PIECE COLLAR, *and* STANDING COLLAR: INTERFACING.)

Complete the garment so it is ready for the collar application. If you have not already done so, stay-stitch the neck edge. Clip the neck seam allowance at 1-inch intervals to facilitate the joining of garment and collar (a).

With right sides together, pin and/or baste the collar to the garment along the neck seam line. Stitch. Secure the stitching at both ends. Trim and grade the seam allowances, making the collar seam allow-

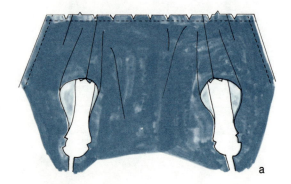

ance wider. Trim diagonally across the corners and at all cross seams (b).

Press the neck seam allowances open over a curve of the tailor's ham. Then press them into the collar. Bring the folded edge of the facing to the neck seam line. Pin in place and slip-stitch (c).

Attach hooks and eyes *(see* HOOK AND EYE ON EDGES THAT ABUT): two sets to the inside of the collar stand (d), another set for the turned-down portion of a fold-over collar (e).

STANDING FELL SEAM. *See* SELF-BOUND SEAM.

STAND OF COLLAR. The amount a collar rises from neckline to roll line. *See* COLLAR.

STAND POCKET. *See* SINGLE-WELT POCKET.

STAY. A length of tape, binding, or ribbon applied to a seam to prevent its stretching or to reinforce one subjected to stress. *(See* TAPED SEAM.) A lining stay applied to the underside of drapes, cowls, shirring, localized pleating, or gathering holds such fullness to a planned shape. *(See* COWL; BLOUSON; STAY FOR PLEATED AREA; STAY FOR SHIRRED AREA.)

In all designs that call for a stay, fit the stay first. It is the relation of the stay to the figure that produces the correct fit of the garment. A lining stay is cut to fit the basic un-full shape of the garment section or, sometimes, to fit the body. The fullness is stitched or tacked to this undercover control.

STAY BUTTON. *See* REINFORCING BUTTON.

STAY FOR PLEATED AREA. Needed when both layers of a pleat have been trimmed away to reduce bulk. *See* PLEAT STAY.

Cut the stay of lining material as wide and as deep as the garment in the area to be stayed plus seam allowances. If necessary, shape the stay to fit the area by darts, seams, or general outline.

Turn under or edge-finish one or both edges of the stay depending on the location. Pin and baste the stay to the wrong side of the area. Where possible, include the stay in the construction seams. Slip-stitch or tack the free edge to the top of the pleats (b).

STAY FOR SHIRRED AREA. Use the same method as stay for pleated area (q.v.). Slip-stitch the stay to the last row of the gathering.

STAY STITCHING. A line of machine stitching in the seam allowance close to the seam line. It fixes the length, shape, and grain of a cut edge. When a curved edge needs to be clipped for better fit or for ease in joining it to a straight one, make the stay stitching right on the seam line.

Use any thread and 8 stitches to the inch. These are generally small enough to stay the edge and large enough for easy removal should that be necessary. Otherwise, the stay stitching may remain permanently in the seam allowance.

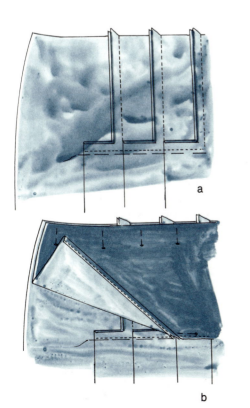

a

b

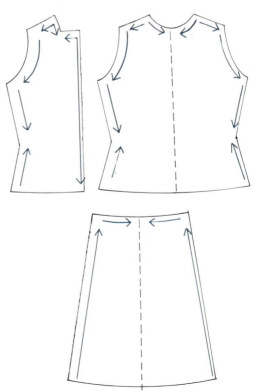

To preserve the grain, stay stitching must be directional. The rule is: stitch from a high point to a low one, from a wide point to a narrow one. The latter takes precedence over the former.

Never make a continuous line of stay stitching around a corner. Break the thread at the end of a row of stitching and begin again in the new direction (a).

On a curve, stitch from the highest point to the lowest point. Break the thread, start the second half of the curve at its highest point, and stitch to the lowest one, where it will meet the previous line of stay stitching. Break the thread (b).

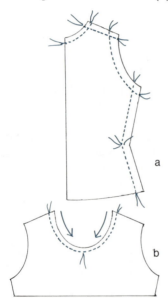

Just to make sure that your stitching has in no way affected the original size and shape of the section, compare your stay-stitched edge with the comparable edge of the pattern. Pull up the thread on any stretched edge. Clip the stitching in a few places to release a pulled-up edge. Stay stitching must preserve the line of an edge, not distort it.

What to Stay-Stitch: All curved and angled edges. If the fabric tends to ravel, it is wise to stay-stitch even straight edges.

What Not to Stay-Stitch: Edges that will eventually be eased into others. For instance: a sleeve cap must be eased into

the armhole. It does not get stay-stitched but the armhole itself does, to preserve its curved line.

Edges that get stretched to fit others. For example: collar necklines are stretched slightly to fit the garment neck seam. They do not get stay-stitched, but the garment neckline does.

In each of the above instances, it is the *fixed edge* that *does* get the stay stitching, while the *edge to be eased or stretched does not.*

The hemline of a garment is not stay-stitched. It, too, must be eased into the adjoining area. Hidden edges that don't join another section do not need stay stitching. For instance: the outer edges of facings.

True bias is not stay-stitched. Its charm is its hang and drape. It should not be restricted with stay stitching.

Stay stitching may seem a tedious task and you may be tempted to skip it. Don't: in the handling during construction it is easy to stretch and pull the fabric out of shape. You certainly wouldn't want that.

STEAM BASTING. A technique used to fuse interfacings to garment fabrics. With the iron set for steam, touch the tip of it lightly at a few strategic points to anchor the fusible interfacing in place for the fusing.

STITCHED AND OVERCAST HEM EDGE. A nonbulky, inconspicuous finish for fabrics that ravel.

Make a row of machine stitching 1/4 inch from the raw edge. Use a large stitch if the hem will require easing. If not, use a stitch indicated for the fabric.

Using the machine stitching as a guide, overcast the edge by hand or by machine. Fasten hem to garment with a blind hemming or blind catch stitch.

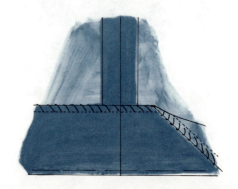

STITCHED AND PINKED EDGE FINISH.
A double guarantee for no raveling. *See*
EDGE FINISHES.

**STRAIGHTEN CUT ENDS OF FABRIC
(CROSS, HORIZONTAL GRAIN).** *See*
GRAIN ESTABLISHED IN KNIT FABRIC; GRAIN ES-
TABLISHED IN WOVEN FABRIC.

**STRAIGHTEN VERTICAL (LENGTH-
WISE) GRAIN OF FABRIC.** *See* GRAIN ES-
TABLISHED IN KNIT FABRIC; GRAIN ESTABLISHED IN
WOVEN FABRIC.

STRAIGHT HEMMING STITCH. *See* VERTI-
CAL HEMMING STITCH.

STRAIGHT OF GOODS. Another way of
saying straight grain of fabric. *See also*
GRAIN; GRAIN MARKING ON PATTERN.

STRAIGHT PLACKET BAND (Ending at
the Neckline with or without a Collar).
Stay-stitch the placket opening on the garment just inside the seam line. Slash
through the center if necessary. Clip to
each corner. Apply a strip of interfacing to
the wrong side of each placket band (a). If
bound buttonholes are to be used, construct them on the overlap band.

With right sides together, fold each
band and its facing. Pin and/or baste, then
stitch across each upper edge. Leave the
lower ends free. Press, trim, and grade the
seam allowances. Snip diagonally across
the corners. Press the seams open over the
point presser. Turn each band to the right
side and carefully work out the corners
(b).

With right sides together, pin and/or
baste one long edge of each band to the
placket opening. The finished edge is at
the top. Stitch and press (c). Trim and
grade the seam allowances. Press them
open first, then toward the band. Turn under the remaining long edge of each facing
and slip-stitch it to the band (d).

Slip the lower end of the underlap band
through the opening to the underside.
With right sides together, pin and/or baste
the lower edge of the band to the seam
allowance of the placket. Stitch across the
band (a). Press the seam flat, then down.

a

b

c

d

At the lower edge of the overlap, trim,
turn under the seam allowances and slip-
stitch the facing to the band (b). Press.

Finish the underside of any bound buttonholes. Make machine buttonholes
through the overlap band. Lap the upper
band over the lower, matching centers.
Slip-stitch the lower edge of the overlap

band in place along the seam line (c). Sew buttons in place on the underlap band. *See also* TAILORED PLACKET.

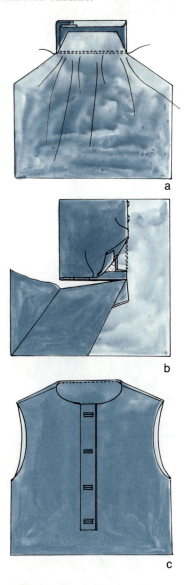

STRAPLESS DRESS. One that ends just above the bust line, leaving the shoulders and neck bare.

A *fitted strapless dress* may be supported from the waistline by featherboning (q.v.) placed over its seams or darts (a). An elasticized bodice is another solution (b). *(See* ELASTICIZED SHIRRING.) The bodice may be fitted tightly against the body at its upper edge without any further help or, if this makes you nervous, run a narrow elastic through a casing across the back (c).

STRAP SEAM. A decorative device for hiding a seam. Make a plain seam on the garment on either the wrong or right side. Trim the seam allowance and press it open. Make the strap as follows: cut a strip of fabric twice the width of the finished strap. Turn under the edges until they just meet. Join the edges with permanent diagonal basting. Place the strap over the garment, matching its seam to the garment seam. Topstitch each edge close to or in from the fold. Include the strap in all cross seams.

STRAP SLEEVE. Designed to give the illusion of width to the shoulder line (a). In this sleeve the shoulder section of the bodice is cut in one with the sleeve cap (b). When the sleeve is set, the epaulet or strap appears as a narrow yoke across the top of the shoulders.

Apart from narrowing it or widening it in the usual way to fit the shoulder, changing the strap otherwise is tampering with the design. Should you need to make any alterations in the pattern at the sleeve cap, cut the strap from the sleeve, make the change, and Scotch-tape it back to position.

In fitting, center the strap on the normal

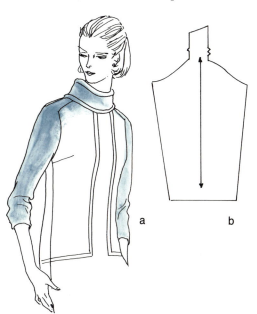

shoulder line. Use the seams that join the strap to the bodice for fitting. Preserve the shape of the strap by making any necessary adjustments on the bodice.

To Set and Stitch the Strap Sleeve: Stay-stitch the shoulder point where strap and sleeve cap join (a). Stitch and press open the seams of bodice and sleeves.

With right sides together, set, pin, and baste the sleeve into the armhole, matching sleeve and bodice seams, notches, and shoulder markings (b). With the sleeve side up, start the machine stitching at one shoulder point and stitch the underarm seam of the sleeve to the other shoulder point. Break the thread. Pull both sets of thread ends through to one side and tie in a square knot.

Slash the seam allowance of the strap to the shoulder marking. Pin and baste the strap to the bodice at the front and back

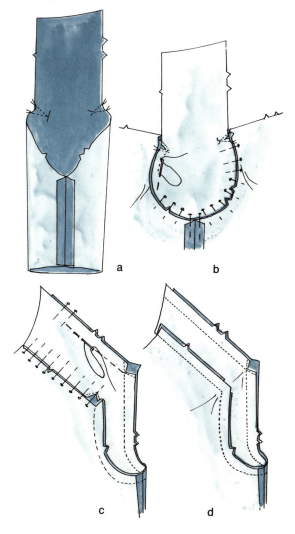

seams (c). Start the machine stitching at one shoulder point, bringing the needle down into the fabric at the end of the underarm seam for a perfect corner. Stitch to the neck. Repeat on the other side of the strap (d).

Clip the underarm seam allowances at intervals. Press them into the sleeve. Press the strap seam allowances toward the strap.

STRETCH FABRICS. Many fabrics of natural fibers have a degree of stretch because of the elasticity of the fiber itself or because of the type of weave or knit construction. Stretch fabrics are specifically planned for stretch. They are woven or knit with a resilient fiber that permits them to expand when worn—either lengthwise (warp), crosswise (filler), or in both directions (two-way stretch)—and to recover when the garments are not being worn. While the largest proportion of stretch fabrics are made of synthetic fibers, stretch characteristics can be added to any of the natural fibers.

Stretch fabrics come with varying degrees of stretch, in various textures, in a variety of print and plain surfaces, in a range of colors. Many of them are given wash-and-wear, crease-resistant, and water-repellent qualities. Most of all, while fitting so trimly, they provide comfort in action. No wonder they are being used increasingly for fashionable clothes.

Working with Stretch Fabrics (See also SPANDEX and POWER NET).

Be sure the *stretch goes in the direction you want it to go.* You can't tell the stretch by simply looking; the fabric may look the same lengthwise or crosswise. Test it.

Use lengthwise stretch for pants, slacks, or jumpsuits. Use crosswise stretch across the shoulders in blouses, shirts, dresses, jackets, coats, skirts, and shorts. Use two-way stretch for swimsuits, girdles, and the like. Don't reverse the grain or use a pattern that requires lengthwise stretch for a crosswise stretch fabric.

Select a *pattern for stretch fabric* in your usual size and make your usual pattern corrections. Patterns for stretch fabrics are built on body measurements without ease. Ease of movement is supplied by the stretch quality of the fabric.

Preshrink washable fabrics, following the laundering instructions that come with the fabric. Or roll in a damp towel, cover with a sheet of plastic, and allow it to absorb the moisture for a few hours. Dry. If the fabric is dry-cleanable, send it to the cleaner's for preshrinking.

Before layout and cutting, stretch the fabric taut, then let it relax on a flat surface until it has completely recovered. To prevent undesirable stretching, work on a flat surface and do not let the fabric hang over the edge of the cutting surface. Support it in some way.

Lay the pattern pieces on the fabric in the direction of the desired stretch. Place pins perpendicular to the direction of the stretch. Use fine, sharp pins and pin often. Cut with sharp shears in the same way as for regular fabric.

Mark with nonwax chalk, tailor's tacks, or dressmaker's tracing paper and tracing wheel. Test the markings on a scrap of fabric.

Interface in the same way as for regular fabric but make sure that the interfacing has some stretch, is preshrunk before construction, and that care is compatible with the stretch fabric. Use stretch linings or underlinings. (Lightweight tricot is suggested.) If necessary, cut the interfacing on the bias for some stretch.

Baste the garment for a *fitting.* Fit, allowing some "give" in the direction of the stretch grain. Follow the rules for fitting grain, outline seams, and style lines (see FITTING).

While the general rule for *thread* is to use the same fiber as that of the fabric, in this case choose which one seems most appropriate for your particular garment—and is available. Some experts prefer mercerized cotton thread, which is supple and comes in the greatest range of colors. Silk thread has some natural elasticity. Synthetic thread is strongest. (Nylon thread provides a minimum of seam breakage.)

For stitching, use ball-point needles (hand and machine) in a size suited to the fabric. Use a balanced tension, a medium stitch, and medium pressure. If stitches break, loosen the tension slightly. Clip bastings at 4-inch intervals to allow for stretching the fabric while machine-stitching.

Use a stretch stitch (q.v.). Where stretch is undesirable, use a straight stitch. Where stretching is not needed, place seam tape in the seam. *(See* TAPED SEAMS.)

In starting the stitching, hold fast the ends of the thread for the first two or three stitches. This prevents the fabric from being pulled into the needle opening on the throat plate. Stitch the fabric "under tension" *(see* TAUT STITCHING) at a slow to medium speed. Backstitch at each end of the stitching. To make sure it won't break in wearing, test the stitching on a scrap of fabric by stretching the seam to the fullest amount. Make any necessary adjustments.

Choose a type of *stretch seam* (q.v.) suitable to the fabric and the style of the garment. Trim, grade, clip, notch all seam allowances as necessary.

Press carefully with the steam iron on a medium setting. Do not iron. Because of its gliding motion, ironing tends to stretch and ripple the fabric.

Insert *zippers* in the usual manner. Be careful not to stretch the fabric when installing zippers or it will ripple.

Buttonholes may be bound or machine-worked. Stabilize the area with a patch of fusible knit interfacing.

For *edge finishes,* use any of the zigzag or stretch overedge stitches.

Blindstitch a *hem* by hand or by machine.

STRETCH SEAMS. Used for stretch fabrics. Standard seams can also be used for stretch seams. The difference is in the use of stretch stitches (q.v.).

Plain Seam. With right sides together, stitch the seam with a straight stretch stitch or a narrow zigzag stitch. Finger pressing is adequate in most instances, particularly when the seam allowances are topstitched. When pressing is used, set the

iron for low heat. For topstitching, use any of the multistretch stitches *(see* STRETCH STITCHES). The stitching may be centered over the seam (a) or a double row, one on each side of the seam (b).

Welt Seam. Stitch a plain stretch seam. Press both seam allowances to one side. Topstitch through all thicknesses—garment and seam allowances. Use any of the multistretch stitches (c).

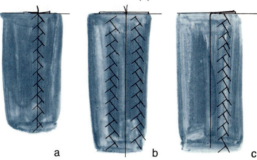

a   b   c

Overlap Seam. Mark the seam lines. Overlap them. Topstitch, using any of the plain stretch or multistretch stitches. The seam line is at the center of the stitch pattern. Trim away excess seam allowances on both sides of the fabric (a).

Abutted Seam. Bring both edges together. Join with any of the multistretch stitches (b). The meeting edges are at the center of the stitch pattern.

Fagoted Seam. Place both edges to be joined such a distance apart that each stitch will catch an edge (c).

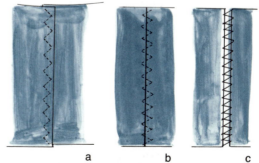

a   b   c

Straight-Stitched Seam. A degree of stretch is possible in a straight-stitched seam by using a short stitch and stretching as you sew. While the stitches may hold for a slight stretch, they will not have the elasticity of stretch stitches. There may be times, however, when straight stitching is preferable to stretch stitching, which may be too heavy for soft, lightweight fabrics.

STRETCH STITCHES. Many of today's sewing machines offer a number of stretch stitches from plain to super. They are produced by the coordinated motions of needle and feed in a pattern formation that is cam-controlled, as in zigzag stitching. They provide suppleness, elasticity, and durability. Since they are so interesting in design, they can double as decorative stitches as well as functional ones.

Stretch stitches look and function best when sewed at the length and width recommended by the sewing machine manufacturer. *(See your sewing machine instruction book.)* However, they can be modified for particular uses. Experiment on a scrap of fabric until you get the result you want. The patterns and numbers of stretch stitches vary with the make of the machine.

TYPES OF STRETCH STITCHES

Straight Stretch Stitch (a). A feature of some sewing machines. It puts 3 stitches in one place, 2 forward, 1 in reverse. It is used for stitching plain, pressed-open seams, which may be double-stitched.

Short, Narrow, Zigzag Stitch (b). Does well in the absence of stretch stitches. It offers more elasticity than a straight stitch but not as much as the more complex stretch stitches. It is used for plain seams and is lost in the thickness of the material when the seam is pressed open.

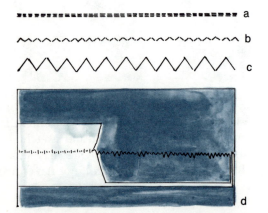

Wide-Open Zigzag Stitch (c). Can be used as an edge finish as well as a reinforcement for seams, facings, hems.

Combination Wide and Narrow Zigzag Stitches (d). Used for very elastic fabrics such as those used in sportswear.

The multistretch stitches have several stitches between the two sides of the zigzag. If one stitch breaks, the fabric is still held fast by the other stitches. They are used for finishing and flattening seams, hems, edges, and for topstitching seams in spandex and power net fabrics.

Types of Multistretch Stitches: Multistretch Stitch (a), Multistitch Zigzag (Serpentine Stitch) (b), Featherstitch (c), Superstretch Stitch (d).

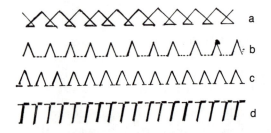

Overedge or overlook stretch stitches have a great degree of elasticity and are a perfect finish for edges in stretch fabrics. Because they go over an edge as well as into the material, they can also be used for stitching and finishing at the same time.

Types of Overedge or Overlock Stretch Stitches: Overlock Stitch (a), Overedge Stitch (b), Overedge Stretch Stitch (c), Slant Overedge (d).

The Blindstitches are the reverse of simple overedge stitches. They, too, provide a degree of elasticity useful for finishing edges as well as blindstitching hems.

Types of Blindstitches: Blindstitch (a); Elastic Blindstitch (b).

With all these possibilities, you should have no hesitancy about stitching stretch fabrics.

VˇVˇVˇVˇVˇVˇVˇVˇVˇVˇV a

WWWWWWWWWWWW b

STRETCH WAISTBAND. *See* ELASTIC DECORATIVE WAISTBAND.

STRETCHY SEAMS. If the fabric you are sewing is inclined to stretch while stitching, stabilize the seam with a strip of tissue paper placed under it, over it, or both. Stitch through fabric and paper. Tear away the paper when the seam is completed.

STRIP BAND. This is a length of knit banding used as finish for a low neckline, crew neck, mock turtleneck, or turtleneck. *See listing for each.*

Strip bands of slightly stretchy knits can be shaped to match the curve of the neck-

Designed for Stripes

line before applied. Very stretchy knit bands for higher necklines are shaped to the neck while being applied. These require a zipper opening.

STRIPES. Used creatively, stripes can be very effective in a garment. Consider the decorative possibilities of vertical, horizontal, diagonal, or chevron placement on all or part of the garment. It matters not whether the fabric is printed, woven, or knit. A ribbed fabric or a wide wale fabric is treated as a striped one. *(See illustration on page 455.)*

The choice of pattern is an important consideration in the use of stripes. Avoid complicated patterns. They can produce confusing results. "Not Suitable for Stripes" is an admonition to be taken seriously. In such designs stripes cannot be properly matched at the darts and seams. If a pattern is designed for stripes or can be used for stripes, there will be a sketch or picture of it on the pattern envelope.

See DIAGONAL PRINTS OR WEAVES. *See also* PLAIDS. The same rules apply to stripes as to plaids. Stripes are easier because there is only one direction to consider.

STRIPES: HEMLINES. *See* PLAIDS: HEMLINES.

STRIPES: MATCHING SEAMS. *See* PLAIDS: SEAMS. *See also* JOINING MATCHING CROSS SEAMS, PLAIDS, STRIPES, AND CHECKS *and so on.*

STRIPES: PLACEMENT ON FABRIC. *See* PLAIDS: LAYOUT. The same general rules apply.

Pin all stripes at intervals so upper and underlayers match. Both balanced and unbalanced stripes can be used either horizontally, vertically, or diagonally regardless of how the fabric appears on the bolt.

If stripes are used horizontally, the lengthwise grain line is placed at right angles to the stripe (a) and all vertical seams and darts are matched.

If stripes are used vertically (b), the lengthwise grain line is placed parallel to a stripe or on a stripe (c). For a center fold, fold the fabric through the center of the stripe. If the center is on a seam, place the seam line at the center of a pair of matching stripes.

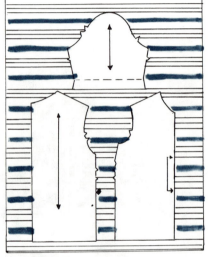

a

Place the sleeve so it matches the front armhole seam line at the notch.

It is sometimes possible (depending on the size and shaping of the pattern and the nature of the stripes) to make vertical stripes continuous around the body. How-

b

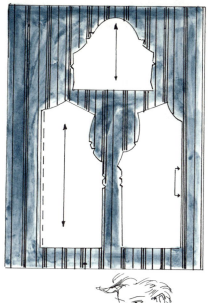

c

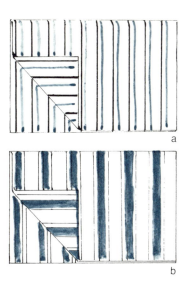

a

b

d

ever, where there are shaped seams, the stripes may or may not match or form chevrons. A *chevron* is best worked with even stripes meeting at an identical angle (d).

Unbalanced stripes require a "With Nap" (directional) layout whether they are used horizontally or vertically. *See* STRIPES: TEST FOR EVENNESS OR UNEVENNESS.

STRIPES: TEST FOR EVENNESS OR UNEVENNESS.

Fold the fabric in half lengthwise with the right side outside. Fold back one corner of the fabric. If the stripes match lengthwise as well as cross-wise, they are even (balanced) (a). If the stripes do not match lengthwise and cross-wise, they are uneven (unbalanced) (b).

STRIPES: ZIPPER IN. *See* ZIPPER IN PLAID, STRIPED, OR CHECKED MATERIAL.

STRIP METHOD OF ELIMINATING HAIR CANVAS (and other heavy interfacing materials) from construction seams. *(See illustration on page 458.)*

Cut 1¼-inch-wide strips of lightweight fabric (organza, lawn, or similar material). Use the facing pattern as a cutting guide. Or use a length of preshrunk tape or seam binding swirled to shape where necessary.

Cut the interfacing sections, mark the seam lines, and join at the shoulders with lapped or abutted seams. Place and pin the strip over the interfacing with all outside edges aligned and inner edges over the seam line (a). Stitch just inside the seam line toward the garment with either two rows of straight stitching or one row of zigzag stitching. Trim away the interfacing close to the stitching (b).

Place the interfacing unit in position on the wrong side of the garment, matching shoulder seams and markings. Pin and baste. Join with other garment sections (such as facing), including the strip (tape or seam binding) rather than the interfacing in the seam. Trim the strip close to the stitching. Trim and grade the other seam allowances (c).

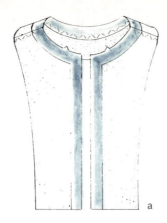

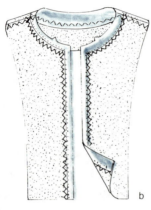

Alternate methods for eliminating hair canvas from construction seams are the fold-back method, the catch-stitched method, the taping method. *See listing for each.*

STUD BUTTON. Like the detachable shank button (q.v.), the stud button is an ornamental button used for a fastening. The only difference between the two is that the stud button, like a stud, has its eye or toggle attached to the shank.

SUBSTRUCTURE. A shape built right into a garment by means of interfacings and underlinings.

SUSPENSION TACK. *See* SWING TACK.

SWIMSUITS OF SPANDEX FABRIC. In selecting a pattern, check the back of the envelope for fabric suggestions. Most tight swimsuits require two-way stretchable knits only. Choose the same size pattern as for nonstretchable fabrics. Check your overall body measurements with those of the pattern. Make the necessary adjustments on pattern front and back.

Place the pattern on the fabric with the greater stretch across the pattern (around the body). Use 1/4-inch seam allowances. Don't clip into them for marking.

All seams are stress seams. Use a row of narrow zigzag stitching on the seam line and a row of wider zigzag stitching close to it within the seam allowance, stretching the fabric slightly while stitching. Trim excess fabric.

The kind, amount, and method of insertion of elastic at the neck, armhole, leg edges, and under the bra assembly, when used, as well as lining, interfacing, and crotch reinforcement depend on the style and the pattern for the swimsuit. Follow the pattern directions. *See also* STRETCH FABRICS *and* SPANDEX.

SWING TACK (SUSPENSION TACK). Made of several long, loose stitches that link together any two separate parts of a garment while allowing a certain amount of movement.

Take a tiny stitch on one part, then another directly opposite on the part to be joined. Pull up the thread to the desired length. Repeat, making two or three stitches between the layers. Fasten the thread.

When a swing tack is in a hidden position, this is sufficient. In an exposed position, use a French tack (q.v.), a variation of the swing tack.

TAB. A small flap attached at one end and used as a part of a fastening or decoration. It is constructed like a flap (q.v.).

TAB CLOSURE. *See* POCKET TAB.

TACKS. Stitches used to join thicknesses of fabric on the inside of the garment, to reinforce points of stress on the outside of the garment, and for marking. Inside tacks are done so as to be inconspicuous from the right side. Since outside tacks are very much in evidence, they are made as decorative as possible. Marking tacks are temporary, while swing tacks are permanent.

Tacks come in considerable variety to meet a range of needs. *See listings for the following:* ARROWHEAD TACK; BAR TACK; BLANKET-STITCH TACK; CATCH-STITCH TACK; CROSS-STITCH TACK; CROW'S-FOOT TACK; FRENCH TACK; HEAVY-DUTY TACK; PLAIN-STITCH TACK; SIMPLIFIED TAILOR'S TACKS; SWING TACK; TAILOR'S TACKS.

TAILOR BASTING. Long diagonal basting stitches (q.v.) used in tailoring to hold together interfacing or underlining and outer fabric.

TAILORED COLLAR. In general, the techniques for collar construction are interchangeable in men's and women's tailoring. What determines the method used are the style, the fabric, and the lining insertion. *See* LINING A TAILORED MAN'S GARMENT; SHAWL COLLAR; TAILORED NOTCHED COLLAR; TAILORED SHAWL COLLAR.

The two collars traditionally associated with tailoring are the *notched collar* (a) and the *shawl collar* (b). In the notched collar, part of the garment rolls back to form lapels. A separate collar is set on the neckline and lapels a little distance in from the ends to form the notch. In the shawl collar, the entire collar is part of the garment front.

The seam that joins right and left collars of the shawl collar is at the center back. No seaming is visible from the front. In the notched collar, the seam line that joins collar to lapels is visible from the front. The collar may or may not have a center back seam.

Whether the collar is all in one piece or in two pieces and whether the joining seam is visible or invisible do not matter. The collar is thought of as a unit that extends from the center back to the break— the point at which the collar rolls back to form the lapel.

The real test of tailoring ability is how one handles the tailored collar and lapels. It isn't that the techniques are so difficult, it's just that they take time: time to put in those hundreds of tiny hand stitches—all invisible, all important; time to test and shape and mold. You may go full speed ahead on other tailoring techniques, but the perfection of collar and lapel takes time.

Adjusting the Collar Pattern. Place a line of thread tracing (q.v.) at the neck seam line of the garment after it has been stitched and pressed. This is placed just above the neckline tape *(see listing for* TAPED SEAMS: TAPE NOT INCLUDED IN A SEAM*)*. Measure the length of the neck seam line from the center back to the point at which the collar joins the lapel. Measure the neck seam line of the undercollar pattern from center back to the point where the collar joins the lapel.

Compare the pattern measurement with the garment measurement. The undercollar pattern (half the total collar) should measure 1/4 inch less in length than the garment neckline. (A whole collar measures 1/2 inch less in length than a garment neckline.) Stretching the collar to fit the jacket or coat neckline produces a better roll and a slightly deeper stand. When a collar neckline just fits the garment neckline, there is less stand.

Make any necessary adjustments to the collar pattern. Up to a seam allowance may be added or subtracted at center back. If the pattern is cut with a center back seam, this is easy enough. Add or decrease at the seam line. When a collar is cut in one piece, slash the pattern at the center back. To increase, spread the slashed sections and insert the needed amount. To decrease, overlap the necessary amount and pin or Scotch-tape.

Do not make too large an alteration in any one place. This distorts the shape of the style line. When more than a seam allowance adjustment is needed, slash and spread in several places, or slash and overlap in several places. This is necessary to preserve the overall shape of the collar.

Adjustment may be balanced: that is, the same amount at the neckline as at the style line. Or it may be made in one place only: change at the neckline but not at the style line. Or retain the neckline measurement but change the style line. *See also* COLLAR ROLL ALLOWANCE.

TAILORED COLLAR: FITTING. The collar should fit in length at the neckline, the roll line, and the style line. It should fit in depth at the stand and the fall. *(See* COLLAR TERMINOLOGY.*)* These two dimensions— length and depth—are so interrelated that to change one often means an automatic change in the other.

It is best not to cut out the collar until the rest of the garment has been assembled and its fit has been tested in muslin or in interfacing material. (The latter is better because it gives a truer picture of how the collar will mold around the neck.) Changes made in fitting at the shoulder and any seams or darts that enter the neckline will affect the fit of the collar. *(See below: Testing the Fit of the Undercollar.)*

Using the adjusted undercollar as a guide, trace the alterations on the upper and undercollar patterns.

TESTING THE FIT OF THE UNDERCOLLAR

The real burden of fit falls upon the undercollar. The upper collar is just so much decoration.

Cut the undercollar interfacing from the

corrected undercollar pattern. *(See* TAILORED COLLAR, *Adjusting the Collar Pattern.)* Mark all seam lines with pencil or dressmaker's carbon.

When there is a center back seam, overlap the seam lines of the interfacing. Place pins at right angles to the seam for easy fitting (a). Stay-stitch the collar neckline. Clip its seam allowance at the neck edge in a sufficient number of places to provide the necessary spread for fitting (b). Remember that the collar fits at the seam line and not at the cut edge.

Overlap the collar interfacing on the garment, matching neck seam lines. Pin. Place the pins directly on the seam line (c).

Note: It is impossible to get a true fitting unless the collar is *overlapped* on the garment.

Match the center backs. Match each point on the lapel where the collar joins it. Stretch the collar neckline between these fixed points to fit the garment neckline. Turn the collar to wearing position (d).

Try on the garment. If you plan to use shoulder pads, slip them into position. Their presence or absence will affect the fit of the collar at the style line. Pin the center front closed from the top button down.

Examine the collar for fit. Adjust as necessary.

Collar Fitting for Depth. After the test undercollar has been pinned to the garment neckline, test it for depth.

The *stand of the collar* should be neither too high nor too low for your neck (a). When a change is indicated, unpin the neckline seam. If the stand is *too high,* lower it by adding length to the collar neckline. Ease the collar neckline to fit the garment neckline. If the stand is *too low,* raise it by shortening the length of the collar neckline. Stretch the collar neckline to fit the garment neckline. Adjustments are generally made on the center back.

The *fall* of the collar should completely cover the neckline seam plus at least 1/2 inch (b). When the stand of the collar fits well around the neck yet discloses the neckline seam, add depth at the style line (c).

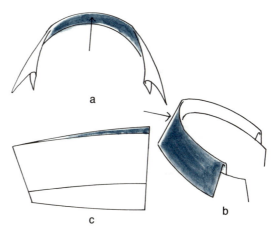

Collar Fitting for Length. The *neckline* has been made to fit by adjusting the collar pattern for length.

The *roll line* extends from the center back to the break of the lapel. It should fit without any strain. Nor should it stand away from the neck unless the collar is designed that way. Adjust the length of the collar at the roll line by using any center back seam allowance (when there is one) to add or subtract. When there is no center back seam, slash, spread, and fill in with more material to add length or slash and overlap or tuck the excess to reduce length.

The *style line* should lie smoothly around the shoulders without pulling, rippling, or poking out at the center back. Add or subtract to the length at any existing back seam. When there is no center back seam, slash, spread, and fill in with more material to add length or slash and overlap or tuck the excess to reduce the length.

To Establish the Roll Line

When you are satisfied with the fit of the undercollar, mark the roll line with pins from the center back to the break of the collar at the front closing (a). Work on one side—the one easiest for you to reach. Remove the garment. Transfer the roll-line marking to the other side of the collar and the other lapel. This will make both sides identical. Substitute a chalk or pencil marking or a line of basting for the pins along the roll line (b).

but mainly by pressing to shape (blocking) over one of several shaping devices. *(See* COLLAR PRESS PADS.)

Shaping the Collar in Construction. Fold the pad-stitched undercollar along the roll line (a). Place the folded undercollar over an appropriate curve of a press pad. Steam the fall of the collar (b). Do not press a crease in the roll line—the collar must really *roll* along this line.

Allow the undercollar to dry in position. A few pins will help to hold it in place on the blocking pad. Remove the collar from the press pad when dry.

Steam-press the inside curve of the collar stand to eliminate any rippling or puckering of the pad stitching (c).

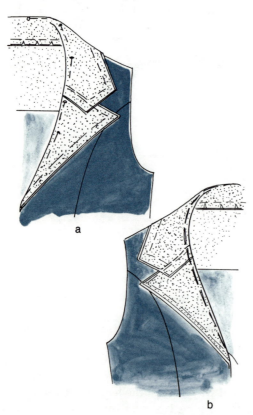

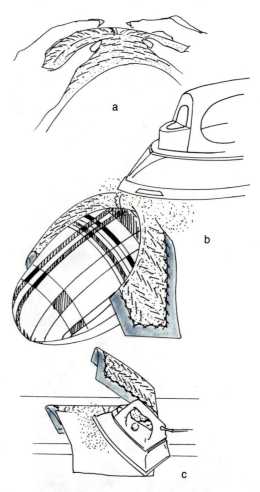

TAILORED COLLAR: PRESSING AND BLOCKING. Though cut flat, a collar is meant to fit around the neck. This rounded contour is achieved partly by pad stitching

Shaping the Completed Collar. When the upper and undercollars have been joined, steam-press all outside edges over a protective cloth. Turn the collar to wearing position. Mold it over the appropriate curve of the blocking device used previously. Press its stand, removing all rippling that may form on the inside curve. Allow the collar to dry in position.

There will be still another pressing and shaping *when the collar has been attached* to the garment neckline and lapel. With the collar in wearing position, place a rolled-up towel under the collar and lapels. Steam-press by holding the iron slightly above them, letting the steam alone set the roll line of collar and lapels. Allow them to dry in position. Pressing a sharp crease in the roll line is optional. *See* TAILORED LAPEL: PRESSING.

TAILORED LAPEL. The lapel is an integral part of the classic notched collar. It is treated like the collar in that it is pad-stitched, pressed to shape, and faced. In traditional tailoring, it is taped along the outside edges and under the roll line.

For pad stitching, *see* PAD STITCHING: TAILORED LAPEL.

For roll line, *see* TAILORED COLLAR: FITTING.

For taping, *see* TAPED ROLL LINE OF LAPEL *and* TAPING METHOD OF ELIMINATING HAIR CANVAS FROM OUTSIDE SEAMS.

Facing and pressing are dealt with immediately following.

TAILORED LAPEL: FACING APPLIED.

By Machine Stitching. Stitch the facing to the front edge of the garment from the hem to the point at which the collar joins the lapel. Clip the seam allowance at this point and at the break of the collar. The former clip is necessary for the collar setting; the latter, for the change of direction at the turnback of the lapel.

Use all tailoring techniques for easing, trimming, grading, pressing, and the handling of the enclosed seams.

By Hand Stitching. It is advisable in some fabrics to attach the lapel facing by hand rather than by machine.

Machine-stitch the facing to the garment as far as the break of the collar. Treat as an enclosed (encased) seam (q.v.). Trim,

clip, and fold the remaining garment seam allowances over the lapel interfacing. Miter the corners. Fasten the catch stitching (a). Turn under the seam allowances of the facing, allowing for the positioning of the joining seam on the underside (b). Place the facing over the lapel and fasten with slip stitches (c).

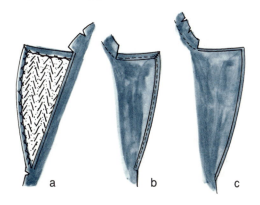

TAILORED LAPEL: PRESSING. A tailored lapel is distinguished by its thin, flat edge and its natural roll.

In Construction. After the lapel has been pad-stitched and taped, position it over the tailor's ham. Steam-press and set the lapel roll (a).

When Completed. With right side up, place the entire front, including the lapel, over a suitable curve of the tailor's ham or coat-and-jacket press board (q.q.v.). Steam-press over a protective cloth (b).

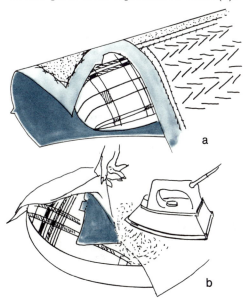

For a soft effect, roll the lapel to position and lightly steam-press. In men's tailoring and women's man-tailored garments, the roll line is often pressed into a sharp crease, starting several inches above the turnback of the lapel and continuing into the collar.

TAILORED NOTCHED COLLAR. Constructed in one of a number of ways depending on the character of the fabric, the kind of interfacing, the method by which the collar is attached to the garment, and whether the construction is by hand or by machine. In tailoring for men, this can be further complicated by the sewing procedure, in turn determined by the construction of the inside pocket and the method of inserting the lining.

Whatever the variations, cut out both undercollar and upper collar and the interfacing from the adjusted pattern. (See TAILORED COLLAR, *Adjusting the Collar Pattern.*) If there is a center back seam, join it. Apply the interfacing and pad-stitch it. Trim all interfacing seam allowances to the seam line.

When the collar is to be attached to the garment by machine (Method 1), upper collar and undercollar are each joined to the garment and facing neck edges before they are joined.

When the collar is to be attached to the garment by hand (Method 2), clip and turn up the undercollar neck edge seam allowance over the interfacing and catch-stitch in place before joining upper collar and undercollar. Following are the most frequently used of the various methods for joining the upper collar and undercollar.

METHOD 1

Machine-Stitch Method for Soft, Loosely Woven, Ravelly Fabrics. Machine-stitch the upper collar to the interfaced undercollar around all but the finished neck edge. That must be left open (a). Use all tailoring techniques for easing, stitching, trimming, grading, and pressing. (See ENCLOSED [ENCASED] SEAM.) Decide whether to topstitch (and when) or to understitch the enclosed seam.

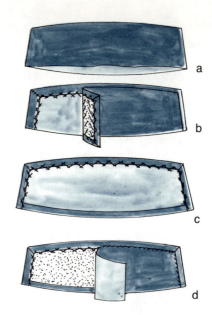

In general, curved style lines are easier to stitch by machine than are those that call for sharp corners. Often when dealing with menswear worsted or heavy coatings, turning corners while allowing enough fullness for easing can present a stitching problem. With such fabrics, it is wiser to attach the upper collar successfully by hand than to botch the collar with imperfect machine stitching.

METHOD 2

Hand-Stitch Method for Hard-to-Ease Fabrics. Trim all undercollar seam allowances 3/8 to 1/2 inch. Turn all undercollar seam allowances over the interfacing and catch-stitch to position, clipping as necessary. Miter the seam allowances of the undercollar at the corners.

Turn under and baste the seam allowances of the upper collar, allowing enough ease so joining seam will not show. When seam allowances are narrow enough, fold the corners neatly away from the edges. Or miter the corners of the upper collar seam allowances. Pin the undercollar to position over the upper collar. Slip-stitch all edges but the neck edge (b).

METHOD 3

Excellent Method for Heavy or Pile Fabrics. Trim all undercollar seam allowances—fabric as well as interfacing. Pin the trimmed interfaced undercollar to the upper collar, placing its raw edges along the upper collar seam lines. Baste to position, this to be removed when the collar is completed. Or permanently catch-stitch lightly to the upper collar, making certain that no stitches come through to the right side (c).

If you are lucky enough to be working with an underlined collar rather than an interfaced one, catch-stitch the undercollar to the underlining.

Miter the corners of the upper collar seam allowances. Trim, press the seam allowances open, and turn them to the right side, covering the edges of the undercollar. Catch-stitch the raw edges of the upper collar to the undercollar.

This is a particularly good way to handle a velvet upper collar. In fact, this method produces such a neat, flat collar that it is a desirable one for many bulky fabrics.

METHOD 4

Flattest Collar of All. Underline or interface the upper collar but *do not pad-stitch.* Miter the seam allowances at the corners of the upper collar. Trim, press open, and turn to the right side. Catch-stitch all raw edges to the underlining or interfacing.

Cut an undercollar of felt or melton cloth. Trim away 3/8 inch of all seam allowances, leaving 1/4 inch for an overlap. Place the undercollar against the seam allowance of the upper collar. Attach with slant hemming stitches (d).

To Attach Collar to Garment

This may be done by a hand-stitching or machine-stitching method. It's easier, quicker, more accurate, flatter, and neater to join the tailored collar to the garment with hand stitching. By this method, results are so spectacular that you may not want to go back to the strictly machine-stitching methods suggested in most pattern directions.

Hand-Stitching Method. Complete the collar and lapel. Working from the right

side, overlap the finished edge of the undercollar on the seam line of the garment neck edge. The garment seam allowance will slip into the opening of the collar.

Pin at each point where collar joins lapel. Pin at center back. Stretch the collar neckline to fit the garment neckline. Do not include the front facing or the upper collar in either the pinning or the stitching. Make sure that both ends of the collar are the same size. Make sure that both lapels are the same size.

Use a single strand of matching thread. Anchor it at one point where collar and lapel meet with over-and-over stitches and work to the opposite point, securing the thread in the same manner. Attach the undercollar to the garment with verticle hemming stitches (a). The stitches are tiny, close together, and strong. They are meant to hold the collar intact for the life of the garment.

Turn to the inside of the garment. Trim, clip, and turn down the loose neck-edge seam allowance of the garment over the neckline tape or the interfacing. Press it open with the tip of the iron. Fasten with either permanent basting or with catch stitching (b). Trim away the seam allow-

ance bulk where collar and lapel join, with diagonal snips. Trim and clip the seam allowances of the upper collar and facing.

Turn to the right side. Fold back the collar to wearing position and pin (c). Turn each lapel to wearing position and pin (d). This will ensure enough length on the upper surface for the roll of collar and lapel.

Turn under the seam allowance of the upper collar into the collar. Turn under the seam allowance of the lapel into the lapel. The folds of collar and lapel meet at the neck seam line. Pin or baste to position (a).

When There Is No Back Facing. Clip the collar seam allowance at the shoulder (the end of the front facing). Bring it down over the neckline tape or the interfacing from one shoulder to the other, clipping as necessary to make it lie flat. Fasten with either permanent basting or with catch stitching (b). The lining will cover this.

When There Is a Back Neck Facing. Attach it to the front facing at the shoulder seams, making any needed adjustments.

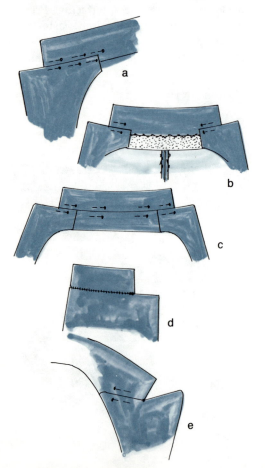

Press the seam allowances open. Trim, clip, and turn under the entire collar seam allowances into the collar and the entire front and back facing seam allowances into the facing. Pin to position (c).

Remove the pins that are holding the collar and lapels in their rolled-back positions. Using a single strand of matching thread, secure its end with several strong over-and-over stitches on the underside of the collar where it joins the lapel (d). Bring the needle through to the right side at the seam line between the folds of collar and facing (e). Slip-stitch the collar to the facing through the folds. Don't draw up the stitches too tightly. When the stitching is completed, secure the end of the thread with several strong over-and-over stitches on the underside.

Machine-Stitching Method. With right sides together, pin, then stitch the pad-stitched undercollar to the garment along the neck seam line. Clip, notch, and trim the seam allowances. Clip the garment seam allowance at the end of the collar (a). Press the seam allowances open over a tailor's ham. Catch-stitch them to the interfacings if this will ensure that they lie flat.

With right sides together, pin, then stitch the upper collar to the garment facings along the neck-edge seam lines. Clip, notch, and trim the seam allowances. Press them open over a tailor's ham. Clip the front facing at the end of the collar (b).

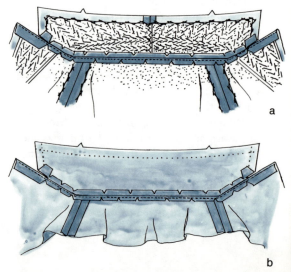

With right sides together, pin, then baste the front facings and upper collar to the garment and undercollar. Match the markings that indicate the junction of collar and lapels. Ease the fullness on the upper surfaces. Turn down the collar seam allowances at the junction of collar and lapels. Pin them out of the way to facilitate the stitching of upper collar and undercollar.

Starting at the center back of the collar, stitch along the outer edges of the upper collar and undercollar to the junction of collar and lapels. Pull the thread ends through to one side and tie them in a square knot. Stitch the second side in the same way, overlapping a few stitches at the beginning of the stitching (a).

Turn up the facing seam allowances at the junction of collar and lapels and pin them out of the way to facilitate the stitching of the lapels and front facing. Stitch one front facing to the garment, starting at the dot that indicates the junction of collar and lapel. Pull the thread ends through to one side and tie them in a square knot. Stitch the second facing in the same way (b).

Trim, clip, and notch the seam allowances as necessary. Grade them. Free all corners and junctions of collar and lapels of bulk (c). Press the seam allowances open over a point presser. Turn to the right side, working out the corners carefully.

To Complete the Collar Construction

After the collar and facings have been attached to the garment, roll all joining seams along the outer edges to the underside. Hold them in place with either edge basting or diagonal basting (q.q.v.). Understitch or topstitch the edges (q.q.v.). Remove the bastings.

Try on the garment or place it over a dress form. Roll back the collar and lapels to wearing position. Pin the garment closed at the first button. Pin, then baste

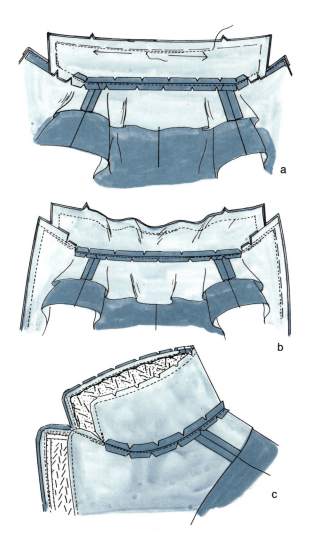

all thicknesses along the roll line of collar and lapels (a). Remove the garment.

To make sure that the upper collar and facing will always stay in place, anchor them. Gently lift the joined upper collar and facing, separating them from the undercollar and garment. Tack the seam allowances of the former to the seam allowances of the latter (b).

Press the outer edges in a manner appropriate for the fabric. Press and block both collar and lapel to shape.

TAILORED PLACKET (FRENCH PLACKET, SHIRT PLACKET). The familiar tailored opening of shirts, blouses, dresses, sleeves. In this placket, a band (often shaped) overlaps a straight band for a decorative closing, usually topstitched. The pattern for the bands may be in one or two pieces.

On the garment, mark the placket opening. Designate which edge is underlap, which overlap. In women's clothing, the right side is overlap, the left underlap; in

boy's and men's clothing just the reverse. In a sleeve placket, the underlap is attached to the back edge—that is, the one closest to the underarm seam.

THE TWO-PIECE PATTERN

Stay-stitch the placket opening just inside the marked seam line. Slash through the center and clip to each corner (a).

To Construct the Underlap: Press the seam allowance of its long unnotched edge to the underside and trim it to half its width (b). Pin the right side of the underlap to the wrong side of the appropriate placket edge, matching notches and aligning seam lines. Stitch. Trim the seam allowances (c). Press toward the underlap.

Fold the underlap to the right side, bringing it up through the clipped corner. Pin the folded edges over the stitching. Edgestitch close to the fold through all thicknesses (d). Secure the stitching at the end of the placket.

Flip up the triangular piece at the end of the placket opening and pin it to the end of the underlap. Stitch along the stitching line across the base of the triangle. Taper the ends of the underlap with two diagonal cuts (e).

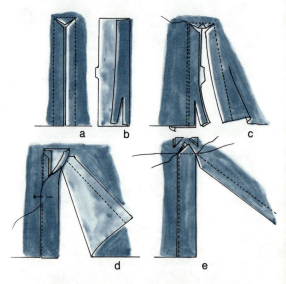

To Construct the Overlap: Turn in the seam allowance on the long unnotched edge and baste close to the fold. Trim the seam allowance (a).

Fold the overlap with right sides together. Pin and stitch the shaped end, both sides of which should match (b). Trim and grade the seam allowances. Taper toward the point. Turn, working out the point carefully with a bodkin or blunt needle (c). Press.

Pin the right side of the overlap's extended edge to the wrong side of the placket, aligning seam lines. Match notches and raw edges. Stitch (d). Trim and grade the seam allowances. Press toward the overlap.

Pin the basted edge of the overlap to the seam. Topstitch close to the basted and folded edges, ending the rows of stitching opposite each other at the beginning of the shaped edge. Pull thread ends through to the underside and tie in a square knot. Keep the underlap free. Baste the raw edges together (e).

With the overlap directly over the underlap, pin the shaped end to position. Topstitch close to the finished edges and across the overlap band (f).

THE ONE-PIECE PATTERN

In this type of pattern, both underlap and overlap are cut in one piece. Once stitched to the placket opening like a facing, the bands are constructed on the same principle as the two-piece pattern. Careful marking of both garment and one-piece bands is important.

Interface each band. Turn in the seam allowances on the sides and the lower end of the overlap band, folding in the fullness at the corner. Baste close to the folds (a). Trim the seam allowances and press.

Pin the right side of the one-piece bands to the wrong side of the garment, aligning

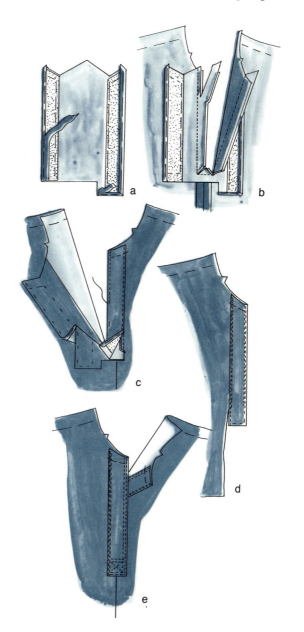

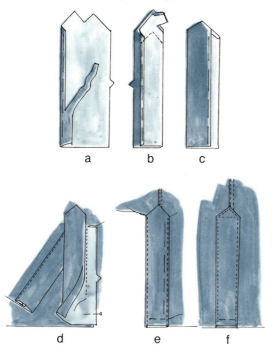

Tailored plackets vary in design. They may have rectangular, rounded, or pointed ends. The topstitching may be done in single or double rows.

seam lines as marked. Stitch, pivoting at the corners of the placket. Slash between the stitching and clip diagonally to each corner. Trim the seam allowances (b).

Turn the one-piece bands to the outside. Press the long seams toward the bands and press the lower end down.

Fold the underlap band to the right side along the fold line, bringing its basted edge over the seam. Baste the upper edges together. Topstitch close to the folded edges (c).

Fold the overlap band to the right side along the fold line, placing its basted edge over the seam. Topstitch close to the folded edges, ending at the points where the lower decorative topstitching pattern begins. Pull the thread ends through to the underside and tie them in square knots. Keep the underlap free. Baste the upper edges together (d).

Pin and baste the overlap band to position over the underlap band. Topstitch close to the remaining outer edges and along the designated stitching lines (e).

TAILORED SET-IN SLEEVE. Constructed in much the same way as any other set-in sleeve (q.v.) except that there is more shape either built into the design of the sleeve, blocked into the sleeve cap, or added at the sleeve cap for support.

There are three basic types of tailored sleeves: a one-piece sleeve with an underarm seam typical of "dressy" suits or coats; a variation of the one-piece sleeve in which the seam is at the back of the arm; and a two-piece sleeve with seams at front and back that join an overarm section to an underarm section. The latter two sleeve types are the ones more frequently used in tailored sleeves. Their seaming provides opportunity for a vent closing (q.v.). *See also* SET-IN SLEEVE TYPES.

In tailored garments, most standard sleeves are cut generously enough to fit most arms. The styling provides sufficient fullness to accommodate moderate variations in girth. Unless you have an unusually heavy or thin arm, this is one measurement you may want to let stand as it is in the pattern. Should you need to make

any alterations, *see* SET-IN SLEEVE: PATTERN CORRECTIONS.

Length of Tailored Sleeve. With arm bent, a suit sleeve should just cover the bend of the wrist. In a man-tailored suit, the length of the sleeve exposes 1/2 inch of the shirt cuff. A coat sleeve ends just above the first thumb joint. *See all listings under* SET-IN SLEEVE. *See also* SLEEVE CAP UNDERLINING; SLEEVE HEAD; *and* SQUARE-FRONT SHOULDER PADS.

TAILORED SHAWL COLLAR. Because it is a soft, rolled collar, the tailored shawl collar is handled like any other shawl collar (q.v.). Should you wish a firmer look, lightly pad-stitch the undercollar from center back to break of collar.

TAILORING. If you can make a dress you can also make a suit or coat. The methods used for dressmaking are also used for tailoring. The additional techniques for tailoring *(see appropriate individual listings)* supply all the skills needed for advanced dressmaking. Furthermore, the techniques are interchangeable for men's and women's tailoring. *See also* CLASSIC TAILORING; UNCONSTRUCTED ("SOFT," UNSTRUCTURED) TAILORING.

TAILORING FOR MEN. While tailoring methods are essentially the same for men's and women's clothing, there are a number of differences. These are dictated by the considerable wear and more subtle shaping of men's clothing. Often these differences are merely familiar tailoring methods used in a different sequence or applied in a different context. They involve the choice of fabric, the considerable interfacing, the fitting, the fly front, the collar application, the lining insertion, and the trouser waistband. *See the listing for each.*

The traditional men's jackets and coats are never underlined nor are men's trousers ever lined. This means that the fabric of which they are made must have sufficient body to maintain its shaping through years of considerable hard wear. Developed especially for this purpose are the menswear woolens and worsteds. The more loosely woven tweeds and woolens make more casual suits and coats. Extremely popular with many are the easy-care fabrics of synthetic fibers, either alone or in combination with natural fibers.

TAILOR'S BUTTONHOLE. Made with an "eyelet" nearest the finished edge of the garment to reinforce the point of stress. The shank of the button pulls against this end.

Mark the length of the buttonhole and the position of the eyelet. Center the eyelet at the outer end of the buttonhole (a). Slash the opening. Make the eyelet in any of the following ways: punch it out with an embroidery stiletto or an awl or make several 1/16-inch diagonal clips to form a circle with sharp-pointed trimming scissors. Trim away the excess fabric to form a perfect circlet about 1/8 inch in diameter.

With matching thread, overcast the cut edges with 1/16-inch overcasting stitches to prevent raveling (b). Pad the slit with a strand of gimp, linen, or cotton thread (No. 10 pearl), or with buttonhole twist of the same color as the garment fabric. Use a length of padding thread twice the length of the buttonhole plus several inches. Fasten the strand at the bar end of the buttonhole on a pin. Carry it across each side of the slash and around the eyelet as you work the buttonhole (c).

Using a 30-inch length of buttonhole thread, slip a knotted end between the outer fabric and the facing at the bar end of the buttonhole. Work the buttonhole stitch over the padding. Fan the stitches around the eyelet. Finish with a bar at the other end (d). Trim away the excess padding thread. Bring the buttonhole thread through to the underside and fasten.

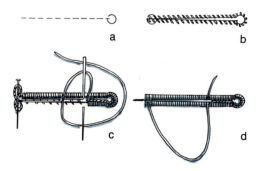

TAILOR'S CHALK. Makes safe, quick, easy markings. The chalky kind that can be brushed off or ironed out is preferable to the waxy kind, which requires cleaning fluid to remove. The chalky kind can also be used on all fabrics, including synthetics, while the waxy kind is generally used on hard-surfaced woolens in tailoring.

Tailor's chalk comes in wedges (with a plastic holder if so desired) in several colors or in pencil form in white and pastel colors. When sharpened to a point, the latter makes a fine thin line.

How to Use the Tailor's Chalk. Use a chalk pencil with a fine point in a color that will show on the fabric. Perforate the pattern in enough places to indicate a dart, seam, or spot marking. Use any suitable sharp instrument such as an orange stick or an embroidery stiletto. Be careful not to mar the fabric when you punch the hole.

Place a pin through each perforation, being sure to make it go through both thicknesses of fabric. Place a cross mark in the area caught by the pin on the upper side of the material (a), and then flip both the pattern and material over and mark the underside of the area as well. Or push the pin through the center of the perforation through both thicknesses of fabric (b). Draw a chalk circle around the spot where the pin enters (upper side) and emerges (under side) from the fabric.

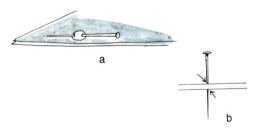

TAILOR'S HAM. The most all-purpose shaping device, so called because it is shaped like a ham. Somewhere on its rounded surface there is a curve that will match most shaped sections of a garment. There are several tailor's hams commercially available. You can make your own of 1/2 yard of material to the dimensions in the illustration.

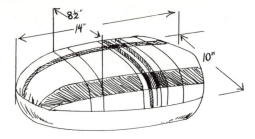

Cut two bias egg-shaped pieces of heavy, firmly woven material—silesia, pocketing, duck, drill, unbleached muslin, or wool. For an especially useful ham, cut one side of smooth material, the other of nubby or napped material. Preshrink the fabric. Dart the broader end for even more shaping. Machine-stitch the two thicknesses, leaving a 5-inch opening. *Pack very tightly* with hardwood sawdust until the ham is quite hard. It cannot hold its shape unless it is. (Some sewers use old nylon stockings for the stuffing. Commerical hams are stuffed with cotton waste or wool scraps.) *(See* PRESSING EQUIPMENT, *Why Wood?)* Turn under the seam allowance of one side of the opening and lap it over the opposite edge. Hem securely.

TAILOR'S HEM. A blindstitched hem (q.v.), the neatest, flattest, most invisible way of attaching a hem.

The true tailor's hem has no edge finish —simply the cut edge of nonravelly material. Used this way, it is reserved for garments to be lined.

TAILOR'S PRESS BOARD. A table-top piece of pressing equipment. Made of hardwood, it has a number of differently curved edges as well as straight and pointed edges. It is a sort of all-purpose combination of tailor's ham and edge and point presser. It comes with a padded cover for when soft edges are indicated. *See* PRESSING CURVED SEAMS *and* PRESSING WORSTED.

TAILOR'S TACKS. Thread markings for points or spots that need to be matched.

Use a double thread of contrasting color. Puncture a perforation in the pattern at the spot to be marked so the thread is not involved with the tissue.

Take a stitch through both thicknesses of the cloth, leaving a 1-inch end. Take another stitch in the same place, making a 1-inch loop. Repeat, making a double loop. Cut the thread, leaving a 1-inch end.

Carefully separate the two layers of cloth until a stitch appears on each outer side (a). This will hold the tufts in place. Clip the thread between the layers. This produces tufts on the right side of the fabric (b). Carefully remove the pattern.

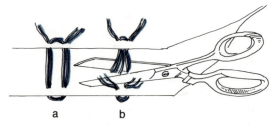

a   b

The trick in successful tailor's tacks is not to cut the loops until the layers of fabric have been separated. If you cut them before, the tufts will pull out as you separate the two thicknesses.

If the fabric is too thick to make tailor's tacks through both layers, make them through the upper layer first. Push the needle through the center of the first tacks to mark the position of those on the underside. Make the tailor's tacks where indicated on the undersurface. *See* MARKING METHODS.

TAPE. A narrow strip of firmly woven cotton, linen, or rayon used to stay seams and reinforce those subject to stress or stretching.

There are several types. Woven-edge seam binding, firm and nonstretchable, has many uses in dressmaking. Twill tape is used especially in tailoring. Bias rayon or cotton bindings come in varying widths with edges prefolded. They are suitable for curved edges or straight ones that require a little more give than seam binding or twill tape may provide. *See* SEAM BINDING; BIAS BINDING; TWILL TAPE.

TAPED FOLD LINE. Any fold line that needs to be stayed is taped. For instance, the fold line of a vent or hem when it is not interfaced, or the fold line of a knit or other stretchy fabric at a facing cut in one with the garment or at a placket.

Cut the necessary length of preshrunk tape. Align one edge of the tape with the fold line. (The other edge rests in the seam allowance or foldback.) Pin or baste to position. Fasten both edges of the tape to the garment with small, invisible slant hemming or catch stitches (q.q.v.). Use a single length of matching thread. Lift only one thread of the outer fabric. Keep the stitches "easy."

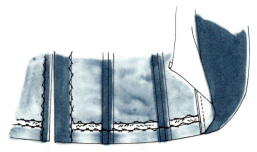

TAPED ROLL LINE OF LAPEL. Measure the lapel roll line from neckline to front seam line. Cut a length of preshrunk tape to this measurement minus 1/4 to 1/2 inch. (Some schools of tailoring end the taping

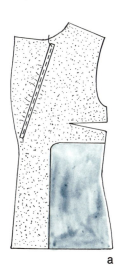
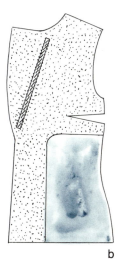

a   b

one third of the way up from the front edge.)

Align the outer edge of the tape with the roll line of the lapel. The rest of the tape extends inward, toward the garment. This setting stays the roll line but does not interfere with the roll. Starting at the neckline seam, pin or baste the tape flat for a distance of about 4 inches. Pull the remainder of the tape taut. Pin or baste to position (a). This tends to throw the lapel back into a soft roll.

Pad-stitch both edges of the tape and, after removing the pins or basting, down the middle of the tape (b).

For taping the outside edges of the lapel, *see* TAPING METHOD OF ELIMINATING HAIR CANVAS FROM OUTSIDE SEAMS.

TAPED SEAM. Which seams are stayed depends on the character of the fabric and the styling and fit of the garment. Those most usually stayed are the shoulder, the neckline, and the waistline. However, tape should be used in any seam if there is the possibility of strain or stretch as at an armhole.

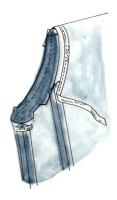

When tape is used to stabilize a seam, use a woven-edge or twill tape 1/4 to 1/2 inch wide. If the seam requires some give, use bias tape. Preshrink the tape. Cut it to the exact length of the seam.

TAPE INCLUDED IN A SEAM

Straight Seam. Cut the preshrunk tape to the necessary length. Center it over the seam line of *one* layer of fabric. Pin or baste. Stitch the seam with the tape side up through all thicknesses (a).

Curved Seam. Preshape the tape. Center it over the seam line. Pin or baste it in position and stitch through all thicknesses with the tape side up (b).

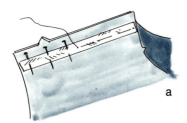

a

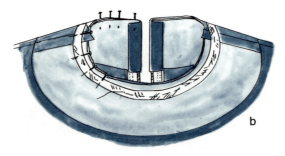

b

TAPE NOT INCLUDED IN A SEAM
Place the tape in the seam allowance with one edge beside the seam line. Stitch along the edge closest to the seam through the seam allowances (a). Trim the seam allowances even with the tape.

a

b

TAPE UNDER A TOPSTITCHED SEAM
This method is used to stabilize a seam, especially in knits. Use a wide tape. Center it over the opened seam allowances on the wrong side. Baste each edge through the seam allowance and the garment. Topstitch each side of the seam, including the tape in the stitching (b). Trim the seam allowances even with the tape.

Bias tape provides flexibility and prevents seam slippage in raschel and other open-structured or stretchy knits.

Cut a length of rayon bias tape through the center (a). Open the fold and place it over the seam line. Stitch through the crease of the tape and the seam line of the garment (b). The seam may be a plain seam pressed open. Or refold the tape toward the seam allowances. Trim the seam allowances even with the tape. Press them all in the same direction. Finish with a row of zigzag or overedge stitching through the tape and seam allowances (c).

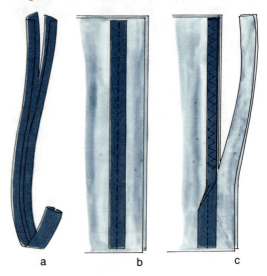

a   b   c

TAPE FASTENERS. *See* SNAP TAPE; HOOK AND EYE TAPE; NYLON TAPE FASTENERS.

TAPE GUARD (LINGERIE STRAP GUARD). Available commerically or make your own of narrow tape, seam binding, or ribbon.

Sew the socket half of a snap to the underside of the shoulder seam. Place it about 3/4 inch from the center of the shoulder toward the neck edge.

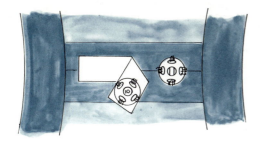

Cut a 2¼-inch length of tape. Turn under ½ inch of the tape and sew the ball half of the snap to the underside. Turn under ¼ inch of the other end of the tape and sew it to the shoulder seam toward the sleeve edge.

TAPING METHOD OF ELIMINATING HAIR CANVAS FROM OUTSIDE SEAMS OF TAILORED GARMENT.

Trim away ¾ inch of the hair canvas interfacing at the neck, lapel, and front edges. Preshrink a length of ⅜-inch twill or cotton tape to cover all your needs. If you are proficient in its use, you may use the narrower ¼-inch tape.

Cut a length of tape to fit the entire neckline from the tip of one lapel to the other (a). Cut a length of tape to fit each lapel-and-front edge. In a curved-bottom style line, bring the tape to the end of the interfacing (b). When the entire front sec-

tion is interfaced, bring the tape to the side or underarm seam (c). Pull the tape taut between the top and bottom buttons and around any lower curved style line (d). This tends to hold the garment against the body. (Taut means the tape is cut ¼ to ½ inch shorter than the actual measurement and is stretched to fit.) Tape is preshaped to fit any curved edge and is pressed smooth on all straight edges.

Apply the tape so the outer edge clears the seam line and rests on the outer fabric. The inner edge lies on the interfacing. The tape straddles the cut edge of the interfacing (a). Pin or baste to position. Apply the curved neck tape in the same way. Miter the tape at the corners (b) or overlap the cut ends.

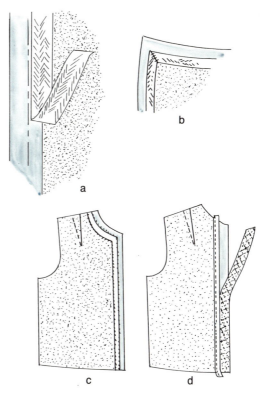

Using a single matching thread, hem the outside edge of the tape to the outer fabric with tiny, "easy," invisible hemming stitches, lifting only a single thread of the fabric at a time. Hem the inner edge of the tape to the interfacing (c). Catch only the interfacing. Do not come through to the garment fabric.

When joining garment sections, stitch *beside* the tape, not through it.

In some cases, it is possible to stitch the inner edge of the tape to the interfacing by machine before applying the interfacing to the outer (fashion) fabric (d). *See* STRIP METHOD OF ELIMINATING HAIR CANVAS FROM CONSTRUCTION SEAMS. However, be very sure that all needed adjustments (occasioned by the precise matching of seams and darts of fashion fabric and supporting material) have been made before the tape is set. *See also* CATCH-STITCH METHOD, FOLD-BACK METHOD.

TAUT STITCHING. A useful technique for stitching knits, bias, stretch, and synthetic fabrics. It also prevents seam puckering.

Pull the fabric evenly both behind the needle and in front of it as it feeds into the machine. Fingers exert a vertical pull on the seam.

THREAD. Because your garment is literally held together by a thread, it is very important that it be the right thread for the fabric. Ideally, the thread should be of the same fiber as the fabric so that it has the same tensile strength and elasticity. Use cotton thread for cotton fabrics; they are both vegetable fibers. Use synthetic thread, such as polyester, for synthetic fabrics; they are both man-made fibers. Use silk thread for silk and wool fabrics; they are both animal fibers.

In tailoring, use silk thread for all construction seams; it provides the necessary strength to hold the seams together for the life of the garment. Because of its elasticity, it can be molded with the fabric in shaped areas. Use mercerized cotton thread for all handwork. Its dull finish blends with the dull, dry finish of most woolens, particularly in places where the stitching is visible.

If silk thread in a matching color is hard to find (it grows increasingly so), use a good grade of mercerized cotton thread instead. In fact, you are safer with cotton thread for all sewing, since synthetic fibers may produce skipped stitches (q.v.).

Because thread works up a bit lighter than it appears on the spool, it is generally better to select a color that looks a shade or two darker than the fabric. However, if light striking the fabric produces a sheen and makes the color appear lighter (as in satin fabrics), select a color of thread a shade lighter than the fabric. The color on the spool may be a bit misleading. It is best to test a strand of the thread against your fabric. For multicolored prints or plaids, choose the dominant color. For tweeds or other mixed colors, choose the color tonality rather than attempting to match one of the colors.

Consider the weight of the fabric, too, in selecting your thread. Obviously, you would not sew a sheer fabric with a heavy thread; it would show as well as produce a bumpy appearance. Nor would you use a lightweight thread on a heavy fabric; it would not hold. Choose a weight of thread compatible with the weight of the fabric. It should imbed itself in the texture of the cloth.

The fineness or coarseness of thread is designated either by number (the higher the number, the finer the thread) or by letter (A, fine, to D, heavy). For hand sewing, thread may be strengthened by running it through beeswax. This is also a good way to prevent tangling and knotting.

For hand and machine sewing, thread the needle with the end cut from the spool. Don't tear thread. Those wispy filaments left by an uneven tear make it difficult to thread the needle.

There appears to be a thread for just about every purpose from toughest utility to finest decorative.

THREAD CARRIERS. This type of belt carrier (q.v.) is primarily used in garments of lightweight material. When made of thread that matches the garment in color, these loops are barely visible. Work as a thread chain (q.v.), a bullion-stitch loop (q.v.), or as several strands of thread covered with blanket stitches like a French tack (q.v.).

Buttonhole twist is stronger, but sewing thread run through beeswax may also be used. Make the carrier slightly longer than the width of the belt so it will pass through easily. The loop is centered over a cross seam when there is one.

THREAD CHAIN. A series of interlocking loops producing a chain that can serve many purposes—as a belt carrier, a thread eye, swing snap, button loop, French tack, and the like.

Use buttonhole twist, embroidery floss, silk thread, or a double thread of mercerized cotton run through beeswax. Fasten the thread securely on the underside with several short backstitches at the beginning point of the chain. Bring the thread through to the right side. Take a tiny (1/16-inch) stitch through the garment and draw the thread through to the surface so it forms a loop. Use either fingers or a crochet hook to crochet the chain.

With the Crochet Hook. Slip the hook through the loop. Wrap the thread around the hook. Draw it up tightly against the previous loop. Repeat until the chain is the desired length (a).

With Fingers. Hold the loop open with thumb and forefinger of the left hand while the right hand holds the supply thread taut with thumb and index finger (b). Using the second finger of the left hand like a crochet hook, pull the supply thread through the loop to form a new one (c). (The loops must be large enough for the fingers to reach through.) Draw up each new loop tightly against the previous one (d). Repeat to the desired length of the chain.

By Either Method. Finish by bringing the threaded needle through the last loop. Draw up the thread tightly to lock the chain. Fasten the end of the chain in a way appropriate for its use.

THREAD CHAIN GUARD (LINGERIE STRAP GUARD). Sew the socket half of a snap to the underside of the shoulder seam. Place it about 3/4 inch from the center of the shoulder toward the neck edge. Fasten the thread to one hole of the ball with several whipping stitches. Work a thread chain (q.v.) for 1 1/2 inches, or just long enough to enclose the lingerie straps comfortably. Fasten it to the shoulder seam toward the sleeve edge with several small backstitches. *See also* TAPE GUARD.

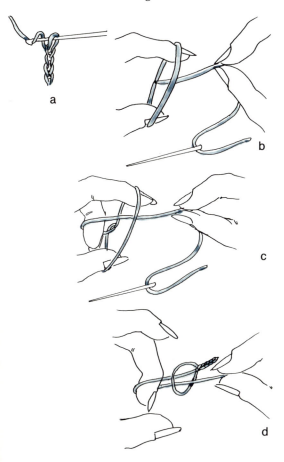

THREAD EYE. Used as a substitute for a metal eye in an exposed position. Since thread is not as strong as metal, use it only in areas where there is not too much strain. Use heavy-duty thread or buttonhole twist in a matching color.

The most usual and by far the strongest is the blanket-stitch eye (q.v.). The bullion-stitch loop (q.v.) can also function as a thread eye, as can a thread chain (q.v.).

A straight eye (a) is just long enough to accommodate the hook without pulling it

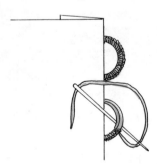

a   b

into a round eye or loop. The length of a round eye (b) depends on its use.

THREAD LOOPS. Similar to round thread eyes (q.v.). Thread loops are often used with buttons on dresses and blouses. Not only are they a more delicate touch than fabric loops or bound buttonholes, but there is no inner construction to show through transparent fabric.

Finish the closing edge. Determine the size and spacing of the loops and mark along the edge with pins or basting thread.

Use a single strand of matching thread. Fasten it on the underside of the material and bring the needle to the right side at the top marking for the loop. Take a stitch in the edge at the bottom marking, leaving a loop large enough to slip easily over the button. Make two or three more such stitches, drawing them up evenly. Work blanket or buttonhole stitches (q.q.v.) over the strands until they are completely covered. Secure the thread on the underside. Press the loops flat over a damp cloth to stiffen them and keep them from twisting.

THREAD TRACING (GUIDE BASTING). *(See* BASTING.) A line of uneven basting with long stitches on the right side of the garment and short stitches on the wrong side. It is generally made through a single thickness of fabric. Thread tracing is a useful way to transfer to the right side those markings made on the wrong side with dressmaker's carbon paper and tracing wheel.

There are many places throughout the construction of a garment where thread tracings are used to outline or designate the position of a pocket or decorative feature, a center line, a fold line, the roll line of a collar, and the like.

Use a single or double strand of thread, unknotted at the end. Start and end the stitching with backstitches.

TIE BELT. One of the simplest belts to make is the straight, turned belt tied in a bow, knot, or loop.

Determine the length of the belt—waist measurement plus the amount of the loop, knot, or bow. Cut a strip of fabric (self- or contrasting) on either straight or bias grain, twice the finished width by the length of the belt plus seam allowances.

Depending on the fabric used, the design of the garment, or one's preference, the belt may be free of stiffening, be interfaced only to that portion that encircles the waist (a), or be interfaced throughout. The interfacing may be as soft or stiff as you wish.

To stiffen a washable belt, use a washable interfacing or an extra layer of self-fabric. To stiffen a nonwashable belt, use any interfacing that will provide the chosen effect. *(See* BELT INTERFACED.)

If the fabric is bulky or heavy or if there is insufficient material for a double width, face the belt with lightweight fabric, grosgrain ribbon, or French belting in the same way in which one would a waistband (q.v.).

Fold the belt lengthwise with right sides inside. Pin and stitch carefully without twisting, keeping lengthwise and crosswise grains at right angles. Off-grain pulling and wrinkling disfigure a belt. Stitch across both ends and along the long edge, leaving an opening at the center for turning (a). Measure for even width throughout the length.

Press seams open over a pointed dowel stick or a hand-held point presser (q.v.) inserted in the opening. Trim seam allowances 1/8 to 1/4 inch. Free corners of bulk. Turn to the right side through the opening, being sure to work out the corners. Turn in

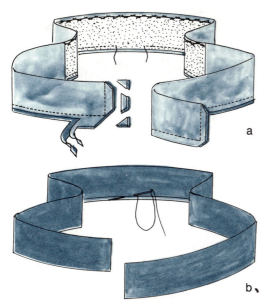

Cut the collar in one piece and fold it lengthwise. If there is unsufficient fabric for this or if the tie is shaped, cut the collar in two pieces—collar and facing.

When interfacing is used, it is generally the collar only that gets interfaced. Cut out the interfacing. Trim away all its seam allowances. If a two-piece collar, attach the interfacing to the collar with catch stitching along the seam lines. If a one-piece collar, catch-stitch along the neck seam line and tack along the fold line.

With right sides inside, stitch each tie to the point where it will join the garment. Leave the neck edge free. Clip the seam allowance at the point where collar and garment meet (a). Trim and grade the seam allowances. Free all corners of bulk. Turn

the seam allowances at the opening and slip-stitch (b). Edge-baste. Press.

Topstitching when the belt is completed adds firmness.

This same method works for shaped or contour tie belts.

TIE COLLAR. A turnover (a) or standing collar (b) that ends in a tie.

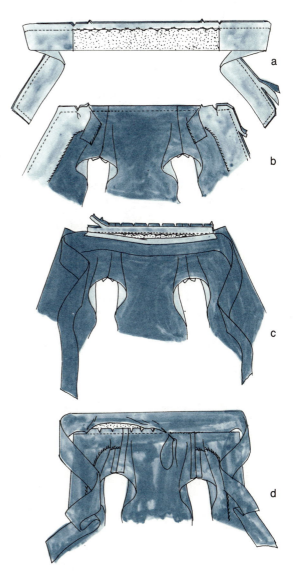

the collar and ends to the right side, working out any corners carefully.

Stitch the front facing to the garment to the point where it meets the collar. Clip to the stitching (b). Trim and grade the seam allowances. Free the corners of bulk. Turn and press. Baste the garment and facing neck edges together.

Pin, baste, then stitch the interfaced edge of the collar to the garment (c). *Note:* the collar joins the garment a little beyond center front, allowing space to tie the knot. Trim, grade, and clip the seam allowances. Press them toward the collar. Turn under the seam allowances of the open edge of the collar (facing) and bring the fold to the seam line. Slip-stitch in place (d).

TIE TACK. *See* SWING TACK.

TIE THREAD ENDS. A way of securing thread at the end of a line of machine stitching where a precise end is necessary. Back-and-forth lock stitching may not be accurate enough in some places. Even if it is, the several rows of stitching it produces may leave the area too stiff.

Draw up the thread so both ends are on the underside. Tie in a square knot: right over left, left over right.

TIGHT ARMHOLE. *See* ARMHOLE PATTERN CORRECTIONS.

TIGHT NECKLINE. *See* NATURAL NECKLINE PATTERN CORRECTIONS.

TOPSTITCHED HEM. A decorative finish for a narrow or wide hem.

Mark, turn up, and baste the hemline close to the fold. Edge-finish the upper edge of the hem. Make certain that the grain lines of hem and garment are aligned or the rows of topstitching will be pulled off-grain. Topstitch from the right side. Use as few or as many rows of topstitching (q.v.) as is consistent with the design of the garment.

TOPSTITCHED WAISTBAND. The procedure for this construction is the reverse of that for the standard waistband.

Stitch the right side of the under band to the wrong side of the skirt or pants (a).

a   b

Trim, grade, and clip the seam allowances. Press them open, then into the band.

Fold the all-in-one-piece band or turn the separate band-and-facing waistband so the right sides are together. Stitch across the ends. Press the seam allowances open over the point presser. Grade them. Free the corners of bulk.

Turn the band to the right side. Fold the all-in-one band lengthwise along the fold line, keeping it even from seam to fold. Pin or baste to position. When upper and under bands have been joined by a seam, roll it to the underside. Press and baste to position.

Turn under the seam allowance of the loose edge. Overlap the folded edge of the band on the right side of the garment, covering the seam line. Pin or baste to position. Topstitch through all thicknesses (b). Sew on the fastenings.

TOPSTITCHED WINDOW BUTTONHOLE. (For use on Ultrasuede, Leather, or Leatherlike Fabrics.)

On the wrong side of the fabric, mark the location and opening of the buttonhole with pencil or chalk. (To ensure uniformity when there is more than one buttonhole, use a buttonhole stencil [q.v.] for tracing the opening.) Cut it out with a sharp blade (a). Trim away 1/8 inch of the interfacing along the opening edge so it won't show.

Make the buttonhole lips. *(See* BOUND BUTTONHOLE: WINDOWPANE METHOD.) Center the lips under the opening on the wrong side. Anchor them with basting tape or fusible web.

Topstitching to hold the lips in place permanently (b) may be done now through garment and lips, or through all

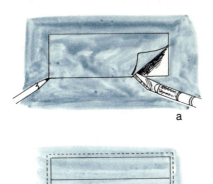

a

b

thicknesses after the facing has been fused on the underside. Remove basting tape.

To finish the underside of the button-hole, a similar opening must be made on the facing directly under the right-side opening. Fuse the facing in place.

TOPSTITCHING. A line of decorative hand or machine stitching that emphasizes the architecture of the design while at the same time holding several layers of material together permanently.

Since it is a feature of the design, use whatever kind of stitching, whatever stitch size, as many rows as close to or as far from the edge as desired, and whatever thread will be most effective. The thread may be matching, contrasting, thick, thin, buttonhole twist, embroidery floss, polyester-spun topstitching thread, single or double strands of mercerized cotton or silk thread.

To create a double thread on a single-needle sewing machine, use the single thread from each of two bobbins set one over the other on the spool holder. On a two-needle sewing machine, use the single thread from each of two spools set on the two spindles. Thread as usual, through one needle, as if the double were a single thread.

In machine topstitching, the decorative thread is generally used for the upper threading and the thread used for the rest of the garment is used for the bobbin. In styles where the fabric reverses itself—for instance, the front closing and lapel of a tailored garment or a convertible collar—the same decorative thread is used for both bobbin and upper thread.

Use a topstitching needle, size 18 (large eye), or one of the self-threading kind that can take thicker thread. Adjust the tension. When using buttonhole twist, increase the needle tension slightly.

Topstitching may be done when the garment is completed, as it would be around the edges of a finished garment. Often, however, it must be done during construction, either because it is easier or because it is more logical. Your pattern directions will indicate this. In either case, baste all layers of fabric together so they won't slip during the topstitching. One line of basting close to the edge is usually enough. If topstitching is to be more than 1/2 inch or more from the edge, make a second line of basting just outside the topstitching line to prevent off-grain pulling.

There are a number of devices for guaranteeing that the stitching is an even distance from the edge.

Mark with thread tracing.

Mark with gummed tape designed for this purpose.

Use the gauge on the throat plate of the machine.

Use a quilting foot.

In machines with a zigzag stitch, set the bight (needle position) over as far as it will go in either direction that is suitable. Keep the presser foot aligned with the edge of the garment.

When the stitching is finished, draw the ends of the thread through to the wrong side. You may tie them in a square knot. Safer yet, thread a needle with the ends and weave them into the topstitching for a few stitches.

In hand topstitching, one of several stitches may be used including: saddle stitch or seed stitch (q.q.v.).

TRIAL FITTING. *See* TRIAL MUSLIN.

TRIAL LAYOUT. A way of preventing the disaster of cutting for most of the length of fabric only to find, as one nears the end, that there is not quite enough material to finish.

Place the fabric on a flat surface. Line up its straightened edges with the straight edges of the cutting surface. Place the pattern in the position indicated on the layout chart.

Start at one end of the fabric. Support the weight of the rest of the cloth at the other end on the cutting table, an ironing board, or a chair. This prevents the pull on the cloth by its own weight. When the pattern pieces have been temporarily pinned to the material in the end area, fold the finished end to make room on the flat surface for the new part.

Place the grain of the pattern parallel to the selvage of the material. Place the pattern pieces close to each other. Spaces between may result in a shortage of as much as five or six crucial inches. This could mean the difference between being able to get the pattern out of the length of cloth and not.

Arrange the pattern pieces so that, if any fabric is left, it will be in one usable piece, either at an end or in the middle. You may find use for a larger piece—a hat, bag, scarf, or trimming. Otherwise you may accumulate pounds of unusable scrap.

Since this is only a trial, use as few pins as will give the information you want. If changes need to be made, it won't take hours to unpin. If the trial layout reveals there is not enough material, there are a number of things you can do.

Make smaller seam allowances and/or a narrower hem. Piece the material. Face or trim in another color or fabric. Combine with another texture: suede, real or make-believe; leather; knitted sections. Eliminate the cloth waistband of the skirt or pants. Use another material for the waistband or its facing. Consider a fabric-faced waistline (q.v.) instead. Eliminate or change some detail. For instance, patch pockets could become bound pockets or welt pockets, both of which take less material.

If you are impossibly short of fabric, give up. Get another pattern with fewer pattern pieces and less detail. Or buy more material (if you can get it).

TRIAL MUSLIN. Mathematical calculations and pattern corrections alone cannot guarantee the fine fit of a garment. They can only provide an approximation of your figure needs. There is this to consider, too: becomingness of style, ease of movement, posture, and individualized shaping can only be truly judged in cloth. Since only minor changes can be made once the garment cloth is cut, a test garment can save a lot of grief.

Do you always need to make a test garment? If you are sure of a particular style, know from experience how to adjust the pattern, have sufficient material to recut if necessary, have sufficient seam allowance to borrow in emergencies, then the test may not be necessary. But if you have any doubts at all about the style or the fitting, or have insufficient fabric to afford the luxury of mistakes, then do make a trial muslin.

The best general test material is muslin, bleached or unbleached, in a weight comparable to that of the fashion fabric. Any other solid-color material of similar weight will do as well. A plain surface will clearly show all seams, darts, and style details. All fitting adjustments will be highly visible.

If the fabric of the garment-to-be is sheer or if the design calls for drapery, use a soft, lightweight fabric for testing, like voile or batiste.

If the garment is to be of knit fabric, test fabric should be a knit, too, since knits fit differently from the way woven cloth does. Use an inexpensive tricot.

For testing the leathers or leather look-alikes, use a nonwoven material that best simulates the texture of your projected garment.

Since you will not be cutting out the entire pattern and since there may be discrepancies in width between the test fabric and the fashion fabric, you will need to devise your own layout chart. *See* LAYOUT CHART OF YOUR OWN DEVISING.

The test garment is a shell with no double thicknesses anywhere. You will not need facings, pockets, or applied trimmings unless they are essential for the completion of a pattern unit. Use the undercollar only, cut on the suggested grain.

Lay out, cut, and mark your test fabric with as much care as you would your fashion fabric. *See* PATTERN PREPARED FOR CUTTING; FABRIC PREPARED FOR CUTTING; CUTTING OUT A GARMENT; MARKING METHODS.

Put the trial muslin together. The quickest way to get the effect of the finished garment without actually stitching it is to *overlap and pin* all seam lines. Pinning gives the information we want. It is so much faster and easier to unpin and repin than to rip stitching and then join the muslin again.

Work with the marked side up. Clip all curved seams; otherwise you will be fitting on the outside edges rather than the fitting lines. Take full seam allowances.

Generally pins are placed lengthwise along the seam. If necessary, they may be placed at right angles to the seam to facilitate a turnover, as at the center back of the undercollar. Use whatever direction won't stab you when trying on the garment.

Pin up all hems to get the general effect of the garment and to determine whether any further changes in length are necessary.

In *testing pants,* basting rather than pinning is advisable. Baste the inseams first. Baste the crotch seam. Clip the crotch seam allowance. Pin the outseams. Baste the waistband in place. (It is hard to judge the fit of pants without suspending them from something; the same is true of a skirt.)

Now let's see how the muslin looks and fits! You must make allowances for the difference between your test fabric and your chosen fabric, but you can quickly tell whether the style is a good one for you. Many a sewer has been known to abandon a pattern upon seeing herself in the muslin and finding how impossible it is to make it fit with even a modest degree of flattery.

Study the muslin for line, proportion, fullness; size; shoulders, neckline, collar; set of sleeves. Decide whether you will keep all the style details or eliminate some of them.

Fitting is fitting whether it be in your test material or in your chosen fabric. All the elements that constitute good fit for one are the same for the other. *See* FITTING.

When the test garment has been fitted to your satisfaction, any *corrections* made on it *must be transferred to the pattern.* It's the paper pattern one uses for the cutting out of the fashion fabric, not the test fabric. That can be too easily forced out of size or shape or off grain in an effort to make it fit the fabric. You can't play tricks with paper. Since it won't budge, the cutting is accurate.

Wherever you have made a change, mark both edges of the new seam line with colored chalk or pencil. You may add your own notches wherever they will prove helpful in reassembling the parts of the pattern. For instance, you may need a new shoulder marking on the sleeve cap if you have made any change from its original position. The repositioning of a seam or the relocation of a dart makes the original notches invalid.

Take the muslin apart. Draw new seam or dart lines to correct any "jumpiness" of the pin markings. Straight lines can be drawn with a ruler. Curved lines can be traced from the original pattern or drawn with an appropriate drafting instrument.

Study the corrected pattern. You may find that the right and left sides are not identical. If the difference is slight, it may simply mean that it has been too difficult by eye to fit both sides alike. In this case, balance the changes, center the darts and equalize them.

If the difference is great, both left and right sides must be considered. It will simplify matters considerably if you use the larger size for cutting so that you will always have enough material to work with. (This is because patterns generally come to you in halves to be cut in twos or on a fold.) Use the smaller side as a fitting guide.

Place the paper pattern over the muslin, matching key lines. Trace the corrections so they will be clearly visible. Add paper if necessary. Trim away what is unnecessary. Make your new pattern a complete record of any alterations that will make the garment fit you.

This corrected pattern is used not only for cutting out the fashion fabric but as a basis for adjusting all facings, interfacings, underlining, interlining, and linings.

TRICOT KNIT. A single-, double-, or triple-warp knit construction. Because of the interlocking yarns, the double- and triple-warp knits are runproof while the single knits are not.

Tricot knits are usually made of fine cotton or synthetic yarns: nylon, a blend of nylon and acetate, or triacetate. Some stretch tricot fabrics contain spandex yarns, which provide some light figure control. Surfaces may be smooth, satinlike, crepelike, or napped. Fine vertical ribs are visible on the right side while flat, herringbone courses appear on the wrong side.

Tricots are produced in 108-inch widths, often cut into narrower widths for easy handling. They range in weight from sheer to heavy. Many have soft draping qualities that make them appropriate for lingerie and loungewear. (*See* LINGERIE: TRICOT KNIT.) Some appear as backing for laminated fabrics.

The *sheer tricots* resemble chiffon and are used for the outer layers of nightgowns and peignoirs, for underlining lace sections, for insertions, and for edge trims.

Medium-weight tricots are used for panties, slips, nightgowns, pajamas, chemises, underlayers of sheer-topped nightgowns and peignoirs or any other lingerie designed for a two-layer construction.

Heavy tricots are used for robes, pajamas, and opaque slips.

Brushed nylon tricots are suitable for warm robes and pajamas.

Treat tricot as a knit (q.v.).

TRIM A CORNER. *See* CORNER TRIMMED.

TRIM A DART. Deep darts or darts in medium-to-heavy fabrics require trimming.

After stitching, slash the dart open as far as the points of a pair of sharp trimming scissors will go—about 1/2 inch short of the dart point; more or less as necessary. Snip across the unslashed end of the dart almost to the seam line. Trim the rest of the dart to a width appropriate for the fabric. Press the dart open where slashed and to one side where unslashed.

TRIMS AND TRIMMINGS. When it comes to trims and trimmings, the sky's the limit! In design, there may be some basic rules, but in the end anything goes—if it works.

Trimmings are intended to enrich a design. A little may go a long way to make a fashion point. Too elaborate a trimming may detract or distort the basic structure and style line of a garment. In general, elaborate trims are reserved for simple garments. Simple trims are all that is necessary on elaborate garments. Whatever the trim, it should be consistent with the style lines of the garment and the already ornamented surface of the fabric.

Don't be limited by the obvious sources of trims. Investigate those of upholstery and drapery departments, millinery supplies—hardware stores, if desirable—anywhere you can come across a bit of this or that which may enhance what you are making.

Trimming may be incorporated in the construction of the garment or it may be applied after it is completed.

TROUSER BELT LOOPS. Made of trouser fabric cut on straight grain in the same way as other fabric carriers (q.v.).

Each strip is twice the width of the finished carrier plus seam allowances. The finished width is usually between ³/₈ and ³/₄ inch. The wider carriers are necessary to support the weight of heavy belts. Each loop is equal in length to the finished waistband (generally between 1³/₈ and 1³/₄ inches) plus seam allowances plus enough extra ease for the belt to pass through easily. *See* BELT CARRIERS. To attach, *see* TROUSER WAISTBAND.

TROUSER CREASE LINES. *See* PRESSING PANTS.

TROUSER CUFFS. To cuff or not to cuff trousers depends largely on the weight of the fabric.

Trouser cuffs on lightweight material weights the fabric so the trouser leg hangs straight. Sports slacks, though of lightweight material, are exceptions. Cuffs on them could end up being a depository for sand, grass, or gravel.

Heavier materials (tweeds, for instance) hang well on their own and look better without cuffs.

When the Pattern Design Includes Cuffs. Make all the pattern corrections necessary in the waist-to-crotch area. Fold the cuff in the pattern as designated. Mea-

sure the inseam and outseam of the pants leg. Adjust as necessary.

Cut the trousers from the adjusted pattern. Mark the hemline of the trousers, the fold line, and turnup line of the cuff (a).

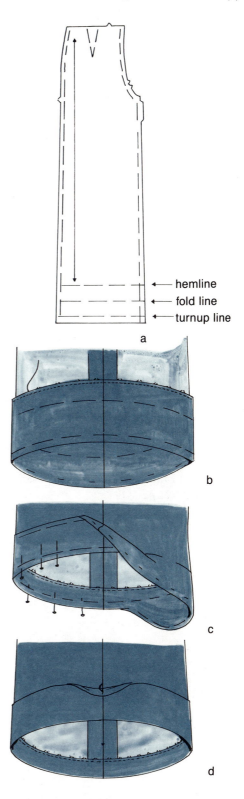

a

b

c

d

Stitch the trouser seams and press the seam allowances open. Trim them below the cuff fold line to half width. Edge-finish the cut edge of the trousers as desired.

Turn the hem allowance to the wrong side along the fold line. Baste close to the folded edge. Fasten the hem allowance to the pant legs in a tailor's hem, a machine blindstitched hem (q.q.v.) or a line of regular machine stitching (b). The latter will not show when the cuff is turned.

Turn the garment right side out. Form the cuff by turning it up along the marked turnup line. Pin, then baste close to the fold through all thicknesses (c). Press lightly. To hold the cuff in place, make a French tack (q.v.) between the cuff and the trouser leg at the seams, 1/2 inch below the top edge of the cuff (d). Remove all bastings and press.

To Add Cuffs to a Pattern (that does not include them): Decide on the depth of the cuff. Double the measurement and add a hem allowance that is 1/2 inch less than the cuff width.

Tape a length of paper to the hemline of the trousers. Measure down from the hemline the cuff width and mark the fold line. Measure down an equal amount and mark the turnup line of the cuff. Measure down the amount of the hem allowance and draw the cutting line.

Shape the cuff slightly at the fold line, adding enough width to allow for a smooth turnup over the trouser leg. *(See* TURNBACK CUFF.*)*

Fold the pattern to position for the cuff along the fold line and the turnup line. Draw the seam lines for the cuff, making them extensions of the trouser seam lines. Add seam allowances. Open out the pattern.

This method will work equally well on straight or shaped trousers.

TROUSER CURTAIN. A pleat at the lower edge of the waistband lining falling below the waistline seam. It conceals the stitching and pocket construction at the waistline.

There is a commercially available as-semblage called men's waistbanding that consists of lining, interfacing, and trouser curtain.

To Make Your Own Trouser Curtain: Cut a waistband lining, making it 2 1/2 inches wider than the finished waistband. Baste the interfacings to the wrong side of the lining. Baste along the pleat roll line at the lower long edge of the interfaced lining—about 1 1/2 inches from the raw edge (a). Turn under the long edge along the roll line, baste (b), then press. Leave the top edge of the pleat open for a standard application. *(See* TROUSER WAISTBAND WITH TROUSER CURTAIN.*)* Or baste along the top edge of the pleat and include both thicknesses in the waistband seam.

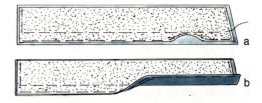

TROUSER HEMS. Set the trouser hems so they touch the shoes in front without breaking and reach the heel seams in back.

Turn up the trouser hems and baste at the folded edges. Measure and trim the hems evenly to a depth of 2 inches. Overcast the raw hem edges and attach to the trousers in a tailor's hem (q.v.). Or turn under and edge-stitch the raw edges and attach to the trouser legs with blindstitches. Press on the right side, protecting the fabric as necessary. *See also* TROUSER CUFFS.

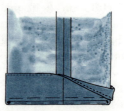

TROUSERS WITH TAILORED WAISTBAND. *(See* TROUSER WAISTBAND.*)* Cut the waistbands of trouser fabric on the lengthwise grain. Make each as long as the measurement from the edge of the fly front to the center back plus seam allowances. This will make them different lengths for right and left sides.

Cut two interfacing pieces the length and width of the waistbands on bias grain. Use any firm interfacing material (heavy canvas, buckram, or the like). Special waistband interfacings are available in a variety of widths and textures, either washable or dry-cleanable. Trim off the front and center back seam allowances on each one.

Cut a facing for each waistband of lining or pocketing to the same length and width as each waistband. This, too, may be cut on the bias for easy fit around the waist.

Baste the interfacing pieces to the underside of the right and left waistbands (a). Make the belt carriers (q.v.) and position them on the right side of the interfaced waistband, keeping all raw edges even at the top and bottom (b). Baste to position.

With right sides together, pin the facings to the waistbands along the upper edges only. Machine-stitch (c). Trim and grade all seam allowances. Press toward the facing.

Open out the waistband and facing. With the facing side up, understitch it to the graded seam allowances close to the seam line (d). Turn the facing to the inside, setting the seam down 1/4 inch from the fold, and press.

The tops of the pockets may be caught in the waistline seam but a preferable method (since it avoids bulk in the seam) is to fold them down and pin them out of the way (a).

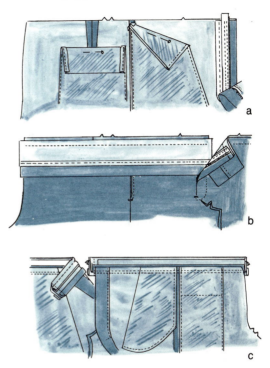

Open out the facings. Pin the waistbands to the trousers, easing pants to fit the waistbands. Machine-stitch (b).

Turn the pockets to position and baste the top edges over the waistline seam. Machine-stitch the pockets through the center of the waist seam allowances. Trim and grade them.

With right sides of facing and waistband together, stitch across the fly ends (c). Trim and grade the seam allowances. Clip diagonally across the corners. Turn and press.

Pin and stitch each trouser leg on the inseam from hem to crotch. Press the seams open. With right sides together, pin and stitch the crotch seam (q.v.) from the base of the fly, along the center back seam, and continuing through the waistband and its opened-out facing (a). This makes it easier to make any waist alterations. Often the top 1 to 1 1/4 inches of the back seam is left open in a "V" shape for comfort.

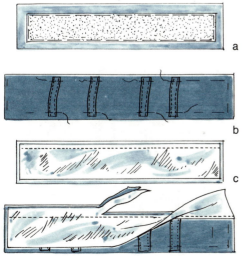

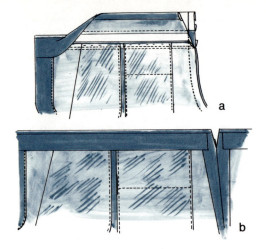

Turn the facing to the inside. Turn under the seam allowance of the loose edge. Position it over the waistline seam and slip-stitch or topstitch in the seam groove (b).

TROUSER WAISTBAND. While methods of construction of trouser waistbands may vary, they all have the following in common. They are made in two pieces—a right and a left waistband. Each consists of an outer layer of pants fabric, a tough, non-stretchable interfacing, a lining (facing) of pocketing or similar closely woven material. In addition, there may also be a stiffener and a trouser curtain. Each of these layers may be cut individually and assembled. Or the waistband may be constructed with men's waistbanding, a commercially available assemblage. *See* TROUSERS WITH TAILORED WAISTBAND; TROUSER WAISTBAND WITH MEN'S WAISTBANDING; TROUSER WAISTBAND WITH TROUSER CURTAIN. *See also* TROUSER WAISTBAND WITH ELASTIC.

TROUSER WAISTBAND WITH ELASTIC. A no-roll, woven spandex functioning as both facing and interfacing can be used in trousers of knit fabric. The elastic is sold by the yard in 1½- to 2½-inch widths. The width of the available elastic determines the width of the waistband.

Cut left and right waistbands of trouser fabric. Make them 1¼ inches wider (two seam allowances) than the elastic. The length of the waistband equals the waistline seam of each half of the trousers plus

an extension on the left waistband equal to the zipper fly facing and a seam allowance on the right waistband.

Cut the elastic the length of each waistband, minus the zipper facing on the left and minus both seam allowances at center back. If the front edge has an extension, cut the elastic only to the fly stitching line.

With right sides up, lap the ribbed edge of the elastic ¼ inch over the long edge of each waistband. Use a small zigzag or stretch stitch (a). With right sides together, stitch each waistband to the trousers. Trim and grade the seam allowances.

Turn the elastic to the inside, bringing the joining seam ¼ inch below the fold. On the *left front,* trim away the elastic over the zipper (b). Fold the facing extension to the underside. Turn under all seam allowances and slip-stitch (c). On the *right front,* turn the elastic to the outside. With right sides of waistband and elastic together, stitch across the end in a line with the edge of the trouser front (d). Trim and grade the seam allowances. Turn to the right side.

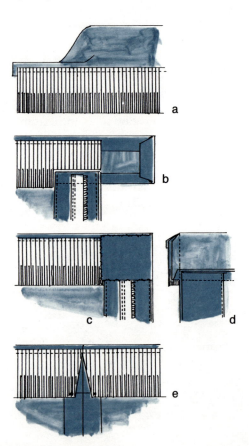

Open out the waistband and elastic at the center back. Stitch the back crotch seam, leaving the elastic unstitched. Turn the elastic to the inside in a wearing position. Turn in the ends of the elastic on a diagonal and tack to the seam allowances (e). Hand-stitch all inside free edges in place.

TROUSER WAISTBAND WITH MEN'S WAISTBANDING. (See TROUSER WAISTBAND.)

Cut the waistband sections of trouser fabric. Make the length equal to the waist seam line of left and right trouser sections plus seam allowances, and 1¼ inches wider than the facing part of the waistbanding.

Cut the men's waistbanding (comes with pleat) the same length as the waistband sections.

With right sides together, stitch each waistband section to each trouser section. Grade all seam allowances and press toward the waistband. Turn under ½ inch of the facing part of the waistbanding and press.

Sandwich the top of the waistband between the facing and interfacing. Pin in place. Topstitch close to the folded edge of the facing (a). Repeat for the other half of the waistband.

With right sides of waistbanding and waistband together, stitch across each front end. Grade the seam allowances. Snip diagonally across the corners (b). Turn to the right side and press.

Open out the waistbanding at center back. Stitch the crotch seam, starting at the top fold of the waistband. Press seam allowances open, continuing into the unstitched waistbanding (c). With right sides of waistband and waistbanding together, stitch across each back edge in the seam-line crease (d). Grade seam allowances. Clip diagonally across corners. Turn to the right side and press.

From the right side of the garment, stitch in the seam groove, making certain that the facing pleat is out of the way (e). Tack the pleat to the pockets and seam allowances around the trousers.

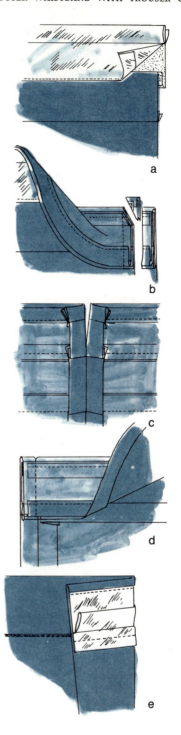

TROUSER WAISTBAND WITH TROUSER CURTAIN.
Cut the left and right waistbands of trouser material. If men's waistbanding is used, make the waistbands the width of the waistbanding minus curtain but plus seam allowances.

When used, make and position the belt loops on the right side of the waistband, keeping all raw edges even at top and bottom. (See TROUSERS WITH TAILORED WAISTBAND.) Baste to position.

On Men's Waistbanding. Turn under the seam allowance on the top edge of the facing. (Facing and interfacing are open at this end.) Position the top of the trouser waistband between the layers of facing and interfacing, lapping the fold of the facing 1/4 inch below the fold line of the waistband. With the facing side up, topstitch close to the folded edge of the facing through all thicknesses—facing, interfacing, and waistband (a).

a

b

a

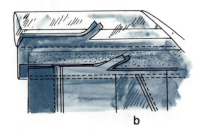

b

On Waistbanding of Your Own Make. With right sides together, pin and stitch the unfolded long edge of the facing to the top of the trouser waistband (b).

On Both Types. With right sides of waistband and facing or waistbanding together, stitch across the ends. Trim and grade the seam allowances. Clip diagonally across the corners (a).

Turn the facing to the inside. Baste it in place. It may be held in place permanently by machine-stitching on the right side through all thicknesses directly in the groove of the waistband seam (b) or by hand blindstitching on the underside along the waistline seam.

Fasten the trouser curtain to both edges of the side pockets and to the center of a back pocket.

TUBING: SELF-FILLED. A soft type in which the seam allowances are used for padding in place of cord, which produces a firm tubing. (See CORDED TUBING.)

Cut a 1- to 1¼-inch bias strip of sufficient length. Fold the strip lengthwise with right sides inside. Stitch to a width slightly wider than the desired width of the finished tubing. A degree of stretching occurs when the bias tubing is turned to the right side, thereby narrowing it somewhat. Make the beginning and ending of the tubing a little wider for easy turning.

Trim the seam allowances to a width a little wider than the finished tubing. A thin fabric requires wider seam allowances to fill the tube while heavy fabrics need narrower seam allowances. Pile fabrics like velveteen must be trimmed closely: pulling pile against pile makes the turning extremely difficult. Whatever the fabric, trim the first inch of the seam allowance quite close to the stitching to make it easier to start the turning against the self-fabric.

There are several ways of *turning the tubing to the right side.*

With a Blunt Needle or Bodkin. Thread the needle or bodkin with a short length of buttonhole twist or heavy-duty thread. Fasten it to one end of the tubing at the seam. Push the bodkin (or needle) through the tubing with the eye entering first (a).

Work needle and thread through the tubing as it gradually reverses itself to the right side (b).

a   b

With the Loop (TUBING) Turner (q.v.). With its hinged clasp first, push the turner through the tube to the opposite end. Pull the turner back slightly until the hook of the clasp catches some of the fabric (a).

With the clasp closing as you do so, draw the turner through the tube, reversing it to the right side (b).

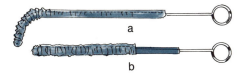

a

b

TUBULAR CORDING. *See* CORDED TUBING.

TUCKED SEAM: STRAIGHT OR CURVED.

Straight. Fold under one seam allowance and press. Overlap the folded edge on the other, matching raw edges and seam lines. Pin and/or baste. Topstitch on the right side an even distance from the fold (a).

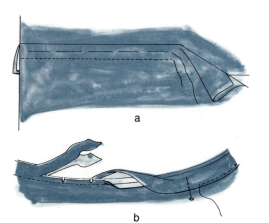

a

b

Curved. Face the curved edge of the top section. Grade the seam allowances, clip or notch as necessary, press the seam open. Turn the facing to the inside, rolling the joining seam to the underside, and press (b). Overlap the faced edge on the under section, matching seam lines. Pin and/or baste. Topstitch an even distance from the faced edge.

TUCK GAUGE. For accurate marking of tucks. Cut a strip of cardboard about a ruler's width and long enough to measure from the fold of one tuck to the fold of another plus an inch or so at the end. Cut the first notch to indicate the depth of the tuck, the second notch to indicate the fold of the next tuck.

Fold the first tuck as marked. Place the top of the gauge on the fold. Using the first notch as a guide, make a row of basting stitches parallel to the fold. Slide the gauge along as you stitch.

Using the second notch as a guide for the fold of the next tuck, mark it with a line of basting. Or, having determined the position of the next tuck with the gauge, draw a thread for the fold line instead of basting. *(See* TUCKS: MARKING.) Fold the tuck on the newly established fold line. Using the first notch of the gauge once more, mark the depth of the next tuck. Continue the procedure for each subsequent tuck. The basting acts as a guide for the stitching.

TUCKS. Stitched folds of fabric used to hold fullness in place or for purely decorative reasons. They may be very narrow, quite wide, or any width between. They may be used singly, in clusters, or in a series. The series may be of uniform or graduated width. Apart from the design, the beauty of tucks depends largely on accuracy in marking and stitching.

While generally done on the lengthwise grain of the fabric, which is firmer, tucks may also be made on the crosswise grain or on the bias. The latter two call for more careful handling because of the stretch factor. Nor need the tucks always be straight; they may be curved.

Often, it is simpler to pretuck the fabric before cutting. This would be true when working with plaids or striped material or when tucks are desired though the pattern doesn't call for them. *See* BIAS TUCKS; BLIND TUCKS; CORDED TUCKS; CROSS TUCKS; CURVED TUCKS; DART TUCK; OVERHANDED TUCKS; PIN TUCKS; RELEASED TUCK; SCALLOPED TUCKS; SHELL TUCKS; SPACED TUCKS; TUCKS WITH EDGINGS; TUCKS IN PLAID OR STRIPED FABRIC; TUCKS WHEN THE PATTERN DOESN'T CALL FOR THEM; TUCKED SEAM: STRAIGHT OR CURVED.

TUCKS IN PLAID OR STRIPED FABRIC.
Fold the fabric into tucks to take best advantage of the lines and colors of the material. Pin or baste to position. Cut from an untucked pattern and proceed as usual. *(See* TUCKS *and* TUCKS WHEN THE PATTERN DOESN'T CALL FOR THEM.)

TUCKS: MARKING. There are a number of methods for marking the position and depth of tucks, depending on whether they are to be formed on the outside or the underside of the garment and whether it is the fold lines or the stitching lines that are to be marked. Use the method that is easiest for you (considering the number of tucks to be marked) and that is most appropriate for the fabric. Use whatever measuring device will prove helpful. This may be a tuck gauge (q.v.), the throat plate markings of the sewing machine, a quilter-guide bar, a tucker, or an edgestitcher.

The most time-consuming method is to mark both stitching lines with tailor's tacks or thread tracing, but there are some fabrics on which no other method is safe.

The easiest method is to mark the first tuck from the pattern and the subsequent ones by the use of one of the measuring devices mentioned above. It also takes less time to mark the fold lines from the pattern and the depth of the tuck with a measuring device than to mark both stitching lines.

The following method is an accurate fold-line marking for sheer and lightweight fabrics. Pull a lengthwise or crosswise thread along the fold line of the tuck for its length. Fold along the drawn thread. It will be invisible in this position. Mark the depth of the tuck with a measuring device.

TUCKS: PIECING. If one width (or length) is not sufficient for all the tucks, piece the fabric.

Fold under and baste the tuck at the end

of the cloth for an overlap. Place it over the end of the under section of fabric, matching stitching lines. Pin and stitch along the tuck stitching line. Trim away any excess fabric on the underside, leaving a narrow seam allowance.

TUCKS: PRESSING. Press each tuck in the direction of the stitching from the right side but on the underside of the fold. Press all tucks in the direction in which they will be worn from the wrong side.

If right-side pressing is needed, use a press cloth. To prevent tuck imprints, use strips of brown wrapping paper as a cushion. *(See* PRESSING: PREVENT IMPRINTS.)

TUCKS: STITCHING. Fold the tuck along the fold line (when that is marked) or match the stitching lines (when they are marked). Pin and/or baste.

In right-side tucks, stitch from the side that will be seen. When tucks are balanced on either side of a center, this will mean reversing the direction of the stitching on one side.

For most purposes, use matching thread or a color that blends. For decorative purposes, use a contrasting color.

When stitching by hand, use very small running stitches (a). When stitching by machine, stitch beside the basting that marks the depth of the tuck (b). Use a balanced tension and a shorter stitch. Straight stitches are the ones generally used (c). For

a

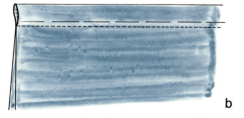

b

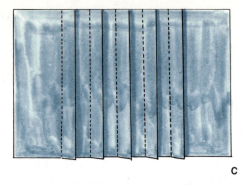

c

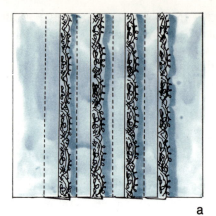

a

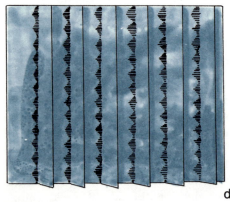

d

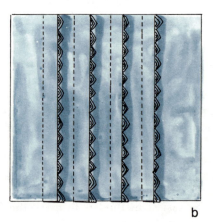

b

fancier tucks, use one of the decorative stitch patterns on the machine (d). It is a good idea to make a sample tuck so all adjustments can be made before working on the garment.

TUCKS WHEN THE PATTERN DOESN'T CALL FOR THEM. Determine the width of each tuck and the spacing between tucks. Multiply by the number of tucks to estimate the necessary yardage. Pretuck the fabric. Place the untucked pattern on the tucked fabric, taking best advantage of the tucking. Cut out the pattern section and proceed as usual. *See also* TUCKS *and* TUCKS IN PLAID OR STRIPED FABRIC.

TUCKS WITH EDGINGS. Tucks of themselves are a decorative feature of a design, but they can be further enhanced with lace edging (a) or rickrack (b).

Make a series or cluster of narrow tucks, leaving sufficient space between them for the width of the edging. Slip the edging under the fold of the tuck. Pin or baste to position. Stitch close to the fold. *See also* TUCKS.

TUNNEL OR SELF-SHANK BUTTON. A tunnel or hole is drilled through the base of the button. *See* BUTTON SHANK OR STEM.

TURNBACK BAND CUFF. A straight separate band of fabric makes a fine cuff. It may be cut on straight or bias grain, though the latter shapes better around the sleeve. Both are constructed in the same way. *See* BIAS CUFF.

TURNBACK CUFF. A cuff that rolls back to cover the base of the sleeve. It can be an extension of the sleeve, a separate band, or a shaped cuff.

The circumference of a cuff at its outer edge (fold line or seam) should be somewhat larger than the sleeve to which it is to be attached so that the cuff will stand away from the sleeve. How much circumference ease depends on the thickness of the material. Start with 1/2 inch and adjust as necessary.

To negotiate the turnback, there also should be sufficient length from the outside edge (style line) to the inside edge. The amount necessary depends on the weight and texture of the fabric.

In addition, the cuff itself should be larger than its facing to assure sufficient material to encircle the sleeve smoothly. Once more, the amount necessary depends on the weight and texture of the fabric.

Mark the turnback line of the cuff with thread tracing. In a one-piece cuff, mark the fold line as well. Apply the interfacing. *See* CUFF INTERFACING.

The construction of the turnback cuff will vary with the type. *See* TURNBACK BAND CUFF; TURNBACK CUFF: EXTENSION OF THE SLEEVE; TURNBACK SHAPED CUFF.

TURNBACK CUFF: EXTENSION OF THE SLEEVE.

The extension eliminates an extra seam and fits closely.

Before stitching the sleeve seam, mark the hemline, the fold line, and the turnback line of the cuff with thread tracing. Apply the cuff interfacing (a).

With right sides together, stitch the underarm seam of the sleeve and cuff. Press the seam allowances open and trim them below the fold line to half width. Finish the cuff edge in an appropriate manner (b). Turn the sleeve hem to the inside along the fold line (c). Baste close to the fold.

Turn the sleeve to the right side along the turnback line, allowing sufficient material for the roll. Pin, then baste through all thicknesses (a). Blind-hem the inside free edge to the sleeve (b). Remove all bastings. Press lightly.

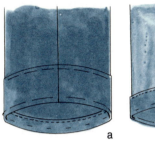 

VARIATIONS OF THIS CUFF

A *separate extension*, constructed in the same way, can be joined to the sleeve with a hemline seam (a). Press the seam allowances open.

A *separate facing* for either the sleeve extension or the separate extension provides opportunity for change of color, texture, or grain. Cut the pattern apart on the fold line. Add a seam allowance to each cut edge (b).

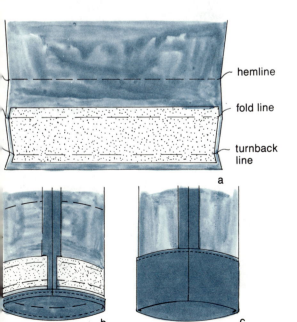

hemline
fold line
turnback line

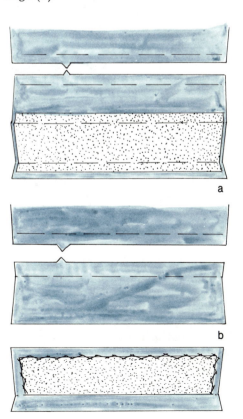

TURNBACK SHAPED CUFF. The shape may be anything from rounded or pointed edges to multishaped or scalloped style lines. Because of its shaped edges, this cuff requires a facing.

Construct the cuff (a). *(See* CUFF INTERFAC-ING *and* CUFF CONSTRUCTION.)

Stitch the sleeve seam and press it open. Slip the cuff over the right side of the sleeve, raw edges of sleeve and cuff matching. Baste in place just inside the seam line (b).

Finish the edges with a strip of bias binding (c) or a facing (d). Slip the facing or bias binding over the cuff and sleeve. Pin or baste in position. Stitch through all thicknesses along the seam line. Trim and grade the seam allowances. Press toward the facing or bias. Understitch the facing.

Roll the cuff to the outside and the facing or bias to the inside of the sleeve, favoring the cuff so the seam is hidden on the underside. Blindstitch the facing or hem the binding to the sleeve.

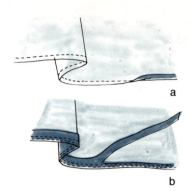

a second row of stitching close to the first. Trim away the excess fabric as close as possible to the stitching (b).

In *sheer fabrics,* use small stitches (15 to 20 per inch) and strips of tissue paper under the stitching where necessary to keep the fabric from stretching or puckering. Tear away the paper when the stitching is completed. *See also* EDGE FINISHES.

TURNED-UP HEM. This is the most usual type of hem and the one generally provided by a pattern. The hem allowance (an extension of the garment) is turned to the inside and stitched by hand (most often) or by machine. In some cases the hem may also be secured by fusing.

The pin-marked hemline arrived at in the hem setting (q.v.) is the fold line of the

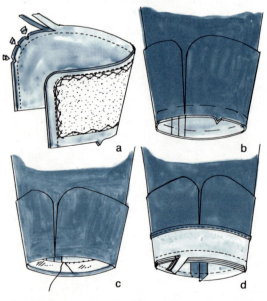

TURNED AND TOPSTITCHED HEM EDGE. One suitable for firm or sheer, nonravelly fabrics.

Run a line of machine stitching along the designated hemline. Turn up the hem along the line of stitching. Machine-stitch around the edge close to the fold (a). Make

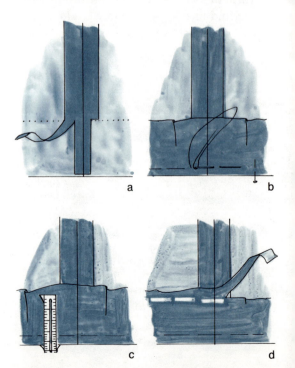

hem. Correct any irregularities in the pin marking. If you plan to sew the hem immediately and if they do not leave hole marks, the pins may remain. If not, substitute a line of thread tracing for the pins.

To reduce bulk in the hem area, trim the seam allowances to half width from the raw edge of the garment to the hemline (a).

Turn the hem to the inside of the garment along the marked hemline. Fix the fold line with pins placed at right angles and close to the fold. If pins will leave hole marks (better test your material), baste close to the fold with a fine needle and thread (b).

Using a gauge or ruler, measure an even distance from the fold line (c). Mark with chalk, pencil, or pins, depending on the color and texture of the fabric. Add a narrow seam allowance if you plan to use an edge finish that requires it. Trim the excess material (d).

Measuring and marking the hem depth is facilitated by working over an ironing board. Slip the garment over it wrong side out as if for pressing and proceed.

Ease out any fullness at the hem edge. (See HEM-EDGE FULLNESS REMOVED.) Finish the hem edge in any manner appropriate for the style and the fabric.

Pin the hem to the garment at all seam lines, center, and suitable intervals between. Distribute any fullness evenly between pins. As far as possible, match the grain of the hem and that of the skirt. Fasten the hem to the garment with hemming stitches (q.v.) or blindstitches (q.v.).

You'll be happy to learn that it's actually preferable to put up a hem with the least number of stitches that will do so securely. Since the stitches are never visible (or should not be), you do not need to perform as if you were in an embroidery contest.

TURTLENECK. A high turnover collar that hugs the throat. *See* BIAS TURNOVER COLLAR; RIBBED BANDING.

TWILL TAPE. A sturdy cotton tape woven in a herringbone design. It is used mainly for staying and strengthening seams. In tailoring, it is also used as a method of eliminating hair canvas from outside seams (q.v.).

Twill tape comes in black and white, in 1/4-inch, 3/8-inch, 1/2-inch, 3/4-inch, and 1-inch widths. The first three are those most generally used in clothing construction.

Tape should be preshrunk before use. Immerse it in hot water and let stand until it has thoroughly absorbed the moisture— about when the water cools. Allow it to dry naturally. It can be pressed to shape when used.

TWO-FABRICS REVERSIBLE. *See* DOUBLE-FACED FABRIC. In the two-fabrics reversible, two identical garments are completed separately, then joined on all outside edges.

Use the same pattern for both outside and inside garments. Stitch all seams and darts as usual since they will be concealed when the separate garments are joined. Interfacing is optional. Press and shape each of the two single layers. Stitch one collar to each neckline. Stitch one cuff to each sleeve. Stitch the sleeves into each of the layers.

For an Untrimmed Edge. Place the right sides of both completed garments together. Pin carefully. Stitch all except the hem edges. Press open, trim, and grade the seam allowances. Clip and notch as necessary. Turn to the right side.

With the outside seam directly on the edge, baste both layers together. Since both sides are to be used, there is no permanent underside, therefore it is unnecessary to observe the usual tailoring technique of favoring the upper layer.

Inside the two garments, join the sleeves and side seams with long, loose permanent basting stitches in the same way that a lining is attached to a garment.

Set the hem. Add seam allowances. Trim the excess. Turn under both seam allowances toward each other and slip-stitch along the edge. Baste so the outside seam is directly on the edge.

Press the garment carefully, using the

pounding block for a crisp edge wherever possible or desirable.

To hold all layers in place, finish with one or two rows of decorative top-stitching.

For a Trimmed Edge. Place the wrong sides of both completed garments together with raw edges aligned. Pin and/or baste the layers together on all outside edges. Machine-stitch through both thicknesses close to the seam line. Trim away the seam allowances of the outside edges. Apply binding (q.v.) or braid.

TWO-PIECE BACK INTERFACING PATTERN.

Because the movement of the arms is forward and the interfacing should not restrict this motion, many people prefer a two-piece back interfacing to the more usual one-piece type. Use muslin or any other lightweight woven interfacing material.

Trace the upper portion (waistline and above) of the complete back pattern. (If there are seams, overlap them to form a whole back.) Mark a point 1 inch to the side of the center back (either seam line or fold). Mark a point 2½ to 3 inches below the underarm seam line on the side farthest from your first point. Draw a curved line connecting these two points. If there are shoulder or neck darts in the original pattern, trace them on the interfacing pattern. Trace the grain line (a). Cut out the pattern. Place it on a double thickness of interfacing material and cut it out. Mark all seam lines and darts.

Construct any darts. Position the interfacing on the wrong side of the garment, aligning the outside edges and overlapping it at center back. Baste the interfacing to the garment around all outside edges (b). Proceed with the construction.

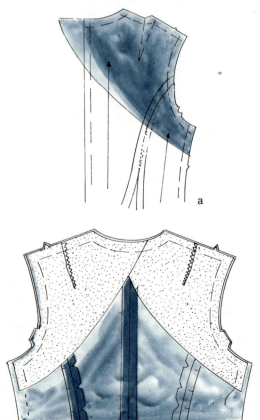

TWO-PIECE COLLAR.

One in which upper collar (collar) and undercollar (facing) are cut separately.

Cut out the collar and its facing. Remember to make the collar just slightly larger so that the joining seam may be rolled to the underside. Cut out the interfacing and apply it to the upper collar or undercollar as the fabric requires. (See COLLAR INTERFACING.)

With right sides together, pin, baste, then stitch both sections (upper and under) on all outside edges but leave the neck edge open. Press the seam allowances open; trim and grade them. Free corners of bulk. Clip or notch curved edges as necessary.

Turn the collar to the right side. Carefully work out corners. Press all outside edges, rolling the seam to the underside. To help keep the seam in place, understitch the enclosed seam allowances either by hand or by machine. End the stitching 1 inch each side of the corners. Or topstitch an even distance from the finished edge.

Attach the two-piece collar to the garment according to type—flat, rolled, or standing (q.q.v.). See also TAILORED NOTCHED COLLAR.

TWO-PIECE GUSSET. See GUSSET.

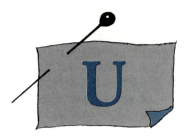

ULTRASUEDE. A polyester, nonfibrous polyurethane fabric that looks and feels like suede. From the standpoint of design and construction, it can be handled like the leather it resembles or like the wash-and-wear fabric that it is.

ULTRASUEDE: BUTTONHOLES. The type of buttonhole used for an Ultrasuede garment depends on whether the seams are constructed by the standard method or the flat (overlap) method. *(See* ULTRASUEDE: SEAMS.)

Appropriate for Standard-Method Garments: Machine-worked buttonholes, bound buttonholes, windowpane bound buttonholes. *See listing for each.*

Appropriate for Flat-Method Garments: Machine-worked buttonholes (q.v.).

Particularly Associated with Ultrasuede Garments: Reinforced slash buttonholes and topstitched windowpane buttonholes (q.q.v.).
To ensure that all are uniform, use a buttonhole stencil (q.v.) to trace the length and width of each buttonhole in a series. To finish the underside of all buttonholes (except those machine-made), locate the buttonhole opening on the facing. Using the buttonhole stencil, place, trace, and cut out a rectangular opening over the finished buttonhole and fuse to position with fusible web. If the buttonhole calls for it, top-stitch through all thicknesses—garment, lips of buttonhole, and facing.

ULTRASUEDE: COLLARS AND LAPELS. These may be constructed by the standard method or the flat method. *(See* ULTRASUEDE: SEAMS *and* ULTRASUEDE: INTERFACINGS.)

With right sides together, stitch the undercollar to the neck edge of the garment.

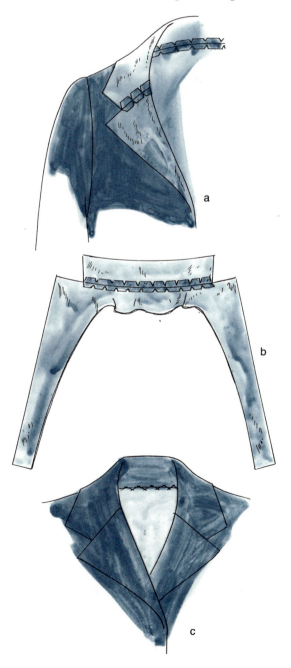

Clip and press the seam allowances open (a). With right sides together, stitch the upper collar to the facing. Clip and press the seam allowances open (b).

With right sides together, place the upper collar/facing over the undercollar/garment. Pin or baste along all outer edges, allowing sufficient ease on the upper collar, lapel, and front of garment so the joining seam may be rolled to the underside when the collar/facing is turned to the right side. Treat the seam as an enclosed (encased) seam (q.v.). Turn the collar to wearing position (c). *(See COLLAR ROLL ALLOWANCE.)* Loosely tack the collar to the garment along the neckline seam. *(See COLLAR and TAILORED NOTCHED COLLAR.)*

FLAT METHOD

Trim the seam allowances from the outside edges of the upper collar and undercollar, the front and lapel except at the neck edge.

Overlap and stitch the undercollar to the neck-edge seam line. Trim the garment seam allowance close to the stitching (a). Overlap and stitch the upper collar to the facing at the neck edge. Trim the lapel seam allowance close to the stitching (b).

With wrong sides together, place the upper collar/facing over the undercollar/garment, aligning and basting the neckline seams. Turn the collar and lapel to wearing position. *(See COLLAR ROLL ALLOWANCE.)* Note that the underlayer will extend slightly beyond the edge of the upper layer be-

cause of the roll of collar and lapel. Trim away any excess fabric.

Slip strips of fusible web between the layers of the collar, lapel, and front edges (c). Steam-press, using a press cloth. Topstitch around all outside edges (d).

ULTRASUEDE: HEMS. These may be simply the cut hem without any further finishing, a hem faced by the flat method *(see* ULTRASUEDE: SEAMS*)* and topstitched, or a regulation, turned-up hem, fused, topstitched, or both.

ULTRASUEDE: INTERFACING. Use fusible, Pellon, or similar interfacing where indicated for single thickness and fusible web for double thicknesses—hems, facings, stand of collar, and lapel. *(See FUSIBLE*

INTERFACING FOR UNSTRUCTURED TAILORED GAR-
MENTS.)

Because Ultrasuede has considerable
body of itself, particularly in areas of
double thicknesses, which is where one
would normally use an interfacing, use a
lighter-weight interfacing than one would
use for a similar-weight woven or knit
fabric. Since fusing will change the texture
of Ultrasuede on the right side, use it sparingly and on surfaces that won't show.
Safety lies in the use of Pellon or similar
interfacing, which in no way alters the
surface of the fabric. *See* FUSIBLES; FUSIBLE
WEB; ULTRASUEDE: PRESSING.

ULTRASUEDE: LAYOUT, CUTTING,
MARKING. Use the layout and fold of
material most advantageous for the
yardage. The fabric may be cut double. Pin
the edges with fine pins (glass-headed pins
are excellent) in the seam allowances. Or
use small strips of basting tape or paper
clips at intervals along the edge to hold the
fabric in place.

Determine the nap and mark its direction on the wrong side of the fabric with
arrows. The layout is directional—neck to
hem. As with velvets, place the pattern
sections with nap running up for richer
color; with nap running down for a softer,
frostier color.

Rather than pin the grain line, anchor it
with lead dressmaker's weights (q.v.) or
with any other safe object heavy enough
to hold the pattern in place. Use fine pins
placed in the seam allowances. Avoid pinning within the interior of the pattern section. If absolutely necessary to do so, remove the pins as soon as the section is cut
out.

Cut with long, even slashes, using long,
bent-handled sharp shears. Cut notches
away from the cutting line.

Marking may be done with a soft lead
pencil or chalk on the wrong side of the
fabric. It is possible to use a washable
dressmaker's tracing paper and a blunt
tracing wheel. Whatever the marking,
don't exert enough pressure to leave a
mark on the right side. For right-side
marking, use silk thread and a fine needle.

ULTRASUEDE LINED. Lining an Ultra-
suede garment is optional but a lining does
lend a touch of luxury. It also makes it
easier to slide the garment on and off. Particularly is this true of a tailored jacket or
coat.

If you plan to wash your Ultrasuede
garment, choose a washable lining. If the
construction of the garment requires dry
cleaning, use a dry-cleanable lining.

The construction and insertion of the
lining are the same as for other garments.
See LINING.

ULTRASUEDE: PATTERN SELECTION.
Because it so closely resembles suede,
one's impulse is to choose a pattern suitable for leather. It's a natural selection and
works well. However, one need not be so
limited. Do remember that Ultrasuede is,
after all, a fabric and can be treated like
one. Almost any style will do. Consider
the surprise element of using this leather
look-alike in a more adventurous, un-
characteristic style. Choose as simple or as
intricate a pattern as you can handle.

While Ultrasuede can be gathered,
pleated, ruffled, smocked, quilted, it cannot be eased readily (for instance, at a
sleeve cap). Select patterns that require a
minimum of easing or remove some of the
ease.

Where possible, look for styles in which
seams rather than darts do the shaping.
Shaping seams provide more subtle fit and
are easier to handle than darts, which tend
to produce bulges in Ultrasuede.

Kimono, raglan, or dropped-shoulder
sleeves are easier to sew than set-in
sleeves.

ULTRASUEDE: POCKETS. Construct
pockets in Ultrasuede by the same methods as for fabric. Use either the standard or
the flat method *(see* ULTRASUEDE: SEAMS*)* for
stitching bound, welt, flap, and patch
pockets. When pockets are constructed by
the flat method, utilize the topstitching for
fastening the pocket to the garment wherever possible. Topstitching may require
stopping and starting the stitching at stra-

tegic points rather than one continuous line of stitching.

ULTRASUEDE: PRESSING.

Ultrasuede needs lots of steam for pressing but at a synthetic setting on the iron. However, steam alone will not flatten seams and darts stitched by the standard method. *(See* ULTRASUEDE: SEAMS.)

The easiest way to flatten a seam or opened dart is with a pounding block (q.v.) or wooden mallet. "Spank" the fabric while it is still moist from the steaming. To prevent seam imprints, press over a seam roll (q.v.) or strips of brown wrapping paper under the seam allowances. *(See* PRESSING: PREVENT IMPRINTS.) Don't expect the sharp, crisp flattening you would get in a hard-surfaced woolen fabric, but you can get quite a good flat seam. *(See* PRESSING WORSTED, HARD-SURFACED, OR FIRMLY WOVEN WOOLENS.)

Another method of flattening the seams and darts is with strips of fusible web placed under the seam allowances. (Make the strips narrower than the seam allowances.) Steam-press lightly with just enough pressure to flatten but not so much as to fuse the two thicknesses. Before they dry, lift the seam allowances and remove the web. Steam-press lightly once more.

Or use strips of fusible web to flatten seam and dart allowances and to hold hems and facings in place permanently with or without further stitching.

Fusing the seam allowances to the garment changes the texture of the Ultrasuede on the right side. Should that happen, or should seam imprints occur, lift the seam allowances, press the section under them. Restore the nap on the right side by a light brushing with a toothbrush. Sometimes even a light brushing with fingertips works well.

To seal pin or needle holes, steam-press and lightly brush up the nap.

Use whatever of your general pressing equipment (q.v.) applies. Use all the usual precautions for preserving the napped surface of the Ultrasuede. *See* PRESSING *(general suggestions);* PRESSING NAPPED FABRIC; PRESSING RAISED-SURFACE FABRIC.

ULTRASUEDE: SEAMS.

Use the standard method or the flat (overlap) method for stitching. *(See* ULTRASUEDE: STITCHING.)

STANDARD METHOD

Ultrasuede garments make up handsomely by this method. They are not the least bit bulkier than any other cloth of comparable weight and texture.

To Stitch Seam Allowances: Stitch in the regulation (right-sides-together) manner and press them open. To hold them in place, seam allowances may be fused, topstitched, or both.

To Stitch Darts: Fuse a 1/2-inch square or round patch of sheer fusible material at the dart point. This both reinforces it and prevents "bubbling." In this material particularly, your stitching must be done so there is a *gradual blending* rather than a sharp bulge at the dart point. *(See* SINGLE-POINTED DART *and* DOUBLE-POINTED CONTOUR DART.) Clip the thread ends and tie them in a square knot. Clip, trim, and press the darts open over a tailor's ham (q.v.). *(See also* PRESSING DARTS *and* ULTRASUEDE: PRESSING.)

Stitch all facings by the regulation enclosed (encased) seam construction (q.v.). If topstitching is to be used, trim and grade the seam allowances, keeping them within the topstitched area. It is especially important to observe all techniques of trimming, clipping, notching, grading, freeing corners of bulk, and pressing.

THE FLAT (OVERLAP) METHOD

By this method, all seams are overlapped and topstitched. The seam allowances of all faced and outer edges are trimmed away, aligned, and topstitched. Hems may be raw (cut) edges, with or without a facing. No finish is necessary, though often desirable.

Knowing this, it is possible to save some fabric by eliminating or diminishing the seam allowances of all such edges.

Stitching the Seams. Trim away the seam allowance from the overlap edge. Trim back the seam allowance of the underlap edge to 3/8 inch or any other prede-

termined width, depending on where the topstitching is to be (a).

In an overlap method, one would naturally think in terms of working from the right side, where the overlap actually occurs. To do so the position of the overlap would have to be marked on the right side of the underlap material. Since it takes considerable marking for an accurate overlap line, it is safer (and much easier) to work in reverse on the underside.

On the Overlap. Working on the *underside,* mark a line 3/8 inch (or whatever you've decided on) from the cut edge. Use a soft lead or chalk pencil. Bring the cut edge of the underlap to this line. Slip a 1/4-inch strip of fusible web between the two (b). Steam-press lightly to position—just enough to hold the two in place for topstitching.

On the Right Side. Make a line of topstitching close to the cut edge of the overlap. Make a second line of topstitching 1/4 inch or more from the first (c).

Lap fronts over backs. If there is an underarm section, lap the front and back sections over the underarm sections. Generally, yoke seams are overlapped on adjoining sections. While the direction of the overlap is not crucial, being consistent is.

COMBINATIONS OF STANDARD AND FLAT METHODS

Combinations of the two methods are perfectly acceptable. For instance, even though the rest of the garment may be stitched by the flat method, the following are better done by the standard method: darts, armhole seams of set-in sleeves (other than shirt sleeves), the gorge line of collar and lapel, the sleeve underarm seam, and pants inseams. In the latter two, it is much easier than sewing both seams of a tube by the flat method. Pants are also more comfortable if the crotch seam is stitched by the standard method.

ULTRASUEDE: SET-IN SLEEVE. This sleeve is set and stitched by the standard method even if the rest of the garment is stitched by the flat method. *(See* ULTRASUEDE: SEAMS.)

Because Ultrasuede does not ease readily, remove some of the ease in the sleeve cap. *(See* SET-IN SLEEVE CAP EASE.) Stitch the underarm seam and press. Gather the cap. Set and stitch the sleeve into the armhole in the usual manner. *(See* SET-IN SLEEVE: SETTING *and* SET-IN SLEEVE: STITCHING.)

It is sometimes helpful to stay the shape of the cap with a strip of bias binding, pressed open to full width and long enough to fit the cap (about 8 to 9 inches). Place on the wrong side of the sleeve cap, aligning the edges of cap and binding. Pin and baste just inside the seam line. The bias also makes it a bit easier to draw up gathering into a cap shape.

Alternative Method. Treat like a shirt sleeve (q.v.). Remove some of the ease in the sleeve cap. Gather it slightly. Set the sleeve into the armhole before stitching the underarm seam in both sleeve and garment. It is easier to topstitch the armhole seam if handled in this way.

ULTRASUEDE: STITCHING. While silk thread, 100% polyester thread, or polyester-core thread are usually recommended, mercerized cotton thread works just as well.

Use fine machine and hand needles. For the construction seams, use 10 to 12 stitches per inch. Smaller stitches will perforate the material as if it were paper and it can be torn just as easily along the perforations. Avoid back-and-forth lock stitching, which tends to weaken (or even tear) the fabric. Use an eased tension and the taut-stitching technique (q.v.). Stitch slowly, a little at a time.

ULTRASUEDE: TRIAL FITTING. This is a must. You should have as clear an idea as possible of how the garment will fit. While it is possible to repin and even to restitch without damage to the material, the amount of change is limited once the fabric is cut.

Make a shell of *nonwoven fabric* that incorporates your usual pattern corrections. This best simulates the nonease of Ultrasuede. Pin the shell together. Follow the rules for fitting other garments but be sure to allow sufficient ease. *(See* FITTING.*)*

Transfer all adjustments to the tissue pattern that is used for cutting.

ULTRASUEDE WAISTBAND. May be applied by either the standard or the flat method. *(See* ULTRASUEDE: SEAMS.*)*

ULTRASUEDE YARDAGE. Because the fabric is expensive, you will want to figure closely, but remember that you must use a "With Nap" layout.

If you plan to use the flat method of construction *(see* ULTRASUEDE: SEAMS*)*, you can save inches by trimming away part or in some cases all of the seam allowances and dispensing with hems.

While pattern pieces are mainly placed in a directional layout, some of them may be tilted off grain (up to 45°) without affecting the drape or making any noticeable color difference. You can save some yardage that way.

Because the crosswise and bias stretches are similar, bias sections may be cut crosswise to save fabric.

For an exact estimate of yardage, make a trial layout on a cutting board or on paper cut to the width of the Ultrasuede. Make the usual pattern corrections. Trim whatever seam allowances and hems of the tissue pattern you have decided to eliminate.

ULTRASUEDE: ZIPPER. *See* ZIPPER IN ULTRASUEDE.

UNBALANCED PLAIDS. *See* PLAIDS: TEST FOR EVENNESS OR UNEVENNESS; PLAIDS; PLACEMENT OF PATTERN ON FABRIC; *and* PLAIDS: DIRECTIONAL LAYOUT.

UNBALANCED STRIPES. *See* PLAIDS: LAYOUT; STRIPES: PLACEMENT ON FABRIC; STRIPES: TEST FOR EVENNESS OR UNEVENNESS.

UNBLEACHED MUSLIN. A woven, natural-color cotton material that comes in various weights and widths. It is used in clothing construction mainly for testing the fit of a garment. Choose the weight and texture closest to that of the fashion fabric being tested. *See* TRIAL MUSLIN.

UNCONSTRUCTED ("SOFT," UNSTRUCTURED) TAILORING. This method of tailoring achieves its effects by abolishing the inner structure of traditional tailoring, frequently the linings, and often even the facings, seam allowances, and hems. Obviously the fashion fabric must be firm enough to go it alone without the benefit

of underpinnings. Generally, too, machine sewing replaces the laborious hand stitching of classic tailoring.

Such tailoring is a way of getting an effect with a minimum of work and a maximum of speed, in addition to an appealing, comfortable style.

UNDERARM DRESS ZIPPER. If the dress is sleeveless, one may use a neck-type zipper on the underarm seam instead of at a center back or center front opening. If the dress has sleeves and a collar that make a center back (or center front) opening impossible, then use a regulation underarm dress zipper. This zipper has tiny metal bridges that hold the tapes together at the top of the zipper as well as at the bottom. If one is not available, make one. *See* STANDARD ZIPPER CONVERTED TO AN UNDERARM DRESS ZIPPER.

When an underarm dress zipper is set, there is a seam above the zipper and below it, making for a partial opening instead of the complete opening achieved by a neck-type zipper.

The placket opening is generally 1/4 to 1/2 inch longer than the zipper, which may be 9, 10, 12, 14 inches or more. At least 6 inches of the opening is in the skirt. The exact length is determined by how tightly fitted are the bodice and the skirt. In a very snug fit, the placket opening in the bodice may reach almost to the armhole; the placket opening in the skirt may reach to the widest part of the hips. If clipping is required at a tightly fitted curved seam, do this after the zipper is stitched in place. Reinforce any place that will require a clip deeper than 3/8 inch. An alternate method is to face the fitted curved seam with a bias strip.

If the placket intersects a cross seam, make sure the seams are matched. Inaccuracy here makes the placket seam lines uneven in length. Trim the cross-seam allowances to reduce the bulk. Clip the underseam allowance at both ends of the placket opening.

The zipper installation is generally a lapped one (q.v.). Stitching is by hand or by machine.

UNDERARM SEAM. The one that curves down from the front notch of the armhole to the underarm and up to the back notch. Because this is an area of stress, a double seam is advised.

Clip the underarm seam allowances every 1/2 inch almost to the stitching to release it for the comfortable underarm fit of the sleeve (a). Remember that the sleeve fits at the seam line, not at the cut edge. An alternate method for handling this is to clip the seam allowances at the front and back notches and trim the underarm seam allowance close to the rows of stitching (b).

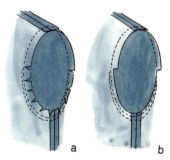

a   b

UNDERCOLLAR. The bottom portion or bottom layer of a collar. It is often referred to as the collar facing. To test the fit of the undercollar, *see* TAILORED COLLAR: FITTING. The same rules would hold for any rolled collar.

UNDERFOLD. A fold lying under another surface; for instance, the turn-under of a pleat.

UNDERLAP. A section of a garment that extends under another; for instance, the edge of a garment closing that lies under its opposite edge, like that of a snapped or buttoned closing.

UNDERLAY. A layer of fabric that lies under another; for instance, the lowest layer (back) of a pleat. It may be a separate piece or part of a larger section.

UNDERLINED HEM. In this hem, the underlining (q.v.) of the garment is carried down to the very edge of the hem and basted to position.

Baste the fold line of the hem through

both outer fabric and underlining. Turn up the underlined hem and trim it to an even depth. There is now a double thickness of underlining to reinforce and weight the hem.

Finish the hem edge in a manner appropriate for the style and fabric. Fasten the hem to the underlining only with catch stitches or hemming stitches. Make sure that no stitches come through to the right side. Remove the basting.

For a less bulky hem, cut off the underlining 1/2 inch beyond the fold line and blindstitch its edge to the hem. Turn up the hem and proceed as above.

UNDERLINING (BACKING). Some fabrics, either alone or interfaced, may not be able to sustain the lines of a design. They need total support. This is supplied by an underlining, commonly called a backing.

The underlining is cut from the same pattern as the outer fabric and applied to its underside. When the two are joined, a new fabric is created that has the surface appeal of the original plus the character of the underlining. For instance, chiffon underlined with crepe is no longer chiffon and no longer crepe; it is crepe-backed chiffon and can be used in an entirely different manner than either crepe or chiffon.

Undoubtedly it may seem more logical to use a firm material to begin with. But then fashion isn't really logical. By the use of an underlining any effect becomes possible and the choice of fabric for design limitless.

Underlining does not need to be used in an entire garment. Underline only those parts that require it for effect. If the underlining proves too heavy or stiff in an area that may need it, use a lighter-weight underlining of the same color. How much or how little you use depends on the fabric and the design of the garment.

Total support is not the only virtue of an underlining. It has other advantages as well. It reinforces seams. It acts as a stay to prevent stretching. An opaque underlining prevents all inner construction details from showing on the outside—seam allowances, darts, interfacings, facings,

pockets, and the like. And it is a wonderful layer to which the hem may be attached without a stitch showing on the right side.

UNDERLINING BOUFFANT OR BELLED SHAPES. Use Method 1 of underlining shirred or gathered designs (q.v.), except that the two layers (outer fabric and underlining) are laid as one layer in soft folds.

UNDERLINING: CONSTRUCTION. There are two methods of handling the underlining. In the first, the two layers—outer fabric and underlining—are treated as one. In the second, the darts (or other fullness) are handled separately in each layer, then the sections are treated as one in the construction seams.

When the layers are handled as one, none of the inner construction shows from the right side. This method is suitable for sheer, lightweight, and medium-weight fabrics and underlining.

When the layers are handled separately, they may be joined with wrong sides together to give the inside of the garment a finished look. By this method, seams won't show but darts may if the fashion fabric is sheer or transparent. To avoid this, the right side of the underlining may be placed against the wrong side of the outer fabric. In doing so, the darts will be visible on the underside of the underlining. This is a method one would use for medium to heavy outer fabric and crisp or springy underlining.

Two Layers Handled as One. Cut the fabric and the underlining from the same pattern. Transfer the pattern markings to the underlining only. Match the centers of both sections, pin, and baste.

For small sections: continue basting or stay-stitching around all outside edges. For large sections: work from the center toward the outer edges, making rows of basting every few inches, then baste around all outside edges.

To stitch a dart: machine-stitch through both thicknesses of material directly down the center, ending at the point. Fold the dart on the line of stitching, smoothing the material away from it. Pin and stitch through all layers. Stitch from the wide end to the dart point, being particularly careful to smooth the fabric at the point and to taper the stitching off the dart point for a perfect blend.

If the finished dart is not too bulky, leave it uncut. If bulky, slash the dart and press it open.

It is very difficult to get a perfectly stitched dart by this method in any but sheer or very lightweight material. For heavier materials, use the method described below.

Two Layers Handled Separately. Cut the fabric and underlining from the same pattern. Transfer the pattern markings to the outer fabric *and* the underlining. Pin and stitch the dart in the outer fabric. Pin and stitch the dart in the backing.

If the finished dart is not too bulky, leave it uncut; if bulky, slash the dart and press it open. When the darts are cut, place them one over the other. If uncut, press the garment dart in one direction, the underlining dart in the opposite direction, to avoid bulk.

Join the outer layer and the underlining with basting. If the garment section has been shaped by darts, it cannot be worked flat as a straight or unshaped section might be. To preserve the shaping, the two are joined over a curve of the tailor's ham. *See* INTERFACING APPLIED TO OUTER FABRIC OF FITTED TAILORED GARMENT.

Both Types. When a soft or lightweight underlining is used, bound buttonholes and bound or applied pockets can be made after the underlining has been applied, using it as a reinforcement for the openings. Heavier or stiffer underlinings are treated in the same way as hair canvas (q.v.).

For underlining garments with fullness, *see* UNDERLINING BOUFFANT OR BELLED SHAPES; UNDERLINING SHIRRED OR GATHERED DESIGNS; UNDERLINING WHEN PLEATS ARE INVOLVED.

UNDERLINING KNITS. Generally knits are not underlined if one wishes to retain the stretch that makes them so appealing.

When an underlining appears necessary, use another knit fabric, like tricot, for the underlining.

Should you wish to disregard the stretch quality of the knit and treat it as a woven fabric, then underline it in the same way as for woven fabric.

For some limited stretch, cut a standard underlining on the bias.

UNDERLINING MATERIALS. Underlining and interfacing materials (q.v.) are used interchangeably. What is underlining in one garment may be interfacing in another. There are no rules. Use your judgment. Underlining may be any weight or any texture that will give the desired effect and that is compatible with the garment in color and care requirements.

UNDERLINING PLUS INTERFACING. If you underline a garment, do you also need an interfacing? That depends on the design and the fabric.

For some soft, loose styles an underlining may be sufficient. A loosely woven or lacy fabric may be underlined first for uniform color and opacity, then interfaced in all the usual places. A closely woven but supple fabric may be firmed up by a combination of interfacing and underlining joined as one layer. Interface the parts you normally would; underline the rest. Join the two by lapped seams (q.v.).

Sometimes several different kinds of supporting material are used in one garment, each performing a specific function in a particular part of the garment.

UNDERLINING SHIRRED OR GATHERED DESIGNS. For a very full effect in sheer or lightweight fabrics, treat outer fabric and underlining as one layer (Method 1). To reduce some of the bulkiness in heavier fabrics, handle each layer separately for fullness, treat as one layer in all construction seams (Method 2).

METHOD 1

Cut the underlining in exactly the same way as the outer fabric. Decide where you want the right side of the underlining in the finished garment. If you wish the color, sheen, or figured surface to show under a sheer outer fabric, place the right side of the underlining against the wrong side of the fashion fabric. If you wish the right side of the underlining against the body, place the layers with the wrong sides together.

Join the outer fabric and underlining. (See UNDERLINING: CONSTRUCTION.) Gather the layers as one fabric. Draw up to the desired degree of fullness. Proceed with the rest of the construction as if one layer.

METHOD 2

Shirr the outer fabric. Cut the underlining to the same dimensions as the outer fabric. Stitch long darts in it to produce a very flared section, one edge of which retains the original fullness while the other equals the length to which the shirring will be drawn. Or cut an underlining to a flared shape.

Join outer fabric and underlining with basting along all outside edges. In this way, the underlining acts as a stay for the fullness, keeping it in place while reducing the bulkiness.

UNDERLINING WHEN PLEATS ARE INVOLVED. Underline unpressed pleats only. Do not underline crisp pleats.

UNDERPOCKET. That part of the pocket that rests against the body or palm of the hand.

UNDERSTITCHING. A line of machine or hand stitching that permanently positions the seam allowances of a garment section and its facing. There are several ways in which this may be done.

After the layers have been stitched and pressed open, the seam allowances trimmed, clipped, notched, and graded, turn the facing to the underside. Press the edges with the seam rolled to the underside. If steam-pressed as in tailoring, allow the garment to dry thoroughly before handling.

In Dressmaking. Open out the facing with the seam allowances directly under it. Stitch the seam allowances to the facing

close to the seam by machine (a) or, in delicate fabrics, by tiny hand stitches (b).

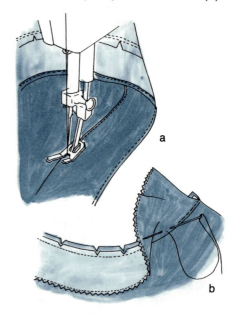

In Tailoring. Edge-baste firmly to hold the pressed seam in position (a). Use either method below. Both are acceptable.

As an enclosed seam: lift the facing gently and fasten the wider seam allowance to the tape or interfacing with either permanent basting or catch stitching (b). This

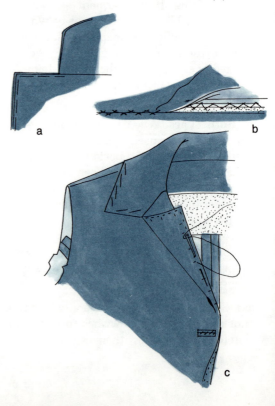

will automatically enclose the narrower seam allowance.

From the outside: hold the seam allowances in place with pickstitches (q.v.) placed 1/8 inch from the edge of an undersurface. Work along the underside of collar and lapel to the break of the collar. Work along the facing edges from the break to the hem (c).

UNIT CONSTRUCTION. A system for assembling a garment by which all that is possible to do on one section is completed before going on to the next step. Most pattern directions, particularly for simple designs, follow a unit work plan. Not only is it easier to work on smaller sections of a garment than on the whole garment, it is also speedier.

UNIT CONSTRUCTION: FACTORY METHOD. This is an alternative work plan when precise fitting isn't necessary, as in children's clothing or utility clothes. *(See* CHILDREN'S CLOTHES.)

UNIT CONSTRUCTION IN CUSTOM DRESSMAKING AND TAILORING.

To Complete Each Unit of Work: Stitch and press all darts and seams within the section. Apply any interfacings and/or underlinings. When the design calls for bound buttonholes, make them now. Machine- or hand-worked buttonholes can be made after the garment is completed. If a zipper is needed, insert it. When the design includes pockets, tabs, and the like, make and apply them. When the style features a collar, make it. An opening, a band, or a cuff is completed before the sleeve is set. A sleeve hem is done after the setting.

Join the Completed Units. When the units are finished as far as it is possible to do so, join them at the side seams and at the shoulders, then proceed with all the circumference operations. On these now tubular units attach the facings. Apply the collar. Set and stitch the sleeves. Stitch the waistline seam of a dress or attach a waistband to a skirt or pants. Set and sew the hems. Add final touches and any necessary handwork. Press as the work progresses.

Fitting. This is done at any time and as many times as necessary. In following the sewing directions that come with a pattern, remember that these directions deal with construction and do not indicate the times and places for fitting. That is left to the sewer. Sometimes it is necessary to reorganize the sewing sequence to include the fittings as needed.

UNLINED GARMENT CONSTRUCTION. Lay out and cut the garment in the same way as a lined garment. In designs with an upper welt or bound pocket, cut an extra-wide front facing to hide it.

For marking, use tailor's chalk, which can be brushed off, or basting thread, which can be removed. Save the dressmaker's carbon paper for areas where it will not show.

As much to protect them as to make them more attractive, all raw edges of darts, seam allowances, facings, and hems should be finished off in some way by hand or by machine. *(See* EDGE FINISHES *and* BIAS BINDING.) If the fabric of the garment is a knit, trim the seam allowances and machine-finish the edges with an overedge stitch.

There is an alternate way of handling the seams and darts in the unlined garment. By this method, the structure of the garment becomes decorative without the addition of applied decoration like bindings. *See* UNLINED GARMENT: SEAMS AND DARTS.

UNLINED GARMENT: SEAMS AND DARTS. Choose any of the seams that appear suitable to the design and fabric. Those most often used are a flat fell seam, welt seam, or double-stitched welt seam. *See listing for each.*

Generally standard darts in unlined garments are stitched by the standard methods and remain uncut. Where necessary to trim, slash, or clip them, the raw edges must be finished off in some way. *(See* EDGE FINISHES.) Darts may also be stitched to resemble a single- or double-stitched welt seam in the same way as darts in a reversible garment made of reversible fabric.

UNLINED JACKET OR COAT. While it may appear so, an unlined garment is not always easier to construct than a lined one. It requires a different but equally demanding construction. A lining can cover a multitude of sewing sins. There is no helpful hiding place in an unlined garment. Everything shows, inside as well as outside. So finish and workmanship must be just about perfect. Still there is no denying its appeal. It is a popular style, especially for knit fabrics.

Choose a simple style with as few seams and darts as possible. (They'll show on the exposed underside.) Patch pockets are more satisfactory than the more intricate welt or bound variety. (That dangling pouch of a pocket is not a particularly attractive sight even though it is on the inside.)

Interfacings are minimal and cut slightly smaller than the facings so they will be unseen. *(See* INTERFACING FOR UNLINED JACKET OR COAT.) Use softer or lighter-weight interfacing than one would normally use for a lined garment. This avoids too much difference in thickness or stiffness between the interfaced parts and the rest of the garment.

The only lining is in the sleeves—the easier to slip them on and off—and if you must, a half lining across the back. Shoulder pads should be covered with self-fabric or a lining fabric of a matching color.

UNPRESSED PLEATS. *See* PLEATS: UNPRESSED.

UNSTRUCTURED ("SOFT") TAILORING. *See* UNCONSTRUCTED ("SOFT," UNSTRUCTURED) TAILORING.

UPPER COLLAR. The top portion or upper layer of a collar, usually referred to as the *collar.*

UPPER POCKET. That part of the pocket that lies over the top of the hand against the outer fabric.

VELOUR. A soft, velvety fabric with thick short pile. It may be woven or knitted of all cotton, all synthetic, or in combination fibers. Velour comes in solid colors, heathers, iridescents, chenilles, stripes, luster yarns, and sculptured effects. Some velours include spandex yarns, making them stretch fabrics.

Treat velour as a pile and/or stretch fabric (q.q.v.).

VELVET. The third dimension of this lovely fabric adds extra dimension to its beauty. There is a richness to its texture and an incomparable way in which it takes the light. When used in soft folds there is a dramatic play of light and shadow. For a very elegant gown or evening suit, one could do no better.

Choose a design with little seaming so the velvety softness is unscarred by seam lines. If there must be buttonholes, hand-worked or machine-made ones are less bulky than bound. Or use a loop-and-button closing. Avoid pockets that slash into the fabric; use only those that can be inserted into an existing seam or applied like a patch pocket. No topstitching—the pressure of the presser foot and the stitching itself mar the fabric.

Determine the direction of the nap and mark it along the selvage. *(See* PILE FABRICS *and* NAPPED FABRICS.) Because pile reflects the light, a directional layout is necessary. There is an additional problem in layout: the shifting movement of the pile in relation to the placement of the pattern. When velvet is folded right sides together, pile against pile has a tendency to stick together like a burr. Though the pattern tissue pinned to the wrong side does not

shift, the fabric "moves." When folded right sides outside, the pile remains stable but the pattern tissue on the pile may shift. To avoid a fold altogether, use a complete pattern placed on the wrong side of the material, opened to full width. Choose whichever method appears easiest for you to handle.

Use fine hand needles rather than pins to set the grain. Remove them as soon as the rest of the pattern is pinned. Use silk pins placed in the seam allowances for the rest of the pattern.

For wrong-side marking, use chalk. For right-side marking, use silk thread. This does not leave its impression on the fabric in the way that cotton thread may.

When basting is necessary, use a fine needle and silk thread. Use backstitches at intervals. This will better hold the fabric in place.

Machine Stitching
Tension: light
Pressure: light
Stitch size: 10 to 12 stitches per inch
Needle: medium
Thread: appropriate for the fiber
Stitch in the direction of the nap. *(See* PILE FABRICS: STITCHING.)

To reduce bulk, face velvet with lightweight lining fabric and tack the facing invisibly to the backing of the fabric. When joining a pile fabric and a plain fabric, machine-stitch with the plain fabric on top.

Press to preserve the pile. *See* PILE FABRICS: PRESSING.

All hand-finishing stitches on the underside are made through the backing of the fabric only. Do not let them come through to the right side. To prevent fraying, finish all raw edges with overedge stitches or binding.

Use an invisible zipper or hand-stitched standard zipper.

Hem Treatment. A turned-up hem will by its nature be soft. Keep it that way with steaming rather than pressing. Don't try for a crisp edge. For an extra-soft, padded look, interface the hem with a bias strip of soft underlining material or lamb's wool padding. *(See* PADDED EDGE.)

Bind the raw edge of the hem with a strip of nylon net or silk(y) seam binding. Tack the hem to the backing of the velvet, using a blindstitch.

Alternatives to a turned-up hem: a hand-rolled hem (q.v.) or a facing (q.v.).

VELVETEEN. A cotton velvet with a short, close pile. The looped warp threads form the pile. Treat like velvet (q.v.).

VENT. A faced opening in a garment for ease. You will find vents in jackets, coats, skirts, sleeves.

In a pattern the vent appears as an extension on a seam (a). One extension (the overlap) is turned under to form a facing; the other remains opened out as an underlap (b).

To Construct the Vent: Mark the fold line of the overlap section, the closing line on the underlap section, and the fold line of the hem of the garment.

Vents are generally interfaced so that they hang properly. If the pattern you are using doesn't provide an interfacing pattern, make your own. When the garment is to be lined, cut the interfacings 1/4 inch wider than the facing and the hem depth. When the garment is to be unlined, make them 1/4 inch narrower. If cut as separate pieces, the hem interfacing is cut on the bias and the vent interfacing on the straight. When hem and vent are cut in one piece make it bias. Use an interfacing material compatible with the fabric of the garment. Pin the interfacing in place along the hemline and the fold line of the overlap facing. Blindstitch or catch-stitch it in place (a).

When bound buttonholes are made in a

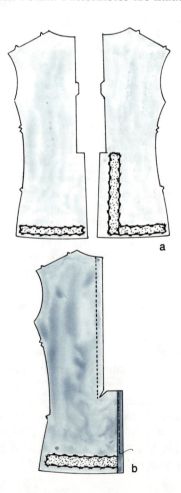

a

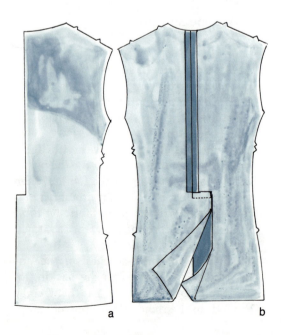

a   b

b

sleeve vent, they are done at this point in the construction.

When the garment is to be unlined, the exposed seams, hem, and vent edges can be finished with bias binding. When the garment is to be lined, turn in the long edge of the underlap extension along its seam line and baste to within several inches of the lower edge.

With right sides of garment sections together, stitch the seam to the marking for the end of the vent. Backstitch so stitching is secure at this point. Clip the seam allowance of the underlap extension so the seam allowance above it can be pressed open while the vent is pressed to one side (b). Complete the construction of the garment. Turn up the hems and attach them in the usual way.

To complete the overlap, grade the facing hem to within a seam allowance of the fold line. Turn the facing to the underside. Turn under the seam allowance of the outer edge. Slip-stitch it to the hem. Blindstitch or catch-stitch the outer edge of the facing to the garment.

To complete the underlap, turn under and baste the remaining long edge of the underlap. Slip-stitch the lower edge to the hem and blindstitch or catch-stitch the outer edge to the underlap.

Alternative Method. Miter the corner of the overlap facing (a). Turn the un-

a

b

derlap hem to the outside along the fold line. With right sides together, stitch the hem to the underlap along the edge (b). Grade the seam allowances and clip diagonally across the corner. Turn the hem to the inside. Turn under the remainder of the long edge and blindstitch or catch-stitch it. Turn up the rest of the hem and attach it.

When a Lining Is Involved at a Vent. Patterns usually provide two different sides for linings at vents—one for the overlap, the other for the underlap. Right and left sides of lining and vent can be confusing since, in construction, the lining is the reverse of the vent.

The safest thing to do is to cut both edges alike as for the vent underlap, which is the larger. With right sides together, stitch the lining sections to the marking for the end of the vent. Secure the stitching. Clip the seam allowance at the end of the stitching. Press it open. Place the lining in position on the garment. Cut away the lining where necessary for underlap and overlap, leaving a seam allowance on each. Turn under the edges of the lining and slip-stitch them to the vent.

VERTICAL GRAIN. In woven fabric, the vertical grain is a lengthwise yarn of the fabric or the selvage. In knit fabric, the vertical grain is a lengthwise rib or wale. *See* GRAIN ESTABLISHED IN KNIT FABRIC; GRAIN ESTABLISHED IN WOVEN FABRIC.

VERTICAL HEMMING STITCH. A strong, stable stitch for joining two thicknesses of material. Also known as a Straight Hemming Stitch.

Work the stitch from right to left. Use a single length of matching thread. The stitch is vertical, at right angles to the edge over which it passes. The needle is slanted and brought up through the edge.

Where a *strong stitch* is needed (for instance, when attaching the undercollar to the neck edge of a tailored garment), insert the needle through both edges in one motion (a). The stitches should be tiny and close together.

When an *invisible stitch* is desirable (as at

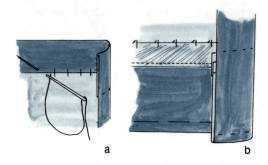

a   b

a hem), lift only one thread of the outer fabric (b). The stitches are ¼ inch to ⅜ inch apart.

The beginning of each next stitch is directly under the ending of the previous stitch. The stitches on the wrong side are vertical; those on the right side are horizontal.

VINYL. *See* LEATHERLIKE FABRICS.

WAFFLE SHIRRING. An interesting texture that can be stitched into smooth-surfaced fabrics.

Shirr on the crosswise grain by hand or by machine, then on the lengthwise grain of the fabric to form a block pattern. In machine shirring (using the gathering foot), use a stitch length short enough to produce only slight fullness.

WAISTBAND. An anchor that holds the fit of skirt or pants in place. It can do the same for a lower edge of a jacket or blouse. The waistband can be unabashedly visible —decorative even—or an inside band, discreetly hidden from view.

The visible waistband (the usual type— straight or contour) is made of three layers: an outside (upper band), an inside (under band), and one between (the interfacing). Any part of a garment that has so many parts has many possibilities for variety in design and fabric.

The upper and under bands can be all of a piece (in a straight band only) or in two pieces, wide or narrow, straight grain or bias. The waistband may be of self-fabric or a contrasting texture, the same color as the garment or a different color. If the fabric is too heavy or too bulky for both upper and under bands, the under band can be made of some lighter-weight material— lining, French belting, or grosgrain ribbon. The interfacing can be firm or rigid. Nor does the waistband have to be inflexible. Stretch waistbands are excellent on knits as well as woven fabrics.

The construction of the waistband may be as simple as the straight, self-fabric bands of many women's skirts (see WAIST-BAND: BASIC METHOD) or as complicated as the two-piece waistband of men's trousers (see TROUSER WAISTBAND). *See also* BIAS WAIST-BAND; CONTOUR WAISTBAND; ELASTIC DECORA-TIVE WAISTBAND; LINING-FACED WAISTBAND; IN-SET WAISTBAND; INSIDE WAISTBAND; RIBBON-FACED WAISTBAND; RIBBON-FACED WAISTLINE; SELVAGE WAISTBAND; TOPSTITCHED WAISTBAND; WAISTBAND CLOSURES; WAISTBAND LENGTH AND WIDTH; WAISTBAND STIFFENERS; WAISTBAND WITH IRON-ON INTERFACING; WAISTBAND WITH PROFES-SIONAL WAISTBANDING.

WAISTBAND: BASIC METHOD. Cut the waistband and its facing. Pin-mark the overlap, underlap, center front, center back, and side seam to match those on the garment waistline. Cut *firm* interfacing from either the upper- or under-band pattern. Trim away the seam allowances.

Place the interfacing over the wrong side of either of the bands. While it is generally the under band or facing that gets interfaced, it often works better if the upper band is interfaced. Pin or baste the interfacing to position. Catch-stitch around all edges (a). *Note:* In the one-piece waistband, one long edge rests against the fold line (b).

When *lightweight interfacing* is used in the waistband, it may be included in the seams. Cut the interfacing the same size as

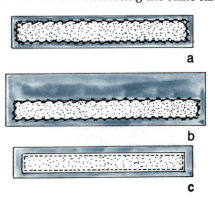

a

b

c

the waistband. Apply it to the waistband like an underlining. Stitch through both waistband and interfacing. Trim the interfacing material close to the seam (c).

If you plan to make a bound buttonhole on the overlap extension, do it now. A machine-made buttonhole is made when the band is finished.

Sewing Sequence for a Waistband with an Extension. Stitch the darts and seams of the garment. Insert the zipper. Attach the band as follows.

With right sides together, pin and/or baste the upper band to the skirt (or pants) along the waist seam line. The extension, be it overlap or underlap, projects beyond the opening (a). Match the markings on the garment and waistband. Ease the garment into the band.

Stitch the waistband to the garment. Trim, grade, and clip the seam allowances. Press them open first, then into the band.

When cut separately, stitch the under band to the upper band along its length. Trim, grade the seam allowances, and press, first open, then toward the band.

Fold the band lengthwise with right sides together, along the fold line in a one-piece band, along the seam in a two-piece band. Stitch across the ends. Press the seam allowances open over a point presser.

Grade the seam allowances and free the corners of bulk.

Turn the band to the right side (b). Fold the all-in-one band lengthwise along the fold line. Make sure that the waistband is even in width from seam to fold along its entire length. Pin or baste to position. When an under band has been stitched to an upper band, roll the joining seam to the underside. Press, then baste to position.

Turn under the seam allowance of the loose edge of the under band and hem or slip-stitch it to the garment along the line of stitching (c).

For an *overlap extension:* make the machine buttonhole. Sew on the button. For an *underlap extension:* sew on hooks and eyes or snaps.

Sewing Sequence for a Waistband Zippered to the Top of the Band. Stitch the darts and seams of the garment. Attach the band to the garment. Insert the zipper to the top of the band (a), observing the usual zipper placement.

In a one-piece band, fold the band to the inside along the fold line. In a two-piece band, attach the under band and turn it to the inside. Turn under the seam allowances at both ends of the under band along the zipper tape. Pin to position. Turn under the seam allowance of the loose, long edge of the under band. Pin to position along the seam (b). Hem or slip-stitch the under band to position (c).

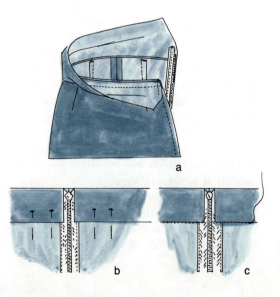

a

b

c

a

b

c

WAISTBAND CARRIERS. *See* FABRIC CARRI-ERS for carrier construction. Waistband carriers are attached to the waistband in one of two ways, depending on the application of the waistband.

METHOD 1

With right sides together, position the end of the carrier along and slightly under the fold line of the waistband (a). Stitch it in place. Press the carrier down over the waistband. Baste the free edge to the waistline seam line (b). Include the carrier in the waistline seam when the band is attached to the garment.

METHOD 2

The reverse of Method 1: the top-stitched waistband. With right sides together, position the carrier on the waistline seam of the garment. Include the carrier in the seam when the waistband facing is stitched to the garment (c). Turn under the seam allowance of the waistband and baste it to position. Press the carrier up over the waistband. Topstitch the lower edge of both waistband and carrier. Fold the carrier turn-under to position along and close to the fold of the waistband.

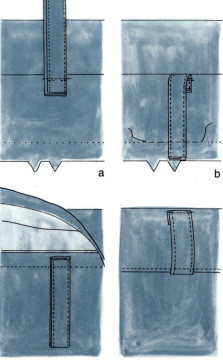

a   b

c   d

Topstitch it to the waistband through all thicknesses (d).

WAISTBAND CLOSURES. The waistband closure may be by overlap, underlap, or simply by bringing a zipper to the top of the waistband.

When an overlap ends flush with the edge of the garment, the underlap must be an extension. For this type of closing, the fasteners are usually hooks and eyes (regular or heavy-duty) or snaps.

Frequently, for design purposes, the overlap is a curved or pointed extension. In this case, it is the underlap that is flush with the edge of the garment. The fastening for this type of closure is generally by button and buttonhole.

Finished extensions, whether on overlap or underlap, are generally 1¼ to 1½ inches in length to provide space for the fasteners and to assure no gapping at the closing.

In *women's garments,* when the garment opening is on the front or left side, the overlap is right over left. (Side closings are generally on the left side.) When the opening is at center back, the overlap is left over right. In *men's garments,* the overlap is left over right.

In either overlap or underlap closures, the zipper is generally put in before the waistband is stitched to the garment. Zippers brought to the top of the waistband can be installed in the seam allowances of the opening and need no extensions. This makes for a very trim closing. *See* ZIPPER IN A BAND AT NECKLINE, WAISTLINE, OR THE LIKE.

WAISTBAND LENGTH AND WIDTH (WOMEN). For men, *see* TROUSER WAISTBAND.

The *length* of a waistband is equal to the waist measurement plus ease plus seam allowances. If you plan to use a closing extension, add 1½ inches. Skirt and pants patterns include waistbands for standard sizes. If your pattern has been altered, the waistband must be altered accordingly. Straight waistbands on altered patterns are often easier to cut by measurement rather than by a corrected pattern.

The *width* of a straight waistband may be

anywhere from 3/4 inch to a maximum of 2 inches. Straight-and-narrow waistbands fit without shaping. When a waistband is more than 2 inches wide, it requires a shaped side seam to fit the indentation of the waist. Contour waistbands, because they are designed to fit the natural contour of the waistline, may be wider.

The width of the *all-in-one-piece waistband* is equal to twice the finished width of the waistband plus two seam allowances. The width for *separate upper and under bands* is equal to the finished width of each band plus two seam allowances.

WAISTBAND—MEN'S TROUSERS. *See* TROUSER WAISTBAND; TROUSER WAISTBAND WITH MEN'S WAISTBANDING; TROUSER WAISTBAND WITH ELASTIC; WAISTBAND WITH IRON-ON INTERFACING; WAISTBAND WITH PROFESSIONAL WAISTBANDING.

WAISTBAND STIFFENERS. Straight or contour waistbands planned as a stable finish to a skirt or pants require some degree of stiffening. How much stiffening is a matter of personal preference. The range is from light to rigid. The following are all possibilities.

If you use any of these, the width of your waistband will be limited by the width of the stiffener: *belting,* a rigid band inserted in belts and waistbands; *professional waistbanding,* a nonroll stiffener; *men's waistbanding,* a preassembled waistband consisting of stiffener, lining, and trouser curtain; *French belting,* which looks like but is stiffer than grosgrain ribbon and less rigid than belting; *grosgrain ribbon,* used as combination facing and light stiffening.

There is no limit to the width of the waistband with these stiffeners: *hair canvas* interfacing or the interfacing used for the rest of the garment in single or double thicknesses; *fusibles (iron-ons),* which come light to sturdy.

WAISTBAND WITH IRON-ON INTERFACING. Use a sturdy iron-on interfacing material cut to the length and width of the waistband (generally sufficient) or the waistband and its facing. Trim away the seam allowances. Place the iron-on on the

wrong side of the waistband with its cut edges on the seam lines. Fuse in place. Construct in the same way as any other interfaced band.

WAISTBAND WITH PROFESSIONAL WAISTBANDING (WOMEN'S). Cut the waistband to waistline measurement plus ease plus seam allowances, by twice the width of the professional waistbanding plus seam allowances. Cut the waistbanding the length of the waistband minus the end seam allowances. Extend it into the underlap or overlap.

With right sides together, pin and stitch the waistband to the waist seam line. Press the seam as stitched (a). Lap the waistbanding over the waistline seam allowances, placing one long edge on the seam. The rest of the banding is up, in the position in which it will be worn. Stitch the edge of the waistbanding to the seam allowances (b). Grade the seam allowances of garment and waistband.

With right sides together, fold the waistband along its fold line. Pin and

a

b

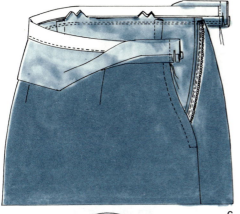

c

d

stitch the ends of the waistband close to but not including the waistbanding (c). Trim and grade the seam allowances. Trim the corner. Turn the waistband to the right side *over the waistbanding.* Turn under the seam allowance of the free edge. Place the turn-under along the seam and slip-stitch (d). Attach fasteners to the ends of the band.

WAISTLINE DART. There are two types of waistline darts—single-pointed and double-pointed. *See listing for each.*

WAISTLINE LOCATED. Ready-to-wear clothes and all commercial patterns are built on the presumption that a "normal" waistline tilts forward slightly. However, in many figures just the opposite is true; the waistline tips backward. For a garment to fit at the waistline (whatever the tilt) without wrinkling, pulling, straining, riding up, sliding down, or dislocation of

seams and darts, the exact line of the waistline must be located.

The natural waistline is located where the indentation of the body makes the circumference smallest. If you are naturally short-waisted or heavy-bosomed, you may want to lower the waistline for a longer, slimmer look. If you are naturally long-waisted or very tall, you may look better when the waistline is raised slightly.

To Locate the Waistline: After all construction seams and darts entering the waistline have been stitched and before a zipper has been installed, try on the garment. Pin the placket closed. Adjust the garment so its seams and darts are in their proper position. While standing, tie a heavy string (or pin a tape measure) snugly in the hollow of the waist or where you would like your waistline to be in the garment. *Caution:* In motion, the waistline appears higher than when one is standing still. For this reason, fit a bodice slightly lower than it is in reality, thereby providing some length ease.

Place a row of pins (use them horizontally) along the bottom of the string or tape around the entire waist. This is easy enough to do for yourself if you have to, though it's helpful to have someone mark the waistline for you.

Remove the garment. Replace the pin markings with a line of thread tracing. This becomes the stitching line for the waistline. Add a seam allowance and trim away any excess fabric.

Standard waistlines in ready-to-wear clothes and commercial patterns are symmetrical—that is, right and left sides are balanced. You may discover upon examination of the waistline marking that your waistline is not symmetrical—right and left sides are different. If the difference is slight, ignore it. It may be the result of inaccurate marking. However, if the difference is pronounced, you must respect it. A bodice, skirt, or waistband attached at your waistline, however unbalanced, will look right, while one attached to the symmetrical-pattern waistline will look all wrong on you.

WAISTLINE STAY. A length of ribbon, French belting, or firmly woven cotton twill tape that holds the waistline as intended by the design in fitted clothes, sheer or stretchy fabric, and styles in which the skirt fabric is heavier than the bodice fabric. A stay can also reduce the strain on a zippered closing.

When There Is No Waistline Seam. Cut 1-inch grosgrain ribbon or French belting to waist measurement plus seam allowance, no ease. The stay should fit snugly. For a finish, turn back the seam allowances at each end and machine-stitch across the ends. Sew hooks and eyes at the finished edges, extending the loops beyond the edge (a).

Attach the stay after the zipper installation. Position it at the waistline with the ends meeting at the center of the zipper. Tack the stay at all seams and darts, leaving the ends free for about 2 inches on either side of the opening for easy fastening (b). Hook the stay before closing the zipper.

When There Is a Waistline Seam, the stay may be attached before or after the zipper is installed.

Stay Attached Before the Zipper Is Installed. Cut a length of ½-inch ribbon or firmly woven cotton twill tape the length of the waistline seam from placket seam line to placket seam line. With skirt seam allowance turned toward the bodice, place the stay over it. Align the edge of the stay with the waistline seam and the ends at the placket seam lines. Pin and/or baste to position.

Drop the bodice into the skirt (right sides together) with both bodice and skirt seam allowances extending out from the garment. Machine-stitch the stay through both seam allowances (a).

Trim the seam allowances to the width of the stay. Grade them, making those of the skirt narrower than the bodice. Edge-finish the seam allowances in ravelly fabric. Press the stay and seam allowances toward the bodice (b).

Insert the zipper, including the stay in the zipper seam.

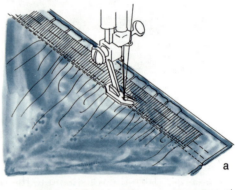

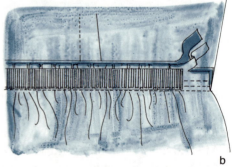

Stay Attached After the Zipper Is Installed. Prepare the stay in the same way as suggested for the preceding no-waistline-seam garment.

Place the stay at the waistline with the lower edge along the seam line. Pin to the waistline seam allowances at the center, side seams, and all darts. Leave free for 2 inches at each side of the zipper (a). Tack securely at these points, going through both seam allowances. Make sure no stitches come through to the right side. Hook the stay before the zipper is closed.

In *a fitted or semifitted tailored garment,* pin the stay around the waistline. Extend the ends 3/4 inch beyond the front facings. Turn under 1/4 inch. Tack in place at front facings or interfacings and all seams and darts with flat catch stitches (b).

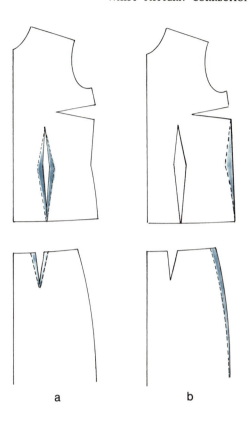

a   b

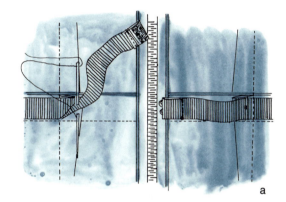

a

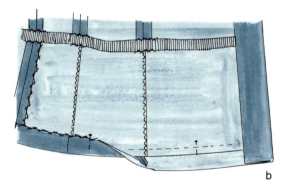

b

WAIST PATTERN CORRECTIONS

Thick Waist. Use less dart (a and b), or add at the side seam (or at any other existing seams).

Slim Waist. Make darts larger or take some off the side seam at the waist or any other existing seams (a and b).

Solid lines in the illustration show correction for thick waist; broken lines, for slim waist.

Swayback. Draw a horizontal slash line from center back to side seam about 2 inches below the waistline. Slash and overlap at center back to the needed amount, tapering to nothing at the side seam. Pin or Scotch-tape to position. Correct the center back line and darts (a).

Or draw a new waistline, dropping it at center back and tapering to nothing at the side seam (b).

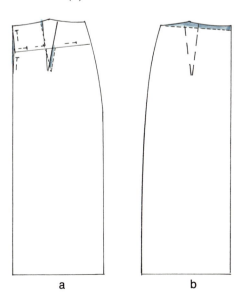

a   b

WEIGHTED TAPE. A length of muslin- or cotton-encased 1/4-inch flat lead weights.

When used at a hem, press the hem first. Place the tape along the fold line of the hem. Tack the casing to the underside of the hem (not the garment) with tiny stitches on the hem and slightly larger ones through the material on the tape between the weights.

A short length of weighted tape tacked to the underside of a cowl drape will hold it in place.

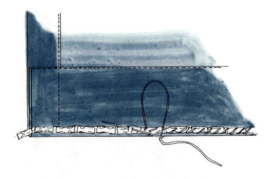

WEIGHTS AT A HEMLINE. You can't depend on gravity alone to hold a hem in place. If a hem is not sufficiently weighted, the entire garment has a tendency to ride up, displacing the seams and darts. For this reason, many hems are interfaced. (See IN-TERFACED HEM.) Some fabrics need more weighting than this or in addition to this. For spot weighting, use dressmaker's weights. For uniform weighting, use weighted tape (q.v.) or chain weights (q.v.).

WELT POCKET. In this pocket, a completely constructed welt is attached to one side of a pocket opening and turned over it to hide the opening in a decorative way. To do this, the welt is placed on the garment for stitching in a position opposite to its final appearance. For instance, a welt destined to turn up from the stitching line (a) is placed in reverse position for stitching (b). In whatever position the welt appears on the garment, the same principle holds (c).

The welt itself is constructed like a flap (q.v.) but, unlike the flap, whose sides

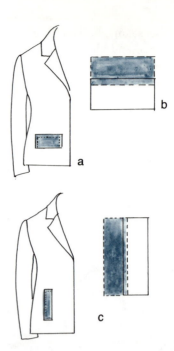

hang free, those of the welt are attached to the garment.

Mark the position of the welt pocket on the right side of the material with thread. Mark the slash line for the opening. Mark the seam line for attaching the welt 1/4 inch away from the slash line (a little more if the thickness of the garment fabric warrants it). Or use the pattern marking for the seam line.

Place the completed welt in position on the right side of the garment, matching the seam line of the lower edge of the welt with the marked seam line of the pocket opening. Pin and/or baste. Stitch through all thicknesses from one end of the welt to the other (a). Do not lock-stitch. It's hard to be so accurate that the lock stitches do not go beyond the welt. Pull the thread ends through to the underside and tie each pair in a square knot. Grade the seam allowances of the welt, trimming them close to the seam line.

Cut the pocket of lining material. Make it equal to the width of the pocket by twice its depth plus seam allowances on all outside edges. Mark the slash line in the center and the seam line the same distance away from it as on the garment marking.

Place the pocket over the welt, right

sides together, sandwiching the welt between the garment and the pocket. Set the
stitching line of the pocket directly over
the stitching line of the welt.

Stitch a rectangle for the pocket opening
(b). This is easier to do if you *turn to the
wrong side,* where the line of stitching that
attached the welt to the garment can be
used as a guideline. Make the first line of
stitching directly over the previous stitching on the welt; stitch across one end for
1/4 to 1/2 inch; make the third side of the
rectangle parallel to the first; stitch across
the second end, making it parallel to the
first end. Turn the last corner and continue
the stitching 1/2 to 1 inch directly over the
first side of the rectangle to secure the
stitching.

Caution: Be sure to start and stop the
stitching two or three stitches *in from* each
end of the welt. This makes the opening of
the pocket a little smaller than the welt.
When turned to its final position, the welt
will completely conceal the opening. Were
you to stitch all the way to the ends, you
would wind up with two conspicuous
gaping holes at the ends of the pocket.

Slash all thicknesses through the center
of the rectangle to within a short distance
of the ends. Clip diagonally to the corners
(c). Turn the pocket to the wrong side by
slipping it gently through the opening.
Pocket and welt will assume their proper
positions. Press the opening carefully.

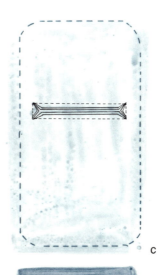

Pin the welt in place and slip-stitch the
ends to the garment (d).

On the underside, pin the upper and
under pockets together. Note that the upper pocket is slightly longer than the underpocket. This is because of the depth of
the opening. Trim it to match the underpocket. Machine-stitch the remaining
sides of the pocket (e).

This method of construction has three
distinct advantages over the usual pattern
directions for construction of a welt:

1. The complete length of the welt is attached securely without involving the
   pocket itself.
2. Because the welt has already been at-

tached, the rectangular opening may safely be made slightly smaller so there are no unsightly holes at the ends that cannot be covered by the welt.

3. When the pocket lining is stitched to the welt and garment from the underside, using the previous line of stitching as a guide, one can be sure it is correctly done. No guessing and no X-ray eyes necessary as when stitching blindly from the right side of the garment.

WELT SEAM. A strong seam used for heavy fabrics.

With right sides together, stitch a plain seam. Trim one seam allowance. Press both seam allowances to one side, the wider enclosing the narrower. On the right side, make a row of decorative topstitching the desired distance from the seam, catching the wider (but not the narrower) of the seam allowances.

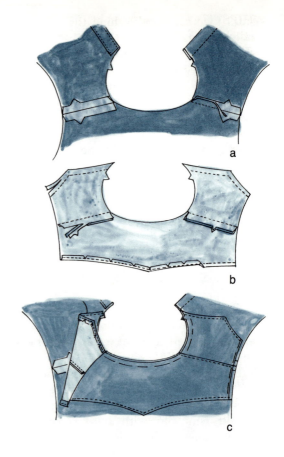

a

b

c

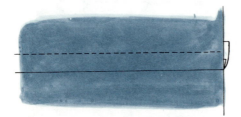

WESTERN SHIRT YOKE. An appliquéd yoke on a shirt that has no yoke.

With wrong sides together, stitch the shoulder seams of the shirt. Press the seam allowances open (a).

With right sides together, stitch the yoke shoulder seams. Trim and grade the seam allowances, making the front seam allowance wider. Press both seam allowances toward the back so the larger encloses the smaller.

Stay-stitch the shaped edges of the yoke in the seam allowance but close to the stitching line. Trim the seam allowances and turn them under on the seam line so no stitching shows. Clip as necessary. Press (b).

Pin and baste the yoke to the right side of the shirt, matching shoulder seams and raw edges of neck and armhole. Topstitch

the yoke first along the shoulder seams, then along the shaped, folded edges (c).

WHIPPED HEM. Similar to a rolled hem (q.v.). Suitable for scarfs, bows, ruffles, flounces, sashes, hems in sheer fabrics.

Stay-stitch ¼ inch below the marked hemline. Trim close to the stitching a few inches at a time to prevent fraying of the entire edge. With wrong side up, roll the edge toward you with thumb and forefinger. Moistening the fingers a little helps the roll. Do a small section at a time—½ to 1 inch (a). Stitch in place with whip-stitches (q.v.) worked over the rolled edge (b). Both stitches and needle are slanted.

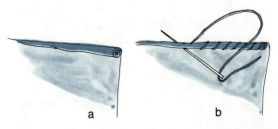

a

b

WHIPSTITCH. A variation of the overhand stitch (q.v.). It is generally used to join two finished edges. The needle enters the fabric at a right angle to the edge, making the stitch itself a slanting one. The thread winds over the edge, enclosing it. Make the stitches very small. They may be placed close together or spaced farther apart depending on the use.

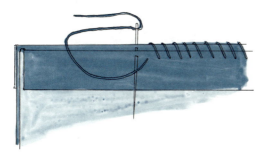

WINDOWPANE METHOD FOR MAKING A BOUND BUTTONHOLE. *See* BOUND BUTTONHOLE: WINDOWPANE METHOD.

WIRE SHANK BUTTON. Wire in the form of an eye is inserted into the loop on the underside. *See* BUTTON SHANK OR STEM; *and* DETACHABLE SHANK BUTTON.

WOOLENS. Fabrics woven from yarns of short, fuzzy, uncombed wool fibers that are twisted together loosely. They cross and intermingle, leaving protruding ends, making a bulky yarn with a soft, fuzzy, fluffy surface. The "country tweeds," fleece, flannel, chinchilla, bouclé, and mohair (among others) are made from such yarns. Since these are supple cloths, they are best used for styles with soft, relaxed, easy lines and unpressed pleats.

The porous surface of woolens makes them good insulators. Stitching, both hand and machine, is hidden in the fuzzy surface.

Woolens show wear and muss easily. However, they generally press well, though nap and pile woolens require special handling. It is comparatively easy to shrink out or ease in fullness of woolens. They can be shaped well but do not hold their shape without the assistance of interfacings and underlinings.

WORK OUT CORNER. This need arises when two layers of fabric have been joined in a cornered seam (q.v.). Turn them to the right side. From the inside, push the corner to position with a blunt-pointed instrument of convenient size. If the corner has been properly stitched, trimmed, and pressed before turning it to the right side, this should produce the desired right angle. If not entirely worked out at the very point, continue from the outside with a blunt-pointed needle or pin.

WORSTEDS. Fabrics woven from long wool fibers combed parallel before spinning, tightly twisted together to give a smooth, dense, compact, firm, hard surface. The weaves are distinctly visible in worsteds. In this group are the gabardines, serges, twills, sharkskins, coverts, glen plaids, houndstooth checks, and other menswear fabrics. These are the fabrics of which the traditional tailored suits and coats are made.

Worsteds can stand hard wear, though they have a tendency to get shiny. The firm, hard surface reduces their insulating quality. Machine and hand stitching is clearly visible on the smooth surface.

Worsteds respond well to pressing but require force for flattening seams and edges. They hold sharp pleats and creases well. It is more difficult to shrink out or ease fullness in them. They can be shaped well and hold their shape without extensive interfacing and with no underlining. They resist wrinkling.

WOVEN AND KNITTED BANDINGS USED AS EXTENSIONS. Cut woven or knitted strips for banding on the grain with the greatest elasticity—bias for wovens, crosswise for knits. Or cut in the same shape as the edge—for instance, a neckline banding. Cut the strip of banding double the desired width plus seam allowances along both long edges and at the ends. On the garment, set the line at the edge for the application of the banding. Add seam allowance.

Join and stitch the ends of the banding

and press the seam allowances open. With right sides outside, press the banding in half lengthwise, using the method deemed best for the material.

With right sides together, pin, then stitch one lengthwise edge of the band to the garment. Grade the seam allowances and press them toward the banding.

In Woven Fabrics. Fold under the seam allowance of the second lengthwise edge and bring the fold to meet the seam line. Pin to position (a). Hem or slip-stitch (b).

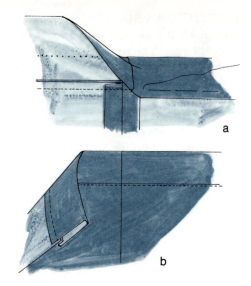

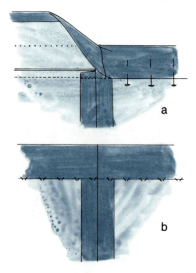

In Knitted Fabrics. Bring the second lengthwise edge flat over the seam line (a) and permanent-baste in place or topstitch from the right side (b).

WRAP STYLES. In these designs, one section of a garment wraps over another. These garments may simply be wrapped and tied or they may be fastened in some other fashion. Wrap styles are understandably popular because of their easy fit.

For fitting, mark the center line of each layer with thread tracing (q.v.). Overlap the upper layer on the under and pin on the center line. Fit on either side of the center toward the side seams. Do not rely on the wrap to produce the size or fullness that may be needed.

WRONG-SIDE MARKINGS. *See* MARKING METHODS.

YARDAGE. The amount of material necessary for a particular garment.

The yardage suggested on the pattern envelope represents the best arrangement of the pattern on a particular width of fabric, for a certain size, with strict respect to how the garment is intended to hang from the smallest to the largest piece. You can be sure considerable experimenting was done before arriving at the yardage estimate. It is not a plot to get you to buy more fabric. It will save a lot of figuring and compromising if you accept the pattern company's suggestion.

Of course, variations are possible. Your fabric may be wider, your figure requirements less. The garment may have been shortened. Perhaps you are using a contrasting collar and cuffs or facings. You may indeed get away with less fabric in a modified layout.

On the other hand, you may need more yardage than the pattern calls for. Additional yardage will be necessary for fabrics not preshrunk or sponged, for straightening the cross grain at both ends, for pattern alterations made for your figure requirements, for the placing, spacing, and matching of surface-design motifs, stripes, checks, plaids, and the directional placement of naps, piles, or bias cuts.

How much more yardage depends on the number and size of the design repeats, the number of pattern sections that need matching, whether the fabric has nap or pile, the directional movement of line,

color, and design. One can only say, "Buy more." (For precise yardage, work out your own layout chart. *See* LAYOUT CHART OF YOUR OWN DEVISING.) When the width of the fabric you've chosen is not included on the pattern envelope, *see the* FABRIC WIDTH CONVERSION CHART.

Don't skimp. A few extra inches may save you hours of time and effort in laying out and cutting your pattern. Not enough fabric may force you to change a design you love to something that doesn't have quite the flair of the original.

YOKE. The fitted portion of a garment, usually at the shoulders or hips. It is a wonderful design device. *(See illustrations on next page.)*

Its seaming may conceal the shaping of the garment (a). It may divide a bodice or skirt into interesting areas (b). Often it provides a smooth, trim area in contrast to fullness in an adjoining area (c). It is a common means of separating a highly decorative area from a very plain one (d).

There are partial yokes, yokes in one with a panel, and yokes in one with a sleeve (d).

A yoke may be attached to the rest of the garment by a plain seam or a lapped seam. Lapped seams are a little more tailored and are easier to make if the yoke has corners, curves, or points.

Yokes in tailored garments are usually interfaced for body and shape retention. Yokes in shirts and dressmaker-type gar-

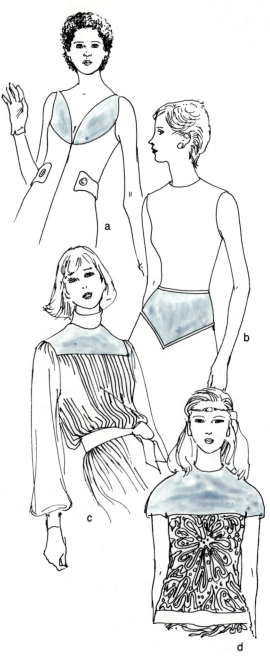

ments are lined rather than interfaced un-less interfacing is necessary for the design.

For types of yoke construction, *see* SHIRT YOKE *and* WESTERN SHIRT YOKE. The same methods may be applied to yokes wher-ever they appear in a garment.

YOKE SLEEVE. In this style, the yoke is cut in one with the shoulder section.

ZIGZAG GATHERED BAND TRIMMING.

An attractive trim that can be used as an alternative to a ruffle trim.

Use a band of self- or contrasting fabric or a length of ribbon. Mark it with zigzag chalk lines or creases as a guide for the gathering. To do this, turn down one end of the strip so the upper lengthwise edge lies at right angles to the grain (a). Press or crease and open out.

Place the right angle of a cardboard rectangle against the crease and draw a chalk line (b) or make a second fold over the cardboard (c); press or crease; open out.

Continue drawing, folding, or creasing in the same way along the length of the

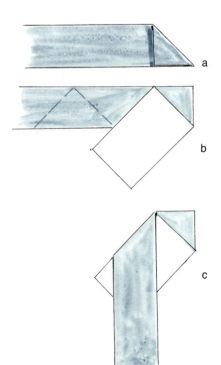

band. Gather along the chalk or crease marks and draw up the thread to the desired fullness (d).

ZIGZAG HEM. Because it prevents fraying, it is suitable for any fabric that ravels. Because it has "give," it is also suitable for fabrics that stretch, like knits.

Make a row of plain or multiple zigzag stitches near the bottom edge of the garment. Use a fine stitch length and the widest possible stitch width. Trim the fabric close to the stitching (a). Fasten the zigzag hem with a blind hemming stitch or, if the

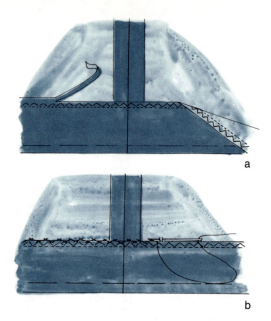

a

b

fabric tends to curl, use a flat catch stitch (b).

ZIGZAG SEAM. An overedge stitch used for a seam in fur and fake fur fabrics.

Trim the seam allowances to 1/8 inch for short-pile fabric, 1/4 inch for long-pile fabric. Baste the seam. Stitch on the designated seam line, using a plain zigzag stitch. The stitching should go over the raw edges to finish and bind them. Use a medium-width, short-length stitch for short piles. Use a wide-width, regular-length stitch for long piles. Test the stitch length, width, and tension on scraps of fabric.

When the seam is completed, work out any hairs caught in the stitching so it disappears in the fabric. Finger-press the seam to one side.

ZIGZAG STITCHING. The advent of the zigzag sewing machine revolutionized home sewing, saving hours of handwork. The stitches themselves are lock stitches that look exactly like their name. They are a series of diagonal stitches with a side-to-side width (bight) and a stitch length (the space between the stitches). From this basic stitch come a great variety of stitches for a great many uses in construction, finishing, and decorative stitching. See the instruction book that comes with your machine.

More thread is used for the diagonal stitches. The stress is not at a single point but across a span. Both these factors allow the stitches more "give" than straight stitching and make them less apt to break. (*See* STRETCH STITCHES.)

For decorative stitching, set the Stitch Pattern Selector for the desired stitch or insert the appropriate cam. For straight-sewing machines without this feature, there is a zigzag attachment that grips and moves the fabric from side to side to form a simple zigzag stitch.

The choices of width and length of zigzag stitches depend on the fabric and the type of construction. The lighter the fabric, the narrower the width and the shorter the stitch. In edge finishes, a wide stitch for ravelly fabrics is best. In decorative stitching, the length and width are determined by the design. In knit fabric, the narrowest of zigzag stitches is effective. You will find many other suggestions for zigzag stitching throughout this text.

Stitch Width. Set the stitch-width regulator for the desired width. The higher the number, the wider the stitch. An "0" setting produces a straight stitch.

Stitch Length. Select as for straight stitching but the stitch appears as a distance between points from side to side rather than in a straight line.

Needle Position. The needle-position selector places the stitches to the right or left of the standard position for straight stitching. This is very helpful as a stitching guide, positioning the stitches a selected distance from an edge or a given line—for instance, in stitching hand-guided machine buttonholes.

Tension. In construction, use properly balanced top and bobbin threads in a degree appropriate for the fabric. In decorative use, the tension can be loosened slightly.

ZIGZAG WIRES. Used as a substitute for featherboning wherever the lines of a garment require a more definite shape and a more rigid support than provided by underlining or shaping seams and darts. Available in 3- to 4-inch lengths.

ZIPPER ADHESIVE TAPE. A double-stick tape with protective covering. It is used in place of basting or pinning on those fabrics that show needle and pin marks.

Strip away the protective covering and press to the fabric. Sew the zipper. Remove the tape.

ZIPPER AT FACED EDGE (Neckline, Waistline, and So On). *See* FACING AT ZIPPERED CLOSING.

ZIPPERED CLOSINGS. One of the greatest inventions of all time must surely be the zipper. Can you imagine what it must have been like in days gone by to get into a dress via dozens and dozens of hooks and eyes or tiny buttons? As if getting into and getting out of clothes by this means wasn't bad enough, imagine the chore of having to sew them all on.

The kind of zipper and how to insert it depends on the design of the garment and the fabric of which it is made. Zipper installations run the gamut—from completely exposed (a) to completely hidden (d), with the standard setting both lapped (b) and centered (c), and the separating (e) and the fly closing (f) in between. *See listing for each.*

The neatest zippered closing is by the use of the invisible zipper (q.v.) in a construction seam. This is comparatively simple and quick to install on the underside of a seam line. No stitching is visible from the right side.

The two standard types of zippered

closings are the lapped (regulation) and the centered (slot seam) (q.q.v.).

If the design is "dressy" and the fabric delicate, looped, or the kind that may catch in the teeth of the zipper when it is closed, use the lapped closing. By this method, the zipper is hidden by a lapped fold. The lap may be to the right or to the left, depending on which is easier for the wearer to use and which is more consistent with the design. Generally an overlap to the right is easier for right-handed people, an overlap to the left for the left-handed. Only one line of stitching is visible in this type of zipper installation.

If the design is geometric or the fabric is heavy or pile, use the centered setting for the zipper. This is also a suitable method for faced or slashed openings, wrist openings, or openings concealed in box or inverted pleats. In the centered closing, the zipper is concealed by two folds of material centered over it. There are two visible lines of stitching, one on each side of the closing.

Generally a seam allowance is sufficient for the application of a zipper. To make very sure there is enough width for the overlap and underlap, cut the placket seam allowances a little wider—3/4 to 7/8 inch instead of the more usual 1/2 or 5/8 inch.

When a zipper is set into a slash in the material rather than into a seam, apply a facing to the slash before setting and stitching the zipper.

In fine custom work, the standard zippers are sewn by hand. Hand stitching holds well and looks prettier than machine stitching. Save the machine-stitched zipper for those garments that will get hard wear and in which the stitching won't show or won't matter.

To Clear the Slide in a Machine Installation: Pull the slide tab down from the top for an inch or so. Stitch the zipper to the depth of the slide pull. Leaving the needle in the fabric, raise the presser foot and pull the slide tab up. Lower the presser foot and continue the stitching. As you come to the end of the second side, stop the stitching an inch or so from the top. Leaving the needle in the fabric, raise the presser foot and slide the tab down to clear the stitching. Lower the presser foot again and continue stitching to the top.

Standard zipper closings may be made by an open method or a closed method. It is easier to do hand-stitched zippers by the open method and machine-stitched zippers by the closed method. *See* CENTERED (SLOT SEAM) ZIPPER *and* LAPPED (REGULATION) ZIPPER.

ZIPPER IN A BAND AT NECKLINE, WAISTLINE, OR THE LIKE. Instead of ending a zipper at neckline or waistline, it can be extended to the top of a band collar or waistband. How this is done depends on whether the band is a double layer or a single layer (as in prepackaged ribbing), whether the zipper installation is one of the standard types or exposed, and whether the placket has or does not have seam allowances.

See ZIPPER IN A DOUBLE BAND WITH SEAM ALLOWANCES AT PLACKET OPENING; ZIPPER IN A DOUBLE BAND WITHOUT SEAM ALLOWANCES AT PLACKET OPENING; ZIPPER IN RIBBED BANDING.

ZIPPER IN A BIAS SEAM. Being stretchy, a bias seam is handled in the same way as a knit. The placket opening is stabilized with stay stitching or a length of woven seam binding before the zipper is set and stitched. *See* ZIPPER IN KNIT FABRIC.

ZIPPER IN A DOUBLE BAND WITHOUT SEAM ALLOWANCES AT PLACKET OPENING. Because of the necessary facing construction, the only possible neat installation is an exposed zipper.

Cut the double band without placket seam allowances. Join its ends temporarily with zigzag stitching in an abutted seam (q.v.) (a). Locate and mark the center line of the placket opening in the garment.

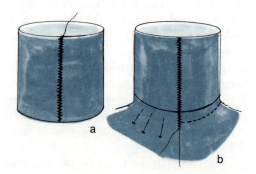

a

b

(The opening is the length of the zipper with the top stop just below the fold line of the band.)

With rights sides together and placket opening lines matching, stitch the band to the garment. Press the seam allowances toward the band (b).

Cut a facing of lightweight material 3 inches wide by the length of the placket plus 2 inches. Mark the center line of the facing. Place the facing over the placket to the fold line of the band, right sides together and center lines matching. Pin. Stitch the facing to the garment 1/8 inch on either side of the center lines and across the bottom of the placket (a).

Slash through the abutted seam of the band and the center line of the placket to within 1/2 inch of the end. Clip diagonally to each corner (b). Turn the facing to the inside and press, rolling the joining seam to the underside (c).

the garment along the fold line. Turn under the seam allowance of the loose, long edge of the under band. Pin to position along the garment seam and across the ends. Hem or slip-stitch the under band to position (b).

In a machine method, machine-stitch from the right side in the well of the seam through all thicknesses.

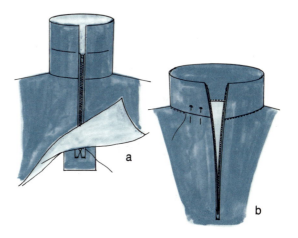

To Stitch Invisibly from the Underside: Slip-baste the edges of the opening to the zipper tape. From the underside, fold back the garment against itself, exposing the zipper tape and the line of previous stitching which attached the facing to the garment.

Using the zipper foot, stitch over the slip basting through the seam allowance, zipper tape, and facing, on both long edges and across the bottom of the placket opening.

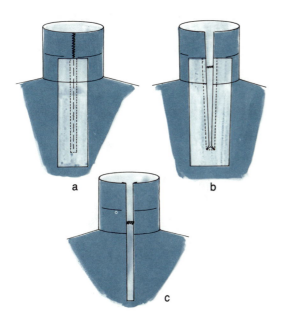

Position the zipper in the opening with the top stop just below the fold line of the band (a). Pin. Either slip-stitch around the exposed zipper, topstitch, or machine-stitch invisibly from the underside. *(See instruction following.)*

Trim away the excess tape at the top of the placket. Fold the band to the inside of

ZIPPER IN A DOUBLE BAND WITH SEAM ALLOWANCES AT PLACKET OPENING. *See* WAISTBAND: BASIC METHOD; SEWING SEQUENCE FOR A WAISTBAND ZIPPERED TO THE TOP OF THE BAND.

Attach the band to the garment. Make sure that the cross seams match. Inaccuracy here will make the placket line uneven in length and the bands unequal in width. Trim the seam allowances at the cross seams to reduce bulk.

With the band extended away from the garment, apply the zipper in the seam allowances. Use a lapped or centered zipper installation (q.q.v.). Position the top stop just below the fold line of the band. Sew by hand or by machine. Trim away the excess tape at the top of the zipper. Fold the band to the inside of the garment along the fold line. Make sure the ends of the band are equal in width.

Turn under the seam allowances to clear the zipper at both ends of the under band along the zipper tape. Pin to position. Turn under the seam allowance of the loose, long edge of the under band. Pin to position along the garment seam. Hem or slipstitch the under band to position. In a machine method, machine-stitch from the right side in the well of the seam through all thicknesses.

ZIPPER IN CHECKED FABRIC. *See* ZIPPER IN PLAID, STRIPED, OR CHECKED MATERIAL.

ZIPPER IN CREPE OR SIMILAR FABRIC. Set and hand-stitch the zipper by the lapped, centered, or invisible zipper installation (q.q.v.). The first two are best done using a tiny half backstitch or prick stitch (q.q.v.). A hand method gives greater control of the crepe, which has a tendency to stretch when machine-stitched.

ZIPPER IN DOUBLE-FACED FABRIC. A centered zipper installation (q.v.) is recommended.

Separate the two layers of fabric at the edges of the placket opening by slicing through the perpendicular threads that join the layers for about 1¼ inches. Turn under the seam allowances of both edges toward each other (to the inside of the fabric). Press lightly.

Sandwich the zipper between the two layers on each side of the opening. Baste through the layers and zipper tape. Topstitch.

ZIPPER IN GARMENT TO BE LAUNDERED. It is a good idea to preshrink the zipper before it is installed to avoid puckering in laundering. If the garment is to be repeatedly laundered, a second preshrinking is an added precaution.

To preshrink the zipper, place it in hot water and allow it to soak for several minutes. Remove it from the water and roll it in a towel to remove the excess moisture. Allow it to air-dry.

ZIPPER IN HIGH-PILE, SHAGGY FABRIC OR FAKE FUR. For an unbulky application, shave or clip the pile from the seam allowance (a). Replace each seam allowance with a length of 1-inch-wide grosgrain ribbon cut 1 inch longer than the placket opening. Overlap the ribbon on the right side of each seam allowance, aligning the edge of the ribbon with the seam line of the fabric. Edgestitch (b). Trim the fabric seam allowances to ¼ inch. Turn the ribbon to the inside and finger-press.

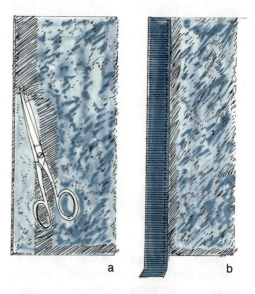

a   b

Open the zipper. Place one side of it face down on the ribbon with the teeth (or coil) directly over the seam line and the bottom stop at the end of the placket opening. Baste and stitch the zipper to the ribbon close to the teeth or coil but leave room for the slide pull to work easily. Repeat for the other side of the zipper. Close the zipper.

On the underside, backstitch the edge of the zipper tape to the ribbon. Catch-stitch the ribbon to the backing of the fabric.

ZIPPER IN KNIT FABRIC. The most satisfactory method of sewing a zipper in knit fabrics is by hand. *(See* ZIPPERED CLOSINGS.*)* It gives infinitely more control than machine stitching when dealing with the stretchiness of knit fabric.

Stabilize the placket opening of moderately stretchy knits by stay-stitching in the seam allowances close to the seam lines. For very stretchy knits, use lengths of woven seam binding on both sides of the opening. Place the seam binding over the seam allowance on the wrong side of the fabric. Stitch close to the seam line.

ZIPPER IN LOW-PILE FABRIC (VELVET, VELVETEEN, AND THE LIKE). Set and hand-stitch the zipper by the lapped, centered, or invisible zipper methods. *See listing for each.*

ZIPPER IN PLAID, STRIPED, OR CHECKED MATERIAL, FABRIC WITH DESIGN MOTIFS OR CROSS SEAMS. When a zipper is installed by hand stitching, one has perfect control in matching cross seams, plaids, stripes, checks, and motifs. It takes a little more work when the stitching is done by machine.

In a machine installation, stitch the first side of the zipper as usual. Fold under the seam allowance of the second side. Using basting tape, tape the fabric to position on the right side, matching *exactly* all cross seams, plaids, stripes, or motifs (a).

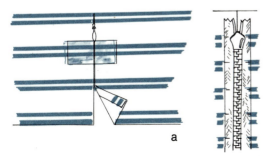

a

b

For the Standard Zipper. Topstitch, then remove the basting tape.

For the Invisible Zipper. Turn to the wrong side. Pencil-mark the zipper tape at each seam line or unit (b). Remove the basting tape from the right side. Open the zipper. Match the markings on the zipper tape with the seams, lines, or motifs of the fabric. Stitch as usual.

ZIPPER IN PLEATED GARMENT. The zipper placement and stitching in a pleated garment should be as inconspicuous as possible and not interfere with the fold or hang of the pleat. Since the placket opening is usually the last seam to be stitched, the last pleat can be made after this and folded so it conceals the zipper installation.

For shaped or seamed pleats, use an invisible zipper installation (q.v.).

For a Box or Inverted Pleat. Position the final seam down the center of the underlay of the pleat. Insert the zipper in the seam by a centered (slot-seam) or invisible zipper installation (q.q.v.).

For a Side or Knife Pleat. Locate the placket where underfold and underlay meet.

Stitch the garment seam, leaving the placket open. Clip the seam allowance of the undersection to the seam line. Turn under the seam allowance to the underside and baste.

From the right side, place the folded edge over the zipper tape with the fold close to the teeth or coil but allow enough room for the pull tab to slide easily. Baste, then machine-stitch (a).

From the underside, place the free edge of the zipper tape over the underfold of the overlapping pleat. Baste the zipper to the underfold, keeping the rest of the pleat free. Machine-stitch the zipper close to the teeth or coil but allow enough room for the slide tab (b).

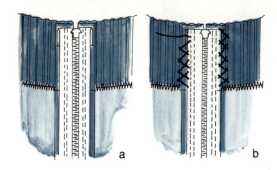

a   b

a

b

ZIPPER IN RIBBED BANDING (Single Layer with Seam Allowance).

Attach the ribbing to the neck edge of the garment.

Use a centered zipper installation (q.v.). Place the top stop just below the top edge of the band. Trim and turn under the upper ends of the zipper tape. Pin and/or baste the zipper to position. Stitch either by hand or by machine, catching the turned-under ends in the stitching (a). Catch-stitch the edges of the zipper tape to the seam allowances of the band (b).

ZIPPER IN SHEER FABRICS. Use a featherweight zipper. If none is available, trim away some of the zipper tape of a standard zipper and overcast the raw edges to prevent raveling. Install by hand, using a prick stitch (q.v.) over just one or two threads on the right side.

ZIPPER IN ULTRASUEDE. The zipper installation in Ultrasuede depends on whether the garment was constructed by the standard method or the flat (overlap) method. *(See* ULTRASUEDE: SEAMS.)

As with other fabrics, the zipper installation may be exposed, separating, invisible, lapped, or centered. *(See listing for each.)* Choose which is consistent with the design of the garment and the method of construction.

Position the zipper with pins, basting (with fine needle and silk thread), basting or masking tape.

INSTALLATION BY THE STANDARD METHOD

The zipper is installed in the same way as in other fabrics. An invisible zipper, hidden in a conventional seam, is easiest of all and looks pretty. In both the lapped and centered installations, the zipper is attached with decorative topstitching that is a continuation of that below the placket opening. In the lapped zipper, the topstitching is along one side of the seam; in the centered zipper, on both sides of the seam.

In either of these installations, *do not* topstitch across the end of the placket. The zipper should hold, but if it will make you feel more secure, fasten the zipper ends on the underside to the seam allowances with catch stitching.

INSTALLATION BY THE FLAT (OVERLAP) METHOD

Exposed Zipper Installation: the same method as that used for any other exposed zipper installation (q.v.) except that an opening for the zipper is cut away on the garment and the facing.

Center the zipper in the opening. Baste, tape, or fuse the Ultrasuede to the zipper tape. Topstitch close to all edges.

Separating Zipper Installation. Use the same method as that used for any other separating zipper installation (q.v.) except that the seam allowances of garment and facing are trimmed away.

Bring the edges of the opening together and fasten on the right side with masking or basting tape. Center the zipper under the opening edges. Fuse the Ultrasuede to the zipper tape or baste. Remove the fastening tape.

Working on the underside, place the facings, when present, over the garment, wrong sides together and opening edges centered over the zipper. Fuse or baste to position.

On the right side, topstitch on both sides of the opening. If desirable, make a second row of topstitching 1/4 inch away from the first.

Lapped Zipper Installation. Trim away the seam allowance of the overlap edge of the garment.

On the overlap, fuse a narrow strip of Ultrasuede to the underside of the placket opening for a facing. Topstitch along the edge (a).

On the underlap, trim away 1/2 inch of the seam allowance of the placket opening, leaving a 1/8-inch extension. Trim the seam allowance below the placket to the predetermined width. Below the opening, mark the seam line on the right side with thread tracing, using silk thread (b).

From the right side, slip the zipper into position on the underlap. Place the 1/8-inch extension of the underlap over the right side of the zipper tape. Allow enough room for the tab slider to work easily. Edgestitch, using the zipper foot (c).

Place the overlap section of the garment over the underlap section, bringing the faced placket edge and the raw edge of the rest of the garment to the seam line of the underlap. Hold in place with basting or masking tape until the stitching is completed.

Baste or fuse the seam below the placket opening. Topstitch the overlap to the underlap below the placket opening, continuing the line of placket edgestitching.

Topstitch the entire length of the garment 1/4 inch away from the previous line of stitching, including the zipper (d). It is this latter stitching that attaches the overlap to the second side of the zipper tape.

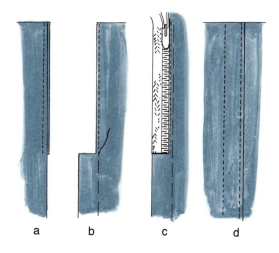

a   b   c   d

ZIPPER: PRESSING OF AREA. *See* PRESSING ZIPPERED AREA.

ZIPPER SHORTENED. If the zipper length you need isn't available, you can shorten a longer one.

To Shorten a Zipper at the Bottom: Make several whipstitches over the coil or chain at the required length (a). For a new bottom stop, sew a large, straight metal eye across the coil or chain and above the whipstitches (b). Trim the zipper and tape about 3/4 inch below the whipstitches.

Instead of whipstitching by hand, it is possible to machine-stitch across a coil zipper. It is also possible to remove the teeth below the end of the placket opening and use a small zipper clamp (if you can get one) as a new bottom stop.

To Shorten a Zipper at the Top: Baste the zipper into place to within 1 inch of the point where you wish the zipper teeth to end. Open the zipper and remove the extra zipper teeth of a chain zipper with a pair of small pliers. For a new top stop, bend two large, straight metal eyes in half and slip them over the tape above the teeth (c). Sew in place securely. Close the zipper. Turn down the tape ends. Cut away the excess tape at an angle and sew in place. *See also* STANDARD ZIPPER CONVERTED TO AN UNDERARM DRESS ZIPPER.

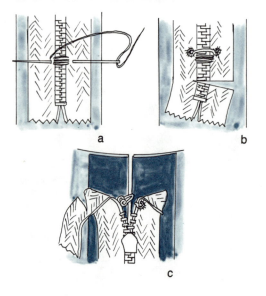

a   b

c

ZIPPER TAIL. Any portion of the zipper that extends below the installed zipper. If the tail is short, stitch each side of the tape to the seam allowance. If the tail is a long one, shorten the zipper (q.v.).

ZIPPER TRIMMED WITH BRAID, RIBBON, OR THE LIKE. *See* EXPOSED ZIPPER WITH TRIMMING.

ZIPPER TYPES. There are three types of zipper: conventional (chain or coil), invisible, and separating. *See individual listings. See also* ZIPPERED CLOSINGS.

ZIPPER UNDERLAY. A protective curtain applied to the underside of the zipper. It avoids catching the zipper on underthings.

The underlay may be a length of 1-inch grosgrain ribbon 1 inch longer than the zipper plus seam allowances. Turn under the seam allowances at top and bottom edges and stitch. Or the underlay may be a 5-inch-wide strip of self-fabric 1 inch longer than the zipper plus seam allowances. With right sides outside, fold the self-fabric strip lengthwise. Edge-finish the bottom and lengthwise edges.

An underlay may be added to skirt or pants before or after the waistband has been attached.

Underlay Added Before the Waistband Is Applied. On the underside, place the underlay over the closed zipper with its top edge aligned with the waistline edge and the lengthwise edge even with the seam allowance edge. Machine-stitch this one long edge of the underlay to only one seam allowance of the placket. Catch-stitch or tack the lower end to the seam allowances (a).

Include the top of the underlay in the waistband seam. Be sure to cut the waistband long enough to extend across the underlay. It is the waistband that holds the underlay in place.

Underlay Added After the Garment Has Been Completed. On the underside, place the ribbon or self-fabric strip over the closed zipper as above, with one end at or above the slider tab. Sew one long edge only to one seam allowance of the placket, using backstitches or running stitches. Catch-stitch or tack the lower end to the seam allowances. Fasten the upper edge with small snaps (b).

a   b